You've only got one life. Make it count.

Your future is filled with fantastic possibilities. And the Navy can help you make them come true.

Imagine virtually unlimited opportunities in 60 high-growth, high-adrenaline positions. In any corner of the world.

The Navy is one of the most exciting ways to explore a bigger universe. Those places that once seemed so far away are now places you'll call home.

Earn money for college. Learn cool, new skills. And experience hands-on training with some of the most advanced technology on the planet.

Experience instant-rush adventures and hands-on challenges. Test your character. Define yourself.

To receive your free video, simply fill out and return the attached card. Or call 1-800-USA-NAVY (872-6289). For an interactive look at the Navy adventure, visit the Life Accelerator™ at navy.com.

accelerate your life™

navy.com   1-800-USA-NAVY

18th EDITION

Scott A. Ostrow

THOMSON

ARCO

Australia • Canada • Mexico • Singapore • Spain • United Kingdom • United States

About The Thomson Corporation and Peterson's

With revenues approaching US$7.2 billion, The Thomson Corporation (www.thomson.com) is a leading global provider of integrated information solutions for business, education, and professional customers. Its Learning businesses and brands (www.thomsonlearning.com) serve the needs of individuals, learning institutions, and corporations with products and services for both traditional and distributed learning.

Peterson's, part of The Thomson Corporation, is one of the nation's most respected providers of lifelong learning online resources, software, reference guides, and books. The Education Supersite^{SM} at www.petersons.com—the Internet's most heavily traveled education resource—has searchable databases and interactive tools for contacting U.S.-accredited institutions and programs. In addition, Peterson's serves more than 105 million education consumers annually.

For more information, contact Peterson's, 2000 Lenox Drive, Lawrenceville, NJ 08648; 800-338-3282; or find us on the World Wide Web at www.petersons.com/about.

ACKNOWLEDGMENTS

Thanks go out to the following organizations for contributing to this book:

U.S. Military Entrance Processing Command, North Chicago, Illinois 60064-3094, for making available the following resource material:

ASVAB 25/26 Student and Parent Guide

ASVAB 25/26 Educator and Counselor Guide

ASVAB 25/26 Counselor Manual

ASVAB Career Exploration Program

ASVAB Technical Manual for the ASVAB 25/26 Career Exploration Program Exploring Careers: The ASVAB Workbook

U.S. Department of Defense, Washington, D.C., for:

     Military Careers

Bureau of Naval Personnel, Washington, D.C., for:

     Tools and Their Uses

     Basic Machines

General Motors Corporation, Detroit, Michigan, for:

     What Makes Autos Run

TABLE OF CONTENTS

WHAT THIS BOOK WILL DO FOR YOU

You are exploring your career options and are scheduled to take the Armed Services Vocational Aptitude Battery (ASVAB). By doing this, you are on the right path to determining your next step in life: college, the military, or a civilian career. A high score on the ASVAB is important for determining your potential for careers in both the military and civilian life.

Preparation for the ASVAB will help you gain the confidence you need to score high. This book will help you reach that goal and determine your strengths and weaknesses in specific subject areas. You can then spend your time wisely and focus on your weak areas by studying the subject reviews. You will also build confidence in your test-taking abilities by taking the four sample test batteries. Knowing the format of the test and feeling at ease on your test day is an important factor for your success.

ASVAB, 18th edition gives you:

- The most up-to-date information for success on the new 2002 version of the test
- The only book available that offers dedicated chapters for each subject test
- Profiles of over 125 military careers
- The most information dedicated to the Armed Forces Qualification Test (AFQT) subject tests.

HOW TO USE THIS BOOK TO ACHIEVE HIGH SCORES

Follow the ten steps listed below to maximize your efforts and make the most of your test preparation.

1. **Read "Introduction to the ASVAB."** This will give you a better understanding of the ASVAB, the different reasons to take the test, when and where you can take it, strategies for preparing for the test, and much more.

2. **Take the first ASVAB test battery.** After completing this test battery, you can evaluate your strengths and weaknesses and record your scores on our Self- Appraisal chart. Don't worry if you do not do well; the first time you take the battery will be the hardest since you are not familiar with it.

3. **Review the areas you need more practice on in the "Strengthening Your Weaknesses" section.** This section provides a dedicated chapter to each ASVAB subject test. You can spend your time wisely and focus on the areas you need to work on and any area that you are unsure of.

4. **Take the second ASVAB test battery.** You should feel more comfortable with this the second time and know what to expect in terms of the test format. Be sure to record your scores in the Self-Appraisal chart on page 24.

5. **Refer back to the review section.** If you need more review in specific areas, go back to the review section to get the help you need.

6. **Take the third ASVAB test battery.** You are gaining familiarity with the test and are striving to surpass your scores from the previous battery. Record your scores in the Self-Appraisal chart and take note of the progress you have made.

7. **Go back to the review section if needed.** The more you study the sections you are unsure of, the more you will learn.

8. **Take the fourth and final ASVAB test battery.** You should feel confident in your progress and knowledge about the test. Record your scores in the Self-Appraisal chart.

9. **Review your progress on the four test batteries you have completed.** You can now go on to " Your ASVAB Scores" to help you determine how the military interprets ASVAB scores.

10. **Turn to "Military Careers" to look for career areas that interest you.** Note that the military careers listed include their civilian counterparts. Also included are the Military Careers Score required for each career.

Don't hesitate to reread the review section or retake one or more of the test batteries. Remember, the more confident you are about the test subjects and the test format, the higher you will score on the ASVAB.

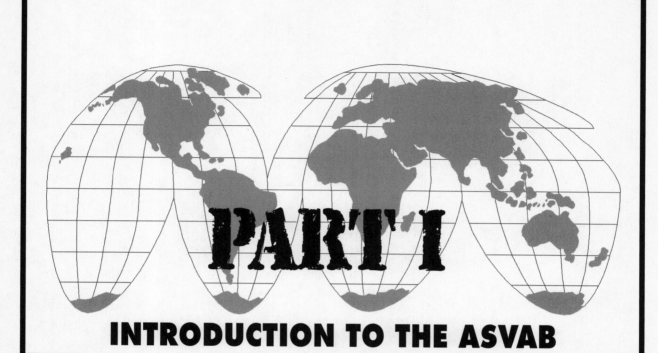

PART I

INTRODUCTION TO THE ASVAB

CHAPTER

GENERAL INFORMATION

If you plan to join the military or want to find out what type of career you are suited for, your first step is to take the Armed Forces Aptitude Battery, or ASVAB. ASVAB is a multiple-aptitude battery consisting of eight to ten subject tests. Over 1.2 million people each year take it to join the military or as part of a student testing program offered in high schools. Its primary purpose is to determine your basic skills and your aptitude for other skills. There are three main versions and purposes for taking the ASVAB:

THE STUDENT ASVAB

The *student* ASVAB, also known as the *institutional* ASVAB, is sponsored by high schools and is offered to all interested students. It was created for high school students in their sophomore, junior, or senior year, or in a post-secondary school, to help identify their abilities. It is a great tool and it has helped many students decide on their future educational or career path. The student ASVAB also helps the military attract well-qualified volunteers for enlistment and to place them in military occupational programs.

Over 1 million people take the student ASVAB each year as part of the military's Career Exploration Program. With this program, students take surveys about their interests, identify personal characteristics, and use their ASVAB scores to match their background to possible careers.

If you choose to take the student ASVAB, you will take the exam with other students at your school. More than likely, there will be one or more military recruiters present as proctors of the exam. This is their sole purpose for being there, and they are prohibited by regulations from actively recruiting during the ASVAB. However, the ASVAB answer sheet contains questions about your plans after high school. Those plans may be attending a two- or four-year college, attending a vocational (or trade) school, or enlisting in the military. If you do well on the ASVAB, military recruiters may contact you regardless of your intended plans. If you list "plans military," you are a prime candidate for enlistment and will be pursued by recruiters from all of the military services. If you do choose to enlist in the military, your student ASVAB scores can be used for qualification for enlistment. Note that your scores remain valid for two years.

THE ENLISTMENT ASVAB

Another form of the ASVAB is referred to as the *enlistment* ASVAB, also known as the *production* ASVAB. This version is given to those pursuing enlistment that either did not take the student version or want to retake the exam in the hope that they will improve their scores. Your enlistment ASVAB scores determine your learning ability and vocational aptitude. Over 500,000 potential recruits take the ASVAB each year.

The enlistment ASVAB is given in one of two places, either at the Military Entrance Processing Station (MEPS) or at a Mobile Examining Team (MET) site. In either place, you take the exam with others who have also decided to join the military. All tests given at the MEPS are computer-adaptive tests (CAT). For more information on the CAT-ASVAB, see *Computer Adaptive Testing*.

Note that your recruiter may arrange for you to take a pre-ASVAB test called the Entrance Screening Test (EST). This pretest is to identify your weaknesses in case you need to review specific subject areas and do additional test preparation before the test.

Student Testing vs. Enlistment Testing

As of July 1, 2002, there are three main differences between these two types of ASVAB.

1. High school officials have the option of administering a "short" version of the ASVAB, known as Short Student ASVAB (SSASVAB). This version contains only those subtests that are used to compute the Armed Forces Qualification Test (AFQT). If your school chooses this option, all test takers are given the shortened version. If you choose to pursue military enlistment, you must take the full-length ASVAB at a later date.

2. The student answer sheets differ from the enlistment answer sheets. They include a section for the "short" version, are a different color, and the personal data order is in a different order from the production answer sheets.

3. The CAT-ASVAB used for enlistment testing, includes two additional test sections: Numerical Operations and Coding Speed. Since those sections may be eliminated in the future check with your recruiter for details.

THE ARMED FORCES CLASSIFICATION TEST (AFCT)

The AFCT, also known as the *in-service* ASVAB, is required when military personnel want to change career fields and do not currently have qualifying ASVAB scores for that career field. The only difference between the AFCT and the ASVAB is the name. At present, the AFCT is given only in the traditional paper-and-pencil version. Also, the two sections that were removed from the paper-and-pencil ASVAB in 2002 are still included in the AFCT. These are: Numerical Operations (NO) and Coding Speed (CS).

TEST CHANGES

On July 1, 2002, the government is making changes to specific versions of the ASVAB. Two subtests from the current ASVAB, Numerical Operations and Coding Speed, are being eliminated from the student ASVAB and the paper-and-pencil version of the enlistment ASVAB. Note that these sections are to remain in the computer-adaptive (CAT) version of the ASVAB and the AFCT until further notice. Check with your recruiter for details.

A change to the paper-and-pencil version of the enlistment ASVAB is the addition of the Assembling Objects section. More information about Assembling Objects is found on pages 22–23.

In addition the removal of the two subtests, there is a new order for the remaining subtests as of July 1, 2002 for the student ASVAB and the paper-and-pencil production ASVAB. Details about the order and test specifics are listed in Subject Tests below.

One additional change does not involve the structure of the test; however, it does affect the way in which it is scored. Because the ASVAB "score" is not a true percentage grade (much like the SAT), renorming of the test scoring, while not changing the test content, will result in making it more difficult to achieve a higher score. For example, obtaining a 50 AFQT at present requires a certain number of correct answers, once the test is renormed the same 50 AFQT will require a greater number of correct responses.

Because the proposed changes involve removing test material, we include a note at the beginning of each Numerical Operations and Coding Speed review section and within the sample test batteries to remind you of the test changes. Be sure to ask your high school guidance counselor or recruiter about the specifics for the test changes, other upcoming changes, and how they relate to your version of the ASVAB.

SUBJECT TESTS

The ASVAB consists of subjects tests designed to measure acquired knowledge, as well as general abilities acquired from interests or hobbies. Listed in the following chart are specifics about the tests and the times allotted for each section.

ASVAB CONTENT

Testing Time	**134 minutes: student ASVAB and paper-and-pencil enlistment ASVAB**
	144 minutes: CAT-ASVAB and AFCT
Administrative Time	**36 minutes**
Total Testing Time	**170 minutes: student ASVAB and paper-and-pencil enlistment ASVAB**
	180 minutes: CAT-ASVAB and AFCT
Total Number of Items	**200: student ASVAB and paper-and-pencil enlistment ASVAB**
	334: CAT-ASVAB and AFCT

TEST	TIME	ITEMS	DESCRIPTION
General Science	11 minutes	25	Measures knowledge of the physical and biological sciences
Arithmetic Reasoning	36 minutes	30	Measures ability to solve arithmetic word problems
Word Knowledge	11 minutes	35	Measures ability to select the correct meaning of words presented in context and to identify the best synonym for a given word
Paragraph Comprehension	13 minutes	15	Measures ability to obtain information from written passages
Mathematics Knowledge	24 minutes	25	Measures knowledge of general mathematics principles, including algebra and geometry
Electronics Information	9 minutes	20	Measures knowledge of electricity, radio principles, and electronics
Auto & Shop Information	11 minutes	25	Measures knowledge of automobiles, tools, and shop terminology and practices
Mechanical Comprehension	19 minutes	25	Measures knowledge of mechanical and physical principles and ability to visualize how illustrated objects work
*Numerical Operations	3 minutes	50	Measures ability to perform arithmetic computations in a speeded context
*Coding Speed	7 minutes	84	Measures ability to use a key in assigning code numbers to words in a speeded context

Numerical Operations and Coding Speed are included on the CAT-ASVAB and AFCT.

You can become more familiar with the ASVAB by getting an overview of the subject tests and the areas that they cover. The list below contains the general contents and purpose of the tests, it shows you what to expect on the tests, and provides you with a better understanding of the content areas covered on the official test battery. The review section of this book, called *Strengthening Your Weaknesses,* contains a chapter for each of the subject areas.

Part 1—General Science (GS)

The General Science test consists of 25 items and covers the material generally taught in junior and senior high school science courses. Most of the questions deal with life science and physical science, with a few questions on earth science. Specifics about what each area covers are:

- Life Science: basic biology, human nutrition, and health
- Physical Science: elementary chemistry and physics
- Earth Science: geology, meteorology, and astronomy

Part 2—Arithmetic Reasoning (AR)

The Arithmetic Reasoning test consists of 30 items and covers basic mathematical problems you may come across in everyday life. These questions are designed to measure general reasoning and the ability to solve mathematical problems.

Part 3—Word Knowledge (WK)

The Word Knowledge test consists of 35 items and is designed to test for ability to understand the meaning of words through synonyms (words having the same or nearly the same meaning as other words). Vocabulary is one of many factors that characterize reading comprehension, but it also provides a good measure of verbal comprehension.

The words used in these synonym questions are used in everyday language. The questions can appear in either of two forms:

1. The key word appears in the stem and is followed by "most nearly means."

2. The key word is used in a sentence.

Part 4—Paragraph Comprehension (PC)

The Paragraph Comprehension test consists of 15 items and is designed to measure ability to obtain information from written material. The reading passages vary in length from one paragraph to several paragraphs and may be used for one or more questions. Each question in this section is to be answered solely on the basis of the information contained in the reading passage.

Part 5—Mathematics Knowledge (MK)

The Mathematics Knowledge test consists of 25 items and is designed to measure general mathematical knowledge. It is a test of your ability to solve problems using high school mathematics, including algebra and some basic geometry. Scrap paper is provided for any figuring you may wish to do.

Part 6—Electronics Information (EI)

The Electronics Information test consists of 20 items dealing with electricity, radio principles, and electronics. This information can be learned through working on radios, working on electrical equipment, reading books, or taking courses.

Part 7—Auto & Shop Information (AS)

The Auto & Shop Information test consists of 25 items and covers the material generally taught in automobile mechanics in vocational-technical schools and in shop instruction. It is designed to measure knowledge of automobiles, tools, and shop terminology and practices.

The automotive information may also be acquired as a hobby or by working with automobiles. The questions generally pertain to diagnosing malfunctions of a car, the use of particular parts on a car, or the meaning of terminology. The shop information may also be acquired as a hobby or through shop experience using a variety of tools and materials.

Part 8—Mechanical Comprehension (MC)

The Mechanical Comprehension test consists of 25 items designed to measure your understanding of mechanical and physical principles. Many of the questions use drawings to illustrate specific principles.

Understanding of these principles comes from observing the physical world, working with or operating mechanical devices, or reading and studying.

Part 9—Numerical Operations (NO)

NOTE: This section is currently on the CAT-ASVAB and AFCT but may be eliminated from upcoming ASVAB tests. Check with your recruiter for details.

The Numerical Operations test contains 50 simple, two-number computations in:
- Addition
- Subtraction
- Multiplication
- Division

All numbers are one- or two-digit whole numbers. This is a speed test that requires you to work as fast as you can without making any mistakes.

Part 10—Coding Speed (CS)

NOTE: This section is currently on the CAT-ASVAB and AFCT but may be eliminated from upcoming ASVAB tests. Check with your recruiter for details.

The Coding Speed test contains 84 questions, each with five options, and is designed to determine your speed and accuracy when finding a number in a table. At the top of each section there is a key that consists of a group of words with a code number for each word. Each question in the subtest is a word taken from the key. From among the options listed for each question, you must find the one that is the correct code number for that word.

This is a speed test that requires you to work as fast as you can without making mistakes.

TEST SCORES

Your ASVAB results are reported by a combination of your test scores, called composite scores. Your composite score measures the following three academic areas:

- Academic ability
- Verbal ability
- Math ability

These composites measure your potential for further formal education and predict performance in general areas requiring verbal and mathematics skills.

If you take the ASVAB in high school, your scores allow you to compare your test performance to a national sample of students at your grade level. This is known as a percentile score. Full details about scoring your ASVAB test are found at the end of this book in *Your ASVAB Results*.

ARMED FORCES QUALIFICATION TEST (AFQT)

Four ASVAB subject tests count toward your AFQT score, which is the score that determines eligibility for enlistment. The composite of the ASVAB subject tests is formed from the following:

Word Knowledge	35 items
Paragraph Comprehension	15 items
Arithmetic Reasoning	30 items
Mathematics Knowledge	25 items

The actual scores you get on your subject tests are considered *raw scores*. The military uses raw scores to compute scoring for specific purposes, such as the AFQT. The equation below shows you how to calculate your AFQT raw score:

(2 × the number correct on Word Knowledge) + (2 × the number correct on Paragraph Comprehension) + the number correct on Arithmetic Reasoning + the number correct on Mathematics Knowledge = AFQT raw score, which is then converted into a percentile score.

Note that if you have a General Equivalency Diploma (GED) or do not have a high school diploma and take the ASVAB for enlistment, the military requires a higher AFQT score. Check with your recruiter for more details about this since each branch of the service has different score requirements.

YOUR ASVAB ANSWER SHEETS

Multiple-Choice Answer Sheets

Machine-rated answer sheets are used by millions of test takers for school admissions, school examinations, scholarships, employment, and military testing. Chances are, you have completed multiple-choice answer sheets when taking the Scholastic Assessment Test (SAT), high school exit level exams, or other school tests.

It is important to be familiar with answer sheets so you accurately record your answers. The points to remember about your ASVAB answer sheets are:

- The response positions are indicated by ovals or circles.
- There are four response positions for each question lettered A, B, C, and D.
- The response positions are numbered consecutively to correspond to the numbers of the questions in the test booklet.

Sample answer sheets are included in this book to make you more comfortable with using them and to give you a feel for the actual test experience.

Different Types of Answer Sheets

The Student ASVAB

The student ASVAB answer sheets are printed solely for the school testing program. Every student taking the test receives an answer sheet packet. The first page of the set is the identification and personal data sheet. This sheet provides space for personal information (name, address, etc.). The remainder of the sheets are for recording your answer choices.

Note that the last page of the answer sheet for the student ASVAB contains a Privacy Act Statement. Students must sign this statement in order to receive their test scores. Check with your guidance counselor to find out if your school shares ASVAB scores with recruiters. If they do share scores and you do not want to be contacted by recruiters, ask your guidance counselor to withhold your scores from the military.

The Enlistment ASVAB

The ASVAB answer sheet packets used in the regular military enlistment program are similar to those answer sheet packets used in the school testing program. The main differences are:

- Order of the personal information
- Number of the test
- Colors of the answer sheets
- Addition of the "short" version answer section on the student version

An important difference in the answer sheet requirements is that students in the school testing program are permitted to take the ASVAB although they may not have a social security number. In the regular enlistment program, all potential enlistees must have a social security number.

FREQUENTLY ASKED QUESTIONS

What is the Armed Services Vocational Aptitude Battery (ASVAB)?

The ASVAB, sponsored by the Department of Defense, is a multi-aptitude test battery consisting of eight to ten individual tests covering General Science, Arithmetic Reasoning, Word Knowledge, Paragraph Comprehension, Mathematics Knowledge, Electronics Information, Auto & Shop Information, and Mechanical Comprehension. If you take the computer-adaptive ASVAB or the AFCT, there are two additional tests covering Numerical Operations and Coding Speed. Your ASVAB results provide scores for each individual test, as well as three academic composite scores—Verbal, Math, and Academic Ability—and two career exploration composite scores.

What is an aptitude?

An aptitude measures your readiness to excel when given the opportunity. This means that you have the ability to learn one type of work or indicate your potential for general training. The ASVAB measures aptitudes that relate to how successful you may be in different jobs.

Why should I take the ASVAB?

As a high school student nearing graduation, or a student in a post-secondary school, or as a recent high school graduate, you are faced with very important career choices. Should you go on to college, technical, or vocational school? Would it be better to enter the job market? Should you consider a military career? As stated above, your ASVAB scores are measures of aptitude. Three of the composite scores measure your aptitude for higher academic learning. The other two general composite scores are provided for career exploration purposes.

The ASVAB is a requirement for entrance into the military. It is also used to determine your eligibility for enlisted occupations.

Anther reason to take the ASVAB is to change career fields when you are already in the military. This is needed if you do not have qualifying ASVAB scores on file for that particular career.

When and where is the ASVAB given?

ASVAB is given once or twice a year at more than 14,000 high schools and post-secondary schools in the United States. It is also given year round at either a Military Entrance Processing Stations (MEPS) or at a Mobile Examining Team (MET) site for anyone interested in enlistment.

Is there a charge or fee to take the ASVAB?

There are no fees for taking any version of the ASVAB.

How long does it take to complete the ASVAB?

It takes approximately 3 hours to complete the ASVAB. This includes the time it takes for you to take the test as well as time for administrative needs (giving instructions, passing out the tests, etc.).

If I want to take the student ASVAB but my school doesn't offer it (or I missed it), what should I do?

If you want to take the ASVAB to join the military, contact your local recruiter to arrange it. If you want to take the student version of the ASVAB for career exploration, you may be able to take it at another school that offers the exam. Ask your guidance counselor to locate a school and make arrangements for you.

How do I find out what my scores mean and how to use them?

If you take the student ASVAB, your scores are given to you, your guidance counselor, and possibly to recruiting services in a report called the ASVAB Student Results Sheet. You will also receive a copy of *Exploring Careers: The ASVAB Workbook* from your guidance counselor. This contains information that will help you understand your ASVAB results and show you how to use them for career exploration. Test results are sent to schools within 30 days of the test date.

If you take the enlistment ASVAB, your recruiter will contact you with your results. Note that CAT-ASVAB results are automatically computed when you finish the test and your score report is printed out. This report contains raw and standard scores for each subject test as well as composite scores. If you qualify for enlistment, you are told the same day when to return for further processing.

Can a high school give the ASVAB test without having scores released to local military recruiters?

Yes. Schools have eight options regarding the release of test information. One option is "Option 8. No release to recruiters." If your school chooses Option 8, recruiters will not receive students' scores. Another option for schools is "Option 1. No special instructions." Under this option, recruiters can obtain scores and use them however they wish. If a school does not select an option, they will automatically be categorized as Option 1. In between Option 1 and Option 8 are other options specifying when recruiters may receive full information or whether they will be given access to phone numbers. Check with your guidance counselor to confirm what option your school selects and if you wish to have your scores withheld from recruiters.

What is a passing score on the ASVAB?

No one "passes" or "fails" the ASVAB. The ASVAB helps you to identify your abilities in different areas and can help you choose a career path. You can also compare your student ASVAB scores to other students at your grade level. If you plan to join the military, you need to meet minimum score requirements that vary from branch to branch. Your enlistment scores also identify your potential for military career areas.

If I take the ASVAB, am I obligated to join the military?

No. Taking the ASVAB does not obligate you to the military in any way.

Is there any relationship between taking the ASVAB and Selective Service registration?

There is no relationship between taking the ASVAB and Selective Service registration. The Selective Service System keeps a list of men from 18 to 25 years old who register to make themselves available in the case of a national emergency for draft purposes. ASVAB information is not available to the Selective Service System.

If I am planning to go to college, should I take the ASVAB?

Yes. ASVAB results provide you with information that can help you determine your capacity for advanced academic education. You can also use your ASVAB results, along with other personal information, to identify areas for career exploration.

If I take the ASVAB in school, can my scores be used if I decide to enlist in the military?

Yes. You can use your ASVAB results for up to two years for military enlistment if you are a junior, a senior, or a post-secondary school student. The military services encourage everyone to finish high school before joining the armed forces.

How long can I use my ASVAB test results for entrance into the military?

If you are a junior, senior, or a post-secondary student, you can use your ASVAB scores for up to two years for military enlistment. If you are a sophomore, you can't use the scores for enlistment and need to take the ASVAB in your junior or senior year or when you apply for military service.

If you take the enlistment ASVAB, your scores are good for two years from your test date.

Should I take the ASVAB if I plan to become a commissioned officer?

Yes. Taking the ASVAB is a valuable experience for any student who wants to become a military officer. The aptitude information you receive could help you in career planning.

Should I take the ASVAB if I am considering entering the Reserve or National Guard?

Yes. The Reserve and National Guard also use the ASVAB for enlistment purposes.

What should I do if a service recruiter contacts me after I take the student ASVAB?

A service recruiter may contact you before you graduate. If you want to learn about the many opportunities available through the military service, arrange for a follow-up meeting. You are under no obligation to the military as a result of taking the ASVAB. If you do decide to meet with a recruiter, we suggest that you read another ARCO book, *Guide to Joining the Military*, which is full of essential information about the enlistment process.

Is the ASVAB administered other than in the school testing program?

Yes. ASVAB is also used in the regular military enlistment program. This version is known as the enlistment ASVAB and is administered at approximately 65 Military Entrance Processing Stations (MEPS) and at over 685 Mobile Examining Team (MET) sites located throughout the United States. Each year, hundreds of thousands of young men and women who are interested in enlisting in the uniformed services (Army, Navy, Air Force, Marines, and Coast Guard), but who did not take the ASVAB while in high school or post-secondary school, are examined and processed at these military stations.

Is the ASVAB used in the regular military enlistment program the same as the student ASVAB?

Yes and no. The enlistment ASVAB given at Military Entrance Processing Stations (MEPS) is a Computerized Adaptive Testing program known as CAT-ASVAB. These tests are not paper-and-pencil tests but are computer administered. An additional section called Assembling Objects is part of the CAT-ASVAB as are the Numerical Operations and Coding Speed sections; these sections are not on the student ASVAB.

The paper-and-pencil enlistment ASVAB given at Mobile Examining Team (MET) sites contains the same subject tests as the student ASVAB.

What is Military Careers?

This is a career information book created by the U.S. Department of Defense. It describes up to 200 enlisted and officer occupations in all of the military services. A condensed version of *Military Careers* is included at the end of this book. High schools who sponsor the ASVAB are sent copies of *Military Careers* for interested students.

Is any special preparation necessary before taking the ASVAB?

Yes. Preparation is required for taking any examination and it is a *must* in order to achieve the best results. Your test scores reflect not only your ability but also the time and effort you put into preparing for the test. The military services use ASVAB to help determine a person's qualification for enlistment and to help indicate the vocational areas for which the person is best suited. Getting the highest score you can increases your career and vocational opportunities.

CHAPTER 2

STRATEGIES FOR PREPARING FOR AND TAKING THE ASVAB

PREPARING FOR THE TEST

To score high on the ASVAB, you should begin preparing for the tests ahead. You can do this by studying subject matter, reviewing sample questions in practice exercises, and by taking practice test batteries. By using the following strategies, you can prepare yourself to achieve the scores you want on your ASVAB test day.

1. **Become familiar with the format of multiple-choice test items**. These items are used exclusively in the Armed Services Vocational Aptitude Battery.

2. **Become familiar with the layout of machine-scored answer sheets**. Know the right way to record your answers in the spaces provided. These standard answer sheets are not complicated if you understand the layout and have practiced blackening the answer space in the correct manner.

3. **Find out what the test will cover**. This book, as well as your school guidance counselor or recruiter, is an excellent source for test-taking tips and strategies as well as information about what type of questions to expect.

4. **Review subject matter covered in the test**. Review the content in the *Strengthening Your Weaknesses* section of this book. This reviews the basics for each subject test.

5. **Take each Specimen Test Battery in this book under actual test conditions**. Answer all questions in these practice tests within the allotted time of the actual test. Refer to the chart of the ASVAB contents in this section that contains the allotted test times for each section.

6. **Check your answers with the answer keys and explanations at the end of each test battery**. For questions answered incorrectly, determine why your original answers are incorrect. Be sure that you also understand the rationale for arriving at the correct answer. This is important to expand your knowledge in the subject areas and have a better understanding of the types of questions that may appear on the test.

7. **Set aside time every day for concentrated study**. Adhere closely to the schedule you set for yourself, and do not waste time with too many breaks.

8. **Study with a friend or a group**. This can be really helpful and may ease the stress of studying. You can also quiz each other on different subjects as needed.

9. **Eliminate distractions**. Studying is easier when there are little or no distractions. Disturbances caused by family and neighbor activities (telephone calls, television, radio, conversations etc.) will work to your disadvantage. Try to find a quiet room to study and, if necessary, use the library.

10. **Keep physically fit**. You cannot study as effectively when you are tired, ill, or tense. Since you are at your mental best when you are in good physical health, make sure you get:

Should You Guess on Test Day?

If you do not know the answer to a multiple-choice test item, should you guess? **Yes!** There is no penalty for incorrect answers on the ASVAB, so it is to your advantage to answer every question. If you can eliminate any answer choices you know are definitely wrong, and can then make your selection from one of the remaining answer choices, you have made an "educated" guess rather than having guessed blindly. You also have increased your probabilities of guessing correctly.

Tips on Guessing

Be sure to remember these three important points when preparing for the ASVAB and making a decision about guessing:

1. Answer all items. There is no penalty for wrong answers.

2. An "educated" guess is better than guessing "blindly."

3. Guessing "blindly" is better than not guessing at all.

TAKING THE TEST

Here are some tips to help you succeed on your test day:

1. **If possible, avoid taking the test when you are tired, ill, injured, or emotionally upset**. Go to bed early the night before the test and get a good night's sleep.

2. **Eat a light meal**. Eating a heavy meal just before the test can make you sleepy and dull your senses.

3. **Bring along all supplies you may need.** This includes a pen, several No. 2 pencils, an eraser, a ruler, etc. Bring eyeglasses if you need them for reading.

4. **Bring a watch to help you budget your time**. Be sure that you know the amount of time you have for each subject test.

5. **Refrain from drinking excessive amounts of liquids**. Don't create the need to waste valuable testing time by going to the rest room during the test. Use the rest room before or after the test, not during the test.

6. **Arrive on time at the test location.** Choose a comfortable seat, if you have a choice, with good lighting and away from possible distractions such as friends, the proctor's desk, the door, open windows, etc.

7. **Inform the proctor of your special needs.** If you are left-handed, have any special physical problem, or have other needs, ask if some arrangements can be made so you can compete equally with the other candidates.

8. **Call uncomfortable conditions to the attention of the person in charge.** This includes the examination room being too cold, too warm, or not well ventilated.

9. **Be confident and calm.** If you follow our study plan of evaluating your strengths and weaknesses, reading the subject reviews of the areas you are unsure of, and completing the four test batteries in this book, you will have the confidence you need to score high on the ASVAB.

10. **Give the test your complete attention.** Block out all other thoughts, pleasant or otherwise, and concentrate solely on the test.

11. **Listen carefully to all instructions.** Read carefully the directions for taking the test and marking the answer sheets. If you don't understand the instructions or directions, raise your hand and ask the proctor for clarification. Failure to follow instructions or misreading directions can only result in a loss of points.

12. **When the signal is given to begin the test, start with the first question.** Don't jump to conclusions. Carefully read the question and all the choices before selecting the answer.

13. **Answer the question as given in the test booklet.** Do not answer what you *believe* the question should be.

14. **Work steadily and quickly but not carelessly.** Be sure to keep an eye on the time so you can complete each section. Note that you will not be permitted to go back and check your answers on the subject tests that you have already completed.

15. **Do not spend too much time on any one question.** If you can't figure out the answer in a few seconds, go on to the next question. If you skip a question, be sure to skip the answer space for that question on the answer sheet. Continue this way through the subject tests, answering only those easy questions that require relatively little time and of which you are sure.

16. **Be sure the question number in the test booklet corresponds to the number of the question you are answering on the answer sheet.** It is a good idea to check the numbers of questions and answers frequently. If you skip a question but fail to skip the corresponding answer blank for that question, all your answers after that will be in the wrong place.

17. **After you have answered every question you know, go back to the more difficult questions you skipped in the subject test and attempt to answer them.** If you are still unsure of the correct answer, eliminate those choices that you know are incorrect and

make an "educated" guess as to which one of the remaining choices is correct. If time does not permit "educated" guessing, guess "blindly" but be sure to answer all questions in the subtest within the allotted time.

18. **If time permits, recheck your answers for errors.** If you find that your first response is incorrect, change it to the correct answer, making sure to erase your initial response completely on the answer sheet. First answers are usually correct. Don't talk yourself out of a correct answer by reading too much into the question. Unless you are sure that you made a mistake the first time around, don't change your answer.

COMPUTERIZED ADAPTIVE TESTING

The CAT-ASVAB is a computerized version of the ASVAB and is available at all Military Entrance Processing Stations (MEPS). It is given to anyone interested in enlisting in Army, Navy, Air Force, Marines, and Coast Guard.

CAT-ASVAB VERSUS THE PAPER-AND-PENCIL TEST

The CAT-ASVAB subtests measure the same abilities as the paper-and-pencil ASVAB subject tests. The only differences are:

- Automotive & Shop Information subject test has been split into two separate tests
- Assembling Objects, a new subject test, has been added
- All subject tests in CAT-ASVAB are adaptive

In the paper-and-pencil ASVAB, all test takers, regardless of their ability, take the same questions. The CAT-ASVAB is adaptive, which means that it tailors questions to the ability level of each test taker. For example, the first test question is given in the middle ability range, not too difficult and not too easy. If it is answered correctly, the next question is more difficult. If the first item is answered incorrectly, the next item is less difficult. The test continues this way until your proficiency level is determined. You will answer questions that are appropriate for your ability level, so you will not waste time answering questions that are too easy or too difficult.

TAKING THE CAT-ASVAB

The computer keyboard used for the CAT-ASVAB has a simple design. Even if you do not have computer experience, you can learn how to take computerized tests after only a brief lesson.

When you arrive for the test session, the test administrator will give you a few instructions and verify your social security number. You will then be directed to an assigned test examination station and seated at a table with a computer monitor and keyboard.

A modified keyboard, similar to the one shown below, is used for the CAT-ASVAB. The keyboard has been modified so that only the keys needed to answer the test questions are labeled. On the main keyboard, all but six keys and the space bar are covered. The modifications include:

- relocating keys A, B, C, D, and E
- labeling the space bar to become ENTER
- relabeling the F1 key to become HELP
- covering all the keys on the numerical keyboard except 0–9

The computer screen begins the programmed orientation session by describing the keyboard and explaining how to use the keys labeled ENTER, A, B, C, D, E, and HELP. You are then given instructions on the following:

- How to answer test items by pressing the response key for the option selected
- Answering every question, even if it means guessing
- How to change answers by pressing another response key before requesting the next question
- Pressing ENTER to verify that the test item was answered and to bring the next item on the screen.

The instructions are clear and simple, and practice is provided until you are comfortable with taking the actual test on the computer.

You should only press the red HELP key if a problem arises that requires the assistance of the test administrator or a monitor. When the HELP key is pressed, subject test timing stops until you return to the test questions. Note that the time spent reading instructions does not count against the subject test time limit either. A practice period is provided until you are ready for the actual tests.

The 12 subject tests that comprise CAT-ASVAB and the order in which they are administered follows.

Title	Time Limit (minutes)	Number of Questions	Type of Test
General Science (GS)	8	16	Power
Arithmetic Reasoning (AR)	39	16	Power
Word Knowledge (WK)	8	16	Power
Paragraph Comprehension (PC)	22	11	Power
Auto Information (AI)	6	11	Power
Numerical Operations	3	50	Speed
Coding Speed	7	84	Speed
Mathematics Knowledge (MK)	18	16	Power
Mechanical Comprehension (MC)	20	16	Power
Electronic Information (EI)	8	16	Power
Shop Information (SI)	5	11	Power
Assembling Objects (AO)	9	16	Power

The first four subject tests (GS, AR, WK, and PC) are administered sequentially. For each of these subject tests, you are first given an easy sample item and instructed to press the correct response key. The screen indicates whether the answer is correct or incorrect. The actual test items follow and you can begin to answer each test item displayed by pressing the appropriate response key (A, B, C, D, or E). You will need to confirm your answers by pressing the ENTER key after each response. The next test item then appears on your computer screen.

The two speed subtests, Numerical Operations (NO) and Coding Speed (CS), are administered next. Number of correct answers in an allotted period of time, rather than a level of difficulty, is used in the two speed subtests to determine test scores. There are multiple test items displayed on the screen only for the Coding Speed (CS) subtest.

Special instructions for these two subtests are first given in a programmed orientation session. Answers are not confirmed by pressing the ENTER key. Instead, the next item appears after a response key (A, B, C, D, or E) is pressed. Answers cannot be changed and all questions must be answered since the computer does not allow you to skip questions

The next six power subject tests (AI, MK, MC, EI, SI, and AO) are administered sequentially. On the Assembling Objects test that measures spatial aptitude, you must determine how an object will look when its parts are mentally assembled. The test has two types of items, both consisting of five pictures. The first picture (left position) shows the parts to be put together; the others show four different ways this might be accomplished. You need to select which one of these is correct.

For example:

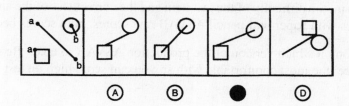

On the first type of item in the figure above, the parts to be assembled are simple geometric figures (lines, squares, rectangles, etc.) that are labeled at one or more points with small letters. By matching corresponding letters on the different parts, you can see where the parts touch when the object is put together properly. Choice C is the correct answer.

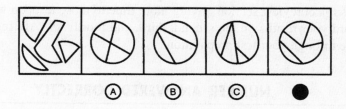

On the second type of item in the figure above, the parts are not labeled. Instead, they fit together like pieces of a puzzle. Choice D is the correct answer.

Assembling Objects test items are suitable for both computerized and paper-and-pencil testing. Future test forms for the High School Testing Program of ASVAB may include Assembling Objects as an added test.

Advantages and Disadvantages of Computerized Adaptive Testing

Advantages

- Length of the test session is reduced.
- The test can be scored immediately.
- Scoring errors are reduced and score accuracy is increased.
- Test security is increased.
- Periodic review and refinement of test items can be done readily.
- Test administration is very flexible, and you do not need to wait for the next scheduled test.

Disadvantages

- You cannot skip around or go back to change an answer.
- You cannot go back and review your answers at the end of the test.

Unlike the paper-and-pencil ASVAB subtest raw scores, CAT-ASVAB subtest raw scores are not equal to the total number of correct answers. CAT-ASVAB subtest scores are computed using formulas that take into account the difficulty of the test item and the correctness of the answer. By equating CAT-ASVAB raw scores with paper-and-pencil ASVAB raw scores, both scores become equivalent.

It is your decision on which version of the production ASVAB to take. Be sure that you choose the version that you feel the most comfortable with so you can score high on test day.

SELF-APPRAISAL CHART

This chart is a great way to see the progress you make after studying the subject review chapters and taking the sample test batteries. Start by recording the test results of the First ASVAB Test Battery. Be sure to read each subject review section, giving more time to those tests on which you scored low. As you take and record your results on the second, third, and fourth ASVAB Test Batteries, you will see the progress made through your test preparation.

NUMBER ANSWERED CORRECTLY

Number of Questions	First Specimen Test Battery	Second Specimen Test Battery	Third Specimen Test Battery
1. General Science	25		
2. Arithmetic Reasoning	30		
3. Word Knowledge	35		
4. Paragraph Comprehension	15		
5. Mathematics Knowledge	25		
6. Electronics Information	20		
7. Auto & Shop Information	25		
8. Mechanical Comprehension	25		
9. Numerical Operations	50		
10. Coding Speed	84		

* Numerical Operations and Coding Speed are included on the CAT-ASVAB and AFCT.

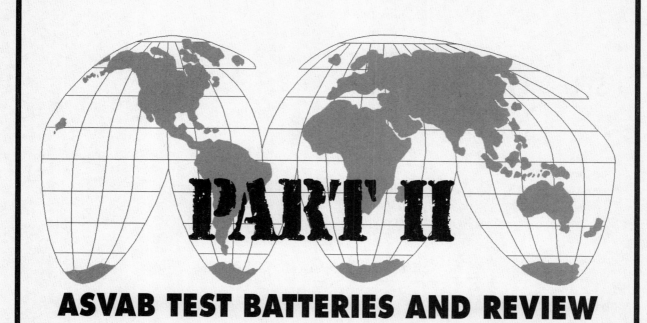

PART II

ASVAB TEST BATTERIES AND REVIEW

FIRST ASVAB SAMPLE TEST BATTERY

You are now ready to take a sample ASVAB test battery to assess your strengths and weaknesses. The scores you get on this sample battery will pinpoint the areas you need to focus on for review and extra practice.

Sample answer sheets and answer keys are included to help you determine your scores. Answer explanations are also provided to give you the reasoning behind each answer. Note that the format of this battery is the same format and content as an actual ASVAB test battery. Follow these guidelines to make the most of this sample test battery:

- Take this test under "real" test conditions (time yourself, take it in a quiet room without distractions, and use the sample answer sheets).

- Time each test carefully and do not go over the time allotted for each section.

- Use the answer keys to get your test scores and to evaluate your performance on each test.

- Record the number of items you answered correctly and incorrectly for each section in the answer chart provided at the end of the battery. Also, record the number of items you want to review further or were unsure about.

- Carefully review and understand the answer explanations to all questions you answered incorrectly.

- Don't forget to review each of the questions that you answered correctly but may not be sure of. This is a necessary step to gain the knowledge and expertise you need to get the highest scores possible on the real ASVAB tests.

- Transfer your scores for each section of the First ASVAB Sample Test Battery to the Self-Appraisal Chart appearing on page 24. This will enable you to track your progress as you continue to prepare for the actual test.

- Use the sample answer sheets provided to record your answers. If you want, you can cut them out to make them easier to use and to simulate actual test conditions.

Specimen Answer Sheet for Answering Parts 1-10
(On the following page)

Part 1: General Science

1.(A)(B)(C)(D)   2.(A)(B)(C)(D)   3.(A)(B)(C)(D)   4.(A)(B)(C)(D)   5.(A)(B)(C)(D)
6.(A)(B)(C)(D)   7.(A)(B)(C)(D)   8.(A)(B)(C)(D)   9.(A)(B)(C)(D)   10.(A)(B)(C)(D)
11.(A)(B)(C)(D)   12.(A)(B)(C)(D)   13.(A)(B)(C)(D)   14.(A)(B)(C)(D)   15.(A)(B)(C)(D)
16.(A)(B)(C)(D)   17.(A)(B)(C)(D)   18.(A)(B)(C)(D)   19.(A)(B)(C)(D)   20.(A)(B)(C)(D)
21.(A)(B)(C)(D)   22.(A)(B)(C)(D)   23.(A)(B)(C)(D)   24.(A)(B)(C)(D)   25.(A)(B)(C)(D)

Part 2: Arithmetic Reasoning

1.(A)(B)(C)(D)   2.(A)(B)(C)(D)   3.(A)(B)(C)(D)   4.(A)(B)(C)(D)   5.(A)(B)(C)(D)
6.(A)(B)(C)(D)   7.(A)(B)(C)(D)   8.(A)(B)(C)(D)   9.(A)(B)(C)(D)   10.(A)(B)(C)(D)
11.(A)(B)(C)(D)   12.(A)(B)(C)(D)   13.(A)(B)(C)(D)   14.(A)(B)(C)(D)   15.(A)(B)(C)(D)
16.(A)(B)(C)(D)   17.(A)(B)(C)(D)   18.(A)(B)(C)(D)   19.(A)(B)(C)(D)   20.(A)(B)(C)(D)
21.(A)(B)(C)(D)   22.(A)(B)(C)(D)   23.(A)(B)(C)(D)   24.(A)(B)(C)(D)   25.(A)(B)(C)(D)
26.(A)(B)(C)(D)   27.(A)(B)(C)(D)   28.(A)(B)(C)(D)   29.(A)(B)(C)(D)   30.(A)(B)(C)(D)

Part 3: Word Knowledge

1.(A)(B)(C)(D)   2.(A)(B)(C)(D)   3.(A)(B)(C)(D)   4.(A)(B)(C)(D)   5.(A)(B)(C)(D)
6.(A)(B)(C)(D)   7.(A)(B)(C)(D)   8.(A)(B)(C)(D)   9.(A)(B)(C)(D)   10.(A)(B)(C)(D)
11.(A)(B)(C)(D)   12.(A)(B)(C)(D)   13.(A)(B)(C)(D)   14.(A)(B)(C)(D)   15.(A)(B)(C)(D)
16.(A)(B)(C)(D)   17.(A)(B)(C)(D)   18.(A)(B)(C)(D)   19.(A)(B)(C)(D)   20.(A)(B)(C)(D)
21.(A)(B)(C)(D)   22.(A)(B)(C)(D)   23.(A)(B)(C)(D)   24.(A)(B)(C)(D)   25.(A)(B)(C)(D)
26.(A)(B)(C)(D)   27.(A)(B)(C)(D)   28.(A)(B)(C)(D)   29.(A)(B)(C)(D)   30.(A)(B)(C)(D)
31.(A)(B)(C)(D)   32.(A)(B)(C)(D)   33.(A)(B)(C)(D)   34.(A)(B)(C)(D)   35.(A)(B)(C)(D)

Part 4: Paragraph Comprehension

1.(A)(B)(C)(D)   2.(A)(B)(C)(D)   3.(A)(B)(C)(D)   4.(A)(B)(C)(D)   5.(A)(B)(C)(D)
6.(A)(B)(C)(D)   7.(A)(B)(C)(D)   8.(A)(B)(C)(D)   9.(A)(B)(C)(D)   10.(A)(B)(C)(D)
11.(A)(B)(C)(D)   12.(A)(B)(C)(D)   13.(A)(B)(C)(D)   14.(A)(B)(C)(D)   15.(A)(B)(C)(D)

Part 5: Mathematics Knowledge

1.Ⓐ Ⓑ Ⓒ Ⓓ   2.Ⓐ Ⓑ Ⓒ Ⓓ   3.Ⓐ Ⓑ Ⓒ Ⓓ   4.Ⓐ Ⓑ Ⓒ Ⓓ   5.Ⓐ Ⓑ Ⓒ Ⓓ
6.Ⓐ Ⓑ Ⓒ Ⓓ   7.Ⓐ Ⓑ Ⓒ Ⓓ   8.Ⓐ Ⓑ Ⓒ Ⓓ   9.Ⓐ Ⓑ Ⓒ Ⓓ   10.Ⓐ Ⓑ Ⓒ Ⓓ
11.Ⓐ Ⓑ Ⓒ Ⓓ   12.Ⓐ Ⓑ Ⓒ Ⓓ   13.Ⓐ Ⓑ Ⓒ Ⓓ   14.Ⓐ Ⓑ Ⓒ Ⓓ   15.Ⓐ Ⓑ Ⓒ Ⓓ
16.Ⓐ Ⓑ Ⓒ Ⓓ   17.Ⓐ Ⓑ Ⓒ Ⓓ   18.Ⓐ Ⓑ Ⓒ Ⓓ   19.Ⓐ Ⓑ Ⓒ Ⓓ   20.Ⓐ Ⓑ Ⓒ Ⓓ
21.Ⓐ Ⓑ Ⓒ Ⓓ   22.Ⓐ Ⓑ Ⓒ Ⓓ   23.Ⓐ Ⓑ Ⓒ Ⓓ   24.Ⓐ Ⓑ Ⓒ Ⓓ   25.Ⓐ Ⓑ Ⓒ Ⓓ

Part 6: Electronics Information

1.Ⓐ Ⓑ Ⓒ Ⓓ   2.Ⓐ Ⓑ Ⓒ Ⓓ   3.Ⓐ Ⓑ Ⓒ Ⓓ   4.Ⓐ Ⓑ Ⓒ Ⓓ   5.Ⓐ Ⓑ Ⓒ Ⓓ
6.Ⓐ Ⓑ Ⓒ Ⓓ   7.Ⓐ Ⓑ Ⓒ Ⓓ   8.Ⓐ Ⓑ Ⓒ Ⓓ   9.Ⓐ Ⓑ Ⓒ Ⓓ   10.Ⓐ Ⓑ Ⓒ Ⓓ
11.Ⓐ Ⓑ Ⓒ Ⓓ   12.Ⓐ Ⓑ Ⓒ Ⓓ   13.Ⓐ Ⓑ Ⓒ Ⓓ   14.Ⓐ Ⓑ Ⓒ Ⓓ   15.Ⓐ Ⓑ Ⓒ Ⓓ
16.Ⓐ Ⓑ Ⓒ Ⓓ   17.Ⓐ Ⓑ Ⓒ Ⓓ   18.Ⓐ Ⓑ Ⓒ Ⓓ   19.Ⓐ Ⓑ Ⓒ Ⓓ   20.Ⓐ Ⓑ Ⓒ Ⓓ

Part 7: Auto & Shop Information

1.Ⓐ Ⓑ Ⓒ Ⓓ   2.Ⓐ Ⓑ Ⓒ Ⓓ   3.Ⓐ Ⓑ Ⓒ Ⓓ   4.Ⓐ Ⓑ Ⓒ Ⓓ   5.Ⓐ Ⓑ Ⓒ Ⓓ
6.Ⓐ Ⓑ Ⓒ Ⓓ   7.Ⓐ Ⓑ Ⓒ Ⓓ   8.Ⓐ Ⓑ Ⓒ Ⓓ   9.Ⓐ Ⓑ Ⓒ Ⓓ   10.Ⓐ Ⓑ Ⓒ Ⓓ
11.Ⓐ Ⓑ Ⓒ Ⓓ   12.Ⓐ Ⓑ Ⓒ Ⓓ   13.Ⓐ Ⓑ Ⓒ Ⓓ   14.Ⓐ Ⓑ Ⓒ Ⓓ   15.Ⓐ Ⓑ Ⓒ Ⓓ
16.Ⓐ Ⓑ Ⓒ Ⓓ   17.Ⓐ Ⓑ Ⓒ Ⓓ   18.Ⓐ Ⓑ Ⓒ Ⓓ   19.Ⓐ Ⓑ Ⓒ Ⓓ   20.Ⓐ Ⓑ Ⓒ Ⓓ
21.Ⓐ Ⓑ Ⓒ Ⓓ   22.Ⓐ Ⓑ Ⓒ Ⓓ   23.Ⓐ Ⓑ Ⓒ Ⓓ   24.Ⓐ Ⓑ Ⓒ Ⓓ   25.Ⓐ Ⓑ Ⓒ Ⓓ

Part 8:Mechanical Comprehension

1.Ⓐ Ⓑ Ⓒ Ⓓ   2.Ⓐ Ⓑ Ⓒ Ⓓ   3.Ⓐ Ⓑ Ⓒ Ⓓ   4.Ⓐ Ⓑ Ⓒ Ⓓ   5.Ⓐ Ⓑ Ⓒ Ⓓ
6.Ⓐ Ⓑ Ⓒ Ⓓ   7.Ⓐ Ⓑ Ⓒ Ⓓ   8.Ⓐ Ⓑ Ⓒ Ⓓ   9.Ⓐ Ⓑ Ⓒ Ⓓ   10.Ⓐ Ⓑ Ⓒ Ⓓ
11.Ⓐ Ⓑ Ⓒ Ⓓ   12.Ⓐ Ⓑ Ⓒ Ⓓ   13.Ⓐ Ⓑ Ⓒ Ⓓ   14.Ⓐ Ⓑ Ⓒ Ⓓ   15.Ⓐ Ⓑ Ⓒ Ⓓ
16.Ⓐ Ⓑ Ⓒ Ⓓ   17.Ⓐ Ⓑ Ⓒ Ⓓ   18.Ⓐ Ⓑ Ⓒ Ⓓ   19.Ⓐ Ⓑ Ⓒ Ⓓ   20.Ⓐ Ⓑ Ⓒ Ⓓ
21.Ⓐ Ⓑ Ⓒ Ⓓ   22.Ⓐ Ⓑ Ⓒ Ⓓ   23.Ⓐ Ⓑ Ⓒ Ⓓ   24.Ⓐ Ⓑ Ⓒ Ⓓ   25.Ⓐ Ⓑ Ⓒ Ⓓ

Part 9: Numerical Operations*

1.(A)(B)(C)(D) 2.(A)(B)(C)(D) 3.(A)(B)(C)(D) 4.(A)(B)(C)(D) 5.(A)(B)(C)(D)
6.(A)(B)(C)(D) 7.(A)(B)(C)(D) 8.(A)(B)(C)(D) 9.(A)(B)(C)(D) 10.(A)(B)(C)(D)
11.(A)(B)(C)(D) 12.(A)(B)(C)(D) 13.(A)(B)(C)(D) 14.(A)(B)(C)(D) 15.(A)(B)(C)(D)
16.(A)(B)(C)(D) 17.(A)(B)(C)(D) 18.(A)(B)(C)(D) 19.(A)(B)(C)(D) 20.(A)(B)(C)(D)
21.(A)(B)(C)(D) 22.(A)(B)(C)(D) 23.(A)(B)(C)(D) 24.(A)(B)(C)(D) 25.(A)(B)(C)(D)
26.(A)(B)(C)(D) 27.(A)(B)(C)(D) 28.(A)(B)(C)(D) 29.(A)(B)(C)(D) 30.(A)(B)(C)(D)
31.(A)(B)(C)(D) 32.(A)(B)(C)(D) 33.(A)(B)(C)(D) 34.(A)(B)(C)(D) 35.(A)(B)(C)(D)
36.(A)(B)(C)(D) 37.(A)(B)(C)(D) 38.(A)(B)(C)(D) 39.(A)(B)(C)(D) 40.(A)(B)(C)(D)
41.(A)(B)(C)(D) 42.(A)(B)(C)(D) 43.(A)(B)(C)(D) 44.(A)(B)(C)(D) 45.(A)(B)(C)(D)
46.(A)(B)(C)(D) 47.(A)(B)(C)(D) 48.(A)(B)(C)(D) 49.(A)(B)(C)(D) 50.(A)(B)(C)(D)

Part 10: Coding Speed*

1.(A)(B)(C)(D) 2.(A)(B)(C)(D) 3.(A)(B)(C)(D) 4.(A)(B)(C)(D) 5.(A)(B)(C)(D)
6.(A)(B)(C)(D) 7.(A)(B)(C)(D) 8.(A)(B)(C)(D) 9.(A)(B)(C)(D) 10.(A)(B)(C)(D)
11.(A)(B)(C)(D) 12.(A)(B)(C)(D) 13.(A)(B)(C)(D) 14.(A)(B)(C)(D) 15.(A)(B)(C)(D)
16.(A)(B)(C)(D) 17.(A)(B)(C)(D) 18.(A)(B)(C)(D) 19.(A)(B)(C)(D) 20.(A)(B)(C)(D)
21.(A)(B)(C)(D) 22.(A)(B)(C)(D) 23.(A)(B)(C)(D) 24.(A)(B)(C)(D) 25.(A)(B)(C)(D)
26.(A)(B)(C)(D) 27.(A)(B)(C)(D) 28.(A)(B)(C)(D) 29.(A)(B)(C)(D) 30.(A)(B)(C)(D)
31.(A)(B)(C)(D) 32.(A)(B)(C)(D) 33.(A)(B)(C)(D) 34.(A)(B)(C)(D) 35.(A)(B)(C)(D)
36.(A)(B)(C)(D) 37.(A)(B)(C)(D) 38.(A)(B)(C)(D) 39.(A)(B)(C)(D) 40.(A)(B)(C)(D)
41.(A)(B)(C)(D) 42.(A)(B)(C)(D) 43.(A)(B)(C)(D) 44.(A)(B)(C)(D) 45.(A)(B)(C)(D)
46.(A)(B)(C)(D) 47.(A)(B)(C)(D) 48.(A)(B)(C)(D) 49.(A)(B)(C)(D) 50.(A)(B)(C)(D)
51.(A)(B)(C)(D) 52.(A)(B)(C)(D) 53.(A)(B)(C)(D) 54.(A)(B)(C)(D) 55.(A)(B)(C)(D)
56.(A)(B)(C)(D) 57.(A)(B)(C)(D) 58.(A)(B)(C)(D) 59.(A)(B)(C)(D) 60.(A)(B)(C)(D)
61.(A)(B)(C)(D) 62.(A)(B)(C)(D) 63.(A)(B)(C)(D) 64.(A)(B)(C)(D) 65.(A)(B)(C)(D)
66.(A)(B)(C)(D) 67.(A)(B)(C)(D) 68.(A)(B)(C)(D) 69.(A)(B)(C)(D) 70.(A)(B)(C)(D)
71.(A)(B)(C)(D) 72.(A)(B)(C)(D) 73.(A)(B)(C)(D) 74.(A)(B)(C)(D) 75.(A)(B)(C)(D)
76.(A)(B)(C)(D) 77.(A)(B)(C)(D) 78.(A)(B)(C)(D) 79.(A)(B)(C)(D) 80.(A)(B)(C)(D)
81.(A)(B)(C)(D) 82.(A)(B)(C)(D) 83.(A)(B)(C)(D) 84.(A)(B)(C)(D)

NOTE: These sections may be eliminated from upcoming ASVAB tests. Check with your high school guidance counselor or recruiter for details.

PART 1: GENERAL SCIENCE

Directions

This is a test of 25 questions to find out how much you know about general science as usually covered in high school courses. Pick the best answer for each question, then blacken the space that has the same number and letter as your choice.

Here are three sample questions.

S1. Water is an example of a

    S1-A   solid.

    S1-B   gas.   Ⓐ Ⓑ ● Ⓓ

    S1-C   liquid.

    S1-D   crystal.

Notice that choice C has been marked for question 1. Now do practice questions 2 and 3 by yourself. Find the correct answer to the question, then mark the space that has the same letter as the answer you picked.

S2. Lack of iodine is often related to which of the following diseases?

    S2-A   Beriberi

    S2-B   Scurvy   Ⓐ Ⓑ Ⓒ Ⓓ

    S2-C   Rickets

    S2-D   Goiter

S3. An eclipse of the sun throws the shadow of the

    S3-A   earth on the moon.

    S3-B   moon on the earth.   Ⓐ Ⓑ Ⓒ Ⓓ

    S3-C   moon on the sun.

    S3-D   earth on the sun.

You should have marked choice D for question 2 and choice B for question 3. If you made any mistakes, erase your mark carefully and blacken the correct answer space. Do this now.

Your score on this test will be based on the number of questions you answer correctly. You should try to answer every question. Do not spend too much time on any one question.

When you begin, be sure to start with question number 1 of Part 1 of your test booklet and number 1 in Part I on your answer form.

DO NOT CONTINUE UNTIL TOLD TO DO SO.

General Science

Time: 11 Minutes—25 Questions

1. Under natural conditions, large quantities of organic matter decay after each year's plant growth has been completed. As a result of such conditions
    - 1-A   many animals are deprived of adequate food supplies.
    - 1-B   soil erosion is accelerated.
    - 1-C   soils maintain their fertility.
    - 1-D   earthworms are added to the soil.

2. The thin, clear layer that forms the outer coat of the eyeball is called the
    - 2-A   pupil.
    - 2-B   iris.
    - 2-C   lens.
    - 2-D   cornea.

3. The most likely reason why dinosaurs became extinct was that they
    - 3-A   were killed by erupting volcanoes.
    - 3-B   were eaten as adults by the advancing mammalian groups.
    - 3-C   failed to adapt to a changing environment.
    - 3-D   killed each other in combat.

4. Which of the following is a chemical change?
    - 4-A   Magnetizing a rod of iron
    - 4-B   Burning one pound of coal
    - 4-C   Mixing flake graphite with oil
    - 4-D   Vaporizing one gram of mercury in a vacuum

5. In the process of manufacturing food, plants
    - 5-A   create energy.
    - 5-B   destroy energy.
    - 5-C   store energy of the sun.
    - 5-D   do not need the energy of the sun.

6. One-celled animals belong to the group of living things known as
    - 6-A   protozoa.
    - 6-B   annelida.
    - 6-C   porifera.
    - 6-D   arthropoda.

7. Spiders can be distinguished from insects by the fact that spiders have
    - 7-A   hard outer coverings.
    - 7-B   large abdomens.
    - 7-C   four pairs of legs.
    - 7-D   biting mouth parts.

8. An important ore of uranium is called
    - 8-A   hematite.
    - 8-B   chalcopyrite.
    - 8-C   bauxite.
    - 8-D   pitchblende.

9. Of the following, the lightest element known on Earth is
    - 9-A   hydrogen.
    - 9-B   oxygen.
    - 9-C   helium.
    - 9-D   air.

10. Of the following gases in the air, the most plentiful is
    - 10-A   argon.
    - 10-B   oxygen.
    - 10-C   nitrogen.
    - 10-D   carbon dioxide.

11. When two forces act on an object in the same direction, the resultant force is equal to the
    - 11-A   difference between the forces.
    - 11-B   product of the forces.
    - 11-C   ratio of the forces.
    - 11-D   sum of the forces.

12. Of the following types of clouds, the ones that occur at the greatest altitude are called
    12-A   cirrus.
    12-B   nimbus.
    12-C   cumulus.
    12-D   stratus.

13. A new drug for treatment of tuberculosis was being tested in a hospital. Patients in Group A actually received doses of the new drug; those in Group B were given only sugar pills. Group B represents
    13-A   a scientific experiment.
    13-B   a scientific method.
    13-C   an experimental error.
    13-D   an experimental control.

14. Of the following, the simple machine that provides a mechanical advantage of 1 is the
    14-A   screw.
    14-B   second-class lever.
    14-C   single fixed pulley.
    14-D   single movable pulley.

15. Radium is stored in lead containers because
    15-A   the lead absorbs the harmful radiation.
    15-B   radium is a heavy substance.
    15-C   lead prevents the disintegration of the radium.
    15-D   lead is cheap.

16. The type of joint that attaches the arm to the shoulder blade is known as a(n)
    16-A   hinge.
    16-B   pivot.
    16-C   immovable.
    16-D   ball and socket.

17. Limes were eaten by British sailors in order to
    17-A   justify their nickname, "limeys."
    17-B   pucker their mouths to resist the wind.
    17-C   satisfy their craving for something acidic.
    17-D   prevent scurvy.

18. The time that it takes for the earth to rotate 45° is
    18-A   1 hour.
    18-B   4 hours.
    18-C   3 hours.
    18-D   10 hours.

19. Of the following glands, the one that regulates the metabolic rate is the
    19-A   adrenal.
    19-B   thyroid.
    19-C   salivary.
    19-D   thymus.

20. All of the following are amphibia EXCEPT
    20-A   the salamander.
    20-B   the frog.
    20-C   the lizard.
    20-D   the toad.

21. Of the following planets, the one that has the shortest revolutionary period around the sun is
    21-A   Earth.
    21-B   Jupiter.
    21-C   Mercury.
    21-D   Venus.

22. The rate of doing work is known as
    22-A   effort.
    22-B   energy.
    22-C   mechanical advantage.
    22-D   power.

23. A circuit breaker is used in many homes instead of a
    23-A   switch.
    23-B   fire extinguisher.
    23-C   fuse.
    23-D   meter box.

24. What is the name of the negative particle that circles the nucleus of the atom?
    24-A   Neutron
    24-B   Meson
    24-C   Proton
    24-D   Electron

25. Which of the following rocks can be dissolved
     with a weak acid?

     25-A   Sandstone
     25-B   Gneiss
     25-C   Granite
     25-D   Limestone

STOP!

IF YOU FINISH BEFORE THE TIME IS UP, YOU MAY CHECK OVER YOUR WORK ON THIS PART ONLY.

PART 2: ARITHMETIC REASONING

Directions

This test has 30 questions about arithmetic. Each question is followed by four possible answers. Decide which answer is correct, then blacken the space that has the same number and letter as your choice. Use your scratch paper for any figuring you wish to do.

Here are two sample questions.

S1. A person buys a sandwich for 90¢, soda for 55¢, and pie for 70¢. What is the total cost?

S1-A	$2.00
S1-B	$2.05
S1-C	$2.15
S1-D	$2.25

Ⓐ Ⓑ Ⓒ Ⓓ

The total cost is $2.15; therefore, choice C is the correct answer.

S2. If 8 workers are needed to run 4 machines, how many workers are needed to run 20 machines?

S2-A	16
S2-B	32
S2-C	36
S2-D	40

Ⓐ Ⓑ Ⓒ Ⓓ

The number needed is 40; therefore, choice D is the correct answer.

Your score on this test will be based on the number of questions you answer correctly. You should try to answer every question. Do not spend too much time on any one question.

Notice that Part 2 begins with question number 1. When you begin, be sure to start with question number 1 in Part 2 of your test booklet and number 1 in Part 2 on your answer form.

DO NOT CONTINUE UNTIL TOLD TO DO SO.

Arithmetic Reasoning

Time: 36 Minutes—30 Questions

1. If a person invests $1,000 at an annual rate of 5%, how much interest will the person have after one year?

    1-A $20
    1-B $50
    1-C $100
    1-D $120

2. If a load of snow contains 3 tons, it will weigh how many pounds?

    2-A   3,000
    2-B   1,500
    2-C   12,000
    2-D   6,000

3. A pint of milk is what part of half a gallon?

    3-A $\dfrac{1}{8}$

    3-B $\dfrac{1}{4}$

    3-C $\dfrac{1}{2}$

    3-D $\dfrac{1}{16}$

4. At the rate of 4 peaches for a half dollar, 20 peaches will cost

    4-A $1.60
    4-B $2.00
    4-C $2.40
    4-D $2.50

5. A student deposited in his savings account the money he had saved during the week. Find the amount of his deposit if he had 10 one-dollar bills, 9 half dollars, 8 quarters, 16 dimes, and 25 nickels.

    5-A $16.20
    5-B $17.42
    5-C $18.60
    5-D $19.35

6. How many minutes are there in 1 day?

    6-A   60
    6-B   1,440
    6-C   24
    6-D   1,440 × 60

7. One year the postage rate for sending 1 ounce of mail first class was increased from 25 cents to 29 cents. The percent of increase in the 29-cent postage rate was most nearly

    7-A   14 percent
    7-B   16 percent
    7-C   18 percent
    7-D   20 percent

8. On a scale drawing, a line $\dfrac{1}{4}$ inch long represents a length of 1 foot. On the same drawing, what length represents 4 feet?

    8-A   1 inch
    8-B   2 inches
    8-C   3 inches
    8-D   4 inches

9. What is the greatest number of half-pint bottles that can be filled from a 10-gallon can of milk?

    9-A   160
    9-B   170
    9-C   16
    9-D   17

10. If 6 men can paint a fence in 2 days, how many men, working at the same uniform rate, can finish it in 1 day?

    10-A   2
    10-B   3
    10-C   12
    10-D   14

11. If 3 apples cost 48¢, how many dozen apples can be bought for $3.84?

11-A   1

11-B $1\frac{1}{2}$

11-C   2

11-D $5\frac{1}{3}$

12. How much time is there between 8:30 a.m. today and 3:15 a.m. tomorrow?

12-A $17\frac{3}{4}$ hrs.

12-B $18\frac{1}{3}$ hrs.

12-C $18\frac{1}{2}$ hrs.

12-D $18\frac{3}{4}$ hrs.

13. A clerk is asked to file 800 cards. If he can file cards at the rate of 80 cards an hour, the number of cards remaining to be filed after 7 hours of work is

13-A   140
13-B   240
13-C   250
13-D   260

14. A woman's weekly salary is increased from $350 to $380. The percent of increase is, most nearly,

14-A   6 percent

14-B $8\frac{1}{2}$ percent

14-C   10 percent

14-D $12\frac{1}{2}$ percent

15. A truck going at a rate of 20 miles an hour will reach a town 40 miles away in how many hours?

15-A   3 hours
15-B   4 hours
15-C   1 hour
15-D   2 hours

16. If a barrel has a capacity of 100 gallons, how many gallons will it contain when it is two fifths full?

16-A   20
16-B   40
16-C   60
16-D   80

17. If a salary of $20,000 is subject to a 20 percent deduction, the net salary is

17-A $14,000
17-B $15,500
17-C $16,000
17-D $18,000

18. If $2,000 is the cost of repairing 100 square yards of pavement, the cost of repairing 1 square yard is

18-A $20
18-B $100
18-C $150
18-D $200

19. A car can travel 24 miles on a gallon of gasoline. How many gallons will be used on a 192-mile trip?

19-A   8
19-B   9
19-C   10
19-D   11

20. If an annual salary of $21,600 is increased by a bonus of $720 and by a service increment of $1,200, the total annual pay is

20-A $22,320
20-B $22,800
20-C $23,320
20-D $23,520

21. A man takes out a $5,000 life insurance policy at a yearly rate of $29.62 per $1,000. What is the yearly premium?

    21-A $90.10
    21-B $100.10
    21-C $126.10
    21-D $148.10

22. On her maiden voyage, the *S.S. United States* made the trip from New York to England in 3 days, 10 hours, and 40 minutes, beating the record set by the *R.M.S. Queen Mary* in 1938 by 10 hours and 2 minutes. How long did it take the *Queen Mary* to make the trip?

    22-A   3 days, 20 hours, 42 minutes
    22-B   3 days, 15 hours, 38 minutes
    22-C   3 days, 12 hours, 2 minutes
    22-D   3 days, 8 hours, 12 minutes

23. Gary bought a shirt for $18.95. He gave the clerk $20.00. How much change should Gary get?

    23-A $2.05
    23-B $1.95
    23-C $1.05
    23-D $.05

24. John bought 20 party favors for $66.00. What was the cost of each one?

    24-A $3.35
    24-B $3.30
    24-C $2.45
    24-D $3.50

25. An inch on a map represents 200 miles. On the same map a distance of 375 miles is represented by

    25-A $1\frac{1}{2}$ inches
    25-B $1\frac{7}{8}$ inches
    25-C $2\frac{1}{4}$ inches
    25-D $2\frac{3}{4}$ inches

26. The number of half-pound packages of tea that can be made up from a box that holds $10\frac{1}{4}$ pounds of tea is

    26-A   5
    26-B $10\frac{1}{2}$
    26-C   20
    26-D $20\frac{1}{2}$

27. A pile of magazines is 4 feet high. If each magazine is $\frac{3}{4}$ of an inch thick, the number of magazines in the pile is

    27-A   36
    27-B   48
    27-C   64
    27-D   96

28. Potatoes are selling at $1.59 for a 5-pound bag. The cost for 10 pounds is

    28-A $1.59 × 10
    28-B $1.59 × 2
    28-C $1.59 × 50
    28-D $1.59 × 5 ÷ 10

29. Five girls each ate 3 cookies from a box containing 2 dozen. What part of a dozen was left?

    29-A $\frac{1}{8}$
    29-B $\frac{1}{4}$
    29-C $\frac{3}{4}$
    29-D $\frac{7}{8}$

30. A folding chair regularly sells for $29.50. How much money is saved if the chair is bought at a 20% discount?

    30-A $4.80

    30-B $5.90

    30-C $6.20

    30-D $7.40

STOP!

IF YOU FINISH BEFORE THE TIME IS UP, YOU MAY CHECK OVER YOUR WORK ON THIS PART ONLY.

PART 3: WORD KNOWLEDGE

Directions

This test has 35 questions about the meanings of words. Each question has an underlined word. You are to decide which one of the four words in the choices most nearly means the same as the underlined word, then mark the space that has the same number and letter as your choice.

Now look at the two sample questions below.

S1. <u>Mended</u> most nearly means   Ⓐ Ⓑ Ⓒ Ⓓ

    S1-A   repaired.

    S1-B   torn.

    S1-C   clean.

    S1-D   tied.

Repaired, choice A, is the correct answer. *Mended* means *fixed* or *repaired. Torn,* choice B, might be the state of an object before it is mended. The repair might be made by tying, choice D, but not necessarily. *Clean,* choice C, is wrong.

S2. It was a <u>small</u> table.   Ⓐ Ⓑ Ⓒ Ⓓ

    S1-A   Sturdy

    S2-B   Round

    S2-C   Cheap

    S2-D   Little

Little means the same as *small,* so choice D is the best one.

Your score on this test will be based on the number of questions you answer correctly. You should try to answer every question. Do not spend too much time on any one question.

When you begin, be sure to start with question number 1 in Part 3 of your test booklet and number 1 in Part 3 on your answer form.

DO NOT CONTINUE UNTIL TOLD TO DO SO.

Word Knowledge

Time: 11 Minutes—35 Questions

1. <u>Double</u> most nearly means
   - 1-A   almost.
   - 1-B   half.
   - 1-C   twice.
   - 1-D   more than.

2. <u>Purchase</u> most nearly means
   - 2-A   charge.
   - 2-B   supply.
   - 2-C   order.
   - 2-D   buy.

3. <u>Hollow</u> most nearly means
   - 3-A   empty.
   - 3-B   brittle.
   - 3-C   rough.
   - 3-D   smooth.

4. The packages were kept in a <u>secure</u> place.
   - 4-A   Distant
   - 4-B   Safe
   - 4-C   Convenient
   - 4-D   Secret

5. <u>Customary</u> most nearly means
   - 5-A   curious.
   - 5-B   necessary.
   - 5-C   difficult.
   - 5-D   common.

6. The clerk was criticized for his <u>slipshod</u> work.
   - 6-A   Slow
   - 6-B   Careful
   - 6-C   Careless
   - 6-D   Original

7. The <u>captive</u> was treated kindly.
   - 7-A   Savage
   - 7-B   Jailer
   - 7-C   Spy
   - 7-D   Prisoner

8. <u>Vegetation</u> most nearly means
   - 8-A   food.
   - 8-B   plant life.
   - 8-C   moisture.
   - 8-D   bird life.

9. <u>Fictitious</u> most nearly means
   - 9-A   imaginary.
   - 9-B   well known.
   - 9-C   odd.
   - 9-D   easy to remember.

10. The policeman <u>consoled</u> the weeping child.
    - 10-A   Found
    - 10-B   Scolded
    - 10-C   Carried home
    - 10-D   Comforted

11. The <u>preface</u> of the book was very interesting.
    - 11-A   Title page
    - 11-B   Introduction
    - 11-C   Table of contents
    - 11-D   Appendix

12. To <u>penetrate</u> most nearly means
    - 12-A   to enter into.
    - 12-B   to bounce off.
    - 12-C   to dent.
    - 12-D   to weaken.

13. <u>Villainous</u> most nearly means
    - 13-A   untidy.
    - 13-B   dignified.
    - 13-C   homely.
    - 13-D   wicked.

14. It is my <u>conviction</u> that you are wrong.
    - 14-A   Guilt
    - 14-B   Imagination
    - 14-C   Firm belief
    - 14-D   Fault

15. <u>Punctual</u> most nearly means
- 15-A   polite.
- 15-B   thoughtful.
- 15-C   proper.
- 15-D   prompt.

16. <u>Juvenile</u> most nearly means
- 16-A   delinquent.
- 16-B   lovesick.
- 16-C   youthful.
- 16-D   humorous.

17. <u>Concisely</u> most nearly means
- 17-A   accurately.
- 17-B   briefly.
- 17-C   fully.
- 17-D   officially.

18. <u>Unite</u> most nearly means
- 18-A   improve.
- 18-B   serve.
- 18-C   uphold.
- 18-D   combine.

19. The foreman <u>defended</u> the striking workers.
- 19-A   Delayed
- 19-B   Shot at
- 19-C   Protected
- 19-D   Informed on

20. The <u>aim</u> of the enlistee was to join the navy.
- 20-A   Bulls-eye
- 20-B   Goal
- 20-C   Duty
- 20-D   Promise

21. <u>Assemble</u> most nearly means
- 21-A   bring together.
- 21-B   examine carefully.
- 21-C   locate.
- 21-D   fill.

22. <u>Merchants</u> most nearly means
- 22-A   producers.
- 22-B   advertisers.
- 22-C   bankers.
- 22-D   storekeepers.

23. <u>Compel</u> most nearly means
- 23-A   tempt.
- 23-B   persuade.
- 23-C   force.
- 23-D   disable.

24. The eagle has a <u>keen</u> eye.
- 24-A   Bright
- 24-B   Shiny
- 24-C   Sharp
- 24-D   Tiny

25. <u>Startled</u> most nearly means
- 25-A   surprised.
- 25-B   chased.
- 25-C   punished.
- 25-D   arrested.

26. <u>Forthcoming</u> events are published daily.
- 26-A   Weekly
- 26-B   Interesting
- 26-C   Social
- 26-D   Approaching

27. <u>Verdict</u> most nearly means
- 27-A   approval.
- 27-B   decision.
- 27-C   sentence.
- 27-D   arrival.

28. <u>Self-sufficient</u> most nearly means
- 28-A   independent.
- 28-B   conceited.
- 28-C   stubborn.
- 28-D   clever.

29. In his hand, the hiker carried a sturdy <u>staff</u>.
- 29-A   Pack
- 29-B   Stick
- 29-C   Loaf
- 29-D   Musical instrument

30. <u>Insignificant</u> most nearly means
- 30-A   unimportant.
- 30-B   unpleasant.
- 30-C   secret.
- 30-D   thrilling.

31. <u>Acquired</u> most nearly means
    31-A   sold.
    31-B   plowed.
    31-C   desired.
    31-D   obtained.

32. <u>Exhaustion</u> most nearly means
    32-A   fear.
    32-B   overconfidence.
    32-C   extreme tiredness.
    32-D   unsteadiness.

33. The door was left <u>ajar</u>.
    33-A   Blocked
    33-B   Locked
    33-C   Unlocked
    33-D   Open

34. <u>Inferior</u> most nearly means
    34-A   noticeable.
    34-B   second-rate.
    34-C   lasting.
    34-D   excellent.

35. The hikers found several <u>crevices</u> in the rocks.
    35-A   Plants
    35-B   Uneven spots
    35-C   Cracks
    35-D   Puddles

STOP!

IF YOU FINISH BEFORE THE TIME IS UP, YOU MAY CHECK OVER YOUR WORK ON THIS PART ONLY.

PART 4: PARAGRAPH COMPREHENSION

Directions

This test contains 15 items measuring your ability to obtain information from written passages. You will find one or more paragraphs of reading material followed by incomplete statements or questions. You are to read the paragraph(s) and select the lettered choice that best completes the statement or answers the question.

Here are two sample questions.

S1. From a building designer's standpoint, three things that make a home livable are the needs of the client, the building site, and the amount of money the client has to spend.

According to the passage, to make a home livable   Ⓐ Ⓑ Ⓒ Ⓓ
- S1-A   the prospective piece of land makes little difference.
- S1-B   it can be built on any piece of land.
- S1-C   the design must fit the owner's income and site.
- S1-D   the design must fit the designer's income.

The correct answer is that the designer must fit the owner's income and site, so choice C is the correct response.

S2. In certain areas, water is so scarce that every attempt is made to conserve it. For instance, on one oasis in the Sahara Desert, the amount of water necessary for each date palm tree has been carefully determined.

How much water is each tree given?   Ⓐ Ⓑ Ⓒ Ⓓ
- S2-A   No water at all
- S2-B   Exactly the amount required
- S2-C   Water only if it is healthy
- S2-D   Water on alternate days

The correct answer is exactly the amount required, so choice B is the correct response.

Your score on this test will be based on the number of questions you answer correctly. You should try to answer every question. Do not spend too much time on any one question.

When you begin, be sure to start with question number 1 in Part 4 of your test booklet and number 1 in Part 4 on your answer form.

DO NOT CONTINUE UNTIL TOLD TO DO SO.

Paragraph Comprehension

Time: 13 Minutes—15 Questions

1. Few drivers realize that steel is used to keep the road surface flat in spite of the weight of buses and trucks. Steel bars, deeply embedded in the concrete, are sinews to take the stresses so that the stresses cannot crack the slab or make it wavy.

   The passage best supports the statement that a concrete road
   1-A   is expensive to build.
   1-B   usually cracks under heavy weights.
   1-C   looks like any other road.
   1-D   is reinforced with other material.

2. Blood pressure, the force that the blood exerts against the walls of the vessels through which it flows, is commonly meant to be the pressure in the arteries. The pressure in the arteries varies with the contraction (work period) and the relaxation (rest period) of the heart. When the heart contracts, the blood in the arteries is at its greatest, or systolic, pressure. When the heart relaxes, the blood in the arteries is at its lowest, or diastolic, pressure. The difference between these pressures is called the pulse pressure.

   According to the passage, which one of the following statements is most accurate?
   2-A   The blood in the arteries is at its greatest pressure during contraction.
   2-B   Systolic pressure measures the blood in the arteries when the heart is relaxed.
   2-C   The difference between systolic and diastolic pressure determines the blood pressure.
   2-D   Pulse pressure is the same as blood pressure.

3. More patents have been issued for inventions relating to transportation than for those in any other line of human activity. These inventions have resulted in a great financial savings to the people and have made possible a civilization that could not have existed without them.

   The one of the following that is best supported by the passage is that transportation
   3-A   would be impossible without inventions.
   3-B   is an important factor in our civilization.
   3-C   is still to be much improved.
   3-D   is more important than any other activity.

4. The Supreme Court was established by Article 3 of the Constitution. Since 1869, it has been made up of nine members—the chief justice and eight associate justices—who are appointed for life. Supreme Court justices are named by the president and must be confirmed by the Senate.

   The Supreme Court
   4-A   was established in 1869.
   4-B   consists of nine justices.
   4-C   consists of justices appointed by the Senate.
   4-D   changes with each presidential election.

5. With the exception of Earth, all of the planets in our solar system are named for gods and goddesses in Greek or Roman legends. This is because the other planets were thought to be in heaven like the gods and our planet lay beneath, like the earth.

   All the planets EXCEPT Earth
   5-A   were part of Greek and Roman legends.
   5-B   were thought to be in heaven.
   5-C   are part of the same solar system.
   5-D   were worshipped as gods.

6. Both the high school and the college should take the responsibility for preparing the student to get a job. Since the ability to write a good application letter is one of the first steps toward this goal, every teacher should be willing to do what he or she can to help the student learn to write such letters.

   The paragraph best supports the statement that
   6-A   inability to write a good letter often reduces one's job prospects.
   6-B   the major responsibility of the school is to obtain jobs for its students.
   6-C   success is largely a matter of the kind of work the student applies for first.
   6-D   every teacher should teach a course in the writing of application letters.

7. Many people think that only older men who have a great deal of experience should hold public office. These people lose sight of an important fact. Many of the founding fathers of our country were comparatively young men. Today more than ever, our country needs young, idealistic politicians.

   The best interpretation of what this author believes is that
   7-A   only experienced men should hold public office.
   7-B   only idealistic men should hold public office.
   7-C   younger men can and should take part in politics.
   7-D   young people don't like politics.

8. The X-ray has gone into business. Developed primarily to aid in diagnosing human ills, the machine now works in packing plants, in foundries, in service stations, and in a dozen ways contributes to precision and accuracy in industry.

   The X-ray
   8-A   was first developed to aid business.
   8-B   is being used to improve the functioning of industry.
   8-C   is more accurate in packing plants than in foundries.
   8-D   increases the output of such industries as service stations.

9. In large organizations, some standardized, simple, inexpensive methods of giving employees information about company policies and rules, as well as specific instructions regarding their duties, is practically essential. This is the purpose of all office manuals of whatever type.

   The paragraph best supports the statement that office manuals
   9-A   are all about the same.
   9-B   should be simple enough for the average employee to understand.
   9-C   are necessary to large organizations.
   9-D   act as constant reminders to the employee of his or her duties.

10. In the relations of man to nature, the procuring of food and shelter is fundamental. With the migration of man to various climates, ever new adjustments to the food supply and to the climate became necessary.

   According to the passage, the means by which man supplies his material needs are
   10-A   accidental.
   10-B   inadequate.
   10-C   limited.
   10-D   varied.

11. Many experiments on the effects of alcohol consumption show that alcohol decreases alertness and efficiency. It decreases self-consciousness and at the same time increases confidence and feelings of ease and relaxation. It impairs attention and judgment. It destroys fear of consequences. Usual cautions are thrown to the winds. Drivers who use alcohol tend to disregard their usual safety practices. Their reaction time slows down; normally quick reactions are not possible for them. They cannot judge the speed of their car or any other car. They become highway menaces.

   The above passage states that the drinking of alcohol makes drivers
   11-A   more alert.
   11-B   less confident.
   11-C   more efficient.
   11-D   less attentive.

12. It is reasonable to assume that drivers may overcome the bad effects of drinking by
   12-A   relying on their good driving habits to a greater extent than normally.
   12-B   waiting for the alcohol to wear off before driving.
   12-C   watching the road more carefully.
   12-D   being more cautious.

Questions 13–15 are based on the passage shown below.

Arsonists are persons who set fires deliberately. They don't look like criminals, but they cost the nation millions of dollars in property loss and sometimes loss of life. Arsonists set fires for many different reasons. Sometimes a shopkeeper sees no way out of losing his business and sets fire to it to collect the insurance. Another type of arsonist wants revenge and sets fire to the home or shop of someone he feels has treated him unfairly. Some arsonists just like the excitement of seeing the fire burn and watching the firefighters at work; arsonists of this type have even been known to help fight the fire.

13. According to the passage above, an arsonist is a person who
  13-A   intentionally sets a fire.
  13-B   enjoys watching fires.
  13-C   wants revenge.
  13-D   needs money.

14. Arsonists have been known to help fight fires because they
  14-A   felt guilty.
  14-B   enjoyed the excitement.
  14-C   wanted to earn money.
  14-D   didn't want anyone hurt.

15. According to the passage above, we may conclude that arsonists
  15-A   would make good firefighters.
  15-B   are not criminals.
  15-C   are mentally ill.
  15-D   are not all alike.

STOP!

IF YOU FINISH BEFORE THE TIME IS UP, YOU MAY CHECK OVER YOUR WORK ON THIS PART ONLY.

PART 5: MATHEMATICS KNOWLEDGE

Directions

This is a test of your ability to solve 25 general mathematical problems. You are to select the correct response from the choices given. Then mark the space on your answer form that has the same number and letter as your choice. Use the scratch paper that has been given to you to do any figuring that you wish.

Now look at the two sample problems below.

S1. If $x + 6 = 7$, then x is equal to   Ⓐ Ⓑ Ⓒ Ⓓ

     S1-A   0

     S1-B   1

     S1-C   −1

     S1-D $\dfrac{7}{6}$

The correct answer is 1, so choice B is the correct response.

S2. What is the area of this square?   Ⓐ Ⓑ Ⓒ Ⓓ

     S2-A   1 square foot

     S2-B   5 square feet

     S2-C   10 square feet

     S2-D   25 square feet

The correct answer is 25 square feet, so choice D is the correct response.

Your score on this test will be based on the number of questions you answer correctly. You should try to answer every question. Do not spend too much time on any one question.

When you are told to begin, be sure to start with question number 1 in Part 5 of your test booklet and number 1 in Part 5 on your answer form.

DO NOT CONTINUE UNTIL TOLD TO DO SO.

Mathematics Knowledge

Time: 24 Minutes—25 Questions

1. If 30 is divided by .06, the result is
   - 1-A   5
   - 1-B   50
   - 1-C   500
   - 1-D   5,000

2. 36 yards and 12 feet divided by 3 =
   - 2-A   40 feet
   - 2-B   124 feet
   - 2-C $12\frac{1}{4}$ yards
   - 2-D   12 yards

3. The cube of 4 is
   - 3-A   12
   - 3-B   32
   - 3-C   64
   - 3-D   128

4. In the formula $l = p + prt$, what does l equal when $p = 500$, $r = 20\%$, $t = 2$?
   - 4-A   10,000
   - 4-B   700
   - 4-C   8,000
   - 4-D   12,000

5. $(x + 3)(x + 3)=$
   - 5-A $x^2 + 9x + 6$
   - 5-B $x^2 + 9x + 9$
   - 5-C $x^2 + 6x + 6$
   - 5-D $x^2 + 6x + 9$

6. $2.4 \times 10^4 =$
   - 6-A   9,600
   - 6-B   2,400
   - 6-C   24,000
   - 6-D   240,000

7. $x^2 \times x^3=$
   - 7-A x^6
   - 7-B x^5
   - 7-C $2x^6$
   - 7-D $2x^5$

8.

   In the figure above, m$\angle AOB = 60°$. If O is the center of the circle, then minor arc AB is what part of the circumference of the circle?
   - 8-A $\frac{1}{2}$
   - 8-B $\frac{1}{3}$
   - 8-C $\frac{1}{6}$
   - 8-D $\frac{1}{8}$

9. In a bag there are red, green, black, and white marbles. If there are 6 red, 8 green, 4 black, and 12 white and one marble is to be selected at random, what is the probability it will be white?
   - 9-A $\frac{1}{5}$
   - 9-B $\frac{2}{5}$
   - 9-C $\frac{4}{15}$
   - 9-D $\frac{2}{15}$

10. A man has T dollars to invest; after he invests $1,000, how much money does he have remaining?

    10-A $T + 1,000$

    10-B $T - 1,000$

    10-C $1,000 - T$

    10-D $1,000T$

11. A rectangular field is 900 yards by 240 yards. What is the largest number of rectangular lots 120 yards by 60 yards that it can be divided into?

    11-A   20

    11-B   60

    11-C   30

    11-D   40

12. $\sqrt{\dfrac{9}{64} + \dfrac{16}{64}} =$

    12-A $\dfrac{5}{8}$

    12-B $\dfrac{7}{64}$

    12-C $\dfrac{5}{64}$

    12-D $\dfrac{25}{64}$

13. If $\dfrac{3}{4}$ of a class is absent and $\dfrac{2}{3}$ of those present leave the room, what fraction of the original class remains in the room?

    13-A $\dfrac{1}{24}$

    13-B $\dfrac{1}{4}$

    13-C $\dfrac{1}{12}$

    13-D $\dfrac{1}{8}$

14. If $a = 3$, then $a^a \cdot a =$

    14-A   9

    14-B   51

    14-C   18

    14-D   81

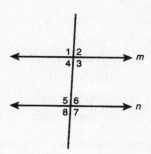

15. In the figure above, lines m and n are parallel and are cut by a transversal. If m$\angle 8 = 80°$, $\angle 3 =$

    15-A   90°

    15-B   100°

    15-C   110°

    15-D   120°

16. If $.04y = 1$, then $y =$

    16-A   .025

    16-B   25

    16-C   .25

    16-D   250

17. $(3 + 2)(6 - 2)(7 + 1) = (4 + 4)(x)$. What is the value of x?

    17-A $13 + 2$

    17-B $14 + 4$

    17-C $4 + 15$

    17-D $8 + 12$

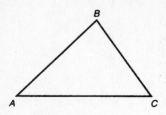

18. Triangle *ABC* is a(n)
    18-A   equilateral triangle.
    18-B   right triangle.
    18-C   scalene triangle.
    18-D   obtuse triangle.

19. From a temperature of 15°, a drop of 21° would result in a temperature of
    19-A   −36°
    19-B   36°
    19-C   −6°
    19-D   −30°

20. A certain highway intersection has had *A* accidents over a ten-year period, resulting in *B* deaths. What is the yearly average death rate for the intersection?
    20-A $A + B - 10$

    20-B $\dfrac{B}{10}$

    20-C $10 - \dfrac{A}{B}$

    20-D $\dfrac{A}{10}$

21. A cube has a volume of 27 cubic inches. What is the surface area?
    21-A   18 square inches
    21-B   36 square inches
    21-C   45 square inches
    21-D   54 square inches

22. $(10^3)^2 =$
    22-A 10^6
    22-B 10^9
    22-C 20^6
    22-D 20^9

23. The sum of the measure of the angles of a pentagon is
    23-A   540°
    23-B   720°
    23-C   900°
    23-D   1,080°

24. $8! = 8 \times 7 \times 6 \times 5 \times 4 \times 3 \times 2 \times 1$
    $4! =$
    24-A 4^4
    24-B   32
    24-C 4^2
    24-D   24

25. If *T* tons of snow fall in 1 second, how many tons fall in *M* minutes?
    25-A $60MT$
    25-B $MT + 60$
    25-C MT

    25-D $\dfrac{60M}{T}$

STOP!

IF YOU FINISH BEFORE THE TIME IS UP, YOU MAY CHECK OVER YOUR WORK ON THIS PART ONLY.

PART 6: ELECTRONICS INFORMATION

Directions

This is a test of your knowledge of electrical, radio, and electronics information. There are 20 questions. You are to select the correct response from the choices given. Then mark the space that has the same number and letter as your choice.

Now look at the two sample questions below.

S1. What does the abbreviation AC stand for?   Ⓐ Ⓑ Ⓒ Ⓓ
   S1-A   Additional charge
   S1-B   Alternating coil
   S1-C   Alternating current
   S1-D   Ampere current

The correct answer is alternating current, so choice C is the correct response.

S2. Which of the following has the least resistance?   Ⓐ Ⓑ Ⓒ Ⓓ
   S2-A   Wood
   S2-B   Silver
   S2-C   Rubber
   S2-D   Iron

The correct answer is silver, so choice B is the correct response.

Your score on this test will be based on the number of questions you answer correctly. You should try to answer every question. Do not spend too much time on any one question.

When you are told to begin, be sure to start with question number 1 in Part 6 of your test booklet and number 1 in Part 6 on your answer form.

DO NOT CONTINUE UNTIL TOLD TO DO SO.

Electronics Information

Time: 9 Minutes—20 Questions

1. The core of an electromagnet is usually
   - 1-A   aluminum.
   - 1-B   brass.
   - 1-C   lead.
   - 1-D   iron.

2. An electrician should consider all electrical equipment "alive" unless he or she definitely knows otherwise. The main reason for this practice is to avoid
   - 2-A   doing unnecessary work.
   - 2-B   energizing the wrong circuit.
   - 2-C   personal injury.
   - 2-D   de-energizing a live circuit.

3. If *voltage* is represented by V, *current* by I, and *resistance* by R, then the one of the following that correctly states Ohm's Law is
   - 3-A $R = V \times I$
   - 3-B $R = \dfrac{I}{V}$
   - 3-C $V = I \times R$
   - 3-D $V = \dfrac{I}{R}$

4. The device used to change AC to DC is a
   - 4-A   frequency changer.
   - 4-B   transformer.
   - 4-C   regulator.
   - 4-D   rectifier.

5.

The reading of the kilowatt-hour meter is
   - 5-A   9672
   - 5-B   1779
   - 5-C   2770
   - 5-D   0762

6. The device that is often used to change the voltage in alternating current circuits is the
   - 6-A   contactor.
   - 6-B   converter.
   - 6-C   rectifier.
   - 6-D   transformer.

7. Electrical contacts are opened or closed when the electrical current energizes the coils of a device called a
   - 7-A   reactor.
   - 7-B   transtat.
   - 7-C   relay.
   - 7-D   thermostat.

8. To determine directly whether finished wire installations possess resistance between conductors and ground, use
   - 8-A   clamps.
   - 8-B   set screws.
   - 8-C   shields.
   - 8-D   a megger.

9.

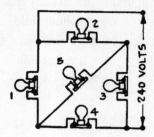

The five lamps shown are each rated at 120 volts, 60 watts. If all are good lamps, lamp 5 will be

9-A   much brighter than normal.

9-B   about its normal brightness.

9-C   much dimmer than normal.

9-D   completely dark.

10. Microfarads are units of measurement usually associated with

10-A   sockets.

10-B   switches.

10-C   capacitors.

10-D   connectors.

11. The three elements of a transistor are

11-A   collector, base, emitter.

11-B   collector, grid, cathode.

11-C   plate, grid, emitter.

11-D   plate, base, cathode.

12. Is it proper procedure to ground the frame of a portable motor?

12-A   No

12-B   No, if it is AC

12-C   Yes, unless the tool is specifically designed for use without a ground

12-D   Yes, if the operation takes place only at less than 150 volts

13. In comparing Nos. 00, 8, 12, and 6 A.W.G. wires, the smallest of the group is

13-A   No. 00

13-B   No. 8

13-C   No. 12

13-D   No. 6

14.

The convenience outlet that is known as a *polarized* outlet is number

14-A   1

14-B   2

14-C   3

14-D   4

15. In a house bell circuit, the push button for ringing the bell is generally connected in the secondary of the transformer feeding the bell. One reason for doing this is to

15-A   save power.

15-B   keep line voltage out of the push button circuit.

15-C   prevent the bell from burning out.

15-D   prevent arcing of the vibrator contact points in the bell.

16.

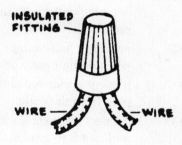

Wires are often spliced by the use of a fitting like the one shown above. The use of this fitting does away with the need for

16-A   skinning.

16-B   cleaning.

16-C   twisting.

16-D   soldering.

17. In order to control a lamp from two different positions, it is necessary to use

17-A   two single-pole switches.

17-B   one single-pole switch and one four-way switch.

17-C   two three-way switches.

17-D   one single-pole switch and two four-way switches.

18. In electronic circuits, the symbol shown below usually represents a

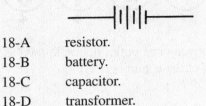

   18-A   resistor.
   18-B   battery.
   18-C   capacitor.
   18-D   transformer.

19.

The sketch shows a head-on view of a three-pronged plug used with portable electrical power tools. Considering the danger of shock when using such tools, it is evident that the function of the U-shaped prong is to

   19-A   ensure that the other two prongs enter the outlet with the proper polarity.
   19-B   provide a half-voltage connection when doing light work.
   19-C   prevent accidental pulling of the plug from the outlet.
   19-D   connect the metallic shell of the tool motor to ground.

20. A compound motor usually has
   20-A   only a shunt field.
   20-B   both a shunt and a series field.
   20-C   only a series field.
   20-D   no brushes.

STOP!

IF YOU FINISH BEFORE THE TIME IS UP, YOU MAY CHECK OVER YOUR WORK ON THIS PART ONLY.

PART 7: AUTO & SHOP INFORMATION

Directions

This test has 25 questions about automobiles, shop practices, and the use tools. Pick the best answer for each question, then blacken the space that has the same number and letter as your choice.

Here are four sample questions.

S1. The most commonly used fuel for running automobile engines is

S1-A   kerosene.   Ⓐ Ⓑ Ⓒ Ⓓ
S1-B   benzine.
S1-C   crude oil.
S1-D   gasoline.

Gasoline is the most commonly used fuel, so choice D is the correct answer.

S2. A car uses too much oil when which parts are worn?

S2-A   Pistons   Ⓐ Ⓑ Ⓒ Ⓓ
S2-B   Piston rings
S2-C   Main bearings
S2-D   Connecting rods

Worn piston rings causes the use of too much oil, so choice B is the correct answer.

S3. The saw shown below is used mainly to cut

S3-A   plywood.   Ⓐ Ⓑ Ⓒ Ⓓ
S3-B   odd-shaped holes in wood.
S3-C   along the grain of the wood.
S3-D   across the grain of the wood.

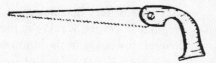

The compass saw is used to cut odd-shaped holes in wood, so choice B is the correct answer.

S4. Thin sheet metal should be cut with

S4-A   ordinary scissors.   Ⓐ Ⓑ Ⓒ Ⓓ
S4-B   a hack saw.
S4-C   tin shears.
S4-D   a jig saw.

Tin shears are used to cut thin sheet metal, so choice C is the correct answer.

Your score on this test will be based on the number of questions you answer correctly. You should try to answer every question. Do not spend too much time on any one question.

When you are told to begin, be sure to start with question number 1 in Part 7 of your test booklet and number 1 in Part 7 on your answer form.

DO NOT CONTINUE UNTIL TOLD TO DO SO.

Auto & Shop Information

Time: 11 Minutes—25 Questions

1. Most automobile engines run according to the
   1-A   rotary cycle.
   1-B   intake-exhaust cycle.
   1-C   four-stroke cycle.
   1-D   two-stroke cycle.

2. The most important rule for a driver to remember in the care of an automobile battery is to
   2-A   make certain that the points are properly adjusted in the spark plugs.
   2-B   burn the headlights or play the radio occasionally while the ignition is turned on.
   2-C   have the battery discharged at regular intervals, weekly in the winter, biweekly in the summer.
   2-D   keep the level of the liquid above the plates.

3. The function of the rotor is to
   3-A   open and close the distributor points.
   3-B   rotate the distributor cam.
   3-C   distribute electricity to the spark plugs.
   3-D   rotate the distributor shaft.

4. A governor is used on an automobile primarily to limit its
   4-A   rate of acceleration.
   4-B   maximum speed.
   4-C   fuel consumption.
   4-D   stopping distance.

5. Automobile headlights are ordinarily connected in
   5-A   parallel.
   5-B   series.
   5-C   diagonal.
   5-D   perpendicular.

6. A fuel injection system on an automobile engine eliminates the necessity for
   6-A   a manifold.
   6-B   a carburetor.
   6-C   spark plugs.
   6-D   a distributor.

7. A mechanic sets the proper electrode gap on a spark plug most accurately if he or she uses a
   7-A   dial gauge.
   7-B   round wire feeler gauge.
   7-C   square wire feeler gauge.
   7-D   conventional flat feeler gauge.

8. When reference is made to the "compression ratio" of an automotive gasoline engine, this is best described as the
   8-A   volume above the piston at top dead center.
   8-B   displacement volume as the piston moves down to bottom dead center.
   8-C   total volume of a cylinder divided by its clearance volume.
   8-D   displacement volume of a cylinder divided by its clearance volume.

9. Reverse flushing of a clogged gasoline engine block and radiator cooling system is done properly by
   9-A   not removing the thermostat from the engine block.
   9-B   connecting the flushing gun at the bottom of the engine block.
   9-C   using air and water.
   9-D   using low pressure steam.

10. Alcohol is put into the radiator of an automobile in cold weather because it

    10-A   lowers the boiling point of the mixture.

    10-B   lowers the freezing point of the mixture.

    10-C   raises the boiling point of the mixture.

    10-D   raises the freezing point of the mixture.

11. The purpose of the ignition coil in a gasoline engine is primarily to

    11-A   raise the current.

    11-B   raise the voltage.

    11-C   smooth the current.

    11-D   smooth the voltage.

12. The tool that is best suited for use with a wood chisel is

    12-A
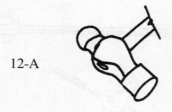

    12-B

    12-C

    12-D
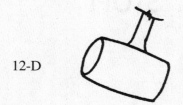

13. An expansion bolt is used to

    13-A   enlarge a hole.

    13-B   fasten into hollow tile.

    13-C   allow for expansion and contraction.

    13-D   fasten into solid masonry.

14. The length of a 10-penny nail, in inches, is

    14-A $2\frac{1}{2}$

    14-B   3

    14-C $3\frac{1}{2}$

    14-D   4

15. Glazier's points are used to

    15-A   hold glass in a wooden window sash.

    15-B   scratch glass so that it can be broken to size.

    15-C   force putty into narrow spaces between glass and sash.

    15-D   remove broken glass from a pane.

16. A wood screw that can be tightened by a wrench is known as a

    16-A   lag screw.

    16-B   carriage screw.

    16-C   Philips screw.

    16-D   monkey screw.

17. The reason that a lubricant prevents rubbing surfaces from becoming hot is that the oil

    17-A   is cold and cools off the rubbing metal surfaces.

    17-B   is sticky, preventing the surfaces from moving over each other too rapidly.

    17-C   forms a smooth layer between the two surfaces, preventing their coming into contact.

    17-D   makes the surfaces smooth so that they move easily over each other.

18. The tool shown above is used to
    18-A   set nails.
    18-B   drill holes in concrete.
    18-C   cut a brick accurately.
    18-D   centerpunch for holes.

19. Wood ladders should not be painted because
    19-A   paint will wear off rapidly due to
                the conditions under which ladders
                are used.
    19-B   ladders are slippery when painted.
    19-C   it is more effective to store the
                ladder in a dry place.
    19-D   paint will hide defects in the
                ladder.

20. The tool shown above is used to measure
    20-A   clearances.
    20-B   wire thickness.
    20-C   inside slots.
    20-D   screw pitch.

21. A lathe would normally be used in making which
    of the following items?
    21-A   A hockey stick
    21-B   A picture frame
    21-C   A bookcase
    21-D   A baseball bat

22. The term "whipping" when applied to rope means
    22-A   binding the ends with cord to
                prevent unraveling.
    22-B   coiling the rope in as tight a ball
                as possible.
    22-C   lubricating the strands with tallow.
    22-D   wetting the rope with water to
                cure it.

23. The set in the teeth of a hand saw primarily
    23-A   prevents the saw from binding.
    23-B   makes the saw cut true.
    23-C   gives the saw a sharper edge.
    23-D   removes the sawdust.

24. Lacquer thinner would most likely be used to
    24-A   clean oil paint from a brush
                immediately after use.
    24-B   rinse a new paint brush before
                using it.
    24-C   clean a paint brush upon which
                paint has hardened.
    24-D   remove paint from the hands.

25. The tool used to measure the depth of a hole is

    25-A

    25-B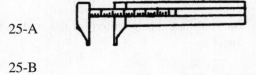

    25-C

    25-D

STOP!

IF YOU FINISH BEFORE THE TIME IS UP, YOU MAY CHECK OVER YOUR WORK ON THIS PART ONLY.

Part 8: Mechanical Comprehension

Directions

This test has 25 questions about mechanical principles. Most of the questions use drawings to illustrate specific principles. Decide which answer is correct and mark the space that has the same number and letter as your choice.

Here are two sample questions.

S1. Which bridge is the strongest? Ⓐ Ⓑ Ⓒ Ⓓ

S2. If all of these objects are the same temperature, which will feel coldest?

Ⓐ Ⓑ Ⓒ Ⓓ

A

B

C

S1-A   A
S1-B   B
S1-C   C
S1-D   All are equally strong.

Choice C is correct.

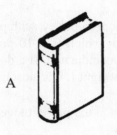
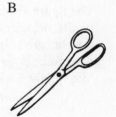

A

B

C

D

S2-A   A
S2-B   B
S2-C   C
S2-D   D

Choice B is correct.

Your score on this test will be based on the number of questions you answer correctly. You should try to answer every question. Do not spend too much time on any one question.

When you are told to begin, be sure to start with question number 1 in Part 8 of your test booklet and number 1 in Part 8 on your answer form.

DO NOT CONTINUE UNTIL TOLD TO DO SO.

Mechanical Comprehension

Time: 19 Minutes—25 Questions

1.

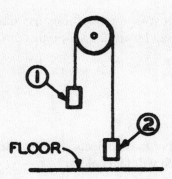

The figure above represents a pulley, with practically no friction, from which two 10-pound weights are suspended as indicated. If a downward force is applied to weight 1, it is most likely that weight 1 will

1-A   come to rest at the present level of weight 2.

1-B   move downward until it is level with weight 2.

1-C   move downward until it reaches the floor.

1-D   pass weight 2 in its downward motion and then return to its present position.

2.

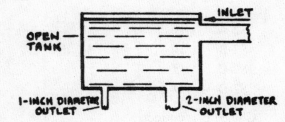

Eight gallons of water per minute are flowing at a given time from the 1-inch outlet in the tank shown. What is the amount of water flowing at that time from the 2-inch outlet?

2-A   64 gallons per minute

2-B   32 gallons per minute

2-C   16 gallons per minute

2-D   2 gallons per minute

3.

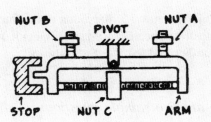

The arm in the figure above is exactly balanced as shown. If nut A is removed entirely, then, in order to rebalance the arm, it will be necessary to turn

3-A   nut C toward the right.

3-B   nut C toward the left.

3-C   nut B up.

3-D   nut B down.

4.   The purpose of an air valve in a heating system is to

4-A   prevent pressure from building up in a room due to the heated air.

4-B   relieve the air from steam radiators.

4-C   allow excessive steam pressure in the boiler to escape to the atmosphere.

4-D   control the temperature in the room.

5.

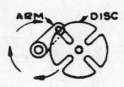

The figure above shows a slotted disc turned by a pin on a rotating arm. One revolution of the arm turns the disc

5-A $\frac{1}{4}$ turn.

5-B $\frac{1}{2}$ turn.

5-C $\frac{3}{4}$ turn.

5-D   one complete turn.

6.

The figure above shows a brass and an iron strip continuously riveted together. High temperatures would probably

6-A   have no effect at all.
6-B   bend the strips.
6-C   separate the strips.
6-D   shorten the strips.

7.

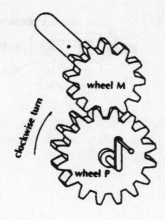

Study the gear wheels in the figure above, then determine which of the following statements is true.

7-A   If you turn wheel M clockwise by means of the handle, wheel P will also turn clockwise.

7-B   It will take the same time for a tooth of wheel P to make a full turn as it will for a tooth of wheel M.

7-C   It will take less time for a tooth of wheel P to make a full turn than it will take a tooth of wheel M.

7-D   It will take more time for a tooth of wheel P to make a full turn than it will for a tooth of wheel M.

8.

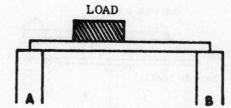

In the figure above, which upright supports the greater part of the load?

8-A   Upright A
8-B   Upright B
8-C   They support it equally
8-D   It cannot be determined

9.

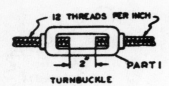

TURNBUCKLE

For the turnbuckle shown, the number of complete turns of Part 1 required to make the ends of the threaded rods meet is

9-A   6
9-B   18
9-C   12
9-D   24

10. When the 100-pound weight is being slowly hoisted up by the pulley, as shown in the figure below, the downward pull on the ceiling to which the pulley is attached is

10-A   50 pounds.
10-B   100 pounds.
10-C   150 pounds.
10-D   200 pounds.

11.

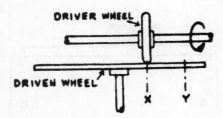

When the driver wheel is moved from location X to location Y, the driven wheel will

11-A   reverse its direction of rotation.
11-B   turn slower.
11-C   not change its speed of rotation.
11-D   turn faster.

12.

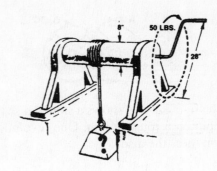

In the diagram above, the axle 8 inches in diameter has attached a handle 28 inches in diameter. If a force of 50 pounds is applied to the handle, the axle will lift a weight of

12-A   224 lbs.
12-B   175 lbs.
12-C   200 lbs.
12-D   88 lbs.

13. The main purpose of expansion joints in steam lines is to

13-A   provide for changes in length of heated pipe.
13-B   allow for connection of additional radiators.
13-C   provide locations for valves.
13-D   reduce breakage of pipe due to minor movement of the building frame.

14. What effort must be exerted to lift a 60-pound weight in the figure of a first-class lever shown below (disregard the weight of the lever in your computation)?

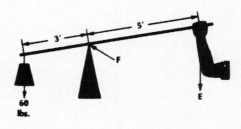

14-A   30 pounds
14-B   36 pounds
14-C   45 pounds
14-D   60 pounds

15.

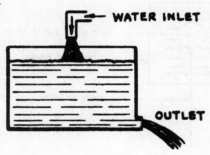

If water is flowing into the tank at the rate of 120 gallons per hour and flowing out of the tank at a constant rate of one gallon per minute, the water level in the tank will

15-A   rise one gallon per minute.

15-B   rise two gallons per minute.

15-C   fall two gallons per minute.

15-D   fall one gallon per minute.

16.

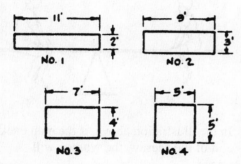

Shown are the bottoms of four bins for storing materials. If the bins are all capable of holding the same amount of any particular material, then the bin whose sides have the least height is the one whose bottom is shown as

16-A   No. 1

16-B   No. 2

16-C   No. 3

16-D   No. 4

17. If the flush tank of a toilet fixture overflows, the fault is likely to be

17-A   failure of the ball to seat properly.

17-B   excessive water pressure.

17-C   defective trap in the toilet bowl.

17-D   waterlogged float.

18.

Which pulley arrangement requires the least force at F in order to lift the weight?

18-A   A

18-B   B

18-C   C

18-D   All three require the same force.

19. In the figure below, the follower is at its highest position between points

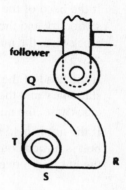

19-A   Q and R.

19-B   R and S.

19-C   S and T.

19-D   T and Q.

20.

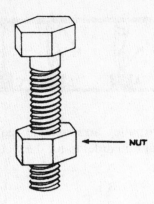

Which of the following statements is true?

20-A   If the nut is held stationary and the head turned clockwise, the bolt will move up.

20-B   If the head of the bolt is held stationary and the nut is turned clockwise, the nut will move down.

20-C   If the head of the bolt is held stationary and the nut is turned clockwise, the nut will move up.

20-D   If the nut is held stationary and the bolt is turned counterclockwise, the nut will move up.

21.

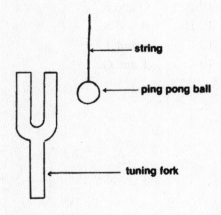

When the tuning fork is struck, the Ping-Pong ball will

21-A   remain stationary.

21-B   bounce up and down.

21-C   hit the tuning fork.

21-D   swing away from the tuning fork.

22.

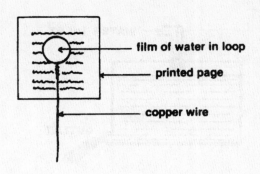

The print looked at through the film of water will

22-A   be too blurred to read.

22-B   look the same as the surrounding print.

22-C   be enlarged.

22-D   appear smaller.

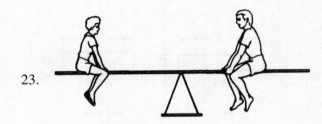

23.

In the illustration above, if the man backs to the end of the seesaw, the woman will

23-A   remain stationary.

23-B   rise in the air.

23-C   hit the ground hard.

23-D   slide to her end of the seesaw.

24. Condensation on cold water pipes is frequently prevented by

24-A   insulating the pipe.

24-B   keeping the temperature of cold water at least 10° above the freezing point.

24-C   keeping the cold water lines near the hot water lines.

24-D   oiling or greasing the outside of the pipe.

25.

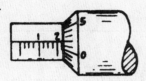

The micrometer above reads

    25-A   .2270
    25-B   .2120
    25-C   .2252
    25-D   .2020

STOP!

IF YOU FINISH BEFORE THE TIME IS UP, YOU MAY CHECK OVER YOUR WORK ON THIS PART ONLY.

PART 9: NUMERICAL OPERATIONS

NOTE: This section is not included on paper-and-pencil versions of ASVAB. It is included on the ASVAB computer-adaptive test (CAT), but may be eliminated in the near future. Check with your recruiter for details.

Directions

This is a test to see how rapidly and accurately you can do 50 simple arithmetic computations. Each problem is followed by four answers, only one of which is correct. Decide which answer is correct, then blacken the space that has the same number and letter as your choice.

Now look at the four example problems below.

S1. $3 \times 3 =$

S1-A	6
S1-B	0
S1-C	9
S1-D	1

Ⓐ Ⓑ Ⓒ Ⓓ

The answer is 9, so choice C is correct.

S3. $5 - 2 =$

S3-A	2
S3-B	3
S3-C	1
S3-D	4

Ⓐ Ⓑ Ⓒ Ⓓ

The answer is 3, so choice B is correct.

S2. $3 + 7 =$

S2-A	4
S2-B	6
S2-C	8
S2-D	10

Ⓐ Ⓑ Ⓒ Ⓓ

The answer is 10, so choice D is correct.

S4. $9 \div 3 =$

S4-A	3
S4-B	6
S4-C	9
S4-D	12

Ⓐ Ⓑ Ⓒ Ⓓ

The answer is 3, so choice A is correct.

This is a speed test, so work as fast as you can without making mistakes. Do each problem as it comes. If you finish before time is up, go back and check your work. When the signal is given, you will turn the page and begin with question 1 in Part 9 of your test booklet and answer space 1 in Part 9 of your answer form.

DO NOT CONTINUE UNTIL TOLD TO DO SO.

Numerical Operations

TIME: 3 Minutes—50 Questions

1. 5 − 3 =
    - 1-A   2
    - 1-B   6
    - 1-C   8
    - 1-D   11

2. 8 − 6 =
    - 2-A   7
    - 2-B   2
    - 2-C   12
    - 2-D   14

3. 12 ÷ 2 =
    - 3-A   10
    - 3-B   3
    - 3-C   4
    - 3-D   6

4. 4 + 6 =
    - 4-A   12
    - 4-B   10
    - 4-C   3
    - 4-D   2

5. 6 × 3 =
    - 5-A   3
    - 5-B   9
    - 5-C   12
    - 5-D   18

6. 9 + 5 =
    - 6-A   14
    - 6-B   4
    - 6-C   13
    - 6-D   16

7. 10 ÷ 5 =
    - 7-A   5
    - 7-B   15
    - 7-C   2
    - 7-D   25

8. 2 × 9 =
    - 8-A   18
    - 8-B   36
    - 8-C   16
    - 8-D   15

9. 8 + 3 =
    - 9-A   13
    - 9-B   12
    - 9-C   11
    - 9-D   15

10. 1 × 6 =
    - 10-A   5
    - 10-B   6
    - 10-C   7
    - 10-D   9

11. 7 − 2 =
    - 11-A   5
    - 11-B   9
    - 11-C   14
    - 11-D   7

12. 5 − 0 =
    - 12-A   0
    - 12-B   1
    - 12-C   5
    - 12-D   10

13. 6 × 7 =
    - 13-A   13
    - 13-B   24
    - 13-C   27
    - 13-D   42

14. 7 + 6 =
    - 14-A   11
    - 14-B   13
    - 14-C   14
    - 14-D   21

15. 8 – 5 =

    15-A   13

    15-B   11

    15-C   4

    15-D   3

16. 6 + 8 =

    16-A   2

    16-B   10

    16-C   12

    16-D   14

17. 4 × 6 =

    17-A   12

    17-B   16

    17-C   24

    17-D   28

18. 3 ÷ 3 =

    18-A   3

    18-B   1

    18-C   0

    18-D   2

19. 2 – 1 =

    19-A   2

    19-B   3

    19-C   0

    19-D   1

20. 4 × 0 =

    20-A   4

    20-B   1

    20-C   16

    20-D   0

21. 9 – 1 =

    21-A   10

    21-B   11

    21-C   9

    21-D   8

22. 4 + 8 =

    22-A   32

    22-B   24

    22-C   12

    22-D   4

23. 5 – 1 =

    23-A   4

    23-B   5

    23-C   6

    23-D   15

24. 9 ÷ 3 =

    24-A   3

    24-B   6

    24-C   9

    24-D   12

25. 4 × 6 =

    25-A   21

    25-B   24

    25-C   26

    25-D   28

26. 7 + 2 =

    26-A   3

    26-B   5

    26-C   9

    26-D   14

27. 8 – 8 =

    27-A   0

    27-B   1

    27-C   8

    27-D   16

28. 15 ÷ 3 =

    28-A   5

    28-B   3

    28-C   12

    28-D   45

29. 2 × 8 =

    29-A   6

    29-B   16

    29-C   18

    29-D   36

30. 1 + 6 =

    30-A   16

    30-B   12

    30-C   7

    30-D   6

31. 40 ÷ 8 =
   - 31-A   4
   - 31-B   5
   - 31-C   6
   - 31-D   8

32. 7 × 6 =
   - 32-A   24
   - 32-B   36
   - 32-C   42
   - 32-D   48

33. 4 + 5 =
   - 33-A   9
   - 33-B   7
   - 33-C   11
   - 33-D   1

34. 6 × 2 =
   - 34-A   8
   - 34-B   4
   - 34-C   36
   - 34-D   12

35. 10 − 8 =
   - 35-A   80
   - 35-B   18
   - 35-C   12
   - 35-D   2

36. 7 ÷ 1 =
   - 36-A   1
   - 36-B   7
   - 36-C   0
   - 36-D   8

37. 9 + 4 =
   - 37-A   11
   - 37-B   13
   - 37-C   15
   - 37-D   17

38. 3 × 8 =
   - 38-A   24
   - 38-B   32
   - 38-C   36
   - 38-D   42

39. 1 + 7 =
   - 39-A   6
   - 39-B   7
   - 39-C   8
   - 39-D   5

40. 6 × 6 =
   - 40-A   12
   - 40-B   18
   - 40-C   36
   - 40-D   66

41. 8 + 9 =
   - 41-A   15
   - 41-B   17
   - 41-C   19
   - 41-D   21

42. 1 + 3 =
   - 42-A   1
   - 42-B   2
   - 42-C   3
   - 42-D   4

43. 2 × 7 =
   - 43-A   5
   - 43-B   9
   - 43-C   12
   - 43-D   14

44. 35 ÷ 7 =
   - 44-A   12
   - 44-B   7
   - 44-C   6
   - 44-D   5

45. 10 − 9 =
   - 45-A   11
   - 45-B   19
   - 45-C   1
   - 45-D   0

46. 3 × 4 =
   - 46-A   12
   - 46-B   7
   - 46-C   5
   - 46-D   1

47. $8 - 6 =$

    47-A   2

    47-B   4

    47-C   12

    47-D   14

48. $8 \div 2 =$

    48-A   6

    48-B   16

    48-C   10

    48-D   4

49. $6 + 7 =$

    49-A   11

    49-B   13

    49-C   15

    49-D   9

50. $9 \div 1 =$

    50-A   8

    50-B   9

    50-C   10

    50-D   11

STOP!

IF YOU FINISH BEFORE THE TIME IS UP, YOU MAY CHECK OVER YOUR WORK ON THIS PART ONLY.

PART 10: CODING SPEED

NOTE: This section is not included on the paper-and-pencil version of the ASVAB. It is included on the ASVAB computer-adaptive test (CAT), but may be eliminated in the near future. Check with your recruiter for details.

Directions

This is a test of 84 items to see how quickly and accurately you can find a number in a table. At the top of each section, there is a number table or "key." The key is a group of words with a code number for each word.

Each question in the test is a word taken from the key at the top. From among the possible answers listed for each question, find the one that is the correct code number for that word.

Look at the sample key and answer the five sample questions below. Note that each of the questions is one of the words in the key. To the right of each question are possible answers listed under the options A, B, C, D, and E.

Sample Questions

Key

| green .... 2715 | man .... 3451 | salt .... 4586 |
| hat .... 1413 | room .... 2864 | tree .... 5972 |

Questions		**Options**				
		A	**B**	**C**	**D**	**E**
S-1.	room	1413	2715	2864	3451	4586
S-2.	green	2715	2864	3451	4586	5972
S-3.	tree	2715	2864	3451	4586	5972
S-4.	hat	1413	2715	2864	3451	4586
S-5.	room	1413	2864	3451	4586	5972

By looking at the key you see that the code number for the first word, "room," is 2864. 2864 is listed under the letter (C), so (C) is the correct answer. The correct answers for the other four questions are (A), (E), (A), and (B).

This is a speed test, so work as fast as you can without making mistakes.

Notice that Part 10 begins at the top of the next answer form. When you begin, be sure to start with question number 1 in Part 10 of your test booklet and number 1 in Part 10 on your answer form.

DO NOT CONTINUE UNTIL TOLD TO DO SO.

Coding Speed

Time: 7 Minutes—84 Questions

Key

bird 7011	egg 1237	jury 2912
pump 3061	stump 8956	car 6300
ghost 9212	maroon 5873	rat 4643
window 6766		

Questions				Options		
		A	**B**	**C**	**D**	**E**
1.	maroon	4643	5873	6766	8956	9212
2.	window	1237	2912	4643	6766	8956
3.	jury	2912	3061	5873	6300	7011
4.	rat	1237	3061	4643	6300	6766
5.	ghost	2912	4643	5873	8956	9212
6.	bird	3061	4643	6300	6766	7011
7.	stump	5873	6300	6766	7011	8956
8.	car	1237	3061	6300	6766	9212
9.	egg	1237	2912	3061	5873	8956
10.	pump	2912	3061	4643	6300	6766
11.	window	3061	6300	6766	7011	9212
12.	rat	3061	4643	5873	6766	8956

Key

blue	5913	dust	9009	hat	8884
money	8648	toe	7277	clown	3761
food	1238	lamp	2212	roast	4650
wish	6702				

Questions		Options				
		A	**B**	**C**	**D**	**E**
13.	clown	1238	2212	3761	8884	9009
14.	wish	3761	4650	5913	6702	7277
15.	roast	2212	4650	6702	8648	8884
16.	blue	1238	2212	3761	4650	5913
17.	roast	1238	3761	4650	7277	8884
18.	dust	3761	5913	6702	8648	9009
19.	food	1238	2212	4650	6702	8648
20.	toe	4650	5913	6702	7277	8884
21.	lamp	2212	3761	6702	8648	8884
22.	money	4650	5913	8648	8884	9009
23.	clown	3761	4650	6702	7277	9009
24.	hat	1238	2212	5913	8648	8884

Key

ant	4848	drama	1981	house	2345
note	3689	tree	8864	bus	9735
fog	6848	laugh	5005	queen	7512
zoo	4584				

Questions		Options				
		A	**B**	**C**	**D**	**E**
25.	laugh	2345	4584	4848	5005	8864
26.	queen	1981	2345	3689	6848	7512
27.	ant	2345	4584	4848	6848	8864
28.	drama	1981	2345	3689	7512	9735
29.	note	1981	3689	4584	8864	9735
30.	fog	3689	4584	4848	6848	8864
31.	tree	4584	4848	6848	8864	9735
32.	bus	1981	2345	3689	7512	9735
33.	house	2345	3689	4584	5005	7512
34.	zoo	2345	4584	4848	6848	8864
35.	note	3689	4848	5005	7512	9735
36.	laugh	2345	3689	5005	6848	7512

Key

art 1066	down 5974	hood 7877
pants 2468	spoon...................... 9060	clue 3682
flower 4003	ice 8880	silence 6969
taxi 1001		

Questions — Options

		A	B	C	D	E
37.	silence	3682	4003	6969	8880	9060
38.	hood	1066	4003	5974	7877	9060
39.	pants	1001	2468	3682	4003	6969
40.	clue	3682	4003	6969	8880	9060
41.	art	1001	1066	4003	7877	8880
42.	down	2468	4003	5974	6969	7877
43.	ice	1001	1066	4003	8880	9060
44.	flower	4003	5974	6969	7877	8880
45.	spoon	2468	3682	6969	8880	9060
46.	down	1066	3682	4003	5974	6969
47.	hood	1001	2468	6969	7877	9060
48.	taxi	1001	1066	4003	8880	9060

Key

angel 7717	eye 6943	gown...................... 3232
joke 8614	nut 9089	brick 1492
flood 5846	ink 4921	llama...................... 2573
red 5487		

Questions — Options

		A	B	C	D	E
49.	flood	1492	4921	5487	5846	6943
50.	gown	2573	3232	6943	8614	9089
51.	joke	1492	4921	5846	7717	8614
52.	nut	1492	2573	3232	8614	9089
53.	angel	2573	4921	6943	7717	8614
54.	ink	1492	4921	6943	7715	8614
55.	red	1492	4912	5487	5846	6943
56.	eye	4921	6943	7717	8614	9089
57.	brick	1492	4912	5846	6943	8614
58.	llama	2573	3232	4921	6943	9089
59.	eye	1492	2573	3232	5846	6943
60.	ink	2573	3232	4921	7717	8614

Key

apple	6080	cone	1787	drum	5489
frown	8932	shoe	9890	bud	2722
devil	4598	ear	3343	roof	7503
train	4672				

Questions		Options				
		A	**B**	**C**	**D**	**E**
61.	devil	4598	4672	5489	8932	9890
62.	ear	1787	2722	3343	5489	6080
63.	frown	2722	4598	5489	7503	8932
64.	drum	3343	4598	4672	5489	9890
65.	bud	1787	2722	4672	6080	7503
66.	roof	1787	2722	5489	7503	8932
67.	train	4598	4672	5489	6080	8932
68.	cone	1787	3343	4598	5489	9890
69.	apple	2722	5489	6080	7503	9890
70.	bud	1787	2722	3343	4598	8932
71.	drum	2722	4598	5489	6080	7503
72.	frown	1787	3343	5489	8932	9890

Key

arch	2641	coin	9559	fuzz	4769
hair	6931	puzzle	8724	battle	1686
dress	5959	green	3480	mud	7777
stew	4162				

Questions		Options				
		A	**B**	**C**	**D**	**E**
73.	puzzle	1686	4769	6931	8724	9559
74.	fuzz	2641	3480	4162	4769	5959
75.	stew	2641	4162	6931	7777	8724
76.	battle	1686	2641	4162	6931	8724
77.	mud	3480	4769	5959	7777	9559
78.	green	1686	3480	4162	6931	8724
79.	coin	2641	4162	5959	7777	9559
80.	arch	2641	4162	4769	6931	8724
81.	dress	1686	4769	5959	8724	9559
82.	hair	4162	4769	5959	6931	7777
83.	puzzle	1686	4162	6931	7777	8724
84.	dress	2641	3480	4162	4769	5959

ANSWER KEY

Use these Answer Keys to determine how many questions you got right on each subject test and to write down the question numbers of those you got wrong or that you are not sure how to answer.

Carefully review and understand the reasoning for each answer, whether you answered it correctly or incorrectly. Note that it is just as important to understand the reasoning for the questions you answered correctly but are unsure of. This will help you gain the knowledge and expertise you need to get the highest score you can on the actual ASVAB tests.

Transfer your scores from each part of the First ASVAB Specimen Test Battery to the Self-Appraisal Chart appearing on page 24. You will be able to see the progress you make as you continue to prepare for the actual test.

Part 1: General Science

Answer Key				
1. C	2. D	3. C	4. B	5. C
6. A	7. C	8. D	9. A	10. C
11. D	12. A	13. D	14. C	15. A
16. D	17. D	18. C	19. B	20. C
21. C	22. D	23. C	24. D	25. D

Items Answered

Incorrectly: ____ ; ____ ; ____ ; ____ ; ____ ; ____ ; ____ ; ____ .

Items Unsure Of: ____ ; ____ ; ____ ; ____ ; ____ ; ____ ; ____ ; ____ .

Total Number Answered Correctly: _____

Part 2: Arithmetic Reasoning

Answer Key				
1. B	2. D	3. B	4. D	5. D
6. B	7. B	8. A	9. A	10. C
11. C	12. D	13. B	14. B	15. D
16. B	17. C	18. A	19. A	20. D
21. D	22. A	23. C	24. B	25. B
26. D	27. C	28. B	29. C	30. B

Items Answered

Incorrectly: _____; _____; _____; _____; _____; _____; _____; _____.

Items Unsure Of: _____; _____; _____; _____; _____; _____; _____; _____.

Total Number Answered Correctly: _____

Part 3: Word Knowledge

Answer Key				
1. C	2. D	3. A	4. B	5. D
6. C	7. D	8. B	9. A	10. D
11. B	12. A	13. D	14. C	15. D
16. C	17. B	18. D	19. C	20. B
21. A	22. D	23. C	24. C	25. A
26. D	27. B	28. A	29. B	30. A
31. D	32. C	33. D	34. B	35. C

Items Answered

Incorrectly: _____; _____; _____; _____; _____; _____; _____; _____.

Items Unsure Of: _____; _____; _____; _____; _____; _____; _____; _____.

Total Number Answered Correctly: _____

Part 4: Paragraph Comprehension

Answer Key				
1. D	2. A	3. B	4. B	5. B
6. A	7. C	8. B	9. C	10. D
11. D	12. B	13. A	14. B	15. D

Items Answered

Incorrectly: _____; _____ ; _____; _____ ; _____; _____ ; _____; _____.

Items Unsure Of: _____ ; _____; _____ ; _____; _____ ; _____ ; _____; _____ .

Total Number Answered Correctly: _____

Part 5: Mathematics Knowledge

Answer key				
1. C	2. A	3. C	4. B	5. D
6. C	7. B	8. C	9. B	10. B
11. C	12. A	13. C	14. D	15. B
16. B	17. D	18. C	19. C	20. B
21. D	22. A	23. A	24. D	25. A

Items Answered

Incorrectly: _____; _____ ; _____; _____ ; _____; _____ ; _____; _____.

Items Unsure Of: _____ ; _____; _____ ; _____; _____ ; _____ ; _____; _____ .

Total Number Answered Correctly: _____

Part 6: Electronics Information

Answer Key				
1. D	2. C	3. C	4. D	5. A
6. D	7. C	8. D	9. D	10. C
11. A	12. C	13. C	14. A	15. B
16. D	17. C	18. B	19. D	20. B

Items Answered

Incorrectly: _____ ; _____ ; _____ ; _____ ; _____ ; _____ ; _____ ; _____ .

Items Unsure Of: _____ ; _____ ; _____ ; _____ ; _____ ; _____ ; _____ ; _____ .

Total Number Answered Correctly: _____

Part 7: Auto & Shop Information

Answer Key				
1. C	2. D	3. C	4. B	5. A
6. B	7. B	8. C	9. C	10. B
11. B	12. D	13. D	14. B	15. A
16. A	17. C	18. B	19. D	20. D
21. D	22. A	23. A	24. C	25. C

Items Answered

Incorrectly: _____ ; _____ ; _____ ; _____ ; _____ ; _____ ; _____ ; _____ .

Items Unsure Of: _____ ; _____ ; _____ ; _____ ; _____ ; _____ ; _____ ; _____ .

Total Number Answered Correctly: _____

Part 8: Mechanical Comprehension

Answer Key				
1. C	2. B	3. A	4. B	5. A
6. B	7. D	8. A	9. C	10. C
11. B	12. B	13. A	14. B	15. A
16. C	17. D	18. A	19. A	20. B
21. D	22. C	23. B	24. A	25. A

Items Answered

Incorrectly: ____; ____; ____; ____; ____; ____; ____; ____.

Items Unsure Of: ____; ____; ____; ____; ____; ____; ____; ____.

Total Number Answered Correctly: _____

Part 9: Numerical Operations

Answer Key				
1. A	2. B	3. D	4. B	5. D
6. A	7. C	8. A	9. C	10. B
11. A	12. C	13. D	14. B	15. D
16. D	17. C	18. B	19. D	20. D
21. D	22. C	23. A	24. A	25. B
26. C	27. A	28. A	29. B	30. C
31. B	32. C	33. A	34. D	35. D
36. B	37. B	38. A	39. C	40. C
41. B	42. D	43. D	44. D	45. C
46. A	47. A	48. D	49. B	50. B

Items Answered

Incorrectly: ____; ____; ____; ____; ____; ____; ____; ____.

Items Unsure Of: ____; ____; ____; ____; ____; ____; ____; ____.

Total Number Answered Correctly: _____

Part 10: Coding Speed

Answer Key				
1. B	2. D	3. A	4. C	5. E
6. E	7. E	8. C	9. A	10. B
11. C	12. B	13. C	14. D	15. B
16. E	17. C	18. E	19. A	20. D
21. A	22. C	23. A	24. E	25. D
26. E	27. C	28. A	29. B	30. D
31. D	32. E	33. A	34. B	35. A
36. C	37. C	38. D	39. B	40. A
41. B	42. C	43. D	44. A	45. E
46. D	47. D	48. A	49. D	50. B
51. E	52. E	53. D	54. B	55. C
56. B	57. A	58. A	59. E	60. C
61. A	62. C	63. E	64. D	65. B
66. D	67. B	68. A	69. C	70. B
71. C	72. D	73. D	74. D	75. B
76. A	77. D	78. B	79. E	80. A
81. C	82. D	83. E	84. E	

Items Answered

Incorrectly: _____; _____; _____; _____; _____; _____; _____; _____.

Items Unsure Of: _____; _____; _____; _____; _____; _____; _____; _____.

Total Number Answered Correctly: _____

NOTE: Sections 9 and 10 are not included on the paper-and-pencil version of the ASVAB. It is included on the ASVAB computer-adaptive test (CAT), but may be eliminated in the near future. Check with your guidance counselor or recruiter for details.

ANSWER EXPLANATIONS

Part 1: General Science

1-C   When organic matter decays, it decomposes into its constituent elements. These elements are returned to the soil, thus increasing its fertility.

2-D   The cornea, a transparent tissue, forms the outercoat of the eyeball covering the iris and pupil.

3-C   The extinction of all sizes and varieties of dinosaurs all over the world can be explained neither by local phenomena nor on a one-by-one basis. The most reasonable assumption is that the dinosaurs failed to adapt and were unable to survive as climatic conditions changed radically.

4-B   Combustion is a chemical process.

5-C   Plants use the energy of the sun to manufacture food.

6-A   Protozoa are one-celled animals. Annelida are worms; porifera are sponges; arthropoda are spiders and crustaceans.

7-C   All spiders have four pairs of legs. True insects have three pairs of legs.

8-D   Uranium is found in pitchblende and other rare metals. Hematite is a source of iron; chalcopyrite is an ore of copper; and bauxite is a source of aluminum.

9-A   The atomic weight of hydrogen is 1.0080, that of helium 4.003, and of oxygen 16.00. Air is not an element, but a mixture of gases.

10-C   Nitrogen constitutes about four fifths of the atmosphere by volume.

11-D   When two forces act in the same direction, the resultant force is equal to the sum of the two forces.

12-A   Cirrus clouds occur at 20,000–40,000 feet and are made up of ice crystals. Nimbus clouds are gray rain clouds; cumulus clouds are fluffy white clouds; and stratus clouds are long, low clouds, generally at altitudes of 2,000–7,000 feet.

13-D   Group B served as the control group. If the condition of patients in Group A were to improve significantly more than that of patients in Group B, scientists might have reason to believe in the effectiveness of the drug.

14-C   A fixed pulley and rope provide a mechanical advantage of one.

15-A   Radiation cannot pass through lead.

16-D   Ball-and-socket joints permit movement in almost all directions.

17-D   Scurvy is a disease caused by a vitamin C deficiency. Limes are rich in vitamin C.

18-C   The earth rotates 360° in 24 hours; therefore, it rotates 45° in 3 hours.

19-B   The thyroid gland regulates the metabolic rate. The adrenal glands secrete hormones that regulate one's reaction to emergencies, among other things. Salivary glands secrete oral saliva. The thymus gland influences growth and development.

20-C   A lizard is a reptile.

21-C   Mercury is closest to the sun; therefore, it has the shortest revolutionary period around the sun.

22-D   Power is the rate or speed of doing work.

23-C   Circuit breakers serve exactly the same function as fuses. Should wires become over heated for any reason, the circuit breaker will "trip," thus breaking the circuit and inter rupting the flow of electricity. Fuse burnout creates the same protective interruption of current.

24-D   An electron is a negative particle. A proton is positively charged; a neutron is neutral and without charge; a meson has both positive and negative charges.

25-D   Limestone, a sedimentary rock composed of calcium carbonate, can be dissolved with a weak acid.

Part 2: Arithmetic Reasoning

1-B   Interest = Principal × Rate

$1,000 × 5% = $1,000 × .05 = $50

2-D   1 ton = 2,000 lbs.;

3 × 2,000 lbs. = 6,000 lbs.

3-B   There are 8 pts. in 1 gal.; therefore, there are 4 pts. in

$\frac{1}{2}$ gal.; 1 pt. $= \frac{1}{4}$ of $\frac{1}{2}$ gal.

4-D   20 peaches are 5 × 4 peaches; 4 peaches cost $.50; 5 × $.50 = $2.50

5-D
$$10 \times \$1.00 = \$10.00$$
$$9 \times \quad .50 = \quad 4.50$$
$$8 \times \quad .25 = \quad 2.00$$
$$16 \times \quad .10 = \quad 1.60$$
$$25 \times \quad .05 = \quad 1.25$$
$$\overline{\quad\quad\quad\quad \$19.35}$$

6-B   60 minutes in one hour; 24 hours in one day; 60 × 24 = 1,440 minutes.

7-B   To find the percent of increase, subtract the original figure from the new figure. Then divide the amount of change by the original figure. 29¢ − 25¢ = 4¢; 4 ÷ 25 = .16 = 16%

8-A $4 \times \frac{1}{4}$ inch = 1 inch

9-A   8 pts. in 1 gal.; 80 pts. in 10 gal.; $160\frac{1}{2}$ pts. in 10 gal.

10-C Common sense will tell you that twice as many men will paint the fence in half the time.

11-C 3 apples cost 48¢, so one apple costs 48 ÷ 3 = 16¢. $3.84 ÷ 16 = 24 apples; 24 = 2 dozen.

12-D

From 8:30 a.m.	12:00 =	11:60
until noon today:	-8:30 =	8:30
		3 hrs. 30 min.
From noon till midnight:		+12 hrs.
From midnight until 3:15 a.m.:		3 hrs. 15 min.
Total time:		18 hours. 45 min.

$$=18\frac{3}{4} \text{ hrs.}$$

13-B 80 cards × 7 hours = 560 cards filed; 800 − 560 = 240 cards remaining.

14-B To find percent of increase, subtract the original figure from the new figure. Then divide the amount of change by the original figure. $380 − $350 = $30; $30 ÷ $350 = .0857 (which is approximately $8\frac{1}{2}\%$).

15-D 40 miles ÷ 20 mph = 2 hrs.

16-B $\dfrac{2}{\cancel{5}} \times \dfrac{\overset{20}{\cancel{100}}}{1} = 40$ gal.

17-C If 20% is deducted, the net salary is 80%. $20,000 × 80% = $20,000 × .80 = $16,000.

18-A $2,000 ÷ 100 = $20

19-A 192 ÷ 24 = 8 gal.

20-D $21,600 + $720 + $1,200 = $23,520

21-D $29.62 × 5 = $148.10

22-A

3 days	10 hrs. 40 min.
	+ 10 hrs. 2 min.
3 days	20 hrs. 42 min.

23-C $20.00 − $18.95 = $1.05

24-B $66.00 ÷ 20 = $3.30

25-B 1 : 200 = x : 375; 200x = 375;

$$x = 375 \div 200 = 1.875 = 1\frac{7}{8} \text{ inches.}$$

26-D $10\frac{1}{4}$ lbs. $\div \frac{1}{2} = \frac{41}{4} \times \frac{2}{1} = 20\frac{1}{2}$ boxes

27-C   4 feet = 48 inches;

$$48 \div \frac{3}{4} = \frac{48}{1} \times \frac{4}{3} = 64 \text{ magazines}$$

28-B   10 pounds = 2×5 pounds, so the cost of 10 pounds is 2 times the cost of 5 pounds.

29-C   There were $2 \times 12 = 24$ cookies. The girls ate $5 \times 3 = 15$ cookies. Therefore, $24 - 15 = 9$

cookies left; $9 = \frac{3}{4}$ dozen.

30-B $\$29.50 \times 20\% = \$29.50 \times .20 = \$5.90$ saved.

Part 3: Word Knowledge

1-C   *Double* means *twofold* or *twice* as much.

2-D   To *purchase* is to *buy* for a price.

3-A   *Hollow* means *empty*.

4-B   *Secure* means *safe,* as in *not exposed to danger.*

5-D   That which is *customary* is *habitual* or established by *common* usage.

6-C   *Slipshod* means *exceedingly slovenly* or *careless.*

7-D   The *captive* is the one who was *captured* and made *prisoner*, regardless of the reason for his capture.

8-B   The term *vegetation* includes all *plant* life.

9-A   *Fictitious* means *imaginary.*

10-D   To *console* is to *comfort.*

11-B   A *preface* is an *introduction.*

12-A   To *penetrate* is to *enter into* or *to pierce.*

13-D   *Villainous* means *wicked* or *evil.*

14-C   One who has a *conviction* is *fully convinced*, and so holds a *firm belief.*

15-D   *Punctual* means *prompt* or *on time.*

16-C   *Juvenile* means *youthful, young,* or *immature.*

17-B   *Concisely* means *briefly*. The word that means "accurately" is "precisely."

18-D   To *unite* is to *put together*, to *combine*, or to *join.*

19-C   To *defend* is to *protect* from harm, verbal or bodily.

20-B   An *aim* is an *intention* or *goal*. To aim is to direct toward the goal.

21-A   To *assemble* is to *congregate,* to *convene*, or to *bring together.*

22-D A *merchant* is one who *sells goods*. A merchant who sells goods from a retail store is a storekeeper.

23-C To *compel* is to *require*, to *coerce*, or to *force*. Compel is a much stronger word than persuade.

24-C *Keen* means *acute, sensitive,* or *sharp*.

25-A *Startled* means *frightened suddenly*, though not seriously, hence *surprised*.

26-D *Forthcoming* means *coming up* or *approaching*.

27-B A *verdict* is a *decision* or *judgment*.

28-A One who is *self-sufficient* is able to accomplish his or her own aims without external aid, and so is *independent*.

29-B The *staff* carried by a hiker is a *stick*. In music, a staff is the horizontal lines and spaces on which music is written.

30-A *Insignificant* means *meaningless* or *unimportant*. The prefix in means *not*, so the word literally means *not significant*.

31-D To *acquire* is to *get* or to *obtain* by any means.

32-C *Exhaustion* is the *using up of energy or resources, extreme tiredness* or *fatigue*.

33-D *Ajar* means *open*.

34-B *Inferior* means of *lower* or *lesser quality, rank,* or *value,* in short, *second-rate*.

35-C A *crevice* is a narrow *opening* or *crack*.

Part 4: Paragraph Comprehension

1-D The first three options are not supported by the passage. The second sentence in the passage states that steel bars, deeply embedded in the concrete, are sinews (a source of strength) to take the stresses.

2-A The third sentence in the passage states that when the heart contracts, the blood in the arteries is at its greatest pressure.

3-B The second sentence states that inventions relating to transportation have made possible a civilization that could not have existed without them. This supports the correct answer—transportation is an important factor in our civilization.

4-B One chief justice plus eight associate justices equals nine justices.

5-B The second sentence states that the other planets were thought to be in heaven.

6-A Step one in the job application process is often the application letter. If the letter is not effective, the applicant will not move on to the next step, and job prospects will be greatly lessened.

7-C The last sentence states that the country needs young, idealistic politicians.

8-B The passage states that the X-ray machine "contributes to precision and accuracy in industry."

9-C The passage states that office manuals are a necessity in large organizations.

10-D The first three options are not supported by the passage. The correct answer is supported by the second sentence, which states, "With the migration of man to various climates, ever new adjustments to the food supply and to the climate became necessary."

11-D The first three options are not supported by the passage. The third sentence in the passage states that the drinking of alcohol impairs attention—making the driver less attentive.

12-B Drinking alcohol causes harmful effects on the driver. The implication is that these effects do not last forever but wear off in time.

13-A The first sentence in the passage states that arsonists set fires deliberately or intentionally.

14-B The last sentence in the passage states that some arsonists just like the excitement of seeing the fire burn and watching the firefighters at work and even helping fight the fire.

15-D The first three options are not supported by the passage. Different types of arsonists mentioned in the passage leads to the conclusion that arsonists are not all alike.

Part 5: Mathematics Knowledge

1-C When dividing by a decimal, move the decimal place in the divisor to the right to create a whole number. Move the decimal point in the dividend to the right the same number of places. Place the decimal point of the quotient directly above the decimal point of the dividend.

$$.06\overline{)30.00} = 500.$$

2-A 36 yards = 108 feet; 108 feet + 12 feet = 120 feet; 120 feet ÷ 3 = 40 feet

3-C $4 \times 4 \times 4 = 64$

4-B $I = 500 + (500 \times .20 \times 2)$

$I = 500 + 200$

$I = 700$

5-D $(x + 3)(x + 3) =$

$$\begin{array}{r} x+3 \\ \times\ \underline{x+3} \\ x^2+3x \\ \underline{+3x+9} \\ x^2+6x+9 \end{array}$$

6-C $2.4 \times 10^4 = 2.4 \times 10,000 = 24,000$

7-B The product of two powers with the same base can be calculated by keeping the base and adding the exponents.

8-C A circle is 360°; 60° is $\frac{1}{6}$ of 360°

9-B   There are $6 + 8 + 4 + 12 = 30$ marbles. $12 \div 30 = .40 = \dfrac{2}{5}$

10-B   If the man uses $1,000 of his T dollars, he has $T - \$1,000$ remaining.

11-C   The field is 900 yds. × 240 yds. = 216,000 sq. yds.

       Each lot is 120 yds. × 60 yds. = 7,200 sq. yds. $216,000 \div 7,200 = 30$ lots

12-A $\sqrt{\dfrac{9}{64} + \dfrac{16}{64}} = \sqrt{\dfrac{25}{64}} = \dfrac{5}{8}$

13-C   If $\dfrac{3}{4}$ are absent, $\dfrac{1}{4}$ are present. If $\dfrac{2}{3}$ of the $\dfrac{1}{4}$ present leave, $\dfrac{1}{3}$ of the $\dfrac{1}{4}$ remain.

       $\dfrac{1}{3} \times \dfrac{1}{4} = \dfrac{1}{12}$ remain in the room.

14-D $3^3 \times 3 = 27 \times 3 = 81$

15-B $\angle 8$ and $\angle 4$ are corresponding angles formed by parallel lines.

       $m\angle 4 = 80°$

       $\angle 3$ and $\angle 4$ are supplementary angles.

       $m\angle 3 = 180 - 80 = 100°$

16-B $.04y = 1$

       $y = 1 \div .04 = 250$

17-D $(3+2)(6-2)(7+1) = (4+4)(x)$

           $(5)(4)(8) = 8x$

              $8x = 160$

                $x = 20 = 8 + 12$

18-C   A triangle with no side of the same length is called scalene.

19-C $15° - 21° = -6°$

20-B   The number of accidents is irrelevant to the question, so A has no place in the equation. B

       (total deaths) × 10 years $= \dfrac{B}{10}$ average deaths per year.

21-D   The cube has 3 edges 3 inches long. Area of one side $= 3 \times 3 = 9$ square inches. There are six sides to a cube. $9 \times 6 = 54$ square inches.

22-A $(10^3)^2 = (10^3)(10^3) = 10^6$

23-A   The sum of the measure of the angles of a convex polygon of n sides $= (n - 2) \times 180°$. A pentagon has 5 sides.

       $(5 - 2) \times 180° = 3 \times 180° = 540°$

24-D   4! (read "four factorial") $= 4 \times 3 \times 2 \times 1 = 24$

25-A   To find how many tons fall in a given number of minutes, multiply the number of tons that fall in one minute by the number of minutes. There are 60 seconds in 1 minute, and *T* tons fall in 1 second. In *M* minutes, the amount of snow that falls is 60 *MT*.

Part 6: Electronics Information

1-D   Soft iron has the property of being easily magnetized or demagnetized. When the current is turned on in an electromagnet, it becomes magnetized. When the current is turned off, the iron loses its magnetism.

2-C   This is a general safety question. Never assume that there is no current in a piece of electrical equipment; the results could be shocking.

3-C   Using algebraic rules, Ohm's Law can be written in three equivalent ways:

$$R = \frac{V}{I}; I = \frac{V}{R} = IR.$$

4-D   A rectifier or diode is a device that changes AC to DC.

5-A   When a kilowatt-hour meter is read, the number that comes just before the indicator is the number that is important. The answer would then be 9672 kWh.

6-D   Converters change DC to AC. Rectifiers change AC to DC. Contactors are remote controlled switches frequently used as part of elevator controls. Transformers change volt ages in AC circuits in accordance with the ratio of the number of turns in the secondary winding to the number of turns in the primary winding.

7-C   A relay works on the principle of an energized coil or an electromagnet. Another device that works by an electromagnet is a solenoid.

8-D   A megger (megohmmeter) is a portable device that produces a voltage. It is used to check for high voltage breakdown of insulation. In this case, it uses a resistance measurement to determine continuity.

9-D   This is the Wheatstone bridge circuit with balanced loads in each of its arms. As there is no voltage across lamp No. 5, it will not be lit.

10-C   The farad is a unit of capacitance. Most capacitors used in electronics are small and their capacitance is only a tiny fraction of a farad. One microfarad is one millionth of a farad.

11-A   Three common elements of the transistor are the emitter, base, and collector.

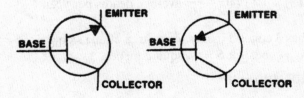

12-C   This is proper safety procedure and should be followed.

13-C   The number on the wires is in reverse order to the amount of current that they can carry. No. 12 is the smallest of the wires.

14-A   The plug can go into the outlet in only one way in a polarized outlet. In the other outlets, the plug can be reversed.

15-B Connecting the bell to a 6- or 12-volt source on the secondary of a transformer is done as a safety precaution. The other way would be dangerous.

16-D This is a mechanical or solderless connector. It does away with the need to solder wires and is found in house wiring.

17-C Two three-way switches will control a lamp from two different positions.

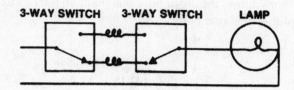

18-B A battery is an assembly of chemical cells. The common 9-volt battery found in transistor radios consists of six 1.5-volt cells connected in series to produce a total of six times 1.5 volts—or 9 volts.

19-D The third prong in the plug is the grounding wire.

20-B A compound motor has two sets of field coils. One is connected in series with the armature. The other is the shunt. It is connected in parallel across the armature.

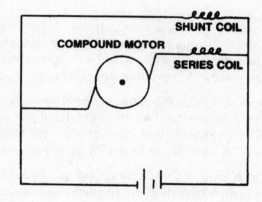

Part 7: Auto & Shop Information

1-C The most popular engine has a four-stroke cycle. The four cycles are intake, compression, power, and exhaust.

2-D The most important rule is to maintain the level of the liquid. This liquid—usually water—acts as an electrolyte, a necessary component when electricity is discharged from a battery. Without it, no electricity will be produced.

3-C The rotor determines which spark plug is to ignite. It is found under the distributor cap. The rotor is connected by a shaft to the engine and is timed to ignite the spark plug at the top of the power stroke.

4-B The governor is a device that is used to limit the maximum speed of an auto. It is used as a safety device.

5-A   Headlights are connected in parallel. In a parallel circuit, if one headlight goes out, the other will still light.

6-B   A fuel injection system eliminates the need for a carburetor by actually forcing the gasoline-air mixture into each one of the cylinders instead of having the gasoline combine with the air in the carburetor and then go through the intake manifold.

7-B   The spark jumps across the arc at only one point on the electrode. A wire gauge gives the best spark plug gap at one point.

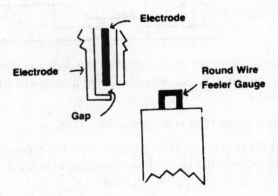

8-C   The clearance volume is the space, at compression, between the top of the piston and the cylinder roof. The total volume is the total space in the cylinder when the piston is at the bottom of the intake stroke. To calculate the compression ratio, divide the total volume by the clearance volume. Many modern engines run at a compression ratio of 8:1.

9-C   Choice C is the best answer. When the engine block and the radiator are clogged, a mechanic wants to remove any foreign material that prevents the antifreeze-water mixture from cooling the engine. Flushing with water and using compressed air remove the blockages. The other methods might not do the job adequately.

10-B   Water freezes at 32°F, or 0°C. Adding alcohol will cause the water to freeze at a lower temperature and will help prevent the engine block from cracking. *Note:* When water freezes it expands, and the pressure created can crack an engine block.

11-B   The ignition coil in a gasoline engine builds up a low voltage current supplied by the battery to the high voltage needed by the spark plugs.

12-D   A wooden mallet is used in woodworking. The other hammers are made of steel. They are too hard and might crack a wood chisel. Choice A is a ball peen hammer, choice B is a straight peen hammer, and choice C is a brick hammer.

13-D   An expansion bolt is put into a hole that has been drilled into solid masonry. The bolt is then tightened, forcing apart the sides of the expansion bolt. This anchors into the concrete.

14-B   A 10-penny nail is 3 inches long. For each 2-penny increase, the length increases by $\frac{1}{2}$ inch. So, a 4-penny nail is $1\frac{1}{2}$ inches long and a 12-penny nail is $3\frac{1}{2}$ inches long.

15-A   Glazier's points are triangular-shaped pieces of metal that are inserted into a window frame to prevent the glass from being pushed out.

16-A The diagram below shows how a lag screw can fit into the head of a wrench.

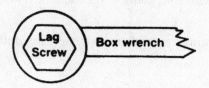

17-C When two pieces of metal rub together, the friction causes a great deal of heat. Oil reduces the friction between the two pieces of metal.

18-B The tool shown is a "star drill." It is hit with a hammer to make a hole in concrete.

19-D One would not be able to see a defect in a painted ladder, such as a knot or a split in the wood. A ladder should *never* be painted.

20-D When a blade in the gauge matches the threads in the screw, the measure is the screw pitch.

21-D A lathe is a machine that rotates a piece of wood in order to create a uniform circular design when the wood is cut with a chisel. A baseball bat is the only round object.

22-A A rope is made from many separate strands of hemp or synthetic fiber, such as nylon. When a rope is cut, the strands can unravel if the ends are not whipped or wrapped with cord.

23-A The set is the angle at which the teeth are bent. It makes the teeth stand out from the rest of the saw and prevents the saw from getting stuck or binding to the stock.

24-C Lacquer thinner is a strong solvent and will dissolve hardened paint.

25-C The flattened part of the tool in choice C rests at the top of the hole and the ruler is then pushed down into the hole until it reaches the bottom. The depth of the hole is then read from the ruler.

Part 8: Mechanical Comprehension

1-C Newton's Law of Motion states that a body at rest will stay at rest unless acted on by an outside force. Conversely, a body in motion stays in motion unless acted on by an outside force. In this picture, both objects are at rest (equilibrium). When an outside force is added to weight 1, the equilibrium changes, moving this weight downward. Because the pulley has practically no friction, the weight strikes the floor.

2-B The volume is dependent on the area of the outlet.

Since $A = \pi r^2$ and $r = \dfrac{d}{2}$, then $A = \pi\left(\dfrac{d^2}{4}\right)$ where A is the area and d is the diameter. The volume is proportional to the diameter squared (d^2). When the volumes of the 1-inch and 2-inch outlets are compared, we see that the latter will produce 4 times as great a volume. If the 1-inch outlet has an 8-gallon flow, then the 2-inch outlet will have a 32-gallon flow.

3-A If nut A were removed, it would be necessary to move nut C to the right to counterbalance the loss of the weight of nut A.

4-B   An air valve on a radiator removes air from the steam pipes. If air is trapped in the pipes, it prevents the steam from going to the radiator. This would prevent the radiator from producing heat.

5-A   Each time the rotating arm makes a complete revolution it moves the slotted disc $\frac{1}{4}$ of a turn.

6-B   The figure shown is a bimetallic strip that works like the wire in a thermostat. High temperatures will cause the metals to heat unevenly. The rivets will keep the strips together, so the only thing that they can do is bend.

7-D   Wheel *P* has 16 teeth; wheel *M* has 12 teeth. When wheel *M* makes a full turn, wheel *P* will still have 4 more teeth to turn. So wheel *P* is slower and will take more time to turn.

8-A   Because the load is closer to upright *A*, it supports more of the load. If the load were directly over *A*, all of the weight would be supported by *A*; then upright *B* could be removed completely.

9-C   The trick with this question is that both of the rods will be pulled in at the same time when the turnbuckle is turned. If it is turned 12 times (12 threads per inch), both rods will be pulled in 1 inch.

10-C   The downward pull equals the 100-lb. weight being hoisted plus the 50-lb. effort. 100 lbs. + 50 lbs. = 150 lbs.

11-B   Imagine the driven wheel as a record. For one rotation of the record, point *y* travels much further than point *x*. It takes more turns of the driver wheel to turn point *y* one complete revolution.

12-B   The diameter of the handle is $3\frac{1}{2}$ times $\left(\frac{28}{8}\right)$ the diameter of the axle. When 50 lbs. of force is applied to the handle, it is multiplied by $3\frac{1}{2}$ times, or, $\frac{28}{8} \times 50 = 175$ lbs.

13-A   When steam flows through pipes, it expands. The pipes would burst if extra space were not provided for expansion and contraction.

14-B   Let *x* = effort that must be exerted. $60 \times 3 = x \times 5$; $180 = 5x$; $x = \frac{180}{5} = 36$

15-A   The water is filling up in the tank at a rate of 120 gallons per hour, or 2 gallons per minute $(\frac{120}{60} = 2)$. The tank is also emptying at a rate of 1 gallon per minute. The net flow is increasing by 1 gallon per minute, because 2 gal./min. input – 1 gal./min. output = 1 gal./min. increase. *Note:* The easiest way to find the answer is to change all measurements to gallons per minute.

16-C   Figure No. 3 has the largest surface area and thus would need the shortest sides. Area = length × width. For No. 3, area = 7 ft. × 4 ft. = 28 sq. ft.

17-D   The water shut-off valve on a flush tank is closed by the force of a lightweight ball rising inside the tank. If this float becomes waterlogged, it will not rise and shut off the water.

18-A The mechanical advantage is calculated by the number of strands supporting the weight. A has 3 strands, B has 2, and C has only 1.

19-A Study the diagram on page 65 and note that the follower is at its highest position between points Q and R.

20-B Clockwise is left to right, so if the nut moves, it follows the threads of the bolt down ward.

21-D When a tuning fork vibrates, it moves currents of air. This vibrating air would cause the Ping-Pong ball to be pushed away.

22-C The film of water inside the loop would form a lens that would enlarge the printing on the page. If you look through a water-filled globe, objects will also appear larger.

23-B If the man moves to the back of the seesaw, his momentum (weight × distance from center) will increase. The woman, who is lighter, will rise in the air.

24-A Insulating the pipes keeps warm moisture-laden air from coming into contact with the cold pipes. This stops condensation.

25-A The measurements that can be made on the micrometer are: a) 2 major divisions and 1 minor division on the ruler-type scale, or $.2 + .025 = .225$; b) 2 minor divisions above 0 on the rotating scale, or $.002$. Summing, we find the final measurement is $.225 + .002 = .227$.

Part 9: Numerical Operations

1-A $5 - 3 = 2$

2-B $8 - 6 = 2$

3-D $12 \div 2 = 6$

4-B $4 + 6 = 10$

5-D $6 \times 3 = 18$

6-A $9 + 5 = 14$

7-C $10 \div 5 = 2$

8-A $2 \times 9 = 18$

9-C $8 + 3 = 11$

10-B $1 \times 6 = 6$

11-A $7 - 2 = 5$

12-C $5 - 0 = 5$

13-D $6 \times 7 = 42$

14-B $7 + 6 = 13$

15-D $8 - 5 = 3$

16-D $6 + 8 = 14$

17-C $4 \times 6 = 24$

18-B $3 \div 3 = 1$

19-D $2 - 1 = 1$

20-D $4 \times 0 = 0$

21-D $9 - 1 = 8$

22-C $4 + 8 = 12$

23-A $5 - 1 = 4$

24-A $9 \div 3 = 3$

25-B $4 \times 6 = 24$

26-C $7 + 2 = 9$

27-A $8 - 8 = 0$

28-A $15 \div 3 = 5$

29-B $2 \times 8 = 16$

30-C $1 + 6 = 7$

31-B $40 \div 8 = 5$

32-C $7 \times 6 = 42$

33-A	$4 + 5 = 9$		**42-D**	$1 + 3 = 4$
34-D	$6 \times 2 = 12$		**43-D**	$2 \times 7 = 14$
35-D	$10 - 8 = 2$		**44-D**	$35 \div 7 = 5$
36-B	$7 \div 1 = 7$		**45-C**	$10 - 9 = 1$
37-B	$9 + 4 = 13$		**46-A**	$3 \times 4 = 12$
38-A	$3 \times 8 = 24$		**47-A**	$8 - 6 = 2$
39-C	$1 + 7 = 8$		**48-D**	$8 \div 2 = 4$
40-C	$6 \times 6 = 36$		**49-B**	$6 + 7 = 13$
41-B	$8 + 9 = 17$		**50-B**	$9 \div 1 = 9$

Part 10: Coding Speed

There is no way to explain the answers to the Coding Speed questions. A few mistakes are inevitable. If you made many mistakes, look to see if they fall into any pattern. Slow down a bit on the next specimen test.

CHAPTER

STRENGTHENING YOUR WEAKNESSES

You completed the first ASVAB Specimen Test and scored yourself on each part of the test. At this point in your ASVAB preparation, you should review your scores to pinpoint your weaknesses. Your next step is knowing what you can do to improve, to achieve your maximum scores, and to enhance your vocational opportunities.

Your test scores reflect a combination of your past learning experiences and the time and effort you put into preparing for the actual ASVAB test. If you have been a "reader," you probably have a good vocabulary and will do well on Word Knowledge and Paragraph Comprehension. If you have spent considerable time in "shop," chances are that you will score high on Auto & Shop Information, Mechanical Comprehension, and Electronics Information. If science has always fascinated you, then you are likely to have more knowledge in this area and will score high in General Science. And if you have always liked math, you probably will do well in Arithmetic Reasoning and Mathematics Knowledge.

It is also a big help to have a feel for the test by:

- Taking sample test batteries
- Timing yourself to the actual times for each test section
- Using the sample answer sheets
- Reviewing material you need extra help in

The basic reviews that follow offer concise yet comprehensive coverage of the subject areas of the ASVAB. It is strongly recommended that you read the basic review for each test and spend extra time studying the reviews for the tests you scored low on. After completing each of the remaining three ASVAB tests, you may find it helpful to return to this review chapter to better understand the answers or the reasoning for getting to the correct answer.

Your efforts preparing for the ASVAB will pay off in higher scores, broader knowledge of the subject matter covered, and better test-taking skills.

GENERAL SCIENCE REVIEW

Since general science covers a great deal of information, we provide only the more important findings and basic concepts of general science that are covered on the ASVAB. This will refresh your memory of what you learned in junior and senior high school science courses.

This review covers the following areas:
- **Life Science:** biology, human nutrition, and health
- **Physical Science:** elementary physics and chemistry
- **Earth Science:** geology, meteorology, and astronomy

Life Science

Classification of Animal and Plant Life

With over a million different kinds of plants and animals living on Earth, there is a need for a system of classification. The system currently in use was developed by Linnaeus and is based on relationships and similarities in structure. The scientific name consists of two terms identifying the genus and species. Note that the first letter of each genus listed below is capitalized and the species is written in small letters.

Homo sapiens: scientific name for man

Escherichia coli: scientific name of the microorganism that inhabits the intestines of man

The classification system has 7 levels. The top level contains the largest number of different kinds of organisms and is called the *kingdom*. The bottom level with the smallest number of different kinds of organisms is called the *species*. The levels are:

1. KINGDOM—contains several related *phyla*

2. PHYLUM—contains several related *classes*

3. CLASS—contains several related *orders*

4. ORDER—contains several related *families*

5. FAMILY—contains several related *genera*

6. GENUS—contains several related *species*

7. SPECIES—contains all organisms with the same characteristics

Scientists have struggled to find the best method of grouping organisms for hundreds of years. The most accepted theory is the five-kingdom system. This includes:

- Animals
- Monerans
- Protists
- Fungi
- Plants

The animal and plant kingdoms are the two principal kingdoms and contain virtually all life. These two kingdoms are described in detail after Figure 1. Brief descriptions of the other three kingdoms are listed below.

Monerans and Viruses

Monerans are very simple one-celled microscopic organisms. They lack internal structures within their cells and have a simple circular molecule of DNA instead of a nucleus. This kingdom includes bacteria and blue-green algae. Many bacteria are known as parasites, which cause diseases (tetanus, gonorrhea, strep throat), or as decomposers, which absorb food from decaying materials or living things. Blue-green algae make their own food by photosynthesizing.

Viruses are a type of life that scientists have difficulty in defining. They do not fit easily into any classification scheme because they do not have a true cell structure. Some scientists describe them as nonliving things, even though they contain protein and nucleic acid. Many human diseases are caused by viruses (polio, influenza, AIDS, herpes, measles, etc.). Viruses cause diseases by using another cell's material to reproduce.

Protists

Protists are microscopic one-celled organisms that have a true nucleus, as well as many other structures found in more complex cells. Protists differ from one another in the way they obtain food. Some depend on other organisms for food, and some can photosynthesize. This kingdom includes protozoa, one-celled algae, and slime molds.

Fungi

Fungi are many-celled organisms with complex cell structure. Their cells lack chloroplasts necessary in photosynthesizing. They are decomposers. This kingdom includes bread molds, mushrooms, and yeasts.

The Plant Kingdom

The two principal plant phyla are the *Bryophyta* and *Tracheophyta*. Bryophytes do not have a vascular system for transporting water, food, and minerals; tracheophytes do have a vascular system.

Figure 1. The five-kingdom system

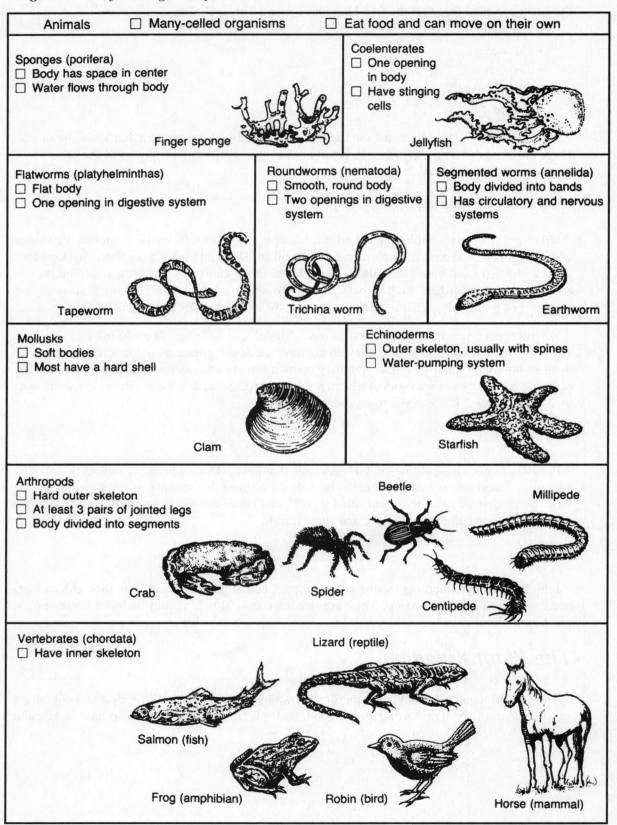

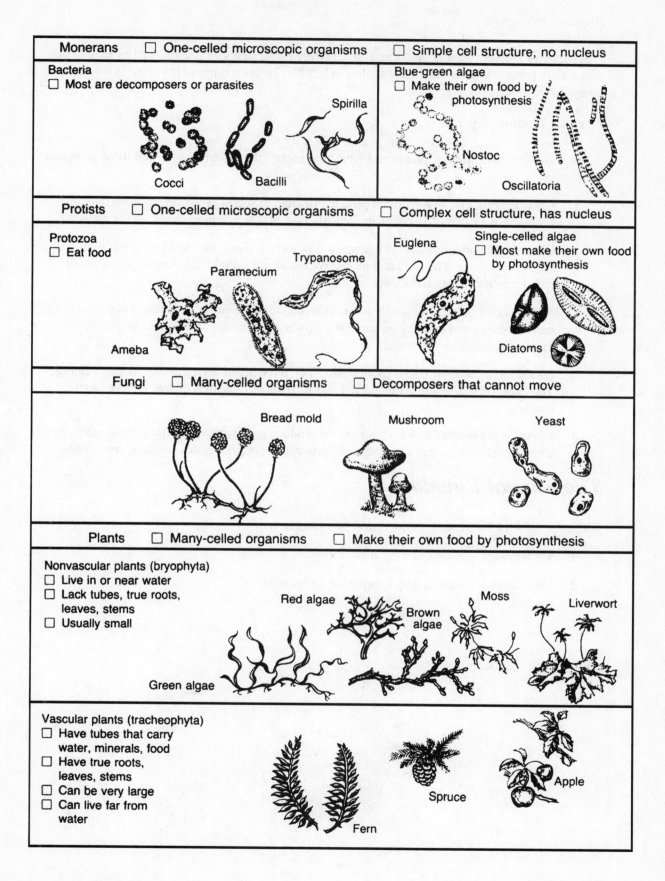

Monerans	☐ One-celled microscopic organisms	☐ Simple cell structure, no nucleus

Bacteria
☐ Most are decomposers or parasites

Spirilla

Cocci   Bacilli

Blue-green algae
☐ Make their own food by photosynthesis

Nostoc

Oscillatoria

Protists	☐ One-celled microscopic organisms	☐ Complex cell structure, has nucleus

Protozoa
☐ Eat food

Trypanosome

Paramecium

Ameba

Euglena

Single-celled algae
☐ Most make their own food by photosynthesis

Diatoms

Fungi	☐ Many-celled organisms	☐ Decomposers that cannot move

Bread mold   Mushroom   Yeast

Plants	☐ Many-celled organisms	☐ Make their own food by photosynthesis

Nonvascular plants (bryophyta)
☐ Live in or near water
☐ Lack tubes, true roots, leaves, stems
☐ Usually small

Red algae   Moss   Liverwort

Brown algae

Green algae

Vascular plants (tracheophyta)
☐ Have tubes that carry water, minerals, food
☐ Have true roots, leaves, stems
☐ Can be very large
☐ Can live far from water

Fern   Spruce   Apple

Phylum Bryophyta

Bryophytes are nonvascular plants and have no true roots, stems, or leaves. As they lack woody tissue, they generally grow only a few inches in height. Common types of bryophytes are mosses, many-celled algae, and liverworts.

Phylum Tracheophyta

Tracheophytes are vascular plants and have true roots, stems, and leaves. The three principal classes are:

1. **Class Filicineae**—Ferns do not produce flowers or seeds. However, spore-producing generations of plants do occur in their life cycles. They require moist, shady areas.

2. **Class Angiospermae**—Angiosperms are flowering plants that produce seeds with protective coverings. The seed and protective tissue are called fruit. Angiosperms are divided into monocots and dicots.

    Monocots have seeds with only one cotyledon, a food-bearing structure. They have long, narrow leaves and parallel veining. The flowering parts are arranged in threes or multiples of three (banana, corn, wheat).

    Dicots have seeds with two cotyledons. They have broad leaves and branched veining. The flowering parts are arranged in fours or fives or multiples of four or five (apple, maple).

3. **Class Gymnospermae**—Gymnosperms produce seed without any protective coverings. Conifers, such as cedar, fir, pine, and spruce, are evergreens that produce seed cones.

The Animal Kingdom

The animal kingdom can be divided into two groups:

1. **Vertebrates**—those that have a backbone

2. **Invertebrates**—those that do not have a backbone

INVERTEBRATES

Phylum	Characteristics
Phylum Porifera	the simplest animals; also called sponges; mostly marine animals that feed on microscopic organisms; porous and lack bony skeletons or tissues. *Examples: sponges*
Phylum Coelenterata	more complex organisms having simple tissues; marine animals *Examples: coral; jellyfish; sea anemone*
Phylum Platyhelminthes	flatworms are the simplest animals with bilateral symmetry and organs; often live as parasites in humans; flat body *Example: tapeworm; liver fluke*
Phylum Nematoda	the roundworms have a digestive tract with two openings; most are parasitic *Example: ascaris; hookworm; trichina*
Phylum Annelida	long, segmented, cylindrical bodies; the only parasitic annelid is the leech *Example: earthworm; leech*
Phylum Mollusca	soft bodies enclosed in a mantle; move by means of a muscular foot; three principle classes: Univalves—single coil shell *Example: snails* Bivalves—two shells connected by a hinge *Example: clams; mussels; oysters; scallops* Head-foot—no shell *Example: squid; octopus*
Phylum Echinodermata	aquatic animals with spiny skins; some have five or more arms that spread out in radial symmetry *Example: starfish; sea urchin; sea cucumber*
Phylum Arthropoda	contains the largest number of animals; segmented bodies covered by an external skeleton; jointed appendages; generally have three distinct body regions (head, chest, and abdomen) *Example: lobster; shrimp; crabs; centipedes; millipedes; spiders; scorpions; insects*

The major classes of anthropoda and their characteristics are:

Crustaceans: have five or more pairs of jointed legs and gills for respiration. The lobster, shrimp, and crab are common crustaceans.

Myriapods: include the centipedes and millipedes. They have long bodies made up of numerous segments with legs on each segment. The centipede has one pair of legs per segment; the millipede has two pairs on each segment.

Arachnids: have two body regions and four pairs of legs. The spider and scorpion are in this class.

Insects: comprise the largest group of arthropods. Insects have three pairs of legs and generally one or two pairs of wings. The ant, bee, butterfly, fly, grasshopper, locust, louse, mosquito, and moth are common insects.

VERTEBRATES

There are five classes of vertebrates in the phylum Chordata.

PHYLUM CHORDATA	
Class	**Characteristics**
Fish	cold-blooded; use internal gills for respiration; uses fins for locomotion *Example: bass; trout; perch; mackerel; shark; etc.*
Amphibians	can live both in the water and on land; cold-blooded; develop lungs in the adult stage *Example: frog; toad; salamander*
Reptiles	cold-blooded; breathe air through lungs; have legs for movement (except snakes); most lay eggs with tough shells *Example: alligator; crocodile; lizard; snake; turtle*
Birds	warm-blooded with feathers and wings; they lay eggs with brittle shells; there are many different kinds of birds with some raised for human consumption *Example: chicken; goose; turkey*
Mammals	warm-blooded with hair or fur on their bodies; they breathe by means of lungs; newborns are fed milk from the mother's mammary glands; mammals are divided into many orders based upon differences in body structure *Examples: duck-bill pltypus; kangaroo; beaver; mouse; rat; squirrel; dolphin; porpoise; whale; cat; dog; fox; lion; wolf; cow; deer; horse; pig; sheep; ape; human; monkey*

The major classes of mammals and their characteristics are:

Monotremes: the most primitive mammals, lay eggs (duck-bill platypus)

Marsupials: carry their young in the pouch on the mother's body (kangaroo)

Rodents: gnawing mammals (beaver, mouse, rat, squirrel)

Flippers: marine mammals with forelimbs that have been modified to flippers (dolphin, porpoise, whale)

Carnivores: have sharp claws and powerful jaws (cat, dog, fox, lion, wolf)

Ungulates: hoofed mammals with teeth adapted for grinding (cow, deer, horse, pig, sheep)

Primates: possess a highly developed brain, stand erect, and have the ability to grasp and hold objects with their two hands (ape, human, monkey)

Humans

Humans are part of the primate order. They are unique in their species in that they have characteristics that set them apart from other primates. These characteristics include:
- Power of speech
- Bi-pedalism, or the ability to walk on two legs instead of four
- Adaptability to almost any environment
- Ability to remember
- Ability to make associations between ideas

Major Systems of the Human Body

The human body is a complex machine that operates in a most effective and precise manner. It consists of several major systems that work together with extreme efficiency.

The Skeletal System

The human skeleton is the supporting framework of the body. It consists of more than 200 bones connected by joints (see Figure 2). The four main types of joints are:

1. *Fixed joints,* as in the skull, hold the bones firmly together.

2. *Hinge joints,* as in the knee and finger, are partly movable and provide some flexibility.

3. *Pivot joints,* as in the elbow, are similar to hinge joints but can also be rotated.

4. *Ball and socket joints,* as in the hip or shoulder, provide greatest flexibility.

The surfaces of joints are lined and cushioned by a flexible material called cartilage. Cartilage is also found in the outer ear and the tip of the nose. Bands of tissue called ligaments support the bones of movable joints.

The Muscular System

This system enables the body to move. The body has more than 600 skeletal muscles that are made up of bundles of striated (or voluntary) muscle fibers. Each end of the muscle is attached to the bone by connective tissue called tendon. Movement results from the contraction of these muscles that always operate in pairs. For example, the contraction of the biceps while the triceps are relaxed causes the elbow to bend; the contraction of the triceps while the biceps are relaxed causes the elbow to straighten (see Figure 3). The skeletal muscles are known as voluntary muscles because they are controlled by the individual through conscious thought.

Figure 2. The human skeleton. Each bone pictured functions in supporting a part of the body.

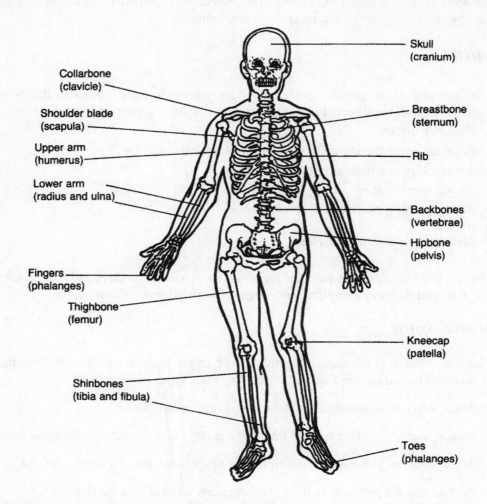

Skull
(cranium)

Collarbone
(clavicle)

Shoulder blade
(scapula)

Upper arm
(humerus)

Lower arm
(radius and ulna)

Breastbone
(sternum)

Rib

Backbones
(vertebrae)

Hipbone
(pelvis)

Fingers
(phalanges)

Thighbone
(femur)

Kneecap
(patella)

Shinbones
(tibia and fibula)

Toes
(phalanges)

Figure 3. Muscles work in pairs. Contraction of the biceps muscle bends the elbow joint. Contraction of the triceps straightens the arm. While one muscle is contracted, the other is relaxed.

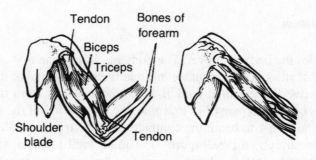

Tendon

Bones of
forearm

Biceps

Triceps

Shoulder
blade

Tendon

Other muscles found in the body are smooth muscle in internal organs and cardiac muscle that enables the heart to pump blood. Smooth and cardiac muscles are known as involuntary muscles because they are not controlled by the individual. They play an important role in maintaining such body functions as circulation, respiration, and digestion.

The Digestive System

The digestive tract is essentially a long, winding tunnel that extends from the mouth to the anus. It includes the mouth, esophagus, stomach, small intestine, large intestine, rectum, and anus (see Figure 4).

Figure 4. The human digestive system

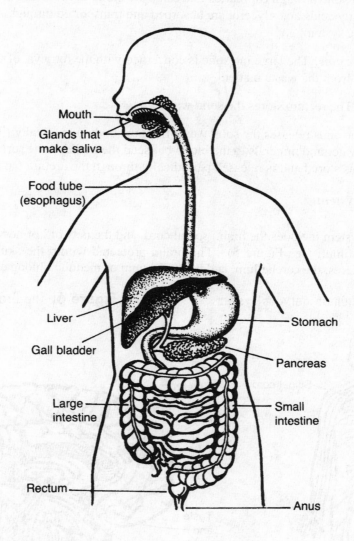

The digestive system controls food intake, digestion, and the absorption of the digested material by the body cells for energy and bodybuilding. The six important steps in digestion are as follows:

1. *Mouth:* The teeth and tongue aid in mechanical digestion. Amylase contained in the saliva acts on the starch.

2. *Stomach:* Food is mixed with acidic gastric juice and pepsin, which acts on the protein.

3. *Small intestine:* The bulk of digestion takes place in the small intestine. The food pulp mixes with alkali and digestive juices manufactured by the pancreas and the liver and is

then released in the duodenum, the beginning of the small intestine. The juice manufactured by the pancreas contains lipase, which changes fat to glycerol and fatty acids; amylase, which changes complex carbohydrates to simple sugars; and trypsins, which change polypeptides to amino acids. Bile produced by the liver aids in the physical digestion by emulsifying fat.

Absorption of all digested substances, except the fatty acids and glycerol, occurs in the small intestine through capillaries that carry the blood to the liver and then to all body cells. Fatty acids and glycerol are absorbed and transported throughout the body by the lymphatic system.

4. *Large intestine:* The large intestine is concerned with the retrieval of water and essential minerals from the waste matter.

5. *Rectum:* The rectum stores the solid waste.

6. *Anus:* The anus releases the solid waste from the body periodically. The kidneys return needed water and minerals to the blood but send the liquid waste (urine) to the bladder, where it is stored and is released periodically through the urethra out of the body.

The Nervous System

The nervous system includes the brain, spinal cord, and the network of nerves. It receives and responds to all stimuli (see Figure 5). The brain, protected within the skull, consists of two cerebral hemispheres, the cerebellum, and the brain stem or medulla oblongata (see Figure 6).

Figure 5. The human nervous system   **Figure 6.** The Brain

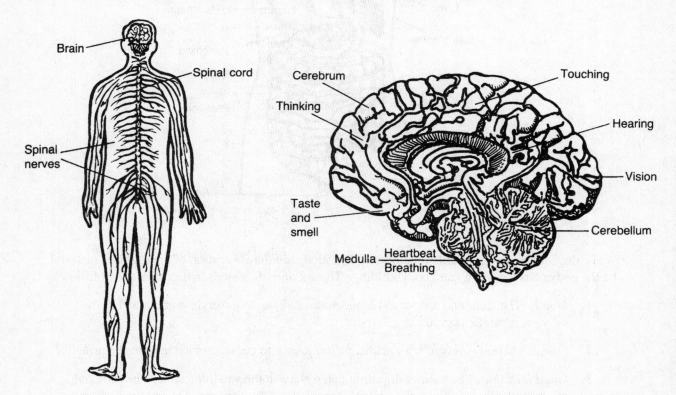

The main components of the nervous systems and their functions are:

- **Cerebrum or forebrain:** major part of the brain and is responsible for many human abilities, such as hearing, seeing, speaking, learning, etc.
- **Cerebellum:** concerned with muscular coordination and is responsible for the coordination of impulses sent out from the cerebrum. It also controls posture and balance.
- **Brain stem:** connects the brain with the spinal cord. It controls several involuntary activities, such as heartbeat rate and breathing rate.
- **Spinal cord:** major connecting center between the brain and the network of nerves. It is also the control center for many simple reflexes.

The Endocrine System

The endocrine system is a group of specialized organs and body tissues that produce, store, and secrete chemical substances. These chemical substances are known as hormones and are chemical regulators that control growth and behavior. They are produced by endocrine glands and the brain controls their release into the bloodstream. When they are released, hormones transfer information and instructions from one set of cells to another (see Figure 7).

The principal endocrine glands are explained in the following chart.

ENDOCRINE GLAND	HORMONE	PROCESS REGULATED
pituitary	1. growth hormone	1. growth of muscle, bone, and other connective tissue
	2. vasopressin	2. increases blood pressure; increases reabsorption of water into blood from kidneys
thyroid	thyroxin	energy release process in the cells
parathyroid	PTH (parathyroid hormone)	nerve impulses and muscle contraction, strength of bones
pancreas	1. insulin	1. regulates the amount of sugar in the blood; speeds up the storage of excess sugar
	2. glucagon	2. speeds up the removal of stored sugar
adrenal glands	adrenaline	readies the body for strenuous physical activity; increases the amount of sugar in the blood
testes	androgens	controls development of sex characteristics of adult males
ovaries	estrogens	controls development of sex characteristics of adult females

Figure 7. The principal endocrine glands in the human body

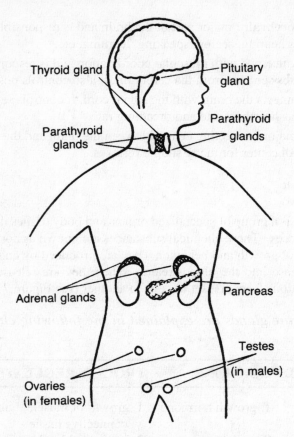

Endocrine organs have no ducts connecting them to specific body parts. The main functions of endocrine organs include:

- Body's growth and development
- Control of the function of various tissues
- Support of pregnancy and other reproductive functions
- Regulation of metabolism

The Circulatory System

The circulatory system's main organ is the heart. It pumps oxygenated blood at high pressure to every part of the body through arteries and capillaries, back to the heart at reduced pressure through small veins and large veins, back to the lungs for oxygenation, and then back to the heart to repeat the cycle.

The heart is a cone-shaped organ that lies in the center of the chest. The lungs are also cone shaped and lie on either side of the heart. The heart has four chambers—the right atrium, the left atrium, the right ventricle, and the left ventricle (see Figure 8).

The nine principal steps in the circulation of blood are as follows:

1. Blood from the body enters the right atrium of the heart.

2. Contraction forces the blood into the right ventricle.

3. Contraction forces the blood into the pulmonary artery, which goes to the lungs.

4. In the lungs, oxygen is picked up and carbon dioxide and water are removed from the blood.

5. Oxygenated blood from the lungs travels through the pulmonary veins to the left atrium.

6. Contraction forces the oxygenated blood into the left ventricle.

7. Strong contraction of the left ventricle forces oxygenated blood into the aorta.

8. Arteries and capillaries carry the oxygenated blood to all blood cells.

9. Blood returns through small veins and then large veins back to the right atrium of the heart.

Figure 8. The circulation of blood through the heart

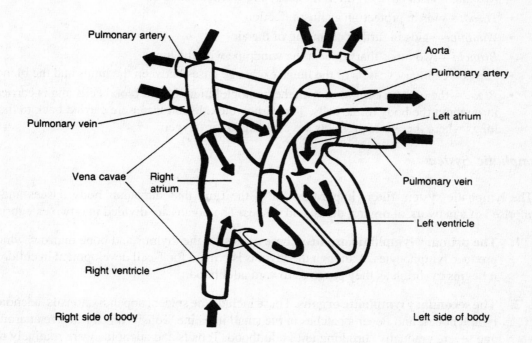

The heartbeat reflects the contraction of the heart. The normal adult heartbeat is about 72 beats per minute. The pulse rate and the heartbeat rate are the same. Each heartbeat consists of two stages. The powerful muscular contraction of the ventricles is the *systolic* stage, when blood is pumped into the aorta. The other stage is the *diastolic*, or rest stage. Blood pressure is the ratio of systolic over diastolic pressure measured in millimeters of mercury. Normal adult blood pressure is about 120/80.

The four principal components of blood are:

1. **Red blood cells (erythrocytes):** carry oxygen and carbon dioxide

2. **White blood cells (leukocytes):** produce antibodies and fight off infections

3. **Platelets:** cell fragments involved in the clotting of blood

4. **Proteins:** involved in blood clotting and antibody production

The Respiratory System

The respiratory system's main function is to breathe air into and out of the lungs while eliminating carbon dioxide. Oxygen diffuses into the blood, while carbon monoxide moves out of the blood via the lungs and out of the body via the mouth or nose. Utilizing oxygen to oxidize the intracellular nutrients releases energy into the body. Exhalation of air rids the body of the waste products of oxidation, carbon dioxide, and water vapor.

The respiratory system consists of the following (see Figure 9):

*   *Nose and nasal cavity*—filter, moisten, and warm inhaled air
*   *Throat*—aids in protection against infection
*   *Windpipe*—aids in further cleansing of the air
*   *Bronchi*—two tubes that connect the windpipe with the lungs
*   *Lungs*—capillary vessels of the lungs exchange gases between the lungs and the blood
*   *Blood*—the oxygen combines with the hemoglobin in the red blood cells and is carried throughout the body to the cells. The carbon dioxide and water are carried back to the lungs where the waste products are exchanged for oxygen.

Lymphatic System

The lymphatic system filters impurities out of the fluid that surrounds body tissues and is comprised of a network of organs, ducts, and tissues. The organs are divided into two categories:

1. **The primary lymphatic organs.** These consist of the thymus and bone marrow, which produce lymphocytes. Although the thymus is critical for T-cell development in children, it begins to shrink as they progress toward adulthood.

2. **The secondary lymphatic organs.** These include the spleen, appendix, tonsils, adenoids, lymph nodes, and Peyer's patches in the small intestine. Tonsils reach full size at around age seven, gradually shrinking until adulthood. Tonsils and adenoids were routinely re moved surgically in the past in most children. Today, tonsils are not removed unless the child experiences repeated infections of the tonsils, known as tonsillitis.

Lymph nodes are mainly clustered in the pelvic area, the neck, and the armpits. They are the lymphatic system's way to fight infection and are connected to one another by lymphatic vessels. White blood cells in the nodes and other secondary organs surround and destroy debris to prevent them from reentering the bloodstream.

Figure 9. Organs of the respiratory system

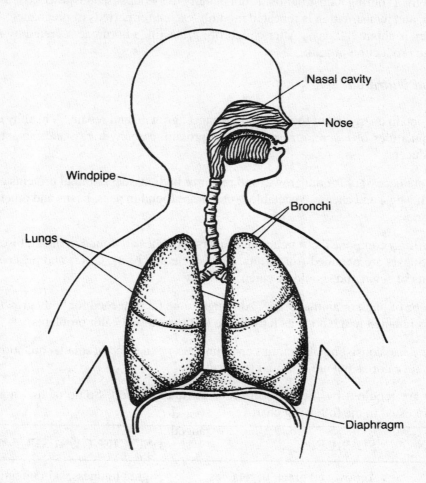

The Excretory System

The excretory system connects to the digestive system and is responsible for the removal of waste substances from the body. The main organs of the excretory system are:

- **Skin:** excretes waste through perspiration
- **Large intestine:** absorbs water from solid food waste
- **Kidneys:** filter blood and excrete waste in the form of urea
- **Liver:** excretes bilirubin
- **Lungs:** excrete carbon dioxide

The Reproductive System

Humans reproduce by the union of male sperm and the female ovum. The male organ ejaculates more than 250 million sperm into the vagina, from which some make their way to the uterus. Ovulation, the release of an egg into the uterus, occurs approximately every 28 days; during the same period the uterus is prepared for the implantation of a fertilized ovum by the action of estrogens. If the sperm unites with a female ovum, a zygote is formed that eventually develops into a fetus. If the sperm fails to unite with the female ovum, other hormones cause the uterine wall to slough off during menstruation. From puberty to menopause, the process of ovulation, and preparation, and menstruation is repeated monthly except for periods of pregnancy. The duration of pregnancy is about 280 days. After childbirth, prolactin, a hormone secreted by the pituitary, activates the production of milk.

Health and Nutrition

Humans obtain energy from food for maintenance, growth, and repair. A healthy diet contains sufficient quantities of *macronutrients*, such as protein, carbohydrates, and fats, since they are energy producers.

Proteins are necessary for the growth and repair of body tissues. Animal proteins are contained in meat, fish, eggs, and cheese. Vegetable proteins are found in peas, beans and other legumes, as well as in grains.

Carbohydrates comprise the starches and sugars. Starches are found in bread, biscuits, cereals, and pasta. Sugars are obtained from fruits, cane sugar, and beets. Cakes and pies contain excessive amounts of sugar and should be eaten sparingly.

Fats may be of plant or animal origin. Although some fat is needed for body growth and repair, excess fat is retained in the body as fatty tissue that can cause health problems.

Micronutrients, consisting of vitamins and minerals, are needed in smaller quantities since they do not contain calories but are essential for health.

Vitamins are required by the body in order to function well. Some of the more important vitamins are listed in the following chart.

VITAMIN	SOURCE	DEFICIENCY RESULT
A	Yellow and green vegetables, eggs, fruits, butter	Night blindness, skin infections
B_1	Whole grain cereals, liver, poultry, peas, beans, pork, eggs	Loss of appetite, beriberi
B_2	Milk, eggs, green vegetables, liver, whole grain cereals	Skin infections, general Weakness
B_{12}	Meat, eggs, dairy products	Anemia
C	Citrus fruits, tomatoes, vegetables	Scurvy
D	Milk, eggs, fish oil	Rickets
E	Green vegetables, meat, wheat germ	Sterility
K	Green vegetables, vegetable oils	Excessive bleeding

Minerals are needed in small quantities for proper metabolic functioning. Mineral salts are chemical compounds containing sodium, calcium, phosphorus, potassium, magnesium, iron, chlorine, fluorine, and iodine.

Fibers are needed for a healthy diet since they provide bulk, which enables the large intestine to carry away body wastes. Water is also essential. The body loses approximately four pints of water a day, which must be replaced. Since most foods contain water, replenishment generally occurs.

A balanced diet requires moderate eating of a variety of foods. Some foods are needed each day from each of the following four major groups:

1. *Milk and Dairy Products.* These foods provide the body with protein, vitamins, and minerals.

2. *Breads and Cereals.* These foods provide energy for the body.

3. *Fruits and Vegetables.* Both raw and cooked fruits and vegetables provide the body with minerals, vitamins, and roughage.

4. *Meats, Poultry, and Fish.* These foods or substitutes, such as eggs, nuts, peas, and beans, supply the body with minerals, vitamins, and proteins.

Human Genetics

Human genetics is the study of heredity, the mechanism by which characteristics are passed from parents to offspring. The three basic laws of heredity were developed by Gregor Mendel in the late eighteenth century. These are:

1. *The Law of Segregation:* individual heredity traits separate in the reproductive cells

2. *The Law of Independent Assortment:* each trait is inherited independently of other traits

3. *The Law of Dominance:* when different traits are crossed, only one trait will be dominant and the other will be recessive.

Every child develops from a fertilized egg (zygote), which contains 23 pairs of chromosomes or a total of 46. Each pair consists of one chromosome from the mother and one from the father (see Figure 10). Each chromosome contains large numbers of hereditary units called genes that determine physical and mental characteristics of the offspring. A gene is a unit of a DNA molecule that carries a code for the production of a specific protein.

Meiosis is a specialized process of cell division in which gametes, also known as sex cells, are produced by sexually mature adults. These gametes are in the haploid stage, they have only one of each pair or half the number of chromosomes. The 23 pairs of chromosomes split into two sets of 23 each. The chromosomes in the nucleus of each gamete is reduced from 46 to 23. At fertilization, the 23 chromosomes from one parent combine with the 23 chromosomes from the other parent to form a new cell with a total of 46 chromosomes. Sexual reproduction by meiosis and fertilization results in great variation among offspring.

Sex Determination

The sex of babies is determined by genes located on the pair of sex chromosomes. In the human female, the two sex chromosomes are alike and are designated as XX. In the male, the sex chromosomes are not alike and are designated as XY.

At fertilization, the zygote or fertilized egg receives an X chromosome from the mother but may receive either an X or Y chromosome from the father (see Figure 10). If the paired chromosomes are XX, the offspring will be female. If the paired chromosomes are XY, the offspring will be male.

Figure 10. Pairing of Chromosomes

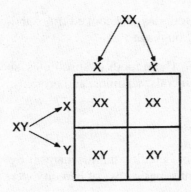

Dominant and Recessive Characteristics

Each person has two genes for each particular characteristic. These genes may be alike or not alike. If the genes are alike, that person is homozygous for that characteristic. If the genes are not alike, the person is heterozygous for that characteristic.

There are many common inherited characteristics and traits of people such as: hair color, eye color, nose size and shape, earlobe, color vision, blood type, and mental ability.

A person's ear shape is determined by the gene received from each parent. To illustrate this, the free earlobe is designated with a capital E in Figure 11 because it is dominant, and the attached earlobe with a small letter e because it is recessive. Consider the following:

- If the genes are alike and the person is homozygous for free earlobes designated by EE, the individual will show free earlobes.
- If the genes are alike and the person is homozygous for attached earlobes designated by ee, the individual will show attached earlobes.
- If the person received an E gene from one parent and an e gene from the other, the person would be heterozygous for ear shape designated by Ee, but would show free earlobes, the dominant form.
- If both parents have a genetic makeup of EE, the offspring will have a genetic makeup of EE and will show free earlobes.
- If both parents have a genetic makeup of ee, the offspring will have a genetic makeup of ee and will show attached earlobes.

If both parents have free earlobes but are heterozygous with a genetic makeup of Ee, the different genetic combinations are:

Figure 11.

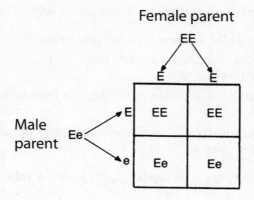

1-EE—homozygous with free earlobes

2-Ee—heterozygous with free earlobes (dominant trait)

1-ee—homozygous with fixed earlobes

If both parents have free earlobes but one is homozygous (EE) and the other is heterozygous (Ee), the different genetic combinations are:

Figure 12.

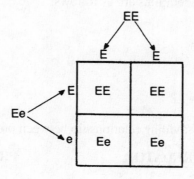

2-EE—homozygous with free earlobes

2-Ee—heterozygous with free earlobes (dominant trait)

Because of this genetic combination, the recessive characteristic does not appear in the second generation but may appear in the third generation depending upon the genetic makeup of both parents and chance.

Ecology

Ecology is the study of the relationship between organisms and their living and physical surroundings. Every plant and animal is a member of a complex system called an ecosystem. In all ecosystems, the following exist as interacting forces:

Producers (green plants): They make their own food via the photosynthesis process.

Consumers (animals): There are three types of consumers:

- Primary consumers, also known as herbivores, eat plants. Samples include grasshoppers, rabbits, and cows.
- Secondary consumers, also called carnivores, are flesh-eaters. These include wolves, snakes, and lions.
- Tertiary consumers, also called omnivores, feed on both herbivores and carnivores. Humans are in this category.

Scavengers: This category feeds on dead organic matter. A vulture is an example of a scavenger.

Decomposers (bacteria and fungi): They break down dead organic matter and release minerals back into the soil.

Important factors that restrict green plants to certain parts of the earth include:

- Temperature
- Soil
- Sunlight
- Water
- Plant eaters

These and additional considerations restrict animals to those parts of the earth where they can survive. Some additional considerations are as follows:

- Food supply
- Mates
- Diseases
- Parasites
- Natural enemies

The food chain is the food-providing relationship between predator and prey. For example:

PREDATOR	PREY
Mammal	Fish
Fish	Amphibian
Amphibian	Arachnid
Arachnid	Insect
Insect	Plant

This entire process is the traditional method of recycling by natural forces. Ecosystems are frequently destroyed because of man's interference. Conservation of natural resources and control of pollution of air, water, and soil will help preserve existing ecosystems.

Biomes

Areas on earth that have similar climate, plants, and animals are called *biomes.* Biomes are permanent ecosytems in a large geographical area. The seven major biomes are:

1. **Arctic Tundra:** Located in the high northern latitudes of the world and is the coldest of all the biomes. There are no deep root systems; the arctic tundra is known for its treeless plains.

2. **Tropical Forests:** Located near the equator and known for high temperatures and constant rainfall.

3. **Deciduous Forests:** Located in eastern North America, northeastern Asia, western and central Europe. Characterized by a modern climate with distinct winters. Its trees have broad leaves that are shed annually.

4. **Taiga:** Located in the broad belt of Eurasia and North America. Contains mostly cold-tolerant evergreen trees. Its seasons are divided into short, moist, and moderately warm summers and cold, dry winters.

5. **Grasslands:** Some locations include North America (the Great Plains) and in the pampas of South America. The grasslands are dominated by grasses rather than large shrubs or trees due to insufficient rainfall.

6. **Deserts:** Deserts cover one-fifth of the earth's surface and are characterized by their high temperatures and lack of sufficient rainfall.

7. **Marine:** This is the largest part of the biosphere, since water covers almost 75 percent of the earth's surface.

Cell Structures and Processes

Cell Structures

Cells are the basic structure of life and develop from other cells. *Protoplasm*, or living material, is contained within tiny cells. These cells differ in size and shape, depending on their function in the body (see Figure 13).

The major parts of cells and their functions are listed below.

1. The **nucleus** is the control center for all cellular activity. Small dark bodies found in the nucleus are called *nucleoli*. The protoplasm within the nucleus is called *nucleoplasm*. Within the nucleoplasm are long, thin fibers called chromatin on which genes are found.

2. The **cytoplasm**, the cells manufacturing area, contains small *vacuoles*, which are storage areas; *mitochondria*, which release the energy for cell operations.

3. **Ribosomes** combine amino acids into proteins. The cytoplasm contains many ribosomes.

4. The **cell membrane** plays an important role in controlling the flow of materials entering and leaving the cell. It is semipermeable and allows only certain materials to enter and leave. The movement of particles from an area of high concentration to an area of lower concentration until equilibrium is reached is termed *diffusion.*

5. **Endoplasmic Reticulum** is a membrane network that extends from the nucleus to the cell membrane. It transports lipids and proteins through the cell.

6. The **Gogi body**, or Golgi apparatus, prepares and stores chemical products produced in the cell and then secretes them outside the cell.

7. **Lysosomes** are sac-like structures that contain release enzymes necessary for intracellular digestion.

8. **Mitochondrians** are the largest organelles in a cell and produce nutrients via cellular respiration to fuel the cell's activities.

Figure 13. Parts of cells

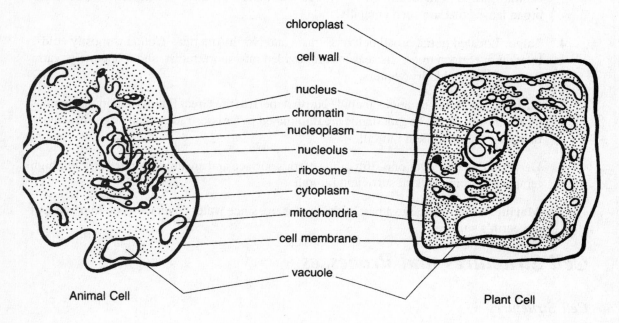

Animal Cell   Plant Cell

chloroplast, cell wall, nucleus, chromatin, nucleoplasm, nucleolus, ribosome, cytoplasm, mitochondria, cell membrane, vacuole

Differences Between Plant and Animal Cells

Although all cells are similar in structure, plant and animal cells do differ. The major differences are as follows:

*   Plant cells have a firm outer boundary called the *cell wall*. This wall supports and protects the plant cell.
*   Vacuoles in the plant cell are much larger than those in the animal cell.
*   Many plant cells contain within the cytoplasm small green structures called chloroplasts. These chloroplasts contain *chlorophyll* that enables the plant cell to make food.

Cell Processes

There are various processes carried out by the living cell. Some major examples are as follows:

- Water is the largest component of the cell protoplasm. Movement or diffusion of water through a semipermeable membrane is known as *osmosis*.
- The total chemical reactions within a living cell, both the building up and the tearing down of complex molecules, is known as the *metabolic* process.
- Cells can also acquire material by engulfing particles. This process is termed *phagocytosis*. The white blood cells protect the body from infection by this method.

Two vital cellular reactions are:

1. *Photosynthesis:* The process by which green plants convert carbon dioxide and water into sugar and oxygen. Both sunlight and chlorophyll are needed for this reaction.

   The chemical reaction for photosynthesis is

   $$6CO_2 + 6H_2O \xrightarrow[\text{chlorophyll}]{\text{sunlight}} C_6H_{12}O_6 + 6O_2$$

Note that six molecules of carbon dioxide combined with six molecules of water to form one molecule of sugar (glucose) and six molecules of oxygen. The energy obtained from the sunlight is stored in the sugar produced.

2. *Respiration:* The reverse of photosynthesis. Both animal and plant cells oxidize glucose to form carbon dioxide and water.

   The chemical reaction for respiration is

   $$C_6H_{12}O_6 + 6O_2 \longrightarrow 6CO_2 + 6H_2O$$

Note that one molecule of sugar (glucose) combined with six molecules of oxygen form six molecules of carbon dioxide and six molecules of water. The energy produced by this reaction is used by the cell.

These are some of the more vital cell processes that enable the cell to carry out essential life activities, such as obtaining food for energy, getting rid of waste materials, obtaining oxygen, and building new material.

Physical Science

Chemistry

Chemistry is the science that deals with the structure, composition, and properties of substances. It is also the study of elements and the compounds they form.

Classification of Matter into Elements and Compounds

Matter is anything that has mass and occupies space, although mass and weight are not the same. Mass is the amount of matter an object contains. Weight is the pull of gravity on that mass.

For example, a 200-pound astronaut may be almost weightless in outer space without any reduction in mass.

Elements

Matter is composed of basic substances known as *elements*. The *atom* is the smallest part of an element that still acts like that element. The atom consists of a nucleus that contains *neutrons* and *protons* in the center. They are surrounded by flying particles called electrons. Atoms are electrically neutral as the positive protons neutralize the negative electrons. The number of electrons outside the nucleus is the same as the number of protons in the nucleus. The neutrons in the nucleus have no charge.

The negatively charged electrons outside the nucleus are arranged in energy levels. When atoms bond to form substances, they complete their outer energy level. The first energy level needs two electrons to be complete, the second energy level needs eight, the third energy level needs eight, etc.

Atomic Numbers

The number of protons in an atom determines its atomic number. The atomic number of hydrogen is one because it has one proton in its nucleus. Helium has an atomic number of two because it has two protons in its nucleus. Carbon has an atomic number of 6; oxygen has an atomic number of 8 (see Figure 14).

Figure 14.

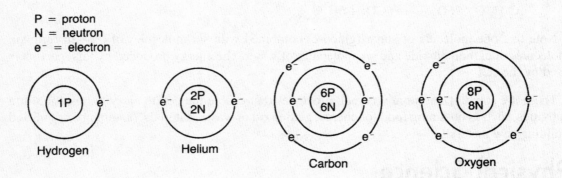

P = proton
N = neutron
e⁻ = electron

Hydrogen   Helium   Carbon   Oxygen

Periodic Table

The periodic table classifies all elements. The elements, listed by increasing atomic number, are arranged in vertical columns called groups or families. Each group contains elements with similar chemical properties (see Figure 15).

Note that hydrogen, lithium, sodium, and potassium, all with one electron in the outermost energy level, are in the same group. Helium, neon, and argon are in the group termed the noble gases. They are rare gases that are completely inert—having completed outermost energy levels.

Figure 15. A left-hand and right-hand portion of the Periodic Table of the Elements

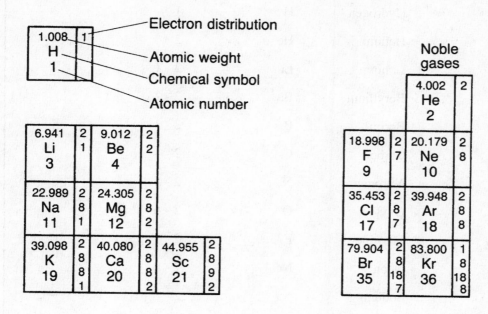

The first 22 elements are listed in the table on page 126. The listing includes the atomic number, name, symbol, and electron distribution within energy levels.

Metals generally have three or fewer electrons in the outermost energy level and tend to give up electrons readily (copper, magnesium, iron, etc.). Nonmetals have five or more electrons in the outermost energy level and tend to hold them tightly (nitrogen, oxygen, chlorine, etc.).

Compounds

Substances composed of atoms of two or more different elements arc called *compounds*. Hydrogen atoms combine with oxygen to form a molecule of water (H_2O). A sodium atom combines with a chlorine atom to form an ionic particle of salt (NaCl). Properties of compounds differ greatly from the properties of the atoms that form the compound. Common salt, a relatively harmless substance, consists of sodium and chlorine, both highly toxic elements. The types of compounds are listed below.

- *Organic* compounds are compounds containing carbon.
- *Hydrocarbons* contain hydrogen and carbon only. Methane, ethylene, acetylene, and propane are hydrocarbons.
- *Carbohydrates* contain only carbon, hydrogen, and oxygen. Common carbohydrates are sugars and starch. Glucose ($C_6H_{12}O_6$) is a simple sugar. Sucrose ($C_{12}H_{22}O_{11}$) or cane sugar is a disaccharide or more complex sugar.
- *Fats* also contain carbon, hydrogen, and oxygen. Fats may be classified as saturated or unsaturated compounds.
- *Proteins* contain carbon, hydrogen, oxygen, and nitrogen. Some proteins contain, in addition, sulfur and phosphorus. Proteins consist of smaller molecules called *amino acids*.

ATOMIC NUMBER	ELEMENT	SYMBOL	ELECTRON DISTRIBUTION
1	Hydrogen	H	1
2	Helium	He	2
3	Lithium	Li	2 - 1
4	Beryllium	Be	2 - 2
5	Boron	B	2 - 3
6	Carbon	C	2 - 4
7	Nitrogen	N	2 - 5
8	Oxygen	O	2 - 6
9	Fluorine	F	2 - 7
10	Neon	Ne	2 - 8
11	Sodium	Na	2 - 8 - 1
12	Magnesium	Mg	2 - 8 - 2
13	Aluminum	Al	2 - 8 - 3
14	Silicon	Si	2 - 8 - 4
15	Phosphorus	P	2 - 8 - 5
16	Sulfur	S	2 - 8 - 6
17	Chlorine	Cl	2 - 8 - 7
18	Argon	Ar	2 - 8 - 8
19	Potassium	K	2 - 8 - 8 - 1
20	Calcium	Ca	2 - 8 - 8 - 2
21	Scandium	Sc	2 - 8 - 9 - 2
22	Titanium	Ti	2 - 8 - 10 - 2

Mixtures

A *mixture* consists of different types of matter near each other but not chemically bound to each other. For example, granite rock has three different crystalline materials dispersed throughout the rock—quartz, feldspar, and mica. They each retain their own unique properties in the mixture.

A *solution* is a mixture in which one type of molecule is dispersed throughout other molecules (sugar and water). The resulting sugar solution has similar properties throughout.

A *suspension* is a mixture in which the dispersed particles are larger than molecules and are dispersed throughout the system. Suspended particles eventually settle out (smoke).

A *colloid* is a mixture containing dispersed particles larger than molecules but small enough not to settle out (gelatin).

Characteristics of Solids, Liquids, and Gases

The three different physical states in which matter normally exists are:

1. *Solids*: A solid has a definite shape and a definite volume. It generally consists of small crystals tightly joined together. The molecular particles in a solid are still in motion but to a much lesser extent. Ice is the solid state of water. Aluminum and copper are solids.

2. *Liquids*: A liquid has a definite volume but takes the shape of its container. Molecular particles in a liquid move about but not rapidly. Mercury is a liquid.

3. *Gases*: A gas has no shape and no definite volume. It is mostly empty space and can readily be expanded or compressed by either pressure or temperature. Particles in a gas move about very rapidly. Steam is the gaseous state of water. Hydrogen and oxygen are gases.

When molecular particles of a substance have little kinetic energy, the substance will be in a solid state. If the solid is heated, the kinetic energy of the molecules increases and the physical state changes from a solid to a liquid (ice to water). The temperature at which a solid substance changes to a liquid is known as its *melting* point.

Further heating will increase the kinetic energy of the molecules still more and the physical state will change from a liquid to a gas (water to steam). The temperature at which a liquid substance changes to a gas is called its *boiling* point.

Lowering the temperature will change a gas to a liquid and a liquid to a solid. The temperature at which a liquid changes to a solid is called the *freezing* point. Movement of particles in matter ceases at absolute zero or –273°C.

Simple Solutions

A solution is a mixture of one substance dissolved in another substance. The substance being dissolved is the *solute*; the substance in which a solute is dissolved is the *solvent*. In a salt solution, the salt (NaCl) is the solute, and water (H_2O) is the solvent.

Solutes may be solids, liquids, or gases. Solvents are generally liquids. Water is the most common solvent. Solutions may be classified according to the relative amounts of solute to solvent.

•   A *dilute* solution contains a relatively small amount of solute dissolved in a large amount of solvent.

- A *concentrated* solution contains a relatively large amount of solute dissolved in a small amount of solvent.

- An *unsaturated* solution is a solution that can still dissolve more solute at the prevailing temperature and pressure.

- A *saturated* solution is one containing the maximum amount of solute that can be dissolved at a given temperature and pressure.

- A *supersaturated* solution is one that contains more solute than it can normally hold at a given temperature.

Acids and Bases

Acids are substances that give up hydrogen ions (H^+) when dissolved in water. Acids react with metals and generally have a sour taste. Some common acids are hydrochloric acid, nitric acid, and sulfuric acid used in industry; acetic acid found in vinegar; lactic acid found in milk; and citric acid found in oranges and lemons.

Bases are substances that give up hydroxyl ions (OH) when dissolved in water. Bases generally contain a metal (the one exception is ammonia). Some common bases are sodium hydroxide (lye) used in making soap and ammonium hydroxide (ammonia) used as a cleaning agent.

When acids and bases react, *neutralization* takes place with the formation of water and a salt.

Hydrochloric acid plus sodium hydroxide yields common salt plus water:

$$HCl + NaOH \longrightarrow NaCl + H_2O$$

The *pH* of a solution is a number within the range of 1 to 14 that indicates the degree of acidity of alkalinity. A pH of 7 indicates a neutral solution; less than 7 shows increased acidity; more than 7 shows increased alkalinity.

Simple Chemical Reactions

Matter may change either by a physical change or by a chemical change. The form, size, or shape of matter is altered in a physical change, but the molecules remain unchanged. Changing water into ice or steam and dissolving sugar in water are examples of physical change. In a chemical change, molecules of new matter are formed that are different from the original matter. The burning of coal or the rusting of iron are examples of chemical change.

A chemical reaction is a reaction in which a chemical change takes place. The molecules that enter the reaction are called *reactants*. The molecules resulting from the reaction are called *products*.

When charcoal burns, the following takes place:

Carbon plus oxygen produces carbon dioxide

$$carbon + oxygen \longrightarrow carbon\ dioxide$$

Using chemical symbols, the formula is:

$$C + O_2 \longrightarrow CO_2$$

This formula is the chemical equation for the oxidation of carbon. One atom of carbon combined with one molecule of oxygen to form one molecule of carbon dioxide.

Using the reaction of hydrogen and oxygen to form water:

$$H_2 + O_2 \longrightarrow H_2O$$

Note that this equation is not balanced, there are two oxygen atoms on the left side and only one oxygen atom on the right.

$$H_2 + O_2 \longrightarrow 2H_2O$$

But now the hydrogen atoms are not balanced. There are 4 hydrogen atoms on the right but only 2 on the left. This is corrected by placing "2" in front of the H_2 on the left side.

$$2H_2 + O_2 \longrightarrow 2H_2O$$

Is the following equation balanced?

$$H_2 + Cl_2 \longrightarrow HCl$$

No, it is not. There are 2 atoms of hydrogen and 2 atoms of chlorine on the left side but only 1 atom of hydrogen and 1 atom of chlorine on the right side.

This equation can be balanced by placing a "2" in front of the HCl.

$$H_2 + Cl \longrightarrow 2HCl$$

There are four types of chemical reactions:

1. *Synthesis:* two or more elements or compounds unite to form one compound:

$$carbon + oxygen \longrightarrow carbon\ dioxide$$
$$C + O_2 \longrightarrow CO_2$$

$$calcium\ oxide + carbon\ dioxide \longrightarrow calcium\ carbonate$$
$$CaO + CO_2 \longrightarrow CaCO_3$$

2. *Decomposition:* a substance breaks down into two or more substances:

Peroxide decomposes into water and oxygen

$$2H_2O_2 \longrightarrow 2H_2O + O_2$$

3. *Single displacement:* one element displaces another in a compound.

$$2KBr + Cl_2 \longrightarrow 2KCl + Br_2$$

Chlorine displaced the bromine in the compound, potassium bromide.

4. *Double displacement:* the positive part of each reactant unites with the negative part of the other reactant.

$$3NaOH + FeCl_3 \longrightarrow 3\ NaCl + Fe(OH)_3$$

Sodium hydroxide reacts with ferric chloride to form sodium chloride and ferric hydroxide.

Measurement

Measurement is an essential part of chemistry. Although the English system of measurement is used in everyday life in the United States, most of the people in the rest of the world, as well as scientists, use the modernized form of the metric system, a decimal system based on tens, multiples of tens, and fractions of tens.

Length

The meter is the standard unit of length in the metric system. The meter (m) may be divided into 100 equal parts called centimeters (cm).

100 cm = 1 m

The meter (m) may also be divided into 1,000 equal parts called millimeters (mm).

1 m = 100 cm = 1,000 mm

1 cm = 10 mm

Distances of considerable length are measured in kilometers (km).

1 km = 1,000 m

Changing from one unit to another is done by simply dividing or multiplying by multiples of 10.

Area

Area is calculated by multiplying length times width. The area of a rectangle 3 meters long and 4 meters wide is 12 square meters.

$$3\ m \times 4\ m = 12\ m^2$$

Volume

Volume is the amount of space an object occupies. If the object is a cube or rectangular solid, the volume is obtained by multiplying length × width × height. The cubic meter is a standard metric unit of volume. However, it is a very large unit containing one million cubic centimeters. The liter (L), equal to 1,000 cubic centimeters, is the metric unit commonly used. The milliliter (ml) is used for measuring still smaller volumes.

1 liter (L) = 1,000 milliliters (ml)

1 ml = 1 cm^3

Mass

The more important units of mass in the metric system are the gram (g), kilogram (kg), and milligram (mg).

1 kg = 1,000 g = 1,000,000 mg

1 g = 1,000 mg

A comparison of the different metric units is shown in the following table.

COMPARISON OF METRIC UNITS			
FACTOR		**METRIC PREFIX**	**SYMBOLS**
× 1,000	kilo-	(kilometer, kiloliter, kilogram)	km, kl, kg
× 100	hecto-	(hectometer, hectoliter, hectogram)	hm, hl, hg
× 10	deka-	(dekameter, dekaliter, dekagram)	dam, dal, dag
× 1		(meter, liter, gram)	m, L, g
× 0.1	deci-	(decimeter, deciliter, decigram)	dm, dl, dg
× 0.01	centi-	(centimeter, centiliter, centigram)	cm, cl, cg
× 0.001	milli-	(millimeter, milliliter, milligram)	mm, ml, mg

Temperature

Temperature is generally measured in scientific work by using the Celsius or centigrade scale. This temperature scale is based on the freezing and boiling points of water. The freezing point is at 0°C; the boiling point is at 100°C.

The Fahrenheit scale, used in everyday activities, is also based on the freezing and boiling points of water. The freezing point is at 32°F; the boiling point is at 212°F.

Use the following formulas to change from one scale to the other:

$$°C = \frac{5}{9}(°F - 32°)$$

$$°F = \frac{9}{5}°C + 32°$$

The Kelvin or absolute scale of temperature is also used in scientific work. This scale starts with absolute zero at –273°C. To change Celsius or centigrade temperature to Kelvin or absolute temperature, add 273°.

$$K = °C + 273°$$

Physics

Physics is the science of matter, energy, and their interactions. These are grouped into many different fields such as mechanics, thermodynamics, magnetism, and electricity.

Force and Work

A *force* is the push or pull that forces an object to change its speed or direction. Weight is the force of gravity on an object. *Work* done on an object is defined as the force exerted on the object times the distance moved in the direction of the force.

If W = work; F = force; and d = distance,

   W = Fd

The unit of work in the British system is expressed in foot-pounds (ft-lb). In the metric system, the unit of work is the newton-meter (n-m) or joule (j).

Power is the rate of doing work.

$$\text{Power} = \frac{\text{Work}}{\text{Time}}$$

If P = Power; W = work; and t = time,

$$P = \frac{W}{t} = \frac{Fd}{t}$$

In the British system, power is expressed in foot-pounds per second or foot-pounds per minute. In the metric system, power is expressed in newton-meters per second or joules or watts. Machine power is generally expressed in *horsepower*. One horsepower is equal to 550 ft-lb/sec.

Newton's Laws

Sir Isaac Newton was an English physicist, philosopher, and mathematician. He formulated the three laws of motion that explain how objects move in response to forces and a law to explain the force of gravity.

1. *Newton's first law of motion* predicts the behavior of objects for which all existing forces are balanced. If the net forces acting on an object is zero, the object will remain at rest or remain moving at a constant velocity. If the force exerted on an object is zero, the object does not necessarily have zero velocity. Without any forces acting on it, including friction, an object in motion will continue to travel at constant velocity. In simpler terms, an object at rest tends to stay at rest, and an object in motion tends to stay in motion with the same speed and in the same direction unless acted upon by an unbalanced force.

2. *Newton's second law of motion* pertains to the behavior of objects for which all existing forces are not balanced. The net force acting on an object equals the product of the mass and

the acceleration of the object. A net force on an object will accelerate it, or change its velocity and the direction of the force in the same as that of the acceleration. The mass (m) of the object is measured in kilograms. Acceleration (a) is measured in meters per second per second. Force (f) is measured in *newtons*. A newton is the force necessary to impart a mass of 1kg an acceleration of 1/m/sec/sec. This theory is illustrated by the following equation: F = ma. Note that this law is also known as the *law of inertia* since the greater the mass of an object, the greater the force needed to overcome it *inertia* (its reluctance to change velocity).

3. *Newton's third law of motion.* An object experiences a force because it is interacting with some other object. When an object exerts force on another object, the second object exerts on the first a force of the same magnitude but in the opposite direction. Simply stated, for every action, there is an equal and opposite reaction.

4. *Newton's law of gravity* states that all objects in the universe attract each other with a force that varies directly as a product of their masses and inversely as square of their separation from each other. The force is known as gravity, the fundamental force responsible for interactions that occur because of mass between particles and matter. Note that the earth, the moon, and planets attraction for objects is known as gravity.

Speed

Speed is a scalar quantity (a quantity that is fully described by a magnitude alone), which refers to how fast an object is moving or the distance an object travels per unit of time. A fast-moving object has a high speed, while a slow-moving object has a low speed. An object with no movement at all has no speed.

$$\text{Speed} = \frac{\text{distance}}{\text{time}}$$

Velocity

Velocity is a vector quantity (a quantity that is fully described by both a magnitude and a direction) that refers to the rate in which an object changes position. *Acceleration* is the rate of change of velocity. Velocity is also called momentum. Note that if an object is very heavy, it will be difficult to stop it or change its direction.

Machines

Machines are devices for transferring energy. Simple machines are generally used in order to change the size or direction of a force.

Machines may be divided into the following classes:
- Lever (see-saw, crowbar, hammer, scissors, pliers, shovel)
- Inclined plane (screw, wedge)
- Wheel and axle (doorknob, steering wheel)
- Pulley (elevator, power shovel)

The jackscrew is actually a combination of the lever and the inclined plane.

$$\text{Efficiency} = \frac{\text{Output Work}}{\text{Input Work}} \times 100$$

The force applied to a machine in order to do the work needed is known as *effort*. The greater the force is applied, the greater the work done. The force that one must overcome is known as *resistance*.

Energy

Energy may be defined as the capacity to do work and can be either kinetic or potential. *Kinetic* energy is the energy possessed by a moving object. *Potential* energy is the work that can be done by an object because of its relative position. Energy is found in many different forms, such as the following:

- Chemical
- Heat
- Electrical
- Light
- Sound
- Mechanical
- Nuclear

Energy is neither created or destroyed but can readily be changed from one form to another. This is known as conservation of energy. For example, chemical energy is changed to electrical energy with the storage battery. Friction may be used to change mechanical energy to heat. The radio may be used to change sound to electrical energy and electrical energy to sound. Note that some energy will be lost in the form of heat when energy is converted.

Heat Transfer

There are three methods by which heat is transferred from one object to another. These are conduction, convection, and radiation.

1. *Conduction* is the simplest method of heat transfer. It is accomplished by direct contact, such as placing your finger on a very hot object. The heat is transferred directly from the very hot object to the skin on your finger. Metals are generally good conductors of heat. Other materials, such as wood or plastic, are poor conductors and are termed *insulators*. Note that many metallic pots and pans have wooden handles that act as heat insulators.

2. *Convection* is the transfer of heat in liquids or gases when heated unevenly. The heated liquid or gas rises and the resulting movement is termed convection.

3. *Radiation* of heat, such as the heat from the sun, is transmitted by electromagnetic waves, which change into heat when they reach their destination.

Basic Electricity

There are two kinds of electric charge. One is positive (+); the other is negative (–). How objects become electrically charged may be explained by *electrons*, negatively charged particles of matter.

When two objects are rubbed together, electrons are taken away from one object and added to the other object. Combing your hair results in electrons moving from your hair to the comb, which then takes on a negative charge.

Protons are positively charged particles. Matter is generally neutral, because it contains an equal number of electrons and protons. The flow of electrons from one place to another results in electric current. Metallic materials allow electrons to flow freely. These materials are called conductors (copper, iron, silver, aluminum, etc.).

Materials that do not allow the free flow of electrons are called insulators (air, rubber, wood, plastic, etc.).

Circuits

An electric circuit is the path along which electrons move from a place where there are many electrons to a place where there are fewer electrons. It consists of many parts, including the power source, conductors, switches, and the appliance or appliances to be operated. The circuits may be in *series* or in *parallel* (see Figure 16 and Figure 17).

In a *series* circuit, all parts are connected in a continuous line, one after another. If any part fails or is switched off, all other parts are turned off. For example, when using series-circuited lights to decorate a Christmas tree, one burnt-out light will cause all the other lights on the tree to become unlit by breaking the flow of electrons in the circuit.

In a *parallel* circuit, the different parts are on separate branches and can be switched off without affecting the parts on the other branches.

There are two kinds of electric circuits:

1. *Direct current* (DC): electrons flow in one direction only. With the dry cell, the electrons move from the negative connector to the positive connector.

2. *Alternating current* (AC): alternating current generated in power stations changes direction many times per second. The electricity produced is by electromagnetic induction resulting from motion in a magnetic field.

Figure 16. This diagram shows a series circuit. If one bulb goes out, all the other bulbs will also go out.

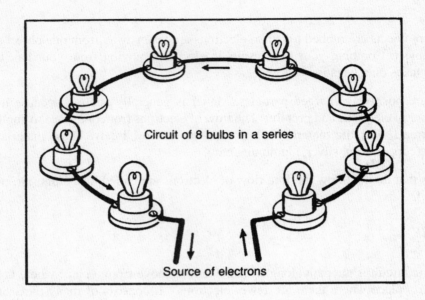

Figure 17. These appliances are arranged in a parallel circuit. You can turn one of them off without affecting the others.

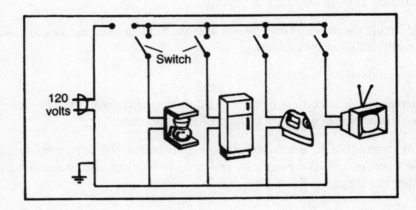

Except for battery-operated electrical systems, such as in the automobile, electrical energy is supplied as alternating current since it can be transmitted through wires at high voltage over great distances, unlike direct current. *Transformers* are used to change the voltage in power lines. *Step-up* transformers raise the voltage; *step-down* transformers reduce the voltage. Voltage supplied to our homes is generally at 110 to 120 volts.

The following terms are used in measuring electricity:

- *Volt:* measures the amount of work done when electrons are moved between two points in an electric circuit.

- *Ampere:* measures the amount of electrons moving past a certain point in a current in one second.

- *Ohm:* the unit of measurement of resistance, which consists of all conditions in an electric circuit that limit the flow of electrons. An electric circuit with a current of 3 amperes and a resistance of 4 ohms would have a voltage of 12. Ohm's law states:

  Volts = Amperes × Ohms

- *Watt:* measures how much electricity is consumed. The amount of electricity used and the length of time used is measured in watt-hours for small amounts of energy or kilowatt-hours for larger amounts. A kilowatt-hour is the amount of energy used in one hour by one kilowatt of power.

- *Ammeter:* used to measure the amount of current in amperes.

- *Voltmeter:* used to measure potential difference in volts.

Fuses and *circuit breakers* are devices that limit current flow. In the fuse, a small section of wire will melt and break the current if a certain amount of electric current passes through it. Current capacity of the fuse is determined by the size (thickness) of the wire. *Circuit breakers* interrupt the flow of current mechanically when the current limit is reached.

Magnetism

Simple magnets have two poles—a north pole and a south pole. If the north poles of two magnets are brought close together, they will repel each other. If the south poles of two magnets are brought together, they will also repel each other.

If the north pole of one magnet is brought close to the south pole of another magnet, they will attract each other (see Figure 18). The force of attraction or repulsion is called magnetic force. The magnetic poles are the two locations on the magnet where magnetic forces are strongest.

The region surrounding the magnet where there is a magnetic force is called the magnetic field. Lines of force extend from one pole to the other pole of the magnet with the greatest force concentrated at the poles (see Figure 19).

When a wire is moved in a magnetic field, current is produced in the wire. This effect, known as *electromagnetic induction*, led to the development of generators. The electric generator produces current that flows in one direction and then in the opposite direction, producing an alternating current.

Figure 18. Like poles repel. Unlike poles attract.

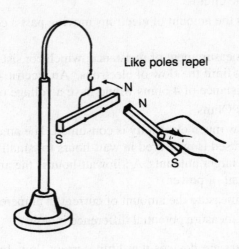

Like poles repel

Figure 19. Lines of force in a magnetic field.

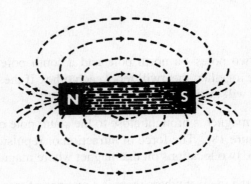

The strength of the magnetic force between two objects increases as the amount of electric charge on these objects increases. The strength of the magnetic charge between the objects decreases as the distance between them increases. Reducing the distance between the two objects by a half results in a magnetic force four times as great. For example, reducing the distance from 100 mm to 50 mm increases the magnetic force fourfold. Similarly, increasing the distance from 100 mm to 200 mm reduces the force to one-fourth the original amount.

The magnetic compass contains a magnetic needle that rotates in a horizontal direction. The compass case is always made of a nonmagnetic substance, usually brass.

Light

Although light possesses many properties of waves (reflection, refraction, etc.), it differs somewhat from other waves. Compared with sound waves, light waves are much faster and can travel through empty space. Light or other waves that can travel through space at very high speed are called electromagnetic waves.

The different types of electromagnetic waves in increasing order of frequency and decreasing wavelength are as follows:

- Ordinary radio waves
- FM and television waves
- Radar and microwaves
- Infrared waves
- Light waves
- Ultraviolet waves
- X-rays
- Gamma waves

Two important characteristics of light are:

1. Light waves generally move in a straight path at approximately 186,000 miles per second.

2. Light may change its direction when moving from one material to another material (for example, from air to water).

Refraction occurs when light waves are bent (change direction) passing from one material into another. Refracted light can cause mirages or false illusions.

Sunlight is a mixture of all the colors of the rainbow—a spectrum. When sunlight is passed through a prism, the colors are separated into a spectrum of red, orange, yellow, green, indigo, and violet.

Reflection occurs when light rays strike a flat mirror and bounce off. The rays striking the mirror are called *incident* rays; those that bounce off are termed *reflected* rays.

Lenses refract light rays in different ways (see Figure 20).

Figure 20. Convex and concave lenses

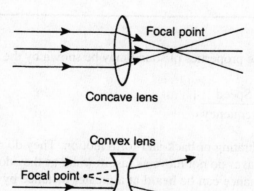

A *convex* lens is so shaped that the edges are thinner than the center. The light rays passing through the prism meet at a certain point. The *focal point* is the point at which the parallel light rays are brought together after being refracted by the lens.

A *concave* lens is so shaped that the edges are thicker than the center. The parallel light rays passing through the prism are spread apart after being refracted by the lens.

Sound

References to sound in physics are really references to *sound waves*. These are waves in gases, liquids, and solids that cannot be transmitted through a vacuum or empty space. There are three important properties of sound waves:

1. *Wavelength* is the distance between high points or between low points and is generally measured in millimeters or centimeters.

2. *Speed* is determined by measuring how fast the waves move. That is, how fast the high point (crest) or low point (trough) moves. Speed is generally measured in meters per second (see Figure 21).

Frequency is determined by measuring the number of waves (crests or troughs) that move past a certain point in one second. The unit of measurement is the hertz (Hz). One hertz is one wave moving past per second.

Figure 21. This diagram shows how speed, frequency, and wavelength are related

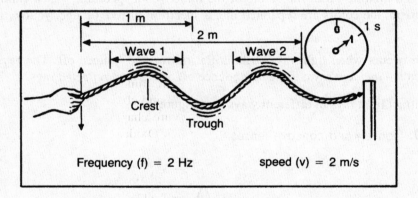

The relationship of these properties of sound may be shown by the formula:

$$\text{Wavelength} = \frac{\text{Speed}}{\text{Frequency}}$$

Sound waves have a vibrating or back-and-forth motion. They do not move as fast in air as in water. Similarly, sound waves do not move as fast in water as they do in wood or metals. A train approaching from the distance can be heard at a greater distance by the noise through the steel rails than by the noise made through the air.

The pitch of sound is closely related to the frequency of the sound waves. A high sound frequency is called a high pitch. The volume, or loudness of a sound, is determined by the amplitude of sound waves. The intensity of sound is expressed on a decibel scale. The amplitude and frequency of sound waves determine the sound intensity.

Earth Science

This section includes several sciences that fall into the earth science. This includes the basics of meteorology and astronomy.

Geology

The earth consists of three layers—the crust, the mantle, and the core.

1. The *crust* is a thin layer and comprises the earth's surface. It varies in thickness from a few miles to perhaps 30 miles.

2. The *mantle* is the thick layer beneath the crust and represents more than 75 percent of the earth's volume. The mantle consists of solid rock. However, the top portion of the mantle has some slight movement.

3. The *core* is the earth's center and comprises almost 20 percent of the earth's volume.

The temperature of the earth's interior is estimated to be between 3,000° C and 4,000° C. This heat is prevented from escaping by the solid rock in the upper mantle and the crust. Cracks in the earth's crust produce *faults*. Earthquakes are caused by the movement of rocks along faults. The waves produced by earthquakes can be recorded by a *seismograph*. The intensity of earthquakes is measured on a 1 to 10 scale called the *Richter* scale.

Rocks

Rocks are pieces of the earth and contain one or more minerals. Rocks differ in size, shape, color, and degree of hardness. The natural mechanical and chemical processes that break rock into smaller pieces are termed *weathering*. Temperature changes, frost action, and plant root growth are common forms of mechanical weathering. Oxidation and action of air pollutants causes chemical weathering.

The natural processes that cause the smaller pieces of rock to be carried away are termed *erosion*. Erosion is generally accomplished by running water, wind, and glaciers.

Based upon their method of formation, the three classes of rock are: igneous, sedimentary, and metamorphic.

Igneous rock is formed by the cooling and hardening of molten material. Granite and pumice are two common igneous rocks.

Sedimentary rock is formed by the joining together of small pieces of rock or sediment deposited when fast-moving streams slow down. The sediment may consist of different sized particles or pieces ranging from mud to gravel. In time, these particles become compressed or cemented together to form sedimentary rock. Shale, sandstone, limestone, and soft coal are common types of sedimentary rock.

Metamorphic rock is formed by changes resulting from great heat, pressure, and time. Both sedimentary and igneous rock may become metamorphosed. Slate, marble, and hard coal are common kinds of metamorphic rock.

Rocks beneath the earth's crust that are heated to the melting point are called *magma*. When the molten magma reaches the earth's surface, it is called *lava*. A *volcano* is the rock formation that results when lava reaches the earth's surface.

Meteorology

- The earth's atmosphere consists of layers of air surrounding Earth's surface. See Figure 22. These gaseous layers are:
- The *troposphere* is the first or innermost layer of the atmosphere and extends five to ten miles above the earth's surface. We live in this layer where virtually all weather changes and cloudiness occur. Most of the air surrounding the earth is found in this layer.
- The second layer is the *stratosphere* and extends up to about 25 to 30 miles above the earth.
- The third layer is the *mesosphere*, which extends to about 50 miles above the earth.
- The fourth or outermost layer is the *thermosphere*, which extends to approximately 350 miles above the earth. Air in this layer is extremely thin.
- The *ionosphere* is the layer between the mesosphere and the thermosphere. This is an important communication zone as it reflects various types of radio waves.

Figure 22. The important layers of the earth's atmosphere. (Note that the heights are not drawn to scale)

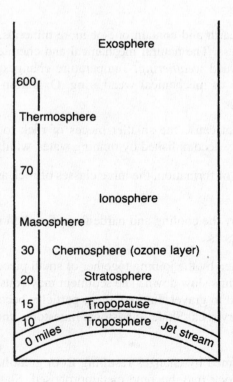

Almost half of the sun's radiation passes through the atmosphere and reaches the earth's surface where it is absorbed by the land and the water of the oceans, which warm the air above them. Land absorbs energy and warms up faster than water. Accordingly, during the daytime, air over land gets warmer than air over water; at night, air over land gets cooler than air over water. These temperature differences cause differences in air density.

The sun's rays strike the earth's surface at different angles. The equator receives direct rays, whereas the regions closer to the poles receive slanted rays. This also affects the air temperatures and causes differences in air density.

Air Pressure

The force with which air presses on the surface of the earth is known as *air pressure*. Cold air is denser and presses down with greater pressure (high pressure). Warm air is less dense and presses down with less pressure (low pressure). Atmospheric pressure is measured by an instrument known as a *barometer*. At sea level, air pressure will normally support 30 inches of mercury. Normal atmospheric pressure is about 15 pounds per square inch at sea level.

Air generally flows from high pressure to low pressure. This air movement is called *wind*. Wind direction is determined by a *weather vane*. Wind velocity is measured by an *anemometer*.

Humidity

The sun's energy evaporates the oceans' water, producing vapor. *Humidity* is the amount of water vapor in air. *Relative humidity* is the amount of moisture in the air compared to the maximum amount it can hold at that temperature. Relative humidity is measured by means of a hygrometer consisting of a wet-and-dry bulb thermometer.

Most people find a relative humidity of 50 to 60 percent at normal room temperature to be quite comfortable. Air is *saturated* when it contains the maximum amount of water vapor it can hold at a given temperature. The temperature at which the relative humidity reaches 100 percent is called the *dew point*, the temperature at which the vapor will begin to condense into a liquid.

Clouds

Clouds have different shapes and sizes. The three basic types of clouds are stratus, cumulus, and cirrus.

1. *Stratus* clouds are broad, flat, low-hanging clouds that blanket the sky. Darkened stratus clouds indicate that rain will soon fall.

2. *Cumulus* clouds are massive clouds having flat bottoms and rounded tops. They resemble white smoke rising from a smokestack and indicate fair weather. When cumulus clouds darken and greatly increase in size, expect heavy rains.

3. *Cirrus* clouds are high, thin, feathery clouds. The presence of such clouds indicates the possibility of rain or snow within a few days.

Air Masses

Air masses have characteristics related to the region where they are formed. Air masses formed over land are dry; those formed over oceans are humid. Air masses formed in the northern regions of the northern hemisphere are cold; those formed at or near the equator are warm.

When two different air masses meet, they do not readily mix but form a boundary of separation called a *front*. When a cold air mass encounters a warm air mass, a cold front is created. The warmer air mass is pushed up causing the formation of cumulus clouds and heavy rain. When a warm air mass encounters a cold air mass, a warm front is created. The warm air passes over the cold air forming cirrus clouds. In time, the clouds thicken and move closer to the earth causing light rain.

Astronomy

Astronomy is the study of the stars, planets, and other heavenly bodies.

The earth's orbit around the sun is termed an ellipse, a slightly flattened circle. As the earth's axis (an imaginary line running through the earth from pole to pole) is not perpendicular but tilted at an angle of $23\frac{1}{2}°$, the North Pole is tilted toward the sun during part of the orbit and tilted away from the sun during another part of the orbit. This explains why daylight and darkness are not of equal length except on the first day of spring (vernal equinox) and the first day of autumn (autumnal equinox).

The earth spins on its axis and makes a complete rotation every 24 hours. It revolves around the sun every $365\frac{1}{4}$ days, necessitating a leap year every four years. The earth revolves and rotates in the same direction from west to east.

The moon is a satellite of the earth. It makes a complete orbit around the earth every $27\frac{1}{3}$ days, turning once on its axis during this period. The moon is the earth's nearest neighbor. A lunar eclipse occurs when the moon moves into the earth's shadow. A solar eclipse occurs when the earth moves into the moon's shadow.

Solar System

The solar system consists of the sun and a multitude of smaller bodies held in orbit by the Sun's huge mass. It is called the *solar system* because the sun's huge mass and its resulting force of gravity controls the movement of these smaller bodies.

The nine planets in the solar system are among its largest bodies. Six of the planets have satellites.

There are four smaller planets closest to the sun frequently called the inner planets. These are:
- Mercury
- Venus

- Earth
- Mars

The five larger planets farthest from the sun are frequently termed the outer planets. They are:
- Jupiter
- Saturn
- Uranus
- Neptune
- Pluto

Some of the small bodies in the solar system collide with the earth. Most of these bodies burn up because of the friction of the earth's atmosphere. These bodies are called *meteors* or "shooting stars." Those that reach the earth's surface are termed *meteorites*.

The *North Star,* or Polaris, is a most important star as it is in direct line with the North Pole of the earth, and therefore appears to remain stationary in the sky. This star has long been used by navigators as a directional guide.

Sample Questions

1. The chief nutrient in lean meat is
   - 1-A   fat.
   - 1-B   starch.
   - 1-C   protein.
   - 1-D   carbohydrates.

2. Which of the following is an invertebrate?
   - 2-A   Starfish
   - 2-B   Pigeon
   - 2-C   Gorilla
   - 2-D   Alligator

3. Substances that hasten chemical reaction time without themselves undergoing change are called
   - 3-A   buffers.
   - 3-B   colloids.
   - 3-C   reducers.
   - 3-D   catalysts.

4. The case of a compass would not be made of
   - 4-A   brass.
   - 4-B   copper.
   - 4-C   plastic.
   - 4-D   steel.

5. An eclipse of the sun throws the shadow of the
      5-A   Moon on the Sun.
      5-B   Moon on the Earth.
      5-C   Earth on the Sun.
      5-D   Earth on the Moon.

Answer Explanations

1-C   Protein is a nutrient found in lean meat. Starch is a form of carbohydrates. Fat may be found in meat, but it is not the chief nutrient in lean meat.

2-A   An invertebrate is an animal that lacks a backbone. Since all birds, mammals, and reptiles have backbones, starfish is the only possible choice.

3-D   Catalysts hasten chemical reaction time without undergoing change.

4-D   Since a compass uses the earth's magnetism to operate, a steel case would interfere in the compass operation.

5-B   A solar eclipse is an obstruction of the sun's rays by the moon. Therefore, the shadow of the moon would be cast on the earth.

ARITHMETIC REASONING REVIEW

The Arithmetic Reasoning section in the ASVAB includes basic math processes like addition, subtraction, multiplication, and division, and applying these computational operations to solve simple math problems you come across in everyday life. The ability to perform basic math operations and to use computational skills to solve simple math problems is needed for activities at work, school, home, in shopping and banking, or engaging in social, community, or recreational activities.

A concise review of basic arithmetic follows. It is provided to refresh your memory about basic math operations and give you practice for the math word problems that are on the ASVAB.

Review of Basic Arithmetic

Whole Numbers

1.	One
10.	Ten
100.	One hundred
1,000.	One thousand
10,000.	Ten thousand
100,000.	One hundred thousand
1,000,000.	One million
10,000,000.	Ten million
100,000,000.	One hundred million
1,000,000,000.	One billion

Always start counting from the decimal point. Note that the value of a digit increases when the digit is moved to the left. Each time it is moved farther to the left of the decimal point, the value of a digit is multiplied by ten. To make it easier to read large numbers (numbers containing four or more digits), commas are placed every three spaces as you go left from the decimal point.

If the decimal point is not shown with the whole number, it is understood to be just to the right of the last digit on the right.

24 means 24.   12,528 means 12,528.

Decimals

.1	One tenth
.01	One hundredth
.001	One thousandth
.0001	One ten-thousandth
.00001	One hundred-thousandth
.000001	One millionth

Always start counting from the decimal point. Note that the value of a digit decreases when the digit in a decimal is moved to the right. The value of the digit is divided by ten each time it is moved one place farther to the right of the decimal point.

Decimals are also known as decimal fractions, since the denominator is either a tenth, hundredth, thousandth, etc.

$$.1 \text{ is } \frac{1}{10} \quad .01 \text{ is } \frac{1}{100} \quad .001 \text{ is } \frac{1}{1000}$$

Fractions

A fraction is a number that indicates one or more equal parts. A fraction has a *numerator*, a *division line*, and a *denominator*.

$$\frac{1}{4} \quad \text{or} \quad 1/4$$

The bottom number (*denominator*) shows the number of equal parts into which the whole has been divided.

The top number (*numerator*) shows how many of these equal parts are in the fraction.

A *proper fraction* has a numerator that is less than the denominator. It is also called a *common fraction* or *fraction*.

$$1/3 \text{ or } \frac{1}{3} \quad 3/4 \text{ or } \frac{3}{4} \quad 7/9 \text{ or } \frac{7}{9}$$

An *improper fraction* has a numerator that is equal to or more than the denominator.

$$3/3 \text{ or } \frac{3}{3} \quad 9/8 \text{ or } \frac{9}{8} \quad 16/15 \text{ or } \frac{16}{15}$$

A *mixed number* consists of a whole number and a fraction.

$$1 \ 1/4 \ \text{or} \ 1\frac{1}{4} \qquad 12 \ 1/2 \ \text{or} \ 12\frac{1}{2}$$

Percent

Percent means hundredth. It may be expressed with the % symbol, as a fraction with a denominator of 100, or as a decimal.

Here is a quick chart to convert percents into fractions and decimals.

Percent	Fraction	Decimal
1%	$\dfrac{1}{100}$	.01
50%	$\dfrac{50}{100}$ or $\dfrac{1}{2}$	.50 or .5
$12\frac{1}{2}\%$	$\dfrac{12.5}{100}$ or $\dfrac{125}{100}$	.125

Addition

Addition is indicated by either the plus (+) sign, the word *plus*, or the word *and*.

Addends are the numbers that are added. The *total* or *sum* is the number obtained by adding all the addends.

Adding Whole Numbers, Decimals, and Dollars and Cents

The numbers to be added are arranged in vertical columns. As additions consist of combining similar units, units must be placed directly under units, tens under tens, hundreds under hundreds, etc. If decimals are to be added, place tenths under tenths, hundredths under hundredths, etc.

		9					$4.32
4	167	82			6.4	$3.85	16.68
21	285	134	23,857	28.7	12.25	6.21	103.14
+153	+310	+2675	+71,204	+34.7	+107.125	+ 4.16	+421.08
178	762	2900	95,061	63.4	125.775	$14.22	$545.22

Note that in vertical additions of dollars and cents, the $ is placed to the left of the top addend and to the left of the total.

Subtraction

Subtraction is indicated by the subtraction sign (–), the word *minus*, the words *take away*, or the words *find the difference between*. There are three parts to a subtraction problem:

Minuend: Placed on the top of the vertical subtraction. It is the number from which another number is taken away.

Subtrahend: Placed below the minuend in vertical subtraction. It is the number that is taken away.

Difference or *remainder:* Result of the subtraction or what is left. This result is put at the bottom in vertical subtraction.

$$
\begin{array}{rl}
581 & \text{minuend} \\
-350 & \text{subtrahend} \\
\hline
231 & \text{remainder or difference}
\end{array}
$$

Subtracting Whole Numbers, Decimals, and Dollars and Cents

As with addition, the numbers in the subtraction are arranged in vertical columns. Units must be placed directly under units, tens under tens, hundreds under hundreds, etc. If there are decimals, place the decimal point directly under the decimal point, tenths under tenths, hundredths under hundredths, etc.

$$
\begin{array}{rrrr}
576 & 385 & 87.647 & \$743.65 \\
-342 & -57 & -8.350 & -418.45 \\
\hline
234 & 328 & 79.297 & \$325.20
\end{array}
$$

Note that in vertical subtraction of dollars and cents, the $ is placed at the left of the minuend and at the left of the answer.

Multiplication

Multiplication is indicated by the multiplication sign (×), the word *multiply*, or the word *times*. There are three main parts to multiplication problems:

1. *Multiplicand:* Number being multiplied.

2. *Multiplier:* Number by which you multiply.

3. *Product:* Answer obtained by multiplying the multiplicand by the multiplier.

$$
\begin{array}{rl}
12 & \text{multiplicand} \\
\times 9 & \text{multiplier} \\
\hline
108 & \text{product}
\end{array}
\qquad
\begin{array}{rl}
483 & \text{multiplicand} \\
\times 24 & \text{multiplier} \\
\hline
1932 & \text{partial product} (4 \times 483) \\
966 & \text{partial product} (2 \times 483) \\
\hline
11592 & \text{product}
\end{array}
$$

Note that when the multiplier consists of more than one digit, the answer obtained by multiplying the multiplicand by each digit of the multiplier is called a *partial product*.

Multiplying Whole Numbers

In the multiplication process, first multiply units, then tens, then hundreds, etc. The answers to each of these separate multiplications are partial products. The final answer or product is obtained by adding all the partial products.

$$
\begin{array}{r}
365 \\
\times 124 \\
\hline
1460 \quad \text{(ones)} \\
730 \quad \text{(tens)} \\
\underline{365} \quad \text{(hundreds)} \\
45,260
\end{array}
$$

Note that the right digit of each partial product is placed in a vertical line with the digit used as a multiplier. The addition of the partial products is made easier by placing the right digit of each succeeding partial product one place farther to the left.

Multiplying Decimals and Dollars and Cents

The multiplication process is the same as that for the whole numbers. However, it requires the additional step of fixing the decimal point in the answer. This is accomplished by counting the total number of digits to the right of the decimal points in both the multiplicand and the multiplier and then fixing the decimal point in the answer by counting off the same total number of places from right to left in the product.

25.6	One digit to the right of the decimal point in the multiplicand plus
× .43	two digits to the right of the decimal point in the multiplier equals
768	three.
1024	Count off three places from right to left in the product to fix the
11.008	decimal point.

$ 325.75	Two digits to the right of the decimal point in the multiplicand plus
× 18	zero digits to the right of the decimal point in the multiplier equals
260600	two.
32575	Count off two from right to left in the product to fix the
$5,863.50	decimal point.

Division

Division is indicated by the division sign (÷), the fraction sign (— or /), the words *divided by*, the short-division symbol)_____ , or the long-division symbol)_____ . Division problems have four parts:

1. *Dividend:* Number being divided.

2. *Divisor:* Number by which you divide.

3. *Quotient:* Answer to division.

4. *Remainder:* Number that is left if division is not exact.

Dividing Whole Numbers

If the divisor is a single-digit number, use either short division or long division. If the divisor has more than one digit, use long division.

Short division

Divisor   3)867   Dividend
             289   Quotient

1. 8 divided by 3 is 2 with a remainder of 2, change 6 to 26.

2. Record the 2 in the quotient under 8.

3. 26 divided by 3 is 8 with a remainder of 2, change 7 to 27.

4. Record the 8 in the quotient under 6.

5. 27 divided by 3 is 9 exactly.

To check if the division is correct, multiply the quotient by the divisor. If no error was made, the product should be the same as the dividend.

Check: 289
          ×3
          867

Long division

$$
\begin{array}{r}
35 \\
26{\overline{)910}} \\
-78 \\
\hline
130 \\
-130 \\
\hline
0
\end{array}
$$

1. Estimate 91 divided by 26 as 3.

2. Record the 3 in the quotient over 1 and multiply 26 by 3.

3. Record the product 78 under 91.

(If the product is greater than 91, it means that 3 is too large and that a lesser number should be used.)

4. Subtract the 78 from the 91 and record the 13.

(If the difference is more than 26, it means that 3 is too small and that a greater number should be estimated.)

5. Bring down the next digit (0 in this case) and join it to the difference.

6. Estimate 130 divided by 26 as 5.

7. Record the 5 in the quotient over the 0 and multiply 26 by 5.

8. Record the product under 130.

9. Subtract 130 from 130.

10. The difference is 0 so there is no remainder.

Check: 35
            ×26
            210
            70
            910

Dividing Decimals

To divide a decimal by a whole number, proceed as if the dividend were a whole number. Then fix the decimal point in the quotient directly in line with the decimal point in the dividend.

$$8)\overline{385.04}$$
$$48.13$$

$$
\begin{array}{r}
48.13 \\
8{\overline{\smash{\big)}\,385.04}} \\
\underline{-32} \\
65 \\
\underline{-64} \\
10 \\
\underline{-8} \\
24 \\
\underline{-24} \\
0
\end{array}
$$

Check: 48.13
            $\times$ 8
            385.04

To divide by a decimal, first rename the divisor as a whole number by moving the decimal point to the right of the last digit on the right. Then move the decimal point in the dividend to the right the same number of places. If necessary, add zeros. Finally, complete the division as you ordinarily would with a whole number as a divisor.

$.6\overline{)2.4}$	is changed to	$6\overline{)24}$
$.6\overline{)24.}$	is changed to	$6\overline{)240}$
$2.4\overline{)3.12}$	is changed to	$24\overline{)31.2}$
$2.46\overline{)3.198}$	is changed to	$246\overline{)319.8}$
$.005\overline{)30.}$	is changed to	$5\overline{)30000}$

Note that in all the above changes, the quotient is unchanged as both the divisor and the dividend are multiplied by the same amount.

Decimal division is also used when the division involves dollars and cents or just cents alone.

$$\frac{\$9.60}{3} = \$3.20 \qquad \frac{\$.75}{15} = \$.05$$

Note that when dollars or cents are divided by a number, the answer is in dollars or cents.

$$\frac{\$150}{\$5} = 30 \qquad \frac{\$5.50}{\$.25} = 22$$

Note that when dollars are divided by dollars or when dollars and cents are divided by dollars and cents, the answer is a number.

Sample Questions

The following sample questions illustrate some of the question types in the Arithmetic Reasoning subtest that deal with the application of the four basic arithmetic operations just covered. Answers and explanations are located on pages 164–168.

Addition

1. 75 + 49 =

    The sum is
    - 1-A   114
    - 1-B   124
    - 1-C   125
    - 1-D   225

2. The sum of $51.75, $172.50, $39.00, $8.54, and $0.09 is
    - 2-A $116.64
    - 2-B $171.78
    - 2-C $261.89
    - 2-D $271.88

Subtraction

3. Subtract: 57,697
    $$-9,748$$

    The remainder is
    - 3-A   40,945
    - 3-B   47,949
    - 3-C   48,949
    - 3-D   67,445

4. Subtract $987.59 from $1,581.06. The difference is
    - 4-A $593.47
    - 4-B $603.47
    - 4-C $693.47
    - 4-D $694.47

5. Add $72.07 and $31.54, and then subtract $25.75. The correct answer is
    - 5-A $77.86
    - 5-B $82.14
    - 5-C $88.96
    - 5-D $129.36

Multiplication

6. Multiply
$$\begin{array}{r} 36 \\ \times 8 \\ \hline \end{array}$$

The product is
6-A   246
6-B   262
6-C   288
6-D   368

7. Multiply 312.77 by .04 and round the result to the nearest hundredth.
7-A   12.51
7-B   12.511
7-C   12.518
7-D   12.52

Division

8. Divide 5)455

The quotient is
8-A   81
8-B   84
8-C   91
8-D   94

9. 7.95 ÷ 0.15 =
9-A   0.53
9-B   5.3
9-C   53
9-D   530

Additional Sample Arithmetic Problems Encountered In Everyday Life

10. Which of the following amounts of money has the greatest value?
10-A   3 quarters
10-B   8 dimes
10-C   15 nickels
10-D   79 pennies

11. Two weeks, five days plus three weeks, four days equals

    11-A   5 weeks, 1 day

    11-B   5 weeks, 2 days

    11-C   6 weeks, 1 day

    11-D   6 weeks, 2 days

12. Subtract: 2 feet, 4 inches

                  −1 foot, 6 inches

    12-A   8 inches

    12-B   10 inches

    12-C   1 foot

    12-D   1 foot, 2 inches

13. Of the 36 students registered in a class, $\frac{2}{3}$ of them are females. How many males are registered in the class?

    13-A   12

    13-B   18

    13-C   24

    13-D   30

14. If a 200-mile trip takes four hours to complete, the average speed is

    14-A   30 miles per hour.

    14-B   40 miles per hour.

    14-C   50 miles per hour.

    14-D   60 miles per hour.

15. How many pounds are in 24 ounces?

    15-A $\frac{1}{2}$

    15-B   1

    15-C $1\frac{1}{2}$

    15-D   2

16. The sales tax of 8% on a purchase of $12.00 is:

    16-A $0.86

    16-B $0.96

    16-C $1.06

    16-D $1.60

17. A dozen oranges costs $1.35. The cost per orange is most nearly:

    17-A   11¢

    17-B   12¢

    17-C   13¢

    17-D   14¢

18. A $75 fund is available for a holiday party. If 75% of the available money is spent for food and beverages, how much is left for other expenses?

    18-A $18.75

    18-B $28.75

    18-C $46.25

    18-D $56.25

19. A certain employee is paid at the rate of $6.74 per hour with time-and-a-half for overtime. The regular work week is 40 hours. During the past week, the employee put in 44 working hours. What were the employee's gross wages for that week?

    19-A $269.60

    19-B $296.56

    19-C $310.04

    19-D $444.84

20. It takes 4 men 14 days to do a certain job. How long should it take 7 men working at the same rate to do the same job?

    20-A   5 days

    20-B   6 days

    20-C   7 days

    20-D   8 days

21. If one quart of floor wax covers 400 square feet, how many gallons of wax are needed to wax the floor of a 6,400-square-foot office?

    21-A   4 gallons

    21-B   8 gallons

    21-C   12 gallons

    21-D   16 gallons

22. A pole 15 feet high casts a shadow 5 feet long. A 6-foot man standing nearby would cast a shadow

    22-A $1\frac{1}{2}$ feet long

    22-B   2 feet long

    22-C $2\frac{1}{2}$ feet long

    22-D   3 feet long

23. If 1 foot of chain costs 17¢, then 4 yards of this chain would cost

    23-A $0.68
    23-B $1.53
    23-C $2.04
    23-D $2.75

24. Tires regularly priced at $44 each are on sale for $37. How much would a truck owner save by buying four tires at the sale price?

    24-A $7
    24-B $28
    24-C $49
    24-D $81

25. How many 32-passenger buses are needed to transport 180 persons?

    25-A   4
    25-B   5
    25-C   6
    25-D   7

26. If a service station greased 270 vehicles in a 31-day period, the daily average of vehicles greased is most nearly

    26-A   6
    26-B   7
    26-C   8
    26-D   9

27. In order to check on a shipment of 500 articles, a sampling of 50 articles was carefully inspected. Of the sample, 4 articles were found to be defective. On this basis, what is the probable percentage of defective articles in the original shipment?

    27-A   .04%
    27-B   4%
    27-C   8%
    27-D   10%

28. If the total area of a four-room apartment is 3,600 square feet, the average area of each room is

    28-A $\frac{1}{4}$ of the total area

    28-B $\frac{1}{3}$ of the total area

    28-C $\frac{1}{2}$ of the total area

    28-D $\frac{3}{4}$ of the total area

Geometry

Area, Perimeter, And Volume

Area

Area is the space enclosed by a plane (flat) figure. A *rectangle* is a plane figure with four right angles. Opposite sides of a rectangle are of equal length and are parallel to each other. To find the area of a rectangle, multiply the length of the base of the rectangle by the length of its height. Area is always expressed in square units.

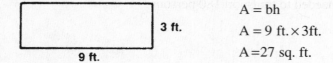

$$A = bh$$
$$A = 9 \text{ ft.} \times 3\text{ft.}$$
$$A = 27 \text{ sq. ft.}$$

A *square* is a rectangle in which all four sides are the same length. The area of a square is found by squaring the length of one side, which is exactly the same as multiplying the square's base by its height.

$$A = s^2$$
$$A = 4 \text{ in.} \times 4 \text{ in.}$$
$$A = 16 \text{ sq. in.}$$

A *triangle* is a three-sided plane figure. The area of a triangle is found by multiplying the base by the altitude (height) and dividing by two.

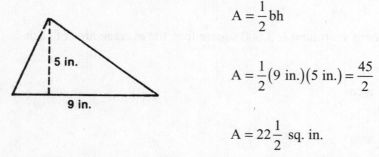

$$A = \frac{1}{2}bh$$

$$A = \frac{1}{2}(9 \text{ in.})(5 \text{ in.}) = \frac{45}{2}$$

$$A = 22\frac{1}{2} \text{ sq. in.}$$

A *circle* is a perfectly round plane figure. The distance from the center of a circle to its rim is its radius. The distance from one edge to the other through the center is its diameter. The diameter is twice the length of the radius.

Pi (π) is a mathematical value equal to approximately 3.14 or $\dfrac{22}{7}$. Pi is frequently used in calculations involving circles. The area of a circle is found by squaring the radius and multiplying it by π.

$A = \pi r^2$

$A = \pi (4 \text{ cm.})^2$

$A = 16\pi$ sq. cm.

You may leave the area in terms of pi unless you are told what value to assign π.

Perimeter

The perimeter of a plane figure is the distance around the outside. To find the perimeter of a polygon (a plane figure bounded by straight lines), just add the lengths of the sides.

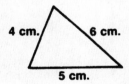

P = 3 in. + 5 in. + 3 in. + 5 in.

= 16 in.

P = 4 cm.+ 6 cm.+ 5 cm.

= 15 cm.

The perimeter of a circle is called the *circumference*. The formula for the circumference of a circle is πd or 2πr, which are both, of course, the same thing.

$C = 2 \cdot 3 \cdot \pi = 6\,\pi$

Volume

The volume of a solid figure is the measure of the space within. To figure the volume of a solid figure, multiply the area by the height or depth.

The volume of a rectangular solid is length × width × height. Volume is always expressed in cubic units.

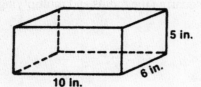

$V = lwh$

$V = (10 \text{ in.})(6 \text{ in.})(5 \text{ in.})$

$V = 300 \text{ cu. in.}$

The volume of a cube is the cube of one side.

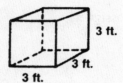

$V = s^3$

$V = (3 \text{ ft.})^3$

$V = 27 \text{ cu. ft.}$

The volume of a cylinder is π times the square of the radius of the base times the height.

$V = \pi r^2 h$

$V = \pi (4 \text{ in.})^2 (5 \text{ in.})$

$V = \pi (16)(5) = 80\pi \text{ cu. in.}$

Sample Questions

Here are sample questions dealing with area, perimeter, and volume. Explanatory answers are located at the end of the Arithmetic Reasoning section.

29. A floor that is 9 feet wide and 12 feet long measures how many square feet?

     29-A   12
     29-B   21
     29-C   108
     29-D   118

30. The area of a room measuring 12 feet by 15 feet is

     30-A   9 square yards
     30-B   12 square yards
     30-C   15 square yards
     30-D   20 square yards

31. The perimeter of a circle that has a radius of 70 feet is most nearly:

    31-A   220 feet

    31-B   440 feet

    31-C   660 feet

    31-D   690 feet

32. Find the perimeter of the square shown below.

1 in.

    32-A   1 inch

    32-B   2 inches

    32-C   3 inches

    32-D   4 inches

33. A swimming pool has an average depth of 4 feet and is 25 feet long and 15 feet wide. What is the volume of the pool?

    33-A   375 cubic feet

    33-B   1,000 cubic feet

    33-C   1,500 cubic feet

    33-D   4,500 cubic feet

34. Find the volume of the cube shown below.

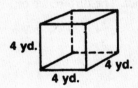

4 yd.   4 yd.   4 yd.

    34-A   12 cubic yards

    34-B   16 cubic yards

    34-C   46 cubic yards

    34-D   64 cubic yards

35. Find the perimeter of the figure shown below.

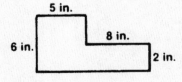

5 in.   8 in.   6 in.   2 in.

    35-A   21 inches

    35-B   25 inches

    35-C   33 inches

    35-D   38 inches

Answers and Explanations

1-B   The sum of the two numbers is 124.

$$
\begin{array}{r}
75 \\
+49 \\
\hline
124
\end{array}
$$

2-D   Arrange the five amounts in proper vertical columns and add. The sum is $271.88.

$$
\begin{array}{r}
\$51.75 \\
172.50 \\
39.00 \\
8.54 \\
+\ 0.09 \\
\hline
\$271.88
\end{array}
$$

3-B   Arrange numbers in proper vertical columns and then subtract. The difference or remainder is 47,949.

$$
\begin{array}{r}
57,697 \\
-9,748 \\
\hline
47,949
\end{array}
$$

4-A   Arrange numbers in proper vertical columns and then subtract. The difference or remainder is $593.47.

$$
\begin{array}{r}
\$1581.06 \\
-987.59 \\
\hline
\$593.47
\end{array}
$$

5-A   This question consists of an addition and a subtraction. The sum of the first two amounts is $103.61. $25.75 from $103.61 gives us an answer of $77.86.

$$
\begin{array}{r}
\$72.07 \\
+31.54 \\
\hline
\$103.61 \\
-25.75 \\
\hline
\$77.86
\end{array}
$$

6-C   The product of the two numbers is 288.

$$\begin{array}{r} 36 \\ \underline{\times 8} \\ 288 \end{array}$$

7-A   Multiply the two numbers and fix the decimal point in the answer to conform with the total number of digits to the right of the decimal points in both the multiplicand and the multiplier. Round off the product to the nearest hundredth.

$$\begin{array}{r} 312.77 \\ \underline{\times\ \ .04} \\ 12.5108 \end{array}$$

8-C   This is simple short division, and the quotient is 91.

$$4\overline{)455}$$
$$91$$

9-C   Rename the divisor as a whole number and move the decimal point in the dividend the same number of places to the right. Complete the division. The quotient is 53.

$$0.15\overline{)7.95} =$$

$$15\overline{)795}$$

$$\begin{array}{r} 53 \\ 15\overline{)795} \\ \underline{-75} \\ 45 \\ \underline{-45} \\ 0 \end{array}$$

10-B   By computing the value of the coins in each option, we find that choice B has the greatest value.

$$3 \times 25¢ = 75¢$$
$$8 \times 10¢ = 80¢$$
$$15 \times 5¢ = 75¢$$
$$79 \times 1¢ = 79¢$$

11-D   The sum of the two time periods is 5 weeks and 9 days, which is equivalent to 6 weeks and 2 days.

2 weeks, 5 days
+3 weeks, 4 days
5 weeks, 9 days

12-B Two feet, four inches is equal to one foot, 16 inches. This amount less one foot, six inches equals 10 inches.

1′16″
−1′6″
10″

13-A Two thirds of 36 is 24, the number of females. This number subtracted from 36 gives the number of males.

14-C Dividing the distance (200) by the number of hours (4) gives the average speed.

15-C There are 16 ounces in a pound; therefore, 24 ounces would be equivalent to one pound, 8 ounces or $1\frac{1}{2}$ pounds.

16-B 8% of $12.00 is 96 cents.

$ 12
×.08
$ .96

17-A The price of a dozen oranges divided by 12 gives the cost per orange. $.1125 to the nearest cent is 11¢.

$$12\overline{)1.3500}$$
            .1125
         −12
          15
         − 12
           30
         − 24
           60
         − 60
            0

18-A The amount of money spent is .75 times $75, which equals $56.25. The fund available minus the amount spent equals the amount left. $75.00 minus $56.25 = $18.75.

19-C $1\frac{1}{2} \times 6.74 = \$10.11$

$6.74 times 40 equals $269.60
$10.11 times 4 equals $\underline{+40.44}$
                          $310.04

20-D 4 men times 14 days equals 56 man-days

7 men times ? equals 56 man-days

56 divided by 7 = 8.

21-A There are four quarts to a gallon. Therefore, 16 quarts divided by 4 equals 4 gallons.

22-B The correct answer is 2 feet.

$15 : 5 :: 6 : x$

$15x = 30$

$x = 2$

23-C The correct answer is $2.04.

4 yards = 12 feet

$1 : .17 :: 12 : x$

$x = 2.04$

24-B $44 minus $37 equals $7, the savings on each tire.

$7 times 4 equals $28, the savings on four tires.

25-C The number of persons to be transported divided by the number of persons the bus can carry will give the number of buses needed. 180 divided by 32 equals 5.6.

26-D The number of vehicles greased divided by the number of days gives the daily average 270/31 = 8.71 The correct answer is 9.

27-C If 4 out of 50 sampled articles were found to be defective, the fraction 4/50 multiplied by 100 equals the percentage of defective articles in the sampling. As 8% of the articles in the sample were found to be defective, the probable percentage of defective articles in the original shipment would also be 8%.

28-A The total area divided by the number of rooms gives the average area of each room. As there are four rooms, the total area divided by four gives the average area of each room.

29-C 9 feet × 12 feet = 108 square feet.

30-D 12 feet = 4 yards; 15 feet = 5 yards; 4 × 5 = 20 square yards.

31-B   Perimeter or circumference = $2\pi r$; $r = 70$ feet; $P = 2 \times \dfrac{22}{7} \times 70$;

$P = 440$ feet.

32-D   Each side is 1 inch. Perimeter = $1 + 1 + 1 + 1 = 4$ inches.

33-C   The volume is obtained by multiplying length times depth times width—25 feet times 4 feet times 15 feet. The answer is 1,500 cubic feet.

34-D   The volume of the cube is the cube of one side. $V = (4 \text{ yds.})^3$. $V = 64$ cubic yards.

35-D   The perimeter = $5 + (6 - 2) + 8 + 2 + 13 + 6 =$

$5 + 4 + 8 + 2 + 13 + 6 = 38$ inches.

WORD KNOWLEDGE REVIEW

The ability to understand other people and to be understood by other people is an important communication skill, both in speaking and in writing. This ability can be measured in a written test by including a section on synonyms—words having the same, or nearly the same, meaning as other words in the language.

Synonym questions are used to test for ability to understand the meaning of words. They are also good indicators of reasoning ability and ability to learn.

The Word Knowledge subtest determines breadth of word knowledge through synonyms. The words used in the synonym questions are those used in everyday language by high school graduates or those who have high school equivalency diplomas. The test questions are four-choice items and appear in either of the two following forms.

Format 1. Complete the definition of a key word.

SAMPLE:

1. Notorious most nearly means
    - 1-A   annoying.
    - 1-B   condemned.
    - 1-C   unpleasant.
    - 1-D   well known.

Notorious means *well known*, which is the same as choice D. Choices A and C are unrelated in meaning since a notorious person may or may not be annoying or unpleasant. Although choice B may be just slightly related in meaning, as *notorious* also implies being widely and unfavorably known, it does not necessarily imply being condemned. Choice D is the only correct answer of the options given.

SAMPLE:

2. To assent means most nearly to
    - 2-A   acquire.
    - 2-B   climb.
    - 2-C   consent.
    - 2-D   participate.

To *assent* means to *express acceptance* or *concurrence*. Choice C is almost the same in meaning. Choices A, B, and D are unrelated in meaning. Choice B is similar in meaning to the word "ascend" but not to "assent."

Choice C is the correct answer.

Format 2. Choose the word that means the same as the key word in a sentence.

SAMPLE:

Choose the lettered word that means most nearly the same as the underlined word as it is used in the sentence.

3.   The <u>rear</u> of the truck should be washed.

     3-A   Back
     3-B   Front
     3-C   Hood
     3-D   Roof

Replace *rear* with each of the choices. The correct choice is the word that does not change the meaning of the sentence. In the question above, the choice that is closest in meaning to the underlined word is *back*. Therefore, choice A is the correct answer.

An excellent method of increasing your vocabulary is by developing and maintaining your own word list. Write down every word you see or hear whose meaning you are not certain of. Look up its meaning in a dictionary and record it next to the word. Then follow up by using the word in a sentence.

A guide to word formation follows. This key to word recognition consists of commonly used prefixes and suffixes, as well as Latin and Greek word stems that have been absorbed into the English language. Use this guide as a reference to increase your knowledge of word meanings, an essential component of verbal ability.

Information about the Word Knowledge test and sample questions with accompanying answer explanations follow the Word Formation section and word parts list. Be sure to study these sections then try the practice questions.

Word Formation—A Key to Word Recognition

Many English words, especially the longer and more difficult ones, are built up out of basic parts or roots. One of the most efficient ways of increasing your vocabulary is to learn some of these parts. Once you know some basic building blocks, you will find it easier to remember words you've learned and to puzzle out unfamiliar ones.

The following chart lists over 150 common word parts. Each part is defined and an example is given of a word in which it appears. Study the chart a small section at a time. When you've learned one of the building blocks, remember to look for it in your reading. See if you can think of other words in which the word part appears. Use the dictionary to check your guesses.

WORD PART	MEANING	EXAMPLE
ab, abs	from, away	*abrade*—to wear off
		absent—away, not present
act, ag	do, act, drive	*action*—a doing
		agent—one who acts for another
alter, altr	other, change	*alternate*—to switch back and forth
am, ami	love, friend	*amorous*—loving
anim	mind, life, spirit	*animated*—spirited
annu, enni	year	*annual*—yearly
ante	before	*antedate*—to occur earlier
anthrop	man	*anthropology*—study of mankind
anti	against	*antiwar*—against war
arbit	judge	*arbiter*—a judge
arch	first, chief	*archetype*—first model
aud, audit, aur	hear	*auditorium*—place where performances are heard
auto	self	*automobile*—self-moving vehicle
bell	war	*belligerent*—warlike
bene, ben	good, well	*benefactor*—one who does good deeds
bi	two	*bilateral*—two-sided
bibli	book	*bibliophile*—book lover
bio	life	*biology*—study of life
brev	short	*abbreviate*—to shorten
cad, cas	fall	*casualty*—one who has fallen
cede, ceed, cess	go, yield	*exceed*—go beyond
		recession—a going backward
cent	hundred	*century*—hundred years
chrom	color	*monochrome*—having one color
chron	time	*chronology*—time order

cide, cis	cut, kill	*suicide*—a self-killing
		incision—a cutting into
circum	around	*circumnavigate*—to sail around
clam, claim	shout	*proclaim*—to declare loudly
clin	slope, lean	*decline*—to slope downward
cogn	know	*recognize*—to know
com, co, col, con	with, together	*concentrate*—to bring closer together
		cooperate—to work with
contra, contro, counter	against	*contradict*—to speak against
		counterclockwise—against the clock's direction
corp	body	*incorporate*—to bring into a body
cosm	order, world	*cosmos*—universe
cre, cresc	grow	*increase*—to grow
cred	trust, believe	*incredible*—unbelievable
culp	blame	*culprit*—one who is to blame
cur, curr, curs	run, course	*current*—presently running
de	away from, down, opposite	*detract*—to draw away from
dec	ten	*decade*—ten years
dem	people	*democracy*—rule by the people
dic, dict	say, speak	*dictation*—a speaking
		predict—to say in advance
dis, di	not, away from	*dislike*—to not like
		digress—to turn away from the subject
doc, doct	teach, prove	*indoctrinate*—to teach
domin	rule	*domineer*—to rule over
du	two	*duo*—a couple
duc, duct	lead	*induct*—to lead in
dur	hard, lasting	*durable*—able to last
equ	equal	*equivalent*—of equal value

ev	time, age	*longevity*—age, length of life
ex, e, ef	from, out	*expatriate*—one who lives outside his native country
		emit—to send out
extra	outside, beyond	*extraterrestrial*—from beyond the earth
fac, fact, fect, fic	do, make	*factory*—place where things are made
		fictitious—made up or imaginary
fer	bear, carry	*transfer*—to carry across
fid	belief, faith	*fidelity*—faithfulness
fin	end, limit	*finite*—limited
flect, flex	bend	*reflect*—to bend back
flu, fluct, flux	flow	*fluid*—flowing substance
		influx—a flowing in
fore	in front of,	*forecast*—to tell ahead of previous time
		foreleg—front leg
form	shape	*formation*—shaping
fort	strong	*fortify*—to strengthen
frag, fract	break	*fragile*—easily broken
fug	flee	*fugitive*—one who flees
gen	birth, kind, race	*engender*—to give birth to
geo	earth	*geology*—study of the earth
grad, gress	step, go	*progress*—to go forward
graph	writing	*autograph*—to write one's own name
her, hes	stick, cling	*adhere*—to cling
		cohesive—sticking together
homo	same, like	*homophonic*—sounding the same
hyper	too much, over	*hyperactive*—overly active
in, il, ig, im, ir	not	*incorrect*—not correct
		ignorant—not knowing
		illogical—not logical
		irresponsible—not responsible

in, il, im, ir	on, into, in	*impose*—to place on
		invade—to go into
inter	between, among	*interplanetary*—between planets
intra, intro	within, inside	*intrastate*—within a state
ject	throw	*reject*—to throw back
junct	join	*juncture*—place where things join
leg	law	*legal*—lawful
leg, lig, lect	choose, gather, read	*legible*—readable
		eligible—able to be chosen
		select—to choose
lev	light, rise	*alleviate*—to make lighter
liber	free	*liberation*—a freeing
loc	place	*location*—place
log	speech, study	*dialogue*—speech for two characters
		psychology—study of the mind
luc, lum	light	*translucent*—allowing some light to pass through
		luminous—shining
magn	large, great	*magnify*—to make larger
mal, male	bad, wrong, poor	*maladjusted*—poorly adjusted
		malevolent—ill-wishing
mar	sea	*marine*—sea-dwelling
ment	mind	*demented*—out of one's mind
meter, metr, mens	measure	*chronometer*—time-measuring device
		commensurate—of equal measure
micr	small	*microwave*—small wave
min	little	*minimum*—least
mis	badly, wrongly	*misunderstand*—to understand wrongly
mit, miss	send	*remit*—to send back
		mission—a sending

mono	single, one	*monorail*—train that runs on a single track
morph	shape	*anthropomorphic*—man-shaped
mov, mob, mot	move	*removal*—a moving away
		mobile—able to move
multi	many	*multiply*—to become many
mut	change	*mutation*—change
nasc, nat	born	*innate*—inborn
		native—belonging by or from birth
neg	deny	*negative*—no, not
neo	new	*neophyte*—beginner
nom	name	*nominate*—to name for office
non	not	*nonentity*—a nobody
nov	new	*novice*—newcomer, beginner
		innovation—something new
omni	all	*omnipresent*—present in all places
oper	work	*operate*—to work
		cooperation—a working together
path, pat, pass	feel, suffer	*patient*—suffering
		compassion—a feeling with
ped, pod	foot	*pedestrian*—one who goes on foot
pel, puls	drive, push	*impel*—to push
phil	love	*philosophy*—love of wisdom
phob	fear	*phobia*—irrational fear
phon	sound	*symphony*—a sounding together
phot	light	*photosynthesis*—synthesis of chemical compounds in plants with the aid of light
poly	many	*polygon*—many-sided figure
port	carry	*import*—to carry into a country
pot	power	*potency*—power
post	after	*postmortem*—after death

pre	before, earlier than	*prejudice*—judgment in advance
press	press	*impression*—a pressing into
prim	first	*primal*—first, original
pro	in favor of, in front of, forward	*proceed*—to go forward
		prowar—in favor of war
psych	mind	*psychiatry*—cure of the mind
quer, quir, quis, ques	ask, seek	*query*—to ask
		inquisitive—asking many questions
		quest—a search
re	back, again	*rethink*—to think again
		reimburse—to pay back
rid, ris	laugh	*deride*—to make fun of
		ridiculous—laughable
rupt	break	*erupt*—to break out
sci, scio	know	*science*—knowledge
		conscious—having knowledge
scrib, script	write	*describe*—to write about
		inscription—a writing on
semi	half	*semiconscious*—half conscious
sent, sens	feel, think	*sensation*—feeling
		sentimental—marked by feeling
sequ, secut	follow	*sequential*—following in order
sol	alone	*desolate*—lonely
solv, solu, solut	loosen	*dissolve*—to loosen the bonds of
		solvent—loosening agent
son	sound	*sonorous*—sounding
spect	look	*inspect*—to look into
		spectacle—something to be looked at
spir	breathe	*respiration*—breathing

stab, stat	stand	*establish*—to make stand, found
string, strict	bind	*restrict*—to bind, limit
stru, struct	build	*construct*—to build
super	over, greater	*superfluous*—overflowing beyond what is needed
tang, ting, tact, tig	touch	*tactile*—of the sense of touch *contiguous*—touching
tele	far	*television*—machine for seeing far
ten, tain, tent	hold	*tenacity*—holding power *contain*—to hold together
term	end	*terminal*—last, ending
terr	earth	*terrain*—surface of the earth
test	witness	*attest*—to witness
therm	heat	*thermos*—container that retains heat
tort, tors	twist	*contort*—to twist out of shape
tract	pull, draw	*attract*—to pull toward
trans	across	*transport*—to carry across a distance
un	not	*uninformed*—not informed
uni	one	*unify*—to make one
vac	empty	*evacuate*—to make empty
ven, vent	come	*convene*—to come together
ver	true	*verity*—truth
verb	word	*verbose*—wordy
vid, vis	see	*video*—means of seeing *vision*—sight
viv, vit	life	*vivid*—lively
voc, vok	call	*provocative*—calling for a response *revoke*—to call back
vol	wish, will	*involuntary*—not willed

Sample Questions

1. <u>Small</u> most nearly means
    1-A   cheap.
    1-B   round.
    1-C   sturdy.
    1-D   little.

2. <u>Impair</u> most nearly means
    2-A   direct.
    2-B   weaken.
    2-C   improve.
    2-D   stimulate.

3. <u>Cease</u> most nearly means
    3-A   stop.
    3-B   start.
    3-C   change.
    3-D   continue.

4. The wind is <u>variable</u> today.
    4-A   Mild
    4-B   Steady
    4-C   Shifting
    4-D   Chilling

5. The student <u>discovered</u> an error.
    5-A   Found
    5-B   Entered
    5-C   Searched
    5-D   Enlarged

6. Do not <u>obstruct</u> the entrance to the building.
    6-A   Block
    6-B   Enter
    6-C   Leave
    6-D   Cross

Answers and Explanations

1-D   *Little* most closely means the same as *small*. The other choices clearly are not related in any way to the word small.

2-B   Of all the choices, *weaken* most closely means the same as *impair*. *Impair* means to *decrease in strength*, *amount*, or *quality*.

3-A   *Stop* most nearly means *cease*. Start and continue are opposites of cease, while change is not related to the word cease.

4-C   The word "shifting" could replace "variable" in this sentence. *Variable* means *changing* or *subject to change*.

5-A   The word "discovered" can be replaced by "found" in this sentence. *Discovered* means *to have uncovered* or *found*.

6-A   Obstruct can be replaced by the word "block." *Obstruct* means to *impede* or *interfere*.

PARAGRAPH COMPREHENSION REVIEW

Reading comprehension, the ability to read and understand written or printed material, is an important verbal skill. The reading material may be in the form of several paragraphs, a single paragraph, or a single sentence. This section includes reading selections that are samples of the type of material that you would be required to read, whether at school, in training, or on the job.

Before you try the samples below, note the eight general suggestions for answering reading comprehension questions. Keep these in mind as you take the sample test batteries in this book as well as on your ASVAB test day.

1. Scan the passage to get the general intent of the reading selection.

2. Reread the passage carefully to understand the main idea and any related ideas.

3. Read each question carefully. Be careful to base your answer on what is stated, implied, or inferred in the reading passage. Do not be influenced by your opinions, personal feelings, or any other information not expressed or implied in the passage.

4. Options that are partly true and partly false are incorrect.

5. Look for such words as *least, greatest, first, not,* etc., appearing in the comprehension question.

6. Be suspicious of options containing words such as *all, always, every, forever, never, none, wholly,* etc.

7. Be sure to consider all options given for the question before selecting your answer.

8. Speed is an important consideration in answering reading comprehension questions. Try to proceed as rapidly as you can without sacrificing careful thinking or reasoning.

When answering Paragraph Comprehension questions, refer back to the paragraph *as often as necessary.* Questions may focus on a particular sentence or phrase within the paragraph. You should refer back to make sure you answer the question correctly instead of trying to answer from memory. Keep in mind that wrong answer choices could be *subtly* wrong. With careful review of the paragraph and the details in the answer choices, it becomes clear which answers are correct and which ones aren't.

Here are samples of the four main types of paragraph comprehension questions you may find on the ASVAB Paragraph Comprehension section of your test. Each type of question is explained, a sample is given, and an explanation of the correct answer is given in detail. Following these are practice questions to try on your own.

The four main type of questions are:

Type 1. Finding specific information or directly stated details contained in the reading passage:

This is a common type of item found in paragraph comprehension tests. It requires the ability to pick out specific facts provided in a passage or, sometimes, the ability to pick out the fact that is not mentioned in a particular passage.

Sample:

There are many signs by which people predict the weather. Some of these have a true basis but many do not. There is, for example, no evidence that it is more likely to storm during one phase of the moon than during another. If it happens to rain on Easter, there is no reason to think that it will rain for the next seven Sundays. The groundhog may or may not see his shadow on Ground-hog Day, but it probably won't affect the weather anyway.

1. Which of the following is *NOT* mentioned as a sign of weather phenomenon?
    1-A   Rain on Easter
    1-B   The phases of the Moon
    1-C   Pain in a person's joints
    1-D   The groundhog's shadow

The correct answer is choice C. The other choices were mentioned in the passage.

Below are some typical "detail" questions:
*   The first toll road in the United States was completed in _____ .
*   Helping to prevent accidents is the responsibility of _____ .
*   The principal reason for issuing traffic summonses is to _____ .
*   The side margins of a typewritten letter are most pleasing when _____ .
*   The reason for maintaining ongoing safety education is that _____ .
*   It would be desirable, when planning a departmental reorganization, to _____ .

Type 2. Recognizing the main idea or concept expressed in the passage.

Although questions of this type may be phrased in different ways, they generally require the ability to summarize the principal purpose or idea expressed in the reading passage. These questions require the ability to analyze and interpret as well as to read and understand the material presented.

Sample:

Specific types of lighting are required at first-class airports by the Department of Commerce. To identify an airport, there must be a beacon of light of not less than 100,000 candlepower, with a beam that properly distributes light up in the air so that it can be seen all around the horizon from an altitude of from 500 to 2,000 feet. All flashing beacons must have a definite Morse code characteristic to aid in identification. Colored lights are required to indicate where safe area for landing ends, red lights being used where landing is particularly dangerous.

2. The best title for this selection is
    2-A   "Landing Areas."
    2-B   "Colored Lights at Airports."
    2-C   "Identification of Airports."
    2-D   "Airport Lighting Requirements."

The correct answer is choice D since every sentence in the paragraph describes a light-ing requirement for airports. The other choices are each mentioned in only one of the four sentences.

Below are other typical "main idea" questions:

*   This paragraph is mainly about _____ .
*   The passage best supports the statement that _____ .
*   The passage means most nearly that _____ .
*   One may conclude from the above statement that _____ .

Type 3. Determining the meaning of certain words as used in context.

The particular meaning of a word as actually used in the passage requires an understanding of the central or main theme of the reading passage, as well as the thought being conveyed by the sentence containing the word in question.

Sample:

The maritime and fishing industries find perhaps 250 applications for rope and cordage. There are hundreds of different sizes, constructions, tensile strengths, and weights in rope and twine. Rope is sold by the pound but ordered by length and is measured by circumference rather than by diameter.

3. In this context, the word "application" means
    3-A   use.
    3-B   description.
    3-C   size.
    3-D   types.

The correct answer is choice A, "use." Try it in the sentence in place of the word "appli-cation;" "use" makes sense in that context and keeps the meaning of the sentence in-tact.

Type 4. Finding implications or drawing inferences from a stated idea.

This type of item requires ability to understand the stated idea and then to reason by logical thinking to the implied or inferred idea. *Implied* means not exactly stated but merely suggested; *inferred* means derived by reasoning. Although these terms are somewhat similar in meaning, *inferred* implies being further removed from the stated idea. Much greater reasoning ability is required to arrive at the proper inference. Because the answer to an inference question will not be found in the passage, it is the most difficult type of comprehension question to answer.

Sample:

The facts, as we see them, on drug use and the dangerous behaviors caused by drugs are that some people do get into trouble while using drugs, and some of those drug users are dangerous to others. Sometimes a drug is a necessary element in order for a person to commit a crime, although it may not be the cause of his or her criminality. On the other hand, the use of a drug sometimes seems to be the only convenient excuse by means of which the observer can account for the undesirable behavior.

4.   The author apparently feels that

      4-A   the use of drugs always results in crime.

      4-B   drugs and crime are only sometimes related.

      4-C   drug use does not always cause crime.

      4-D   drugs are usually an element in accidents and suicides.

The author states that drugs are sometimes a necessary element in a crime but at other times are just an excuse for criminal behavior. Therefore, choice B is the correct answer.

Other typical "inference" questions include any of the following:

- Which of the following is implied by the above passage? _____ .
- Of the following, the most valid implication of the above paragraph is _____ .
- The author probably believes that _____ .
- It can be inferred from the above passage that _____ .
- The best of the following inferences that can be made is that _____ .

Now try the sample Paragraph Comprehension questions that follow. Detailed explanations of the answers are given immediately after each question to help you understand the logic of the answers. Once you feel comfortable with these, continue on to try the next set of sample questions on your own.

1.   Investigations show that activation analysis of wipings taken from a suspect's hands will reveal not only whether he or she has fired a gun recently but also the type of ammunition used, the number of bullets fired, and the hand in which the gun was held.

Activation analysis of wipings taken from the hands of a person suspected of firing a gun can *NOT* be used to reveal the

      1-A   exact time the gun was fired.

      1-B   hand in which the gun was fired.

      1-C   number of bullets fired.

      1-D   type of ammunition used.

The paragraph states that activation analysis can be used to reveal choices B, C, and D. Although activation analysis can reveal whether the suspect fired a gun recently, it can *not* ascertain the exact time the gun was fired; therefore, choice A is correct.

The ability of activation analysis to detect and identify very tiny amounts of certain elements has come to the aid of law-enforcement officers in a variety of ways. Hair even hundreds of years old can be analyzed successfully for arsenic and other residues.

2. English scientists recently found an unusual amount of arsenic in a relic of hair from Napoleon's head. The suspicion now is that he was slowly poisoned to death.

    The case of King Eric XIV of Sweden is similar. When the king's body was exhumed recently, activation analysis showed that his body contained traces of poisonous arsenic.

    Both King Eric XIV of Sweden and Napoleon could have been
    2-A   killed by gunshot.
    2-B   killed in military combat.
    2-C   poisoned by arsenic.
    2-D   poisoned by lead.

    For this question, the possibility of poisoning by arsenic is indicated in paragraphs 2 and 3 for both Napoleon and King Eric XIV. There is nothing in the reading passage suggesting that their deaths were due to gunshot or occurred in military combat; nor is there any reference to poisoning by lead. Choice C is the only correct answer.

3. In spite of the fact that the latitude of Scandinavia corresponds to that of Alaska and Siberia, the climate is surprisingly mild. Even in winter, the temperatures in Scandinavia are often higher than those of Central Europe and sometimes even Southern Europe. The average temperature is higher in Scandinavia than for other places on the same latitude, thanks to the Gulf Stream that washes the Scandinavian Atlantic coastline.

    According to the quotation above, it may be concluded that the latitude of Scandinavia is
    3-A   higher than that of Alaska.
    3-B   lower than that of Siberia.
    3-C   higher than that of Southern Europe.
    3-D   lower than that of Central Europe.

    Nothing in the passage suggests that the latitude is either higher or lower than that of Alaska or Siberia; nor is there any indication that it is lower than that of Central Europe. The implication is that it is higher than that of Southern Europe. Choice C is the correct answer.

Answer the next two questions on the basis of the following passage.

4. It is important for every office to have proper lighting. Inadequate lighting is a common cause of fatigue and tends to create a dreary atmosphere in the office. Appropriate light intensity is essential for proper lighting. It is generally recommended that for "casual seeing" tasks, such as in reception rooms or inactive file rooms, the amount of lighting be 30-foot candles. For "ordinary seeing" tasks, such as reading or for work in active file rooms and mail rooms, the recommended lighting is 100-foot candles. For "very difficult seeing" tasks, such as transcribing, accounting, and business machine use, the recommended lighting is 150-foot candles.

    For copying figures onto a payroll, the recommended lighting is
    4-A   less than 30-foot candles.
    4-B   30-foot candles.
    4-C   100-foot candles.
    4-D   150-foot candles.

5. For this question, it is necessary to determine the proper lighting task for copying figures onto a payroll. This activity requires much more light than for either "casual seeing" or for "ordinary seeing." As it is a "very difficult seeing" task, choice D is the correct answer.

It can be inferred from the passage above that a well-coordinated lighting scheme is likely to result in

   5-A   greater employee productivity.
   5-B   lower lighting costs.
   5-C   more use of natural light.
   5-D   windowless offices.

In this question, there is no mention of lighting costs or the need for windowless offices in the reading passage. Nor is there any suggestion for greater use of natural light. Choices B, C, and D are therefore eliminated. If inadequate lighting is a common cause of fatigue, one can *infer* that proper lighting would eliminate this fatigue element and should result in greater employee productivity. Choice A is the correct answer.

Sample Questions

1. In the relations of man to nature, the procuring of food and shelter is fundamental. With the migration of man to various climates, ever new adjustments to the food supply and to the climate became necessary.

According to the passage, the means by which man supplies his material needs are

   1-A   accidental.
   1-B   inadequate.
   1-C   limited.
   1-D   varied.

2. From a building designer's standpoint, three things that make a home livable are the needs of the client, the building site, and the amount of money the client has to spend.

According to the passage, to make a home livable,

   2-A   it can be built on any piece of land.
   2-B   the design must fit the designer's income.
   2-C   the design must fit the owner's income and site.
   2-D   the prospective piece of land makes little difference.

3. Twenty-five percent of all household burglaries can be attributed to unlocked windows or doors. Crime is the result of opportunity plus desire. To prevent crime, it is each individual's responsibility to

   3-A   provide the desire.
   3-B   provide the opportunity.
   3-C   prevent the desire.
   3-D   prevent the opportunity.

4. In certain areas, water is so scarce that every attempt is made to conserve it. For instance, on one oasis in the Sahara Desert the amount of water necessary for each date palm has been carefully determined.

How much water is each tree given?
4-A   No water at all
4-B   Water on alternate days
4-C   Exactly the amount required
4-D   Water only if it is healthy

Answers and Explanations

1-D   The author talks about "adjustments" to the food supply and climate. Of the available choices, the only word related to adjustment is "varied."

2-C   The author mentions two necessary items; the building site and amount of money available. Choice C is the only answer that contains these two items.

3-D   Choices A and B can be immediately eliminated, and since individuals cannot control the desires of burglars, choice D is the only logical answer.

4-C   The only conclusion that can be drawn from information given is contained in choice C. The author talks about "...the amount of water necessary..." This is the key to the correct answer.

MATHEMATICS KNOWLEDGE REVIEW

The Mathematics Knowledge subtest of the ASVAB deals with the ability to use basic mathematical relationships learned in math courses, such as algebra, geometry, and trigonometry. This subtest tests your knowledge of math principles, concepts, and procedures. This review section can also be considered a continuation of the Arithmetic Reasoning Review given previously. Reread that section as background material for Mathematics Knowledge Review.

Adding Fractions

With the same denominator

Fractions with the same denominator are added directly, as each part represents a part of the same value. Add the numerators and place the sum over the common denominator. If necessary, then simplify to the simplest form.

$$\begin{array}{r} \frac{1}{5} \\[4pt] +\frac{3}{5} \\ \hline \frac{4}{5} \end{array} \qquad \begin{array}{r} \frac{1}{5} \\[2pt] \frac{3}{5} \\[2pt] +\frac{4}{5} \\ \hline \frac{8}{5} = 1\frac{3}{5} \end{array}$$

With different denominators

Fractions with different denominators may not be added directly because parts of different values are involved. They must be renamed as equivalent fractions having the same common denominator. After all the fractions have the same denominator, add the numerators and place the total over the common denominator. If necessary, then simplify to the simplest form.

$$\frac{1}{2}+\frac{1}{4}; \quad \frac{1}{2}+\frac{1}{3}+\frac{3}{4}$$

$$
\begin{array}{cccc}
& & \dfrac{1}{2} & \dfrac{6}{12} \\[6pt]
\dfrac{1}{2} & \dfrac{2}{4} & \dfrac{1}{3} & \dfrac{4}{12} \\[6pt]
+\dfrac{1}{4} & +\dfrac{1}{4} & +\dfrac{3}{4} & +\dfrac{9}{12} \\[6pt]
& \dfrac{3}{4} & & \dfrac{19}{12}=1\dfrac{7}{8}
\end{array}
$$

Adding Mixed Numbers

In adding mixed numbers, first add all the whole numbers, then add all fractions, and then add the sum of the whole numbers to the sum of the fractions.

$$4\frac{1}{4}+3\frac{1}{2}+2\frac{1}{2}$$

$$
\begin{array}{cc}
4\dfrac{1}{4} & 4\dfrac{1}{4} \\[8pt]
3\dfrac{1}{2} & 3\dfrac{2}{4} \\[8pt]
+2\dfrac{1}{2} & +2\dfrac{2}{4} \\[8pt]
& 9+\dfrac{5}{4}=9+1\dfrac{1}{4}=10\dfrac{1}{4}
\end{array}
$$

Adding Percents

As percents are actually fractions with 100 as the same common denominator, they may be added directly.

$$
\begin{array}{ccc}
6\% & & 20\% \\
4\% & 8\% & 25\% \\
+9\% & +17\% & +35\% \\
\hline
19\% & 25\% & 80\%
\end{array}
$$

If fractional parts of a percent are involved in the addition, the addends may be added as decimals or added directly after the fractional parts are renamed with the same common denominator.

$$15\frac{1}{2}\% + 8\frac{1}{4}\%$$

$$
\begin{array}{ccc}
.155 & 15\frac{1}{2}\% & 15\frac{2}{4}\% \\
\underline{+.0825} & \underline{+8\frac{1}{4}\%} & \underline{+8\frac{1}{4}\%} \\
.2375 & & 23\frac{3}{4}\%
\end{array}
$$

Subtracting Fractions

With the same denominator

Fractions with the same denominator may be subtracted directly.

$$\frac{3}{5} - \frac{2}{5} = \frac{1}{5} \qquad \frac{7}{8} - \frac{1}{8} = \frac{6}{8}, \text{ which simplifies to } \frac{3}{4}.$$

With different denominators

Fractions with different denominators are not subtracted directly because parts of different values are involved. They must be renamed as equivalent fractions having the same common denominator. After the fractions have the same denominator, subtract the numerators and place the remainder over the common denominator.

$$\frac{3}{4} - \frac{2}{3} = \frac{9}{12} - \frac{8}{12} = \frac{1}{12} \qquad \frac{4}{5} - \frac{1}{2} = \frac{8}{10} - \frac{5}{10} = \frac{3}{10}$$

Subtracting Mixed Numbers

With the same denominator

If mixed numbers have the same denominator, rename them as improper fractions and subtract directly.

$$4\frac{1}{3} - 2\frac{2}{3} = \frac{13}{3} - \frac{8}{3} = \frac{5}{3} = 1\frac{2}{3}$$

With different denominators

If mixed numbers have different denominators, first rename as improper fractions, then rename as equivalent fractions with the same common denominator and subtract directly.

$$3\frac{1}{3} - 2\frac{3}{4} = \frac{10}{3} - \frac{11}{4} = \frac{40}{12} - \frac{33}{12} = \frac{7}{12}$$

Subtracting Percents

Percents are fractions with 100 as the same common denominator and may be subtracted directly.

$$70\% \text{ minus } 30\% = 40\%$$

If fractional parts of a percent are involved in the subtraction, rename them as decimals.

$$8\frac{1}{4}\% - 5\frac{2}{5}\%$$

$$
\begin{array}{ll}
8\dfrac{1}{4}\% & .0825 \\[2mm]
-5\dfrac{2}{5}\% & \underline{-.0540} \\[2mm]
 & .0285 = 2\dfrac{85}{100}\% = 2\dfrac{17}{20}\%
\end{array}
$$

Multiplying Fractions

With fractions, the product of the numerators divided by the product of the denominators gives the final answer or product.

$$\frac{1}{2} \times \frac{2}{3} = \frac{2}{6}, \text{ which simplifies to } \frac{1}{3}.$$

Dividing a number in the numerator by the same number in the denominator simplifies the computation.

$$\frac{1}{\underset{1}{\cancel{2}}} \times \frac{\overset{1}{\cancel{2}}}{3} = \frac{1}{3}$$

Dividing a common factor is particularly useful when multiplying many fractions.

$$\frac{3}{5} \times \frac{1}{2} \times \frac{2}{3} \times \frac{5}{8} = \frac{3 \times 1 \times 2 \times 5}{5 \times 2 \times 3 \times 8} = \frac{30}{240} = \frac{1}{8}$$

With dividing common factors:

$$\frac{3}{5} \times \frac{1}{2} \times \frac{2}{3} \times \frac{5}{8} = \frac{\overset{1}{\cancel{3}} \times 1 \times \overset{1}{\cancel{2}} \times \overset{1}{\cancel{5}}}{\underset{1}{\cancel{5}} \times \underset{1}{\cancel{2}} \times \underset{1}{\cancel{3}} \times 8} = \frac{1}{8}$$

Note that dividing common factors is permitted when only multiplication is involved.

When multiplying fractions and whole numbers, use the same procedure as when multiplying fractions only. Whole numbers are basically fractions with the whole number as the numerator and one as the denominator.

$$4 = \frac{4}{1} \qquad\qquad 10 = \frac{10}{1} \qquad\qquad 150 = \frac{150}{1}$$

When multiplying a fraction and a whole number, the word *of* means *multiplied* by.

$\frac{1}{2}$ of 48 means $\frac{1}{2} \times \frac{48}{1}$, which equals $\frac{48}{2}$ and equals 24.

Multiplying Mixed Numbers

There are several methods that may be used in multiplying mixed numbers.

When the numbers are small, rename the mixed numbers as improper fractions and then multiply in the usual manner.

$$3\frac{1}{4} \times 16 = \frac{13}{4} \times \frac{16}{1} = \frac{208}{4} = 52$$

$$2\frac{2}{3} \times 1\frac{1}{4} = \frac{8}{3} \times \frac{5}{4} = \frac{40}{12} = \frac{10}{3} = 3\frac{1}{3}$$

$$1\frac{1}{2} \times 2\frac{2}{3} \times 3\frac{3}{4} = \frac{\overset{1}{\cancel{3}}}{\underset{1}{\cancel{2}}} \times \frac{\overset{1}{\cancel{8}}}{\underset{1}{\cancel{3}}} \times \frac{15}{\cancel{4}} = 15$$

When the numbers are large and the fractional parts have exact decimal equivalents, rename the fractional parts as decimals and then multiply.

$$342\frac{1}{4} \times 609\frac{3}{4} = 342.25 \times 609.75$$

$$
\begin{array}{r}
342.25 \\
\times 609.75 \\
\hline
171125 \\
239575 \\
308025 \\
2053500 \\
\hline
208,686.9375
\end{array}
$$

When the numbers are not small and the fractional parts have no exact decimal equivalents, use the partial product method as follows:

$$386\frac{3}{7} \times 245\frac{1}{3}$$

$$386\frac{3}{7}$$

$$\times 245\frac{1}{3}$$

$$\rule{3cm}{0.4pt}$$

$$\frac{3}{21} \qquad \left(\frac{1}{3} \times \frac{3}{7}\right)$$ Find the partial products of

a. the fractional parts of the multiplier and the multiplicand;

$$128\frac{2}{3} \qquad \left(\frac{1}{3} \times 386\right)$$ b. the fractional part of the multiplier and the whole number of the multiplicand;

$$105 \qquad \left(\frac{3}{7} \times 245\right)$$ c. the fractional part of the multiplicand and the whole number of the multiplier;

$$\underline{94,570} \qquad (245 \times 386)$$ d. the whole number part of the multiplier and the whole number part of the multiplicand.

$$94,803\frac{17}{21}$$ Add the partial products and, if necessary, simplify the fractional part of the answer.

Multiplying Percents

Since a percent is actually a fraction with a denominator of 100, they may be multiplied after renaming the percent as a decimal or as a fraction.

$$33\% \times 8\% = .33 \times .08 = .0264 = 2\frac{64}{100}\% = 2\frac{32}{50}\% = 2\frac{16}{25}\%$$

$$75\% \times 50\% = \frac{3}{4} \times \frac{1}{2} = \frac{3}{8} = 37\frac{1}{2}\%$$

Other Multiplication Properties

1. If the multiplier and the multiplicand are interchanged, the product will remain the same.

    $5 \times 4 = 20 \qquad 4 \times 5 = 20$

2. If the numbers being multiplied are associated in different ways, the product will remain the same.

    $3 \times (5 \times 2) = 2 \times (3 \times 5) = 5 \times (2 \times 3)$

3. Multiplying any number by one does not change the number.

    $8 \times 1 = 2 \qquad 1.5 \times 1 = 1.5 \qquad \frac{3}{4} \times 1 = \frac{3}{4}$

4. Zero times any number equals zero.

    $8 \times 0 = 0 \qquad 1.5 \times 0 = 0 \qquad \frac{3}{4} \times 0 = 0$

5. a. To multiply by 10, move the decimal point in the number one place to the right:

    $1.36 \times 10 = 13.6, \; 13.6 \times 10 = 136, \; 136 \times 10 = 1,360$

    b. To multiply by 100, move the decimal point in the number two places to the right.

    $3.61 \times 100 = 361, \; 36.1 \times 100 = 3,610, \; 361 \times 100 = 36,100$

    c. To multiply by 1,000, move the decimal point in the number three places to the right.

$$4.875 \times 1,000 = 4,875$$
$$48.75 \times 1,000 = 48,750$$
$$487.5 \times 1,000 = 487,500$$
$$4,875 \times 1,000 = 4,875,000$$

When multiplying by 10, 100, 1,000, etc., move the decimal point in the number as many places to the right as there are zeros in the multiplier. If necessary, add zero(s) to the product.

Dividing Fractions

With fractions, first multiply by the reciprocal of the divisor.

$\frac{3}{4} \div \frac{1}{2}$ is changed to $\frac{3}{4} \times \frac{2}{1}$, which equals $\frac{6}{4} = 1\frac{1}{2}$

$\frac{2}{3} \div \frac{3}{4}$ is changed to $\frac{2}{3} \times \frac{4}{3}$, which equals $\frac{8}{9}$

$3 \div \frac{3}{4}$ is changed to $\frac{3}{1} \times \frac{4}{3}$, which equals $\frac{12}{3} = 4$

$\frac{1}{4} \div 2$ is changed to $\frac{1}{4} \times \frac{1}{2}$, which equals $\frac{1}{8}$

Dividing Percents

A percent divided by a percent is similar to dividing two fractions with 100 as the common denominator.

$25\% \div 50\%$ is changed to $\frac{25}{100} \times \frac{100}{50}$, which equals $\frac{25}{50} = \frac{1}{2}$

$40\% \div 40\%$ is changed to $\frac{40}{100} \times \frac{100}{40}$, which equals 1

Note that when a percent is divided by a percent, the result is a whole number or a fraction.

$\frac{1}{2} \div 25\%$ is changed to $\frac{1}{2} \times \frac{100}{25}$, which equals $\frac{100}{50} = 2$

$25\% \div \frac{1}{2}$ is changed to $\frac{25}{100} \times \frac{2}{1}$, which equals $\frac{50}{100} = \frac{1}{2}$

Similarly, when a fraction is divided by a percent or a percent is divided by a fraction, the result is also a whole number or a fraction.

Percents may also be renamed to decimal form before division.

$$25\% \div 50\% \text{ is changed to } \frac{.25}{.50}, \text{ which equals } \frac{25}{50} = \frac{1}{2}$$

$$\frac{1}{2} \div 25\% \text{ is changed to } \frac{1}{2} \div .25 = \frac{1}{2} \times \frac{1}{.25} = \frac{1}{.50} = \frac{100}{50} = 2$$

$$25\% \div \frac{1}{2} \text{ is changed to } .25 \div \frac{1}{2} = .25 \times 2 = .50 = \frac{1}{2}$$

Dividing Mixed Numbers

There are several methods that are used to divide mixed numbers.

When the numbers are small, rename the mixed numbers as improper fractions and then divide in the usual manner.

$$2\frac{1}{4} \div 1\frac{1}{2} \text{ is changed to } \frac{9}{4} \div \frac{3}{2}, \text{ which becomes } \frac{9}{4} \times \frac{2}{3} \text{ and equals } \frac{3}{2} = 1\frac{1}{2}$$

$$1\frac{1}{2} \div 2\frac{1}{4} \text{ is changed to } \frac{3}{2} \div \frac{9}{4}, \text{ which becomes } \frac{3}{2} \times \frac{4}{9} \text{ and equals } \frac{2}{3}$$

When the mixed numbers are large and the fractional parts have exact decimal equivalents, rename the fractional parts as decimals and then divide.

$$432\frac{3}{5} \text{ divided by } 156\frac{1}{2} \text{ is changed to } 432.6 \div 156.5$$

$$1565\overline{)4326}$$

When the mixed numbers are large and the fractional parts do not have exact decimal equivalents,

1. multiply both the dividend and the divisor by the denominator of the fraction if only one fraction is involved:

$$475 \div 28\frac{2}{3} = \frac{475 \times 3}{28\frac{2}{3} \times 3} = \frac{475 \times 3}{\frac{86}{3} \times 3} = \frac{1425}{86}$$

$$27\frac{1}{6} \div 39 = \frac{27\frac{1}{6} \times 6}{39 \times 6} = \frac{\frac{163}{6} \times 6}{39 \times 6} = \frac{163}{234}$$

2. multiply both the dividend and the divisor by the least common denominator if two fractions are involved:

$$42\frac{2}{3} \div 12\frac{1}{6} = \frac{42\frac{2}{3} \times 6}{12\frac{1}{6} \times 6} = \frac{\frac{128}{3} \times 6}{\frac{73}{6} \times 6} = \frac{256}{73}$$

Other Division Properties

1. If the division is not exact, the number that is left is the remainder. This remainder becomes the numerator and the divisor becomes the denominator of this common fraction that is added to the quotient:

$$4\overline{)1207}$$
$$301\frac{3}{4}$$

2. The remainder may also be shown as a decimal. The decimal point is placed to the right of the unit digit of the dividend and zero digits are added. Divide to the desired number of decimal places:

$$4\overline{)1207.00}$$
$$301.75$$

3. Dividing any number by one does not change the number:

$$25 \div 1 = 25 \qquad 4.7 \div 1 = 4.7 \qquad \frac{3}{5} \div 1 = \frac{3}{5}$$

4. Dividing by zero is not permissible, as the answer indicated would be infinity.

5. a. To divide by ten, move the decimal point in the number one place to the left:

$$\frac{136}{10} = 13.6 \qquad \frac{13.6}{10} = 1.36 \qquad \frac{1.36}{10} = .136$$

b. To divide by 100, move the decimal point in the number two places to the left:

$$\frac{350}{100} = 3.50 \qquad \frac{35}{100} = 3.5 \qquad \frac{3.5}{100} = .035$$

c. To divide by 1000, move the decimal point in the number three places to the left:

$$\frac{4055}{1000} = 4.055 \qquad \frac{40.55}{1000} = .04055$$

$$\frac{405.5}{1000} = .4055 \qquad \frac{4.055}{1000} = .004055$$

When dividing by 10, 100, 1000, etc., move the decimal point in the number as many places to the left as there are zeros in the divisor. If necessary, use zeros at the left of the dividend.

Factors Of A Product

When two or more numbers are multiplied to produce a certain product, each of the numbers is known as a *factor* of the product.

$1 \times 8 = 8$ (1 and 8 are factors of the product)

$2 \times 4 = 8$ (2 and 4 are factors of the product)

Base

A *base* is a number used as a factor two or more times. $2 \times 2 \times 2$ may be written 2^3, which is read "2 cubed" or "2 to the third power." In the equation $2^3 = 8$, 2 is called the base.

Exponent

The *exponent* is the number that shows how many times the base is to be used as a factor. 10^2 is a short way of writing 10×10. 10 is called the base in 10^2; 2 is called the exponent.

$a^4 = a \times a \times a \times a$ (*a* is the base, 4 is the exponent)

$5^3 = 5 \times 5 \times 5$ (5 is the base, 3 is the exponent)

Power

Power is an expression such as 3^2. 3^2 is the second power of three (3×3) and is equal to 9. 2^4 is the fourth power of two ($2 \times 2 \times 2 \times 2$) and is equal to 16. Note that all the factors of the product are equal.

Reciprocal

If the product of two numbers is 1, either number is called the *reciprocal* of the other number.

4 is the reciprocal of $\frac{1}{4}$; $\frac{1}{4}$ is the reciprocal of 4; $4 \times \frac{1}{4} = 1$. Similarly, $\frac{3}{5}$ is the reciprocal of $\frac{5}{3}$; $\frac{5}{3}$

is the reciprocal of $\frac{3}{5}$; $\frac{3}{5} \times \frac{5}{3} = 1$.

Factorial

The *factorial* of a natural or counting number is the product of that number and all the natural numbers less than it. **4 factorial**, written as 4! = 4 × 3 × 2 × 1 = 24.

Prime Number

A *prime number* is a natural or counting number with exactly two factors namely itself and 1. Examples of prime numbers are 2, 3, 5, 7, 11, 13, 17, etc.

Roots

Square Root

The *square root* of a number is a number that, when raised to the second power, produces the given number. For example, the square root of 16 is 4 because $4^2 = 16$. $\sqrt{}$ is the symbol for square root.

The square roots of the most common perfect squares are given in the table below.

NUMBER	PERFECT SQUARE	NUMBER	PERFECT SQUARE
1	1	10	100
2	4	11	121
3	9	12	144
4	16	13	169
5	25	14	196
6	36	15	225
7	49	20	400
8	64	25	625
9	81	30	900

For example, to find $\sqrt{81}$ note that 81 is the perfect square of 9, or $9^2 = 81$. Therefore, $\sqrt{81} = 9$.

Cube Root

Cube root is the procedure inverse of raising to a cube. If $2^3 = 8$, than $\sqrt[3]{8} = 2$. The cube root of $27 = 3$; $3^3 = 27$.

Algebra

Algebra is the branch of mathematics that focuses on addition, subtraction, multiplication, and division operations applied to variables, or unknowns, instead of specific numbers.

Here are these operations in algebraic form:

Operation	Algebraic Form
Addition: The sum of two numbers	$x + y$
Subtraction: The difference of two numbers	$x - y$
Multiplication: The product of two numbers	$x \times y$ *or* xy
Division: The quotient of two numbers	$\dfrac{x}{y}$

Algebraic Equations

An *equation* states that two quantities are equal. The solution to an equation is a number that can be substituted for the letter, or *variable*, to give a true statement.

For example, in the equation $x + 7 = 10$, if 5 is substituted for x, the equation becomes $5 + 7 = 10$, which is false. If 3 is substituted for x, the equation becomes $3 + 7 = 10$, which is true. Therefore, $x = 3$ is a solution for the equation $x + 7 = 10$.

An equation has been solved when it is transformed or rearranged so that a variable or unknown is on one side of the equal sign and a number is on the other side.

There are two basic principles that are used to transform equations:

1. The same quantity may be added to, or subtracted from, both sides of an equation.

    To solve the equation $x - 3 = 2$, add 3 to both sides:

$$
\begin{aligned}
x - 3 &= 2 \\
+3 \quad & \quad +3 \\
\hline
x \quad &= 5
\end{aligned}
$$

    Adding 3 isolates x on one side and leaves a number on the other side. The solution to the equation is $x = 5$.

To solve the equation $y + 4 = 10$, subtract 4 from both sides (adding -4 to both sides will have the same effect):

$$\begin{array}{rcr} y+4 &=& 10 \\ \underline{-4} & & \underline{-4} \\ y &=& 6 \end{array}$$

The variable has been isolated on one side of the equation. The solution is $y = 6$.

2. Both sides of an equation may be multiplied by, or divided by, the same quantity.

To solve $2a = 12$, divide both sides by 2:

$$\frac{2a}{2} = \frac{12}{2}$$
$$a = 6$$

To solve $\dfrac{b}{5} = 10$, multiply both sides by 5:

$$5 \cdot \frac{b}{5} = 10 \cdot 5$$
$$b = 50$$

To solve equations containing more than one operation:

First, eliminate any number that is being added to or subtracted from the variable.
Then eliminate any number that is multiplying or dividing the variable.

Solve:

$$\begin{array}{rcll} 3x-6 &=& 9 & \\ \underline{+6} & & \underline{+6} & \text{Adding 6 eliminates } -6. \\ 3x &=& 15 & \\ \dfrac{3x}{3} &=& \dfrac{15}{3} & \text{Dividing by 3 eliminates the 3 that is} \\ & & & \quad \text{multiplying the } x. \\ x &=& 5 & \text{The solution to the original equation is} \\ & & & \quad x = 5. \end{array}$$

Geometry

Angles

An *angle* is the figure formed by two rays meeting at a point.

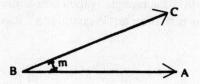

The point B is the *vertex* of the angle and the $\overline{BA}$ and $\overline{BC}$ are the *sides* of the angle. The symbol for an angle is $\angle$.

Types of Angles

1. When two straight lines intersect (cut each other), four angles are formed. If these four angles are equal, each angle is a *right angle* and contains 90°. The symbol ⌐ is used to indicate a right angle, as shown below.

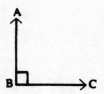

$\angle$ABC is a right angle.

2. An angle less than a right angle is an *acute angle*.

3. If the two sides of an angle extend in opposite directions forming a straight line, the angle is a *straight angle* and contains 180°.

4. An angle greater than a right angle (90°) and less than a straight angle (180°) is an *obtuse angle*.

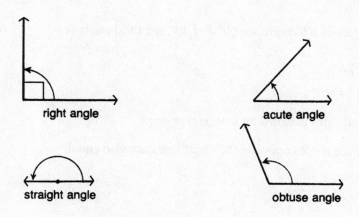

right angle

acute angle

straight angle

obtuse angle

Complementary angles are two angles whose sum is 90°. Each angle is the complement of the other. If an angle contains 30°, its complement contains 60°. If an angle contains $x°$, its complement contains $(90 - x)°$.

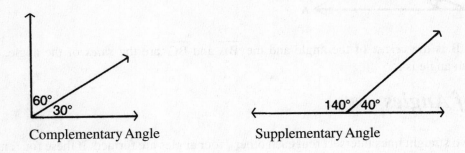

Complementary Angle   Supplementary Angle

Supplementary angles are two angles whose sum is 180°. Each angle is the supplement of the other. If an angle contains 140°, its supplement contains 40°. If an angle contains $x°$, its supplement contains $(180 - x)°$.

Triangles

A *triangle* is a closed, three-sided figure. The following figures are triangles.

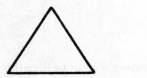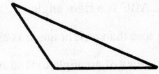

The sum of the three angles of a triangle is 180°.

To find an angle of a triangle given the other two angles, add the given angles and subtract their sum from 180°.

For example, if two angles of a triangle are 60° and 40°, the third angle is

$$180° - (60° + 40°) =$$
$$180° - 100° = 80°$$

A triangle with two equal sides is called an *isosceles triangle.*

In an isosceles triangle, the angles opposite the equal sides are also equal.

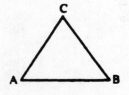

If AC = BC, then m∠A = m∠B

A triangle with all three sides equal is called an *equilateral triangle*.

Each angle of an equilateral triangle is 60°.

A triangle with a right angle is called a *right triangle*.

In a right triangle, the two acute angles are complementary.

In a right triangle, the side opposite *the right angle* is called the *hypotenuse* and is the longest side. The other two sides are called *legs*.

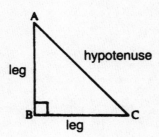

In right triangle ABC, $\overline{AC}$ is the hypotenuse. $\overline{AB}$ and $\overline{BC}$ are the legs.

The *Pythagorean Theorem* states that in a right triangle, the square of the hypotenuse equals the sum of the squares of the legs.

In right triangle ABC: $(AC)^2 = (AB)^2 + (BC)^2$

Circles

A *circle* is a closed plane curve, all points of which are equidistant from a point within called the center.

A complete circle contains 360°.

A *radius* of a circle is a line segment connecting the center with any point on the circle.

A *diameter* of a circle is a line segment connecting any two points on the circle and passing through the center of the circle. The diameter of any circle is twice the radius of that circle.

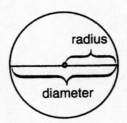

Perimeter

The *perimeter* of a two-dimensional figure is the distance around the figure. The perimeter of a rectangle equals twice the sum of the length and the width.

$$P = 2(l + w)$$
$$P = 2(8 + 4) = 2(12)$$
$$P = 24$$

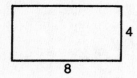

The perimeter of a triangle is the sum of the three sides.

$$P = 7 + 6 + 5 = 18$$

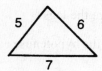

The perimeter of a circle is called the circumference. The circumference of a circle is equal to the product of the diameter multiplied by π.

The formula is $C = \pi d$

Pi (π) is a mathematical value equal to approximately 3.14 or $\dfrac{22}{7}$.

$$C = \pi d$$
$$C = \pi(3) = 3\pi$$

Area

In a two-dimensional figure, the total space within the figure is called the *area*.

Area is expressed in square denominations, such as square inches, square centimeters, or square miles.

The area of a rectangle equals the product of the length (or base) multiplied by the width (or height).

$A = lw$

$A = 9\ ft. \times 3\ ft.$

$A = 27\ sq.\ ft.$

3 ft.

9 ft.

The area of a triangle is equal to one half the product of the base and the height. The height (or altitude) of a triangle is a line drawn from a vertical perpendicular to the opposite side, called the base.

$A = \dfrac{1}{2}bh$

$A = \dfrac{1}{2}(9\ in.)(5\ in.) = \dfrac{45}{2}$

$A = 22\dfrac{1}{2}\ sq.\ in.$

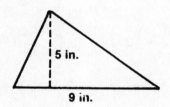

5 in.

9 in.

The area of a circle is equal to the radius squared multiplied by π.

$A = \pi r^2$

$A = \pi(4\ cm.)^2$

$A = 16\pi\ sq.\ cm.$

4 cm.

You may leave the area in terms of pi unless you are told what value to assign π.

Sample Questions

Sample questions illustrating some of the types of questions found in the Mathematics Knowledge subtest follow. Explanatory answers are given at the end of this section and show how the correct answers are obtained.

1. The sum of $2\frac{5}{8}$, $3\frac{3}{16}$, $1\frac{1}{2}$, and $4\frac{1}{4}$ is

     1-A $9\frac{13}{16}$

     1-B $10\frac{7}{16}$

     1-C $11\frac{9}{16}$

     1-D $13\frac{3}{16}$

2. Which fraction is equal to 0.20?

     2-A $\frac{1}{5}$

     2-B $\frac{2}{7}$

     2-C $\frac{3}{16}$

     2-D $\frac{1}{50}$

3. Which of the following fractions is the smallest?

     3-A $\frac{3}{4}$

     3-B $\frac{5}{6}$

     3-C $\frac{7}{8}$

     3-D $\frac{19}{24}$

4. The product of $11\frac{2}{13}$ times $13\frac{7}{9}$ is most nearly

    4-A   152.58

    4-B   152.68

    4-C   153.58

    4-D   153.68

5. The sum of $\sqrt{81}$ and $\sqrt{25}$ is

    5-A   106

    5-B   86

    5-C   24

    5-D   14

6. Find the value of $\left(3\sqrt{2}\right)^2$

    6-A $9\sqrt{2}$

    6-B   18

    6-C   24

    6-D   36

7. $\sqrt[3]{216}$ is equal to

    7-A   6

    7-B   12

    7-C   36

    7-D   72

8. The fourth root of 81 is

    8-A   324

    8-B   27

    8-C   9

    8-D   3

9. The numerical value of 5! is

    9-A   110

    9-B   115

    9-C   120

    9-D   125

10. The numerical value of $\frac{4!}{3!}$ is

    10-A   .75

    10-B   1.25

    10-C   1.33

    10-D   4

11. Which one of the following is a prime number?

    11-A   9
    11-B   11
    11-C   15
    11-D   21

12. The reciprocal of 4 is

    12-A   .25
    12-B   .40
    12-C   1.25
    12-D   1.40

13. 1,000 is equivalent to

    13-A 10^2
    13-B 10^3
    13-C 10^4
    13-D 10^5

14. $10^3 \times 10^4 =$

    14-A 10^7
    14-B 10^{12}
    14-C 100^7
    14-D 100^{12}

15. When +5 is added to –7, the sum is

    15-A   +2
    15-B   –2
    15-C   +12
    15-D   –12

16. Find the product of (–5)(–4)(–3).

    16-A   +12
    16-B   –12
    16-C   +60
    16-D   –60

17. Solve the following: $\dfrac{5}{9}(41+40)-40 =$

    17-A   55
    17-B   5.00
    17-C   22.30
    17-D   73.80

18. If you subtract −1 from +1, the result will be

    18-A   −2
    18-B   −1
    18-C   +1
    18-D   +2

19. If $a + 6 = 7$, then a is equal to

    19-A   0

    19-B $\dfrac{7}{6}$

    19-C   +1
    19-D   −1

20. If $4y = 12$, then $y =$

    20-A $\dfrac{1}{4}$

    20-B $\dfrac{1}{3}$

    20-C   3
    20-D   8

21. If 50% of $x = 66$, then $x =$

    21-A   132
    21-B   99
    21-C   66
    21-D   33

22. $8 \times 8 = 4^x$. Find x.

    22-A   1
    22-B   2
    22-C   3
    22-D   4

23. If $2^{n-3} = 32$, then n equals

    23-A   5
    23-B   6
    23-C   7
    23-D   8

24. What percent of a is b?

   24-A $\dfrac{b}{a}$

   24-B $\dfrac{a}{b}$

   24-C $\dfrac{100b}{a}$

   24-D $\dfrac{100a}{b}$

25. Using the formula $A = P(1 + rt)$, find A when $P = 500$, $r = .03$, and $t = 15$.

   25-A   625
   25-B   725
   25-C   795
   25-D   800

26. If $a = 5b$, then $\dfrac{3}{5}a =$

   26-A $\dfrac{5}{3}b$

   26-B $\dfrac{3}{5}b$

   26-C $3b$

   26-D $\dfrac{b}{3}$

27. If you multiply $x + 3$ by $2x + 5$, what will be the coefficient of x?

   27-A   11
   27-B   10
   27-C   9
   27-D   6

28. $\dfrac{x-2}{x^2-6x+8}$ can be simplified to

   28-A $\dfrac{1}{x-4}$ 28-C $\dfrac{1}{x+4}$

   28-B $\dfrac{1}{x-2}$ 28-D $\dfrac{1}{x+2}$

29. If $2x = 3y$ and $5x + y = 34$, $y =$

    29-A   4

    29-B   5

    29-C   6

    29-D   7

30. Solve for x: $\begin{array}{l} x + y = a \\ x - y = b \end{array}$

    30-A $a + b$

    30-A $a - b$

    30-C $\dfrac{1}{2}(a+b)$

    30-D $\dfrac{1}{2}(a-b)$

31. Solve for x: $\dfrac{x+1}{8} = \dfrac{28}{32}$

    31-A   5

    31-B   6

    31-C   7

    31-D   8

32. If $\dfrac{a}{b} \times \dfrac{b}{c} \times \dfrac{c}{d} \times \dfrac{d}{e} \times x = 1$, then x must be equal to

    32-A $\dfrac{a}{e}$

    32-B $\dfrac{e}{a}$

    32-C $\dfrac{1}{a}$

    32-D $\dfrac{1}{e}$

33. If $\dfrac{a}{b} = \dfrac{3}{4}$, then $12a =$

    33-A $3b$

    33-B $6b$

    33-C $9b$

    33-D $12b$

34. The average of two numbers is A. If one of the numbers is x, the other number is

    34-A $\dfrac{A}{2} - x$

    34-B $\dfrac{A + x}{2}$

    34-C $A - x$

    34-D $2A - x$

35. Two angles that are both equal and supplementary are

    35-A   acute angles.

    35-B   obtuse angles.

    35-C   right angles.

    35-D   straight angles.

36. In one hour, the minute hand of a clock rotates through an angle of

    36-A   45°

    36-B   90°

    36-C   180°

    36-D   360°

37. At 6:00 a.m., the angle between the hands of the clock is

    37-A   90°

    37-B   120°

    37-C   180

    37-D   360°

38. In the triangle given below, if $m\angle B = 90°$,

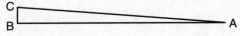

    38-A $\overline{AB}$ is longer than $\overline{AC}$.

    38-B   angle ABC is less than angle ACB.

    38-C $m\angle ABC = m\angle ACB$.

    38-D $m\angle ABC$ is greater than $m\angle ACB$.

39. A circle is inscribed in a square whose side is 6. What is the circumference of the circle in terms of π?

    39-A 3π

    39-B 6π

    39-C 9π

    39-D 12π

40. The hypotenuse of a right triangle whose legs are 5″ and 12″ is

    40-A   7″

    40-B   13″

    40-C   14″

    40-D   17″

41. How many meters will a point on the rim of a wheel travel if the wheel makes 50 rotations and its radius is one meter?

    41-A   314

    41-B   298

    41-C   283

    41-D   157

42. The area of a square is 36 square inches. If the side of this square is doubled, the area of the new square will be

    42-A   72 square inches.

    42-B   144 square inches.

    42-C   216 square inches.

    42-D   244 square inches.

43. The circumference of a circle that has a radius of 70 feet is most nearly

    43-A   440 feet.

    43-B   660 feet.

    43-C   690 feet.

    43-D   15,300 feet.

44. The distance between two points on a graph whose rectangular coordinates are (2,4) and (5,8) is most nearly

    44-A   5.0

    44-B   5.5

    44-C   6.0

    44-D   6.5

45. In triangle ABC, AB = BC and $\overline{AC}$ is extended to D. If angle BCD contains 110°, find the number of degrees in angle B.

    45-A   20°

    45-B   40°

    45-C   60°

    45-D   80°

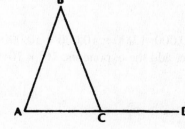

Answers and Explanations

1-C Arrange the numbers in proper vertical columns, then rename fractions as equivalent fractions having the same common denominator and, finally, add.

The sum of $10\dfrac{25}{16}$ is actually $11\dfrac{9}{16}$.

2-A $.2 = \dfrac{2}{10} = \dfrac{1}{5}$

3-A Rename all fractions as 24ths and then compare numerators.

$A = \dfrac{18}{24}$, $B = \dfrac{20}{24}$, $C = \dfrac{21}{24}$, $D = \dfrac{19}{24}$.

4-D Rename the mixed numbers as fractions and then multiply: $\dfrac{145}{13} \times \dfrac{124}{9} = \dfrac{17980}{117} = 153.68$.

5-D $\sqrt{81} = 9$; $\sqrt{25} = 5$; $9 + 5 = 14$

6-B $\left(3\sqrt{2}\right)^2 = 3\sqrt{2} \times 3\sqrt{2} = 9 \times 2 = 18$

7-A $6 \times 6 \times 6 = 216$.

8-D $3 \times 3 \times 3 \times 3 = 81$.

9-C The factorial of 5 is $5 \times 4 \times 3 \times 2 \times 1 = 120$

10-D The factorial of a natural number is the product of that number and all the natural numbers less than it. $4! = 4 \times 3 \times 2 \times 1 = 24$.

$3! = 3 \times 2 \times 1 = 6$

$\dfrac{4!}{3!} = \dfrac{24}{6} = 4$

11-B Of the numbers given, only 11 has no other factor except 1 and itself. $3 \times 3 = 9$; $3 \times 5 = 15$; $7 \times 3 = 21$.

12-A If the product of two numbers is 1, either number is called the reciprocal or multiplicative inverse of the other. For example, since $4 \times \dfrac{1}{4} = 1$, 4 is the reciprocal

of $\dfrac{1}{4}$ and $\dfrac{1}{4}$ is the reciprocal of 4. $\dfrac{1}{4}$ is equivalent to .25.

13-B $10 \times 10 \times 10 = 1,000$.

14-A $10^3 = 1,000$; $10^4 = 10,000$; $1,000 \times 10,000 = 10,000,000$ or 10^7. To multiply numbers of the same base, add the exponents. $10^3 \times 10^4 = 10^{(3+4)} = 10^7$.

15-B To add numbers with different signs, subtract the magnitude of the numbers and use the sign of the number with the greater magnitude.

16-D If there is an odd number of negative factors when multiplying, the product is negative. $(-5)(-4)(-3) = -60$.

17-B $\left(\dfrac{5}{9} \times 81\right) - 40 = 45 - 40 = 5$.

18-D Subtracting -1 from $+1$, change -1 to $+1$ and add to $+1 = +2$.

19-C $a = 7 - 6 = +1$.

20-C $y = \dfrac{12}{4} = 3$.

21-A $\dfrac{1}{2}$ of $x = 66$; $x = 66 \times 2 = 132$.

22-C $8 \times 8 = 64$; $4 \times 4 \times 4 = 64$; $x = 3$.

23-D $2^5 = 32$; $n - 3 = 5$; $n = 8$.

24-C $\dfrac{b}{a} \times 100 = \dfrac{100b}{a}$.

25-B $A = 500(1 + .03 \times 15) = 500(1 + .45) = 500(1.45) = 725$.

26-C $\dfrac{3}{5} \times 5b = 3b$.

27-A
$$x + 3$$
$$2x + 5$$
$$2x^2 + 6x$$
$$\underline{ + 5x + 15}$$
$$2x^2 + 11x + 15$$

28-A The factors of $x^2 - 6x + 8$ are $(x - 4)$ and $(x - 2)$

Therefore, $\dfrac{x - 2}{x^2 - 6x + 8} = \dfrac{x - 2}{(x - 4)(x - 2)} = \dfrac{1}{(x - 4)}$.

29-A Solve for x: $2x = 3y$
$$x = \dfrac{3y}{2}$$

Substitute in the second equation and solve for y:

$$5\left(\frac{3y}{2}\right) + y = 34$$

$$\frac{15y}{2} + y = 34$$

$$15y + 2y = 68$$

$$17y = 68$$

$$y = 4$$

30-C   Add the two equations to eliminate y:

$$x + y = a$$
$$\underline{x - y = b}$$
$$2x = a + b$$

Solve for x:

$$x = \frac{a+b}{2}$$

31-B   Solve for x:

$$\frac{x+1}{8} = \frac{28}{32}$$

$$(x+1)32 = 8 \times 28$$

$$32x + 32 = 224$$

$$32x = 224$$

$$32x = 192$$

$$x = \frac{192}{32} = 6$$

32-B   Divide common factors, and then solve

$$\frac{a}{\cancel{b}} \times \frac{\cancel{b}}{\cancel{c}} \times \frac{\cancel{c}}{\cancel{d}} \times \frac{\cancel{d}}{e} \times x = 1$$

$$\frac{a}{e} \times x = 1$$

$$\frac{ax}{e} = 1$$

$$ax = e$$

$$x = \frac{e}{a}$$

33-C   Solve for a

$$\frac{a}{b} = \frac{3}{4}$$

$$4a = 3b$$

$$a = \frac{3b}{4}$$

$$12a = \overset{3}{\cancel{12}}\left(\frac{3b}{\cancel{4}}\right)$$

$$12a = 9b$$

34-D   Let x = one of the numbers and y = the other number. $\frac{x+y}{2} = A; x + y = 2A; y = 2A - x$.

35-C   If the angles are equal and supplementary, they must be of the same value and add up to 180°. Each is 90° or a right angle.

36-D   In one hour, the minute hand rotates a full circle of 360°.

37-C   At 6:00 a.m., one hand is at 6 and the other is at 12, forming a straight angle or 180°.

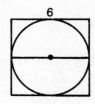

38-D   In this right triangle, angle ABC is a right angle. Each of the other angles in the triangle must be less than 90°. $\overline{AC}$, the hypotenuse, is longer than either leg of the triangle.

39-B   Side = 6; therefore, diameter = 6. Circumference = $\pi \times$ diameter = 6π.

40-B   The Pythagorean Theorem states that for any right triangle, the sum of the square of the legs is equal to the square of the length of the hypotenuse. $5^2 + 12^2 = h^2$, $25 + 144 = h^2$, $h^2 = 169$. $\sqrt{169} = 13$. $h = 13$. The correct answer is 13″.

41-A   If the radius of the wheel is one meter, its diameter is two meters. The circumference is $\pi \times$ diameter = $2 \times 22/7$. The distance traveled is $50 \times 2 \times 22/7 = 100 \times 22/7 = 314$.

42-B   If the area of a square = 36 square inches, the side of the square = 6 inches. If doubled to 12 inches, the area of the new square will be 12 inches by 12 inches = 144 square inches.

43-A   If the radius is 70 feet, the diameter is 140 feet. Circumference = π × diameter =

$140 \times \dfrac{22}{7} = 440$ feet.

44-A   As shown in the graph below, we have a right triangle with one leg of 3 and the other leg of 4. Using the Pythagorean Theorem, the hypotenuse, or the distance between the two points, is obtained as follows: $h^2 = 3^2 + 4^2$; $h^2 = 9 + 16$; $h^2 = 25$;

$h = \sqrt{25}$; $h = 5$.

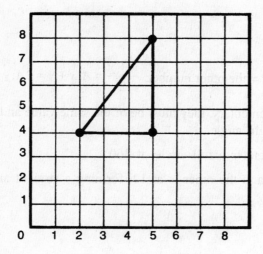

45- B

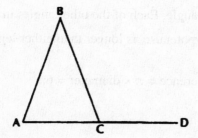

ACD is a straight line. Therefore, if m∠ BCD = 110°, m∠ BCA = 70°. AB = BC. Therefore, triangle ABC is an isosceles triangle and m∠ BAC = m∠ BCA = 70°. The sum of the angles of a triangle = 180°. Therefore, m∠ ABC = 180° – (70° + 70°) = 180° – 140° = 40°.

ELECTRONICS INFORMATION REVIEW

Electricity

Electricity is a form of energy resulting from the existence of charged particles. It is an invisible force that we know about only through the effects it produces. The exact nature of electricity is not known but the laws governing electrical phenomena are clearly understood and defined. The same is true for the laws of gravitation that are known, while the nature of gravity cannot be defined.

In order to understand basic electronic theory, it is important to be familiar with the basics of electricity.

The Movement of Electricity

In many ways electricity in motion is like flowing water, and electrical phenomena can be more easily understood if this analogy is borne in mind. In dealing with the flow of electricity and the flow of water, we consider three factors:

1. Electrical Current: Flow of electricity, usually along a conductor

2. Electrical Pressure: Causes the current to flow

3. Resistance: Regulates the flow of current

Electrical Current

To know about the flow of water in a pipe, determine how many gallons of water flow through the pipe in a second. In exactly the same way, an electrician determines the number of *coulombs* of electricity that flow through a wire in a second. Just as the gallon is a measure of the quantity of water, the coulomb is a measure of the quantity of electricity. There is an abbreviated method of describing the flow of electrical current. An electrician speaks of the *ampere*, which means one coulomb per second, and is thus saved the trouble of saying *"per second"* every time he wants to describe the current flow. Very small currents drawn by electronic devices are frequently measured in terms of milliamperes (ma), or one thousandth of an ampere.

Electrical Pressure

Water pressure is measured in pounds per square inch. There is also a measure of electrical pressure. This electrical pressure has a definite effect upon the number of amperes flowing along a wire. The electrical unit of pressure is the volt. A volt means the same thing in speaking of a current of electricity that a pound-per-square-inch pressure does in speaking of a current of water. Just as a higher pressure is required to force the same current of water through a small pipe than through a large pipe, so a higher electrical pressure is required to force the same current of electricity through a small wire than through a large wire. The voltage (pressure) between two points in an electric circuit is sometimes spoken of as the difference in potential, the drop in potential, or merely the *"drop"* between those two points.

The main distinction between amperes and volts is that the amperes represent the amount of the current flowing through a circuit; the volts represent the pressure causing it to flow.

Electrical Resistance

The electrical unit of resistance is the ohm. A wire has one ohm resistance when a pressure of one volt forces a current of one ampere through it. Ohms are often represented by the symbol: Ω.

Ohm's Law

In any circuit through which a current is flowing, the three following factors are present:

1. The pressure or potential difference, expressed in volts, causing the current to flow

2. The opposition or resistance of the circuit, expressed in ohms, which must be over come

3. The current strength, expressed in amperes, which is maintained in the circuit as a result of the pressure overcoming the resistance. A definite and exact relation exists between three factors: pressure, current strength, and resistance in any circuit, whereby the value of any one factor may always be calculated when the values of the other two factors are known. This relation is known as Ohm's Law. It may be summarized as follows:

The current in any electric circuit is equal to the voltage applied to the circuit, divided by the resistance of the circuit.

Let V =   voltage applied to the circuit expressed in volts

R =   resistance of the circuit, expressed in ohms

I =   current strength in amperes, to be maintained through the circuit

Then, by the above statement of Ohm's Law,

$$\text{Current} = \frac{\text{Voltage}}{\text{Resistance}} \text{ or Amperes} = \frac{\text{volts}}{\text{ohms}} \text{ or } I = \frac{V}{R}$$

Ohm's Law can also be written in the following equivalent forms:

$$V = IR$$
$$I = \frac{V}{R}$$

Electrical Power

The product of the voltage across a device and current flowing through it is defined as the power consumed by the device. The power consumed by a device that draws one ampere when one volt is applied to it is one watt.

$$P = VI$$

where P = power in watts, V = volts, and I = amperes.

The Circuit

Electricity is not as simple as water; it cannot be piped from one point to another. In order to flow, electricity must be sent along a closed circuit. Except through a generator or a battery cell, electricity always flows from a higher to a lower level. The higher level or positive is marked +, and the lower level or negative is marked –, in order to indicate the direction in which the current is flowing. A given point is + to all points below its level, and – to all points above its level.

If any of the wires leading from the + to the – terminal is broken, the current cannot flow, for the circuit has been interrupted and is incomplete.

Measurements

There are different ways to determine measurements for currents, pressure, and electrical resistance.

Measuring Electrical Current

In order to find out how much current is flowing through an electric circuit, insert a current meter into the circuit so that all the current that you wish to measure flows through the meter. A current meter called an ammeter measures an electric current and is read in amperes. The ammeter must be of very low resistance in order not to hinder the current and must be handled carefully since it is very delicate.

Measuring Electrical Pressure

When it is necessary to measure the pressure causing an electric current to flow through a circuit, the terminals of a *voltmeter* are tapped on to that circuit in such a way that the voltmeter is made to register not current but pressure. The method of attaching a voltmeter is different from that used in attaching an ammeter. The ammeter becomes a part of the circuit; the voltmeter does not become a part of the circuit.

Measuring Electrical Resistance

In order to find the resistance of an electrical component, the voltmeter reading is divided by the ammeter reading, or an ohmmeter or "megger" is used.

Regulating and Controlling Electrical Current

By inserting or removing resistance from a circuit, you regulate and control the current required for various electrical purposes. An adjustable resistance, or any apparatus for changing the resistance without opening the circuit, is called a *rheostat*. The function of a rheostat is to absorb electrical energy. This energy, which appears as heat, is wasted instead of performing any useful work.

The Effects of a Current

A current of electricity is believed to be a transfer of electrons through a circuit, and since these carriers are so minute, a direct measurement of them is impractical. Consequently, the effects it produces, all of which are commercially utilized, measure an electric current. The effects manifested by a current of electricity are:

Heating Effect

Every wire, that conducts a current of electricity becomes heated to some extent as a result of the current because the best conductors offer some opposition (resistance) to the flow of the current. It is in overcoming this resistance that the heat is developed. If the wire is large in a cross-sectional area and the current is small, the heat developed will be so small in amount as not to be recognized by the touch. Nevertheless, the wire releases some heat energy. On the other hand, with a small wire and a large current, it becomes quite hot.

Magnetic Effect

A wire carrying a current of electricity deflects a magnetic needle. When the wire is insulated and coiled around an iron core, the current magnetizes the core.

Chemical Effect

Electrical current is capable of decomposing certain chemical compounds when it is passed through them, breaking up the compounds into their constituent parts. In the production of electrical energy by a simple primary cell, electrolytic decomposition takes place inside the cell when the current is flowing. Electroplating, or the art of deposing a coating of metal upon any object, is based upon the principles of electrolytic decomposition.

Physiological Effect

A current of electricity passed through the body produces muscular contractions that are due to the physiological effects of an electrical current. Electrotherapeutics deals with the study of this effect.

The Dynamo and Electromagnetic Induction

The electrical generator and the electric motor are intimately related. The term dynamo is applied to machines that convert either mechanical energy into electrical energy or electrical energy into mechanical energy by utilizing the principles of electromagnetic induction. A dynamo is called a generator when mechanical energy supplied in the form of rotation is converted into electrical energy. When the energy conversion takes place in the reverse order, the dynamo is called a motor. Thus, a dynamo is a reversible machine capable of operation as a generator or motor as desired.

The generator consists fundamentally of a number of loops of insulated wires revolving in a strong magnetic field in such a way that these wires cut across the lines of magnetic force. This cutting of the lines of force sets up an electromotive force along the wires.

Wherever there is an electric current present, there is also present a magnetic field. It is not true that wherever a magnetic field exists, there also exists an electric current, in the ordinary sense; but you can say that wherever a conductor moves in a magnetic field in such a way as to cut lines of force, an electromotive force is set up. It is on this principle that the electric generator works.

Alternating Current (AC) and Direct Current (DC)

A direct or continuous current flows always in the same direction. In many cases it has a constant strength for definite periods of time. A pulsating current has a uniform direction, but the current strength varies. Most direct current generators furnish pulsating current; but since the pulsations are very small, the current is practically constant.

An alternating current of electricity is one that changes its direction of flow at regular intervals of time. These intervals are usually much shorter than one second. During an interval, the current strength is capable of varying in any way. In practice, the strength rises and then falls smoothly. Most electricity today comes in the form of alternating current since high voltage can more easily be obtained with alternating current than with direct current. High voltages are much more cheaply transmitted over power lines than are low voltages.

The alternating current (AC) supplied to our homes ordinarily changes its direction of flow 60 times per second. The term used to describe the frequency with which a current changes its direction of flow per second is the Hertz (Hz). House current, therefore, has a frequency of 60 Hz.

Basic Electronic Theory

Electronic devices and systems frequently operate at very high frequencies. These high frequencies are measured in terms of kilohertz (KHz), which represents a thousand Hz, or in megahertz (MHz), which represents a million Hz.

Some representative frequencies used by electronic systems are
- AM radio broadcasts: 535 KHz to 1,605 KHz
- FM radio broadcasts: 88 MHz to 108 MHz
- TV Channel 2: 54 MHz
- Radar: 400 MHz to 100,000 MHz

Visible light is an ultrahigh frequency form of radiation that occurs at frequencies in the order of a billion MHz.

Impedance

The flow of AC is impeded not only by a circuit's resistance but also by its reactance. Reactance is due to the presence of capacitance and inductance. *Capacitive* reactance and *inductive* reactance are both measured in ohms (Ω). The total of the resistances and reactances in an AC circuit is called its impedance.

Some kinds of electrical circuits, especially those used in electronics, require particular values of capacitive or inductive reactance to function properly. Electronic components such as capacitors, typically rated in microfarads (MFD), and inductors, typically rated in millihenries (MH), are introduced in circuits as required to offer capacitive and inductive reactances.

Rectification

Electronic circuits are frequently used to change alternating current to direct current. These circuits, called rectifiers, usually contain solid-state semiconductor diodes that conduct electricity in only one direction. The current output of the diodes contains ripples that are smoothed into a steady DC output by means of filters consisting of combinations of inductors and capacitors.

Transistors

The transistor is another solid-state device frequently found in electronic circuits. It consists of two types of semiconductor material, N-type and P-type. An NPN transistor consists of P-type material sandwiched between two sections of N-type material. Another version is called a PNP transistor and consists of N-type material sandwiched between two sections of P-type material. Each transistor has an emitter, a collector, and a base section. The common symbolic representations of transistors are as follows.

Figure 1. Transistors

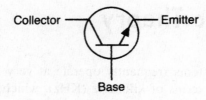

NPN Transistor

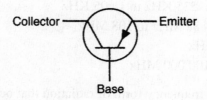

PNP Transistor

Electronic Circuits

Some of the other common symbols used to represent components of electronic circuits are as follows.

Figure 2. Symbols for electronic circuit components

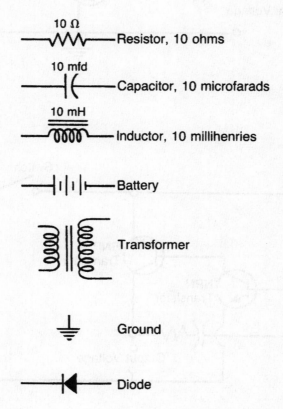

These elements are combined to create typical electronics circuits, such as:

Figure 3. Half wave filtered rectifier

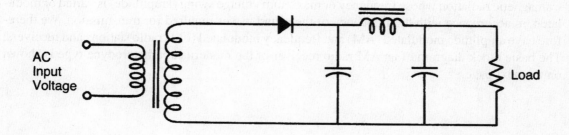

Figure 4. NPN transistor amplifier

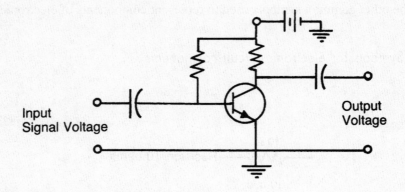

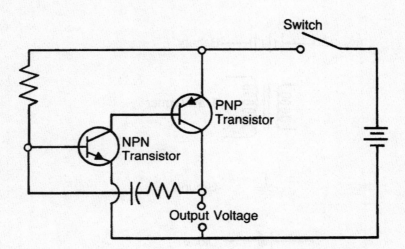

Communications Electronics

Combinations of basic electronic circuits make up complex communications systems. Block diagrams, such as the one below, can help you to understand these systems by defining basic components within an overall complex system. Radio transmitters send out high-frequency electromagnetic radiation whose frequency or maximum voltage swing (amplitude) is varied or modulated, in accordance with the frequency of the sound waves required for transmission. We therefore have amplitude modulated (AM) and frequency modulated (FM) radio stations and receivers. The basic block diagram of an AM radio receiver of the modern superheterodyne type is shown on the next page.

Figure 5. Superheterodyne AM receiver

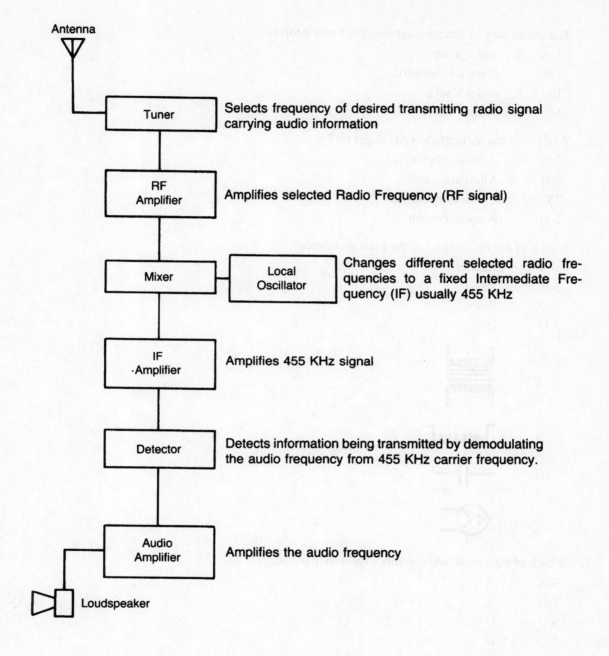

Antenna

Tuner — Selects frequency of desired transmitting radio signal carrying audio information

RF Amplifier — Amplifies selected Radio Frequency (RF signal)

Mixer — **Local Oscillator** — Changes different selected radio frequencies to a fixed Intermediate Frequency (IF) usually 455 KHz

IF Amplifier — Amplifies 455 KHz signal

Detector — Detects information being transmitted by demodulating the audio frequency from 455 KHz carrier frequency.

Audio Amplifier — Amplifies the audio frequency

Loudspeaker

Sample Questions

1. The safest way to run an extension cord to a lamp is
   - 1-A   under a rug.
   - 1-B   along a baseboard.
   - 1-C   under a sofa.
   - 1-D   behind a sofa.

2. What does the abbreviation AC stand for?
   - 2-A   Additional charge
   - 2-B   Alternating coil
   - 2-C   Alternating current
   - 2-D   Ampere current

3. Which of the following has the least resistance?
   - 3-A   Rubber
   - 3-B   Silver
   - 3-C   Wood
   - 3-D   Iron

A

B

C

D

4. Which of the above is the symbol for a transformer?
   - 4-A   A
   - 4-B   B
   - 4-C   C
   - 4-D   D

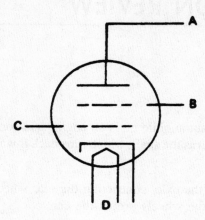

5. In the schematic vacuum tube illustrated above, the cathode is element

    5-A   A

    5-B   B

    5-C   C

    5-D   D

6. Flux is used in the process of soldering together two conductors in order to

    6-A   provide a luster finish.

    6-B   prevent oxidation when the connection is heated.

    6-C   maintain the temperature of the soldering iron.

    6-D   prevent the connection from becoming overheated.

Answers and Explanations

1-B   The safest place to run an extension cord to protect against fire hazard is along the base-board. Running an extension cord near furniture or under a rug increases the potential of a fire in case of an electrical short.

2-C   AC, Alternating Current, is the type of current that is used to operate household appliances as opposed to DC (Direct Current).

3-B   Since silver is the best conductor of electricity it also has the least resistance.

4-A   Diagram A is the symbol for a transformer.

5-D   Element D represents the cathode in the illustration of the vacuum tube.

6-B   The process of soldering causes oxidation on the connections being heated. Flux is added to the process in order to prevent oxidation from occurring.

AUTO & SHOP INFORMATION REVIEW

Basic Auto Information*

It is easy to see that the very least we need to make an automobile go is an engine and some means of connecting the engine to the wheels. The engine turns the shaft, which runs back toward the rear wheels.

It has a gear on the end, which meshes with a gear on the axle, connecting the rear wheels together. As the first shaft turns, it rotates the axle and the wheels propel the car.

If there were no hills around and we didn't want to go very fast and didn't want to turn any corners, this arrangement might work. But in an actual automobile, we have some more parts between the engine and the wheels. From here on, we're going to take them up one by one and try to explain what they are and what they do.

Engine

The power of an automobile engine comes from the burning of a mixture of gasoline and air in a small, enclosed space. When this mixture burns, it expands greatly and pushes out in all directions. It happens so quickly that we sometimes call it an explosion. This push or pressure can be used to move a part of the engine, and the movement of this part is eventually transmitted back to the wheels to drive the car.

Looking at an engine under the hood of an automobile, it seems to be a complicated sort of thing with hundreds of pieces and attachments and what-nots. But we can forget about most of these for the present and consider only the basic parts.

Cylinders and Pistons

First, we must have a cylinder. This is something like a tall metal can, or a pipe closed at one end. In fact, some of the early automobiles used cast iron pipes for cylinders.

Inside the cylinder we have a piston. This is a plug that is close-fitting but can slide up and down easily. It is the part of the engine that is moved by the expanding gases, being driven down on each power impulse or explosion.

Connecting Rod and Crankshaft

Now, we must find some way to change that up-and-down motion to rotary motion in order to propel the car. For this we have a connecting rod and crankshaft. The crankshaft is a shaft with an off-set portion, the crank, which describes a circle as the shaft rotates. The top end of the connecting rod is fastened to the piston, so it goes up and down in a straight line. The bottom end is fastened to the crank, so that end has to go around in a circle as the piston moves up and down.

*The "Basic Auto Information" section is based on *What Makes Autos Run*.

On one end of the crankshaft is a heavy wheel called the flywheel. If we turn a grindstone or emery wheel rapidly by hand, and then let go, the wheel will keep on rotating. This is the same action as the flywheel. It keeps the engine turning between power impulses.

These are the basic parts of an engine; but what we have shown here would make only a single-cylinder engine. Most automobile engines today have four or more cylinders. They can be arranged in one straight row, which we call an in-line engine, or in two rows set at an angle, descriptively called a V-type engine. In either case we have only one crankshaft, but it has a number of cranks instead of only one. With a number of cylinders the flywheel does not have such a big job to do because the power impulses occur more often and thus keep the crankshaft turning.

Valves

This basic engine we have put together so far has no way of getting the fuel-air mixture into it or burned gases out of it. We need some "doors," which in this case we call valves. Two holes are cut in the top of the cylinder, one for intake and one for exhaust. Metal discs are arranged to fit tightly over the holes to close them, but when pushed down they open the holes to allow passage of the gases through them. They work very much like the familiar stopper in a washbowl but turned upside down.

The valves are controlled by rocker arms and rods, which are moved by a camshaft. This is a shaft with cams or bumps on it—one bump for each valve—which push up on the rods to open the valves. The camshaft is driven by the crankshaft, at one-half speed. The cams are accurately shaped and located, and the shaft rotates at just the proper speed, as the valves must open and close at exactly the right moment.

Carburetor

In order to produce power, the engine needs a supply of gasoline and air mixed in the proper proportions. The carburetor does the mixing job. Gasoline is pumped from the tank to the carburetor by the fuel pump. This operates in much the same manner as the old-fashioned water pump, each stroke pushing a little fuel on to the carburetor where it goes first to the float chamber.

Air enters the carburetor through the air cleaner, being pulled in by the pumping action of the engine pistons working in the cylinders. This air flows through a venturi (a reduced passage in the carburetor) at high speed, then past the end of a tube leading from the float chamber. This sucks out the fuel into the air stream, breaking the liquid up into a fine mist and mixing it thoroughly with the air. An atomizer, or garden sprayer, works in a similar manner. Then the fuel and air mixture goes on into the engine, the amount being controlled by a throttle valve at the base of the carburetor, which is opened or closed by movement of the accelerator pedal.

A good mixture for burning in an engine is about 15 pounds of air to 1 pound of gasoline. Air being so much lighter than gasoline, this means that for every gallon of gasoline we burn, we use enough air to fill a room 10 feet square and more than 10 feet high. We call them gasoline engines, but it is easy to see that in some ways air plays the more important part.

Spark Plug

Now we have everything we need to make an engine run except something to start the mixture burning in the cylinder. Any kind of a spark will do it. In a cigarette lighter we make a spark by friction against a special metal. In an engine we do it electrically. A spark plug is inserted in the top of each cylinder, and a spark is created by electricity jumping across the gap between the two electrodes of the plug.

Battery

A battery furnishes the electricity, but several additional pieces of equipment are necessary for a complete ignition system. The coil and the breaker cooperate to develop a very high voltage, and the distributor is responsible for getting the high voltage electricity to the right spark plug at the right time.

All of this must take place very rapidly. In an eight-cylinder engine driving a car 55 miles per hour, the ignition system would have to furnish about 7,350 sparks per minute, or 123 each second. And it must do this at exactly the right time and without a miss.

The reason the valve mechanism and ignition system must perform their duties at just the right time is that an engine operates with a certain definite cycle of events—over and over again, at a high rate of speed. Now that we have all the necessary parts of an engine, we can see how it actually works.

Four Cylinder Engines

Most automobile engines are four-cycle engines. This means they operate on a four-stroke cycle, taking four strokes of the piston—down, up, down, up—for one complete cycle of events.

On the first stroke, the intake valve is open and the piston moves down, pulling in the fuel-air mixture until the cylinder is full. This is the *intake stroke*.

Then the intake valve closes and the piston starts up on the *compression stroke*. It squeezes the mixture into a small space at the top of the cylinder, which increases the pressure in the cylinder to almost 200 pounds per square inch.

Between the second and third strokes, ignition or firing takes place. The spark, jumping the gap of the spark plug, ignites the mixture of fuel and air squeezed at the top of the cylinder. In burning, the mixture, of course, gets very hot and tries to expand in all directions. The pressure rises to about 600 or 700 pounds per square inch. The piston is the only thing that can move, so the expanding gases push it down to the bottom of the cylinder. This is the *power stroke*.

The fuel is burned and the energy in the gases has been used up in pushing the piston downward. Now it is necessary to clear these burned gases out of the cylinder to make room for a new charge. On the *exhaust stroke*, the exhaust valve opens and the piston pushes the gases out through the opening.

The cycle continues through the same series of actions. The crankshaft is going around continuously while the piston is going up and down, but we should note that it is only on the power stroke that the piston is driving it around. On the other three strokes, the crankshaft is driving the piston.

There is one power stroke to every two revolutions of the crankshaft. This is for each cylinder, of course; with an eight-cylinder engine there are four power strokes for each revolution.

It is a fundamental fact of internal combustion engines that the more we compress the mixture, the harder we squeeze it, the more power we get from it. Compression ratio is a measure of how much we squeeze the mixture. If the cylinder holds 100 cubic inches when the piston is all the way down in its lowest position and 10 cubic inches when the piston is up as far as it can go, we say the compression ratio is 10:1. The mixture has been compressed into a space 1/10 as large as it originally occupied. Fifty years ago, 4:1 was a common figure for the compression ratio of automobile engines. This has increased over the years, and today compression ratios range upward of 8:1.

If we did not have a cooling system our engine would not last very long. The usual way of cooling the engine is to put water jackets around the hottest parts. Water is constantly circulated through these by a small pump. The heat of the cylinder makes the water hot, and it then goes to the radiator where it is cooled by the outside air passing through. Then it starts back to the engine again to do more cooling. It is actually very much like a steam or hot water heating system in a home. The engine is our boiler that heats up the water, which then goes to a radiator where it gives up its heat to the air.

Lubrication System

We also need a lubrication system for our engine. If all the rotating and reciprocating parts were running metal against metal, with no film of oil between them, they would soon heat up and stick. The friction would also make it harder for the parts to turn. So we have a reservoir of oil in the crankcase, where a pump forces it to the bearings and more critical points in the engine. Some of it flows through tubes and some through passages drilled in the crankshaft and connecting rods. The lubrication system might be compared to the water system in a house. The liquid is forced from one central place through pipes to many different locations where it is needed.

Electric Motor

We must have some way of starting the engine. It has to be turning over before it can run under its own power, and we give it this initial start by means of an electric motor. This is somewhat similar to the motor in our vacuum cleaner or washing machine. It runs on electricity from the battery, and the starter switch is similar to the electric wall switch that turns on the lights in our home.

Alternator

There is one more important piece of electrical equipment: the alternator. It looks something like the starter motor, but its job is just the opposite. Instead of taking electricity from the battery to start the engine, the alternator is driven by the engine and generates electric current, which feeds back into the battery to keep it charged for starting. The alternator also supplies power for the ignition system, lights, radio, and other electrical units.

Emissions Systems

There are three major pollutants that are emitted from automobiles into the atmosphere:

1. **Hydrocarbons:** Hydrocarbons, which we can think of as essentially unburned gasoline, come from the exhaust pipe and the engine's crankcase as a result of the combustion process. They also enter the atmosphere from the carburetor and the fuel tank through an evaporation process.

2. **Carbon monoxide:** Carbon monoxide (CO) results from partially burned fuel when rich fuel/air mixtures do not allow complete combustion all the way to carbon dioxide (CO).

3. **Oxides of nitrogen:** Oxides of nitrogen, on the other hand, are gases formed during combustion due to the high temperatures.

Today's cars have built-in systems designed to reduce the three major pollutants emitted from these sources. The systems may vary somewhat between different makes of cars, but they all work to perform the same job: reducing emissions of hydrocarbons, carbon monoxide, and oxides of nitrogen. Let's see what the systems are and what they do.

The first emission control applied to automobile engines was called the positive crankcase ventilation (PCV) system. This system, introduced in the early 1960s, is still in use today. During the "compression strokes" of the pistons, small amounts of gasoline vapors are forced past the piston rings from the combustion chamber and into the engine crankcase. These infinitesimal amounts of vapors expelled each engine cycle would add up to significant quantities of hydrocarbon (HC) emissions if they were allowed to enter the atmosphere. They don't, however, because the PCV system directs these vapors back to the intake system so that they are burned in the combustion chambers.

There is another system, air injection, that helps control hydrocarbon and carbon monoxide emissions in the exhaust. Air is injected by a pump into the engine's exhaust ports to cause further burning of the hot gasoline vapors before they pass out the exhaust pipe.

Figure 1. Air injection system

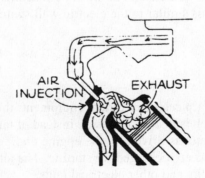

A *catalytic converter*, was first introduced on most 1975 model cars made in the U.S. This emission control system oxidizes HC and CO into harmless water vapor and carbon dioxide as the exhaust gases pass through a canister containing pellets that are coated with a catalyst material. A catalyst promotes chemical reactions, allowing them to take place at much lower than normal temperatures and more rapidly than a chemical reaction ordinarily would proceed. In the case of the catalytic converter emission control system, this means that catalysts allow more nearly complete oxidation of hydrocarbons and carbon monoxide at a much lower temperature than ordinary "burning."

Figure 2. Catalytic converter

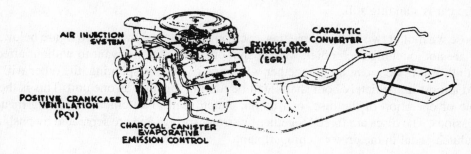

The catalytic converter has played a major role in reducing the emission of hydrocarbons and carbon monoxide from exhaust pipes into the atmosphere. It has also promoted improved fuel economy and has helped engineers "tune" the engine for a more pleasant car to drive.

Although the present catalytic converter, an oxidizing converter, does an excellent job in controlling HC and CO emissions, it isn't effective in controlling oxides of nitrogen (NOx), the third type of pollutant in exhaust gases. Oxides of nitrogen are different from HC and CO because they will not burn to harmless combustion products. Instead, control of NOx in the engine exhaust usually requires measures to prevent its formation.

Oxides of nitrogen are formed any time you have very high temperatures in the oxidation process (usually above 3,000° F, or 1,090° C) when air is used to provide the oxygen. Air contains 79% nitrogen and 21% oxygen, so you could say the air burns.

The formation of NOx in an engine is minimized by diluting the fuel/air mixture entering the combustion chamber. This helps reduce the peak combustion temperature. One system being used to control NOx emission is called Exhaust Gas Recirculation (EGR). With this system, small quantities of exhaust gases are recirculated back into the intake system of the engine to dilute the fuel/air mixture. Engineers are also looking at a "Three-Way Closed Catalyst Loop System" in which all three pollutants can be removed from the exhaust gases by a single catalytic converter. Such a system has been used already in a limited number of production cars.

To reduce hydrocarbons that evaporate from the carburetor and the fuel tank when the engine is not running, there's a system that vents gasoline vapors into a canister filled with carbon granules. These granules act like a sponge and soak up the fumes and store them while the car is parked. When the engine starts up, the fumes are fed back to the engine and burned.

Further control of exhaust emissions was brought about within the engine by:
- Changing the shape of the combustion chambers
- Using a leaner air-fuel ratio (more air in the mixture that goes to the cylinders for combustion)
- Regulating the temperature of the air entering the carburetor
- Increasing the speed at which the engine idles
- Modifying spark timing for stop-and-go driving

These changes to the engine all combine to help achieve more complete combustion and decrease exhaust emissions.

Drive System

The first thing needed in the drive system is a device that completely disconnects the engine from the rear wheels and the rest of the power transmission system. This allows the engine to run when the car is standing still.

Suppose we mount two ordinary pie tins, each on a shaft, as shown in the figure below. As long as they are not touching each other, we can spin one as fast as we want to without affecting the other at all. But if we move them together when one of them is spinning, the other will begin to turn and almost immediately both shafts will be turning together as one unit. This is the general principle of operation of the disc, or friction, clutch used in automobiles having manual shift transmissions. The discs are forced together by strong springs and are separated by pushing down on the clutch pedal in the driver's compartment.

Cars equipped with automatic transmissions do not have a friction clutch or clutch pedal. We will discuss those shortly, but first we will cover the manual shift type transmission and drive system.

Figure 3. Drive system

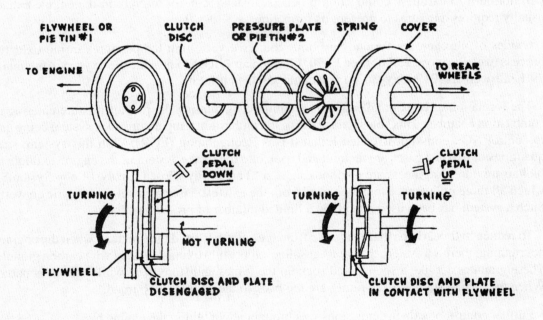

Transmissions

A transmission enables us to change the speed of the engine in relation to the speed of the rear wheels by functioning as a system of gears. Suppose we have a small gear with 12 teeth driving a larger gear with 24 teeth. When the first gear has made one complete revolution, we might say that it has gone a distance equivalent to 12 teeth. The second one has gone around the same distance—12 teeth—but this means only one half a revolution for the larger gear. So this second gear and the shaft it is fastened to always turn at one half the speed of the first gear and its shaft.

Figure 4. Gear system

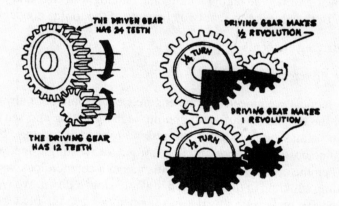

In a manual shift automobile transmission, we have several combinations of gears arranged so that we can select the one we want to use at any moment. For low gear, or first, a small gear on the engine shaft drives a large gear on another shaft. This reduces the speed and increases the twisting force. Then a small gear on the second shaft drives a large gear on the drive shaft that goes to the rear axle. This reduces the speed and increases the twist still more, giving a ratio of about 3:1 for starting up or heavy pulling.

When the car has started, we need less twisting force to turn the rear wheels and we would like more speed. For intermediate or second gear, we use the same first pair of gears as in low. We disconnect the second pair, however, and drive through two other gears. These are arranged with the larger one driving the smaller, so there is less overall speed reduction than in first gear, about $1\frac{2}{3}$:1.

Most of the time while we are driving we need no reduction at all in the transmission. This is third, or high gear, and the engine shaft is connected directly to the drive shaft. They both revolve at the same speed, that is a 1:1 ratio.

One very important requirement of a transmission is to provide means to make a car back up. Reverse gear is very much like first, giving about the same ratio and using the same four gears. It also uses a fifth gear, however, which causes the drive shaft to turn in the opposite direction.

This makes a complete manual shift transmission of the conventional type, with three speeds forward and one reverse. The gears are mounted in a metal case filled with oil to lubricate the gears and bearings. The various speeds are selected by moving a gearshift in the driver's compartment.

Many manual transmissions today have four or five speeds, sometimes called overdrive. In these higher gear ratios, the engine is actually turning slower than the drive shaft and rear axle. With the high gear ratios and lower engine speeds, fuel economy can be significantly improved.

Automatic Transmissions

Most cars built today have some form of automatic transmission, which eliminates the clutch and the need to shift gears manually to obtain the right gear ratios. There are various types, but most of them are similar in the way they affect the driving of the car.

They usually have a hydraulic drive of some sort. The type that is in wide use today is the three-element torque converter. Imagine taking a doughnut, slicing it in two, and putting blades on the inside of each half. Both halves represent two elements of the torque converter:

1. Pump (or driving element)

2. Turbine (or driven element)

The pump is mechanically connected to the engine's crankshaft, so it always rotates when the engine runs. When the engine is started, the pump begins rotating and sends oil, spinning in a clockwise direction, against the blades of the turbine to start it turning. The spinning oil has energy that the turbine absorbs and converts into torque, or twisting force, which then is sent to the rear wheels. When the oil leaves the turbine it spins in a counterclockwise direction, and if it went back to the pump spinning in this direction it would slow it down. We would lose any torque that had been gained. To make sure this doesn't happen, we use the blades of the stator, which does not rotate (not just yet, anyway), to change the direction of the oil flow so it spins again in a clockwise direction. When the oil now enters the pump it adds to the torque the pump receives from the engine, the pump starts to turn faster, and we start to obtain torque multiplication. The cycle of oil going from the pump to the turbine, then through the stator, and back to the pump is repeated over and over until the car reaches a speed where torque multiplication is no longer needed. When this happens, the stator starts to turn freely (it's fixed to rotate only clockwise). The pump and turbine then rotate at nearly the same speed and act like a fluid coupling, or clutch. We now have a situation similar to high gear in a manual shift transmission where the engine crankshaft is connected directly to the driveshaft and both revolve at nearly the same speed. The stator stops rotating when torque multiplication is needed.

The turbine is connected by a shaft to a gear transmission located behind the converter. The transmission usually used contains planetary gear sets and provides the desired number of forward speed gear ratios automatically. These gear ratios may also be selected manually for greater engine braking or exceptionally hard pulling. A reverse gear and neutral are also provided. The planetary type of gear transmission has its gears in mesh at all times. Gear ratios for different driving conditions are obtained using hydraulic controls that cause friction bands and clutches to grab and hold certain gears of the set stationary while the others rotate.

Figure 5. Hydraulic torque converter

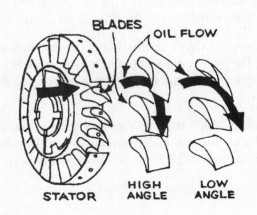

Hydraulic torque converters can have variations in the design of their basic components. Some elements may have their blades set at a fixed angle to the flow of oil. Others may have blades that are hydraulically operated to provide varying blade angles automatically. For example, a stator could have a low angle for maximum efficiency during the average operating range of the transmission and a high angle for increased acceleration and performance (when more torque is needed at the rear wheels). There also are variations in the way the components are arranged in hydraulic torque converters. Some have two stators, others have multiple sets of pump and turbine blades. Differences can exist, too, in the way the planetary gears are combined with the pump, turbine, and stator elements.

Under ordinary circumstances, however, these variations will not make a great deal of difference to the driver of the car. He still will find no clutch pedal and will have no shifting to do, except when he wants to back up. And for forward driving, all he has to do is step on the accelerator to go and the brake pedal to stop.

Rear Axle

From the transmission the propeller shaft, or drive shaft, goes back to the rear axle. This is simply a solid or tubular steel shaft. The universal joint allows the rear axle to move up or down in relation to the transmission without bending or breaking the shaft. It is something like the gimbals of a compass on a boat, which allows the compass to remain level at all times no matter how the boat rolls or pitches.

In the rear axle we have two sets of gears. The first, ring gear and pinion, is simply to transmit the power around a corner. It enables the propeller shaft to drive the axle shafts, which are at right angles to it. The old-fashioned ice cream freezer has a set of gears to do the same thing.

When we turn a corner the outside wheel has to travel farther than the inside wheel, and so it has to go faster during that time. We have a set of gears called the differential to take care of this. The differential consists of two small bevel gears on the ends of the axle shafts meshed with two bevel gears (for simplicity we show only one) mounted in the differential frame. This frame is fastened solidly to the ring gear. When the car is going straight ahead, the frame and the gears all rotate as a unit, with no motion between one another. But when the car is turning, one wheel wants to go faster than the other, so the gears on the axle shafts rotate relative to the other small gear. If the ring gear were stationary, one axle would turn frontward and the other one backward. But inasmuch as the ring gear is turning the whole unit, it means that one axle is turning faster than the ring gear and the other is turning slower by the same amount. This can be carried to the point where one wheel is stationary and the other one is turning at twice ring gear speed, which is the situation we sometimes get when one wheel is on a slippery spot and the other isn't. Some cars, however, can be equipped with a limited slip differential, a type of differential that allows the major driving force to go to the wheel having greater traction.

Figure 6.

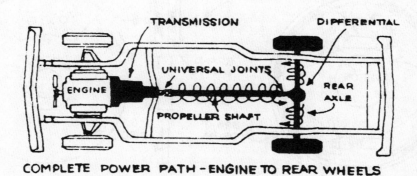

COMPLETE POWER PATH – ENGINE TO REAR WHEELS

The Axle Shafts

The axle shafts, of course, drive the wheels and make the car move, which is the point we have been getting to all this time. We now have a complete rear wheel drive system, just as outlined at the beginning. Power starts at the engine and eventually gets to the rear wheels after passing through various mechanisms so that it will arrive there in the proper form.

There also are cars today that have front wheel drive. The same basic components are used as for the rear wheel drive system, but all the components are arranged up front of the driver. The power flow from the engine is to the front wheel axle shafts. Instead of the rear wheels pushing the car forward, the front wheels pull the car along.

Brakes

There is one more part of the car we should mention before we are through. We have shown how we get the car to move, but another very important point is to be able to stop it.

Brakes are provided for this purpose. There is one in each of the four wheels, and they are simply a method of applying friction to the rotating wheels to stop them. It is like rubbing a stick against the rim of a child's wagon wheels.

Two types of brake systems can be found on today's cars:

1. Drum brake

2. Disc brake

Figure 7. Brake systems

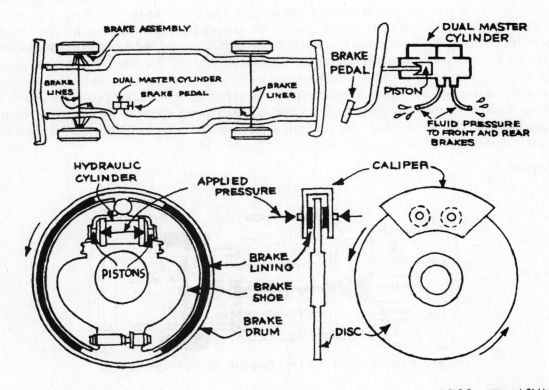

In the drum brake system, two stationary brake shoes covered with a special friction material, called brake lining, are forced outward by hydraulic pressure against the inside of a metal drum that rotates with the wheel. A system of steel tubes filled with a special hydraulic brake fluid runs from a master cylinder to each brake. When the driver steps on the brake pedal, pressure is built up in the master cylinder and this pressure is transmitted through the tubes, called brake lines, to pistons located inside a hydraulic cylinder in each wheel. The pistons move outward and push the shoes against the brake drum. As a safety feature, today's cars have a dual master cylinder that provides two independent hydraulic systems, one for the front wheels and one for the rear.

In the disc brake system, the brake lining is bonded to brake shoes positioned on each side of a rotating disc located in the wheel. When the brake pedal is applied, hydraulic pressure transmitted from the dual master cylinder causes a caliper to clamp the opposing shoes against the disc (it's like taking your thumb and forefinger and squeezing them together against a rotating plate).

The brake is a friction device that converts work into heat, and the amount of heat created by the brakes during a fast stop from high speed is amazing. Because of this, proper cooling of the brakes is an important consideration during their design.

Basic Shop Information*

Common Hand Tools

Tools are designed to make a job easier and enable you to work more efficiently and are a craftsman's best friend. Here are examples of tools by category.

Striking Tools

Hammers, mallets, and sledges are used to apply a striking force.

* Condensed from *Tools and Their Uses*, Bureau of Naval Personnel

Hammers

Figure 8. Hammers, mallets, and sledges

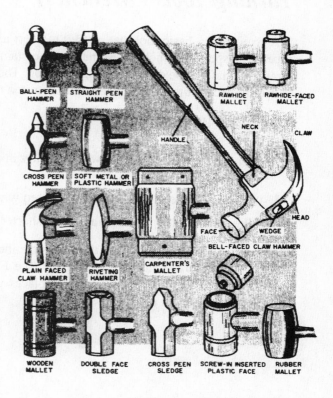

Carpenter's Hammer. The primary use of the carpenter's hammer is to drive or draw (pull) nails. Note the names of the various parts of the hammer shown in Figure 8. The carpenter's hammer has either a curved or straight claw. The face may be either bell-faced or plain-faced, and the handle may be made of wood or steel.

Machinist's Hammer. Machinist's hammers are used mostly by people who work with metal or who work around machinery. These hammers are distinguished from carpenter's hammers by a variable-shaped peen, rather than a claw, at the opposite end of the face. The ball-peen hammer is probably most familiar to you. It has a ball that is smaller in diameter than the face. It is therefore useful for striking areas that are too small for the face to enter.

Machinist's hammers may be further divided into hard-face and soft-face classifications. The hard-faced hammer is made of forged tool steel, while the soft-faced hammer has a head made from brass, lead, or a tightly rolled strip of rawhide. Plastic-tipped hammers, or solid plastic with a lead core for added weight, are becoming increasingly popular.

Mallets and Sledges

The mallet is a short-handled tool used to drive wooden-handled chisels, gouges, or wooden pins or to form or shape sheet metal where hard-faced hammers would mar or injure the finished work. Mallet heads are made from a soft material, usually wood, rawhide, or rubber.

The sledge is a steel-headed, heavy-duty driving tool that can be used for a number of purposes. Short-handled sledges are used to drive bolts, driftpins, and large nails and to strike cold chisels and small hand rock drills. Long-handled sledges are used to break rock and concrete; to drive spikes, bolts, or stakes; and to strike rock drills and chisels.

Turning Tools (Wrenches)

A wrench is a basic tool that is used to exert a twisting force on bolt heads, nuts, studs, and pipes. The special wrenches designed to do certain jobs are, in most cases, variations of the basic wrenches that will be described in this section. The size of any wrench used on bolt heads or nuts is determined by the size of the opening between the jaws of the wrench.

Open-End Wrenches

Solid, nonadjustable wrenches with openings in one or both ends are called open-end wrenches.

Usually they come in sets of from six to ten wrenches with sizes ranging from $\frac{5}{16}$ to 1 inch. Wrenches with small openings are usually shorter than wrenches with large openings.

Open-end wrenches may have their jaws parallel to the handle or at angles anywhere up to 90 degrees. The average angle is 15 degrees (see Figure 9). This angular displacement variation permits selection of a wrench suited for places where there is room to make only a part of a complete turn of a nut or bolt.

Figure 9. Open-end wrenches

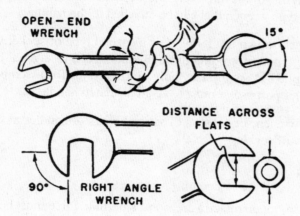

Box Wrenches

Box wrenches (see Figure 10) are safer than open-end wrenches since there is less likelihood they will slip off the work. They completely surround or box a nut or bolt head. The most frequently used box wrench has 12 points or notches arranged in a circle in the head and can be used with a minimum swing angle of 30 degrees. Six- and eight-point wrenches are used for heavy, 12 for medium, and 16 for light duty only.

Figure 10. 12-point box-end wrench

One disadvantage of the box-end wrench is the loss of time that occurs whenever a craftsman has to lift the wrench off and place it back on the nut in another position in case there is insufficient clearance to spin the wrench in a full circle.

Combination Wrench

After a tight nut is broken loose, it can be unscrewed much more quickly with an open-end wrench than with a box wrench. This is where a combination box-open end wrench (see Figure 11) comes in handy. You can use the box end for breaking nuts loose or for snugging them down and the open end for faster turning.

The box-end portion of the wrench can be designed with an offset in the handle. Notice in the figure below how the 15-degree offset allows clearance over nearby parts.

Figure 11. Combination wrench

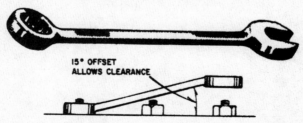

Socket Wrench

The socket wrench is one of the most versatile wrenches in the toolbox. Basically, it consists of a handle and a socket type wrench that can be attached to the handle.

The "Spintite" wrench shown in Figure 12 is a special type of socket wrench. It has a hollow shaft to accommodate a bolt protruding through a nut, has a hexagonal head, and is used like a screwdriver. It is supplied in small sizes only and is useful for assembly and electrical work. When used for the latter purpose, it must have an insulated handle.

A complete socket wrench set consists of several types of handles along with bar extensions, adapters, and a variety of sockets.

Torque Wrenches

There are times when, for engineering reasons, a definite force must be applied to a nut or bolt head. In such cases a torque wrench must be used. For example, equal force must be applied to all the head bolts of an engine. Otherwise, one bolt may bear the brunt of the force of internal combustion and ultimately cause engine failure.

The three most commonly used torque wrenches are the deflecting beam, dial indicating, and micrometer setting types (see Figure 13).

Figure 12. Socket set components

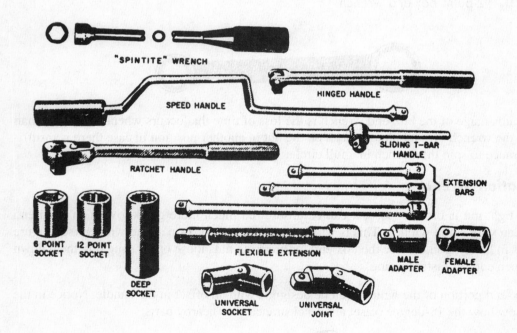

Figure 13. Torque wrenches

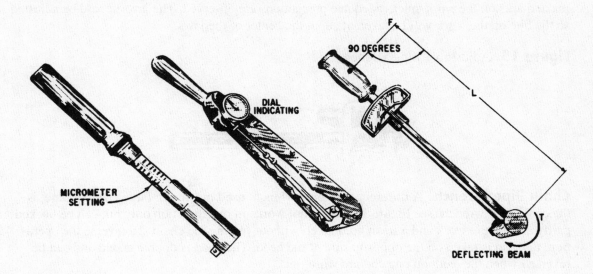

Adjustable Wrenches

A handy all-round wrench that is generally included in every toolbox is the adjustable open-end wrench. This wrench is not intended to take the place of the regular solid open-end wrench. In addition, it is not built for use on extremely hard-to-turn items. Its usefulness is achieved by being capable of fitting odd-sized nuts. This flexibility is achieved although one jaw of the adjustable open-end wrench is fixed because the other jaw is moved along a slide by a thumbscrew adjustment (see Figure 14). By turning the thumbscrew, the jaw opening may be adjusted to fit various sizes of nuts.

Adjustable wrenches are available in varying sizes ranging from 4–24 inches in length. The size of the wrench selected for a particular job is dependent upon the size of nut or bolt head to which the wrench is to be applied. As the jaw opening increases, the length of the wrench increases.

Figure 14. Adjustable wrenches

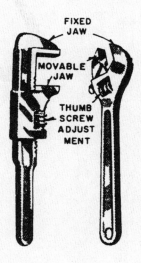

Pipe Wrench (Stillson). When rotating or holding round work, an adjustable pipe wrench (Stillson) may be used (see Figure 15). The movable jaw on a pipe wrench is pivoted to permit a gripping action on the work. This tool must be used with discretion, as the jaws are serrated and always make marks on the work unless adequate precautions are observed. The jaws should be adjusted so the bite on the work will be taken at about the center of the jaws.

Figure 15. Adjustable pipe wrench

Chain Pipe Wrench. A different type pipe wrench, used mostly on large sizes of pipe, is the chain pipe wrench (see Figure 16). This tool works in one direction only but can be backed partly around the work and a fresh hold taken without freeing the chain. To reverse the operation, the grip is taken on the opposite side of the head. The head is double ended and can be reversed when the teeth on one end are worn out.

Strap Wrench. The strap wrench (see Figure 17) is similar to the chain pipe wrench but uses a heavy web strap in place of the chain. This wrench is used for turning pipe or cylinders where you do not want to mar the surface of the work. To use this wrench, the webbed strap is placed around the cylinder and passed through the slot in the metal body of the wrench. The strap is then pulled up tight and as the mechanic turns the wrench in the desired direction, the webbed strap tightens further around the cylinder. This gripping action causes the cylinder to turn.

Figure 17. Strap wrench

Figure 16. Chain pipe wrench

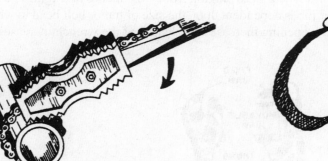

Spanner Wrenches

Many special nuts are made with notches cut into their outer edge. For these nuts a hook spanner (see Figure 18) is required. This wrench has a curved arm with a lug or hook on the end. This lug fits into one of the notches of the nut and the handle turned to loosen or tighten the nut. This spanner may be made for just one particular size of notched nut, or it may have a hinged arm to adjust it to a range of sizes.

Another type of spanner is the pin spanner. Pin spanners have a pin in place of a hook. This pin fits into a hole in the outer part of the nut. Face pin spanners are designed so that the pins fit into holes in the face of the nut.

Setscrew Wrenches (Allen and Bristol)

In some places it is desirable to use recessed heads on setscrews and capscrews. One type (Allen) is used extensively on office machines and in machine shops. The other type (Bristol) is used infrequently.

Figure 18. General-purpose spanner wrenches

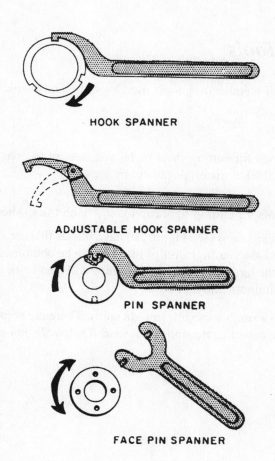

HOOK SPANNER

ADJUSTABLE HOOK SPANNER

PIN SPANNER

FACE PIN SPANNER

Recessed head screws usually have a hex-shaped (six-sided) recess. To remove or tighten this type of screw requires a special wrench that will fit in the recess. This wrench is called an Allen-type wrench. Allen-type wrenches, are made from hexagonal L-shaped bars of tool steel (see Figure 19). They range in size up to $\frac{3}{4}$ inch. When using the Allen-type wrench make sure you use the correct size to prevent rounding or spreading the head of the screw. A snug fit within the recessed head of the screw is an indication that you have the correct size.

The Bristol wrench is made from round stock. It is also L-shaped, but one end is fluted to fit the flutes or little splines in the Bristol setscrew (see Figure 19).

Figure 19. Allen and Bristol type wrenches

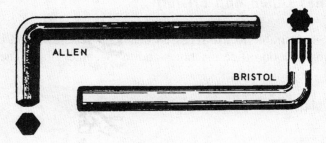

Metal Cutting Tools

There are many types of metal cutting tools used by skilled mechanics.

Snips and Shears

Snips and shears are used for cutting sheet metal and steel of various thicknesses and shapes. Normally, the heavier or thicker materials are cut by shears.

One of the handiest tools for cutting light (up to $\frac{1}{16}$ inch thick) sheet metal is the hand snip (tip snips). The straight *hand snips* (see Figure 20) have blades that are straight and cutting edges that are sharpened to an 85-degree angle. Snips like this can be obtained in different sizes ranging from the small 6-inch to the large 14-inch snip. Tip snips will also work at slightly heavier gauges of soft metals such as aluminum alloys.

It is hard to cut circles or small arcs with straight snips. There are snips especially designed for circular cutting. They are called circle snips. *Hawks-Bill snips. Trojan snips,* and *avian snips.*

Figure 20. Snips

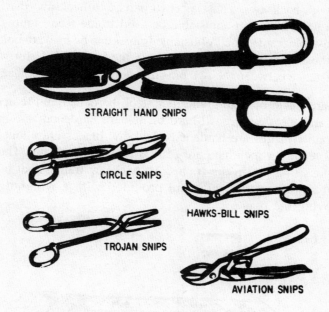

STRAIGHT HAND SNIPS

CIRCLE SNIPS

HAWKS-BILL SNIPS

TROJAN SNIPS

AVIATION SNIPS

Bolt Cutters

Bolt cutters (see Figure 21) are giant shears with very short blades and long handles. The handles are hinged at one end. The cutters are at the ends of extensions that are jointed in such a way that the inside joint is forced outwards when the handles are closed, thus forcing the cutting edges together with great force.

Bolt cutters are made in lengths of 18 to 36 inches. The larger ones will cut mild steel bolts and rods up to one-half inch. The material to be cut should be kept as far back in the jaws as possible. Never attempt to cut spring wire or other tempered metal with bolt cutters. This will cause the jaws to be sprung or nicked.

Adjusting screws near the middle hinges provide a means for ensuring that both jaws move the same amount when the handles are pressed together. Keep the adjusting screws just tight enough to ensure that the cutting edges meet along their entire length when the jaws are closed. The hinges should be kept well oiled at all times.

Figure 21. Bolt cutters

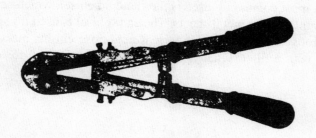

Hacksaws

Hacksaws are used to cut metal that is too heavy for snips or bolt cutters. Thus, metal bar stock can be cut readily with hacksaws. There are two parts to a hacksaw: the frame and the blade. Common hacksaws have either an adjustable or solid frame (see Figure 22). Most hacksaws found are of the adjustable frame type. Adjustable frames can be made to hold blades from 8 to 16 inches long, while those with solid frames take only the length blade for which they are made. This length is the distance between the two pins that hold the blade in place.

Hacksaw blades are made of high-grade tool steel, hardened and tempered. There are two types, the all-hard and the flexible. All-hard blades are hardened throughout, whereas only the teeth of the flexible blades are hardened. Hacksaw blades are about one-half inch wide, have from 14 to 32 teeth per inch, and are from 8 to 16 inches long. The blades have a hole at each end that hooks to a pin in the frame. All hacksaw frames that hold the blades either parallel or at right angles to the frame are provided with a wingnut or screw to permit tightening or removing the blade.

Figure 22. Hacksaws

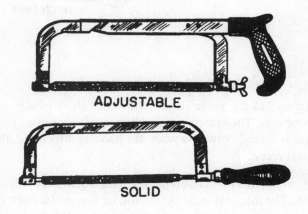

ADJUSTABLE

SOLID

Chisels

Chisels are tools that can be used for chipping or cutting metal. They will cut any metal that is softer than the materials of which they are made. Chisels are made from a good grade tool steel and have a hardened cutting edge and beveled head. Cold chisels are classified according to the shape of their points, and the width of the cutting edge denotes their size. The most common shapes of chisels are flat (cold chisel), cape, round nose, and diamond point (see Figure 23).

The type of chisel most commonly used is the flat cold chisel, which serves to cut rivets, split nuts, chip castings, and cut thin metal sheets. The cape chisel is used for special jobs like cutting keyways, narrow grooves, and square corners. Round-nose chisels make circular grooves and chip inside corners with a fillet. Finally, the diamond point is used for cutting V-grooves and sharp corners.

Files

A toolkit is not complete unless it contains an assortment of files. There are a number of different types of files in common use, and each type may range in length from 3 to 18 inches.

Grades. Files are graded according to the degree of fineness and according to whether they have single- or double-cut teeth. The difference is apparent when you compare the files in Figure 24A.

Figure 23. Types of points on metal cutting chisel

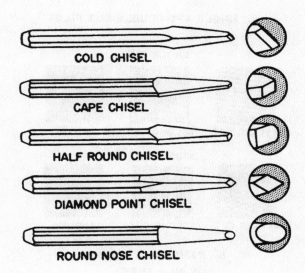

COLD CHISEL

CAPE CHISEL

HALF ROUND CHISEL

DIAMOND POINT CHISEL

ROUND NOSE CHISEL

Single-cut files have rows of teeth cut parallel to each other. These teeth are set at an angle of about 65 degrees with the centerline. You will use single-cut files for sharpening tools, finish filing, and drawfiling. They are also the best tools for smoothing the edges of sheet metal.

Files with crisscrossed rows of teeth are double-cut files. The double cut forms teeth that are diamond-shaped and fast cutting. You will use double-cut files for quick removal of metal and for rough work.

Files are also graded according to the spacing and size of their teeth or their coarseness and fineness. Some of these grades are pictured in Figure 24B. In addition to the three grades shown, you may use some *dead smooth* files, which have very fine teeth, and some rough files with very coarse teeth. The fineness or coarseness of file teeth is also influenced by the length of the file. (The length of a file is the distance from the tip to the heel and does not include the tang (see Figure 24C).) When you have a chance, compare the actual size of the teeth of a 6-inch, single-cut smooth file and a 12-inch, single-cut smooth file. You will notice the 6-inch file has more teeth per inch than the 12-inch file.

Shapes. Files come in different shapes. Therefore, in selecting a file for a job, the shape of the finished work must be considered. Some of the cross-sectional shapes are shown in Figure 24D.

Triangular files are tapered (longitudinally) on all three sides. They are used to file acute internal angles and to clear out square corners. Special triangular files are used to file saw teeth.

Figure 24. File information

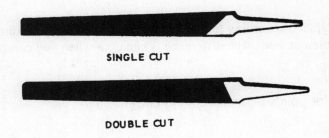

SINGLE CUT

DOUBLE CUT

A. SINGLE AND DOUBLE-CUT FILES

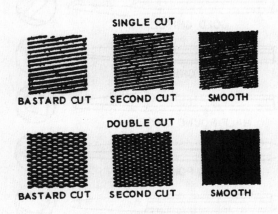

SINGLE CUT

BASTARD CUT   SECOND CUT   SMOOTH

DOUBLE CUT

BASTARD CUT   SECOND CUT   SMOOTH

B. DESIGN AND SPACING OF FILE TEETH

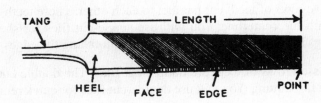

TANG   LENGTH

HEEL   FACE   EDGE   POINT

C. FILE NOMENCLATURE.

SQUARE   TRIANGULAR   ROUND

HALF ROUND   MILL   FLAT

D. CROSS-SECTIONAL SHAPES OF FILES

Mill files are tapered in both width and thickness. One edge has no teeth and is known as a *safe edge*. Mill files are used for smoothing lathe work, drawfiling, and other fine, precision work. Mill files are always single-cut.

Flat files are general-purpose files and may be either single-or double-cut. They are tapered in width and thickness. *Hard* files, not shown, are somewhat thicker than flat files. They taper slightly in thickness, but their edges are parallel. The flat or hard files most often used are the double-cut for rough work and the single-cut, smooth file for finish work.

Square files are tapered on all four sides and are used to enlarge rectangular-shaped holes and slots. *Round* files serve the same purpose for round openings. Small round files are often called "rattail" files.

The *half round* file is a general-purpose tool. The rounded side is used for curved surfaces and the flat face on flat surfaces. When you file an inside curve, use a round or half round file whose curve most nearly matches the curve of the work.

Twist Drills

The most common tool for making holes in metal is the twist drill. It consists of a cylindrical piece of steel with spiral grooves. One end of the cylinder is pointed, while the other end is shaped so that it may be attached to a drilling machine. The grooves, usually called flutes, may be cut into the steel cylinder, or the flutes may be formed by twisting a flat piece of steel into a cylindrical shape.

The principal parts of a twist drill are the body, the shank, and the point (see Figure 25). The dead center of a drill is the sharp edge at the extreme tip end of the drill. It is formed by the intersection of the cone-shaped surfaces of the point and should always be in the exact center of the axis of the drill. The point of the drill should not be confused with the dead center. The point is the entire cone-shaped surface at the end of the drill.

Figure 25. Twist drill nomenclature

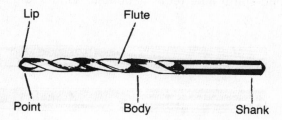

The lip or cutting edge of a drill is that part of the point that actually cuts away the metal when drilling a hole. It is ordinarily as sharp as the edge of a knife. There is a cutting edge for each flute of the drill.

The lip clearance of a drill is the surface of the point that is ground away or relieved just back of the cutting edge of the drill. The strip along the inner edge of the body is called the margin. It is the greatest diameter of the drill and extends the entire length of the flute. The diameter of the margin at the shank end of the drill is smaller than the diameter at the point. This allows the drill to revolve without binding when drilling deep holes.

Countersinks

Countersinking is the operation of beveling the mouth of a hole with a rotary tool called a countersink (see Figure 26). The construction of the countersink is similar to the twist drill. There are four cutting edges, which are taper-ground, to the angle marked on the body.

A countersink is used primarily to set the head of a screw or rivet flush with the material in which it is being placed. Countersinks are made in a number of sizes. One size usually takes care of holes of several different sizes. That is, the same countersink can be used for holes from $\frac{1}{4}$ to $\frac{1}{2}$ inch in diameter. Remove only enough metal to set the screw or rivet head flush with the material. If you remove too much material the hole will enlarge and weaken the work.

Select the countersink with the correct lip angle to correspond with the screw or rivet head being used. This type of countersink can be turned by any machine that will turn a twist drill.

Figure 26. Countersink

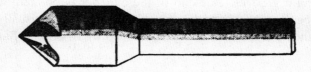

Reamers

Reamers are used to enlarge and true a hole. The reamer consists of three parts—the body, the shank, and the blades. The shank has a square tang to allow the reamer to he held with a wrench for turning. The main purpose of the body is to support the blades.

Figure 27. Above solid spiral flute reamer; Bottom: solid straight flute reamer

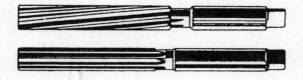

Reamers of the types shown in Figure 27 are available in any standard size. They are also available in size variations of .001 inch for special work. A solid straight flute reamer lasts longer and is less expensive than the expansion reamer. However, the solid spiral flute reamer is preferred by craftsmen because it is less likely to chatter.

For general purposes, an expansion reamer (see Figure 28) is the most practical. This reamer can usually be obtained in standard sizes from $\frac{1}{4}$ inch to 1 inch, by 32nds. It is designed to allow the blades to expand $\frac{1}{32}$ of an inch. For example, the $\frac{1}{4}$-inch expansion reamer will ream a $\frac{1}{4}$- to $\frac{9}{32}$-inch hole. A $\frac{9}{32}$-inch reamer will enlarge the hole from $\frac{9}{32}$ to $\frac{5}{16}$ of an inch. This range of adjustment allows a few reamers to cover sizes up to 1 inch.

Figure 28. Expansion reamer

Punches

A hand punch (see Figure 29) is a tool that is held in the hand and struck on one end with a hammer. The part held in the hand is usually octagonal shaped, or it may be knurled. This prevents the tool from slipping around in the hand. The other end is shaped to do a particular job.

The center punch, is used for marking the center of a hole to be drilled. If you try to drill a hole without first punching the center, the drill will "wander" or "walk away" from the desired center. Automatic center punches are useful for layout work. They are operated by pressing down on the shank by hand. An inside spring is compressed and released automatically, striking a blow on the end of the punch. The impression is light, but adequate for marking, and serves to locate the point of a regular punch when a deeper impression is required.

Drift punches, sometimes called "starting punches," have a long taper from the tip to the body. They arc that way to withstand the shock of heavy blows. They may be used for knocking out rivets after the heads have been chiseled off or for freeing pins that are "frozen" in their holes.

After a pin has been loosened or partially driven out, the drift punch may be too large to finish the job. The follow-up tool to use is the *pin punch*. It is designed to follow through the hole without jamming. Always use the largest drift or pin punch that will fit the hole. These punches usually come in sets of three to five assorted sizes. Both of these punches will have flat points, never edged or rounded.

Figure 29. Punches

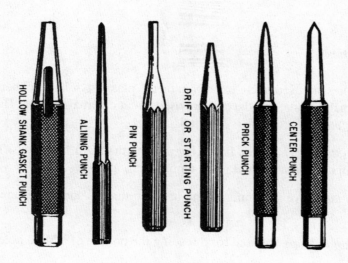

For assembling units of a machine, an *alignment* (aligning) punch is invaluable. It is usually about 1 foot long and has a long gradual taper. Its purpose is to line up holes in mating parts.

Hollow metal cutting punches are made from hardened tool steel. They are made in various sizes and are used to cut holes in light gauge sheet metal.

Figure 30. Types of common taps

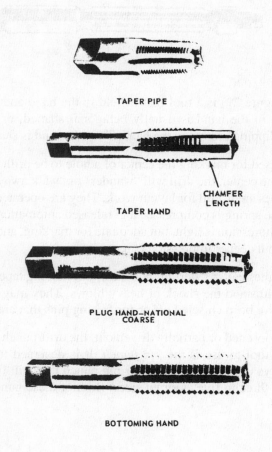

TAPER PIPE

TAPER HAND

CHAMFER LENGTH

PLUG HAND–NATIONAL COARSE

BOTTOMING HAND

Taps and Dies

Taps and dies are used to cut threads in metal, plastics, or hard rubber. The taps arc is used for cutting internal threads, and the dies are used to cut external threads. The most common taps are shown in Figure 30.

The *taper (starting) hand tap* has a chamfer length of 8 to 10 threads. These taps are used when starting a tapping operation and when tapping through holes.

Plug hand taps have a chamfer length of 3 to 5 threads and are designed for use after the taper tap.

Bottoming hand taps are used for threading the bottom of a blind hole. They have a very short chamfer length of only 1 to $1\frac{1}{2}$ threads for this purpose. This tap is always used after the plug tap has already been used. Both the taper and plug taps should precede the use of the bottoming hand tap.

Pipe taps are used for pipefittings and other places where extremely tight fits are necessary. The tap diameter, from end to end of threaded portion, increases at the rate of $\frac{3}{4}$ - inch per foot. All the threads on this tap do the cutting, as compared to the straight taps where only the nonchamfered portion does the cutting.

Dies are made in several different shapes and are of the solid or adjustable type. The *square pipe die* (see Figure 31) will cut American Standard Pipe Thread only. It comes in a variety of sizes for cutting threads on pipe with diameters of $\frac{1}{8}$ to 2 inches.

Figure 31. Types solid dies

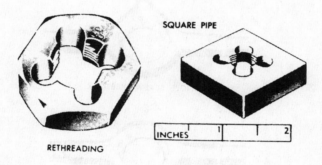

A *rethreading* die (see Figure 32) is used principally for dressing over bruised or rusty threads on screws or bolts. It is available in a variety of sizes for rethreading American Standard Coarse and Fine Threads. These dies are usually hexagonal in shape and can be turned with a socket, box, open-end, or any wrench that will fit. Rethreading dies are available in sets of 6, 10, 14, and 28 assorted dies in a case.

Figure 32. Types of adjustable dies

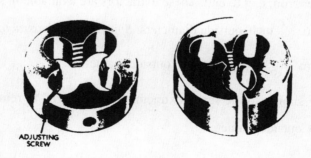

Round split adjustable dies (shown above) are called "Button" dies and can be used in either hand diestocks or machine holders. The adjustment in the screw adjusting type is made by a fine-pitch screw that forces the sides of the die apart or allows them to spring together. The adjustment in the open adjusting types is made by means of three screws in the holder, one for expanding and two for compressing the dies. Round split adjustable dies are available in a variety of sizes to cut American Standard Coarse and Fine Threads, special form threads, and the standard sizes of threads that are used in Britain and other European countries. For hand threading, these dies are held in diestocks (see Figure 33). One type of die stock has three pointed screws that will hold round dies of any construction, although it is made specifically for open adjusting-type dies.

Figure 33. Diestocks

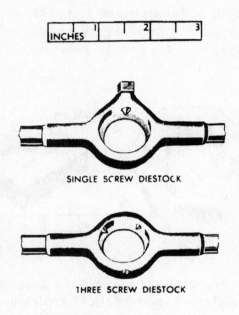

Screw and Tap Extractors

Screw extractors are used to remove broken screws without damaging the surrounding material or the threaded hole. Tap extractors are used to remove broken taps. Some screw extractors are straight, having flutes from end to end. These extractors are available in sizes to remove broken screws having $\frac{1}{4}$ to $\frac{1}{2}$ inch outside diameters. *Spiral tapered extractors* are sized to remove screws and bolts from $\frac{3}{16}$ to $2\frac{1}{8}$ inches outside diameter.

Tap extractors are similar to the screw extractors and are sized to remove taps ranging from $\frac{3}{16}$ to $2\frac{1}{8}$ inches outside diameter.

To remove a broken screw or tap with a spiral extractor first drill a hole of proper size in the screw or tap. The size hole required for each screw extractor is stamped on it. The extractor is then inserted in the hole and turned counterclockwise to remove the defective component.

Pipe and Tubing Cutters and Flaring Tools

Pipe cutters (see Figure 34) are used to cut pipe made of steel, brass, copper, wrought iron, and lead. Tube cutters are used to cut tubing made of iron, steel, brass, copper, and aluminum. The essential difference between pipe and tubing is that tubing has considerably thinner walls. Flaring tools (see Figure 35) are used to make single or double flares in the ends of tubing.

Figure 34. Pipe and tubing cutters

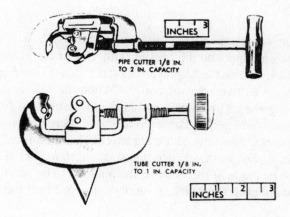

Figure 35. Single flaring tool

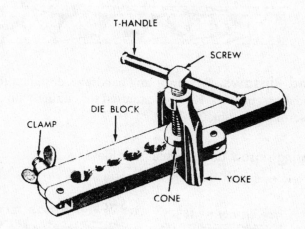

Woodcutting Hand Tools

A person working with wood uses a large variety of hand tools and should be familiar with these tools, their proper names, the purpose for which they are used, and how to keep them in good condition.

Figure 36. Nomenclature of a handsaw

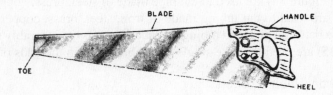

Handsaws

The most common carpenter's handsaw consists of a steel blade with a handle at one end. The blade is narrower at the end opposite the handle. This end of the blade is called the "point" or "toe." The end of the blade nearest the handle is called the "heel" (see Figure 36). One edge of the blade has teeth, which act as two rows of cutters. When the saw is used, these teeth cut two parallel grooves close together. The chips (saw-dust) are pushed out from between the grooves (kerf) by the beveled part of the teeth. The teeth are bent alternately to one side or the other, to make the kerf wider than the thickness of the blade. This bending is called the "set" of the teeth (see Figure 37). The number of teeth per inch, the size and shape of the teeth, and the amount of set depend on the use to be made of the saw and the material to be cut. Carpenter's handsaws are described by the number of points per inch. A number stamped near the handle gives the number of points of the saw.

Figure 37. "Set" of hand saw teeth

Crosscut Saws and Ripsaws. Woodworking handsaws designed for general cutting consist of ripsaws and crosscut saws. Ripsaws are used for cutting with the grain and crosscut saws are for cutting across the grain.

Figure 38. Comparing ripsaw and crosscut-saw teeth

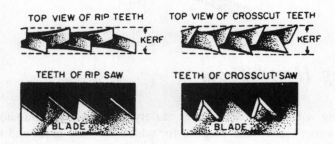

The major difference between a ripsaw and a crosscut saw is the shape of the teeth. A tooth with a square-faced chisel-type cutting edge, like the ripsaw tooth (see Figure 38), does a good job of cutting with the grain (called ripping) but a poor job of cutting across the grain (called crosscutting). A tooth with a beveled, knife-type cutting edge, like the crosscut-saw tooth (see Figure 39), does a good job of cutting across the grain but a poor job of cutting with the grain.

Special Purpose Saws. The more common types of saws used for special purposes are shown in Figure 39. The *backsaw* is a crosscut saw designed for sawing a perfectly straight line across the face of a piece of stock. A heavy steel backing along the top of the blade keeps the blade perfectly straight.

The *dovetail saw* is a special type of backsaw with a thin, narrow blade and a chisel-type handle.

The *compass saw* is a long, narrow, tapering ripsaw designed for cutting out circular or other nonrectangular sections from within the margins of a board or panel. A hole is bored near the cutting line to start the saw. A *keyhole saw* is simply a finer, narrower compass saw. The *coping saw* is used to cut along curved lines.

Figure 39. Special saws

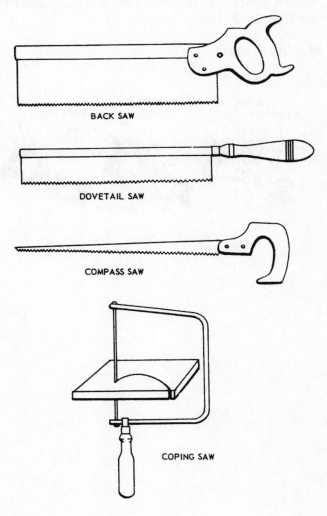

BACK SAW

DOVETAIL SAW

COMPASS SAW

COPING SAW

Planes

The plane is the most extensively used of the hand shaving tools. Most of the lumber handled by anyone working with wood is dressed on all four sides, but when performing jobs such as fitting doors and sash and interior trim work, planes must be used.

Bench and block planes are designed for general surface smoothing and squaring. Other planes are designed for special types of surface work.

The principal parts of a bench plane and the manner in which they are assembled are shown in Figure 40. The part at the rear that you grasp to push the plane ahead is called the handle; the part at the front that you grasp to guide the plane along its course is called the knob. The main body of the plane, consisting of the bottom, the sides, and the sloping part that carries the plane iron, is called the frame. The bottom of the frame is called the sole, and the opening in the sole, through which the blade emerges, is called the mouth. The front end of the sole is called the toe; the rear end, the heel.

There are three types of bench planes (see Figure 41): *the smooth plane*, the *jack plane*, and the *jointer plane* (sometimes called the *fore plane* or the *gage plane*). All are used primarily for shaving and smoothing with the grain; the chief difference is the length of the sole. The sole of the smooth plane is about 9 inches long, the sole of the jack plane about 14 inches long, and the sole of the jointer plane from 20–24 inches long.

Figure 40. Parts of a bench plane

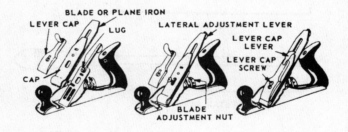

Figure 41. Types of bench planes and block plane

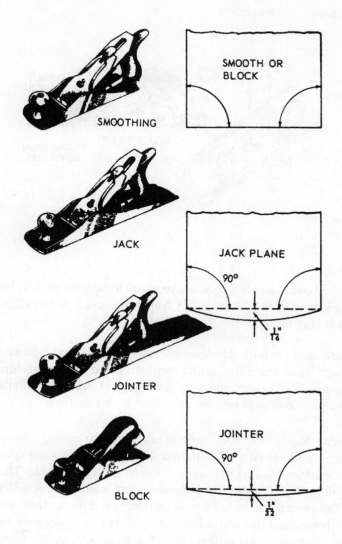

The longer the sole of the plane is, the more uniformly flat and true the planed surface will be. Consequently, which bench plane you should use depends upon the requirements with regard to surface trueness. The smooth plane is, in general, a smoother only; it will plane a smooth but not an especially true surface in a short time. It is also used for cross-grain smoothing and squaring of end stock.

The jack plane is the general "jack-of-all-work" of the bench plane group. It can take a deeper cut and plane a truer surface than the smooth plane. The jointer plane is used when the planed surface must meet the highest requirements with regard to trueness. A *block plane* and the names of its parts are shown in Figure 42. Note that the plane iron in a block plane does not have a plane iron cap and also that, unlike the iron in a bench plane, the iron in a block plane goes in bevel-up.

The block plane, which is usually held at an angle to the work, is used chiefly for cross-grain squaring of end stock. It is also useful, however, for smoothing all plane surfaces on very small work.

Figure 42. Block plane nomenclature

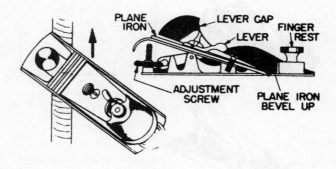

Boring Tools

When working with wood, you are frequently required to bore holes. It is important, therefore, that you know the proper tools used for this job. Auger bits and a variety of braces and drills are used extensively for boring purposes.

Auger Bits. Bits are used for boring holes for screws, dowels, and hardware; as an aid in mortising (cutting a cavity in wood for joining members); and in shaping curves and for many other purposes. Like saws and planes, bits vary in shape and structure with the type of job to be done. Some of the most common bits are described in this section.

Auger bits are screw-shaped tools consisting of six parts: the cutter, screw, spur, twist, shank, and tang (see Figure 43). The twist ends with two sharp points called the spurs, which score the circle, and two cutting edges, which cut shavings within the scored circle. The screw centers the bit and draws it into the wood. The threads of the screw are made in three different pitches: steep, medium, and fine. The steep pitch makes for quick boring and thick chips, and the fine or slight pitch makes for slow boring and fine chips. For end-wood boring, a steep- or medium-pitch screw bit should be used because end wood is likely to be forced in between the fine screw threads, and that will prevent the screw from taking hold. The twist carries the cuttings away from the cutters and deposits them in a mound around the hole.

Figure 43. Nomenclature of an auger bit

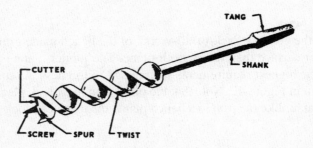

The sizes of auger bits are indicated in sixteenths of an inch and are stamped on the tang (see Figure 44). A number 10 stamped on the tang means $\frac{10}{16}$ or $\frac{5}{8}$ inches, number 5 means $\frac{5}{16}$ inches, and so on. The most common woodworker's auger bit set ranges in size from $\frac{1}{4}$ to 1 inch.

Figure 44. Size markings on auger bits

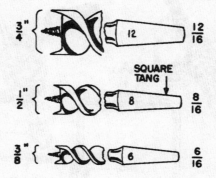

Ordinary auger bits up to 1 inch in diameter are from 7–9 inches long. Short auger bits that are about $3\frac{1}{2}$ inches inches long are called *dowel* bits.

Expansive auger bits have adjustable cutters for boring holes of different diameters (see Figure 45). Expansive bits are generally made in two different sizes. The larger size has three cutters and bores holes up to 4 inches in diameter. A scale on the cutter blade indicates the diameter of the hole to be bored.

Figure 45. Expansive bit

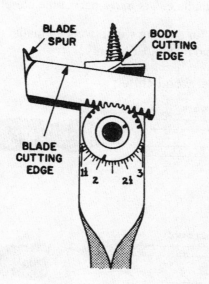

Braces and Drills. The auger bit is the tool that actually does the cutting in the wood; however, it is necessary that another tool be used to hold the auger bit and give you enough leverage to turn the bit. The tools most often used for holding the bit are the carpenter's brace, breast drill, and push drill (see Figure 46).

Figure 46. Brace and drill

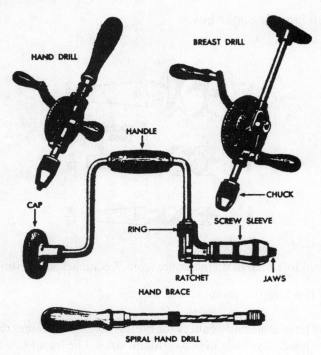

Wood Chisels

A *wood chisel* is a steel tool fitted with a wooden or plastic handle. It has a single beveled cutting edge on the end of the steel part, or blade. According to their construction, chisels may be divided into two general classes: *tang chisels*, in which part of the chisel enters the handle, and *socket chisels*, in which the handle enters into a part of the chisel (see Figure 47).

A *socket chisel* is designed for striking with a wooden mallet (never a steel hammer), while a tang chisel is designed for hand manipulation only.

Figure 47. Tang and socket wood chisels

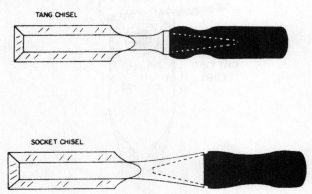

Wood chisels are also divided into types, depending upon their weights and thicknesses, the shape or design of the blade, and the work they are intended to do.

The shapes of the more common types of wood chisels are shown in Figure 48. The *firmer chisel* has a strong, rectangular-cross-section blade, designed for both heavy and light work. The blade of the *paring chisel* is relatively thin and is beveled along the sides for the fine paring work. The butt chisel has a short blade, designed for work in hard-to-get-at places.

The *butt chisel* is commonly used for chiseling the *gains* (rectangular depressions) for the *butt* hinges on doors; hence the name. The *mortising chisel* is similar to a socket firmer but has a narrow blade, designed for chiseling out the deep, narrow mortises for mortise-and-tenon joints. This work requires a good deal of levering out of chips; consequently, the mortising chisel is made extra thick in the shaft to prevent breaking.

A *framing chisel* is shaped like a firmer chisel but has a very heavy, strong blade designed for work in rough carpentry.

Figure 48. Shapes of common types of wood chisels

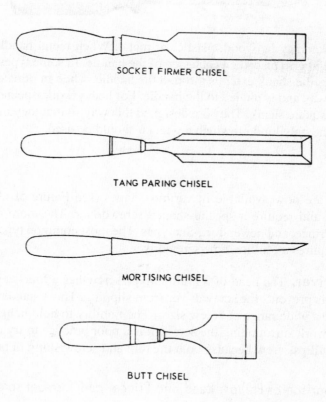

SOCKET FIRMER CHISEL

TANG PARING CHISEL

MORTISING CHISEL

BUTT CHISEL

Screwdrivers

A screwdriver is one of the most basic of basic hand tools.   It is designed for one function only: to drive and remove screws.

Standard

There are three main parts to a standard screwdriver (see Figure 49). The portion you grip is called the handle, the steel portion extending from the handle is the shank, and the end that fits into the screw is called the blade. The steel shank is designed to withstand considerable twisting force in proportion to its size, and the tip of the blade is hardened to keep it from wearing.

Standard screwdrivers are classified by size, according to the combined length of the shank and blade. The most common sizes range in length from $2\frac{1}{2}$ to 12 inches. There are many screwdrivers smaller and some larger for special purposes. The diameter of the shank and the width and thickness of the blade are generally proportionate to the length, but again there are special screwdrivers with long thin shanks, short thick shanks, and extra wide or extra narrow blades.

Figure 49. Screwdriver parts

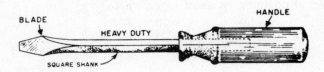

Screwdriver handles may be wood, plastic, or metal. When metal handles are used, there is usually a wooden hand grip placed on each side of the handle. In some types of wood- or plastic-handled screwdrivers the shank extends through the handle, while in others the shank enters the handle only a short way and is pinned to the handle. For heavy work, special types of screwdrivers are made with a square shank. They are designed this way so that they may be gripped with a wrench, but this is the only kind on which a wrench should be used.

Recessed

Recessed screws are now available in various shapes (see Figure 50). They have a cavity formed in the head and require a special-shaped screwdriver. The more common include the Phillips, Reed and Prince, and newer Torq-Set types. The most common type found is the Phillips head screw. This requires a Phillips-type screwdriver.

Phillips Screwdriver. The head of a Phillips-type screw has a four-way slot into which the screwdriver fits. This prevents the screwdriver from slipping. Three standard-sized Phillips screwdrivers handle a wide range of screw sizes. Their ability to hold helps to prevent damaging the slots or the work surrounding the screw. It is a poor practice to try to use a standard screwdriver on a Phillips screw because both the tool and screw slot will be damaged.

Figure 50. Comparison of Philips, Reed and Prince, and Torq-Set screwheads

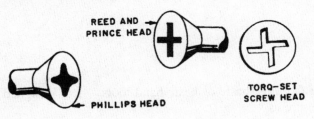

Reed and Prince Screwdriver. Reed and Prince screwdrivers (see Figure 51) are not interchangeable with Phillips screwdrivers. Therefore, always use a Reed and Prince screwdriver with Reed and Prince screws and a Phillips screwdriver with Phillips screws, or a ruined tool or ruined screwhead will result.

Figure 51.

The Phillips screwdriver has about 30-degree flukes and a blunt end, while the Reed and Prince has 45-degree flukes and a sharper, pointed end. The Phillips screw has beveled walls between the slots; the Reed and Prince, straight, pointed walls. In addition, the Phillips screw slot is not as deep as the Reed and Prince slot.

"Torq-Set" Screws. "Torq-Set" machine screws (offset cross-slot drive) have recently begun to appear in new equipment. The main advantage of the newer type is that more torque can be applied to its head while tightening or loosening than any other screw of comparable size and material without damaging the head of the screw.

Offset Screwdrivers

An offset screwdriver (see Figure 52) may be used where there is not sufficient vertical space for a standard or recessed screwdriver. Offset screwdrivers are constructed with one blade forged in line and another blade forged at right angles to the shank handle. Both blades are bent 90 degrees to the shank handle. By alternating ends, most screws can be seated or loosened even when the swinging space is very restricted. Offset screwdrivers are made for both standard and recessed head screws.

Figure 52. Offset driver

Figure 53. Ratchet and driver

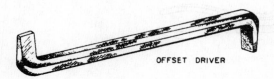

OFFSET DRIVER

RATCHET AND SPIRAL DRIVER

Ratchet Screwdriver

For fast easy work, the ratchet screwdriver (see Figure 53) is extremely convenient, as it can be used one-handed and does not require the bit to be lifted out of the slot after each turn. It may be fitted with either a standard type bit or a special bit for recessed heads. The ratchet screwdriver is most commonly used by the woodworker for driving screws in soft wood.

Pliers

Pliers are used for cutting purposes as well as holding and gripping small articles in situations where it may be inconvenient or impossible to use hands (see Figure 54).

Combination pliers are handy for holding or bending flat or round stock. The *long-nosed pliers* are less rugged and break easily if you use them on heavy jobs. Long-nosed pliers commonly called needle-nose pliers are especially useful for holding small objects in tight places and for making delicate adjustments. The round-nosed kind are handy when you need to crimp sheet metal or form a loop in a wire. *Diagonal cutting pliers*, commonly called "diagonals" or "dikes," are designed for cutting wire and cotter pins close to a flat surface and are especially useful in the electronic and electrical fields. *Duckbill pliers* are used extensively in aviation areas.

Figure 54. Pliers

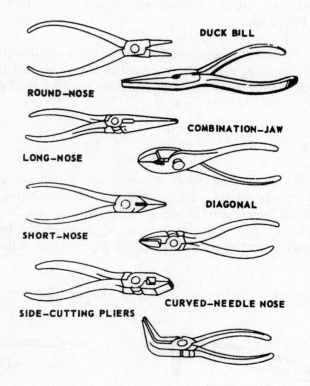

Slip-Joint Pliers

Slip-joint pliers (see Figure 55) are pliers with straight, serrated (grooved) jaws, and the screw or pivot with which the jaws are fastened together may be moved to either of two positions, in order to grasp small- or large-sized objects better.

To spread the jaws of slip-joint pliers, first spread the ends of the handles apart as far as possible. The slip-joint, or pivot, will now move to the open position. To close, again spread the handles as far as possible, then push the joint back into the closed position.

Figure 55. Slip-joint pliers

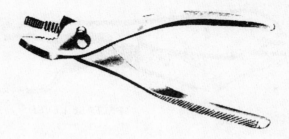

Slip-joint combination pliers (see Figure 56) are pliers similar to the slip-joint pliers just described but with the additional feature of a side cutter at the junction of the jaws. This cutter consists of a pair of square cut notches, one on each jaw, which act like a pair of shears when an object is placed between them and the jaws are closed.

Figure 56. Slip-joint combination pliers

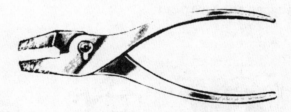

The cutter is designed to cut material such as soft wire and nails. To use the cutter, open the jaws until the cutter on either jaw lines up with the other. Place the material to be cut as far back as possible into the opening formed by the cutter, and squeeze the handles of the pliers together. Do not attempt to cut hard material such as spring wire or hard rivets with the combination pliers. To do so will spring the jaws; and if the jaws are sprung, it will be difficult thereafter to cut small wire with the cutters.

Wrench (Vise-Grip) Pliers

Vise-grip pliers (see Figure 57) can be used for holding objects regardless of their shape. A screw adjustment in one of the handles makes them suitable for several different sizes. The jaws of vise-grips may have standard serrations, such as the pliers just described, or may have a clamp-type jaw. The clamp-type jaws are generally wide and smooth and are used primarily when working with sheet metal.

Vise-grip pliers have an advantage over other types of pliers in that you can clamp them on an object and they will stay. This will leave your hands free for other work.

Figure 57. Vise-grip pliers

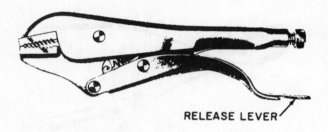

RELEASE LEVER

Vises and Clamps

Vises (see Figure 58) are used for holding work when it is being planed, sawed, drilled, shaped, sharpened, or riveted or when wood is being glued. Clamps are used for holding work that cannot be satisfactorily held in a vise because of its shape and size or when a vise is not available. Clamps are generally used for light work.

Figure 58. Common types of bench vises

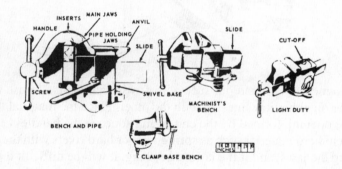

A *machinist's bench vise* is a large steel vise with rough jaws that prevent the work from slipping. Most of these vises have a swivel base with jaws that can be rotated, while others cannot be rotated. A similar light duty model is equipped with a cutoff. These vises are usually bolt-mounted onto a bench.

The *bench and pipe vise* has integral pipe jaws for holding pipe from $\frac{3}{4}$ to 3 inches in diameter. The maximum working main jaw opening is usually 5 inches, with a jaw width of 4 to 5 inches. The base can be swiveled to any position and locked. These vises are equipped with an anvil and are also bolted onto a workbench.

The *clamp base vise* usually has a smaller holding capacity than the machinist's or the bench and pipe vise and is usually clamped to the edge of a bench with a thumbscrew. These vises can be obtained with a maximum holding capacity varying between $1\frac{1}{2}$ and 3 inches. These vises normally do not have pipe holding jaws.

The *blacksmith's vise* (see Figure 59) is used for holding work that must be pounded with a heavy hammer. It is fastened to a sturdy workbench or wall, and the long leg is secured into a solid base on the floor.

Figure 59. Blacksmith's and pipe vises

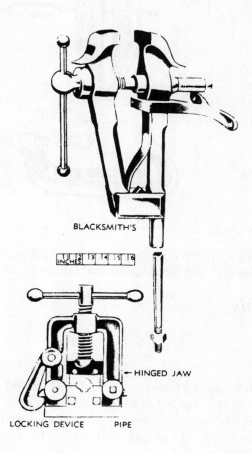

The *pipe vise* (see Figure 59) is specially designed to hold round stock or pipe. The vise shown has a capacity of 1 to 3 inches. One jaw is hinged so that the work can be positioned and then the jaw brought down and locked. This vise is also used on a bench. Some pipe vises are designed to use a section of chain to hold down the work. Chain pipe vises range in size from $\frac{1}{8}$- to $2\frac{1}{2}$ -inch pipe capacity up to $\frac{1}{2}$- to 8-inch pipe capacity.

A *C-clamp* (see Figure 60) is shaped like the letter C. It consists of a steel frame threaded to receive an operating screw with a swivel head. It is made for light, medium, and heavy service in a variety of sizes.

Figure 60. C-clamp and hand screw clamp

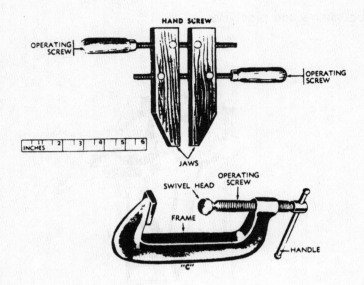

A *hand screw clamp* (see Figure 60) consists of two hard maple jaws connected with two operating screws. Each jaw has two metal inserts into which the screws are threaded.

Measuring Tools

Rules and Tapes

There are many different types of measuring tools in use. Where exact measurements are required, a micrometer caliper (mike) is used. Such a caliper, when properly used, gives measurements to within .001 of-an-inch accuracy. On the other hand, where accuracy is not extremely critical, the common rule or tape will suffice for most measurements.

Figure 61. Some common types of rules

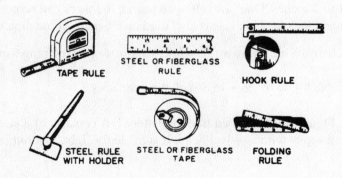

Figure 61 shows some of the types of rules and tapes commonly used. Of all measuring tools, the simplest and most common is the steel rule. This rule is usually 6 or 12 inches in length, although other lengths are available. Steel rules may be flexible or nonflexible, but the thinner the rule, the easier it is to measure accurately because the division marks are closer to the work.

Generally a rule has four sets of graduations, one on each edge of each side. The longest lines represent the inch marks. On one edge, each inch is divided into 8 equal spaces, so each space represents $\frac{1}{8}$ inch. The other edge of this side is divided into sixteenths. The $\frac{1}{4}$-inch and $\frac{1}{2}$-inch marks are commonly made longer than the smaller division marks to facilitate counting, but the graduations are not, as a rule, numbered individually, as they are sufficiently far apart to be counted without difficulty. The opposite side is similarly divided into 32 and 64 spaces per inch, and it is common practice to number every fourth division for easier reading.

There are many variations of the common rule. Sometimes the graduations are on one side only, sometimes a set of graduations is added across one end for measuring in narrow spaces, and sometimes only the first inch is divided into 64ths, with the remaining inches divided into 32nds and 16ths.

A metal or wood folding rule may be used for measuring purposes. These folding rules are usually 2 to 6 feet long. The folding rules cannot be relied on for extremely accurate measurements because a certain amount of play develops at the joints after they have been used for a while.

Steel tapes are made from 6 to about 300 feet in length. The shorter lengths are frequently made with a curved cross section so that they are flexible enough to roll up but remain rigid when extended. Long, flat tapes require support over their full length when measuring, or the natural sag will cause an error in reading.

Flexible-rigid tapes are usually contained in metal cases into which they wind themselves when a button is pressed or into which they can be easily pushed. A hook is provided at one end to hook over the object being measured so one person can handle it without assistance. On some models, the outside of the case can be used as one end of the tape when measuring inside dimensions.

Simple Calipers

Simple calipers are used in conjunction with a scale to measure diameters. The calipers most commonly used are shown in Figure 62.

Outside calipers for measuring outside diameters are bowlegged; those used for inside diameters have straight legs with the feet turned outward. Calipers are adjusted by pulling or pushing the legs to open or close them. Fine adjustment is made by tapping one leg slightly on a hard surface to close them or by turning them upside down and tapping on the joint end to open them.

Figure 62. Simple calipers—noncalibrated

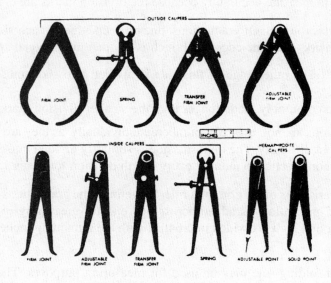

Spring-joint calipers have the legs joined by a strong spring hinge and linked together by a screw and adjusting nut. For measuring chamfered cavities (grooves) or for use over flanges, transfer calipers are available. They are equipped with a small auxiliary leaf attached to one of the legs by a screw. The measurement is made as with ordinary calipers; then the leaf is locked to the leg.

Slide Caliper

The main disadvantage of using ordinary calipers is that they do not give a direct reading of a caliper setting. As explained earlier, you must measure a caliper setting with a rule. To overcome this disadvantage, use slide calipers (see Figure 63). This instrument is occasionally called a *caliper rule*.

Figure 63. Caliper square (slide caliper)

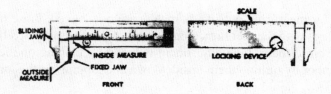

Slide calipers can be used for measuring outside, inside, and other dimensions. One side of the caliper is used as a measuring rule, while the scale on the opposite side is used in measuring outside and inside dimensions. Graduations on both scales are in inches and fractions thereof. A locking screw is incorporated to hold the slide caliper jaws in position during use. Stamped on the frame are two words, "IN" and "OUT." These are used in reading the scale while making inside and outside measurements, respectively.

To measure the outside diameter of round stock or the thickness of flat stock, move the jaws of the caliper into firm contact with the surface of the stock. Read the measurement at the reference line stamped OUT.

While measuring the inside diameter of a hole or the distance between two surfaces, insert only the rounded tips of the caliper jaws into the hole or between the two surfaces. Read the measurement on the reference line stamped IN.

Note that two reference lines are needed if the caliper is to measure both outside and inside dimensions and that they are separated by an amount equal to the outside dimension of the rounded tips when the caliper is closed.

Pocket models of slide calipers are commonly made in 3-inch and 5-inch sizes and are graduated to read in 32nds and 64ths. Pocket slide calipers are valuable when extreme precision is not required. They are frequently used for duplicating work when the expense of fixed gauges is not warranted.

Vernier Caliper

A *vernier caliper* (see Figure 64) consists of an L-shaped member with a scale engraved on the long shank. A sliding member is free to move on the bar and carries a jaw that matches the arm of the L. The vernier scale is engraved on a small plate that is attached to the sliding member.

Perhaps the most distinct advantage of the vernier caliper over other types of calipers is the ability to provide very accurate measurements over a large range. It can be used for both internal and external surfaces. Pocket models usually measure from zero to 3 inches, but sizes are available all the way to 4 feet. In using the vernier caliper, you must be able to measure with a slide caliper and be able to read a vernier scale.

Figure 64. Vernier caliper

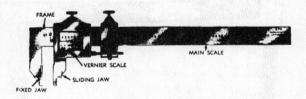

Micrometer

In much wider use than the vernier caliper is the *micrometer*, commonly called the "mike." It is important that a person who is working with machinery or in a machine shop thoroughly understand the mechanical principles, construction, use, and care of the micrometer. Figure 65 shows an outside micrometer caliper with the various parts clearly indicated. Micrometers are used to measure distances to the nearest .001 of an inch. The measurement is usually expressed or written as a decimal, so you must know the method of writing and reading decimals.

Figure 65. Nomenclature of an outside micrometer caliper

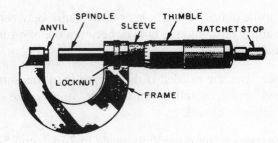

Types

There are three types of micrometers that are commonly used: the outside micrometer caliper (including the screw thread micrometer), the inside micrometer, and the depth micrometer. The outside micrometer is used for measuring outside dimensions, such as the diameter of a piece of round stock. The screw thread micrometer is used to determine the pitch diameter of screws. The inside micrometer is used for measuring inside dimensions; for example, the inside diameter of a tube or hole, the bore of a cylinder, or the width of a recess. The depth micrometer is used for measuring the depth of holes or recesses.

Figure 66. Carpenter's square

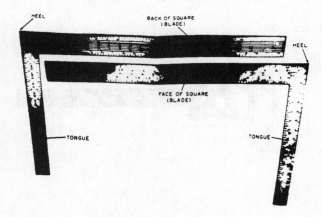

Squares

Squares are primarily used for testing and checking trueness of an angle or for laying out lines on materials. Most squares have a rule marked on their edge. As a result they may also be used for measuring. There are several types of squares commonly used.

Carpenter's Square

The size of a carpenter's steel square (see Figure 66) is usually 12 × 8 inches, 24 × 16 inches, or 24 × 18 inches. The flat sides of the blade and the tongue are graduated in inches and fractions of an inch. (The square also contains information that helps to simplify or eliminate the need for computations in many woodworking tasks.) The most common uses for this square are laying out and squaring up large patterns and for testing the flatness and squareness of large surfaces. Squaring is accomplished by placing the square at right angles to adjacent surfaces and observing if light shows between the work and the square.

One type of carpenter's square (framing) has additional tables engraved on the square. With the framing square, the craftsman can perform calculations rapidly and lay out rafters, oblique joints, and stairs.

Try Square

The *try square* (see Figure 67) consists of two parts at right angles to each other: a thick wood or iron stock and a thin, steel blade. Most try squares are made with the blades graduated in inches and fractions of an inch. The blade length varies from 2 to 12 inches. This square is used for setting or checking lines or surfaces that have to be at right angles to each other.

Figure 67. Common try square

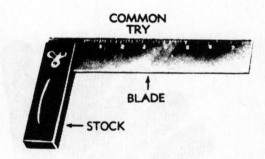

Sliding T-Bevel

The sliding T-bevel (see Figure 68) is an adjustable try square with a slotted beveled blade. Blades are normally 6 to 8 inches long. The sliding T-bevel is used for laying out angles other than right angles and for testing constructed angles such as bevels. These squares are made with either wood or metal handles.

Figure 68. Sliding T-bevel

Miscellaneous Gages

There are a number of miscellaneous gages. The depth gage, feeler gage, thread gage, dividers, and plumb bob are among some of the gages that will be discussed here.

Depth Gage

A depth gage is an instrument for measuring the depth of holes, slots, counterbores, and recesses and the distance from a surface to some recessed part.

Thickness (Feeler) Gage

Thickness (feeler) gages are used for checking and measuring small openings such as contact point clearances, narrow slots, etc. These gages are made in many shapes and sizes, and, as shown in Figure 69, thickness gages can be made with multiple blades (usually 2 to 26). Each blade is a specific number of thousandths of an inch thick. This enables the application of one tool to the measurement of a variety of thicknesses. Some thickness gage blades are straight, while others are bent at 45 and 90 degree angles at the end. Thickness gages can also be grouped so that there are several short and several long blades together. Before using a feeler gage, remove any foreign matter from the blades. You cannot get a correct measurement unless the blades are clean.

Figure 69. Thickness gages

Thread Gage

Thread gages (screw-pitch gages) are used to determine the pitch and number of threads per inch of threaded fasteners (See Figure 70). They consist of thin leaves whose edges are toothed to correspond to standard thread sections.

The number of threads per inch is indicated by the numerical value on the blade that is found to fit the unknown threads. Using this value as a basis, correct sizes of nuts, bolts, tap cutters, and die cutters are selected for use.

Figure 70. Screw pitch gage

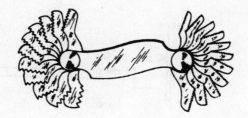

Wire Gage

The *wire gage* shown in Figure 71 is used for measuring the diameters of wires or the thickness of sheet metal. This gage is circular in shape with cutouts in the outer perimeter. Each cutout gages a different size from No. 0 to No. 36. Examination of the gage will show that the larger the gage number, the smaller the diameter or thickness.

Marking Gages

A marking gage is used to mark off guidelines parallel to an edge, end, or surface of a piece of wood or metal. It has a sharp spur or pin that does the marking.

Figure 71. Using a wire gage to measure wire and sheet metal

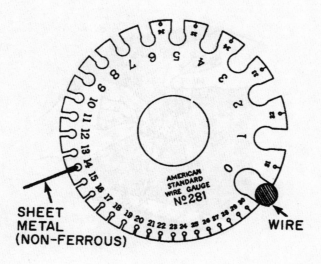

Marking gages (see Figure 72) are made of wood or steel. They consist of a graduated beam about 8 inches long on which a head slides. The head can be fastened at any point on the beam by means of a thumbscrew. The thumbscrew presses a brass shoe tightly against the beam and locks it firmly in position. The steel pin or spur that does the marking projects from the beam about $\frac{1}{16}$ inch .

Figure 72. Marking gages

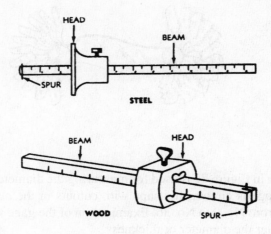

Dividers

Dividers (see Figure 73) are useful instruments for transferring measurements and are frequently used in scribing arcs and circles in layout work.

Figure 73. Setting a divider to a desired radius

Plumb Bob

A *plumb bob* (see Figure 74) is a pointed, tapered brass or bronze weight that is suspended from a cord for determining the vertical or plumb line to or from a point on the ground. Common weights for plumb bobs are 6, 8, 10, 12, 14, 16, 18, and 24 oz. A plumb bob usually has a detachable tip so that if the tip should become damaged it can be renewed without replacing the entire instrument.

Figure 74. Plumb bob

The plumb bob is used in carpentry to determine true verticality when erecting vertical uprights and corner posts of framework. Surveyors use it for transferring and lining up points.

Levels

Levels are tools designed to prove whether a plane or surface is true horizontal or true vertical. Some precision levels are calibrated so that they will indicate in degrees, minutes, and seconds the angle inclination of a surface in relation to a horizontal or vertical surface.

The level is a simple instrument consisting of a liquid, such as alcohol or chloroform, partially filling a glass vial or tube so that a bubble remains. The tube is mounted in a frame, which may be aluminum, wood, or iron. Levels are equipped with one, two, or more tubes. One tube is built in the frame at right angles to another. The tube indicated in Figure 75 is slightly curved, causing the bubble to seek always the highest point in the tube. On the outside of the tube are two sets of graduation lines separated by a space. Leveling is accomplished when the air bubble is centered between the graduation lines.

Figure 75. Horizontal and vertical use of level

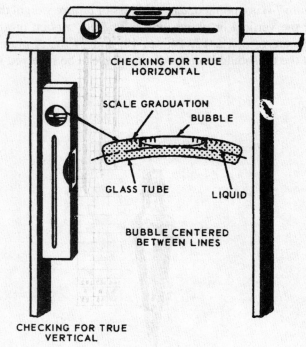

Fastening Components

Woodworking Fasteners

Nails

Nails achieve their fastening or holding power when they displace wood fibers from their original position. The pressure exerted against the nail by these fibers, as they try to spring back to their original position, provides the holding power.

The usual type of shank is round, but there are various special-purpose nails with other types of shanks. Nails with square, triangular, longitudinally grooved, and spirally grooved shanks have a much greater holding power than smooth round wire nails of the same size.

The lengths of the most commonly used nails are designated by the *penny* system. The abbreviation for the word "penny" is the letter "d." Thus, the expression "a 2d nail" means a two-penny nail. The penny sizes and corresponding length and thicknesses (in gage sizes) of the common nails are shown in Figure 76. The thickness of a nail increases and the number of nails per pound decrease with the penny size.

Figure 76. Common nail sizes

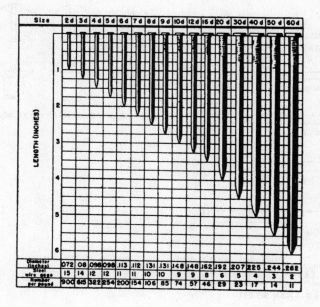

Nails larger than 20d are called spikes and are generally designated by their length in inches (such as 5 inches or $6\frac{1}{2}$ inches); nails smaller than 2d are designated in fractions of an inch instead of in the penny system.

Shown below are the more common types of wire nails. The *brad* and the *finish* nail both have a deep countersink head that is designed to be "set" below the surface of the work. These nails are used for interior and exterior trimwork where the nails are "set" and puttied to conceal their location. The *casing* nail is used for the same purpose, but because of its flat countersink head, it may be driven flush and left that way.

The other nails shown in Figure 77 are all flat-headed, without countersinks. One of these flat-headed nails (called the *common* nail) is one of the most widely used in general wood construction. Nails with large flat heads are used for nailing roof paper, plaster board, and similar thin or soft materials. *Duplex* or *double-headed* nails are used for nailing temporary structures, such as scaffolds, which are eventually to be dismantled. When using the double-headed nail, it is driven to the lowest head so that it can be easily drawn at a later time.

Figure 77. Nail varieties   **Figure 78.** Woodscrew heads

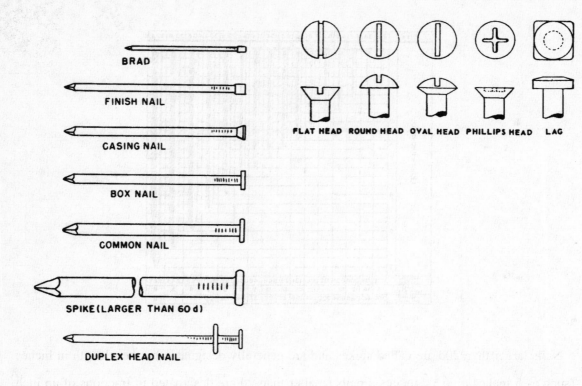

Wood Screws

Screws have several advantages over nails. They may be easily withdrawn at any time without injury to the material. They also hold the wood more securely, can be easily tightened, and, generally, are neater in appearance. Wood screws are designated by material, type of head (see Figure 78), and size.

Most wood screws are made of steel or brass, but other metals are used as well. Cost or special purpose application will determine the selection of the material to be used.

The size of an ordinary wood screw is indicated by the length and body diameter (unthreaded part) of the screw. Figure 79 shows the nomenclature and the three most common types of wood screws. Notice that the length is always measured from the point to the greatest diameter of the head.

Body diameters are designated by gauge numbers, running from 0 (for about a $\frac{1}{16}$ -in. diameter) to 24 (for about a $\frac{3}{8}$ -in. diameter).

Designation of length and gauge number appear as "1¼-9". This means a No. 9 screw is 1¼ inches long.

Figure 79. Nomenclature and types of woodscrews

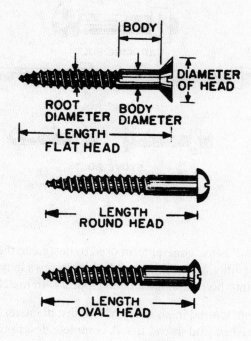

Metal Fastening Devices

Many mechanisms and devices are held together with metal fasteners. Only the more commonly used fasteners will be discussed here.

Metal parts can be fastened together with various fastening devices, such as rivets, bolts, screws, etc. Rivets provide a more permanent type of fastening, whereas bolts and screws are used to fasten together parts that may have to be taken apart later.

Bolts

A *bolt* is distinguished from a wood screw by the fact that it does not thread into the wood but goes through and is held by a nut threaded onto the end of the bolt. Figure 80 shows four common types of bolts used in woodworking. *Stove* bolts are rather small, ranging in length from $\frac{3}{8}$ to 4 inches and in body diameter from $\frac{1}{8}$ to $\frac{3}{8}$ inch . *Carriage and machine bolts* run from $\frac{3}{4}$ to 20 inches long and from $\frac{3}{16}$ to $\frac{3}{4}$ inch in diameter. (The carriage bolt has a square section below the head, which is imbedded in the wood to prevent the bolt from turning as the nut is drawn up.) The machine bolt has a hexagon or square head, which is held with a wrench to prevent it from turning.

Figure 80. Bolts

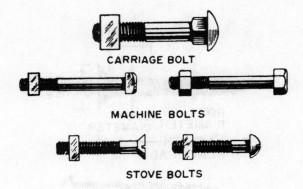

CARRIAGE BOLT

MACHINE BOLTS

STOVE BOLTS

Machine Screws

The term "machine screw" is the general term used to designate the small screws that are used in tapped holes for the assembly of metal parts. Machine screws may also be used with nuts, but usually, they are screwed into holes that have been tapped with matching threads.

Machine screws are manufactured in a variety of lengths, diameters, pitches (threads per inch), materials, head shapes, finishes, and thread fits. A complete description of machine screws must include these factors. For example, " $\frac{1}{2}$ inch, 8-32, round head, brass, chromium-plated, machine screw." The first number is the length of the screw. Let's examine some of these other factors.

Diameter and Pitch The diameters of American Standard machine screws are expressed in gage numbers or fractions of an inch. In the preceding paragraph, the "8-32" means that the screw gage is No. 8 and that it has 32 threads per inch. Note, particularly, that the "eight" and "thirty-two" are two separate numbers, indicating two individual measurements; they are never to be pronounced "six-thirty-seconds" or written as a fraction such as $\frac{6}{32}$.

Materials and Finishes

Most machine screws are made of steel or brass. They may be plated to help prevent corrosion. Other special machine screws made of aluminum or Monel metal are also obtainable. The latter metal is highly resistant to the corrosive action of salt water.

Head Shapes

A variety of common and special machine screw head shapes are shown in Figure 81. Some of the heads require special tools for driving and removing. These special tools are usually included in a kit that comes with the machine or installation on which the screws are used.

Figure 81. Machine screw and capscrew heads

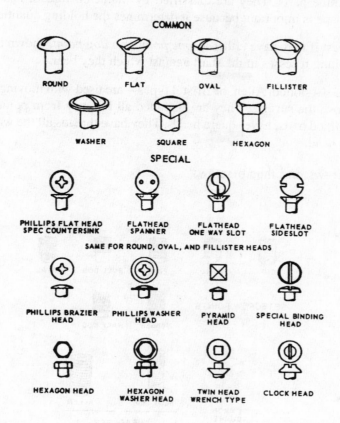

Capscrews

Capscrews perform the same functions as machine screws but come in larger sizes for heavier work. Sizes range up to 1 inch in diameter and 6 inches in length.

Capscrews are usually used without nuts. They are screwed into tapped holes and are sometimes referred to as tap bolts. Capscrews may have square, hex, flat, button, or fillister heads. Fillister heads are best for use on moving parts when such heads are sunk into counterbored holes. Hex heads are usually used where the metal parts do not move.

The strongest capscrews are made of alloy steel and can withstand great stresses, strains, and shearing forces. Capscrews made of Monel metal are often specified on machinery that is exposed to salt water. Some capscrews have small holes through their heads. A wire, called a *safety wire*, is run through the holes of several capscrews to keep them from coming loose.

Setscrews

Setscrews are used to secure small pulleys, gears, and cams to shafts and to provide positive adjustment of machine parts. They are classified by diameter, thread, head shape, and point shape. The point shape is important because it determines the holding qualities of the setscrew.

Setscrews hold best if they have either a *cone point* or a *dog point*, shown in Figure 82. These points fit into matching recesses in the shaft against which they bear.

Headless setscrews—slotted, Allen, or Bristol types—are used with moving parts because they do not stick up above the surface. They are threaded all the way from point to head. *Common setscrews*, used on fixed parts, have square heads. They have threads all the way from the point to the shoulder of the head.

Figure 82. Setscrews and thumb screws

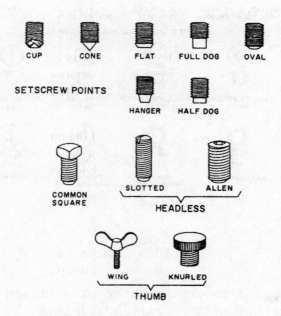

Thumb screws are used for setscrews, adjusting screws, and clamping screws. Because of their design they can be loosened or tightened without the use of tools.

Nuts

Square and hexagonal nuts are standard but they are supplemented by special nuts (see Figure 83). One of these is the *jam nut*, used above a standard hex nut to lock it in position. It is about half as thick as the standard hex nut and has a washer face.

Figure 83. Common kinds of nuts

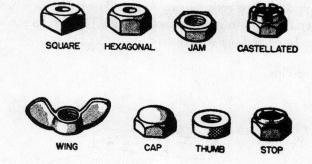

Castellated nuts are slotted so that a safety wire or *cotter key* may be pushed through the slots and into a matching hole in the bolt. This provides a positive method of preventing the nut from working loose. For example, you will see these nuts used with the bolts that hold the two halves of an engine connecting rod together.

Wing nuts are used where the desired degree of tightness can be obtained by the fingers. *Cap nuts* are used where appearance is an important consideration. They are usually made of chromium plated brass. *Thumb nuts* are knurled, so they can be turned by hand for easy assembly and disassembly.

Elastic stop nuts are used where it is imperative that the nut does not come loose. These nuts have a fiber or composition washer built into them that is compressed automatically against the screw threads to provide holding tension. They are used extensively on radio equipment, sound equipment, fire control equipment, and aircraft.

Washers

Figure 84 shows the types of washers in common use. *Flat washers* are used to back up bolt heads and nuts and to provide larger bearing surfaces. They prevent damage to the surfaces of the metal parts.

Split lock washers are used under nuts to prevent loosening by vibration. The ends of these spring-hardened washers dig into both the nut and the work to prevent slippage.

Shakeproof lock washers have teeth or lugs that grip both the work and the nut. Several patented designs, shapes, and sizes are obtainable.

Figure 84. Washers

Keys and Pins

Cotter keys (see Figure 85) are used to secure screws, nuts, bolts, and pins. They are also used as stops and holders on shafts and rods. *Square keys* and *woodruff keys* are used to prevent hand wheels, gears, cams, and pulleys from turning on a shaft. These keys are strong enough to carry heavy loads if they are fitted and seated properly.

Figure 85. Keys and Pins

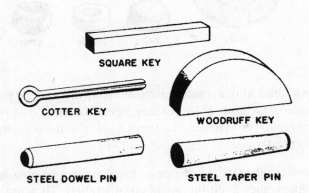

Taper pins are used to locate and position matching parts. They are also used to secure small pulleys and gears to shafts. They usually have a taper of $\frac{1}{4}$ inch per foot. Holes for taper pins must be reamed with tapered reamers. If this is not done the taper pin will not fit properly.

Figure 86. Types of cotter pins

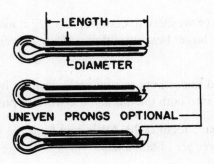

Dowel pins are used to position and align the units or parts of an assembly. One end of a dowel pin is chamfered, and it is usually .001 to .002 inch greater in diameter than the size of the hole into which the pin will be driven.

Cotter Pins. Some cotter pins are made of low-carbon steel, while others consist of stainless steel, and thus are more resistant to corrosion. Regardless of shape or material, all cotter pins are used for the same general purpose—safetying.

Dimension perimeters of a cotter pin are shown in Figure 86. Whenever uneven prong cotter pins are used, the length measurement is to the end of the shortest prong.

Rivets

Rivets are used extensively as a fastening device in aircraft. They are also used to join metal sheets when brazing, welding, or locking techniques will not provide a satisfactory joint.

Rivet Types

The major types of rivets used extensively include the standard type and pop rivets. Standard rivets must be driven using a bucking bar, whereas the pop rivets have a self heading capability and may be installed where it is impossible to use a bucking bar.

- **Standard Rivets.** Wherever possible, rivets should be made of the same material as the material they join. They are classified by lengths, diameters, and their head shape and size. Some of the standard head shapes are shown in Figure 87 below.

Selection of the proper length of a rivet is important. Should too long a rivet be used, the formed head will be too large, or the rivet may bend or be forced between the sheets being riveted. Should too short a rivet be used, the formed head will be too small or the riveted material will be damaged. The length of the rivet should equal the sum of the thickness of the metal plus $1\frac{1}{2}$ times the diameter of the rivet.

Figure 87. Some common types of rivets

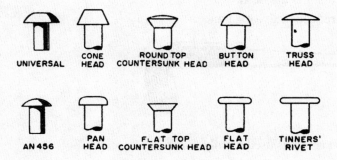

- **Pop Rivets.** Pop rivets have two advantages compared to standard rivets in that they can be set by one person and also be used for blind fastening. This means that they can be used when there is limited or no access to the reverse side of the work.

Sample Questions

1. A fuel injection system on an automobile engine eliminates the necessity for
   - 1-A   a manifold.
   - 1-B   a carburetor.
   - 1-C   spark plugs.
   - 1-D   a distributor.

2. A car uses too much oil when which parts are worn?
   - 2-A   Pistons
   - 2-B   Piston rings
   - 2-C   Main bearings
   - 2-D   Connecting rods

3. The function of the rotor is to
   - 3-A   distribute the electricity to the spark plugs.
   - 3-B   open and close the distributor points.
   - 3-C   rotate the distributor cam.
   - 3-D   rotate the distributor shaft.

4. What happens if cylinder head torquing is not done in proper sequence?
   - 4-A   It warps the piston rings.
   - 4-B   It cracks the intake manifold.
   - 4-C   It distorts the head.
   - 4-D   It reduces valve clearance.

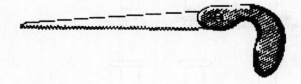

5. The saw shown above is used mainly to cut
   - 5-A   across the grain of the wood.
   - 5-B   along the grain of the wood.
   - 5-C   plywood.
   - 5-D   odd-shaped holes in wood.

6. Sheet metal should be cut with
   - 6-A   household scissors.
   - 6-B   a hack saw.
   - 6-C   tin shears.
   - 6-D   a jig saw.

7. A lathe would normally be used in making which of the following items?

  7-A   A baseball bat
  7-B   A bookcase
  7-C   A hockey stick
  7-D   A picture frame

8. What tool is shown to the right?

  8-A   Countersink
  8-B   Keyhole saw
  8-C   Hole saw
  8-D   Grinding saw

Answers and Explanations

1-B Fuel injected engines utilize injectors to spray the fuel mixture into the combustion chamber rather than using a carburetor to mix the fuel and air.

2-B Piston rings carry small amounts of oil to coat the cylinders. Normally the oil is not allowed to enter the combustion chamber. When piston rings are worn they allow oil through to be burned during the combustion process.

3-A The rotor turns inside the distributor connecting the charge from the coil to the spark plug at the exact time required to complete the combustion process.

4-C Improper torque may cause distorting of the head because one side of the head may be too tight while the other side is not tight enough. This may also result in improper dissipation of heat also causing the head to warp.

5-D The saw pictured is a "compass saw," which is used to cut circular or other nonrectangular shapes in wood.

6-C Sheet metal work is best done using tin shears. While a hacksaw or jigsaw may work you will wind-up with distorted metal. Household scissors just won't "cut it."

7-A A lathe is a machine used to make objects that are made of one solid piece of material and usually has a rounded shape, such as table legs and baseball bats.

8-C A hole saw uses a drill bit like instrument to start the hole and then a rounded "saw" blade to cut the actual hole.

MECHANICAL COMPREHENSION REVIEW

Levers

The simplest machine, and perhaps the one that you are most familiar with, is the *lever*. A seesaw is a familiar example of a lever in which one weight balances the other.

There are three basic parts in all levers:

1. *fulcrum* (F), a force

2. *effort* (E)

3. *resistance* (R)

Look at the lever in Figure 1. You see the pivotal point F (fulcrum); the effort (E), which you apply at a distance A from the fulcrum; and a resistance (R), which acts at a distance from the fulcrum. Distances A and a are the lever arms.

Figure 1. A simple lever

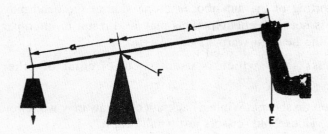

Classes of Levers

The three classes of levers are shown in Figures 2 and 3. The location of the fulcrum (the fixed or pivot point) with relation to the resistance (or weight) and the effort determines the lever class.

First-Class Levers

In the first-class lever (see Figure 2A), the fulcrum is located between the effort and the resistance. As mentioned earlier, the seesaw is a good example of the first-class lever. The amount of weight and the distance from the fulcrum can be varied to suit the need. Crowbars, shears, and pliers are common examples of this class of lever.

Figure 2. First- and second-class levers

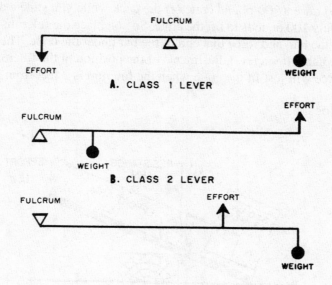

Second-Class Levers

The second-class lever (see Figure 2B) has the fulcrum at one end; the effort is applied at the other end. The resistance is somewhere between these two points.

Both first- and second-class levers are commonly used to help in overcoming big resistances with a relatively small effort.

Third-Class Levers

There are occasions when you will want to speed up the movement of the resistance even though you have to use a large amount of effort. Levers that help you accomplish this are third-class levers. As shown in Figure 2C, the fulcrum is at one end of the lever and the weight or resistance to be overcome is at the other end, with the effort applied at some point between. You can always spot third-class levers because you will find the effort applied between the fulcrum and the resistance. Look at Figure 3. It is easy to see that while point E is moving the short distance, e, the resistance, R, has been moved a greater distance, r. The speed of R must have been greater than that of E, since R covered a greater distance in the same length of time.

Figure 3. A third-class lever

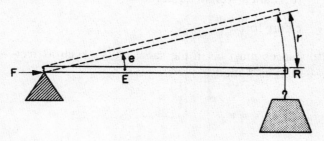

One convenient thing about machines is that you can determine in advance the forces required for their operation, as well as the forces they will exert. Consider for a moment the first-class lever. Suppose you have an iron bar, like the one shown in Figure 3. This bar is 9 feet long, and you want to use it to raise a 300-pound crate off the deck while you slide a dolly under the crate. But you can exert only 100 pounds to lift the crate. So you place the fulcrum—a wooden block—beneath one end of the bar, and force that end of the bar under the crate. Then you push down on the other end of the bar. After a few adjustments of the position of the fulcrum, you will find that your 100-pound force will just fit the crate when the fulcrum is 2 feet from center of the crate.

Figure 4. Easy does it

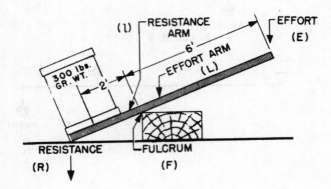

This leaves a 6-foot length of bar from the fulcrum to the point where you push down. The 6-foot portion is three times as long as the distance from the fulcrum to the center of the crate. But you lifted a load three times as great as the force you applied—3 × 100 = 300 pounds. Here is an indication of a direct relationship between lengths of lever arms and forces acting on those arms.

You can state this relationship in general terms by saying the length of the effort arm is the same number of times greater than the length of the resistance arm as the resistance to be overcome is greater than the effort you must apply. Writing these words as a mathematical equation, it looks like this:

$$\frac{L}{I} = \frac{R}{E}$$

in which

L	=	length of effort arm
I	=	length of resistance arm
R	=	resistance weight or force
E	=	effort force

Remember that all distances must be in the same units—such as feet—and all forces must be in the same units—such as pounds.

Mechanical Advantage

There is another thing about first-class and second-class levers that you have probably noticed by now. Since they can be used to magnify the applied force, they provide positive mechanical advantages. The third-class lever provides what's called a fractional mechanical advantage, which is really a mechanical disadvantage. You use more force than the force of the load you lift.

$$\text{MECHANICAL ADVANTAGE} = \frac{\text{RESISTANCE}}{\text{EFFORT}}$$

or

$$\text{M.A.} = \frac{R}{E}$$

Mechanical advantage of levers may also be found by dividing the length of the effort arm A by the length of the resistance arm a. Stated as a formula, this reads:

$$\text{MECHANICAL ADVANTAGE} = \frac{\text{EFFORT ARM}}{\text{RESISTANCE ARM}}$$

$$\text{M.A.} = \frac{A}{a}$$

Block and Tackle

Blocks, also known as pulleys, are simple machines that have many uses. Remember how your mouth hung open as you watched movers taking a piano out of a fourth story window? The guy on the end of the tackle eased the piano safely to the sidewalk with a mysterious arrangement of blocks and ropes.

You rig a block-and-tackle to make some of your work easier. Learn the names of the parts of the block shown in Figure 5. Look at the single block and see some of the ways you can use it. If you lash a single block to a fixed object—an overhead, a yardarm, or a bulkhead—you give yourself the advantage of being able to pull from a convenient direction.

Figure 5. Look it over   **Figure 6.** No Advantage

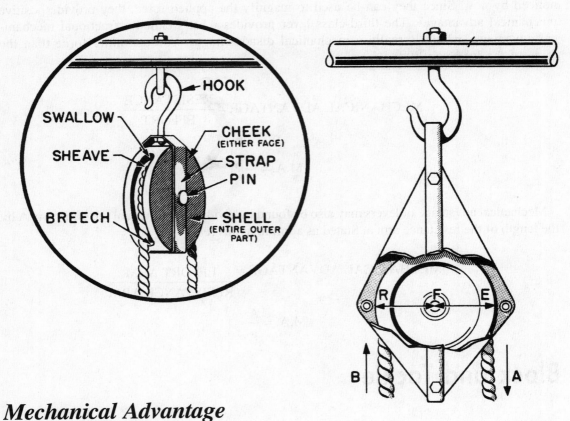

Mechanical Advantage

With a single fixed sheave, the force of your down-pull on the fall must be equal to the weight of the object being hoisted. You can't use this rig to lift a heavy load or resistance with a small effort; you can change only the direction of your pull.

A single fixed block is really a first-class lever with equal arms. The arms EF and FR are equal; hence, the mechanical advantage is one. When you pull down at A with a force of one pound, you raise a load of one pound at B. A single fixed block does not magnify force nor speed (see Figure 6).

Figure 7. A runner

You can, however, use a single block-and-fall to magnify the force you exert. Notice, in Figure 7 that the block is not fixed, and that the fall is doubled as it supports the 200-pound cask. When rigged this way, a single block-and-fall is called a runner. Each half of the fall carries one half of the total load, or 100 pounds. Thus, by the use of the runner, the person is lifting a 200-pound cask with a 100-pound pull. The mechanical advantage is two. Check this by the formula:

$$\text{M.A.} = \frac{R}{E} = \frac{200}{100}, \text{ or } 2$$

The single movable block in this setup is really a second-class lever (see Figure 8). Your effort, E, acts upward upon the arm, EF, which is the diameter of the sheave. The resistance, R, acts downward on the arm, FR, which is the radius of the sheave. Since the diameter is twice the radius, the mechanical advantage is two.

But, when the effort at E moves up two feet, the load at R is raised only about one foot. That's one thing to remember about blocks and falls—if you are actually getting a mechanical advantage from the system, the length of rope that passes through your hands is greater than the distance that the load is raised. However, if you can lift a big load with a small effort, you don't care how much rope you have to pull.

The person in Figure 7 is in an awkward position to pull. If he had another single block handy, he could use it to change the direction of the pull, as in Figure 9. This second arrangement is known as a gun tackle purchase. Because the second block is fixed, it merely changes the direction of pull—and the mechanical advantage of the whole system remains two.

You can arrange blocks in a number of ways, depending on the job to be done and the mechanical advantage you want to get. For example, a luff tackle consists of a double block and a single block, rigged as in Figure 10. Notice that the weight is suspended by the three parts of rope that extend from the movable single block. Each part of the rope carries its share of the load. If the crate weighs 600 pounds, then each of the three parts of the rope supports its share—200 pounds. If there's a pull of 200 pounds downward on rope B, you will have to pull down with a force of 200 pounds on A to counterbalance the pull on B. Neglecting the friction in the block, a pull of 200 pounds is all that is necessary to raise the crate. The mechanical advantage is:

$$\text{M.A.} = \frac{R}{E} = \frac{600}{200} = 3$$

Figure 8. It's 2 to 1

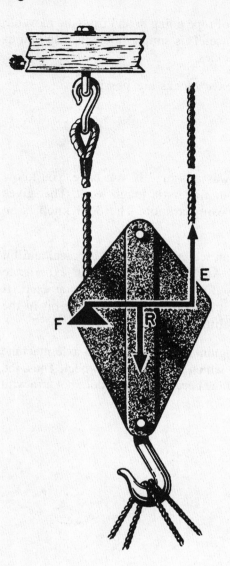

Figure 9. A gun tackle

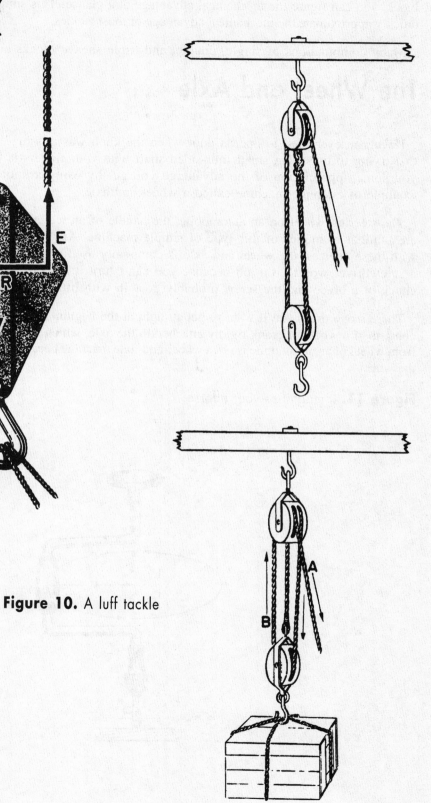

Figure 10. A luff tackle

Here's a good tip. If you count the number of the parts of rope going to and from the movable block, you can figure the mechanical advantage at a glance. This simple rule will help you to quickly approximate the mechanical advantage of most tackles.

Many combinations of single, double, and triple sheave blocks are possible.

The Wheel and Axle

Have you ever tried to open a door when the knob was missing? If you have, you know that trying to twist that small four-sided shaft with your fingers is tough work. That gives you some appreciation of the advantage you get by using a knob. The door knob is an example of a simple machine called a wheel and axle.

The steering wheel on an automobile, the handle of an ice cream freezer, a brace, and bit are familiar examples of this type of simple machine. As you know from your experience with these devices, the wheel and axle is commonly used to multiply the force you exert. If a screwdriver won't do a job because you can't turn it, you stick a screwdriver bit in the chuck of a brace and the screw probably goes in with little difficulty.

There's one thing you'll want to get straight at the beginning. The wheel-and-axle machine consists of a wheel or crank rigidly attached to the axle, which turns with the wheel. Thus, the front wheel of an automobile is not a wheel-and-axle machine because the axle does not turn with the wheel.

Figure 11. It magnifies your effort

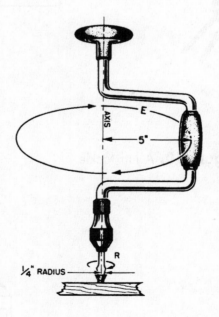

Mechanical Advantage

How does the wheel-and-axle arrangement help to magnify the force you exert? Suppose you use a screwdriver bit in a brace to drive a stubborn screw (see Figure 11). Your effort is applied on the handle, which moves in a circular path, the radius of which is 5 inches. If you apply a 10-pound force on the handle, how big a force will be exerted against the resistance at the screw?

Assume the radius of the screwdriver blade is $\frac{1}{4}$ inch. You are really using the brace as a second-class lever—see Figure 11. The size of the resistance that can be overcome can be found from the following formula in which

L   =   radius of the circle through which the handle turns

I   =   one-half the width of the edge of the screwdriver blade

R   =   force of the resistance offered by the screw

E   =   force of effort applied on the handle

$$\frac{L}{I} = \frac{R}{E}$$

Substituting in the formula and solving:

$$\frac{5}{1/4} = \frac{R}{10}$$

$$R = \frac{5 \times 10}{1/4}$$

$$= 5 \times 10 \times 4$$

$$= 200 \ lb.$$

This means that the screwdriver blade will tend to turn the screw with a force of 200 pounds. The relationship between the radii or the diameters, or the circumferences of the wheel and axle, tells you how great a mechanical advantage you can get.

Moment of Force

In a number of situations, you can use the wheel-and-axle to speed up motion. The rear-wheel sprocket of a bike, along with the rear wheel itself, is an example. When you are pedaling, the sprocket is fixed to the wheel, so the combination is a true wheel-and-axle machine. Assume that the sprocket has a circumference of 8 inches, and the wheel circumference is 80 inches. If you turn the sprocket at a rate of one revolution per second, each sprocket tooth moves at a speed of 8 inches per second. Since the wheel makes one revolution for each revolution made by the sprocket, any point on the tire must move through a distance of 80 inches in one second. So, for every 8-inch movement of a point on the sprocket, you have moved a corresponding point on the wheel through 80 inches.

Since a complete revolution of the sprocket and wheel requires only one second, the speed of a point on the circumference of the wheel is 80 inches per second, or ten times the speed of a tooth on the sprocket. *NOTE: Both sprocket and wheel make the same number of revolutions per second so the speed of turning for the two is the same.*

Here is an idea that you will find useful in understanding the wheel and axle, as well as other machines. You probably have noticed that the force you apply to a lever tends to turn or rotate it about the fulcrum. You also know that a heave on a fall tends to rotate the sheave of the block and that turning the steering wheel of a car tends to rotate the steering column. Whenever you use a lever, or a wheel and axle, your effort on the lever arm or the rim of the wheel tends to cause a rotation about the fulcrum or the axle in one direction or another. If the rotation occurs in the same direction as the hands of a clock, that direction is called clockwise. If the rotation occurs in the opposite direction from that of the hands of a clock, the direction of rotation is called counterclockwise. A glance at Figure 12 will make clear the meaning of these terms.

You have already seen that the result of a force acting on the handle of the carpenter's brace depends not only on the amount of that force but also on the distance from the handle to the center of rotation. From here on you'll know this result as a moment of force, or a torque (pronounced tork). Moment of force and torque have the same meaning.

Figure 12. Directions of rotation

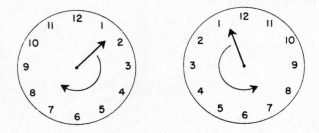

The Inclined Plane and the Wedge

The Barrel Roll

You have probably watched a driver load barrels on a truck. The truck is backed up to the curb. The driver places a long double plank or ramp from the sidewalk to the tailgate, and then rolls the barrel up the ramp. A 32-gallon barrel may weigh close to 300 pounds when full, and it would be quite a job to lift one up into the truck. Actually, the driver is using a simple machine called the inclined plane. You have seen the inclined plane used in many situations. Cattle ramps, a mountain highway, and the gangplank are familiar examples.

The inclined plane permits you to overcome a large resistance by applying a relatively small force through a longer distance than the load is raised (see Figure 13). Here you see the driver easing the 300-pound barrel up to the bed of the truck, three feet above the sidewalk. He is using a plank nine feet long. If he didn't use the ramp at all, he'd have to apply a 300-pound force straight up through the three-foot distance. With the ramp, however, he can apply his effort over the entire nine feet of the plank as the barrel is slowly rolled up to a height of three feet. It looks, then, as if he could use a force only three-ninths of 300, or 100 pounds, to do the job. And that is actually the situation.

Figure 13. An inclined plane

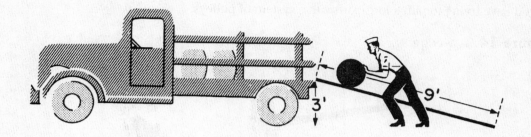

Here's the formula.

$$\frac{L}{I} = \frac{R}{E}$$

in which

L	=	Length of the ramp, measured along the slope
I	=	Height of the ramp
R	=	Weight of object to be raised or lowered
E	=	Force required to raise or lower object

Now apply the formula to this problem.

In this case, L = 9 feet; I = 3 feet; and R = 300 pounds. By substituting these values in the formula, you get

$$\frac{9}{3} = \frac{300}{E}$$
$$9E = 900$$
$$E = 100 \text{ pounds}$$

Since the ramp is three times as long as its height, the mechanical advantage is three. You find the theoretical mechanical advantage by dividing the total distance through which your effort is exerted by the vertical distance through which the load is raised or lowered.

The Wedge

You have probably used wedges. The wedge is a special application of the inclined plane. Abe Lincoln used a wedge to help him split logs into rails for fences. The blades of knives, axes, hatchets, and chisels act as wedges when they are forced into a piece of wood. The wedge is two inclined planes, set base-to-base. By driving the wedge full-length into the material to be cut or split, the material is forced apart a distance equal to the width of the broad end of the wedge (see Figure 14).

Long, slim wedges give high mechanical advantage. For example, the wedge of Figure 14 has a mechanical advantage of six. Their greatest value, however, lies in the fact that you can use them in situations where other simple machines won't work. Imagine the trouble you'd have trying to pull a log apart with a system of pulleys.

Figure 14. A wedge

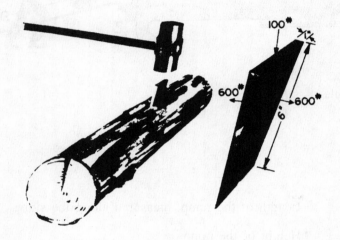

The Screw

A Modified Inclined Plane

The screw is a simple machine that has many uses. The vise on a workbench, the screw clamps used to hold a piece of furniture together, and many automobile jacks make use of the great mechanical advantage of the screw.

A screw is a modification of the inclined plane. Cut a sheet of paper in the shape of a right triangle—an inclined plane. Wind it around a pencil, as in Figure 15. Then you can see that the screw is actually an inclined plane wrapped around a cylinder. As the pencil is turned, the paper is wound up so that its hypotenuse forms a spiral thread similar to the thread on the screw shown at the right. The pitch of the screw, and of the paper, is the distance between identical points on the same threads, and measured along the length of the screw.

The Jack

In order to understand how the screw works, look at Figure 16. Here you see a jackscrew of the type that is used to raise a house or a piece of heavy machinery. The jack has a lever handle with a length *r*. If you pull the lever handle around one turn, its outer end has described a circle. The circumference of this circle is equal to 2p. (You remember that p equals 3.14, or $\frac{22}{7}$.) That is the distance, or the lever arm, through which your effort is applied.

Figure 15. A screw is an inclined plane in spiral form

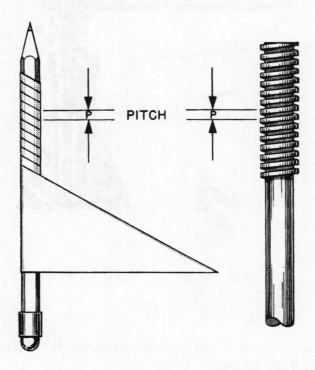

At the same time, the screw has made one revolution, and in doing so has been raised a height equal to its pitch p. You might say that one full thread has come up out of the base. At any rate, the load has been raised a distance p.

Remember that the theoretical mechanical advantage is equal to the distance through which the effort or pull is applied, divided by the distance the resistance or load is moved.

Assuming a 2-foot—24″—length for the lever arm, and a $\frac{1}{4}$-inch pitch for the thread, you can find the theoretical mechanical advantage by the formula

$$\text{M.A.} = \frac{2\pi r}{p}$$

in which

r = length of handle = 24 inches

p = pitch, or distance between corresponding points on successive threads = $\frac{1}{4}$ inch

Figure 16. A jack screw

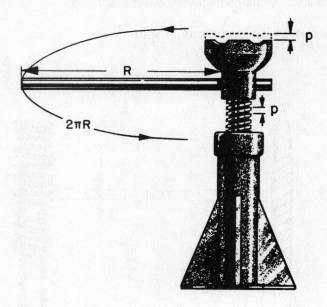

Substituting

$$\text{T.M.A.} = \frac{2 \times 3.14 \times 24}{1/4} = \frac{150.72}{1/4} = 602.88$$

A 50-pound pull on the handle would result in a theoretical lift of 50×602 or about 30,000 pounds. Fifteen tons for fifty pounds.

But jacks have considerable friction loss. The threads are cut so that the force used to overcome friction is greater than the force used to do useful work. If the threads were not cut this way, if no friction were present, the weight of the load would cause the jack to spin right back down to the bottom as soon as the handle is released.

The Micrometer

In using the jack, you exerted your effort through a distance of $2\pi r$, or 150 inches, in order to raise the screw $\frac{1}{4}$ inch . It takes a lot of circular motion to get a small amount of straight-line motion from the head of the jack. You will use this point to advantage in the micrometer, which is a useful device for making accurate small measurements, measurements of a few thousandths of an inch.

In Figure 17, you see a cutaway view of a micrometer. The thimble turns freely on the sleeve, which is rigidly attached to the micrometer frame. The spindle is attached to the thimble and is fitted with screw threads, which move the spindle and thimble to the right or left in the sleeve when the thimble is rotated. These screw threads are cut 40 threads to the inch. Hence, one turn of the thimble moves the spindle and thimble $\frac{1}{40}$ inch. This represents one of the smallest divisions on the micrometer. Four of these small divisions make $\frac{4}{40}$ of an inch, or $\frac{1}{10}$ inch. Thus, the distance from 0 to 1 or 1 to 2 on the sleeve represents $\frac{1}{10}$ or 0.1 inch.

Figure 17. A micrometer

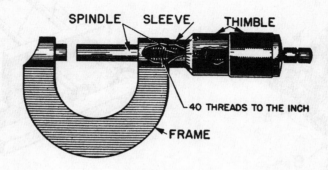

Gears

Did you ever take a clock apart to see what made it tick? Of course you came out with some parts left over when you got it back together again. And they probably included a few gear wheels. Gears are used in many machines. Frequently the gears are hidden from view in a protective case filled with grease or oil, and you may not see them.

An eggbeater gives you a simple demonstration of the three things that gears do. They can change the direction of motion; increase or decrease the speed of the applied motion; and magnify or reduce the force that you apply. Gears also give you a positive drive. There can be, and usually is, creep or slip in a belt drive. But gear teeth are always in mesh, and there can be no creep or slip.

Follow the directional changes in Figure 18. The crank handle is turned in the direction indicated by the arrow—clockwise, when viewed from the right. The 32 teeth on the large vertical wheel A mesh with the 8 teeth on the right-hand horizontal wheel B, which rotates as indicated by the arrow. Notice that as B turns in a clockwise direction, its teeth mesh with those of wheel C and cause wheel C to revolve in the opposite direction. The rotation of the crank handle has been transmitted by gears to the beater blades, which also rotate.

Figure 18. A simple arrangement gear   **Figure 19.** Spur gears coupling two parallel shafts

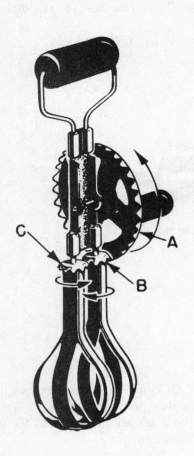

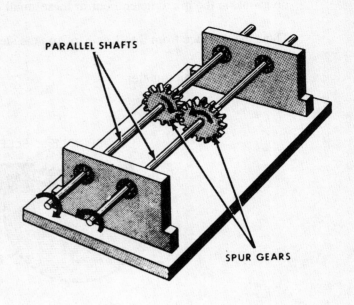

Now figure out how the gears change the speed of motion. There are 32 teeth on gear A and 8 teeth on gear B. But the gears mesh, so that one complete revolution of A results in four complete revolutions of gear B. And since gears B and C have the same number of teeth, one revolution of B results in one revolution of C. Thus, the blades revolve four times as fast as the crank handle.

Previously, you learned that third-class levers increase speed at the expense of force. The same thing happens with this eggbeater. The magnitude of the force is changed, and the force required to turn the handle is greater than the force applied to the frosting by the blades. Therefore, a mechanical advantage of less than one results.

Types of Gears

When two shafts are not lying in the same straight line, but are parallel, motion can be transmitted from one to the other by means of spur gears. This setup is shown in Figure 19.

Spur gears are wheels with mating teeth cut in their surfaces so that one can turn the other without slippage. When the mating teeth are cut so that they are parallel to the axis of rotation, as shown in Figure 19, the gears are called straight spur gears.

When two gears of unequal size are meshed together, the smaller of the two is usually called a pinion. By unequal size, we mean an unequal number of teeth causing one gear to be of a larger diameter than the other. The teeth, themselves, must be of the same size in order to mesh properly.

The most commonly used type is the straight spur gear, but quite often you'll run across another type of spur gear called the helical spur gear.

In helical gears, the teeth are cut slantwise across the working face of the gear. One end of the tooth, therefore, lies ahead of the other. In other words, each tooth has a leading end and a trailing end. A look at these gears in Figure 20 shows you how they're constructed.

In the straight spur gears, the whole width of the teeth comes in contact at the same time. But with helical (spiral) gears, contact between two teeth starts first at the leading ends and moves progressively across the gear faces until the trailing ends are in contact. This kind of meshing action keeps the gears in constant contact with one another. Therefore, less lost motion and smoother, quieter action is possible. One disadvantage of this helical spur gear is the tendency of each gear to thrust or push axially on its shaft. It is necessary to put a special thrust bearing at the end of the shaft to counteract this thrust. Figure 20 also shows you three other gear arrangements in common use.

Figure 20. Gear types

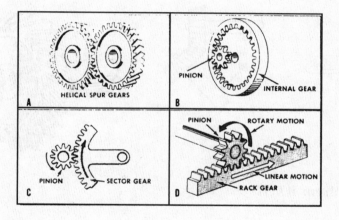

The internal gear in Figure 20B has teeth on the inside of a ring, pointing inward toward the axis of rotation. An internal gear is always meshed with an external gear, or pinion, whose center is offset from the center of the internal gear. Either the internal or pinion gear can be the driver gear, and the gear ratio is calculated the same as for the other gears—by counting teeth.

Often, only a portion of a gear is needed where the motion of the pinion is limited. In this case the sector gear (Figure 20C) is used to save space and material. The rack and pinion in Figure 20D are both spur gears. The rack may be considered as a piece cut from a gear with an extremely large radius. The rack-and-pinion arrangement is useful in changing rotary motion into linear motion.

The Bevel Gear

So far, most of the gears you've learned about transmit motion between parallel shafts. But when shafts are not parallel (at an angle), another type of gear is used—the bevel gear. This type of gear can connect shafts lying at any given angle because they can be beveled to suit the angle.

Figure 21A shows a special case of the bevel gear—the miter gear. A pair of miter gears is used to connect shafts having a 90-degree angle, which means the gear faces are beveled at a 45-degree angle.

You can see in Figure 21B below how bevel gears are designed to join shafts at any angle. Gears cut at any angle other than 45 degrees are called just plain bevel gears.

The gears shown in Figure 21 are called straight bevel gears, because the whole width of each tooth comes in contact with the mating tooth at the same time. However, you'll also run across spiral bevel gears with teeth cut so as to have advanced and trailing ends. Figure 22 shows you what spiral bevel gears look like. They have the same advantages as other spiral (helical) gears—less lost motion and smoother, quieter operation.

Figure 21. Bevel gears   **Figure 22.** Spiral bevel gears

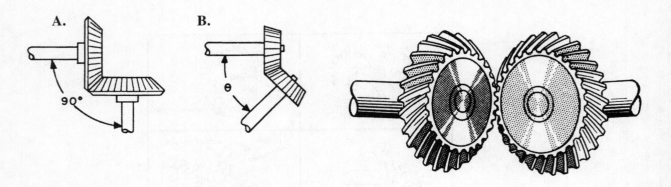

The Worm and Worm Wheel

Worm and worm-wheel combinations, like those in Figure 23, have many uses and advantages. But it's better to understand their operating theory before learning of their uses and advantages.

Figure 23A shows the action of a single-thread worm. For each revolution of the worm, the worm wheel turns one tooth. Thus, if the worm wheel has 25 teeth the gear ratio is 25:1.

Figure 23. Worm gears

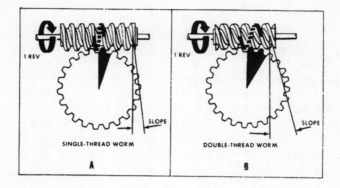

Figure 23B shows a double-thread worm. For each revolution of the worm in this case, the worm wheel turns two teeth. That makes the gear ratio 25:2 if the worm wheel has 25 teeth.

Likewise, a triple-threaded worm would turn the worm wheel three teeth per revolution of the worm.

Changing Direction with Gears

No doubt you know that the crankshaft in an automobile engine can turn in only one direction. If you want the car to go backward, the effect of the engine's rotation must be reversed. This is done by a reversing gear in the transmission not by reversing the direction in which the crankshaft turns.

Changing Speed

As you've already seen in the eggbeater, gears can be used to change the speed of motion. Another example of this use of gears is found in your clock or watch. The mainspring slowly unwinds and causes the hour hand to make one revolution in 12 hours. Through a series—or train—of gears, the minute hand makes one revolution each hour, while the second hand goes around once per minute.

Magnifying Force with Gears

Gear trains are used to increase the mechanical advantage. In fact, wherever there is a speed reduction, the effect of the effort you apply is multiplied. Look at the cable winch in Figure 24. The crank arm is 30 inches long, and the drum on which the cable is wound has a 15-inch radius. The small pinion gear has 10 teeth, which mesh with the 60 teeth on the internal spur gear. You will find it easier, to figure the mechanical advantage of this machine if you think of it as two machines.

First, figure out what the gear and pinion do for you. The theoretical mechanical advantage of any arrangement of two meshed gears can be found by the following formula:

$$\text{M.A. (theoretical)} = \frac{T_o}{T_a}.$$

in which

T_o =   number of teeth on driven gear

T_a =   number of teeth on driver gear

In this case, $T_o = 60$ and $T_a = 10$. Then,

$$\text{M.A. (theoretical)} = \frac{T_o}{T_a} = \frac{60}{10} = 6$$

Figure 24. This magnifies your effort

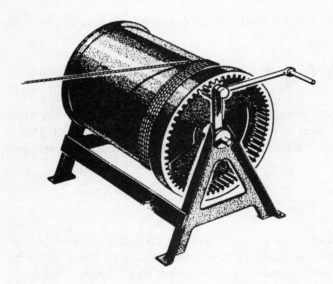

Now, for the other part of the machine, which is a simple wheel-and-axle arrangement consisting of the crank arm and the drum. The theoretical mechanical advantage of this can be found by dividing the distance the effort moves—$2\pi R$—in making one complete revolution, by the distance the cable is drawn up in one revolution of the drum—$2\pi r$.

$$\text{M.A. (theoretical)} = \frac{2\pi R}{2\pi r} = \frac{R}{r} = \frac{30}{15} = 6$$

You know that the total, or overall, theoretical mechanical advantage of a compound machine is equal to the product of the mechanical advantages of the several simple machines that make it up. In this case, you considered the winch as being two machines—one having an M. A. of 6, and the other an M. A. of 2. Therefore, the overall theoretical mechanical advantage of the winch is 6 × 2, or 12. Since friction is always present, the actual mechanical advantage may be only 7 or 8. Even so, by applying a force of 100 pounds on the handle, you could lift a load of 700 or 800 pounds.

Work

Measurement

You know that machines help you to do work. But just what is work? Work doesn't mean simply applying a force.

Work, in the mechanical sense of the term, is done when a resistance is overcome by a force acting through a measurable distance.

Notice that two factors are involved—force and movement through a distance. The force is normally measured in pounds, and the distance in feet. Work, therefore, is commonly measured in units called foot-pounds. You do one foot-pound of work when you lift a one-pound weight through a height of one foot. But—you also do one foot-pound of work when you apply one pound of force on any object through a distance of one foot. Writing this as a formula, it becomes—

$$\underset{\text{(foot-pounds)}}{\text{WORK}} = \underset{\text{(pounds)}}{\text{FORCE}} \times \underset{\text{(feet)}}{\text{DISTANCE}}$$

Thus, if a person lifts a 90-pound bag through a vertical distance of 5 feet, he will do

WORK = 90 × 5 = 450 ft-lb.

There are two points concerning work that you should get straight right at the beginning.

First, in calculating the work done you measure the actual resistance being overcome. This is not necessarily the weight of the object being moved. To make this clear, look at the job being done in Figure 25A. A man is pulling a 900-pound load of supplies 200 feet along the dock. Does this mean that he is doing 900 × 200, or 180,000 foot-pounds of work? Of course not. He isn't working against the pull of gravity—or the total weight—of the load. He's pulling only against the rolling friction of the truck, and that may be as little as 90 pounds. That is the resistance that is being overcome. Always be sure that you know what resistance is being overcome by the effort, as well as the distance through which it is moved. The resistance in one case may be the weight of the object; in another it may be the frictional resistance of the object as it is dragged or rolled along the deck.

Figure 25A. Working against friction

The second point to hold in mind is that you have to move the resistance to do any work on it. If you hold a suitcase for 15 minutes while waiting for a bus, your arm will get tired. However, according to the definition of work, you aren't doing any—because you aren't moving the suitcase. You are merely exerting a force against the pull of gravity on the bag.

You already know about the mechanical advantage of a lever. Now consider it in terms of getting work done easily, look at Figure 25B. The load weighs 300 pounds, and you want to lift it up onto a platform a foot above the floor. How much work must you do on it? Since 300 pounds must be raised one foot, 300×1, or 300 foot-pounds of work must be done. You can't make this weight any smaller by the use of any machine. However, if you use the eight-foot plank as shown, you can do that amount of work, by applying a smaller force through a longer distance. Notice that you have a mechanical advantage of 3, so that a 100-pound push down on the end of the plank will raise the 300-pound crate. How long of a distance will you have to exert that 100-pound push? Neglecting friction—and in this case you can safely do so—the work done on the machine is equal to the work done by the machine. Say it this way:

work put in = work put out

and since work = force × distance, you can substitute *"force times distance"* on each side of the work equation. Thus,

$$F_1 \text{ times } S_1 = F_2 \text{ times } S_2$$

in which

F_1	=	Effort applied, in pounds
S_1	=	Distance through which effort moves, in feet
F_2	=	Resistance overcome, in pounds

S_2 =   Distance resistance is moved, in feet

Now substitute the known values, and you obtain—

100 times S_1 = 300 times 1

S_1 = 3 feet

Figure 25B. Push 'em up

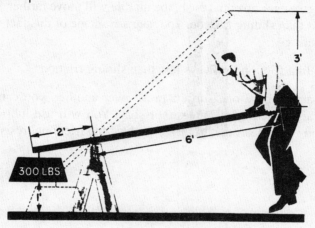

Friction

You are going to push a 400-pound crate up a 12-foot plank, the upper end of which is 3 feet higher than the lower end. You figure out that a 100-pound push will do the job, since the height the crate is to be raised is one-fourth of the distance through which you are exerting your push. The theoretical mechanical advantage is 4. Then you push 100 pounds worth and nothing happens! You've forgotten that there is friction between the surface of the crate and the surface of the plank. This friction acts as a resistance to the movement of the crate—and you must overcome this resistance to move the crate. In fact, you might have to push as much as 150 pounds to move it. Fifty pounds would be used to overcome the frictional resistance, and the remaining 100 pounds would be the useful push that would move the crate up the plank.

Friction is the resistance that one surface offers to its movement over another surface. The amount of friction depends upon the nature of the two surfaces and the forces that hold them together.

In many instances, friction is useful to you. Friction helps you hold back the crate from sliding down the inclined ramp. The cinders you throw under the wheels of your car when it's slipping on an icy pavement increase the friction. You wear rubber-soled shoes in the gym to keep from slipping. And locomotives carry a supply of sand, which can be dropped on the tracks in front of the driving wheels to increase the friction between the wheels and the track. Nails hold structures together because of the friction between the nails and the lumber.

When you are trying to stop or slow up an object in motion, when you want traction, and when you want to prevent motion from taking place, you make friction work for you. But when you want a machine to run smoothly and at high efficiency, you eliminate as much friction as possible by oiling and greasing bearings and honing and smoothing rubbing surfaces.

Wherever you apply force to cause motion, friction makes the actual mechanical advantage fall short of the theoretical mechanical advantage. Because of friction, you have to make a greater effort to overcome the resistance that you want to move. If you place a marble and a lump of sugar on a table and give each an equal push, the marble will move farther. This is because rolling friction is always less than sliding friction. You take advantage of this fact whenever you use ball bearings or roller bearings.

Remember that rolling friction is always less than sliding friction.

When it is necessary to have one surface move over another, you can decrease the friction by the use of lubricants, such as oil, grease, or soap. You will use lubricants on flat surfaces, as well as on ball and roller bearings, to further reduce the frictional resistance and to cut down the wear.

Power

It's all very well to talk about how much work a person can do, but the payoff is how long it takes that person to do it.

Power is the rate of doing work. Thus, power always includes the time element.

By formula, $\text{Power} = \dfrac{\text{Work, in ft-lb.}}{\text{Time, in minutes}}$

Horsepower

You measure force in pounds; distance in feet; work in foot-pounds. What is the common unit used for measuring power? The horsepower. If you want to tell someone how powerful an engine is, you could say that it is so many times more powerful than a man, or an ox, or a horse. But what man, and whose ox or horse? James Watt, the inventor of the steam engine, compared his early models with the horse. By experiment, he found that an average horse could lift a 330-pound load straight up through a distance of 100 feet in one minute. By agreement among scientists, that figure of 33,000 foot-pounds of work done in one minute has been accepted as the standard unit of power, and it is called a horsepower (hp).

Since there are 60 seconds in a minute, one horsepower is also equal to $\dfrac{33,000}{60} = 550$ foot-pounds per second. By formula $\text{Horsepower} = \dfrac{\text{Power (in ft-lb. per min.)}}{33,000}$

Force and Pressure

By this time you should have a pretty good idea of what a force is. A force is a push or a pull exerted on, or by, an object. You apply a force on a machine, and the machine in turn transmits a force to the load. Men and machines, however, are not the only things that can exert forces. If you've been out in a sailboat you know that the wind can exert a force. Further, you don't have to get knocked on your ear more than a couple of times by the waves to get the idea that water, too, can exert a force.

Measuring Forces

You've had a lot of experience in measuring forces. You can estimate or "guess" the weight of a package you're going to mail by "hefting" it. Or you can put it on a scale to find its weight accurately. Weight is a common term that tells you how much force or pull gravity is exerting on the object.

You can readily measure force with a spring scale. An Englishman named Hooke discovered that if you hang a 1-pound weight on a spring, the spring stretches a certain distance. A 2-pound weight will extend the spring just twice as far, and 3 pounds will lengthen it three times as far as the 1-pound weight. Right there is the makings of the spring scale. All you need to do is attach a pointer to the spring, put a face on the scale, and mark on the face the positions of the pointer for various loads in pounds or ounces.

This type of scale can be used to measure the pull of gravity—the weight—of an object, or the force of a pull exerted against friction. Unfortunately, springs get tired, just as you do. When they get old, they don't always snap back to the original position. Hence, an old spring or an overloaded spring will give inaccurate readings.

Honest Weight—No Springs

Because springs do get tired, other types of force-measuring devices are made. Perhaps you've seen the sign, "Honest Weight—No Springs," on some scales. Scales of this type are shown in Figure 26. They are applications of first-class levers. The one shown in Figure 26A is the simplest type. Since the distance from the fulcrum to the center of each platform is equal, the scale is balanced when equal weights are placed on the platforms. With your knowledge of levers, you will be able to figure out how the steelyard shown in Figure 26B operates.

Figure 26. Balances

A   B

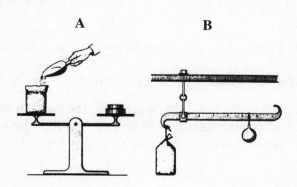

Pressure

Have you ever tried to walk on crusted snow that would break through when you put your weight on it? But you could walk on the same snow if you put on snowshoes. Further, you know that snowshoes do not reduce your weight—they merely distribute it over a larger area. In doing this, they reduce the pressure per square inch. Figure out how that works. If you weigh 160 pounds, that weight, or force, is more or less evenly distributed by the soles of your shoes. The area of the soles of an average man's shoes is roughly 60 square inches. Each one of those square inches has to carry $160 \div 60 = 2.6$ pounds of your weight. Since 2.6 pounds per square inch is too much for the snow crust, you break through.

When you put on the snowshoes, you distribute your weight over an area of approximately 900 sq. in.—depending, of course, on the size of the snowshoes. Now the force on each one of those square inches is equal to only $160 \div 900 = 0.18$ pound. The pressure on the snow has been decreased, and the snow can easily support you.

Pressure is force per unit area and is measured in pounds per square inch (psi). With showshoes on, you exert a pressure of 0.18 psi. To calculate pressure, divide the force by the area over which the force is applied. The formula is

$$\text{Pressure, in psi} = \frac{\text{Force, in lb.}}{\text{Area, in sq. in.}} \quad \text{Or, } P = \frac{F}{A}$$

To get this idea, follow this problem. A tank for holding fresh water is 10 feet long, 6 feet wide, and 4 feet deep. It holds, therefore, $10 \times 6 \times 4$, or 240 cubic feet of water. Each cubic foot of water weighs about 62.5 pounds. The total force tending to push the bottom out of the tank is equal to the weight of the water—240×62.5, or 15,000 lb. What is the pressure on the bottom?

Since the weight is evenly distributed on the bottom, you apply the formula $P = \dfrac{F}{A}$ and substitute the proper values for F and A. In this case, F = 15,000 lb., and the area of the bottom in square inches is $10 \times 6 \times 144$, since 144 sq. in. = 1 sq. ft.

$$P = \frac{15,000}{10 \times 6 \times 144} = 1.74 \text{ psi}$$

Now work out the idea in reverse. You live at the bottom of the great sea of air that surrounds the earth. Because the air has weight—gravity pulls on the air, too—the air exerts a force on every object that it surrounds. Near sea level that force on an area of 1 square inch is roughly 15 pounds. Thus, the air pressure at sea level is about 15 psi. The pressure gets less and less as you go up to higher altitudes.

With your finger, mark out an area of one square foot on your chest. What is the total force that tends to push in your chest? Again, use the formula $P = \dfrac{F}{A}$. Now substitute 15 psi for P, and for A use 144 sq. in. Then, F = 144 × 15, or 2,160 lb. The force on your chest is 2,160 lb. per square foot—more than a ton pushing against an area of 1 sq. ft. If there were no air inside your chest to push outward with the same pressure, you'd be squashed flat.

Measuring Pressure

Fluids, which include both liquids and gases, exert pressure. A fluid at rest exerts equal pressure in all directions.

In many jobs, it is necessary to know the pressure exerted by gas or a liquid. For example, it is important at all times to know the steam pressure inside of a boiler. One device to measure pressure is the Bourdon gage, shown in Figure 27. Its working principle is the same as that of those snakelike paper tubes that you get at a New Year's party. They straighten out when you blow into them.

In the Bourdon gage there is a thin-walled metal tube, somewhat flattened, and bent into the form of a C. Attached to its free end is a lever system that magnifies any motion of the free end of the tube. The fixed end of the gage ends in a fitting that is threaded into the boiler system so that the pressure in the boiler will be transmitted to the tube. Like the paper "snake," the metal tube tends to straighten out when the pressure inside it is increased. As the tube straightens, the pointer is made to move around the dial. The pressure, in psi, may be read directly on the dial.

Air pressure and pressures of steam and other gases, and fluid pressures in hydraulic systems, are generally measured in pounds per square inch. For convenience, however, the pressure exerted by water is commonly measured in pounds per square foot.

Figure 27. The Bourdon gage

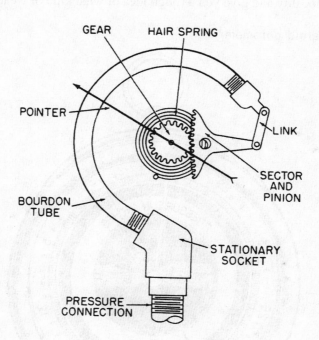

The Bourdon gage is a highly accurate but rather delicate instrument and can be very easily damaged. In addition, it develops trouble where pressure fluctuates rapidly. To overcome this, another type of gage, the Schrader, was developed. The Schrader gage is not as accurate as the

Bourdon but is sturdily constructed and quite suitable for ordinary hydraulic pressure measurements. It is especially recommended for fluctuating loads. In the Schrader gage, a piston is directly actuated by the liquid pressure to be measured, and moves up a cylinder against the resistance of a spring, carrying a bar or indicator with it over a calibrated scale. In this manner, all levers, gears, cams, and bearings are eliminated, and a sturdy instrument can be constructed.

Where accurate measurements of comparatively slight pressures are desired, a diaphragm type gage may be used. Diaphragm gages give sensitive and reliable indications of small pressure differences.

The Barometer

To the average person, the chief importance of weather is as an introduction to general conversation. But at sea and in the air, advance knowledge of what the weather will do is a matter of great concern to all hands. Operations are planned or cancelled on the basis of weather predictions. Accurate weather forecasts are made only after a great deal of information has been collected by many observers located over a wide area.

One of the instruments used in gathering weather data is the barometer. Remember, the air is pressing on you all the time. So-called normal atmospheric pressure is 14.7 psi. But as the weather changes, the air pressure may be greater or less than normal. If the air pressure is low in the area where you are, you know that air from one or more of the surrounding high-pressure areas is going to move in toward you. Moving air—or wind—is one of the most important factors in weather changes. In general, if you're in a low-pressure area you may expect wind, rain, and storms, while a high-pressure area generally enjoys clear weather. The barometer can tell you the air pressure in your locality and give you a rough idea of what kind of weather may be expected.

Figure 28. An aneroid barometer

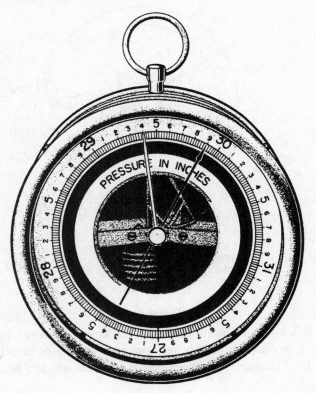

The aneroid barometer, shown in Figure 28, is an instrument that measures air pressure. It contains a thin-walled metal box from which most of the air has been pumped. A pointer is mechanically connected to the box by a lever system. If the pressure of the atmosphere increases, it tends to squeeze in the sides of the box. This squeeze causes the pointer to move toward the high-pressure end of the scale. If the pressure decreases, the sides of the box expand outward. This causes the pointer to move toward the low-pressure end of the dial.

Machine Elements and Basic Mechanisms

Machine Elements

Any machine, however simple, utilizes one or more basic machine elements or mechanisms in its makeup. In this section, we will take a look at some of the more familiar elements and mechanisms commonly used in machinery and equipment.

Bearings

Previously, we saw that whenever two objects rub against each other, friction is produced. If the surfaces are very smooth, there will be little friction; if either or both are rough, there will be more friction. *Friction* is the resistance to any force that tends to produce motion of one surface over another. When you are trying to start a loaded hand truck rolling, you have to give it a hard tug (to overcome the resistance of static friction) to get it started. Starting to slide the same load across the floor would require a harder push than starting it on rollers. That is because rolling friction is always less than sliding friction. To take advantage of this fact, rollers or bearings are used in machines to reduce friction. Lubricants on bearing surfaces reduce the friction even further.

A bearing is a support and guide that carries a moving part (or parts) of a machine and maintains the proper relationship between the moving part or parts and the stationary part. It usually permits only one form of motion, as rotation, and prevents any other. There are two basic types of bearings: sliding type (plain bearings), also called friction or guide bearings, and antifrictional type (roller and ball bearings).

Sliding Type (Plain) Bearings

In bearings of this type, a film of lubricant separates the moving part from the stationary part. There are three types of sliding motion bearings in common use: reciprocal motion bearings, journal bearings, and thrust bearings.

Reciprocal motion bearings provide a bearing surface on which an object slides back and forth. They are found on steam reciprocating pumps, where connecting rods slide on bearing surfaces near their connections to the pistons. Similar bearings are used on the connecting rods of large internal-combustion engines, and in many mechanisms operated by cams.

Journal bearings are used to guide and support revolving shafts. The shaft revolves in a housing fitted with a liner. The inside of the liner, on which the shaft bears, is made of babbitt metal or similar soft alloy (antifriction metal) to reduce friction. The soft metal is backed by a bronze or a copper layer, and that has a steel back for strength. Sometimes the bearing is made in two halves and is clamped or screwed around the shaft. It is also called a laminated sleeve bearing.

Thrust bearings are used on rotating shafts, such as those supporting bevel gears, worm gears, propellers, and fans. They are installed to resist axial thrust or force and to limit axial movement. They are used chiefly on heavy machinery.

Antifrictional or Roller and Ball Bearings

You may have had first-hand acquaintance with ball bearings when you were a child. They were what made your roller skates, skateboard, or bicycle wheels spin freely. If any of the little steel balls came out and were lost, your wheels screeched and groaned. The balls or rollers were of hard, highly-polished steel. The typical bearing consisted of two hardened steel rings (called *races*), the hardened steel balls or rollers, and a *separator*. The motion occurred between the race surfaces and the rolling elements. Ball bearings of this type have since been replaced by more modern antifrictional bearings.

Springs

Springs are elastic bodies (generally metal) that can be twisted, pulled, or stretched by some force and that have the ability to return to their original shape when the force is released. Springs used in machinery are generally made of metal—usually steel, though some are of phosphor bronze, brass, or other alloys. A part that is subject to constant spring thrust or pressure is said to be *spring loaded*. (Some components that appear to be spring-loaded are actually under hydraulic or pneumatic pressure or are moved by weights.)

Functions of Springs

Springs are used for many purposes, and one spring may serve more than one purpose. Listed below are some of the more common of these functional purposes. As you read them, try to think of at least one familiar application of each.

- To store energy for part of a functioning cycle
- To force a component to bear against, to maintain contact with, to engage, to disengage, or to remain clear of, some other component
- To counterbalance a weight or thrust (gravitational, hydraulic, etc.). Such springs are usually called equilibrator springs.
- To maintain electrical continuity
- To return a component to its original position after displacement
- To reduce shock or impact by gradually checking the motion of a moving weight
- To permit some freedom of movement between aligned components without disengaging them. These are sometimes called takeup springs.

Types of Springs

As you read different books, you will find that authors do not agree on classification of types of springs. The names are not as important as the types of work they can do and the loads they can bear. We may say there are three basic types: flat; spiral; and helical or coil.

Flat springs include various forms of elliptic or leaf springs (see Figure 29A(1 & 2)), made up of flat or slightly curved bars, plates, or leaves, and special flat springs (see Figure 29A(3)). A special flat spring is made from a flat strip or bar into whatever shape or design is calculated to be best suited for its position and purpose.

Spiral springs are sometimes called clock or power springs (see Figure 29B), and sometimes coil springs. A well-known example is a watch or clock spring, which is wound (tightened) and then gradually releases the power as it unwinds. Although there is good authority for calling this spring by other names, to avoid confusion we shall consistently call it *spiral*.

Helical springs, often called spiral, but not in this text (see Figure 29), are probably the most common type of spring. They may be used in compression (29D1), extension or tension (see Figure 29D2), or torsion (see Figure 29D3). A spring used in compression tends to shorten in action, while a tension spring lengthens in action. Torsion springs are made to transmit a twist instead of a direct pull and operate by coiling or uncoiling action.

In addition to straight helical springs, cone, double cone, keg, and volute springs are also classed as helical. These are usually used in compression. A cone spring (see Figure 29D4), often called a valve spring because it is frequently used in valves, is shaped by winding the wire on a tapered mandrel instead of a straight one. A double cone spring (not illustrated) is composed of two cones joined at the small ends, and a keg spring (not illustrated) is two cone springs joined at their large ends.

Figure 29. Types of springs

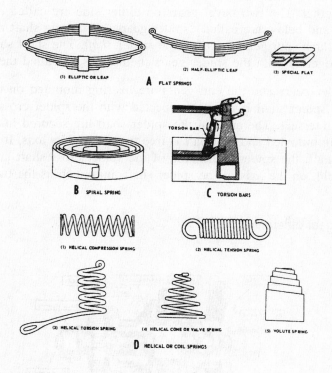

Volute springs (see Figure 29D5) are conical springs made from a flat bar, which is so wound that each coil partially overlaps the adjacent one. The width (and thickness) of the material gives it great strength or resistance.

A conical spring can be pressed flat so it requires little space, and it is not likely to buckle sidewise.

Torsion bars (see Figure 29C) are straight bars that are acted on by torsion (twisting force). The bar may be circular or rectangular in cross section, or less commonly in other shapes. It may also be a tube.

Basic Mechanisms

The Gear Differential

A gear differential is a mechanism that is capable of adding and subtracting mechanically. To be more precise, it adds the total revolution of two shafts—or subtracts the total revolutions of one shaft from the total revolutions of another shaft—and delivers the answer by positioning a third shaft. The gear differential will add or subtract any number of revolutions, or very small fractions of revolutions, continuously and accurately. It will produce a continuous series of answers as the inputs change.

Figure 30 is a cutaway drawing of a bevel gear differential showing all its parts and how they are related to each other. Grouped around the center of the mechanism are four bevel gears, meshed together. The two bevel gears on either side are called *end gears*. The two bevel gears above and below are called "spider gears." The long shaft running through the end gears and the three spur gears is called the *spider shaft*. The short shaft running through the spider gears, together with the spider gears themselves, is called the *spider*.

Each of the spider gears and the end gears are bearing mounted on their shafts and are free to rotate. The spider shaft is rigidly connected with the spider cross shaft at the center block where they intersect. The ends of the spider shaft are secured in flanges or hangers, but they are bearing mounted and the shaft is free to rotate on its axis. It follows then that to rotate the spider shaft, the spider, consisting of the spider cross shaft and the spider gears, must tumble, or spin, on the axis of the spider shaft, inasmuch as the two shafts are rigidly connected.

Figure 30. Bevel gear differential

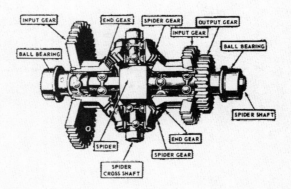

The three spur gears shown in Figure 30 are used to connect the two end gears and the spider shaft to other mechanisms. They may be of any convenient size. Each of the two input spur gears is attached to an end gear. An input gear and an end gear together are called a *side* of a differential. The third spur gear is the output gear, as designated in Figure 30. This is the only gear that is pinned to the spider shaft. All of the other gears, both bevel and spur, in the differential are bearing mounted.

Linkages

A linkage may consist of either one or a combination of the following four basic parts:

1. Rod, shaft, or plunger

2. Lever

3. Rocker arm

4. Bell crank

These parts combined are used to transmit limited rotary or linear motion. To change direction of a motion, cams are used with the linkage.

Lever-type linkages are used in equipment that has to be opened and closed; for instance, valves in electric-hydraulic systems, gates, clutches, clutch-solenoid interlocks, etc. Rocker arms are merely a variation, or special use, of levers.

Bell cranks are used primarily to transmit motion from a link traveling in one direction to another link, which is to be moved in a different direction. The bell crank is mounted on a fixed pivot, and the two links are connected at two points in different directions from the pivot. By properly locating the connection points, the output links can be made to move in any desired direction.

All linkages require occasional adjustments or repair, particularly when they become worn. To make the proper adjustments, a person must be familiar with the basic parts that constitute a linkage. Adjustments are normally made by lengthening or shortening the rods and shafts by means of a clevis or turnbuckle.

Couplings

In a broad sense, the term *coupling* applies to any device that holds two parts together. Line shafts that are made up of several shafts of different lengths may be held together by any of several types of shaft couplings. When shafts are very closely aligned, the sleeve coupling may be used. It consists of a metal tube slit at each end. The slit ends enable the clamps to fasten the sleeve securely to the shaft ends. With the clamps tightened, the shafts are held firmly together and turn as one shaft. The sleeve coupling also serves as a convenient device for making adjustments between units. The weight at the opposite end of the clamp from the screw is merely to offset the weight of the screw and clamp arms. By distributing the weight more evenly, shaft vibration is reduced.

A universal joint is the answer when two shafts not in the same plane must be coupled. Universal joints may have various forms. They are used in nearly all types and classes of machinery. An elementary universal joint, sometimes called a Hooke joint (see Figure 31), consists of two U-shaped yokes fastened to the ends of the shafts to be connected. Within these yokes is a cross-shaped part that holds the yokes together and allows each yoke to bend, or pivot, one with respect to the other. With this arrangement, one shaft can drive the other even though the angle between the two is as great as 25 degrees from alignment. Figure 32 shows a ring and trunnion type of universal joint. This is merely a slight modification of the old Hooke joint. This type is commonly used in automobile drive shaft systems. Two, and sometimes three, are utilized. Another type of universal joint is used where a smoother torque transmission is desired and less structural strength is required. This is the Bendix-Weiss universal joint (see Figure 33). In this type of joint, four large balls transmit the rotary force, with a smaller ball as a spacer. With the Hooke type of universal joint, a whipping motion occurs as the shafts rotate—the amount of whip depends on the degree of shaft misalignment. The Bendix-Weiss joint does not have this disadvantage; it transmits rotary motion with a constant angular velocity. This type of joint is both more expensive to manufacture and of less strength than the Hooke types, however.

Figure 31. Universal joint (Hooke type)   **Figure 32.** Ring and trunnion universal joint

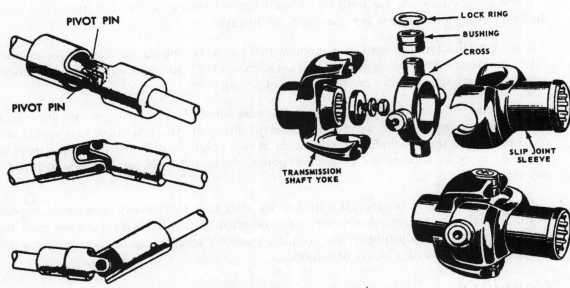

Figure 33. Bendix-Weiss universal joint

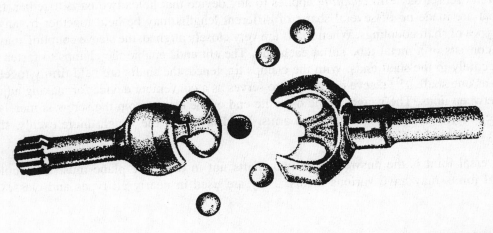

Cam and Cam Followers

A cam is a specially shaped surface, projection, or groove whose movement with respect to a part in contact with it (cam follower) drives the cam follower in another movement in response. A cam may be a projection on a revolving shaft (or on a wheel) for the purpose of changing the direction of motion from rotary to up-and-down, or vice versa. It may be a sliding piece or a groove to impart an eccentric motion. Some cams do not move at all but cause a change of motion in the contacting part. Cams are not ordinarily used to transmit power in the sense that gear trains are. They are generally used to modify mechanical movement, the power for which is furnished through other means. They may control other mechanical units, or lock together or synchronize two or more engaging units.

Clutches

Types

A clutch is a form of coupling that is designed to connect or disconnect a driving and a driven member for stopping or starting the driven part. There are two general classes of clutches—positive clutches and friction clutches.

Positive clutches have teeth that interlock. The simplest is the jaw or claw type (see Figure 34A), which is usable only at low speeds. The spiral claw or ratchet type (see Figure 34B) cannot be reversed. An example of a clutch is seen in bicycles—it engages the rear sprocket with the rear wheel when the pedals are pushed forward and lets the rear wheel revolve freely when the pedals are stopped.

Friction clutches. The object of a *friction clutch* is to connect a rotating member to one that is stationary, to bring it up to speed, and to transmit power with a minimum of slippage. Figure 34C shows a cone clutch commonly used in motor trucks. They may be single-cone or double-cone. Figure 34D shows a disc clutch, also used in autos. A disc clutch may also have a number of plates (multiple-disc clutch). In a series of discs, each driven disc is located between two driving discs. You may have had experience with a multiple-disc clutch on your car. The Hele-Shaw clutch is a combined conical-disc clutch (see Figure 34E). The groove permits circulation of oil, and cooling. Single-disc clutches are frequently dry clutches (no lubrication); multiple-disc clutches may be dry or wet (lubricated or run in oil).

Magnetic clutches are a recent development in which the friction surfaces are brought together by magnetic force when the electricity is turned on (see Figure 34F). The induction clutch transmits power without contact between driving and driven members.

Pneumatic and hydraulic clutches are used on diesel engines and transportation equipment (see Figure 34G).

Figure 34. Types of clutches.

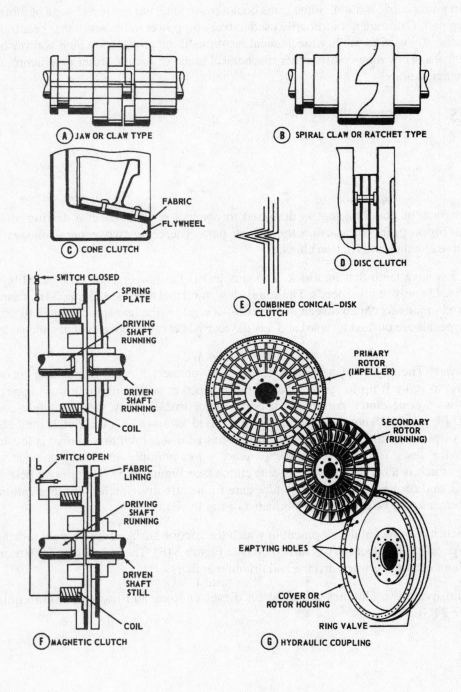

Sample Questions

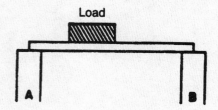

Load

1. Which post holds up the greater part of the load?

    1-A   Post A
    1-B   Post B
    1-C   Both equal
    1-D   Not clear

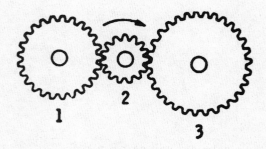

2. Which of the other gears is moving in the same direction as gear 2?

    2-A   Gear 1
    2-B   Gear 3
    2-C   Neither of the other gears
    2-D   Both of the other gears

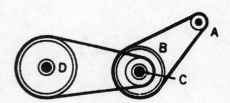

3. In this arrangement of pulleys, which pulley turns fastest?

    3-A   A
    3-B   B
    3-C   C
    3-D   D

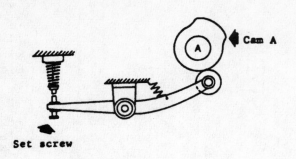

4. As cam A makes one complete turn, the setscrew will hit the contact point

    4-A   once.

    4-B   twice.

    4-C   three times.

    4-D   not at all.

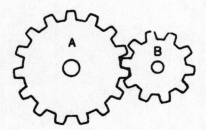

5. When gear A makes 14 revolutions, how many revolutions will gear B make?

    5-A   21

    5-B   17

    5-C   14

    5-D   9

6. If all of the following objects are at room temperature, which will feel coldest?

    6-A   Book

    6-B   Metal spoon

    6-C   Wooden chest

    6-D   Blanket

7. Liquid is being transferred from the barrel to the bucket by
    7-A   suction in the hose.
    7-B   fluid pressure in the hose.
    7-C   air pressure on top of the liquid.
    7-D   capillary action.

Answer Explanations

1-A   The weight is distributed more on the side of post A. Therefore, it is holding up the greatest part of the load.

2-C   Because of the way the gears are meshed, both gear 1 and gear 3 will move in the opposite direction of gear 2.

3-A   Pulley A is the smallest gear. Therefore, it must turn faster (make more revolutions per minute).

4-A   The single lobe on cam A will cause the setscrew to hit the contact point once during the cam's revolution.

5-A   Since gear A has 15 teeth and gear B has 10 teeth, gear A is 1.5 the size of gear B. Therefore, $14 \times 1.5 = 21$.

6-B   Metal will feel coldest out of paper, wood, and the fabric of a blanket.

7-D   Capillary action is the correct method to transfer liquid from the barrel to the bucket.

NUMERICAL OPERATIONS REVIEW

NOTE: This section may be eliminated from upcoming ASVAB tests. Check with your high school guidance counselor or recruiter for details.

The Numerical Operations section of the ASVAB test consists of 50 very simple arithmetic questions that must be answered in only 3 minutes. Speed is a very important factor since you only have about $3\frac{1}{2}$ seconds for each test item.

Do not attempt to compute these answers using pencil and scrap paper since it takes too much time. Instead, solve each problem in your head. If you are not sure of an answer, guess and go on to the next question. Do not skip any questions, since you will not have time to go back to fill in unanswered spaces. Since a wrong answer will not count against you, it does not hurt to guess.

Most people cannot complete all 50 questions in the 3 minutes allowed. Do not be upset if you cannot finish; just answer as many questions as you can. The four basic arithmetic operations are equally represented in this subtest. All questions are simple two-number problems and all numbers are either one- or two-digit whole numbers. The four basic arithmetic operations and their types of equations are:

1. Addition: indicated by the plus (+) sign

    12 + 5 =

2. Subtraction: indicated by the minus (–) sign

    9 – 3 =

3. Multiplication: indicated by the multiplication (×) sign

    8 × 4 =

4. Division: indicated by the division (÷) sign

    24 ÷ 6 =

Remember that Numerical Operations is a speed test. You must rapidly read the question, quickly determine the correct answer, immediately blacken the corresponding space on your answer sheet, and then go on to the next question and repeat the operation, working as fast as you can without making mistakes for the entire 3 minute period.

The following are 50 sample questions similar to those on the actual ASVAB test. Make believe that it is the real test. Time yourself or have someone time you to see how many questions you can answer within the allotted time of 3 minutes. An answer key is located after the questions.

1. 4 + 6 =
    1-A   8
    1-B   10
    1-C   12
    1-D   14

2. 8 − 5 =
    2-A   3
    2-B   4
    2-C   13
    2-D   17

3. 14 − 7 =
    3-A   3
    3-B   7
    3-C   8
    3-D   11

4. 12 ÷ 2 =
    4-A   4
    4-B   6
    4-C   8
    4-D   10

5. 1 + 1 =
    5-A   0
    5-B   1
    5-C   2
    5-D   11

6. 6 × 5 =
    6-A   11
    6-B   20
    6-C   25
    6-D   30

7. 6 + 6 =
    7-A   0
    7-B   1
    7-C   6
    7-D   12

8. 4 × 3 =
    8-A   7
    8-B   9
    8-C   12
    8-D   18

9. 12 ÷ 3 =
    9-A   3
    9-B   4
    9-C   15
    9-D   36

10. 4 × 5 =
    10-A   9
    10-B   12
    10-C   16
    10-D   20

11. 9 + 3 =
    11-A   3
    11-B   9
    11-C   12
    11-D   27

12. 7 + 5 =
    12-A   12
    12-B   14
    12-C   25
    12-D   35

13. 3 − 3 =
    13-A   0
    13-B   1
    13-C   2
    13-D   3

14. 7 + 6 =
    14-A   11
    14-B   12
    14-C   13
    14-D   14

15. $6 \div 2 =$
   - 15-A   3
   - 15-B   4
   - 15-C   8
   - 15-D   12

16. $4 \times 2 =$
   - 16-A   2
   - 16-B   4
   - 16-C   6
   - 16-D   8

17. $7 - 7 =$
   - 17-A   0
   - 17-B   1
   - 17-C   10
   - 17-D   14

18. $5 + 3 =$
   - 18-A   2
   - 18-B   8
   - 18-C   10
   - 18-D   15

19. $18 \div 6 =$
   - 19-A   3
   - 19-B   4
   - 19-C   12
   - 19-D   24

20. $1 - 1 =$
   - 20-A   0
   - 20-B   1
   - 20-C   2
   - 20-D   4

21. $3 \div 3 =$
   - 21-A   0
   - 21-B   1
   - 21-C   3
   - 21-D   9

22. $0 + 5 =$
   - 22-A   0
   - 22-B   1
   - 22-C   4
   - 22-D   5

23. $14 \div 2 =$
   - 23-A   7
   - 23-B   12
   - 23-C   16
   - 23-D   28

24. $2 \times 10 =$
   - 24-A   5
   - 24-B   12
   - 24-C   20
   - 24-D   22

25. $0 \times 3 =$
   - 25-A   0
   - 25-B   1
   - 25-C   3
   - 25-D   30

26. $8 - 4 =$
   - 26-A   2
   - 26-B   4
   - 26-C   10
   - 26-D   12

27. $7 \times 4 =$
   - 27-A   11
   - 27-B   28
   - 27-C   31
   - 27-D   35

28. $16 \div 4 =$
   - 28-A   4
   - 28-B   8
   - 28-C   12
   - 28-D   20

29. $15 \div 5 =$
   - 29-A   1
   - 29-B   3
   - 29-C   10
   - 29-D   20

30. $10 + 2 =$
   - 30-A   4
   - 30-B   5
   - 30-C   8
   - 30-D   12

31. $3 - 2 =$
    31-A   0
    31-B   1
    31-C   5
    31-D   6

32. $0 + 0 =$
    32-A   0
    32-B   1
    32-C   2
    32-D   3

33. $9 \times 4 =$
    33-A   13
    33-B   33
    33-C   36
    33-D   46

34. $2 - 1 =$
    34-A   1
    34-B   2
    34-C   3
    34-D   5

35. $14 - 12 =$
    35-A   2
    35-B   4
    35-C   24
    35-D   26

36. $5 \times 5 =$
    36-A   1
    36-B   10
    36-C   15
    36-D   25

37. $6 \times 6 =$
    37-A   12
    37-B   30
    37-C   36
    37-D   42

38. $11 \div 1 =$
    38-A   1
    38-B   10
    38-C   11
    38-D   12

39. $20 \div 2 =$
    39-A   10
    39-B   12
    39-C   18
    39-D   22

40. $9 - 1 =$
    40-A   3
    40-B   5
    40-C   6
    40-D   8

41. $8 \times 4 =$
    41-A   2
    41-B   12
    41-C   22
    41-D   32

42. $12 - 7 =$
    42-A   5
    42-B   7
    42-C   9
    42-D   11

43. $4 \times 8 =$
    43-A   4
    43-B   12
    43-C   32
    43-D   36

44. $3 + 8 =$
    44-A   5
    44-B   11
    44-C   21
    44-D   24

45. $13 + 1 =$
    45-A   12
    45-B   13
    45-C   14
    45-D   15

46. $7 \times 5 =$
    46-A   12
    46-B   25
    46-C   35
    46-D   45

47. 2 + 8 =

    47-A   4

    47-B   6

    47-C   8

    47-D   10

48. 2 + 9 =

    48-A   5

    48-B   7

    48-C   11

    48-D   18

49. $5 \div 1 =$

    49-A   1

    49-B   4

    49-C   5

    49-D   6

50. $30 \div 5 =$

    50-A   3

    50-B   4

    50-C   5

    50-D   6

Answer Key

1-B	2-A	3-B	4-B	5-C
6-D	7-D	8-C	9-B	10-D
11-C	12-A	13-A	14-C	15-A
16-D	17-A	18-B	19-A	20-A
21-B	22-D	23-A	24-C	25-A
26-B	27-B	28-A	29-B	30-D
31-B	32-A	33-C	34-A	35-A
36-D	37-C	38-C	39-A	40-D
41-D	42-A	43-C	44-B	45-C
46-C	47-D	48-C	49-C	50-D

CODING SPEED REVIEW

NOTE: This section may be eliminated from upcoming ASVAB tests. Check with your high school guidance counselor or recruiter for details.

Ability to understand and use simple coding is often required by both civilian and military personnel. The numerical index in filing arranges records based on code numbers. The Dewey decimal classification in libraries uses code numbers to arrange nonfiction books on the library shelves. Coding is also used on price tags of merchandise sold in retail stores.

The Coding Speed section of the ASVAB tests for skill in using simple codes quickly and accurately. It is a speed test requiring you to match four-digit numbers with commonly used words listed in a key as quickly and accurately as possible.

The subtest consists of 84 items, which must be answered in only 7 minutes. Speed is very important, since you only have about five seconds for each test item. Most people are not able to complete all 85 items in 7 minutes. Do not be upset if you cannot finish within the allotted time. Just answer as many questions as you can.

Before each set of questions you will find a "key." The key consists of ten words listed in alphabetical order. Each word has a four-digit code number assigned to it.

In the set of questions you will find the same ten words, scrambled and sometimes repeated. Following each word in the test are *five* answer choices in columns labeled "A" to "E." The answer choices are four-digit numbers and are in ascending order. In other words, the lowest number is always in column A, the next higher number is in column B, and so on to the highest number in column E. First, look at the word. Then find the correct code number among the choices, and mark the letter of the column in which you found the correct code number on your answer sheet.

To illustrate, try the sample test items on the next page. Tips on finding the correct codes and an answer key are listed beneath the questions.

Sample Questions

Key

game ... 6456	hat 1413	man 3451	salt 4586
green ... 2715	house ... 2859	room ... 2864	tree 5972

Questions		Options				
		A	B	C	D	E
1.	room	1413	2715	2864	3451	4586
2.	green	2715	2864	3451	4586	5972
3.	tree	1413	2715	3451	4586	5972
4.	hat	1413	2715	3451	4586	5972
5.	room	1413	2864	3451	4586	5972
6.	house	1413	2859	4586	5972	6456
7.	man	2715	2864	3451	4586	5972
8.	game	2859	2864	4586	5972	6456
9.	salt	2859	2864	3451	4586	5972
10.	tree	2864	3451	4586	5972	6456

Note that each of the questions is one of the words in the key table. To the right of each question are possible answers listed under the letters A, B, C, D, and E. The word in Question 1 is *room*. By looking at the key, you will see that the code number for *room* is 2864. Of the five possible answers for Question 1, 2864 is listed under C, so C would be marked on the answer form for Question 1. As you can see, the correct answer for 2 *green* is A, 3 *tree* is E, 4 *hat* is A, 5 *room* is B, 6 *house* is B, 7 *man* is C, 8 *game* is E, 9 *salt* is D, and 10 *tree* is D.

Answer Key				
1-C	2-A	3-E	4-A	5-B
6-B	7-C	8-E	9-D	10-D

Coding is not only a test of your memory and your eye-hand coordination, it is a test of your working speed. Quickly read the question, determine the correct answer, immediately blacken the corresponding space on your answer sheet, and go on to the next question and repeat this process again, working as fast as you can without making mistakes during the 7-minute period.

The following are additional sample questions similar to those on the actual ASVAB. Make believe that it is the real test. Since you are given 7- minutes to answer 84 questions, your allotted time for 12 questions is one minute per question. Time yourself or have someone time you to see how many of the 12 questions you can answer within the allotted time of one minute.

The answer key appears at the end of the set of 12 sample questions.

Key

| bargain ...... 8385 | game .... 6456 | knife .... 7150 | owner ....6227 | sofa........... 9645 |
| chin .... 8930 | house .... 2859 | music .... 1117 | point ....4703 | sunshine ... 7489 |

Questions		Options					
		A	B	C	D	E	
1.	game	6456	7150	8385	8930	9645	1 (A) (B) (C) (D)
2.	knife	1117	6456	7150	7489	8385	2 (A) (B) (C) (D)
3.	bargain	2859	6227	7489	8385	9645	3 (A) (B) (C) (D)
4.	chin	2859	4703	8385	8930	9645	4 (A) (B) (C) (D)
5.	house	1117	2859	6227	7150	7489	5 (A) (B) (C) (D)
6.	sofa	7150	7489	8385	8930	9645	6 (A) (B) (C) (D)
7.	owner	4703	6227	6456	7150	8930	7 (A) (B) (C) (D)
8.	music	1117	2859	7489	8385	9645	8 (A) (B) (C) (D)
9.	knife	6227	6456	7150	7489	8385	9 (A) (B) (C) (D)
10.	sunshine	4703	6227	6456	7489	8930	10 (A) (B) (C) (D)
11.	chin	1117	2859	4703	7150	8930	11 (A) (B) (C) (D)
12.	point	1117	4703	6227	6456	7150	12 (A) (B) (C) (D)

Answer Key

1-A	2-C	3-D	4-D	5-B
6-E	7-B	8-A	9-C	10-D
11-E	12-B			

Note that in the set of 12 sample questions, only the first two digits of the four-digit number is needed to identify the word. In such case, it would save time and effort to check the first two digits only instead of the entire number.

SECOND ASVAB TEST BATTERY

You completed your first battery, pinpointed your strengths and weaknesses, completed subject reviews, and are now prepared to take another sample test battery. Keep in mind that the more test batteries you take, the more confident you will be on your actual test day.

Here are the guidelines again to help you make the most of this sample test battery:

- Take this test under "real" test conditions (time yourself, take it in a quiet room without distractions, and use the sample answer sheets).

- Time each test carefully and do not go over the time allotted for each section.

- Use the answer keys to get your test scores and to evaluate your performance on each test.

- Record the number of items you answered correctly and incorrectly for each section in the answer chart provided at the end of the battery. Also, record the number of items you want to review further or were unsure about.

- Carefully review and understand the answer explanations to all questions you answered incorrectly.

- Don't forget to review each of the questions that you answered correctly but may not be sure of. This is a necessary step to gain the knowledge and expertise you need to get the highest scores possible on the real ASVAB tests.

- Transfer your scores for each section of the First ASVAB Sample Test Battery to the Self-Appraisal Chart appearing on page 24. This will enable you to track your progress as you continue to prepare for the actual test.

- Use the sample answer sheets provided to record your answers. If you want, you can cut them out to make them easier to use and to simulate actual test conditions.

Specimen Answer Sheet for Answering Parts 1–10
(On the following page)

Part 1: General Science

1. Ⓐ Ⓑ Ⓒ Ⓓ   2. Ⓐ Ⓑ Ⓒ Ⓓ   3. Ⓐ Ⓑ Ⓒ Ⓓ   4. Ⓐ Ⓑ Ⓒ Ⓓ   5. Ⓐ Ⓑ Ⓒ Ⓓ
6. Ⓐ Ⓑ Ⓒ Ⓓ   7. Ⓐ Ⓑ Ⓒ Ⓓ   8. Ⓐ Ⓑ Ⓒ Ⓓ   9. Ⓐ Ⓑ Ⓒ Ⓓ   10. Ⓐ Ⓑ Ⓒ Ⓓ
11. Ⓐ Ⓑ Ⓒ Ⓓ   12. Ⓐ Ⓑ Ⓒ Ⓓ   13. Ⓐ Ⓑ Ⓒ Ⓓ   14. Ⓐ Ⓑ Ⓒ Ⓓ   15. Ⓐ Ⓑ Ⓒ Ⓓ
16. Ⓐ Ⓑ Ⓒ Ⓓ   17. Ⓐ Ⓑ Ⓒ Ⓓ   18. Ⓐ Ⓑ Ⓒ Ⓓ   19. Ⓐ Ⓑ Ⓒ Ⓓ   20. Ⓐ Ⓑ Ⓒ Ⓓ
21. Ⓐ Ⓑ Ⓒ Ⓓ   22. Ⓐ Ⓑ Ⓒ Ⓓ   23. Ⓐ Ⓑ Ⓒ Ⓓ   24. Ⓐ Ⓑ Ⓒ Ⓓ   25. Ⓐ Ⓑ Ⓒ Ⓓ

Part 2: Arithmetic Reasoning

1. Ⓐ Ⓑ Ⓒ Ⓓ   2. Ⓐ Ⓑ Ⓒ Ⓓ   3. Ⓐ Ⓑ Ⓒ Ⓓ   4. Ⓐ Ⓑ Ⓒ Ⓓ   5. Ⓐ Ⓑ Ⓒ Ⓓ
6. Ⓐ Ⓑ Ⓒ Ⓓ   7. Ⓐ Ⓑ Ⓒ Ⓓ   8. Ⓐ Ⓑ Ⓒ Ⓓ   9. Ⓐ Ⓑ Ⓒ Ⓓ   10. Ⓐ Ⓑ Ⓒ Ⓓ
11. Ⓐ Ⓑ Ⓒ Ⓓ   12. Ⓐ Ⓑ Ⓒ Ⓓ   13. Ⓐ Ⓑ Ⓒ Ⓓ   14. Ⓐ Ⓑ Ⓒ Ⓓ   15. Ⓐ Ⓑ Ⓒ Ⓓ
16. Ⓐ Ⓑ Ⓒ Ⓓ   17. Ⓐ Ⓑ Ⓒ Ⓓ   18. Ⓐ Ⓑ Ⓒ Ⓓ   19. Ⓐ Ⓑ Ⓒ Ⓓ   20. Ⓐ Ⓑ Ⓒ Ⓓ
21. Ⓐ Ⓑ Ⓒ Ⓓ   22. Ⓐ Ⓑ Ⓒ Ⓓ   23. Ⓐ Ⓑ Ⓒ Ⓓ   24. Ⓐ Ⓑ Ⓒ Ⓓ   25. Ⓐ Ⓑ Ⓒ Ⓓ
26. Ⓐ Ⓑ Ⓒ Ⓓ   27. Ⓐ Ⓑ Ⓒ Ⓓ   28. Ⓐ Ⓑ Ⓒ Ⓓ   29. Ⓐ Ⓑ Ⓒ Ⓓ   30. Ⓐ Ⓑ Ⓒ Ⓓ

Part 3: Word Knowledge

1. Ⓐ Ⓑ Ⓒ Ⓓ   2. Ⓐ Ⓑ Ⓒ Ⓓ   3. Ⓐ Ⓑ Ⓒ Ⓓ   4. Ⓐ Ⓑ Ⓒ Ⓓ   5. Ⓐ Ⓑ Ⓒ Ⓓ
6. Ⓐ Ⓑ Ⓒ Ⓓ   7. Ⓐ Ⓑ Ⓒ Ⓓ   8. Ⓐ Ⓑ Ⓒ Ⓓ   9. Ⓐ Ⓑ Ⓒ Ⓓ   10. Ⓐ Ⓑ Ⓒ Ⓓ
11. Ⓐ Ⓑ Ⓒ Ⓓ   12. Ⓐ Ⓑ Ⓒ Ⓓ   13. Ⓐ Ⓑ Ⓒ Ⓓ   14. Ⓐ Ⓑ Ⓒ Ⓓ   15. Ⓐ Ⓑ Ⓒ Ⓓ
16. Ⓐ Ⓑ Ⓒ Ⓓ   17. Ⓐ Ⓑ Ⓒ Ⓓ   18. Ⓐ Ⓑ Ⓒ Ⓓ   19. Ⓐ Ⓑ Ⓒ Ⓓ   20. Ⓐ Ⓑ Ⓒ Ⓓ
21. Ⓐ Ⓑ Ⓒ Ⓓ   22. Ⓐ Ⓑ Ⓒ Ⓓ   23. Ⓐ Ⓑ Ⓒ Ⓓ   24. Ⓐ Ⓑ Ⓒ Ⓓ   25. Ⓐ Ⓑ Ⓒ Ⓓ
26. Ⓐ Ⓑ Ⓒ Ⓓ   27. Ⓐ Ⓑ Ⓒ Ⓓ   28. Ⓐ Ⓑ Ⓒ Ⓓ   29. Ⓐ Ⓑ Ⓒ Ⓓ   30. Ⓐ Ⓑ Ⓒ Ⓓ
31. Ⓐ Ⓑ Ⓒ Ⓓ   32. Ⓐ Ⓑ Ⓒ Ⓓ   33. Ⓐ Ⓑ Ⓒ Ⓓ   34. Ⓐ Ⓑ Ⓒ Ⓓ   35. Ⓐ Ⓑ Ⓒ Ⓓ

Part 4: Paragraph Comprehension

1. Ⓐ Ⓑ Ⓒ Ⓓ   2. Ⓐ Ⓑ Ⓒ Ⓓ   3. Ⓐ Ⓑ Ⓒ Ⓓ   4. Ⓐ Ⓑ Ⓒ Ⓓ   5. Ⓐ Ⓑ Ⓒ Ⓓ
6. Ⓐ Ⓑ Ⓒ Ⓓ   7. Ⓐ Ⓑ Ⓒ Ⓓ   8. Ⓐ Ⓑ Ⓒ Ⓓ   9. Ⓐ Ⓑ Ⓒ Ⓓ   10. Ⓐ Ⓑ Ⓒ Ⓓ
11. Ⓐ Ⓑ Ⓒ Ⓓ   12. Ⓐ Ⓑ Ⓒ Ⓓ   13. Ⓐ Ⓑ Ⓒ Ⓓ   14. Ⓐ Ⓑ Ⓒ Ⓓ   15. Ⓐ Ⓑ Ⓒ Ⓓ

Part 5: Mathematics Knowledge

1. Ⓐ Ⓑ Ⓒ Ⓓ   2. Ⓐ Ⓑ Ⓒ Ⓓ   3. Ⓐ Ⓑ Ⓒ Ⓓ   4. Ⓐ Ⓑ Ⓒ Ⓓ   5. Ⓐ Ⓑ Ⓒ Ⓓ
6. Ⓐ Ⓑ Ⓒ Ⓓ   7. Ⓐ Ⓑ Ⓒ Ⓓ   8. Ⓐ Ⓑ Ⓒ Ⓓ   9. Ⓐ Ⓑ Ⓒ Ⓓ   10. Ⓐ Ⓑ Ⓒ Ⓓ
11. Ⓐ Ⓑ Ⓒ Ⓓ   12. Ⓐ Ⓑ Ⓒ Ⓓ   13. Ⓐ Ⓑ Ⓒ Ⓓ   14. Ⓐ Ⓑ Ⓒ Ⓓ   15. Ⓐ Ⓑ Ⓒ Ⓓ
16. Ⓐ Ⓑ Ⓒ Ⓓ   17. Ⓐ Ⓑ Ⓒ Ⓓ   18. Ⓐ Ⓑ Ⓒ Ⓓ   19. Ⓐ Ⓑ Ⓒ Ⓓ   20. Ⓐ Ⓑ Ⓒ Ⓓ
21. Ⓐ Ⓑ Ⓒ Ⓓ   22. Ⓐ Ⓑ Ⓒ Ⓓ   23. Ⓐ Ⓑ Ⓒ Ⓓ   24. Ⓐ Ⓑ Ⓒ Ⓓ   25. Ⓐ Ⓑ Ⓒ Ⓓ

Part 6: Electronics Information

1. Ⓐ Ⓑ Ⓒ Ⓓ   2. Ⓐ Ⓑ Ⓒ Ⓓ   3. Ⓐ Ⓑ Ⓒ Ⓓ   4. Ⓐ Ⓑ Ⓒ Ⓓ   5. Ⓐ Ⓑ Ⓒ Ⓓ
6. Ⓐ Ⓑ Ⓒ Ⓓ   7. Ⓐ Ⓑ Ⓒ Ⓓ   8. Ⓐ Ⓑ Ⓒ Ⓓ   9. Ⓐ Ⓑ Ⓒ Ⓓ   10. Ⓐ Ⓑ Ⓒ Ⓓ
11. Ⓐ Ⓑ Ⓒ Ⓓ   12. Ⓐ Ⓑ Ⓒ Ⓓ   13. Ⓐ Ⓑ Ⓒ Ⓓ   14. Ⓐ Ⓑ Ⓒ Ⓓ   15. Ⓐ Ⓑ Ⓒ Ⓓ
16. Ⓐ Ⓑ Ⓒ Ⓓ   17. Ⓐ Ⓑ Ⓒ Ⓓ   18. Ⓐ Ⓑ Ⓒ Ⓓ   19. Ⓐ Ⓑ Ⓒ Ⓓ   20. Ⓐ Ⓑ Ⓒ Ⓓ

Part 7: Auto & Shop Information Review

1. Ⓐ Ⓑ Ⓒ Ⓓ   2. Ⓐ Ⓑ Ⓒ Ⓓ   3. Ⓐ Ⓑ Ⓒ Ⓓ   4. Ⓐ Ⓑ Ⓒ Ⓓ   5. Ⓐ Ⓑ Ⓒ Ⓓ
6. Ⓐ Ⓑ Ⓒ Ⓓ   7. Ⓐ Ⓑ Ⓒ Ⓓ   8. Ⓐ Ⓑ Ⓒ Ⓓ   9. Ⓐ Ⓑ Ⓒ Ⓓ   10. Ⓐ Ⓑ Ⓒ Ⓓ
11. Ⓐ Ⓑ Ⓒ Ⓓ   12. Ⓐ Ⓑ Ⓒ Ⓓ   13. Ⓐ Ⓑ Ⓒ Ⓓ   14. Ⓐ Ⓑ Ⓒ Ⓓ   15. Ⓐ Ⓑ Ⓒ Ⓓ
16. Ⓐ Ⓑ Ⓒ Ⓓ   17. Ⓐ Ⓑ Ⓒ Ⓓ   18. Ⓐ Ⓑ Ⓒ Ⓓ   19. Ⓐ Ⓑ Ⓒ Ⓓ   20. Ⓐ Ⓑ Ⓒ Ⓓ
21. Ⓐ Ⓑ Ⓒ Ⓓ   22. Ⓐ Ⓑ Ⓒ Ⓓ   23. Ⓐ Ⓑ Ⓒ Ⓓ   24. Ⓐ Ⓑ Ⓒ Ⓓ   25. Ⓐ Ⓑ Ⓒ Ⓓ

Part 8: Mechanical Comprehension Review

1. Ⓐ Ⓑ Ⓒ Ⓓ   2. Ⓐ Ⓑ Ⓒ Ⓓ   3. Ⓐ Ⓑ Ⓒ Ⓓ   4. Ⓐ Ⓑ Ⓒ Ⓓ   5. Ⓐ Ⓑ Ⓒ Ⓓ
6. Ⓐ Ⓑ Ⓒ Ⓓ   7. Ⓐ Ⓑ Ⓒ Ⓓ   8. Ⓐ Ⓑ Ⓒ Ⓓ   9. Ⓐ Ⓑ Ⓒ Ⓓ   10. Ⓐ Ⓑ Ⓒ Ⓓ
11. Ⓐ Ⓑ Ⓒ Ⓓ   12. Ⓐ Ⓑ Ⓒ Ⓓ   13. Ⓐ Ⓑ Ⓒ Ⓓ   14. Ⓐ Ⓑ Ⓒ Ⓓ   15. Ⓐ Ⓑ Ⓒ Ⓓ
16. Ⓐ Ⓑ Ⓒ Ⓓ   17. Ⓐ Ⓑ Ⓒ Ⓓ   18. Ⓐ Ⓑ Ⓒ Ⓓ   19. Ⓐ Ⓑ Ⓒ Ⓓ   20. Ⓐ Ⓑ Ⓒ Ⓓ
21. Ⓐ Ⓑ Ⓒ Ⓓ   22. Ⓐ Ⓑ Ⓒ Ⓓ   23. Ⓐ Ⓑ Ⓒ Ⓓ   24. Ⓐ Ⓑ Ⓒ Ⓓ   25. Ⓐ Ⓑ Ⓒ Ⓓ

Part 9: Numerical Operations

1. Ⓐ Ⓑ Ⓒ Ⓓ 2. Ⓐ Ⓑ Ⓒ Ⓓ 3. Ⓐ Ⓑ Ⓒ Ⓓ 4. Ⓐ Ⓑ Ⓒ Ⓓ 5. Ⓐ Ⓑ Ⓒ Ⓓ
6. Ⓐ Ⓑ Ⓒ Ⓓ 7. Ⓐ Ⓑ Ⓒ Ⓓ 8. Ⓐ Ⓑ Ⓒ Ⓓ 9. Ⓐ Ⓑ Ⓒ Ⓓ 10. Ⓐ Ⓑ Ⓒ Ⓓ
11. Ⓐ Ⓑ Ⓒ Ⓓ 12. Ⓐ Ⓑ Ⓒ Ⓓ 13. Ⓐ Ⓑ Ⓒ Ⓓ 14. Ⓐ Ⓑ Ⓒ Ⓓ 15. Ⓐ Ⓑ Ⓒ Ⓓ
16. Ⓐ Ⓑ Ⓒ Ⓓ 17. Ⓐ Ⓑ Ⓒ Ⓓ 18. Ⓐ Ⓑ Ⓒ Ⓓ 19. Ⓐ Ⓑ Ⓒ Ⓓ 20. Ⓐ Ⓑ Ⓒ Ⓓ
21. Ⓐ Ⓑ Ⓒ Ⓓ 22. Ⓐ Ⓑ Ⓒ Ⓓ 23. Ⓐ Ⓑ Ⓒ Ⓓ 24. Ⓐ Ⓑ Ⓒ Ⓓ 25. Ⓐ Ⓑ Ⓒ Ⓓ
26. Ⓐ Ⓑ Ⓒ Ⓓ 27. Ⓐ Ⓑ Ⓒ Ⓓ 28. Ⓐ Ⓑ Ⓒ Ⓓ 29. Ⓐ Ⓑ Ⓒ Ⓓ 30. Ⓐ Ⓑ Ⓒ Ⓓ
31. Ⓐ Ⓑ Ⓒ Ⓓ 32. Ⓐ Ⓑ Ⓒ Ⓓ 33. Ⓐ Ⓑ Ⓒ Ⓓ 34. Ⓐ Ⓑ Ⓒ Ⓓ 35. Ⓐ Ⓑ Ⓒ Ⓓ
36. Ⓐ Ⓑ Ⓒ Ⓓ 37. Ⓐ Ⓑ Ⓒ Ⓓ 38. Ⓐ Ⓑ Ⓒ Ⓓ 39. Ⓐ Ⓑ Ⓒ Ⓓ 40. Ⓐ Ⓑ Ⓒ Ⓓ
41. Ⓐ Ⓑ Ⓒ Ⓓ 42. Ⓐ Ⓑ Ⓒ Ⓓ 43. Ⓐ Ⓑ Ⓒ Ⓓ 44. Ⓐ Ⓑ Ⓒ Ⓓ 45. Ⓐ Ⓑ Ⓒ Ⓓ
46. Ⓐ Ⓑ Ⓒ Ⓓ 47. Ⓐ Ⓑ Ⓒ Ⓓ 48. Ⓐ Ⓑ Ⓒ Ⓓ 49. Ⓐ Ⓑ Ⓒ Ⓓ 50. Ⓐ Ⓑ Ⓒ Ⓓ

Part 10: Coding Speed

1. Ⓐ Ⓑ Ⓒ Ⓓ 2. Ⓐ Ⓑ Ⓒ Ⓓ 3. Ⓐ Ⓑ Ⓒ Ⓓ 4. Ⓐ Ⓑ Ⓒ Ⓓ 5. Ⓐ Ⓑ Ⓒ Ⓓ
6. Ⓐ Ⓑ Ⓒ Ⓓ 7. Ⓐ Ⓑ Ⓒ Ⓓ 8. Ⓐ Ⓑ Ⓒ Ⓓ 9. Ⓐ Ⓑ Ⓒ Ⓓ 10. Ⓐ Ⓑ Ⓒ Ⓓ
11. Ⓐ Ⓑ Ⓒ Ⓓ 12. Ⓐ Ⓑ Ⓒ Ⓓ 13. Ⓐ Ⓑ Ⓒ Ⓓ 14. Ⓐ Ⓑ Ⓒ Ⓓ 15. Ⓐ Ⓑ Ⓒ Ⓓ
16. Ⓐ Ⓑ Ⓒ Ⓓ 17. Ⓐ Ⓑ Ⓒ Ⓓ 18. Ⓐ Ⓑ Ⓒ Ⓓ 19. Ⓐ Ⓑ Ⓒ Ⓓ 20. Ⓐ Ⓑ Ⓒ Ⓓ
21. Ⓐ Ⓑ Ⓒ Ⓓ 22. Ⓐ Ⓑ Ⓒ Ⓓ 23. Ⓐ Ⓑ Ⓒ Ⓓ 24. Ⓐ Ⓑ Ⓒ Ⓓ 25. Ⓐ Ⓑ Ⓒ Ⓓ
26. Ⓐ Ⓑ Ⓒ Ⓓ 27. Ⓐ Ⓑ Ⓒ Ⓓ 28. Ⓐ Ⓑ Ⓒ Ⓓ 29. Ⓐ Ⓑ Ⓒ Ⓓ 30. Ⓐ Ⓑ Ⓒ Ⓓ
31. Ⓐ Ⓑ Ⓒ Ⓓ 32. Ⓐ Ⓑ Ⓒ Ⓓ 33. Ⓐ Ⓑ Ⓒ Ⓓ 34. Ⓐ Ⓑ Ⓒ Ⓓ 35. Ⓐ Ⓑ Ⓒ Ⓓ
36. Ⓐ Ⓑ Ⓒ Ⓓ 37. Ⓐ Ⓑ Ⓒ Ⓓ 38. Ⓐ Ⓑ Ⓒ Ⓓ 39. Ⓐ Ⓑ Ⓒ Ⓓ 40. Ⓐ Ⓑ Ⓒ Ⓓ
41. Ⓐ Ⓑ Ⓒ Ⓓ 42. Ⓐ Ⓑ Ⓒ Ⓓ 43. Ⓐ Ⓑ Ⓒ Ⓓ 44. Ⓐ Ⓑ Ⓒ Ⓓ 45. Ⓐ Ⓑ Ⓒ Ⓓ
46. Ⓐ Ⓑ Ⓒ Ⓓ 47. Ⓐ Ⓑ Ⓒ Ⓓ 48. Ⓐ Ⓑ Ⓒ Ⓓ 49. Ⓐ Ⓑ Ⓒ Ⓓ 50. Ⓐ Ⓑ Ⓒ Ⓓ
51. Ⓐ Ⓑ Ⓒ Ⓓ 52. Ⓐ Ⓑ Ⓒ Ⓓ 53. Ⓐ Ⓑ Ⓒ Ⓓ 54. Ⓐ Ⓑ Ⓒ Ⓓ 55. Ⓐ Ⓑ Ⓒ Ⓓ
56. Ⓐ Ⓑ Ⓒ Ⓓ 57. Ⓐ Ⓑ Ⓒ Ⓓ 58. Ⓐ Ⓑ Ⓒ Ⓓ 59. Ⓐ Ⓑ Ⓒ Ⓓ 60. Ⓐ Ⓑ Ⓒ Ⓓ
61. Ⓐ Ⓑ Ⓒ Ⓓ 62. Ⓐ Ⓑ Ⓒ Ⓓ 63. Ⓐ Ⓑ Ⓒ Ⓓ 64. Ⓐ Ⓑ Ⓒ Ⓓ 65. Ⓐ Ⓑ Ⓒ Ⓓ
66. Ⓐ Ⓑ Ⓒ Ⓓ 67. Ⓐ Ⓑ Ⓒ Ⓓ 68. Ⓐ Ⓑ Ⓒ Ⓓ 69. Ⓐ Ⓑ Ⓒ Ⓓ 70. Ⓐ Ⓑ Ⓒ Ⓓ
71. Ⓐ Ⓑ Ⓒ Ⓓ 72. Ⓐ Ⓑ Ⓒ Ⓓ 73. Ⓐ Ⓑ Ⓒ Ⓓ 74. Ⓐ Ⓑ Ⓒ Ⓓ 75. Ⓐ Ⓑ Ⓒ Ⓓ
76. Ⓐ Ⓑ Ⓒ Ⓓ 77. Ⓐ Ⓑ Ⓒ Ⓓ 78. Ⓐ Ⓑ Ⓒ Ⓓ 79. Ⓐ Ⓑ Ⓒ Ⓓ 80. Ⓐ Ⓑ Ⓒ Ⓓ
81. Ⓐ Ⓑ Ⓒ Ⓓ 82. Ⓐ Ⓑ Ⓒ Ⓓ 83. Ⓐ Ⓑ Ⓒ Ⓓ 84. Ⓐ Ⓑ Ⓒ Ⓓ

PART 1: GENERAL SCIENCE

Directions

This is a test of 25 questions to find out how much you know about general science as usually covered in high school courses. Pick the best answer for each question, then blacken the space on your answer form that has the same number and letter as your choice.

Here are three sample questions.

S1. Water is an example of a   Ⓐ Ⓑ Ⓒ Ⓓ
    S1-A   solid.
    S1-B   gas.
    S1-C   liquid.
    S1-D   crystal.

Now look at the section of your answer sheet labeled Part 1, *"Practice."* Notice that answer space C has been marked for question 1. Now do practice questions 2 and 3 by yourself. Find the correct answer to the question, then mark the space on your answer form that has the same letter as the answer you picked. Do this now.

S2. Lack of iodine is often related to which of the following diseases?   Ⓐ Ⓑ Ⓒ Ⓓ
    S2-A   Beriberi
    S2-B   Scurvy
    S2-C   Rickets
    S2-D   Goiter

S3. An eclipse of the sun throws the shadow of the   Ⓐ Ⓑ Ⓒ Ⓓ
    S3-A   earth on the moon.
    S3-B   moon on the earth.
    S3-C   moon on the sun.
    S3-D   earth on the sun.

You should have marked choice D for question 2 and choice B for question 3. If you made any mistakes, erase your mark carefully and blacken the correct answer space. Do this now.

Your score on this test will be based on the number of questions you answer correctly. You should try to answer every question. Do not spend too much time on any one question.

When you begin, be sure to start with question number 1 of Part 1 of your test booklet and number 1 in Part 1 on your answer form.

DO NOT CONTINUE UNTIL TOLD TO DO SO.

General Science

Time: 11 Minutes—25 Questions

1. Citrus fruits include
   1-A   apples.
   1-B   bananas.
   1-C   oranges.
   1-D   peaches.

2. What temperature is shown on a Fahrenheit thermometer when a centigrade thermo-meter reads 0°?
   2-A   −40°
   2-B   −32°
   2-C   0°
   2-D   32°

3. The major chemical constituent of a cell, by weight, is
   3-A   protein.
   3-B   ash.
   3-C   water.
   3-D   carbohydrates.

4. Which of the following is NOT a viral disease?
   4-A   Measles
   4-B   Mumps
   4-C   Smallpox
   4-D   Syphilis

5. Alcoholic beverages contain
   5-A   wood alcohol.
   5-B   isopropyl alcohol.
   5-C   glyceryl alcohol.
   5-D   grain alcohol.

6. The air around us is composed mostly of
   6-A   carbon.
   6-B   nitrogen.
   6-C   hydrogen.
   6-D   oxygen.

7. The process that is responsible for the continuous removal of carbon dioxide from the atmosphere is
   7-A   respiration.
   7-B   oxidation.
   7-C   metabolism.
   7-D   photosynthesis.

8. Ringworm is caused by a(n)
   8-A   alga.
   8-B   fungus.
   8-C   bacterium.
   8-D   protozoan.

9. Light passes through the crystalline lens in the eye and focuses on the
   9-A   cornea.
   9-B   iris.
   9-C   pupil.
   9-D   retina.

10. Saliva contains an enzyme that acts on
   10-A   carbohydrates.
   10-B   proteins.
   10-C   minerals.
   10-D   vitamins.

11. The vitamin that helps coagulation of the blood is
   11-A   C
   11-B   E
   11-C   D
   11-D   K

12. Of the following, the part of a ship that gives it stability by lowering the center of gravity is the
   12-A   bulkhead.
   12-B   keel.
   12-C   anchor.
   12-D   prow.

13. To reduce soil acidity, a farmer should use
   13-A   lime.
   13-B   phosphate.
   13-C   manure.
   13-D   peat moss.

14. Which of the following minerals is restored to the soil by plants of the pea and bean family?

    14-A   Sulfates

    14-B   Carbonates

    14-C   Nitrates

    14-D   Phosphates

15. Bacteria of decay help

    15-A   deplete soil.

    15-B   enrich soil.

    15-C   form oxygen.

    15-D   form water.

16. Of the following, the food that contains the largest amount of vitamin C is

    16-A   carrots.

    16-B   sweet potatoes.

    16-C   lima beans.

    16-D   tomatoes.

17. The cyclotron is used to

    17-A   measure radioactivity.

    17-B   measure the speed of the earth's rotation.

    17-C   split atoms.

    17-D   store radioactive energy.

18. The earth completes one trip around the sun approximately every

    18-A   24 hours.

    18-B   52 weeks.

    18-C   7 days.

    18-D   30 days.

19. A person is more buoyant when swimming in salt water than in fresh water because

    19-A   he keeps his head out of salt water.

    19-B   salt coats his body with a floating membrane.

    19-C   salt water has greater tensile strength.

    19-D   salt water weighs more than an equal volume of fresh water.

20. A volcanic eruption is caused by

    20-A   sunspots.

    20-B   pressure inside the earth.

    20-C   nuclear fallout.

    20-D   boiling lava.

21. The scientific name of an organism consists of its

    21-A   family and class.

    21-B   genus and species.

    21-C   order and family.

    21-D   species and kingdom.

22. The energy in the storage battery of a car is transformed from

    22-A   chemical to electrical energy.

    22-B   electrical to mechanical energy.

    22-C   heat to mechanical energy.

    22-D   mechanical to electrical energy.

23. A yardstick can usually be balanced by placing a finger beneath the point marked

    23-A   14 inches.

    23-B   16 inches.

    23-C   18 inches.

    23-D   20 inches.

24. When two forces act on an object in opposite directions, the resultant force is equal to the

    24-A   difference between the forces.

    24-B   ratio of the forces.

    24-C   product of the forces.

    24-D   sum of the forces.

25. The moon is a

    25-A   star.

    25-B   satellite.

    25-C   planetoid.

    25-D   planet.

STOP!

IF YOU FINISH BEFORE THE TIME IS UP, YOU MAY CHECK OVER YOUR WORK ON THIS PART ONLY.

PART 2: ARITHMETIC REASONING

Directions

This test has 30 questions about arithmetic. Each question is followed by four possible answers. Decide which answer is correct, then blacken the space on your answer form that has the same number and letter as your choice. Use your scratch paper for any figuring you wish to do.

Here are two sample questions.

S1. A person buys a sandwich for 90¢, soda for 55¢, and pie for 70¢. What is the total cost?   Ⓐ Ⓑ Ⓒ Ⓓ

S1-A	$2.00
S1-B	$2.05
S1-C	$2.15
S1-D	$2.25

The total cost is $2.15; therefore, choice C is the correct answer.

S2. If 8 workers are needed to run 4 machines, how many workers are needed to run 20 machines?   Ⓐ Ⓑ Ⓒ Ⓓ

S2-A	16
S2-B	32
S2-C	36
S2-D	40

The number needed is 40; therefore, choice D is the correct answer.

Your score on this test will be based on the number of questions you answer correctly. You should try to answer every question. Do not spend too much time on any one question.

Notice that Part 2 begins with question number 1. When you begin, be sure to start with question number 1 in Part 2 of your test booklet and number 1 in Part 2 on your answer form.

DO NOT CONTINUE UNTIL TOLD TO DO SO.

Arithmetic Reasoning

Time: 36 Minutes—30 Questions

1. A man owned 75 shares of stock worth $50 each. The corporation declared a dividend of 8%, payable in stock. How many shares did he then own?

   1-A   81 shares
   1-B   90 shares
   1-C   91 shares
   1-D   95 shares

2. If a scow is towed at the rate of 3 miles an hour, how many hours will be needed to tow the scow 28 miles?

   2-A   10 hours 30 minutes
   2-B   9 hours 20 minutes
   2-C   12 hours
   2-D   9 hours 15 minutes

3. If a fire truck is 60 feet away from a hydrant, it is how many feet nearer to the hydrant than a truck that is 100 feet away?

   3-A   60 feet
   3-B   50 feet
   3-C   40 feet
   3-D   20 feet

4. A clerk spent his 35-hour work week as follows: $\frac{1}{5}$ of his time in sorting mail; $\frac{1}{2}$ of his time in filing letters; and $\frac{1}{7}$ of his time in reception work. The rest of his time was devoted to messenger work. The percentage of time spent on messenger work by the clerk during the week was most nearly

   4-A   6%
   4-B   14%
   4-C   10%
   4-D   16%

5. A dealer bought some bicycles for $4,000. He sold them for $6,200, making $50 on each bicycle. How many bicycles were there?

   5-A   40
   5-B   43
   5-C   38
   5-D   44

6. Many American cars feature speedometers that show kilometers per hour. If you are required to drive 500 miles, and you know that one kilometer is approximately $\frac{5}{8}$ of a mile, how many kilometers would you cover in that journey?

   6-A   625
   6-B   800
   6-C   850
   6-D   1,000

7. Six gross of special drawing pencils were purchased for use in a department. If the pencils were used at the rate of 24 a week, the maximum number of weeks that the 6 gross of pencils would last is

   7-A   6 weeks.
   7-B   24 weeks.
   7-C   12 weeks.
   7-D   36 weeks.

8. A stock clerk had 600 pads on hand. He then issued $\frac{3}{8}$ of his supply of pads to Division X, $\frac{1}{4}$ to Division Y, and $\frac{1}{6}$ to Division Z. The number of pads remaining in stock is

   8-A   48
   8-B   240
   8-C   125
   8-D   475

9. During a sale, records that normally cost $6.98 each were priced at 2 for $12.50. Pete bought 4 records at the sale price. How much money did he save by buying the 4 records on sale?

    9-A $2.98
    9-B $2.92
    9-C $2.50
    9-D $1.46

10. A student must walk 2 miles to get to school. If she walks at an average of 3 miles per hour, how many minutes should it take her to walk to school?

    10-A   40
    10-B   20
    10-C   50
    10-D   45

11. Two sailors traveled by bus from one point to another. The trip took 15 hours, and they left their point of origin at 8 a.m. What time did they arrive at their destination?

    11-A   11 a.m.
    11-B   10 p.m.
    11-C   11 p.m.
    11-D   12 a.m.

12. A team won 8 of the 24 games it played in one season. What percent of the games did it win?

    12-A $33\frac{2}{3}\%$

    12-B $33\frac{1}{3}\%$

    12-C   50%
    12-D   16%

13. A man deposited a check for $1,000 to open an account. Shortly after that, he withdrew $941.20. How much did he have left in his account?

    13-A $56.72
    13-B $58.80
    13-C $59.09
    13-D $60.60

14. A shopper bought 4 pillow cases that cost $4.98 apiece, 2 fitted sheets that cost $8.29 apiece, and 2 flat sheets that cost $8.09 apiece. What was her total bill?

    14-A $52.58
    14-B $51.68
    14-C $52.68
    14-D $21.36

15. The wage rate in a certain trade is $8.60 an hour for a 40-hour week and $1\frac{1}{2}$ times the base pay for overtime. An employee who works 48 hours in a week earns

    15-A $447.20
    15-B $498.20
    15-C $582.20
    15-D $619.20

16. The temperature yesterday at noon was 68.5 degrees. Today at noon it was 59.9 degrees. What was the difference in temperature?

    16-A   8.4 degrees
    16-B   8.5 degrees
    16-C   8.6 degrees
    16-D   8.7 degrees

17. A pole 12 feet high has a shadow 4 feet long. A nearby pole is 24 feet high. How long is its shadow?

    17-A   4 feet
    17-B   8 feet
    17-C   12 feet
    17-D   16 feet

18. A woman bought a new color television with a $40 down payment and 16 monthly payments of $20 each. What was the total cost of the television?

    18-A $450
    18-B $360
    18-C $320
    18-D $280

19. A man paid $42.30 for gasoline in May, $38.60 in June, and $43.00 in July. What was his average monthly cost for gasoline?

    19-A $40.45

    19-B $41.30

    19-C $61.95

    19-D $123.90

20. A skier started a fire in the fireplace. Each log she put on burned for a half-hour. If she started with a supply of 10 logs, for how many hours could the fire burn?

    20-A   5 hours

    20-B $8\frac{1}{2}$ hours

    20-C   10 hours

    20-D   7 hours

21. To go from Poughkeepsie, New York, to West Palm Beach, Florida, you must travel 1,400 miles. If you can average a driving speed of 50 miles an hour, how many hours must you drive to make this trip?

    21-A   25

    21-B   28

    21-C   30

    21-D $27\frac{1}{2}$

22. Mrs. Jones wishes to buy 72 ounces of canned beans for the least possible cost. Which of the following should she buy?

    22-A   Six 12-ounce cans at 39¢ per can

    22-B   Seven 10-ounce cans at 34¢ per can

    22-C   Three 24-ounce cans at 79¢ per can

    22-D   Two 25-ounce cans at 62¢ per can

23. On a certain day the temperature ranged from −2°F to 10°F. What is the difference between the high and low temperatures for that day?

    23-A   6°

    23-B   8°

    23-C   10°

    23-D   12°

24. Fred had a coupon worth $2.00 toward the purchase of 1 record. Each record cost $5.98, and Fred bought 2 records. How much did Fred have to pay?

    24-A $3.98

    24-B $7.96

    24-C $9.96

    24-D $10.98

25. An officer traveled 1,200 miles in 20 hours. How many miles per hour did she average?

    25-A   45

    25-B   60

    25-C   50

    25-D   65

26. A boy sold $88.50 worth of stationery. If he received a $33\frac{1}{3}$% commission, what was the amount of his commission?

    26-A $29.50

    26-B $40.00

    26-C $50.00

    26-D $62.50

27. What is the shortest board a man must buy in order to cut 3 sections from it, each 4 feet 8 inches long?

    27-A   12 feet

    27-B   14 feet

    27-C   16 feet

    27-D   18 feet

28. A girl bought a sweater for $21.00, a blouse for $14.98, and a scarf for $4.97. What was the total cost of her purchases?

    28-A $35.50

    28-B $40.85

    28-C $30.85

    28-D $40.95

29. Don and Frank started from the same point and drove in opposite directions. Don's rate of travel was 50 miles per hour. Frank's rate of travel was 40 miles per hour. How many miles apart were they at the end of 2 hours?

    29-A   90
    29-B   160
    29-C   140
    29-D   180

30. A decorator went to a department store and ordered curtains for 5 windows. One pair of curtains cost $14.28; 2 pairs cost $33.26 apiece; and the remaining 2 pairs cost $65.38 apiece. What was the retail cost of the 5 pairs of curtains?

    30-A $211.46
    30-B $211.56
    30-C $112.92
    30-D $110.82

STOP!

IF YOU FINISH BEFORE THE TIME IS UP, YOU MAY CHECK OVER YOUR WORK ON THIS PART ONLY.

PART 3: WORD KNOWLEDGE

Directions

> This test has 35 questions about the meanings of words. Each question has an under-lined word. You are to decide which one of the four words in the choices most nearly means the same as the underlined word, then mark the space on your answer form that has the same number and letter as your choice.

Now look at the two sample questions below.

S1. <u>Mended</u> most nearly means   Ⓐ Ⓑ Ⓒ Ⓓ
    S1-A   repaired.
    S1-B   torn.
    S1-C   clean.
    S1-D   tied.

Repaired, choice A, is the correct answer. *Mended* means *fixed* or *repaired. Torn,* choice B, might be the state of an object before it is mended. The repair might be made by *tying,* choice D, but not necessarily. *Clean,* choice C, is wrong.

S2. It was a <u>small</u> table.   Ⓐ Ⓑ Ⓒ Ⓓ
    S1-A   Sturdy
    S2-B   Round
    S2-C   Cheap
    S2-D   Little

Little means the same as *small,* so choice D is the best one.

Your score on this test will be based on the number of questions you answer correctly. You should try to answer every question. Do not spend too much time on any one question.

When you begin, be sure to start with question number 1 in Part 3 of your test booklet and number 1 in Part 3 on your answer form.

DO NOT CONTINUE UNTIL TOLD TO DO SO.

Word Knowledge

Time: 11 Minutes—35 Questions

1. <u>Revenue</u> most nearly means
   - 1-A   taxes.
   - 1-B   income.
   - 1-C   expenses.
   - 1-D   produce.

2. <u>Convene</u> most nearly means
   - 2-A   meet.
   - 2-B   debate.
   - 2-C   agree.
   - 2-D   drink.

3. The machine has <u>manual</u> controls.
   - 3-A   Self-acting
   - 3-B   Simple
   - 3-C   Hand-operated
   - 3-D   Handmade

4. <u>Deportment</u> most nearly means
   - 4-A   attendance.
   - 4-B   intelligence.
   - 4-C   neatness.
   - 4-D   behavior.

5. <u>Prior</u> most nearly means
   - 5-A   personal.
   - 5-B   more urgent.
   - 5-C   more attractive.
   - 5-D   earlier.

6. <u>Grimy</u> most nearly means
   - 6-A   ill-fitting.
   - 6-B   poorly made.
   - 6-C   dirty.
   - 6-D   ragged.

7. <u>Approximate</u> most nearly means
   - 7-A   mathematically correct.
   - 7-B   nearly exact.
   - 7-C   remarkable.
   - 7-D   worthless.

8. The man <u>survived</u> his three sisters.
   - 8-A   Outlived
   - 8-B   Envied
   - 8-C   Excelled
   - 8-D   Destroyed

9. She is a <u>competent</u> worker.
   - 9-A   Busy
   - 9-B   Capable
   - 9-C   Friendly
   - 9-D   Good-natured

10. All service was <u>suspended</u> during the emergency.
    - 10-A   Turned back
    - 10-B   Checked carefully
    - 10-C   Regulated strictly
    - 10-D   Stopped temporarily

11. The <u>territory</u> is too large for one platoon to defend.
    - 11-A   Region
    - 11-B   Swamp
    - 11-C   Ranch
    - 11-D   Beach

12. <u>Huge</u> most nearly means
    - 12-A   ugly.
    - 12-B   tall.
    - 12-C   wide.
    - 12-D   immense.

13. <u>Prevented</u> most nearly means
    - 13-A   allowed.
    - 13-B   suggested.
    - 13-C   hindered.
    - 13-D   urged.

14. Mail will be <u>forwarded</u> to our new address.

    14-A   Sent

    14-B   Returned

    14-C   Canceled

    14-D   Received

15. The room was <u>vacant</u> when we arrived.

    15-A   Quiet

    15-B   Dark

    15-C   Available

    15-D   Empty

16. <u>Irritating</u> most nearly means

    16-A   nervous.

    16-B   unsuitable.

    16-C   annoying.

    16-D   noisy.

17. The cyclist pedaled at a <u>uniform</u> rate.

    17-A   Increasing

    17-B   Unchanging

    17-C   Unusual

    17-D   Very slow

18. <u>Power</u> most nearly means

    18-A   size.

    18-B   ambition.

    18-C   force.

    18-D   success.

19. They reached the <u>shore</u> in a landing barge.

    19-A   Gulf

    19-B   Coast

    19-C   Inlet

    19-D   Alien

20. <u>Flexible</u> most nearly means

    20-A   pliable.

    20-B   rigid.

    20-C   weak.

    20-D   athletic.

21. <u>Comprehend</u> most nearly means

    21-A   hear.

    21-B   listen.

    21-C   agree.

    21-D   understand.

22. <u>Instructor</u> most nearly means

    22-A   expert.

    22-B   assistant.

    22-C   teacher.

    22-D   foreman.

23. <u>Commended</u> most nearly means

    23-A   reprimanded.

    23-B   praised.

    23-C   promoted.

    23-D   blamed.

24. <u>Revolving</u> most nearly means

    24-A   rocking.

    24-B   working.

    24-C   vibrating.

    24-D   turning.

25. <u>Alert</u> most nearly means

    25-A   watchful.

    25-B   busy.

    25-C   helpful.

    25-D   honest.

26. The computer did not <u>function</u> yesterday.

    26-A   Finish

    26-B   Stop

    26-C   Operate

    26-D   Overheat

27. <u>Hazard</u> most nearly means

    27-A   damage.

    27-B   choice.

    27-C   opportunity.

    27-D   danger.

28. <u>Blemish</u> most nearly means

    28-A   color.

    28-B   insect.

    28-C   flaw.

    28-D   design.

29. The reply will be <u>conveyed</u> by messenger.

    29-A   Carried

    29-B   Guarded

    29-C   Refused

    29-D   Damaged

30. <u>Pedestrian</u> most nearly means
   - 30-A   passenger.
   - 30-B   street-crosser.
   - 30-C   walker.
   - 30-D   traffic light.

31. <u>Attorney</u> most nearly means
   - 31-A   banker.
   - 31-B   lawyer.
   - 31-C   foot doctor.
   - 31-D   accountant.

32. <u>Obsolete</u> most nearly means
   - 32-A   out of date.
   - 32-B   broken down.
   - 32-C   as good as new.
   - 32-D   improved.

33. The classroom has <u>stationary</u> desks.
   - 33-A   Heavy
   - 33-B   Carved
   - 33-C   Written-upon
   - 33-D   Not movable

34. We heard the <u>steady</u> ticking of the clock.
   - 34-A   Noisy
   - 34-B   Eerie
   - 34-C   Tiresome
   - 34-D   Regular

35. The letter <u>emphasized</u> two important ideas.
   - 35-A   Introduced
   - 35-B   Overlooked
   - 35-C   Contrasted
   - 35-D   Stressed

STOP!

IF YOU FINISH BEFORE THE TIME IS UP, YOU MAY CHECK OVER YOUR WORK ON THIS PART ONLY.

PART 4: PARAGRAPH COMPREHENSION

Directions

This test contains 15 items measuring your ability to obtain information from written passages. You will find one or more paragraphs of reading material followed by incomplete statements or questions. You are to read the paragraph(s) and select the lettered choice that best completes the statement or answers the question.

Here are two sample questions.

S1. From a building designer's standpoint, three things that make a home livable are the needs of the client, the building site, and the amount of money the client has to spend.

According to the passage, to make a home livable   Ⓐ Ⓑ Ⓒ Ⓓ
- S1-A   the prospective piece of land makes little difference.
- S1-B   it can be built on any piece of land.
- S1-C   the design must fit the owner's income and site.
- S1-D   the design must fit the designer's income.

The correct answer is that the design must fit the owner's income and site, so choice C is the correct response.

S2. In certain areas, water is so scarce that every attempt is made to conserve it. For instance, on one oasis in the Sahara Desert the amount of water necessary for each date palm tree has been carefully determined.

How much water is each tree given?   Ⓐ Ⓑ Ⓒ Ⓓ
- S2-A   No water at all
- S2-B   Exactly the amount required
- S2-C   Water only if it is healthy
- S2-D   Water on alternate days

The correct answer is exactly the amount required, so choice B is the correct response.

Your score on this test will be based on the number of questions you answer correctly. You should try to answer every question. Do not spend too much time on any one question.

When you begin, be sure to start with question number 1 in Part 4 of your test booklet and number 1 in Part 4 on your answer form.

DO NOT CONTINUE UNTIL TOLD TO DO SO.

Paragraph Comprehension

Time: 13 Minutes—15 Questions

1. The lead-acid storage battery is used for storing energy in its chemical form. The battery does not actually store electricity but converts an electrical charge into chemical energy that is stored until the battery terminals are connected to a closed external circuit. When the circuit is closed, the battery's chemical energy is transformed back into electrical energy and, as a result, current flows through the circuit.

   According to this passage, a lead-acid battery stores
   - 1-A   current.
   - 1-B   electricity.
   - 1-C   electric energy.
   - 1-D   chemical energy.

2. A good or service has value only because people want it. Value is an extrinsic quality wholly created in the minds of people and is not intrinsic in the property itself.

   According to this passage, it is correct to say that an object will be valuable if it is
   - 2-A   beautiful.
   - 2-B   not plentiful.
   - 2-C   sought after.
   - 2-D   useful.

3. You can tell a frog from a toad by its skin. In general, a frog's skin is moist, smooth, and shiny while a toad's skin is dry, dull, and rough or covered with warts. Frogs are also better at jumping than toads are.

   You can recognize a toad by its
   - 3-A   great jumping ability.
   - 3-B   smooth, shiny skin.
   - 3-C   lack of warts.
   - 3-D   dry, rough skin.

4. The speed of a boat is measured in knots. One knot is equal to a speed of one nautical mile an hour. A nautical mile is equal to 6,080 feet, while an ordinary mile is 5,280 feet.

   According to the passage, which of the following statements is true?
   - 4-A   A nautical mile is longer than an ordinary mile.
   - 4-B   A speed of 2 knots is the same as 2 miles per hour.
   - 4-C   A knot is the same as a mile.
   - 4-D   The distance a boat travels is measured in knots.

5. There are only two grooves on a record—one on each side. The groove is cut in a spiral on the surface of the record. For stereophonic sound, a different sound is recorded in each wall of the groove. The pick-up produces two signals, one of which goes to the left-hand speaker and one to the right-hand speaker.

Stereophonic sound is produced by

   5-A cutting extra grooves in a record.

   5-B recording different sounds in each wall of the groove.

   5-C sending the sound to two speakers.

   5-D having left- and right-hand speakers.

6. It is a common assumption that city directories are prepared and published by the cities concerned. However, the directory business is as much a private business as is the publishing of dictionaries and encyclopedias. The companies financing the publication make their profits through the sales of the directories themselves and through the advertising in them.

The paragraph best supports the statement that

   6-A the publication of a city directory is a commercial enterprise.

   6-B the size of a city directory limits the space devoted to advertising.

   6-C many city directories are published by dictionary and encyclopedia concerns.

   6-D city directories are sold at a cost to local residents and businessmen.

7. Although rural crime reporting is spottier and less efficient than city and town reporting, sufficient data has been collected to support the statement that rural crime rates are lower than those in urban communities.

The paragraph best supports the statement that

   7-A better reporting of crime occurs in rural areas than in cities.

   7-B there appears to be a lower proportion of crime in rural areas than in cities.

   7-C cities have more crime than towns.

   7-D no conclusions can be drawn regarding crime in rural areas because of inadequate reporting.

8. Iron is used in making our bridges and skyscrapers, subways and steamships, railroads and automobiles, and nearly all kinds of machinery—besides millions of small articles, from the farmer's scythe to the tailor's needle.

The paragraph best supports the statement that iron

   8-A is the most abundant of the metals.

   8-B has many different uses.

   8-C is the strongest of all metals.

   8-D is the only material used in building skyscrapers and bridges.

9. Most solids, like most liquids, expand when heated and contract when cooled. To allow for this, roads, sidewalks, and railroad tracks are constructed with spacing between sections so that they can expand during the hot weather.

    If roads, sidewalks, and railroad tracks were not constructed with spacing between sections,

    9-A   nothing would happen to them when the weather changed.

    9-B   they could not be constructed as easily as they are now.

    9-C   they would crack or break when the weather changed.

    9-D   they would not appear to be even.

10. Twenty-five percent of all household burglaries can be attributed to unlocked windows or doors. Crime is the result of opportunity plus desire.

    To prevent crime, it is each individual's responsibility to

    10-A   provide the desire.

    10-B   provide the opportunity.

    10-C   prevent the desire.

    10-D   prevent the opportunity.

Questions 11 and 12 are based on the following passage.

When demand for new buildings rises sharply, prices of such buildings usually increase rapidly while construction invariably lags behind. The relation of supply to demand is one of the factors that may greatly influence prices. When demand for new buildings suddenly declines, their prices fall because the available supply cannot be immediately curtailed.

11. According to the above passage, a sharp increase in demand for new buildings usually results in

    11-A   fewer new buildings in proportion to buyers.

    11-B   a proportionate increase in construction.

    11-C   more builders of new buildings.

    11-D   more sellers.

12. When there is a sudden drop in the demand for new buildings, the immediately resulting effect on their prices is attributable mainly to the

    12-A   cessation in new construction.

    12-B   curtailment in the supply of such buildings.

    12-C   reduction in new construction.

    12-D   static condition in the supply of such buildings.

Questions 13–15 are based on the passage shown below.

A large proportion of the people behind bars are not convicted criminals, but people who have been arrested and are being held until their trial in court. Experts have often pointed out that this detention system does not operate fairly. For instance, a person who can afford to pay bail usually will not get locked up. The person must show up in court when he is supposed to; otherwise, he will forfeit his bail. Sometimes, one who can show that he is a stable citizen with a job and a family will be released on "personal recognizance." The result is that the well-to-do, the employed, and the family men can often avoid the detention system. Those who do wind up in detention tend to be the poor, the unemployed, the single, and the young.

13. According to the passage above, people who are put behind bars
    13-A   are almost always dangerous criminals.
    13-B   include many innocent people who have been arrested by mistake.
    13-C   are often people who have been arrested but have not yet come to trial.
    13-D   are all people who tend to be young and single.

14. The passage says that the detention system works unfairly against people who are
    14-A   rich.
    14-B   married.
    14-C   old.
    14-D   unemployed.

15. When someone is released on "personal recognizance," this means that
    15-A   the judge knows that he is innocent.
    15-B   he does not have to show up for a trial.
    15-C   he has a record of previous convictions.
    15-D   he does not have to pay bail.

STOP!

IF YOU FINISH BEFORE THE TIME IS UP, YOU MAY CHECK OVER YOUR WORK ON THIS PART ONLY.

PART 5: MATHEMATICS KNOWLEDGE

Directions

This is a test of your ability to solve 25 general mathematical problems. You are to select the correct response from the choices given. Then mark the space on your answer form that has the same number and letter as your choice. Use the scratch paper that has been given to you to do any figuring that you wish.

Now look at the two sample problems below.

S1. If $x + 6 = 7$, then x is equal to   Ⓐ Ⓑ Ⓒ Ⓓ

S1-A   0

S1-B   1

S1-C   −1

S1-D $\dfrac{7}{6}$

The correct answer is 1, so choice B is the correct response.

S2. What is the area of this square?   Ⓐ Ⓑ Ⓒ Ⓓ

S2-A   1 square foot

S2-B   5 square feet

S2-C   10 square feet

S2-D   25 square feet

The correct answer is 25 square feet, so choice D is the correct response.

Your score on this test will be based on the number of questions you answer correctly. You should try to answer every question. Do not spend too much time on any one question.

When you are told to begin, be sure to start with question number 1 in Part 5 of your test booklet and number 1 in Part 5 on your answer form.

DO NOT CONTINUE UNTIL TOLD TO DO SO.

Mathematics Knowledge

Time: 24 Minutes—25 Questions

1. A box contains 3 black, 4 red, and 5 white marbles. If one marble is to be picked at random, what is the probability that it will be red?

    1-A $\dfrac{1}{5}$

    1-B $\dfrac{1}{2}$

    1-C $\dfrac{1}{3}$

    1-D $\dfrac{1}{4}$

2.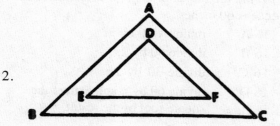

    In the figure above, the sides of $\triangle ABC$ are respectively parallel to the sides of $\triangle DEF$. If the complement of C is 40, then the complement of F is

    2-A   20°
    2-B   50°
    2-C   40°
    2-D   60°

3. The sum of the measure of the angles of a hexagon is

    3-A   540°
    3-B   720°
    3-C   900°
    3-D   1,080°

4. If: $A^2 + B^2 = A^2 + X^2$, then B equals

    4-A $\pm X$
    4-B $X^2 - 2A^2$
    4-C $\pm A$
    4-D $A^2 + X^2$

5. If $6 + x + y = 20$ and $x + y = k$, then $20 - k =$

    5-A   6
    5-B   0
    5-C   14
    5-D   20

6. $\sqrt{75} =$

    6-A $3\sqrt{5}$
    6-B $5\sqrt{3}$
    6-C $5\sqrt{15}$
    6-D $15\sqrt{5}$

7. $\sqrt{960}$ is a number between

    7-A   20 and 30
    7-B   60 and 70
    7-C   80 and 90
    7-D   30 and 40

8.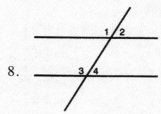

    If $m\angle 2 = 80$, $m\angle 4 =$

    8-A   80°
    8-B   100°
    8-C   120°
    8-D   None of the above

9. $\dfrac{10^4}{10} =$

   9-A 10^3

   9-B 10^4

   9-C 20^3

   9-D 20^4

10. $\angle 1$ and $\angle 2$ form a linear pair and therefore are supplementary angles. If $m\angle 1 = 7x - 6$ and $m\angle 2 = 5x + 18$, $\angle 2 =$

   10-A   78°

   10-B   82°

   10-C   85°

   10-D   88°

11. If $x = y$, find the value of $8 + 5(x - y)$.

   11-A $8 + 5x - 5y$

   11-B $8 + 5xy$

   11-C $13x - 13y$

   11-D 8

12.

Triangle R is 3 times triangle S.

Triangle S is 3 times triangle T.

If triangle S = 1, what is the sum of the three triangles?

   12-A $2\dfrac{1}{3}$

   12-B $3\dfrac{1}{3}$

   12-C $4\dfrac{1}{3}$

   12-D   6

13. How many different combinations of jackets and pants are possible from a wardrobe that contains 3 jackets and 5 pairs of pants?

   13-A   3

   13-B   5

   13-C   8

   13-D   15

14. Divide 1.672 by .08

   14-A   200.9

   14-B   20.9

   14-C   2.9

   14-D   .29

15. If $D = R \times T$, then $R =$

   15-A $D \times T$

   15-B $T \div R$

   15-C $T - D$

   15-D $D \div T$

16. To find the radius of a circle whose circumference is 60 inches

   16-A   multiply 60 by π.

   16-B   divide 60 by 2π.

   16-C   divide 30 by 2π.

   16-D   divide 60 by π and extract the square root of the result.

17. Which is NOT a prime number?

   17-A   23

   17-B   37

   17-C   87

   17-D   53

18. A is older than B. With the passage of time

   18-A   the ratio of the ages of A and B remains unchanged.

   18-B   the ratio of the ages of A and B increases.

   18-C   the ratio of the ages of A and B decreases.

   18-D   the difference in their ages varies.

19. If you multiply $x + 3$ by $2x + 5$, what will the coefficient of x be?

    19-A   3
    19-B   6
    19-C   9
    19-D   11

20. $(x + 3)(x + 2)$

    20-A $x^2 + 5x + 5$
    20-B $x^2 + 5x + 6$
    20-C $x^2 + 6x + 5$
    20-D $x^2 + 6x + 6$

21. The perimeter of a rectangle is 90. One side of the rectangle is twice the length of the other. What is the length of the longer side?

    21-A   20
    21-B   25
    21-C   30
    21-D   35

22.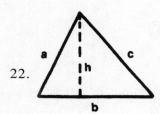

The area of the figure above can be determined by the formula

    22-A $ac \div b$

    22-B $\dfrac{1}{2}bh$

    22-C $bc \div a$

    22-D bh^2

23. If psychological studies of college students show K percent to be emotionally unstable, the number of college students not emotionally unstable per 100 college students is

    23-A $100 - K$
    23-B $1 - K$
    23-C $K - 1$
    23-D $100 \div K$

24. A cog wheel having 8 cogs plays into another cog wheel having 24 cogs. When the small wheel has made 42 revolutions, how many has the larger wheel made?

    24-A   14
    24-B   16
    24-C   20
    24-D   10

25. A quadrilateral is a square only if

    25-A   it has four right angles.
    25-B   it has at least one pair of parallel sides.
    25-C   it has four right angles and four equal sides.
    25-D   both pairs of its opposite sides are parallel.

STOP!

IF YOU FINISH BEFORE THE TIME IS UP, YOU MAY CHECK OVER YOUR WORK ON THIS PART ONLY.

PART 6: ELECTRONIC INFORMATION

Directions

This is a test of your knowledge of electrical, radio, and electronics information. There are 20 questions. You are to select the correct response from the choices given. Then mark the space on your answer form that has the same number and letter as your choice.

Now look at the two sample questions below.

S1. What does the abbreviation AC stand for?   Ⓐ Ⓑ Ⓒ Ⓓ
   S1-A   Additional charge
   S1-B   Alternating coil
   S1-C   Alternating current
   S1-D   Ampere current

The correct answer is alternating current, so choice C is the correct response.

S2. Which of the following has the least resistance?   Ⓐ Ⓑ Ⓒ Ⓓ
   S2-A   Wood
   S2-B   Silver
   S2-C   Rubber
   S2-D   Iron

The correct answer is silver, so choice B is the correct response.

   Your score on this test will be based on the number of questions you answer correctly. You should try to answer every question. Do not spend too much time on any one question.

   When you are told to begin, be sure to start with question number 1 in Part 6 of your test booklet and number 1 in Part 6 on your answer form.

DO NOT CONTINUE UNTIL TOLD TO DO SO.

Electronics Information

Time: 9 Minutes—20 Questions

1. In lights controlled by three-way switches, the switches should be treated and put in as

   1-A   flush switches.
   1-B   single pole switches.
   1-C   three double pole switches.
   1-D   three pole switches.

2. When working on live 600-volt equipment where rubber gloves might be damaged, an electrician should

   2-A   work without gloves.
   2-B   carry a spare pair of rubber gloves.
   2-C   reinforce the fingers of the rubber gloves with rubber tape.
   2-D   wear leather gloves over the rubber gloves.

3. A "mil" measures

   3-A   an eighth of an inch.
   3-B   a millionth of an inch.
   3-C   a thousandth of an inch.
   3-D   a ten-thousandth of an inch.

4.
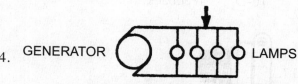

GENERATOR   LAMPS

EACH LAMP TAKES 1 AMPERE

The current in the wire at the point indicated by the arrow is

   4-A   1 ampere.
   4-B   2 amperes.
   4-C   3 amperes.
   4-D   4 amperes.

5. If a fuse of higher than the required current rating is used in an electrical circuit,

   5-A   better protection will be afforded.
   5-B   the fuse will blow more often since it carries more current.
   5-C   serious damage may result to the circuit from overload.
   5-D   maintenance of the large fuse will be higher.

6. The electrical contacts in the tuner of a television set are usually plated with silver. Silver is used to

   6-A   avoid tarnish.
   6-B   improve conductivity.
   6-C   improve appearance.
   6-D   avoid arcing.

7. The following equipment is required for a "2-line return-call" electric bell circuit:

   7-A   2 bells, 2 metallic lines, 2 ordinary push buttons, and one set of batteries.
   7-B   2 bells, 2 metallic lines, 2 return-call push buttons, and 2 sets of batteries.
   7-C   2 bells, 2 metallic lines, 2 return-call push buttons, and one set of batteries.
   7-D   2 bells, 2 metallic lines, one ordinary push button, one return-call push button, and one set of batteries.

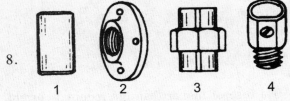

8.

    1   2   3   4

The standard coupling for rigid electrical conduit is

8-A   1
8-B   2
8-C   3
8-D   4

9. Metal cabinets used for lighting circuits are grounded to

9-A   eliminate electrolysis.
9-B   ensure that the fuse in a defective circuit will blow.
9-C   reduce shock hazard.
9-D   simplify wiring.

10. Low Potential is a trade term that refers to

10-A   700 volts.
10-B   600 volts or less.
10-C   1,200 volts.
10-D   900 volts.

11. The purpose of having a rheostat in the field circuit of a DC shunt motor is to

11-A   control the speed of the motor.
11-B   minimize the starting current.
11-C   limit the field current to a safe value.
11-D   reduce sparking at the brushes.

12. A polarized plug generally has

12-A   two parallel prongs of the same size.
12-B   prongs at an angle with one another.
12-C   magnetized prongs.
12-D   prongs marked plus and minus.

13.

The reading of the kilowatt-hour meter is

13-A   7972
13-B   1786
13-C   2786
13-D   6872

14. Commutators are found on

14-A   mercury rectifiers.
14-B   DC motors.
14-C   circuit breakers.
14-D   alternators.

15. Neutral wire can be quickly recognized by the

15-A   greenish color.
15-B   bluish color.
15-C   natural or whitish color.
15-D   black color.

16. The term that is NOT applicable in describing the *construction* of a microphone is

16-A   dynamic.
16-B   carbon.
16-C   crystal.
16-D   feedback.

17.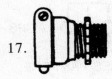

The fitting shown is used in electrical construction to

17-A   clamp two adjacent junction boxes together.
17-B   act as a ground clamp for the conduit system.
17-C   attach a flexible metallic conduit to a junction box.
17-D   protect exposed wires where they pass through a wall.

18. A good magnetic material is
    18-A   copper.
    18-B   iron.
    18-C   tin.
    18-D   brass.

19. Rosin is a material generally used
    19-A   in batteries.
    19-B   for high voltage insulation.
    19-C   as a dielectric.
    19-D   as a soldering flux.

20. The letters RHW when applied to electrical wire indicate the wire
    20-A   has a solid conductor.
    20-B   has rubber insulation.
    20-C   is insulated with paper.
    20-D   has lead sheath.

STOP!

IF YOU FINISH BEFORE THE TIME IS UP, YOU MAY CHECK OVER YOUR WORK ON THIS PART ONLY.

PART 7: AUTO & SHOP INFORMATION

Directions

This test has 25 questions about automobiles, shop practices, and the use of tools. Pick the best answer for each question, then blacken the space on your answer form that has the same number and letter as your choice.

Here are two sample questions.

S1. A car uses too much oil when which parts are worn?   Ⓐ Ⓑ Ⓒ Ⓓ

S2-A   Pistons
S2-B   Piston rings
S2-C   Main bearings
S2-D   Connecting rods

Worn piston rings causes the use of too much oil, so choice B is the correct answer.

S2. The saw shown to the right is used mainly to cut   Ⓐ Ⓑ Ⓒ Ⓓ

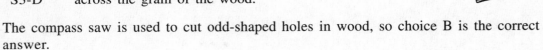

S3-A   plywood.
S3-B   odd-shaped holes in wood.
S3-C   along the grain of the wood.
S3-D   across the grain of the wood.

The compass saw is used to cut odd-shaped holes in wood, so choice B is the correct answer.

Your score on this test will be based on the number of questions you answer correctly. You should try to answer every question. Do not spend too much time on any one question.

When you are told to begin, be sure to start with question number 1 in Part 7 of your test booklet and number 1 in Part 7 on your answer form.

DO NOT CONTINUE UNTIL TOLD TO DO SO.

Auto & Shop Information

Time: 11 Minutes—25 Questions

1. An engine, such as is most often used in automobiles, is called a(n)
   1-A   diesel engine.
   1-B   external-combustion engine.
   1-C   internal-combustion engine.
   1-D   three cycle engine.

2. In the four-stroke cycle gasoline engine, the sequence of the steps in each cylinder to complete a cycle is which one of the following?
   2-A   Intake stroke, power stroke, compression stroke, exhaust stroke
   2-B   Intake stroke, compression stroke, exhaust stroke, power stroke
   2-C   Intake stroke, exhaust stroke, compression stroke, power stroke
   2-D   Intake stroke, compression stroke, power stroke, exhaust stroke

3. Vapor-lock in a gasoline engine is most likely due to
   3-A   an over-rich gas-air mixture.
   3-B   fuel forming bubbles in the gas line.
   3-C   a tear in the fuel pump diaphragm.
   3-D   the carburetor being clogged with dirt.

4. When the level of the liquid in a battery gets too low, it is necessary to put in some more
   4-A   battery acid.
   4-B   hydroxide.
   4-C   water.
   4-D   antifreeze.

5. After brakes have been severely overheated, what should be checked for?
   5-A   Water condensation in brake fluid
   5-B   Glazed brake shoes
   5-C   Wheels out of alignment
   5-D   Crystallized wheel bearings

6. A good lubricant for locks is
   6-A   graphite.
   6-B   grease.
   6-C   mineral oil.
   6-D   motor oil.

7. If the "charge and discharge" indicator, whether a meter or a light, suddenly indicates "discharge" while a car is in normal operation, it is best that the car be
   7-A   stopped immediately and then be towed in for repairs.
   7-B   stopped immediately and have a new battery installed on the spot.
   7-C   driven as usual and the incident ignored.
   7-D   driven to the nearest garage for inspection and repair.

8. Manifolds are used to conduct
   8-A   gases out of an engine only.
   8-B   gases into an engine only.
   8-C   gases into or out of an engine.
   8-D   heat into the piston.

9. What forces fuel from the carburetor into the cylinder?
   9-A   The fuel pump
   9-B   Atmospheric pressure
   9-C   Temperature difference
   9-D   The distributor

10. The most probable cause of a complete loss of oil pressure while driving is
    10-A   a crankcase oil level that is too low.
    10-B   a crankcase oil level that is too high.
    10-C   the use of too thick an oil.
    10-D   dirty oil.

11. To test for leaks around the intake manifold of an idling engine, the mechanic would most likely use
    11-A   soap bubbles.
    11-B   talc powder.
    11-C   oil.
    11-D   heavy grease.

12. If the intake manifold of a gasoline engine is warped to the extent that it leaks, the engine will most likely tend to
    12-A   check out with a vacuum gauge as running on a rich mixture.
    12-B   miss on one cylinder.
    12-C   perform better on acceleration.
    12-D   have a fast idle.

13. The type of screwdriver that will develop the greatest turning force is a
    13-A   screwdriver-bit and brace.
    13-B   straight handle with ratchet.
    13-C   standard straight handle.
    13-D   spiral push-type.

14.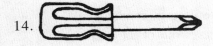

    The tool shown above is used to
    14-A   ream holes in wood.
    14-B   countersink holes in soft metals.
    14-C   turn Phillips-head screws.
    14-D   drill holes in concrete.

15. A jointer plane is
    15-A   used for making close fits.
    15-B   used for heavy rough work.
    15-C   usually less than 12 inches long.
    15-D   used for squaring of end-stock.

16. A number 10 wood screw is
    16-A   thicker than a number 6.
    16-B   longer than a number 6.
    16-C   shorter than a number 6.
    16-D   thinner than a number 6.

17. Paint is "thinned" with
    17-A   linseed oil.
    17-B   varnish.
    17-C   turpentine.
    17-D   gasoline.

18.

    The tool shown above is
    18-A   an offset wrench.
    18-B   a box wrench.
    18-C   a spanner wrench.
    18-D   an open end wrench.

19. What is used to fasten ceramic tiles to walls?
    19-A   Putty
    19-B   Caulking
    19-C   Plaster of Paris
    19-D   Mastic

20. With which of these screw heads do you use an "Allen" wrench?
    20-A
    20-B
    20-C
    20-D   ✳

21. When sanding wood by hand, best results are usually obtained in finishing the surface when the sanding block is worked
    21-A   across the grain.
    21-B   in a diagonal to the grain.
    21-C   in a circular motion.
    21-D   with the grain.

22. A 6-point saw is one that
    22-A   weighs 6 ounces per foot.
    22-B   is made of no. 6 gauge steel.
    22-C   has 6 teeth per inch.
    22-D   has 6 styles of teeth for univer-
            sal work.

23. A brad is similar in shape to a
    23-A   box nail.
    23-B   finishing nail.
    23-C   common nail.
    23-D   tack.

24. The carpenter's "hand screw" is

    24-A

    24-B

    24-C

    24-D

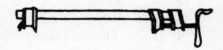

25. Of the following tools, the one that is least like
    the others is
    25-A   brace and bit.
    25-B   plane.
    25-C   draw-knife.
    25-D   spoke-shave.

STOP!

IF YOU FINISH BEFORE THE TIME IS UP, YOU MAY CHECK OVER YOUR WORK ON THIS PART ONLY.

PART 8: MECHANICAL COMPREHENSION

Directions

This test has 25 questions about mechanical principles. Most of the questions use drawings to illustrate specific principles. Decide which answer is correct and mark the space on your separate answer form that has the same number and letter as your choice.

Here are two sample questions.

S1. Which bridge is the strongest?   Ⓐ Ⓑ Ⓒ Ⓓ

S1-A   A
S1-B   B
S1-C   C
S1-D   All are equally strong.

Choice C is correct.

S2. If all of these objects are the same temperature, which will feel coldest?   Ⓐ Ⓑ Ⓒ Ⓓ

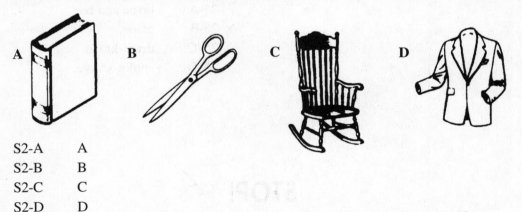

S2-A   A
S2-B   B
S2-C   C
S2-D   D

Choice B is correct.

Your score on this test will be based on the number of questions you answer correctly. You should try to answer every question. Do not spend too much time on any one question.

When you are told to begin, be sure to start with question number 1 in Part 8 of your test booklet and number 1 in Part 8 on your answer form.

DO NOT CONTINUE UNTIL TOLD TO DO SO.

Mechanical Comprehension

Time: 19 Minutes—25 Questions

1.

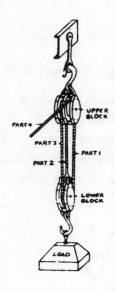

When a load is hoisted by means of the tackle shown above, the part that remains stationary is

1-A   the load.
1-B   the lower block.
1-C   the lower hook.
1-D   the upper block.

2.

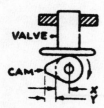

The figure above shows a cam and a valve. For each cam revolution, the vertical valve rise equals distance

2-A   Y.
2-B   X.
2-C   X plus Y.
2-D   twice X.

3.

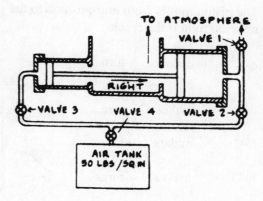

If all valves are closed at the start, in order to have air pressure from the tank move the pistons to the right, the valves to be opened are

3-A   2 and 4.
3-B   2, 3, and 4.
3-C   1 and 2.
3-D   1, 3, and 4.

4. Automatic operation of a sump pump is controlled by the

4-A   pneumatic switch.
4-B   float.
4-C   foot valve.
4-D   centrifugal driving unit.

5.

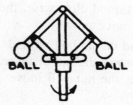

The figure above shows a governor on a rotating shaft. As the shaft speeds up, the governor balls will

5-A   move down.
5-B   move upward and inward.
5-C   move upward.
5-D   move inward.

6.

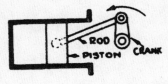

The figure above shows a crank and piston. The piston moves from mid-position to the extreme right if the crank

6-A   makes a $\frac{1}{2}$ turn.

6-B   makes a $\frac{3}{4}$ turn.

6-C   makes 1 turn.

6-D   makes $1\frac{1}{2}$ turns.

7.

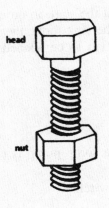

Referring to the figure above, which one of the following statements is true?

7-A   If the nut is held stationary and the head turned clockwise, the bolt will move down.

7-B   If the head of the bolt is held stationary and the nut is turned clockwise, the nut will move down.

7-C   If the head of the bolt is held stationary and the nut is turned clockwise, the nut will move up.

7-D   If the nut is held stationary and the head turned counterclockwise, the bolt will move up.

8.

Which hydraulic press requires the least force to lift the weight?

8-A   A

8-B   B

8-C   C

8-D   All three require the same force.

9.   The try-cocks of steam boilers are used to

9-A   act as safety valves.

9-B   empty the boiler of water.

9-C   test steam pressure in the boiler.

9-D   find the height of water in the boiler.

10.

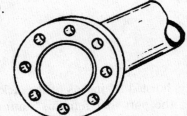

In the case of the standard flanged pipe shown, the maximum angle through which it would be necessary to rotate the pipe in order to line up the holes is

10-A   22.5°

10-B   45°

10-C   30°

10-D   60°

11.

The force F needed to balance the lever is, in pounds, most nearly

11-A   7.5

11-B   12.5

11-C   10

11-D   15

12.

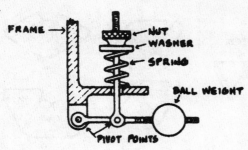

If the ball and spring mechanism are balanced in the position shown, the ball will move upward if

12-A   the nut is loosened.

12-B   the ball is moved away from the frame.

12-C   the nut is loosened and the ball moved away from the frame.

12-D   the nut is tightened.

13.

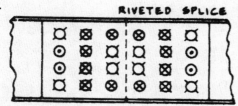

In the structural steel splice, the different types of rivets are shown by different symbols. The number of different types of rivets is

13-A   6

13-B   4

13-C   5

13-D   3

14. The main purpose of baffle plates in a furnace is to

14-A   change the direction of flow of heated gases.

14-B   retard the burning of gases.

14-C   increase combustion rate of the fuel.

14-D   prevent escape of flue gases through furnace openings.

15.

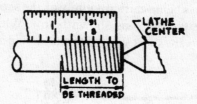

A very light cut (trace) is being measured as a check before cutting the thread on the lathe. The number of threads per inch shown is

15-A   12

15-B   14

15-C   13

15-D   15

16. A characteristic of a rotary pump is

16-A   a rapidly rotating impeller that moves the liquid through the discharge piping.

16-B   two gears, meshed together and revolving in opposite directions that move the liquid to the discharge pipe.

16-C   valves that are required on the discharge side of the pump.

16-D   it is usually operated at high speeds up to 3,600 rpm.

17.

In the diagram above, pulley A drives a system of pulleys. Pulleys B and C are keyed to the same shaft. Use the following diameters in your computations: A = 1 inch; B = 2 inches; $C = \frac{1}{2}$ inch ; and D = 4 inches. When pulley A runs at an rpm of 2,000, pulley D will make

17-A   125 rpm.

17-B   500 rpm.

17-C   250 rpm.

17-D   8,000 rpm.

18. The weight is being carried entirely on the shoulders of the two persons shown below. Which person bears the most weight on the shoulder?

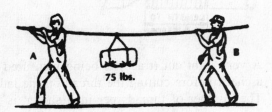

18-A   A
18-B   B
18-C   Both are carrying the same weight.
18-D   It cannot be determined.

19. In the figure shown below, what force must be applied to the 6-inch file scraper to pry up the lid of the paint can? Assume that the average force holding the lid is 50 pounds (disregard weight of file scraper.

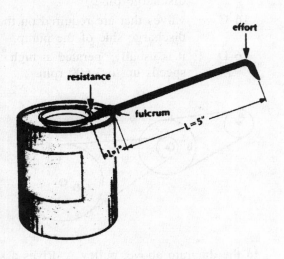

19-A   10 pounds
19-B   20 pounds
19-C   30 pounds
19-D   40 pounds

20.

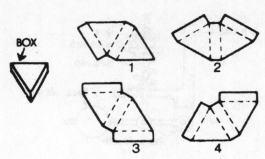

The flat sheet metal pattern that can be bent along the dotted lines to form the completely closed triangular box is

20-A   1
20-B   3
20-C   2
20-D   4

21. Neglecting friction, what is the mechanical advantage in using a single fixed pulley shown to the right?

21-A   1
21-B   2
21-C   3
21-D   4

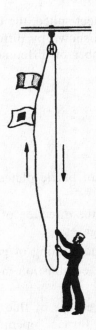

22.

If the block on which the lever is resting is moved closer to the brick, the brick will be

22-A   easier to lift and will be lifted higher.

22-B   harder to lift and will be lifted higher.

22-C   easier to lift but will not be lifted as high.

22-D   harder to lift and will not be lifted as high.

23.

A

B

C

D

If all of these objects are the same temperature, which will feel coldest?

23-A   A

23-B   B

23-C   C

23-D   D

24. In the figure shown below, one complete revolution of the windlass drum will move the weight up

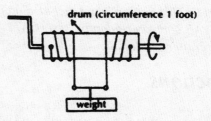

24-A   6 inches.

24-B   12 inches.

24-C   18 inches.

24-D   24 inches.

25.

If both cyclists pedal at the same rate on the same surface, the cyclist in front will

25-A   travel at the same speed as the cyclist behind.

25-B   move faster than the cyclist behind.

25-C   move more slowly than the other cyclist.

25-D   have greater difficulty steering.

STOP!

IF YOU FINISH BEFORE THE TIME IS UP, YOU MAY CHECK OVER YOUR WORK ON THIS PART ONLY.

PART 9: NUMERICAL OPERATIONS

NOTE: This section is not included on paper-and-pencil versions of ASVAB. It is included on the ASVAB computer-adaptive test (CAT), but may be eliminated in the near future. Check with your recruiter for details.

Directions

This is a test to see how rapidly and accurately you can do 50 simple arithmetic computations. Each problem is followed by four answers, only one of which is correct. Decide which answer is correct, then blacken the space on your answer form which has the same number and letter as your choice.

Now look at the four example problems below.

S1. $3 \times 3 =$ ⒶⒷⒸⒹ

    S1-A   6
    S1-B   0
    S1-C   9
    S1-D   1

The answer is 9, so choice C is correct.

S2. $3 + 7 =$ ⒶⒷⒸⒹ

    S2-A   4
    S2-B   6
    S2-C   8
    S2-D   10

The answer is 10, so choice D is correct.

S3. $5 - 2 =$ ⒶⒷⒸⒹ

    S3-A   2
    S3-B   3
    S3-C   1
    S3-D   4

The answer is 3, so choice B is correct.

S4. $9 \div 3 =$ ⒶⒷⒸⒹ

    S4-A   3
    S4-B   6
    S4-C   9
    S4-D   12

The answer is 3, so choice A is correct.

This is a speed test, so work as fast as you can without making mistakes. Do each problem as it comes. If you finish before time is up, go back and check your work. When the signal is given, you will turn the page and begin with question 1 in Part 9 of your test booklet and answer space 1 in Part 9 of your answer form.

DO NOT CONTINUE UNTIL TOLD TO DO SO.

Numerical Operations

Time: 3 Minutes—50 Questions

1. 60 ÷ 10 =
   - 1-A   5
   - 1-B   6
   - 1-C   10
   - 1-D   16

2. 5 − 2 =
   - 2-A   3
   - 2-B   6
   - 2-C   7
   - 2-D   9

3. 3 × 4 =
   - 3-A   7
   - 3-B   12
   - 3-C   15
   - 3-D   21

4. 8 − 6 =
   - 4-A   12
   - 4-B   5
   - 4-C   4
   - 4-D   2

5. 4 + 8 =
   - 5-A   6
   - 5-B   10
   - 5-C   12
   - 5-D   14

6. 6 × 8 =
   - 6-A   24
   - 6-B   48
   - 6-C   42
   - 6-D   36

7. 3 + 9 =
   - 7-A   12
   - 7-B   11
   - 7-C   13
   - 7-D   14

8. 7 + 8 =
   - 8-A   12
   - 8-B   15
   - 8-C   17
   - 8-D   19

9. 3 × 8 =
   - 9-A   5
   - 9-B   13
   - 9-C   24
   - 9-D   32

10. 16 ÷ 2 =
    - 10-A   8
    - 10-B   12
    - 10-C   9
    - 10-D   6

11. 9 × 3 =
    - 11-A   21
    - 11-B   25
    - 11-C   27
    - 11-D   29

12. 3 + 4 =
    - 12-A   1
    - 12-B   7
    - 12-C   9
    - 12-D   11

13. 10 − 6 =
    - 13-A   4
    - 13-B   8
    - 13-C   14
    - 13-D   16

14. 1 + 5 =
    - 14-A   0
    - 14-B   4
    - 14-C   5
    - 14-D   6

15. 4 × 2 =

15-A   6
15-B   16
15-C   12
15-D   8

16. 49 ÷ 7 =

16-A   6
16-B   7
16-C   8
16-D   9

17. 3 × 10 =

17-A   7
17-B   13
17-C   15
17-D   30

18. 8 − 0 =

18-A   8
18-B   0
18-C   1
18-D   80

19. 5 + 8 =

19-A   11
19-B   12
19-C   13
19-D   15

20. 7 − 6 =

20-A   5
20-B   1
20-C   11
20-D   13

21. 8 − 3 =

21-A   5
21-B   11
21-C   12
21-D   13

22. 2 × 2 =

22-A   2
22-B   4
22-C   6
22-D   8

23. 6 ÷ 1 =

23-A   16
23-B   15
23-C   7
23-D   6

24. 6 ÷ 2 =

24-A   12
24-B   8
24-C   4
24-D   3

25. 4 + 5 =

25-A   25
25-B   20
25-C   11
25-D   9

26. 7 × 8 =

26-A   56
26-B   48
26-C   42
26-D   72

27. 9 + 6 =

27-A   13
27-B   14
27-C   15
27-D   16

28. 8 ÷ 2 =

28-A   4
28-B   7
28-C   1
28-D   6

29. 7 − 1 =

29-A   8
29-B   0
29-C   7
29-D   6

30. 8 ÷ 8 =

30-A   8
30-B   0
30-C   16
30-D   1

31. 2 × 9 =

    31-A   17
    31-B   19
    31-C   18
    31-D   16

32. 7 + 3 =

    32-A   4
    32-B   10
    32-C   13
    32-D   11

33. 30 ÷ 3 =

    33-A   33
    33-B   11
    33-C   12
    33-D   10

34. 6 + 8 =

    34-A   14
    34-B   15
    34-C   17
    34-D   19

35. 9 + 2 =

    35-A   10
    35-B   7
    35-C   11
    35-D   12

36. 1 × 5 =

    36-A   5
    36-B   1
    36-C   6
    36-D   10

37. 9 ÷ 3 =

    37-A   3
    37-B   8
    37-C   9
    37-D   18

38. 4 × 8 =

    38-A   24
    38-B   28
    38-C   32
    38-D   42

39. 5 ÷ 5 =

    39-A   25
    39-B   10
    39-C   5
    39-D   1

40. 7 − 4 =

    40-A   11
    40-B   9
    40-C   6
    40-D   3

41. 4 − 0 =

    41-A   0
    41-B   4
    41-C   1
    41-D   5

42. 1 × 2 =

    42-A   1
    42-B   2
    42-C   3
    42-D   4

43. 16 ÷ 4 =

    43-A   4
    43-B   8
    43-C   12
    43-D   20

44. 9 × 9 =

    44-A   99
    44-B   0
    44-C   72
    44-D   81

45. 5 + 7 =

    45-A   11
    45-B   2
    45-C   12
    45-D   13

46. 10 − 4 =

    46-A   4
    46-B   6
    46-C   8
    46-D   14

47. 4 + 7 =

    47-A   3

    47-B   21

    47-C   12

    47-D   11

48. 9 × 5 =

    48-A   45

    48-B   47

    48-C   55

    48-D   36

49. 20 ÷ 2 =

    49-A   40

    49-B   22

    49-C   18

    49-D   10

50. 8 − 7 =

    50-A   56

    50-B   15

    50-C   5

    50-D   1

STOP!

IF YOU FINISH BEFORE THE TIME IS UP, YOU MAY CHECK OVER YOUR WORK ON THIS PART ONLY.

PART 10: CODING SPEED

NOTE: This section is not included on paper-and-pencil versions of ASVAB. It is included on the ASVAB computer-adaptive test (CAT), but may be eliminated in the near future. Check with your recruiter for details.

Directions

This is a test of 84 items to see how quickly and accurately you can find a number in a table. At the top of each section, there is a number table or "key." The key is a group of words with a code number for each word.

Each question in the test is a word taken from the key at the top. From among the possible answers listed for each question, find the one that is the correct code number for that word.

Look at the sample key and answer the five sample questions below. Note that each of the questions is one of the words in the key. To the right of each question are possible answers listed under the options A, B, C, D, and E.

Sample Questions

Key

green 2715	man 3451	salt 4586
hat 1413	room 2864	tree 5972

Questions		Options				
		A	**B**	**C**	**D**	**E**
S-1.	room	1413	2715	2864	3451	4586
S-2.	green	2715	2864	3451	4586	5972
S-3.	tree	2715	2864	3451	4586	5972
S-4.	hat	1413	2715	2864	3451	4586
S-5.	room	1413	2864	3451	4586	5972

By looking at the key you see that the code number for the first word, "room," is 2864. 2864 is listed under the letter (C), so (C) is the correct answer. The correct answers for the other four questions are (A), (E), (A), and (B).

This is a speed test, so work as fast as you can without making mistakes.

Notice that Part 10 begins at the top of the next answer form. When you begin, be sure to start with question number 1 in Part 10 of your test booklet and number 1 in Part 10 on your answer form.

DO NOT CONTINUE UNTIL TOLD TO DO SO.

Coding Speed

Time: 7 Minutes—84 Questions

Key

button 5266	dawn 9745	gold 8351	love 2456	pot 7007
chop 1817	flu 3838	iris 4658	mail 6234	puppy ... 6606

Questions		Options				
		A	**B**	**C**	**D**	**E**
1.	button	2456	4658	5266	6234	8351
2.	puppy	1817	2456	5266	6234	6606
3.	gold	1817	3838	6234	8351	9745
4.	mail	2456	4658	5266	6234	8351
5.	flu	3838	5266	6234	6606	9745
6.	iris	2456	4658	5266	6234	8351
7.	pot	3838	5266	6606	7007	9745
8.	chop	1817	3838	6234	6606	8351
9.	love	2456	4658	5266	6234	9745
10.	iris	1817	3838	4658	6234	7007
11.	dawn	2456	3838	6234	6606	9745
12.	mail	2456	4658	6234	8351	9745

Key

axle 5614	club 1090	lamp 6686	muffin 3939	trip 8968
baby 9846	guitar 4379	mop 2545	noose 7867	waste ... 4886

Questions		Options				
		A	**B**	**C**	**D**	**E**
13.	guitar	3939	4379	4886	6686	7867
14.	waste	1090	2545	3939	4379	4886
15.	axle	4379	4886	5614	6686	8968
16.	mop	1090	2545	4379	7867	9846
17.	trip	3939	4886	6686	8968	9846
18.	lamp	2545	3939	4886	5614	6686
19.	club	1090	4379	4886	5614	7867
20.	muffin	2545	3939	4379	7867	8968
21.	noose	4379	5614	7867	8968	9846
22.	lamp	1090	3939	4886	6686	8968
23.	baby	4379	4886	6686	7867	9846
24.	noose	1090	6686	7867	8968	9846

Key

aunt 7959	deer 8812	hail 1929	judge 5761	mark 6776
couch 4790	dove 1918	iron 2458	ladle 3344	pistol ...9434

Questions			Options		
		A	**B**	**C**	**D**	**E**
25.	pistol	1918	1929	4790	7959	9434
26.	iron	1929	2458	3344	6776	7959
27.	mark	3344	4790	5761	6776	7959
28.	judge	1918	1929	2458	4790	5761
29.	ladle	2458	3344	6776	7959	9434
30.	couch	4790	5761	6776	8812	9434
31.	deer	1918	2458	5761	7959	8812
32.	aunt	3344	5761	7959	8812	9434
33.	pistol	1929	3344	4790	7959	9434
34.	dove	1918	1929	2458	3344	4790
35.	mark	4790	6776	7959	8812	9434
36.	hail	1929	2458	5761	6776	7959

Key

coach 4589	eagle 5583	lunch 2024	oven 1418	stable .. 3377
coal 9260	gun 1118	marble 6874	root 6943	top 7337

Questions			Options		
		A	**B**	**C**	**D**	**E**
37.	marble	2024	4589	5583	6874	6943
38.	stable	1418	3377	5583	7337	9260
39.	eagle	1118	2024	3377	5583	6874
40.	lunch	1118	1418	2024	6943	9260
41.	oven	1418	3377	4589	6943	7337
42.	coal	2024	4589	6874	6943	9260
43.	root	5583	6874	6943	7337	9260
44.	coach	1118	2024	3377	4589	6874
45.	top	1418	3377	5583	6943	7337
46.	gun	1118	1418	4589	7337	9260
47.	eagle	2024	3377	5583	6943	7337
48.	root	1418	2024	6943	7337	9260

Key

| bed | 4814 | doll | 9086 | fence | 2026 | girl | 8797 | kick | 7546 |
| coat | 3765 | elbow | 5511 | gift | 1683 | index | 6904 | lump | 2826 |

Questions		Options			
	A	**B**	**C**	**D**	**E**
49. index	2026	2826	3765	6904	9086
50. coat	1683	3765	4814	5511	7546
51. lump	2826	3765	6904	7546	8797
52. fence	1683	2026	4814	5511	6904
53. kick	1683	3765	6904	7546	8797
54. doll	2026	2826	6904	8797	9086
55. bed	4814	5511	7546	8797	9086
56. elbow	1683	4814	5511	6904	7546
57. gift	1683	2026	3765	4814	6904
58. girl	2826	3765	6904	7546	8797
59. coat	1683	2026	2826	3765	4814
60. kick	2026	2826	3765	4814	7546

Key

| air | 1230 | cabin | 5254 | edge | 6010 | goose | 4656 | knee | 3369 |
| brush | 8800 | day | 1010 | fate | 7946 | island | 9064 | lever | 2125 |

Questions		Options			
	A	**B**	**C**	**D**	**E**
61. island	1010	3369	7946	8800	9064
62. goose	1230	2125	4656	5254	6010
63. knee	2125	3369	5254	7946	8800
64. fate	1010	1230	3369	4656	7946
65. brush	2125	4656	5254	8800	9064
66. lever	1010	1230	2125	6010	8800
67. cabin	3369	4656	5254	7946	9064
68. edge	1230	2125	4656	6010	8800
69. air	1230	3369	5254	7946	9064
70. knee	1010	1230	2125	3369	4656
71. cabin	1230	2125	3369	4656	5254
72. day	1010	1230	6010	8800	9064

Key

bell 5458	dash 4844	fuss 4363	iron 9100	mug 7613
cable 1058	echo 1978	height 2984	jewel 6877	tub 3439

Questions		**Options**				
		A	**B**	**C**	**D**	**E**
73.	height	1058	1978	2984	7613	9100
74.	jewel	1978	4844	5458	6877	7613
75.	bell	2984	3439	4363	4844	5458
76.	dash	2984	3439	4363	4844	6877
77.	cable	1058	1978	6877	7613	9100
78.	fuss	3439	4363	4844	5458	7613
79.	mug	2984	4363	5458	6877	7613
80.	echo	1978	2984	5458	7613	9100
81.	tub	3439	4363	4844	6877	7613
82.	iron	1058	1978	4363	7613	9100
83.	bell	1978	2984	5458	6877	7613
84.	dash	4363	4844	5458	7613	9100

STOP!

IF YOU FINISH BEFORE THE TIME IS UP, YOU MAY CHECK OVER YOUR WORK ON THIS PART ONLY.

ANSWER KEY

Use these answer keys to determine how many questions you answered correctly on each part and to list those items that you answered incorrectly or that you are not sure how to answer.

Be certain to review carefully and understand the rationale for arriving at the correct answers for all questions you answered incorrectly, as well as those you answered correctly but are unsure of. This is absolutely essential in order to acquire the knowledge and expertise necessary to obtain the maximum scores possible on the actual ASVAB tests.

Transfer the scores you obtained on each part of the Second ASVAB Specimen Test to the Self-Appraisal Chart appearing on page 24. This will enable you to see the progress made as you continue to prepare for the actual test.

Part 1—General Science

Answer Key				
1. C	2. D	3. C	4. D	5. D
6. B	7. D	8. B	9. D	10. A
11. D	12. B	13. A	14. C	15. B
16. D	17. C	18. B	19. D	20. B
21. B	22. A	23. C	24. A	25. B

Items Answered Incorrectly: _____ ; _____ ; _____ ; _____ ; _____ ; _____ ; _____ ; _____ .

Items Unsure Of: ____ ; __ ; __ ; __ ; __ ; __ ; __ ; __ .

Total Number Answered Correctly: _____ .

Part 2—Arithmetic Reasoning

Answer Key				
1. A	2. B	3. C	4. D	5. D
6. B	7. D	8. C	9. B	10. A
11. C	12. B	13. B	14. C	15. A
16. C	17. B	18. B	19. B	20. A
21. B	22. A	23. D	24. C	25. B
26. A	27. B	28. D	29. D	30. B

Items Answered Incorrectly: ____ ; ___ ; ____ ; ___ ; ____ ; ____ ; ___ ; ____ .

Items Unsure Of: ___ ; __ ; __ ; __ ; __ ; __ ; __ ; __ .

Total Number Answered Correctly: ___ .

Part 3—Word Knowledge

Answer Key				
1. B	2. A	3. C	4. D	5. D
6. C	7. B	8. A	9. B	10. D
11. A	12. D	13. C	14. A	15. D
16. C	17. B	18. C	19. B	20. A
21. D	22. C	23. B	24. D	25. A
26. C	27. D	28. C	29. A	30. C
31. B	32. A	33. D	34. D	35. D

Items Answered Incorrectly: ____ ; ___ ; ____ ; ___ ; ____ ; ____ ; ___ ; ____ .

Items Unsure Of: ___ ; __ ; __ ; __ ; __ ; __ ; __ ; __ .

Total Number Answered Correctly: _____ .

Part 4—Paragraph Comprehension

Answer Key				
1. D	2. C	3. D	4. A	5. B
6. A	7. B	8. B	9. C	10. D
11. A	12. D	13. C	14. D	15. D

Items Answered Incorrectly: _____; _____; _____; _____; _____; _____; _____; _____.

Items Unsure Of: _____; ___; ___; ___; ___; ___; ___; ___.

Total Number Answered Correctly: ___.

Part 5—Mathematics Knowledge

Answer Key				
1. C	2. C	3. B	4. A	5. A
6. B	7. D	8. A	9. A	10. D
11. D	12. C	13. D	14. B	15. D
16. B	17. C	18. C	19. D	20. B
21. C	22. B	23. A	24. A	25. C

Items Answered Incorrectly: _____; _____; _____; _____; _____; _____; _____; _____.

Items Unsure Of: _____; ___; ___; ___; ___; ___; ___; ___.

Total Number Answered Correctly: _____.

Part 6—Electronics Information

Answer Key				
1. B	2. D	3. C	4. B	5. C
6. B	7. B	8. A	9. C	10. B
11. A	12. B	13. D	14. B	15. C
16. D	17. C	18. B	19. D	20. B

Items Answered Incorrectly: ____; ____ ; ____; ____ ; ____; ____; ____; ____ .

Items Unsure Of: ____; ___; ___; ___; ___; ___; ___; ___ .

Total Number Answered Correctly: ____ .

Part 7—Auto & Shop Information

Answer Key				
1. C	2. D	3. B	4. C	5. B
6. A	7. D	8. C	9. B	10. A
11. C	12. D	13. A	14. C	15. A
16. A	17. C	18. D	19. D	20. C
21. D	22. C	23. B	24. B	25. A

Items Answered Incorrectly: ____; ____ ; ____; ____ ; ____; ____; ____; ____ .

Items Unsure Of: ____; ___; ___; ___; ___; ___; ___; ___ .

Total Number Answered Correctly: ____ .

Part 8—Mechanical Comprehension

Answer Key				
1. D	2. A	3. D	4. B	5. C
6. B	7. C	8. A	9. D	10. A
11. C	12. D	13. B	14. A	15. C
16. B	17. A	18. A	19. A	20. B
21. A	22. C	23. D	24. B	25. B

Items Answered Incorrectly: ____ ; ____ ; ____ ; ____ ; ____ ; ____ ; ____ ; ____ .

Items Unsure Of: ____ ; __ ; __ ; __ ; __ ; __ ; __ ; __ .

Total Number Answered Correctly: ___ .

Part 9—Numerical Operations

Answer Key				
1. B	2. A	3. B	4. D	5. C
6. B	7. A	8. B	9. C	10. A
11. C	12. B	13. A	14. D	15. D
16. B	17. D	18. A	19. C	20. B
21. A	22. B	23. D	24. D	25. D
26. A	27. C	28. A	29. D	30. D
31. C	32. B	33. D	34. A	35. C
36. A	37. A	38. C	39. D	40. D
41. B	42. B	43. A	44. D	45. C
46. B	47. D	48. A	49. D	50. D

Items Answered Incorrectly: ____ ; ____ ; ____ ; ____ ; ____ ; ____ ; ____ ; ____ .

Items Unsure Of: ____ ; __ ; __ ; __ ; __ ; __ ; __ ; __ .

Total Number Answered Correctly: _____ .

Part 10—Coding Speed

Answer Key				
1. C	2. E	3. D	4. D	5. A
6. B	7. D	8. A	9. A	10. C
11. E	12. C	13. B	14. E	15. C
16. B	17. D	18. E	19. A	20. B
21. C	22. D	23. E	24. C	25. E
26. B	27. D	28. E	29. B	30. A
31. E	32. C	33. E	34. A	35. B
36. A	37. D	38. B	39. D	40. C
41. A	42. E	43. C	44. D	45. E
46. A	47. C	48. C	49. D	50. B
51. A	52. B	53. D	54. E	55. A
56. C	57. A	58. E	59. D	60. E
61. E	62. C	63. B	64. E	65. D
66. C	67. C	68. D	69. A	70. D
71. E	72. A	73. C	74. D	75. E
76. D	77. A	78. B	79. E	80. A
81. A	82. E	83. C	84. B	

Items Answered Incorrectly: _____ ; ____ ; ____ ; ____ ; ____ ; ____ ; ____ ; ____ .

Items Unsure Of: ____ ; __ ; __ ; __ ; __ ; __ ; __ ; __ .

Total Number Answered Correctly: ____ .

ANSWER EXPLANATIONS

Part 1—General Science

1-C   Citrus fruits include lemons, limes, oranges, and grapefruits.

2-D   Water freezes at 0° on a centigrade or Celsius thermometer. Water freezes at 32° Fahrenheit.

3-C   The major chemical constituent of a cell by importance is protein but by weight it is water.

4-D   Syphilis is caused by the spirochete *Treponema pallidum*. The spirochete is a type of bacteria.

5-D   Wood alcohol is methyl alcohol, which is extremely toxic; drinking it may cause blindness. Isopropyl alcohol is rubbing alcohol. Glyceryl alcohol is an industrial solvent.

6-B   Nitrogen constitutes about four fifths of the earth's atmosphere, by volume.

7-D   By the process of photosynthesis, green plants remove carbon dioxide from the atmosphere and replace it with oxygen.

8-B   Ringworm is a skin disease caused by a fungus.

9-D   Light enters the eye through the pupil (the opening in the center of the iris), travels through the transparent crystalline lens, then travels through the vitreous humor (eyeball), and finally focuses on the retina.

10-A   The salivary glands secrete the enzyme ptyalin, which acts on carbohydrates.

11-D   Vitamin K is useful in the coagulation of blood. Vitamin C prevents scurvy; vitamin E maintains muscle tone and aids in fertility; and vitamin D prevents rickets.

12-B   A bulkhead is a wall; the anchor keeps the ship from moving; and the prow is the front of the ship.

13-A   Lime is highly alkaline.

14-C   Bacteria on the roots of legumes, plants that include peas and beans, serve to fixate free nitrogen and return it to the soil as nitrates.

15-B   Decay bacteria decompose organic compounds of dead organisms to inorganic compounds, which enrich the soil.

16-D   All vegetables contain some vitamin C, and yellow vegetables contain more vitamin C than green ones. However, citrus fruits contain far more vitamin C than any vegetables, and tomatoes are citrus fruits.

17-C   The cyclotron is the machine that splits atoms.

18-B   It takes the earth one year to complete an orbit of the sun. A year contains 365 days, or 52 weeks.

19-D   The weight of the salt water displaced by a human body is greater than the weight of fresh water displaced by that same body. Because the water displaced is heavier, the body is proportionally lighter and is more buoyant.

20-B   Boiling lava erupts from a volcano. The force that causes the eruption is pressure inside the earth.

21-B   The scientific name of an organism consists of the genus and the species.

22-A   The dry cell and the storage battery are devices in which chemical reactions produce electricity.

23-C   The 18″ mark is at the center of the yardstick and at the center of gravity. The forces on it are balanced at that point.

24-A   When two forces act on an object in opposite directions, the resultant force produced is equal to the difference between the two forces.

25-B   The moon is a satellite of the earth.

Part 2—Arithmetic Reasoning

1-A   8% of 75 = 6 shares; 75 shares + 6 shares = 81 shares

2-B   28 miles ÷ 3 mph $= 9.33$ hrs. $= 9\frac{1}{3}$ hrs. $= 9$ hrs. 20 min.

3-C   100 ft. − 60 ft. = 40 ft.

4-D   The number of hours in the clerk's work week is irrelevant. Figure the percent of his time that he spent at the enumerated tasks. The difference between that percent and his full week (100%) is the percent of his time spent on messenger work.

$$\frac{1}{5} = \frac{14}{70}$$

$$\frac{1}{2} = \frac{35}{70}$$

$$\frac{1}{7} = \frac{10}{70}$$

$$\frac{59}{70} = .84 = 84\%;\ 100\% - 84\%$$

$$= 16\% \text{ on messenger work}$$

5-D $6,200 − $4,000 = $2,200 is the amount he made. $2,200 ÷ $50 (profit on each bicycle) = 44 bicycles sold.

6-B   Rename the miles as kilometers by dividing them by $\frac{5}{8}$.

$$500 \text{ miles} \div \frac{5}{8} = \frac{\overset{100}{\cancel{500}}}{1} \times \frac{8}{\cancel{5}} = 800 \text{ kilometers}$$

7-D There are 144 pencils in a gross; $144 \times 6 = 864$ pencils in all. $864 \div 24 = 36$ weeks' worth of pencils.

8-C $\dfrac{3}{8} = \dfrac{9}{24}$

$\dfrac{1}{4} = \dfrac{6}{24}$

$\dfrac{1}{6} = \dfrac{4}{24}$

$\overline{\phantom{\dfrac{1}{6}}}$

$\dfrac{19}{24}$ of the pads were issued;

$$\frac{5}{24} \text{ remained} \frac{5}{\underset{1}{\cancel{24}}} \times \frac{\overset{25}{\cancel{600}}}{1} = 125 \text{ pads remained}$$

9-B The regular cost of 4 records was $6.98 \times 4 = \$27.92$. The sale price of 4 records was $12.50 \times 2 = \$25.00$. $27.92 - \$25.00 = \$2.92$

10-A 1 hour = 60 minutes. At 3 miles per hour, the student covers 1 mile every 20 minutes. Therefore, she will need 40 minutes to walk 2 miles.

11-C 8 a.m. + 15 hours = 23 o'clock = 11 p.m.

12-B Express the relationship of games won to games played as a fraction: $\dfrac{8}{24}$.

Reduce to lowest terms: $\dfrac{8}{24} = \dfrac{1}{3}$

Then convert to a percent:

$\dfrac{1}{3} = .33\overline{3} = 33\dfrac{1}{3}\%$

13-B $1,000.00 - \$941.20 = \$58.80$

14-C $\$4.98 \times 4 = \$19.92$

$\$8.29 \times 2 = \$16.58$

$\underline{+\$8.09 \times 2 = \$16.18}$

$\$52.68$

15-A   48 − 40 = 8 hours overtime

Salary for 8 hours overtime:

$$1\frac{1}{2} \times \$8.60 \times 8 = \frac{3}{\cancel{2}_1} \times \$8.60 \times \cancel{8}^4$$

$$= \$103.20$$

Salary for 40 hours regular time:

$$\$8.60 \times 40 = \$344.00$$

Total salary = \$344.00 + \$103.20

$$= \$447.20$$

16-C   68.5° − 59.9° = 8.6°

17-B   Let x = length of shadow of nearby pole.

$$12 : 4 = 24 : x$$
$$12x = 96$$
$$x = 8 \text{ feet.}$$

18-B   Multiply the number of monthly payments by amount to be paid each month:
16 × \$20 = \$320. Add the down payment to the total of monthly payments:

\$320 + \$40 = \$360.

19-B   Add the three monthly totals, then divide by 3 to find the average monthly cost:

$$\begin{array}{r} \$42.30 \\ 38.60 \\ + \ \underline{43.00} \\ \$123.90 \end{array} \qquad \$123.90 \div 3 = \$41.30$$

20-A $10 \times \dfrac{1}{2}$ hours = 5 hours

21-B   1,400 miles ÷ 50 mph = 28 hours

22-A   Only choices A and C represent 72 ounces. 6 × \$.39 = \$2.34, which is less than
3 × \$.79 = \$2.37

23-D   From −2°F to 0°F = 2°

From 0°F to 10°F = 10°

10° + 2° = 12°

24-C   Fred paid \$5.98 − \$2.00 = \$3.98 for one record, plus \$5.98 for the second record, totaling \$9.96.

25-B   Rate = Distance ÷ Time 1,200 miles ÷ 20 hours = 60 mph

26-A $33\frac{1}{3}\% = \frac{1}{3}$; $\$88.50 \times \frac{1}{3} = \$29.50$

27-B 4 ft. 8 in. × 3 = 12 ft. 24 in. = 14 ft.

28-D $21.00 + $14.98 + $4.97 = $40.95

29-D Don drove 50 miles × 2 hours = 100 miles. Frank drove 40 miles × 2 hours = 80 miles. Since they drove in opposite directions, add the two distances to learn that they were 180 miles apart.

30-B $\$14.28 \times 1 = \$14.28$
$33.26 \times 2 = \;\;66.52$
$+\underline{65.38 \times 2 = 130.76}$
$\$211.56$

Part 3—Word Knowledge

1-B *Revenue* means *income*. Taxes produce revenue but they are not in themselves revenue.

2-A To *convene* is to *assemble* or to *meet*. When people convene they often debate, agree, and/or drink.

3-C *Manual*, as opposed to automatic or mechanical, means hand-operated.

4-D *Deportment* means *behavior* or *conduct*.

5-D *Prior* means *previous* or *earlier*.

6-C Grimy and ragged often go together, but *grimy* means *dirty*.

7-B *Approximate* means *nearly* exact.

8-A To *survive* is to *live beyond the life or existence of another*, in short, to *outlive*.

9-B *Competent* means *qualified* or *capable*.

10-D To *suspend* is to *stop temporarily*.

11-A A *territory* is a *large expanse of land or water*, a *region*.

12-D *Huge* means *very large, enormous,* or *immense*.

13-C To *prevent* is to *keep from happening* or to *hinder*.

14-A To *forward* is to *transmit* or to *send on*.

15-D *Vacant* means *unfilled* or *empty*.

16-C To *irritate* is to *incite impatience or displeasure*, to *exasperate*, or to *annoy*.

17-B *Uniform* means *all the same, consistent,* or *unchanging*.

18-C *Power* is *strength* or *force*. All the other choices are attributes that might help one to attain power.

19-B The *shore* is the *land bordering a body of water*—in other words, the *coast*.

20-A *Flexible* means *capable of being adapted, elastic,* or *pliable.*

21-D To *comprehend* is to *grasp the meaning of* or to *understand.*

22-C To *instruct* is to *teach*; an *instructor* is a *teacher.*

23-B To *commend* is to *recommend as worthy of notice* or to *praise.*

24-D To *revolve* is to *turn around* or to *rotate.*

25-A To be *alert* is to be *wide awake* and *watchful.*

26-C To *function* is to *operate* or to *work.*

27-D A *hazard* is a *risk, peril,* or *danger.*

28-C A *blemish* is a *mark of deformity,* a *defect,* or a *flaw.*

29-A To *convey* is to *transmit,* to *transport,* or to *carry.*

30-C A *pedestrian* is a *foot traveler,* a *walker.* Pedestrians walk across the street.

31-B An *attorney* is a *lawyer.*

32-A *Obsolete* means *no longer in use* or *out-of-date.*

33-D *Stationary* means *fixed in one place, not movable.*

34-D *Steady* means *constant* and *regular.*

35-D To *emphasize* is to *stress.*

Part 4—Paragraph Comprehension

1-D The second sentence in the passage states that the battery converts an electrical charge into chemical energy that is stored until the battery terminals are connected to a closed external circuit.

2-C The first sentence states that a good or service has value only because people want it.

3-D The second sentence states that a toad's skin is both dry and rough.

4-A The last sentence states that a nautical mile is equal to 6,080 feet, while an ordinary mile is 5,280 feet. Accordingly, a nautical mile is longer than an ordinary mile.

5-B The third sentence states that for stereophonic sound, a different sound is recorded in each wall of the groove.

6-A The business of publishing city directories is a private business operated for profit. As such, it is a commercial enterprise.

7-B The passage says that enough data has been collected to draw the conclusion that the rural crime rates are lower than those in urban communities.

8-B The passage lists many different uses for iron.

9-C The spaces allow roads, sidewalks, and railroad tracks to expand in the summer and contract in winter without cracking or breaking.

10-D The second sentence states that crime is the result of opportunity plus desire. Accordingly, to prevent crime, it is each individual's responsibility to prevent the opportunity.

11-A The first sentence states that when there is a sharp rise in demand for new buildings, construction invariably lags behind; that is, there are fewer new buildings in proportion to buyers.

12-D The last sentence states that when there is a sudden drop in the demand for new buildings their prices fall because the available supply cannot be curtailed.

13-C The first sentence states that a large proportion of the people behind bars are not criminals but people who are being held until their trial in court.

14-D The last sentence states that those who do wind up in detention tend to be the poor, the unemployed, the single, and the young.

15-D The passage states that one who can show that he is a stable citizen with a job and a family will be released on "personal recognizance" and can often avoid the detention system without paying bail.

Part 5—Mathematics Knowledge

1-C There are 12 marbles in the box. 4 out of 12 are red = 1 out of 3 are red. The probability of picking a red marble is $\frac{1}{3}$.

2-C If the sides are parallel, the angles are congruent.

3-B A hexagon has 6 sides. $(n - 2) \times 180° = (6 - 2) \times 180° = 720°$.

4-A Subtract A^2 from both sides of the equation: $B^2 = X^2$, therefore $B = \pm X$.

5-A $6 + x + y = 20$

$x + y = 14 = k$; now substitute

$20 - 14 = 6$

6-B $\sqrt{75} = \sqrt{3 \times 25} = 5\sqrt{3}$

7-D The first step in finding a square root is grouping the digits into pairs, starting at the decimal point. If necessary, place a 0 to the left of the first digit to create a pair. Each pair represents one digit in the square root. The square root of 960 is a two-digit number in the 30s because the square root of 09 is 3.

8-A $\angle 2$ and $\angle 1$ are supplementary angles. $m\angle 1 = 100°$. $\angle 1$ and $\angle 4$ are supplementary. $m\angle 4 = 80°$.

9-A $\dfrac{10^4}{10} = \dfrac{10000}{10} = 1000 = 10^3$

The base remains unchanged.

10-D $7x - 6 + 5x + 18 = 12x + 12 = 180°$

$12x = 180° - 12 = 168°$

$x = 14$

$5 \times 14 + 18 = 70 + 18 = 88°$

11-D $8 + 5(x - y) = 8 + 5x - 5y$

Since $x = y$, $5x = 5y$ and $5x - 5y = 0$

Substituting: $8 + 0 = 8$

12-C $S = 1$

$R = 3 \times 1$

$+T = \dfrac{1}{3}$

$\overline{\qquad}$

$4\dfrac{1}{3}$

13-D   Each jacket can be worn with 5 pairs of pants. $3 \times 5 = 15$

14-B   When the divisor is a decimal, move the decimal point to the right until the divisor becomes an integer. Move the decimal point in the dividend to the right the same number of spaces. Place the decimal point in the quotient directly above the decimal point in the dividend.

$$.08\overline{)1.672} = 20.9$$

15-D   You must do the same thing to both sides of an equation. To find R, you must divide the right side of the equation by T ($R \times T \div T = R$). Therefore, you must also divide the left side of the equation by T ($D \div T$). The equation then reads $R = D \div T$.

16-B $C = 2\pi r$

$60 = 2\pi r$ (Divide both sides by 2π)

$r = 60 \div 2\pi$

17-C   87 can be divided by 3 as well as by 1 and itself.

18-C   Pick a pair of ages and try for yourself. A is 2; B is 4; the ratio of their ages is 2 : 4 or 1 : 2. In two years, A is 4 and B is 6. The ratio of their ages is 4 : 6 or 2 : 3.

19-D

$x + 3$

$\times 2x + 5$

$\overline{\qquad}$

$2x^2 + 6x$

$\quad 5x + 15$

$\overline{\qquad}$

$2x^2 + 11x + 15$

20-B

$$x + 3$$
$$\underline{\times\ x + 2}$$
$$x^2 + 3x$$
$$\underline{\quad\quad 2x + 6}$$
$$x^2 + 5x + 6$$

21-C Let x equal shorter side; $2x$ equals length of longer side. $6x = 90$; $x = 15$;   longer side = $2x = 30$.

22-B The formula for the area of a triangle is one half the base times the height.

23-A "Percent" means out of 100. If K percent are emotionally unstable, then K out of 100 are emotionally unstable. The remainder, $100 - K$, are not unstable.

24-A The larger wheel is 3 times the size of the smaller wheel, so it makes one third the revolutions.

$$42 \div 3 = 14$$

25-C By definition, a square must have four equal sides and four right angles.

Part 6—Electronics Information

1-B A three-way switch is a single-pole double-throw switch or two single-pole switches.

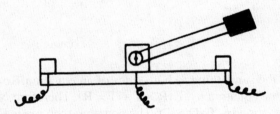

2-D Leather gloves offer the best protection over the rubber gloves. The leather can withstand severe conditions before it will tear. The rubber acts as insulation.

3-C A "mil" is short for milli or 1/1,000 of an inch.

4-B The formula for determining the current in a parallel circuit is: $I_t = I_1 + I_2 + I_3 + ... I_n$. The current going through the lamps is 1 amp + 1 amp = 2 amps.

5-C Never use a fuse having a higher rating than that specifically called for in the circuit. A fuse is a safety device used to protect a circuit from serious damage caused by too high a current.

6-B Silver is a much better conductor of electricity than copper. However, gold is also used for tuner contacts because it will not tarnish. Silver can tarnish.

7-B A "2-line return-call" electric bell circuit would have 2 bells, 2 metallic lines, 2 return-call push buttons, and 2 sets of batteries. It might look like this:

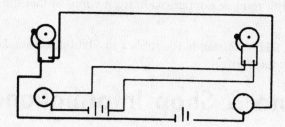

8-A   Figure 1, a connector, is used to join two sections of aluminum pipe conduit.

9-C   Grounding a fixture is a safety precaution used to lessen the chance of shock.

10-B   In electrical terms, potential or E.M.F. is the voltage. Electricians consider any voltage of 600 volts or less to be low potential.

11-A   A rheostat regulates the amount of voltage to the motor. The more voltage to a motor, the faster it will turn.

12-B   A polarized plug is used so that the plug can only go into the receptacle in one way. The prongs are at an angle to one another.

13-D   When reading an electric meter, you read the lower number just before the pointer. This meter would show 6872 kilowatt hours.

14-B   In a DC motor, the commutators are the metal contact points that the brushes come into contact with.

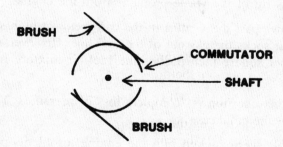

15-C   The neutral wire is whitish in color; the hot lead is black; and the ground wire is green.

16-D   Carbon, crystal, and dynamic are all types of microphones. Feedback is a condition caused when sound coming from a speaker is fed back into a microphone, causing noise.

17-C   This type of connector will join a flexible metallic conduit to a junction box. The wire is secured by tightening the compression screw. The locknut is tightened to secure the connector to the junction box.

18-B   Good magnetic metals are iron, steel, nickel, and cobalt. Iron is the only one mentioned here.

19-D   Rosin is used to remove copper-oxide from wires so that the solder can join the copper wires.

20-B   In the letters RHW, R stands for rubber insulation, H stands for heat resistant, and W stands for waterproof.

Part 7—Auto & Shop Information

1-C   Automobiles use internal combustion engines. Gasoline is exploded inside a cylinder to produce power.

2-D   The four strokes of an internal combustion engine are the intake stroke, the compression stroke, the power stroke, and the exhaust stroke.

3-B   Vapor-lock usually occurs when the gasoline in the gas line has turned to vapor and the carburetor does not get enough gasoline.

4-C   Batteries in a car are refilled with distilled water. The other chemicals either will not work or will damage the battery.

5-B   Overheating the brake shoe will cause the brake material to glaze and become slippery. Slippery brakes are dangerous because they take longer to stop a car.

6-A   Graphite, which is powdered carbon, is very slippery and will not bind the small springs and metal parts of a lock.

7-D   Usually when an alarm light goes on, the best procedure is to stop the car immediately. However, the discharge light shows that the battery is not charging and if the car is stopped it may not start again. If the engine is running, there is enough electricity being made to get the car to a gas station; do not turn off the ignition until you get there.

8-C   The intake manifold conducts the gas-air mixture to the cylinders and the exhaust manifold gets rid of the waste products from the engine.

9-B   When air flows past the venturi in the carburetor at high speed, a low pressure area is created that sucks the gas out of the fuel line. However, normal air pressure (about 15 pounds per square inch pushes the fuel-air mixture from the carburetor to the cylinders.

10-A   The key to this question is "complete loss of pressure." This would be caused by a lack of oil in the crankcase.

11-C   If soap or talc were sucked into the engine, problems might arise. Heavy grease might not be taken in by a small leak. Oil can be burned in the engine if it were used to indicate a leak around the intake manifold.

12-D   If the intake manifold is warped, air would seep in. The carburetor would get a lean mixture of too much air and not enough gas. The engine would then run at a fast idle.

13-A   By placing a screwdriver at the end of a brace, you will have a much wider turning arc than by just using an ordinary screwdriver. The wider the turning arc, the more force that the screwdriver will exert. Screwdrivers with wide handles exert more force than those with narrow handles.

14-C   This is a Phillips-head screwdriver. It will turn Phillips-head screws with this shape:

15-A   A jointer plane is used for planing wood when close tolerances are required.

16-A   The number on the box of wood screws tells the thickness. The higher the number, the thicker the screw. A number 10 wood screw will be thicker than a number 6 wood screw.

17-C   Paint is made thinner or easier to apply by diluting it with turpentine. Linseed oil and varnish are not used as paint thinners.

18-D   The opened face on this tool shows that it is an open-end wrench.

19-D   Mastic, a glue, is applied to a wall with a serrated applicator. Then, the tiles are pressed into the mastic.

20-C   An "Allen" wrench is hexagonal and will fit into screw C.

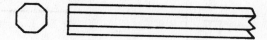

21-D   The smoothest finish can be obtained by sanding the wood with the grain.

22-C   The number of points on a saw tells the number of teeth per inch. For example, a 6-point saw has 6 teeth per inch and a 22-point saw has 22 teeth per inch.

23-B   A brad is similar to a finishing nail in that both nails do not have flat heads and can be countersunk into the wood.

24-B   The carpenter's "hand screw" is shown in Figure B.

25-A   A brace and bit are used to drill holes while the other tools are used to smooth down wood.

Part 8—Mechanical Comprehension

1-D   Because the upper block is connected to an immovable hook, it must remain stationary.

2-A   The distortion of the cam causes the valve to rise when contact is made. The amount of this distortion is the length Y.

3-D   To move the pistons to the right, valves 1, 3, and 4 must be open. Valve 4 permits the air to enter the system; valve 3 allows the air to hit the left side of the piston; and valve 1 is an exhaust channel for the air.

4-B   When the water level rises past the safe area, the float turns on the sump pump. When the level of water in the sump pump goes down, the float also goes down and will shut off the sump pump.

5-C   The centrifugal force acts to pull the balls outward. Since the two balls are connected to a yolk around the center bar, this outward motion pulls the balls upward.

6-B   The piston is now in part of the compression stroke; $\frac{1}{4}$ turn will move it to full compression; $\frac{1}{2}$ more turn will move it to the end of the power stroke. Adding $\frac{1}{4} + \frac{1}{2} = \frac{3}{4}$ turn.

7-C   To tighten the bolt, turn it counterclockwise. To tighten the nut on the bolt the reverse is true—turn it clockwise.

8-A   Pressure is defined as $\frac{\text{Force}}{\text{Area}}$. For a given force, 20 lbs., the smaller the area, the greater the pressure produced. The smallest area is at position A, requiring the least force to lift the weight.

9-D   The try-cocks show the level of the water inside the boiler. They use the principle that water seeks its own level in a system.

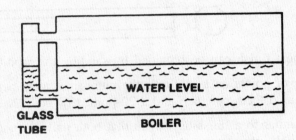

10-A There are 8 holes in the circular cross-section of the flanged pipe. All circles have 360°. Thus, each hole is separated by 360°/8 or 22.5°/hole.

11-C The sum of the moments must be zero.

Summing around the fulcrum we have:

(6 ft. × 5 lbs.) + (3 ft. × 10 lbs.) = 6 ft. × F

Combining terms, we get: 60 (ft. – lbs.) = 6 ft. × F

Dividing both sides by 6: 10 lbs. = F

12-D The ball will move up if the arm holding it is pulled up. This will happen when the nut is tightened.

13-B There are only 4 different types of symbols shown in the pictures:

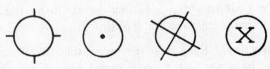

14-A To increase the efficiency of heating gas, baffles cause gases to mix more thoroughly and thereby to come in closer contact with the heating elements in a furnace.

15-C The problem here is that only part of a ruler is shown. Count 4 units on the 8th scale. This corresponds to $6\frac{1}{2}$ threads on the length to be threaded. Doubling the $6\frac{1}{2}$ threads (in $\frac{1}{2}$ inch) we get 13 threads in 1 inch.

16-B Two gears, moving together, turn in opposite directions. Liquid is thus forced through the pipe.

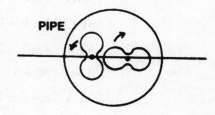

17-A The larger the pulley, the more distance it must cover, and therefore, the smaller the rpm. If A turns at 2,000 rpm, B (twice as large) turns at 1,000 rpm; C is attached to B and turns at the same rate. Finally, D (8 times larger than C) turns at 1,000/8 or 125 rpm.

18-A The weight is not centered but is closer to A. The distance from the center of the load to A is less than the distance from the center of the load to B. Therefore, A would support the greater part of the load.

19-A Let x = force that must be applied.

$$50 \times 1 = x \times 5; 50 = 5x; x = \frac{50}{5} = 10 \text{ lbs.}$$

20-B Figure 3, when folded on the dotted lines, forms the congruent triangles necessary to construct a closed triangular box.

21-A A single fixed pulley is actually a first-class lever with equal arms. The mechanical advantage, neglecting friction, is 1.

22-C If the block is moved toward the brick, the moment for a given force exerted will increase (being further from the force), making it easier to lift; the height will be made smaller, hardly raising the brick when moved to the limit (directly underneath it).

23-D The metal key has the highest conductivity. Metals are the best conductors of heat. The other choices can be used as insulators.

24-B One complete revolution will raise the weight 1 foot or 12 inches.

25-B The formula for circumference of a wheel is $C = 2\pi r$. The wheel radius of the bike in front is larger. One revolution of the larger wheel will cover a greater linear distance along the road in a given period of time.

Part 9—Numerical Operations

1-B	$60 \div 10 = 6$		**26-A**	$7 \times 8 = 56$
2-A	$5 - 2 = 3$		**27-C**	$9 + 6 = 15$
3-B	$3 \times 4 = 12$		**28-A**	$8 \div 2 = 4$
4-D	$8 - 6 = 2$		**29-D**	$7 - 1 = 6$
5-C	$4 + 8 = 12$		**30-D**	$8 \div 8 = 1$
6-B	$6 \times 8 = 48$		**31-C**	$2 \times 9 = 18$
7-A	$3 + 9 = 12$		**32-B**	$7 + 3 = 10$
8-B	$7 + 8 = 15$		**33-D**	$30 \div 3 = 10$
9-C	$3 \times 8 = 24$		**34-A**	$6 + 8 = 14$
10-A	$16 \div 2 = 8$		**35-C**	$9 + 2 = 11$
11-C	$9 \times 3 = 27$		**36-A**	$1 \times 5 = 5$
12-B	$3 + 4 = 7$		**37-A**	$9 \div 3 = 3$
13-A	$10 - 6 = 4$		**38-C**	$4 \times 8 = 32$
14-D	$1 + 5 = 6$		**39-D**	$5 \div 5 = 1$
15-D	$4 \times 2 = 8$		**40-D**	$7 - 4 = 3$
16-B	$49 \div 7 = 7$		**41-B**	$4 - 0 = 4$
17-D	$3 \times 10 = 30$		**42-B**	$1 \times 2 = 2$
18-A	$8 - 0 = 8$		**43-A**	$16 \div 4 = 4$
19-C	$5 + 8 = 13$		**44-D**	$9 \times 9 = 81$
20-B	$7 - 6 = 1$		**45-C**	$5 + 7 = 12$
21-A	$8 - 3 = 5$		**46-B**	$10 - 4 = 6$
22-B	$2 \times 2 = 4$		**47-D**	$4 + 7 = 11$
23-D	$6 \div 1 = 6$		**48-A**	$9 \times 5 = 45$
24-D	$6 \div 2 = 3$		**49-D**	$20 \div 2 = 10$
25-D	$4 + 5 = 9$		**50-D**	$8 - 7 = 1$

Part 10—Coding Speed

There is no way to explain the answers to the Coding Speed questions; they are either right or wrong. If you still find yourself making many mistakes, try to develop a new strategy on the next specimen test.

CHAPTER

THIRD ASVAB TEST BATTERY

ow that you have completed two test batteries, you should be feeling more confident about taking the ASVAB. You have keyed in on your strengths and weaknesses and have reviewed the subject material you need. This third test battery is another practice run through of the ASVAB.

Here are the guidelines again to help you make the most of this sample test battery:

- Take this test under "real" test conditions (time yourself, take it in a quiet room without distractions, and use the sample answer sheets).
- Time each test carefully and do not go over the time allotted for each section.
- Use the answer keys to get your test scores and to evaluate your performance on each test.
- Record the number of items you answered correctly and incorrectly for each section in the answer chart provided at the end of the battery. Also, record the number of items you want to review further or were unsure about.
- Carefully review and understand the answer explanations to all questions you answered incorrectly.
- Don't forget to review each of the questions that you answered correctly but may not be sure of. This is a necessary step to gain the knowledge and expertise you need to get the highest scores possible on the real ASVAB tests.
- Transfer your scores for each section of the First ASVAB Sample Test Battery to the Self-Appraisal Chart on page 24. This will enable you to track your progress as you continue to prepare for the actual test.
- Use the sample answer sheets provided to record your answers. If you want, you can cut them out to make them easier to use and to simulate actual test conditions.

Specimen Answer Sheet for Answering Parts 1–10
(On the following page)

Part 1: General Science

1. Ⓐ Ⓑ Ⓒ Ⓓ 2. Ⓐ Ⓑ Ⓒ Ⓓ 3. Ⓐ Ⓑ Ⓒ Ⓓ 4. Ⓐ Ⓑ Ⓒ Ⓓ 5. Ⓐ Ⓑ Ⓒ Ⓓ
6. Ⓐ Ⓑ Ⓒ Ⓓ 7. Ⓐ Ⓑ Ⓒ Ⓓ 8. Ⓐ Ⓑ Ⓒ Ⓓ 9. Ⓐ Ⓑ Ⓒ Ⓓ 10. Ⓐ Ⓑ Ⓒ Ⓓ
11. Ⓐ Ⓑ Ⓒ Ⓓ 12. Ⓐ Ⓑ Ⓒ Ⓓ 13. Ⓐ Ⓑ Ⓒ Ⓓ 14. Ⓐ Ⓑ Ⓒ Ⓓ 15. Ⓐ Ⓑ Ⓒ Ⓓ
16. Ⓐ Ⓑ Ⓒ Ⓓ 17. Ⓐ Ⓑ Ⓒ Ⓓ 18. Ⓐ Ⓑ Ⓒ Ⓓ 19. Ⓐ Ⓑ Ⓒ Ⓓ 20. Ⓐ Ⓑ Ⓒ Ⓓ
21. Ⓐ Ⓑ Ⓒ Ⓓ 22. Ⓐ Ⓑ Ⓒ Ⓓ 23. Ⓐ Ⓑ Ⓒ Ⓓ 24. Ⓐ Ⓑ Ⓒ Ⓓ 25. Ⓐ Ⓑ Ⓒ Ⓓ

Part 2: Arithmetic Reasoning

1. Ⓐ Ⓑ Ⓒ Ⓓ 2. Ⓐ Ⓑ Ⓒ Ⓓ 3. Ⓐ Ⓑ Ⓒ Ⓓ 4. Ⓐ Ⓑ Ⓒ Ⓓ 5. Ⓐ Ⓑ Ⓒ Ⓓ
6. Ⓐ Ⓑ Ⓒ Ⓓ 7. Ⓐ Ⓑ Ⓒ Ⓓ 8. Ⓐ Ⓑ Ⓒ Ⓓ 9. Ⓐ Ⓑ Ⓒ Ⓓ 10. Ⓐ Ⓑ Ⓒ Ⓓ
11. Ⓐ Ⓑ Ⓒ Ⓓ 12. Ⓐ Ⓑ Ⓒ Ⓓ 13. Ⓐ Ⓑ Ⓒ Ⓓ 14. Ⓐ Ⓑ Ⓒ Ⓓ 15. Ⓐ Ⓑ Ⓒ Ⓓ
16. Ⓐ Ⓑ Ⓒ Ⓓ 17. Ⓐ Ⓑ Ⓒ Ⓓ 18. Ⓐ Ⓑ Ⓒ Ⓓ 19. Ⓐ Ⓑ Ⓒ Ⓓ 20. Ⓐ Ⓑ Ⓒ Ⓓ
21. Ⓐ Ⓑ Ⓒ Ⓓ 22. Ⓐ Ⓑ Ⓒ Ⓓ 23. Ⓐ Ⓑ Ⓒ Ⓓ 24. Ⓐ Ⓑ Ⓒ Ⓓ 25. Ⓐ Ⓑ Ⓒ Ⓓ
26. Ⓐ Ⓑ Ⓒ Ⓓ 27. Ⓐ Ⓑ Ⓒ Ⓓ 28. Ⓐ Ⓑ Ⓒ Ⓓ 29. Ⓐ Ⓑ Ⓒ Ⓓ 30. Ⓐ Ⓑ Ⓒ Ⓓ

Part 3: Word Knowledge

1. Ⓐ Ⓑ Ⓒ Ⓓ 2. Ⓐ Ⓑ Ⓒ Ⓓ 3. Ⓐ Ⓑ Ⓒ Ⓓ 4. Ⓐ Ⓑ Ⓒ Ⓓ 5. Ⓐ Ⓑ Ⓒ Ⓓ
6. Ⓐ Ⓑ Ⓒ Ⓓ 7. Ⓐ Ⓑ Ⓒ Ⓓ 8. Ⓐ Ⓑ Ⓒ Ⓓ 9. Ⓐ Ⓑ Ⓒ Ⓓ 10. Ⓐ Ⓑ Ⓒ Ⓓ
11. Ⓐ Ⓑ Ⓒ Ⓓ 12. Ⓐ Ⓑ Ⓒ Ⓓ 13. Ⓐ Ⓑ Ⓒ Ⓓ 14. Ⓐ Ⓑ Ⓒ Ⓓ 15. Ⓐ Ⓑ Ⓒ Ⓓ
16. Ⓐ Ⓑ Ⓒ Ⓓ 17. Ⓐ Ⓑ Ⓒ Ⓓ 18. Ⓐ Ⓑ Ⓒ Ⓓ 19. Ⓐ Ⓑ Ⓒ Ⓓ 20. Ⓐ Ⓑ Ⓒ Ⓓ
21. Ⓐ Ⓑ Ⓒ Ⓓ 22. Ⓐ Ⓑ Ⓒ Ⓓ 23. Ⓐ Ⓑ Ⓒ Ⓓ 24. Ⓐ Ⓑ Ⓒ Ⓓ 25. Ⓐ Ⓑ Ⓒ Ⓓ
26. Ⓐ Ⓑ Ⓒ Ⓓ 27. Ⓐ Ⓑ Ⓒ Ⓓ 28. Ⓐ Ⓑ Ⓒ Ⓓ 29. Ⓐ Ⓑ Ⓒ Ⓓ 30. Ⓐ Ⓑ Ⓒ Ⓓ
31. Ⓐ Ⓑ Ⓒ Ⓓ 32. Ⓐ Ⓑ Ⓒ Ⓓ 33. Ⓐ Ⓑ Ⓒ Ⓓ 34. Ⓐ Ⓑ Ⓒ Ⓓ 35. Ⓐ Ⓑ Ⓒ Ⓓ

Part 4: Paragraph Comprehension

1. Ⓐ Ⓑ Ⓒ Ⓓ 2. Ⓐ Ⓑ Ⓒ Ⓓ 3. Ⓐ Ⓑ Ⓒ Ⓓ 4. Ⓐ Ⓑ Ⓒ Ⓓ 5. Ⓐ Ⓑ Ⓒ Ⓓ
6. Ⓐ Ⓑ Ⓒ Ⓓ 7. Ⓐ Ⓑ Ⓒ Ⓓ 8. Ⓐ Ⓑ Ⓒ Ⓓ 9. Ⓐ Ⓑ Ⓒ Ⓓ 10. Ⓐ Ⓑ Ⓒ Ⓓ
11. Ⓐ Ⓑ Ⓒ Ⓓ 12. Ⓐ Ⓑ Ⓒ Ⓓ 13. Ⓐ Ⓑ Ⓒ Ⓓ 14. Ⓐ Ⓑ Ⓒ Ⓓ 15. Ⓐ Ⓑ Ⓒ Ⓓ

Part 5: Mathematics Knowledge

1. Ⓐ Ⓑ Ⓒ Ⓓ   2. Ⓐ Ⓑ Ⓒ Ⓓ   3. Ⓐ Ⓑ Ⓒ Ⓓ   4. Ⓐ Ⓑ Ⓒ Ⓓ   5. Ⓐ Ⓑ Ⓒ Ⓓ
6. Ⓐ Ⓑ Ⓒ Ⓓ   7. Ⓐ Ⓑ Ⓒ Ⓓ   8. Ⓐ Ⓑ Ⓒ Ⓓ   9. Ⓐ Ⓑ Ⓒ Ⓓ   10. Ⓐ Ⓑ Ⓒ Ⓓ
11. Ⓐ Ⓑ Ⓒ Ⓓ   12. Ⓐ Ⓑ Ⓒ Ⓓ   13. Ⓐ Ⓑ Ⓒ Ⓓ   14. Ⓐ Ⓑ Ⓒ Ⓓ   15. Ⓐ Ⓑ Ⓒ Ⓓ
16. Ⓐ Ⓑ Ⓒ Ⓓ   17. Ⓐ Ⓑ Ⓒ Ⓓ   18. Ⓐ Ⓑ Ⓒ Ⓓ   19. Ⓐ Ⓑ Ⓒ Ⓓ   20. Ⓐ Ⓑ Ⓒ Ⓓ
21. Ⓐ Ⓑ Ⓒ Ⓓ   22. Ⓐ Ⓑ Ⓒ Ⓓ   23. Ⓐ Ⓑ Ⓒ Ⓓ   24. Ⓐ Ⓑ Ⓒ Ⓓ   25. Ⓐ Ⓑ Ⓒ Ⓓ

Part 6: Electronics Information

1. Ⓐ Ⓑ Ⓒ Ⓓ   2. Ⓐ Ⓑ Ⓒ Ⓓ   3. Ⓐ Ⓑ Ⓒ Ⓓ   4. Ⓐ Ⓑ Ⓒ Ⓓ   5. Ⓐ Ⓑ Ⓒ Ⓓ
6. Ⓐ Ⓑ Ⓒ Ⓓ   7. Ⓐ Ⓑ Ⓒ Ⓓ   8. Ⓐ Ⓑ Ⓒ Ⓓ   9. Ⓐ Ⓑ Ⓒ Ⓓ   10. Ⓐ Ⓑ Ⓒ Ⓓ
11. Ⓐ Ⓑ Ⓒ Ⓓ   12. Ⓐ Ⓑ Ⓒ Ⓓ   13. Ⓐ Ⓑ Ⓒ Ⓓ   14. Ⓐ Ⓑ Ⓒ Ⓓ   15. Ⓐ Ⓑ Ⓒ Ⓓ
16. Ⓐ Ⓑ Ⓒ Ⓓ   17. Ⓐ Ⓑ Ⓒ Ⓓ   18. Ⓐ Ⓑ Ⓒ Ⓓ   19. Ⓐ Ⓑ Ⓒ Ⓓ   20. Ⓐ Ⓑ Ⓒ Ⓓ

Part 7: Auto & Shop Information

1. Ⓐ Ⓑ Ⓒ Ⓓ   2. Ⓐ Ⓑ Ⓒ Ⓓ   3. Ⓐ Ⓑ Ⓒ Ⓓ   4. Ⓐ Ⓑ Ⓒ Ⓓ   5. Ⓐ Ⓑ Ⓒ Ⓓ
6. Ⓐ Ⓑ Ⓒ Ⓓ   7. Ⓐ Ⓑ Ⓒ Ⓓ   8. Ⓐ Ⓑ Ⓒ Ⓓ   9. Ⓐ Ⓑ Ⓒ Ⓓ   10. Ⓐ Ⓑ Ⓒ Ⓓ
11. Ⓐ Ⓑ Ⓒ Ⓓ   12. Ⓐ Ⓑ Ⓒ Ⓓ   13. Ⓐ Ⓑ Ⓒ Ⓓ   14. Ⓐ Ⓑ Ⓒ Ⓓ   15. Ⓐ Ⓑ Ⓒ Ⓓ
16. Ⓐ Ⓑ Ⓒ Ⓓ   17. Ⓐ Ⓑ Ⓒ Ⓓ   18. Ⓐ Ⓑ Ⓒ Ⓓ   19. Ⓐ Ⓑ Ⓒ Ⓓ   20. Ⓐ Ⓑ Ⓒ Ⓓ
21. Ⓐ Ⓑ Ⓒ Ⓓ   22. Ⓐ Ⓑ Ⓒ Ⓓ   23. Ⓐ Ⓑ Ⓒ Ⓓ   24. Ⓐ Ⓑ Ⓒ Ⓓ   25. Ⓐ Ⓑ Ⓒ Ⓓ

Part 8: Mechanical Comprehension

1. Ⓐ Ⓑ Ⓒ Ⓓ   2. Ⓐ Ⓑ Ⓒ Ⓓ   3. Ⓐ Ⓑ Ⓒ Ⓓ   4. Ⓐ Ⓑ Ⓒ Ⓓ   5. Ⓐ Ⓑ Ⓒ Ⓓ
6. Ⓐ Ⓑ Ⓒ Ⓓ   7. Ⓐ Ⓑ Ⓒ Ⓓ   8. Ⓐ Ⓑ Ⓒ Ⓓ   9. Ⓐ Ⓑ Ⓒ Ⓓ   10. Ⓐ Ⓑ Ⓒ Ⓓ
11. Ⓐ Ⓑ Ⓒ Ⓓ   12. Ⓐ Ⓑ Ⓒ Ⓓ   13. Ⓐ Ⓑ Ⓒ Ⓓ   14. Ⓐ Ⓑ Ⓒ Ⓓ   15. Ⓐ Ⓑ Ⓒ Ⓓ
16. Ⓐ Ⓑ Ⓒ Ⓓ   17. Ⓐ Ⓑ Ⓒ Ⓓ   18. Ⓐ Ⓑ Ⓒ Ⓓ   19. Ⓐ Ⓑ Ⓒ Ⓓ   20. Ⓐ Ⓑ Ⓒ Ⓓ
21. Ⓐ Ⓑ Ⓒ Ⓓ   22. Ⓐ Ⓑ Ⓒ Ⓓ   23. Ⓐ Ⓑ Ⓒ Ⓓ   24. Ⓐ Ⓑ Ⓒ Ⓓ   25. Ⓐ Ⓑ Ⓒ Ⓓ

Part 9: Numerical Operations

1. Ⓐ Ⓑ Ⓒ Ⓓ   2. Ⓐ Ⓑ Ⓒ Ⓓ   3. Ⓐ Ⓑ Ⓒ Ⓓ   4. Ⓐ Ⓑ Ⓒ Ⓓ   5. Ⓐ Ⓑ Ⓒ Ⓓ
6. Ⓐ Ⓑ Ⓒ Ⓓ   7. Ⓐ Ⓑ Ⓒ Ⓓ   8. Ⓐ Ⓑ Ⓒ Ⓓ   9. Ⓐ Ⓑ Ⓒ Ⓓ   10. Ⓐ Ⓑ Ⓒ Ⓓ
11. Ⓐ Ⓑ Ⓒ Ⓓ   12. Ⓐ Ⓑ Ⓒ Ⓓ   13. Ⓐ Ⓑ Ⓒ Ⓓ   14. Ⓐ Ⓑ Ⓒ Ⓓ   15. Ⓐ Ⓑ Ⓒ Ⓓ
16. Ⓐ Ⓑ Ⓒ Ⓓ   17. Ⓐ Ⓑ Ⓒ Ⓓ   18. Ⓐ Ⓑ Ⓒ Ⓓ   19. Ⓐ Ⓑ Ⓒ Ⓓ   20. Ⓐ Ⓑ Ⓒ Ⓓ
21. Ⓐ Ⓑ Ⓒ Ⓓ   22. Ⓐ Ⓑ Ⓒ Ⓓ   23. Ⓐ Ⓑ Ⓒ Ⓓ   24. Ⓐ Ⓑ Ⓒ Ⓓ   25. Ⓐ Ⓑ Ⓒ Ⓓ
26. Ⓐ Ⓑ Ⓒ Ⓓ   27. Ⓐ Ⓑ Ⓒ Ⓓ   28. Ⓐ Ⓑ Ⓒ Ⓓ   29. Ⓐ Ⓑ Ⓒ Ⓓ   30. Ⓐ Ⓑ Ⓒ Ⓓ
31. Ⓐ Ⓑ Ⓒ Ⓓ   32. Ⓐ Ⓑ Ⓒ Ⓓ   33. Ⓐ Ⓑ Ⓒ Ⓓ   34. Ⓐ Ⓑ Ⓒ Ⓓ   35. Ⓐ Ⓑ Ⓒ Ⓓ
36. Ⓐ Ⓑ Ⓒ Ⓓ   37. Ⓐ Ⓑ Ⓒ Ⓓ   38. Ⓐ Ⓑ Ⓒ Ⓓ   39. Ⓐ Ⓑ Ⓒ Ⓓ   40. Ⓐ Ⓑ Ⓒ Ⓓ
41. Ⓐ Ⓑ Ⓒ Ⓓ   42. Ⓐ Ⓑ Ⓒ Ⓓ   43. Ⓐ Ⓑ Ⓒ Ⓓ   44. Ⓐ Ⓑ Ⓒ Ⓓ   45. Ⓐ Ⓑ Ⓒ Ⓓ
46. Ⓐ Ⓑ Ⓒ Ⓓ   47. Ⓐ Ⓑ Ⓒ Ⓓ   48. Ⓐ Ⓑ Ⓒ Ⓓ   49. Ⓐ Ⓑ Ⓒ Ⓓ   50. Ⓐ Ⓑ Ⓒ Ⓓ

Part 10: Coding Speed

1. Ⓐ Ⓑ Ⓒ Ⓓ   2. Ⓐ Ⓑ Ⓒ Ⓓ   3. Ⓐ Ⓑ Ⓒ Ⓓ   4. Ⓐ Ⓑ Ⓒ Ⓓ   5. Ⓐ Ⓑ Ⓒ Ⓓ
6. Ⓐ Ⓑ Ⓒ Ⓓ   7. Ⓐ Ⓑ Ⓒ Ⓓ   8. Ⓐ Ⓑ Ⓒ Ⓓ   9. Ⓐ Ⓑ Ⓒ Ⓓ   10. Ⓐ Ⓑ Ⓒ Ⓓ
11. Ⓐ Ⓑ Ⓒ Ⓓ   12. Ⓐ Ⓑ Ⓒ Ⓓ   13. Ⓐ Ⓑ Ⓒ Ⓓ   14. Ⓐ Ⓑ Ⓒ Ⓓ   15. Ⓐ Ⓑ Ⓒ Ⓓ
16. Ⓐ Ⓑ Ⓒ Ⓓ   17. Ⓐ Ⓑ Ⓒ Ⓓ   18. Ⓐ Ⓑ Ⓒ Ⓓ   19. Ⓐ Ⓑ Ⓒ Ⓓ   20. Ⓐ Ⓑ Ⓒ Ⓓ
21. Ⓐ Ⓑ Ⓒ Ⓓ   22. Ⓐ Ⓑ Ⓒ Ⓓ   23. Ⓐ Ⓑ Ⓒ Ⓓ   24. Ⓐ Ⓑ Ⓒ Ⓓ   25. Ⓐ Ⓑ Ⓒ Ⓓ
26. Ⓐ Ⓑ Ⓒ Ⓓ   27. Ⓐ Ⓑ Ⓒ Ⓓ   28. Ⓐ Ⓑ Ⓒ Ⓓ   29. Ⓐ Ⓑ Ⓒ Ⓓ   30. Ⓐ Ⓑ Ⓒ Ⓓ
31. Ⓐ Ⓑ Ⓒ Ⓓ   32. Ⓐ Ⓑ Ⓒ Ⓓ   33. Ⓐ Ⓑ Ⓒ Ⓓ   34. Ⓐ Ⓑ Ⓒ Ⓓ   35. Ⓐ Ⓑ Ⓒ Ⓓ
36. Ⓐ Ⓑ Ⓒ Ⓓ   37. Ⓐ Ⓑ Ⓒ Ⓓ   38. Ⓐ Ⓑ Ⓒ Ⓓ   39. Ⓐ Ⓑ Ⓒ Ⓓ   40. Ⓐ Ⓑ Ⓒ Ⓓ
41. Ⓐ Ⓑ Ⓒ Ⓓ   42. Ⓐ Ⓑ Ⓒ Ⓓ   43. Ⓐ Ⓑ Ⓒ Ⓓ   44. Ⓐ Ⓑ Ⓒ Ⓓ   45. Ⓐ Ⓑ Ⓒ Ⓓ
46. Ⓐ Ⓑ Ⓒ Ⓓ   47. Ⓐ Ⓑ Ⓒ Ⓓ   48. Ⓐ Ⓑ Ⓒ Ⓓ   49. Ⓐ Ⓑ Ⓒ Ⓓ   50. Ⓐ Ⓑ Ⓒ Ⓓ
51. Ⓐ Ⓑ Ⓒ Ⓓ   52. Ⓐ Ⓑ Ⓒ Ⓓ   53. Ⓐ Ⓑ Ⓒ Ⓓ   54. Ⓐ Ⓑ Ⓒ Ⓓ   55. Ⓐ Ⓑ Ⓒ Ⓓ
56. Ⓐ Ⓑ Ⓒ Ⓓ   57. Ⓐ Ⓑ Ⓒ Ⓓ   58. Ⓐ Ⓑ Ⓒ Ⓓ   59. Ⓐ Ⓑ Ⓒ Ⓓ   60. Ⓐ Ⓑ Ⓒ Ⓓ
61. Ⓐ Ⓑ Ⓒ Ⓓ   62. Ⓐ Ⓑ Ⓒ Ⓓ   63. Ⓐ Ⓑ Ⓒ Ⓓ   64. Ⓐ Ⓑ Ⓒ Ⓓ   65. Ⓐ Ⓑ Ⓒ Ⓓ
66. Ⓐ Ⓑ Ⓒ Ⓓ   67. Ⓐ Ⓑ Ⓒ Ⓓ   68. Ⓐ Ⓑ Ⓒ Ⓓ   69. Ⓐ Ⓑ Ⓒ Ⓓ   70. Ⓐ Ⓑ Ⓒ Ⓓ
71. Ⓐ Ⓑ Ⓒ Ⓓ   72. Ⓐ Ⓑ Ⓒ Ⓓ   73. Ⓐ Ⓑ Ⓒ Ⓓ   74. Ⓐ Ⓑ Ⓒ Ⓓ   75. Ⓐ Ⓑ Ⓒ Ⓓ
76. Ⓐ Ⓑ Ⓒ Ⓓ   77. Ⓐ Ⓑ Ⓒ Ⓓ   78. Ⓐ Ⓑ Ⓒ Ⓓ   79. Ⓐ Ⓑ Ⓒ Ⓓ   80. Ⓐ Ⓑ Ⓒ Ⓓ
81. Ⓐ Ⓑ Ⓒ Ⓓ   82. Ⓐ Ⓑ Ⓒ Ⓓ   83. Ⓐ Ⓑ Ⓒ Ⓓ   84. Ⓐ Ⓑ Ⓒ Ⓓ

PART 1: GENERAL SCIENCE

Directions

This is a test of 25 questions to find out how much you know about general science as usually covered in high school courses. Pick the best answer for each question, then blacken the space on your answer form that has the same number and letter as your choice.

Here are three sample questions.

S1. Water is an example of a   Ⓐ Ⓑ Ⓒ Ⓓ

     S1-A   solid.

     S1-B   gas.

     S1-C   liquid.

     S1-D   crystal.

Now look at the section of your answer sheet labeled Part 1, "Practice." Notice that answer space C has been marked for question 1. Now do practice questions 2 and 3 by yourself. Find the correct answer to the question, then mark the space on your answer form that has the same letter as the answer you picked. Do this now.

S2. Lack of iodine is often related to which of the following diseases?   Ⓐ Ⓑ Ⓒ Ⓓ

     S2-A   Beriberi

     S2-B   Scurvy

     S2-C   Rickets

     S2-D   Goiter

S3. An eclipse of the sun throws the shadow of the   Ⓐ Ⓑ Ⓒ Ⓓ

     S3-A   earth on the moon.

     S3-B   moon on the earth.

     S3-C   moon on the sun.

     S3-D   earth on the sun.

You should have marked choice D for question 2 and choice B for question 3. If you made any mistakes, erase your mark carefully and blacken the correct answer space. Do this now.

Your score on this test will be based on the number of questions you answer correctly. You should try to answer every question. Do not spend too much time on any one question.

When you begin, be sure to start with question number 1 of Part 1 of your test booklet and number 1 in Part 1 on your answer form.

DO NOT CONTINUE UNTIL TOLD TO DO SO.

General Science

Time: 11 Minutes—25 Questions

1. Which one of the following is NOT a fruit?
   1-A   Potato
   1-B   Tomato
   1-C   Cucumber
   1-D   Green pepper

2. The hammer, anvil, and stirrup bones lie in the
   2-A   knee.
   2-B   hip.
   2-C   ear.
   2-D   elbow.

3. Of the following, a condition NOT associated with heavy cigarette smoking is
   3-A   shorter life span.
   3-B   slowing of the heartbeat.
   3-C   cancer of the lung.
   3-D   heart disease.

4. You are most likely to develop hypothermia when
   4-A   it is very hot and you have nothing to drink.
   4-B   you are bitten by a rabid dog.
   4-C   you fall asleep in the sun.
   4-D   it is very cold and your clothes are wet.

5. If you are caught away from home during a thunderstorm, the safest place to be is
   5-A   in a car.
   5-B   under a tree.
   5-C   in an open field.
   5-D   at the top of a small hill.

6. During a thunderstorm, we see a lightning bolt before we hear the sound of the accompanying thunder chiefly because
   6-A   the eye is more sensitive than the ear.
   6-B   the wind interferes with the sound of the thunder.
   6-C   the storm may be very far away.
   6-D   the speed of light is much greater than the speed of sound.

7. The Kelvin (K) unit is used to measure
   7-A   density.
   7-B   pressure.
   7-C   temperature.
   7-D   time.

8. The number of degrees on the Fahrenheit thermometer between the freezing point and the boiling point of water is
   8-A   100 degrees.
   8-B   212 degrees.
   8-C   180 degrees.
   8-D   273 degrees.

9. An observer on Earth sees the phases of the moon because the
   9-A   moon revolves around the sun.
   9-B   moon revolves around the earth.
   9-C   earth revolves around the sun.
   9-D   moon rotates on its axis.

10. Which of the following diseases is NOT caused by a pathogenic bacteria?
    10-A   Rabies
    10-B   Tetanus
    10-C   Typhoid fever
    10-D   Tuberculosis

11. A vector is used to represent force. The length of the vector indicates its

    11-A   direction.

    11-B   magnitude.

    11-C   magnitude and direction.

    11-D   velocity.

12. Of the following, the statement that best describes a "high" on a weather map is

    12-A   the air extends farther up than normal.

    12-B   the air pressure is greater than normal.

    12-C   the air temperature is higher than normal.

    12-D   the air moves faster than normal.

13. The smallest particle of gold that still retains the characteristics of gold is

    13-A   a molecule.

    13-B   a proton.

    13-C   an electron.

    13-D   an atom.

14. Narcotics may be dangerous if used without supervision, but they are useful in medicine because they

    14-A   increase production of red blood cells.

    14-B   kill bacteria.

    14-C   relieve pain.

    14-D   stimulate the heart.

15. The primary reason why fungi are often found growing in abundance deep in the forest is that

    15-A   it is cooler.

    15-B   it is warmer.

    15-C   they have little exposure to sunlight for photosynthesis.

    15-D   they have a plentiful supply of organic matter.

16. The presence of coal deposits in Alaska shows that at one time Alaska

    16-A   had a tropical climate.

    16-B   was covered with ice.

    16-C   was connected to Asia.

    16-D   was formed by volcanic action.

17. If a person has been injured in an accident and damage to the back and neck is suspected, it is best to

    17-A   roll the person over so that he does not lie on his back.

    17-B   rush the person to the nearest hospital.

    17-C   force the person to drink water to replace body fluids.

    17-D   wait for professional help.

18. A 1,000-ton ship must displace a weight of water equal to

    18-A   500 tons.

    18-B   1,500 tons.

    18-C   1,000 tons.

    18-D   2,000 tons.

19. Vitamin C is also known as

    19-A   citric acid.

    19-B   ascorbic acid.

    19-C   lactic acid.

    19-D   glutamic acid.

20. The temperature of the air falls at night because the earth loses heat by

    20-A   radiation.

    20-B   conduction.

    20-C   convection.

    20-D   rotation.

21. The normal height of a mercury barometer at sea level is

    21-A   15 inches.

    21-B   32 feet.

    21-C   30 inches.

    21-D   34 feet.

22. Nitrogen-fixing bacteria are found in nodules on the roots of the

    22-A   beet.

    22-B   potato.

    22-C   carrot.

    22-D   clover.

23. The vascular system of the body is concerned with

    23-A   respiration.

    23-B   sense of touch.

    23-C   circulation of blood.

    23-D   enzymes.

24. In which of the following types of rocks are most fossils found?

    24-A   Igneous

    24-B   Metamorphic

    24-C   Sedimentary

    24-D   Volcanic

25. If you wish to cut down on saturated fats and cholesterol in your diet, which of the following foods should you avoid?

    25-A   Fish

    25-B   Dry beans and peas

    25-C   Cheese

    25-D   Spaghetti

STOP!

IF YOU FINISH BEFORE THE TIME IS UP, YOU MAY CHECK OVER YOUR WORK ON THIS PART ONLY.

PART 2: ARITHMETIC REASONING

Directions

This test has 30 questions about arithmetic. Each question is followed by four possible answers. Decide which answer is correct, then blacken the space on your answer form that has the same number and letter as your choice. Use your scratch paper for any figuring you wish to do.

Here are two sample questions.

S1. A person buys a sandwich for 90¢, soda for 55¢, and pie for 70¢. What is the total cost?

S1-A	$2.00
S1-B	$2.05
S1-C	$2.15
S1-D	$2.25

Ⓐ Ⓑ Ⓒ Ⓓ

The total cost is $2.15; therefore, choice C is the correct answer.

S2. If 8 workers are needed to run 4 machines, how many workers are needed to run 20 machines?

S2-A	16
S2-B	32
S2-C	36
S2-D	40

Ⓐ Ⓑ Ⓒ Ⓓ

The number needed is 40; therefore, choice D is the correct answer.

Your score on this test will be based on the number of questions you answer correctly. You should try to answer every question. Do not spend too much time on any one question.

Notice that Part 2 begins with question number 1. When you begin, be sure to start with question number 1 in Part 2 of your test booklet and number 1 in Part 2 on your answer form.

DO NOT CONTINUE UNTIL TOLD TO DO SO.

Arithmetic Reasoning

Time: 36 Minutes—30 Questions

1. If pencils are bought at 70 cents per dozen and sold at 3 for 20 cents, the total profit on 6 dozen is
    - 1-A   50 cents.
    - 1-B   60 cents.
    - 1-C   65 cents.
    - 1-D   75 cents.

2. A certain type of siding for a house costs $10.50 per square yard. What does it cost for the siding for a wall 4 yards wide and 60 feet long?
    - 2-A $800
    - 2-B $840
    - 2-C $2,520
    - 2-D $3,240

3. A parcel delivery service charges $9.26 for the first 4 pounds of package weight and an additional $1.06 for each half pound over 4 pounds. What is the charge for a package weighing $6\frac{1}{2}$ pounds?
    - 3-A $2.65
    - 3-B $6.89
    - 3-C $11.91
    - 3-D $14.56

4. A typist uses lengthwise a sheet of paper 9 inches by 12 inches. She leaves a 1-inch margin on each side and a $1\frac{1}{2}$-inch margin on top and bottom. What fractional part of the page is used for typing?
    - 4-A $\dfrac{21}{22}$
    - 4-B $\dfrac{7}{12}$
    - 4-C $\dfrac{5}{9}$
    - 4-D $\dfrac{3}{4}$

5. A carpenter needs 4 boards, each 2 feet 9 inches long. If wood is sold only by the foot, how many feet must he buy?
    - 5-A   9
    - 5-B   10
    - 5-C   11
    - 5-D   12

6. An employee has $\dfrac{2}{9}$ of his salary withheld for income tax. The percent of his salary that is withheld is most nearly
    - 6-A   16%
    - 6-B   18%
    - 6-C   20%
    - 6-D   22%

7. On a blueprint in which 2 inches represents 5 feet, the length of a room measures $7\frac{1}{2}$ inches. The actual length of the room is

   7-A $12\frac{1}{2}$ feet.

   7-B $7\frac{1}{2}$ feet.

   7-C $15\frac{3}{4}$ feet.

   7-D $18\frac{3}{4}$ feet.

8. During a 25% off sale, an article sells for $375. What was the original price of this article?
   8-A $93.75
   8-B $468.75
   8-C $500
   8-D $575

9. The total length of fencing needed to enclose a rectangular area 46 feet by 34 feet is
   9-A   26 yards, 1 foot.

   9-B $26\frac{2}{3}$ yards.

   9-C   52 yards, 2 feet.

   9-D $53\frac{1}{3}$ yards.

10. A piece of wood 35 feet 6 inches long was used to make 4 shelves of equal length. The length of each shelf was

   10-A   9 feet, $1\frac{1}{2}$ inches.

   10-B   8 feet, $10\frac{1}{2}$ inches.

   10-C   7 feet, $10\frac{1}{2}$ inches.

   10-D   7 feet, $1\frac{1}{2}$ inches.

11. A team won 2 games and lost 10. The fraction of its games won is correctly expressed as

   11-A $\frac{1}{6}$

   11-B $\frac{1}{5}$

   11-C $\frac{4}{5}$

   11-D $\frac{5}{6}$

12. What is the simple interest on $600 at 8% for 2 years?
   12-A $48
   12-B $64
   12-C $96
   12-D $108

13. A change purse contained 3 half dollars, 8 quarters, 7 dimes, 6 nickels, and 9 pennies. Express in dollars and cents the total amount of money in the purse.
   13-A $3.78
   13-B $4.32
   13-C $3.95
   13-D $4.59

14. How much does a salesperson earn for selling $68 worth of writing paper if she is paid a commission of 40% on her sales?
   14-A $20.40
   14-B $25.60
   14-C $22.80
   14-D $27.20

15. If a certain job can be performed by 18 clerks in 26 days, the number of clerks need to perform the job in 12 days is
   15-A   24
   15-B   30
   15-C   39
   15-D   52

16. A carton contains 9 dozen file folders. If a clerk removes 53 folders, how many folders are left in the carton?

    16-A   37
    16-B   44
    16-C   55
    16-D   62

17. A man had $25.00. He saw some ties that cost $4.95 apiece. How many of these ties could he buy?

    17-A   6
    17-B   7
    17-C   5
    17-D   3

18. A man earns $20.56 on Monday; $32.90 on Tuesday; and $20.78 on Wednesday. He spends half of all that he earns during the three days. How much does he have left?

    18-A $29.19
    18-B $31.23
    18-C $34.27
    18-D $37.12

19. How many packages of candy containing $\frac{3}{4}$ of a pound each can be filled from 15 pounds of candy?

    19-A   10
    19-B   20
    19-C   15
    19-D   25

20. A champion runner ran the 100-yard dash in three track meets. The first time he ran it in 10.2 seconds; the second in 10.4 seconds; and the third in 10 seconds. What was his average time?

    20-A   10.1 seconds
    20-B   10.2 seconds
    20-C   10.3 seconds
    20-D   10.4 seconds

21. A crate containing a tool weighs 12 pounds. If the tool weighs 9 pounds, 9 ounces, how much does the crate weigh?

    21-A   2 pounds, 1 ounce
    21-B   2 pounds, 7 ounces
    21-C   3 pounds, 1 ounce
    21-D   3 pounds, 7 ounces

22. The area of a room measuring 12 feet by 15 feet is

    22-A   9 square yards.
    22-B   12 square yards.
    22-C   15 square yards.
    22-D   20 square yards.

23. A woman purchased a blouse for $10.98. She returned the blouse the next day and selected a better one costing $12.50. She gave the clerk a 5-dollar bill to pay for the difference in price. How much change should she receive?

    23-A $3.58
    23-B $3.48
    23-C $2.52
    23-D $1.52

24. The daily almanac report for one day during the summer stated that the sun rose at 6:14 a.m. and set at 6:06 p.m. Find the number of hours and minutes in the time between the rising and setting of the sun on that day.

    24-A   11 hours, 52 minutes
    24-B   11 hours, 2 minutes
    24-C   12 hours, 8 minutes
    24-D   12 hours, 48 minutes

25. In a 45-minute gym class, 30 boys want to play basketball. Only 10 can play at once. If each player is to play the same length of time, how many minutes should each play?

    25-A   8
    25-B   12
    25-C   15
    25-D   20

26. The library charges 5¢ for the first day and 2¢ for each additional day that a book is overdue. If a borrower paid 65¢ in late charges, for how many days was the book overdue?

    26-A   15
    26-B   21
    26-C   25
    26-D   31

27. How many slices of bread, each weighing 2 ounces, are needed to balance 2 pounds of apples?

    27-A   8
    27-B   12
    27-C   16
    27-D   24

28. If $\frac{1}{2}$ cup of spinach contains 80 calories and the same amount of peas contains 300 calories, how many cups of spinach have the same caloric content as a $\frac{2}{3}$ cup of peas?

    28-A $\frac{2}{5}$

    28-B $1\frac{1}{3}$

    28-C   2

    28-D $2\frac{1}{2}$

29. If it takes 30 minutes to type 6 pages, how many hours will it take to type 126 pages at the same rate?

    29-A   6.3
    29-B   10.5
    29-C   15
    29-D   25

30. A night watchman must check a certain storage area every 45 minutes. If he first checks the area as he begins a 9-hour tour of duty, how many times will he have checked this storage area?

    30-A   10
    30-B   11
    30-C   12
    30-D   13

STOP!

IF YOU FINISH BEFORE THE TIME IS UP, YOU MAY CHECK OVER YOUR WORK ON THIS PART ONLY.

PART 3: WORD KNOWLEDGE

Directions

This test has 35 questions about the meanings of words. Each question has an underlined word. You are to decide which one of the four words in the choices most nearly means the same as the underlined word, then mark the space on your answer form that has the same number and letter as your choice.

Now look at the two sample questions below.

S1. <u>Mended</u> most nearly means   Ⓐ Ⓑ Ⓒ Ⓓ
   S1-A   repaired.
   S1-B   torn.
   S1-C   clean.
   S1-D   tied.

Repaired, choice A, is the correct answer. *Mended* means *fixed* or *repaired. Torn,* choice B, might be the state of an object before it is mended. The repair might be made by *tying,* choice D, but not necessarily. *Clean,* choice C, is wrong.

S2. It was a <u>small</u> table.   Ⓐ Ⓑ Ⓒ Ⓓ
   S1-A   Sturdy
   S1-B   Round
   S1-C   Cheap
   S1-D   Little

Little means the same as *small,* so choice D is the best answer.

Your score on this test will be based on the number of questions you answer correctly. You should try to answer every question. Do not spend too much time on any one question.

When you begin, be sure to start with question number 1 in Part 3 of your test booklet and number 1 in Part 3 on your answer form.

DO NOT CONTINUE UNTIL TOLD TO DO SO.

Word Knowledge

Time: 11 Minutes—35 Questions

1. <u>Superiority</u> most nearly means
   1-A   abundance.
   1-B   popularity.
   1-C   permanence.
   1-D   excellence.

2. <u>Absurd</u> most nearly means
   2-A   disgusting.
   2-B   foolish.
   2-C   reasonable.
   2-D   very old.

3. Be careful, that liquid is <u>inflammable</u>!
   3-A   Poisonous
   3-B   Valuable
   3-C   Explosive
   3-D   Likely to give off fumes

4. <u>Conscious</u> most nearly means
   4-A   surprised.
   4-B   afraid.
   4-C   disappointed.
   4-D   aware.

5. <u>Exhibit</u> most nearly means
   5-A   display.
   5-B   trade.
   5-C   sell.
   5-D   label.

6. We <u>assumed</u> that Jack had been elected.
   6-A   Knew
   6-B   Wished
   6-C   Decided
   6-D   Supposed

7. <u>Counterfeit</u> most nearly means
   7-A   mysterious.
   7-B   false.
   7-C   unreadable.
   7-D   priceless.

8. <u>Expertly</u> most nearly means
   8-A   awkwardly.
   8-B   quickly.
   8-C   skillfully.
   8-D   unexpectedly.

9. <u>Marshy</u> most nearly means
   9-A   swampy.
   9-B   sandy.
   9-C   wooded.
   9-D   rocky.

10. The children pledged <u>allegiance</u> to the flag.
    10-A   Freedom
    10-B   Homeland
    10-C   Protection
    10-D   Loyalty

11. The cashier <u>yearned</u> for a vacation.
    11-A   Begged
    11-B   Longed
    11-C   Saved
    11-D   Applied

12. <u>Summit</u> most nearly means
    12-A   face.
    12-B   top.
    12-C   base.
    12-D   side.

13. The driver <u>heeded</u> the traffic signals.
    13-A   Worried about
    13-B   Ignored
    13-C   Disagreed with
    13-D   Took notice of

14. <u>Vigorously</u> most nearly means
    14-A   sleepily.
    14-B   thoughtfully.
    14-C   energetically.
    14-D   sadly.

15. <u>Imitate</u> most nearly means
    15-A   copy.
    15-B   attract.
    15-C   study.
    15-D   appreciate.

16. The <u>severity</u> of their criticism upset us.
    16-A   Harshness
    16-B   Suddenness
    16-C   Method
    16-D   Unfairness

17. <u>Incredible</u> most nearly means
    17-A   thrilling.
    17-B   convincing.
    17-C   uninteresting.
    17-D   unbelievable.

18. We made a very <u>leisurely</u> trip to California.
    18-A   Roundabout
    18-B   Unhurried
    18-C   Unforgettable
    18-D   Tiresome

19. <u>Gratitude</u> most nearly means
    19-A   thankfulness.
    19-B   excitement.
    19-C   disappointment.
    19-D   sympathy.

20. <u>Familiar</u> most nearly means
    20-A   welcome.
    20-B   dreaded.
    20-C   rare.
    20-D   well known.

21. He had an <u>acute</u> pain in his back.
    21-A   Dull
    21-B   Slight
    21-C   Alarming
    21-D   Sharp

22. <u>Bewildered</u> most nearly means
    22-A   worried.
    22-B   offended.
    22-C   puzzled.
    22-D   delighted.

23. <u>Conclusion</u> most nearly means
    23-A   theme.
    23-B   suspense.
    23-C   end.
    23-D   beginning.

24. She likes the <u>aroma</u> of fresh-brewed coffee.
    24-A   Flavor
    24-B   Warmth
    24-C   Fragrance
    24-D   Steam

25. <u>Nonessential</u> most nearly means
    25-A   damaged.
    25-B   unnecessary.
    25-C   expensive.
    25-D   foreign-made.

26. <u>Amplified</u> most nearly means
    26-A   expanded.
    26-B   summarized.
    26-C   analyzed.
    26-D   shouted.

27. The vase remained <u>intact</u> after it was dropped.
    27-A   Unattended
    27-B   Undamaged
    27-C   A total loss
    27-D   Unmoved

28. Penicillin is a <u>potent</u> drug.
    28-A   Harmless
    28-B   Possible
    28-C   Effective
    28-D   Drinkable

29. <u>Terminate</u> most nearly means
    29-A   continue.
    29-B   go by train.
    29-C   begin.
    29-D   end.

30. The prisoner is a <u>notorious</u> bank robber.
    30-A   Convicted
    30-B   Dangerous
    30-C   Well-known
    30-D   Escaped

31. <u>Fatal</u> most nearly means
    31-A   accidental.
    31-B   deadly.
    31-C   dangerous.
    31-D   beautiful.

32. <u>Indigent</u> people are entitled to food stamps.
    32-A   Poor
    32-B   Lazy
    32-C   Angry
    32-D   Homeless

33. <u>Technique</u> most nearly means
    33-A   computed.
    33-B   engineered.
    33-C   calculation.
    33-D   method.

34. <u>Vocation</u> most nearly means
    34-A   school.
    34-B   examination.
    34-C   occupation.
    34-D   carpentry.

35. One should eat only <u>mature</u> fruits.
    35-A   Edible
    35-B   Washed
    35-C   Ripe
    35-D   Sprayed

STOP!

IF YOU FINISH BEFORE THE TIME IS UP, YOU MAY CHECK OVER YOUR WORK ON THIS PART ONLY.

PART 4: PARAGRAPH COMPREHENSION

Directions

This test contains 15 items measuring your ability to obtain information from written passages. You will find one or more paragraphs of reading material followed by incomplete statements or questions. You are to read the paragraph(s) and select the lettered choice that best completes the statement or answers the question.

Here are two sample questions.

S1. From a building designer's standpoint, three things that make a home livable are the needs of the client, the building site, and the amount of money the client has to spend.

According to the passage, to make a home livable   Ⓐ Ⓑ Ⓒ Ⓓ
- S1-A   the prospective piece of land makes little difference.
- S1-B   it can be built on any piece of land.
- S1-C   the design must fit the owner's income and site.
- S1-D   the design must fit the designer's income.

The correct answer is that the design must fit the owner's income and site, so choice C is the correct response.

S2. In certain areas, water is so scarce that every attempt is made to conserve it. For instance, on one oasis in the Sahara Desert the amount of water necessary for each date palm tree has been carefully determined.

How much water is each tree given?   Ⓐ Ⓑ Ⓒ Ⓓ
- S2-A   No water at all
- S2-B   Exactly the amount required
- S2-C   Water only if it is healthy
- S2-D   Water on alternate days

The correct answer is exactly the amount required, so choice B is the correct response.

Your score on this test will be based on the number of questions you answer correctly. You should try to answer every question. Do not spend too much time on any one question.

When you begin, be sure to start with question number 1 in Part 4 of your test booklet and number 1 in Part 4 on your answer form.

DO NOT CONTINUE UNTIL TOLD TO DO SO.

Paragraph Comprehension

Time: 13 Minutes—15 Questions

1. The prevention of accidents makes it necessary not only that safety devices be used to guard exposed machinery, but also that mechanics be instructed in safety rules that they must follow for their own protection.

    The passage best supports the statement that industrial accidents
    1-A   are always avoidable.
    1-B   may be due to ignorance.
    1-C   usually result from inadequate machinery.
    1-D   cannot be entirely overcome.

2. Just as the procedure of a collection department must be clear-cut and definite, so the various paragraphs of a collection letter must show clear organization, giving evidence of a mind that has a specific end in view.

    The passage best supports the statement that a collection letter should always
    2-A   be divided into several paragraphs.
    2-B   express confidence in the debtor.
    2-C   be brief but courteous.
    2-D   be carefully planned.

3. The rights of an individual should properly be considered of greatest importance in a democracy until the activities of an individual come in conflict with the community interest or with the interest of society.

    According to this passage, in a democracy
    3-A   there is nothing of greater importance than the rights of the individual.
    3-B   there must be no conflict between the interest of the community and the rights of the individual.
    3-C   the rights of the individual are secondary to the interest of the community.
    3-D   the rights of the individual are generally incompatible with the interest of society.

4. Thomas Edison was responsible for over 1,000 inventions in his 84-year life span. Among the most famous of his inventions are the phonograph, the electric light bulb, motion picture film, the electric generator, and the battery.

    According to the passage, Thomas Edison
    4-A   was the most famous inventor.
    4-B   was responsible for 84 inventions.
    4-C   invented many things in his short life.
    4-D   was responsible for the phonograph and motion picture film.

5. Scientists are taking a closer look at the recent boom in the use of wood for heating. Wood burning, it seems, releases high levels of pollutants. It is believed that burning wood produces a thousand times more CO, carbon monoxide, than natural gas does when it burns.

    According to the passage, CO is
    5-A   natural gas.
    5-B   wood.
    5-C   carbon monoxide.
    5-D   heat.

6. The location of a railway line is necessarily a compromise between the desire to build the line with as little expense as possible and the desire to construct it so that its route will cover that over which trade and commerce are likely to flow.

    The route selected for a railway line
    6-A   should be the one over which the line can be built most cheaply.
    6-B   determines the location of commercial centers.
    6-C   should always cover the shortest possible distance between its terminals.
    6-D   cannot always be the one involving the lowest construction costs.

7. A survey to determine the subjects that have helped students most in their jobs shows that type-writing leads all other subjects in the business group. It also leads among the subjects college students consider most valuable and would take again if they were to return to high school.

    The paragraph best supports the statement that
    7-A   the ability to type is an asset in business and in school.
    7-B   students who return to night school take typing.
    7-C   students with a knowledge of typing do superior work in college.
    7-D   success in business is assured those who can type.

8. Direct lighting is the least satisfactory lighting arrangement. The desk or ceiling light with a reflector that diffuses all the rays downward is sure to cause glare on the working surface.

    Direct lighting is least satisfactory as a method of lighting chiefly because
    8-A   the light is diffused causing eye strain.
    8-B   the shade on the individual desk lamp is not constructed along scientific lines.
    8-C   the working surface is usually obscured by the glare.
    8-D   direct lighting is injurious to the eyes.

9. In almost every community, fortunately, there are certain men and women known to be public-spirited. Others, however, may be selfish and act only as their private interests seem to require.

    The paragraph suggests that those citizens who disregard others are
    9-A   needed.
    9-B   found only in small communities.
    9-C   not known.
    9-D   not public-spirited.

10. Unfortunately, specialization in industry creates workers who lack versatility. When a laborer is trained to perform only one task, he or she is almost entirely dependent for employment upon the demand for that particular skill. If anything happens to interrupt that demand, he or she is unemployed.

The paragraph best supports the statement that

10-A   the demand for labor of a particular type is constantly changing.

10-B   the average laborer is not capable of learning more than one task at a time.

10-C   some cases of unemployment are due to laborers' lack of versatility.

10-D   too much specialization is as dangerous as too little.

Questions 11 and 12 are based on the following passage.

Because electric drills run at high speed, the cutting edges of a twist drill are heated quickly. If the metal is thick, the drill point must be withdrawn from the hole frequently to cool it and clear out chips. Forcing the drill continuously into a deep hole will heat it, thereby spoiling its temper and cutting edges. A portable electric drill can be used to drill holes in material too large to handle in a drill press.

11. According to the above passage, overheating a twist drill will

11-A   slow down the work.

11-B   cause excessive drill breakage.

11-C   dull the drill.

11-D   spoil the accuracy of the work.

12. One method of preventing overheating of a twist drill, according to the above passage, is to

12-A   use cooling oil.

12-B   drill a smaller pilot hole first.

12-C   use a drill press.

12-D   remove the drill from the work frequently.

Questions 13–15 are based on the passage shown below.

Many accidents and injuries can be prevented if employees learn to be more careful. Wearing shoes with badly worn soles or open toes can easily lead to foot injuries from tacks, nails, and chair legs. Loose or torn clothing should not be worn near moving machinery. When supplies are stored, they should be placed or piled so that nothing sticks out of the pile.

If an employee is injured, no matter how small the injury, he or she should report it to the supervisor and have the injury treated. A small cut not attended to can easily become infected and can cause more trouble than some injuries that at first seem more serious. It never pays to take chances.

13. According to the passage above, an employee who gets a slight cut should

13-A   have it treated to help prevent infection.

13-B   know that a slight cut becomes more easily infected than a big cut.

13-C   pay no attention to it as it can't become serious.

13-D   realize that it is more serious than any other type of injury.

14. According to the passage, you should NOT wear loose clothing when you are

    14-A   in a corridor.

    14-B   storing supplies.

    14-C   moving chairs.

    14-D   near moving machinery.

15. According to the passage above, it is *not* true that

    15-A   by being more careful, employees can reduce the number of accidents.

    15-B   women should wear shoes with open toes for comfort when working.

    15-C   supplies should be piled so that nothing is sticking out from the pile.

    15-D   if an employee sprains his or her wrist at work he or she should tell the supervisor about it.

STOP!

IF YOU FINISH BEFORE THE TIME IS UP, YOU MAY CHECK OVER YOUR WORK ON THIS PART ONLY.

PART 5: MATHEMATICS KNOWLEDGE

Directions

This is a test of your ability to solve 25 general mathematical problems. You are to select the correct response from the choices given. Then mark the space on your answer form that has the same number and letter as your choice. Use the scratch paper that has been given to you to do any figuring that you wish.

Now look at the two sample problems below.

S1. If $x + 6 = 7$, then x is equal to   Ⓐ Ⓑ Ⓒ Ⓓ

S1-A	0
S1-B	1
S1-C	−1
S1-D	$\frac{7}{6}$

The correct answer is 1, so choice B is the correct response.

S2. What is the area of this square?   Ⓐ Ⓑ Ⓒ Ⓓ

S2-A	1 square foot
S2-B	5 square feet
S2-C	10 square feet
S2-D	25 square feet

The correct answer is 25 square feet, so choice D is the correct response.

Your score on this test will be based on the number of questions you answer correctly. You should try to answer every question. Do not spend too much time on any one question.

When you are told to begin, be sure to start with question number 1 in Part 5 of your test booklet and number 1 in Part 5 on your answer form.

DO NOT CONTINUE UNTIL TOLD TO DO SO.

Mathematics Knowledge

Time: 24 Minutes—25 Questions

1. The cube of 8 is
   - 1-A   128
   - 1-B   256
   - 1-C   512
   - 1-D   None of the above

2. When $2x - 1$ is multiplied by 10, the result is 70. What is the value of x?
   - 2-A   2
   - 2-B   12
   - 2-C   3
   - 2-D   4

3. If the circumference of a circle has the same numbered value as its area, then the radius of the circle must be
   - 3-A   1
   - 3-B   5
   - 3-C   2
   - 3-D   0

4. R is what percent of 1,000?
   - 4-A $.001R$
   - 4-B $1R$
   - 4-C $.01R$
   - 4-D $.1R$

5. A car owner finds he needs 12 gallons of gas for each 120 miles he drives. If he has his carburetor adjusted, he will need only 80% as much gas. How many miles will 12 gallons of gas then last him?
   - 5-A   90
   - 5-B   150
   - 5-C   96
   - 5-D   160

6. The perimeter of a square with side r =
   - 6-A $r^2 + r^2$
   - 6-B $4r$
   - 6-C r^4
   - 6-D   None of the above

7. A quadrilateral is a parallelogram only if
   - 7-A   both pairs of its opposite sides are parallel.
   - 7-B   it has four right angles.
   - 7-C   it has four right angles and four equal sides.
   - 7-D   it has at least one pair of parallel sides.

8.
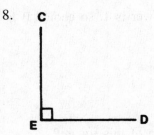

In the diagram above, $\overline{CE} \perp \overline{ED}$. If CE = 7 and ED = 6, what is the shortest distance from C to D?
   - 8-A   6
   - 8-B $4\sqrt{12}$
   - 8-C   7
   - 8-D $\sqrt{85}$

9. 5% of 5% of 100 is
   - 9-A   25
   - 9-B   .25
   - 9-C   2.5
   - 9-D   10

10. If $\frac{3}{8}$ of a number is 96, the number is

    10-A   132
    10-B   36
    10-C   256
    10-D   156

11. A line of print in a magazine article contains an average of 6 words. There are 5 lines to the inch. If 8 inches are available for an article that contains 270 words, how must the article be changed?

    11-A   Add 30 words.
    11-B   Delete 30 words.
    11-C   Delete 40 words.
    11-D   Add 60 words.

12. An angle has a measure five times that of its supplement. What is the measure of the angle?

    12-A   60°
    12-B   75°
    12-C   120°
    12-D   150°

13. If $\frac{2}{3}$ of a jar is filled with water in one minute, how many minutes longer will it take to fill the jar?

    13-A $\frac{1}{4}$

    13-B $\frac{1}{3}$

    13-C $\frac{1}{2}$

    13-D $\frac{2}{3}$

14. If $2 - x = x - 2$, then $x =$

    14-A   –2
    14-B   2
    14-C   0
    14-D $\frac{1}{2}$

15. What is the correct time if the hour hand is exactly $\frac{2}{3}$ of the way between 5 and 6?

    15-A   5:25
    15-B   5:40
    15-C   5:30
    15-D   5:45

16. A square is changed into a rectangle by increasing its length 10% and decreasing its width 10%. Its area

    16-A   remains the same
    16-B   decreases by 10%
    16-C   increases by 1%
    16-D   decreases by 1%

17. If all P are S and no S are Q, it necessarily follows that

    17-A   all Q are S.
    17-B   all Q are P.
    17-C   no P are Q.
    17-D   no S are P.

18. $(x + a)(x + b) =$

    18-A $x^2 + (ab)x + a + b$
    18-B $x^2 + (a + b)x + ab$
    18-C $x^2 + (ab)x + ab$
    18-D $x^2 + (a + b)x + a + b$

19. If $\frac{5}{4}x = \frac{5}{4}$, then $1 - x =$

    19-A $-\frac{5}{4}$

    19-B   1
    19-C   0
    19-D   -1

20. Factor the following:
    $a^2 - 2ab + b^2$

    20-A $(a + b)^2$
    20-B $(a - b)^2$
    20-C $(a^2 + b^2)$
    20-D $(a^2 - b^2)$

21. When 5.1 is divided by 0.017, the quotient is

21-A   30
21-B   300
21-C   3,000
21-D   30,000

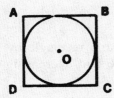

22. The area of circle O is 64π. The perimeter of square ABCD is

22-A   32
22-B   32π
22-C   64
22-D   16

23. The number of digits in the square root of 64,048,009 is

23-A   4
23-B   5
23-C   6
23-D   7

24. If 9 is 9% of x, then $x =$

24-A   .01
24-B   100
24-C   1
24-D   9

25. If a cube has a volume of 64 cubic centimeters, what is the length of an edge?

25-A   4 centimeters
25-B   6 centimeters
25-C   8 centimeters
25-D   10 centimeters

STOP!

IF YOU FINISH BEFORE THE TIME IS UP, YOU MAY CHECK OVER YOUR WORK ON THIS PART ONLY.

PART 6: ELECTRONICS INFORMATION

Directions

This is a test of your knowledge of electrical, radio, and electronics information. There are 20 questions. You are to select the correct response from the choices given. Then mark the space on your answer form that has the same number and letter as your choice.

Now look at the two sample questions below.

S1. What does the abbreviation AC stand for?   Ⓐ Ⓑ Ⓒ Ⓓ
    S1-A   Additional charge
    S1-B   Alternating coil
    S1-C   Alternating current
    S1-D   Ampere current

The correct answer is alternating current, so choice C is the correct response.

S2. Which of the following has the least resistance?   Ⓐ Ⓑ Ⓒ Ⓓ
    S2-A   Wood
    S2-B   Silver
    S2-C   Rubber
    S2-D   Iron

The correct answer is silver, so choice B is the correct response.

Your score on this test will be based on the number of questions you answer correctly. You should try to answer every question. Do not spend too much time on any one question.

When you are told to begin, be sure to start with question number 1 in Part 6 of your test booklet and number 1 in Part 6 on your answer form.

DO NOT CONTINUE UNTIL TOLD TO DO SO.

Electronics Information

Time: 9 Minutes—20 Questions

1. Boxes and fittings intended for outdoor use should be of
    1-A   weatherproof type.
    1-B   stamped steel of not less than No. 16.
    1-C   standard gauge.
    1-D   stamped steel plated with cadmium.

2. A direct-current supply may be obtained from an alternating-current source by means of
    2-A   a frequency changer set.
    2-B   an inductance-capacitance filter.
    2-C   a silicon diode rectifier.
    2-D   None of the above

3. Fuses protecting motor circuits have to be selected to permit a momentary surge of
    3-A   voltage when the motor starts.
    3-B   voltage when the motor stops.
    3-C   current when the motor starts.
    3-D   current when the motor stops.

4. When working near lead acid storage batteries, extreme care should be taken to guard against sparks, essentially to avoid
    4-A   overheating the electrolyte.
    4-B   an electric shock.
    4-C   a short circuit.
    4-D   an explosion.

5. The voltage that will cause a current of 5 amperes to flow through a 20-ohm resistance is
    5-A $\frac{1}{4}$ volt.
    5-B   4 volts.
    5-C   20 volts.
    5-D   100 volts.

6. Receptacles in a house-lighting system are regularly connected in
    6-A   parallel.
    6-B   series.
    6-C   diagonal.
    6-D   perpendicular.

7. The electronic symbol shown below usually represents a

    7-A   resistor.
    7-B   inductor.
    7-C   capacitor.
    7-D   transformer.

8. If a live conductor is contacted accidentally, the severity of the electrical shock is determined primarily by
    8-A   the size of the conductor.
    8-B   the current in the conductor.
    8-C   whether the current is AC or DC.
    8-D   the contact resistance.

9. Locknuts are frequently used in making electrical connections on terminal boards. The purpose of the locknuts is to
    9-A   eliminate the use of flat washers.
    9-B   prevent unauthorized personnel from tampering with the connections.
    9-C   keep the connections from loosening through vibration.
    9-D   increase the contact area at the connection point.

10. If a condenser is connected across the make-and-break contact of an ordinary electric bell, the effect will be to

10-A   speed up the action of the clapper.

10-B   reduce the amount of arcing at the contact.

10-C   slow down the action of the clapper.

10-D   reduce the load on the bell transformer or battery.

11. A material NOT used in the makeup of lighting wires or cables is

11-A   rubber.

11-B   paper.

11-C   lead.

11-D   cotton.

12.

VOLTMETER
GOOD LAMPS   GOOD LAMPS
BURNED OUT LAMP
600 VOLTS

The reading of the voltmeter should be

12-A   600

12-B   300

12-C   120

12-D   0

13. Silver is a better conductor of electricity than copper; however, copper is generally used for electrical conductors. The main reason for using copper instead of silver is its

13-A   cost.

13-B   weight.

13-C   strength.

13-D   melting point.

14. Direct current arcs are "hotter" and harder to extinguish than alternating current arcs, so electrical appliances that include a thermostat are frequently marked for use on "AC only." One appliance that might be so marked because it includes a thermostat is a

14-A   soldering iron.

14-B   floor waxer.

14-C   vacuum cleaner.

14-D   household iron.

15. An alternator is

15-A   an AC generator.

15-B   a frequency meter.

15-C   a ground detector device.

15-D   a choke coil.

16. Operating an incandescent electric light bulb at less than its rated voltage will result in

16-A   shorter life and brighter light.

16-B   brighter light and longer life.

16-C   longer life and dimmer light.

16-D   dimmer light and shorter life.

17.

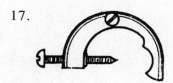

The device shown above is a

17-A   C-clamp.

17-B   test clip.

17-C   battery connector.

17-D   ground clamp.

18. When the electric refrigerator in a certain household kitchen starts up, the kitchen light at first dims considerably and then increases somewhat in brightness while the refrigerator motor is running; the light finally returns to full brightness when the refrigerator shuts off. This behavior of the light shows that most likely the

18-A   circuit wires are too small.

18-B   refrigerator motor is defective.

18-C   circuit fuse is too small.

18-D   kitchen lamp is too large.

19. A circular mil is a measure of electrical conductor
    19-A   length.
    19-B   area.
    19-C   volume.
    19-D   weight.

20. The instrument by which electric power may be measured is a
    20-A   rectifier.
    20-B   scanner drum.
    20-C   ammeter.
    20-D   wattmeter.

STOP!

IF YOU FINISH BEFORE THE TIME IS UP, YOU MAY CHECK OVER YOUR WORK ON THIS PART ONLY.

PART 7: AUTO & SHOP INFORMATION

Directions

This test has 25 questions about automobiles, shop practices, and the use of tools. Pick the best answer for each question, then blacken the space on your answer form that has the same number and letter as your choice.

Here are three sample questions.

S1. The most commonly used fuel for running automobile engines is

    S1-A   kerosene.

    S1-B   benzine.

    S1-C   crude oil.

    S1-D   gasoline.

Ⓐ Ⓑ Ⓒ Ⓓ

Gasoline is the most commonly used fuel, so choice D is the correct answer.

S2. A car uses too much oil when which parts are worn?

    S2-A   Pistons

    S2-B   Piston rings

    S2-C   Main bearings

    S2-D   Connecting rods

Ⓐ Ⓑ Ⓒ Ⓓ

Worn piston rings causes the use of too much oil, so choice B is the correct answer.

S3. The saw shown to the right is used mainly to cut

    S3-A   plywood.

    S3-B   odd-shaped holes in wood.

    S3-C   along the grain of the wood.

    S3-D   across the grain of the wood.

Ⓐ Ⓑ Ⓒ Ⓓ

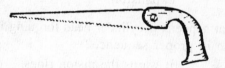

The compass saw is used to cut odd-shaped holes in wood, so choice B is the correct answer.

Your score on this test will be based on the number of questions you answer correctly. You should try to answer every question. Do not spend too much time on any one question.

When you are told to begin, be sure to start with question number 1 in Part 7 of your test booklet and number 1 in Part 7 on your answer form.

DO NOT CONTINUE UNTIL TOLD TO DO SO.

Auto & Shop Information

Time: 11 Minutes—25 Questions

1. Burned engine bearings are due to
   - 1-A   lack of oil in the engine.
   - 1-B   lack of water in the engine.
   - 1-C   too much oil in the engine.
   - 1-D   too much water in the engine.

2. If the temperature gauge indicates the engine is getting overheated,
   - 2-A   allow it to cool down.
   - 2-B   pour cold water in immediately.
   - 2-C   pour hot water in immediately.
   - 2-D   pour in a cooling antifreeze at once.

3. Cam ground pistons are used primarily because
   - 3-A   they can be used in badly worn engines without reboring the cylinders.
   - 3-B   their use increases the compression ratio.
   - 3-C   their use aids in the lubrication of the cylinder walls.
   - 3-D   they eliminate piston slap in engine warm-up and permit expansion.

4. What happens if cylinder head torquing is not done in proper sequence?
   - 4-A   It warps the piston rings.
   - 4-B   It cracks the intake manifold.
   - 4-C   It distorts the head.
   - 4-D   It reduces valve clearance.

5. Water sludge in engine crankcase oil is most usually caused by
   - 5-A   using a low viscosity oil.
   - 5-B   condensation in the crankcase.
   - 5-C   mixing different brands of motor oil.
   - 5-D   using a high viscosity oil.

6. A car slows down, lacks power, and a popping sound can be heard. The trouble is likely to be
   - 6-A   a faulty fuel supply.
   - 6-B   a shorted sparkplug.
   - 6-C   pitted breaker points.
   - 6-D   faulty distributor timing.

7. Setting the spark plug gap opening closer than normally required would probably result in
   - 7-A   smoother idling and increase in top engine speed.
   - 7-B   rougher idling and decrease in top engine speed.
   - 7-C   smoother idling and decrease in top engine speed.
   - 7-D   rougher idling and increase in top engine speed.

8. If a gasoline engine is continued in operation with a voltage regulator unable to check the output voltage of the alternator, the result would most likely be to
   - 8-A   "run down" the battery.
   - 8-B   reverse the current through the voltage coils.
   - 8-C   demagnetize the relay iron core.
   - 8-D   overcharge the battery.

9. Upon dismantling a gasoline engine, it was found that the piston rings were stuck in the grooves, not being free to rotate. This was most likely caused by
   - 9-A   operating the engine with spark setting in advanced position.
   - 9-B   the thermostat maintaining too low an engine temperature.
   - 9-C   dirty or contaminated lubricating oil.
   - 9-D   using the wrong type of spark plugs in the engine.

10. Upon the complete loss of oil pressure while a car is in operation, it is best that the car be

10-A pulled over to the side of the road and the engine stopped immediately for inspection.

10-B pulled over to the side of the road and a repair truck called to install a new oil pump.

10-C driven a few miles to your favorite garage.

10-D driven as usual for the entire day and be dropped off at the garage in the evening.

11. When painting, nail holes and cracks should be

11-A filled with putty before starting.

11-B filled with putty after the priming coat is applied.

11-C filled with paint by careful working.

11-D ignored.

12.

The tool shown above is a

12-A punch.

12-B drill holder.

12-C Phillips-type screwdriver.

12-D socket wrench.

13. The length of a flat head screw is defined as the length

13-A of the threaded portion.

13-B of the shank plus the threaded portion.

13-C of the complete screw.

13-D between the bottom of the head and the point.

14. If the head of a hammer has become loose on the handle, it should properly be tightened by

14-A driving the handle further into the head.

14-B driving a nail alongside the present wedge.

14-C using a slightly larger wedge.

14-D soaking the handle in water.

15. End grain of wood should be sanded

15-A crosswise.

15-B with the grain.

15-C obliquely.

15-D with a circular motion.

16.

The tool shown above is

16-A an Allen-head wrench.

16-B a double scraper.

16-C an offset screwdriver.

16-D a nail puller.

17. To install an expansion shield in a concrete wall, of the following, the proper tool to use is a

17-A bull nose chisel.

17-B star drill.

17-C chrome vanadium alloy cold chisel.

17-D rock wedge.

18. A method that can be used to prevent the forming of "skin" on a partially used can of oil paint is to

18-A turn the can upside down every few months.

18-B pour a thin layer of solvent over the top of the paint.

18-C store the paint in a well-ventilated room.

18-D avoid shaking the can after it has been sealed.

19. Which of the saws is used to make curved cuts?

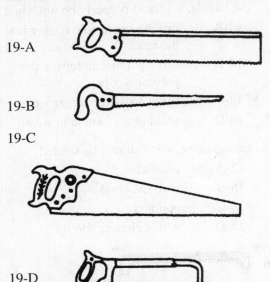

19-A

19-B

19-C

19-D

20. A screw is broken off in a tapped hole. The proper tools to use in removing the broken screw from the hole are

    20-A   hammer and cold chisel.

    20-B   drill and EZY-out.

    20-C   acetylene and oxygen torch.

    20-D   screw driver and pliers.

21. "Blistering" is generally caused by applying paint

    21-A   over a primer that has not completely dried.

    21-B   containing an improper binder for the pigment.

    21-C   that has been thinned too much.

    21-D   over a surface that has excessive moisture.

22. The plane to use in shaping a curved edge on wood is known as

    22-A   jack.

    22-B   spoke shave.

    22-C   smooth.

    22-D   rabbet.

23. The wrench that is used principally for pipe work is

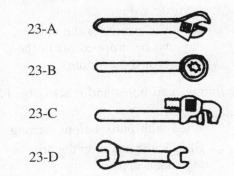

    23-A

    23-B

    23-C

    23-D

24. If an expander is used under an oil ring, it must be

    24-A   of the diagonal joint type.

    24-B   of a rigid type.

    24-C   of the step joint type.

    24-D   of the vented type.

25. A squeegee is a tool that is used in

    25-A   drying windows after washing.

    25-B   cleaning inside boiler surfaces.

    25-C   the central vacuum cleaning system.

    25-D   clearing stoppages in waste lines.

STOP!

IF YOU FINISH BEFORE THE TIME IS UP, YOU MAY CHECK OVER YOUR WORK ON THIS PART ONLY.

PART 8: MECHANICAL COMPREHENSION

Directions

This test has 25 questions about mechanical principles. Most of the questions use drawings to illustrate specific principles. Decide which answer is correct and mark the space on your separate answer form that has the same number and letter as your choice.

Here are two sample questions.

S1. Which bridge is the strongest?

A   B   C

S1-A   A
S1-B   B
S1-C   C   Ⓐ Ⓑ Ⓒ Ⓓ
S1-D   All are equally strong.

Choice C is correct.

S2. If all of these objects are the same temperature, which will feel coldest?   Ⓐ Ⓑ Ⓒ Ⓓ

A   B   C   D

S2-A   A
S2-B   B
S2-C   C
S2-D   D

Choice B is correct.

Your score on this test will be based on the number of questions you answer correctly. You should try to answer every question. Do not spend too much time on any one question.

When you are told to begin, be sure to start with question number 1 in Part 8 of your test booklet and number 1 in Part 8 on your answer form.

DO NOT CONTINUE UNTIL TOLD TO DO SO.

Mechanical Comprehension

Time: 19 Minutes—25 Questions

1.

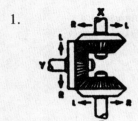

Which of the following is correct if gear Z is turned to the right (R)?

1-A   Gear Y turns L, and gear X turns R.

1-B   Gear Y turns R, and gear X turns R.

1-C   Gear Y turns L, and gear X turns L.

1-D   Gear Y turns R, and gear X turns L.

2.

The figure above represents a water tank containing water. The number 1 indicates an intake pipe and 2 indicates a discharge pipe. Of the following, the statement that is *least* accurate is that the

2-A   tank will eventually overflow if water flows through the intake pipe at a faster rate than it flows out through the discharge pipe.

2-B   tank will empty completely if the intake pipe is closed and the discharge pipe is allowed to remain open.

2-C   water in the tank will remain at a constant level if the rate of intake is equal to the rate of discharge.

2-D   water in the tank will rise if the intake pipe is operating when the discharge pipe is closed.

3.

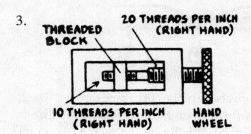

In the figure above, the threaded block can slide in the slot but cannot revolve. If the hand wheel is turned 20 revolutions clockwise, the threaded block will move

3-A   1 inch to the left.

3-B $\frac{1}{2}$ inch to the left.

3-C   1 inch to the right.

3-D $\frac{1}{2}$ inch to the right.

4.

What is the function of A and B in the crankshaft shown in the drawing?

4-A   They strengthen the crankshaft by increasing its weight.

4-B   They make it easier to remove the crankshaft for repairs.

4-C   They are necessary to maintain the proper balance of the crankshaft.

4-D   They hold grease for continuous lubrication of the crankshaft.

5. Sweating usually occurs on pipes that

5-A   contain cold water.

5-B   contain hot water.

5-C   are chrome plated.

5-D   require insulation.

6.

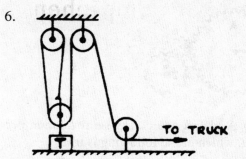

The tank, T, is to be raised as shown by attaching the pull rope to a truck. If the tank is to be raised 10 feet, the truck will have to move

6-A   20 feet.

6-B   40 feet.

6-C   30 feet.

6-D   50 feet.

7.

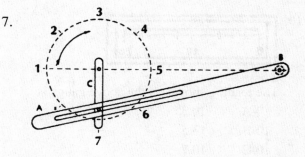

In the diagram above, crank arm C revolves at a constant speed of 400 rpm and drives the lever AB. When lever AB is moving the fastest, arm C will be in position

7-A   1

7-B   6

7-C   5

7-D   7

8. Assume that the color of the flame from a gas stove is bright yellow. To correct this, you should

8-A   close the air flap.

8-B   increase the size of the gas opening.

8-C   increase the gas pressure.

8-D   open the air flap.

9.

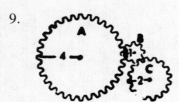

If gear A makes one clockwise revolution per minute, which of the following is true?

9-A   Gear B makes one counter clockwise revolution every 4 minutes.

9-B   Gear C makes two clockwise revolutions every minute.

9-C   Gear B makes four clockwise revolutions every minute.

9-D   Gear C makes one counter clockwise revolution every 8 minutes.

10.

The reading shown on the above gauge is

10-A   10.35

10-B   13.5

10-C   10.7

10-D   17.0

11.

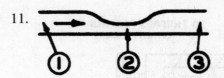

The figure above represents a pipe through which water is flowing in the direction of the arrow. There is a constriction in the pipe at the point indicated by the number 2. Water is being pumped into the pipe at a constant rate of 350 gallons per minute. Of the following, the most accurate statement is that

11-A   the velocity of the water at point 2 is the same as the velocity of the water at point 3.

11-B   a greater volume of water is flowing past point 1 in a minute than is flowing past point 2.

11-C   the velocity of the water at point 1 is greater than the velocity at point 2.

11-D   the volume of water flowing past point 2 in a minute is the same as the volume of water flowing past point 1 in a minute.

12.

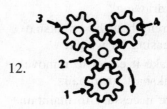

Four gears are shown in the figure above. If gear 1 turns as shown, then the gears turning in the same direction are

12-A   2 and 3.

12-B   2 and 4.

12-C   3 and 4.

12-D   2, 3, and 4.

13.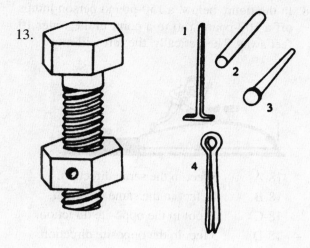

The figure above shows a bolt and nut and four numbered pieces. If all of the pieces are long enough to go through the bolt, and if the circular hole extends through the bolt and through the other side of the nut, which piece must you use to fix the nut in a stationary position?

13-A   1
13-B   3
13-C   2
13-D   4

14. Assume that a gear and pinion have a ratio of 3:1. If the gear is rotating at 300 revolutions per minute, the speed of the pinion in revolutions per minute is most nearly

14-A   100
14-B   900
14-C   300
14-D   1,800

15. The wrecking bar is a first-class lever with curved lever arms. In the figure shown below, what is the theoretical mechanical advantage in using the wrecking bar to tear the crate open?

15-A   3
15-B   4
15-C   5
15-D   6

16.

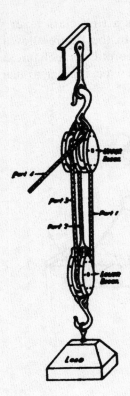

Determine which part of the rope is fastened directly to the block.

16-A   Part 1
16-B   Part 3
16-C   Part 2
16-D   Part 4

17.

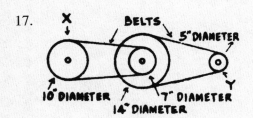

A double belt drive is shown in the figure above. If the pulley marked X is revolving at 100 rpm, the speed of pulley Y is

17-A   800 rpm.
17-B   200 rpm.
17-C   400 rpm.
17-D   25 rpm.

18. In the figure below, a 150-pound person jumps off a 500-pound raft to a point in the water 10 feet away. Theoretically, the raft will move

18-A   5 feet in the same direction.
18-B   10 feet in the same direction.
18-C   1 foot in the opposite direction.
18-D   3 feet in the opposite direction.

19.

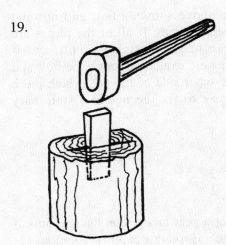

The simple machine pictured above is a form of

19-A   inclined plane.
19-B   pulley.
19-C   spur gear.
19-D   torque.

20.

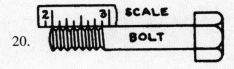

The number of threads per inch on the bolt is

20-A   16
20-B   8
20-C   10
20-D   7

21. In order to open the valve in the figure below once every second, the wheel must rotate at

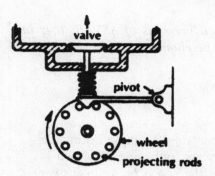

21-A   6 rpm.
21-B   10 rpm.
21-C   20 rpm.
21-D   30 rpm.

22. In order to stop a faucet from dripping, your first act should be to replace the

22-A   cap nut.
22-B   seat.
22-C   washer.
22-D   spindle.

23. In the figure given below, assume that all valves are closed. For air flow from R through G and then through S to M, open

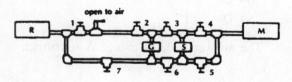

23-A   valves 7, 6, and 5.
23-B   valves 7, 3, and 4.
23-C   valves 7, 6, and 4.
23-D   valves 7, 3, and 5.

24.

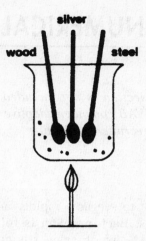

Which spoon is hottest?
24-A   Wood
24-B   Silver
24-C   Steel
24-D   Silver and steel are equally hot.

25.

There are twenty teeth on the front sprocket and ten teeth on the rear sprocket on the bicycle above. Each time the pedals go around, the rear wheel will

25-A   go halfway around.
25-B   go around once.
25-C   go around twice.
25-D   go around four times.

STOP!

IF YOU FINISH BEFORE THE TIME IS UP, YOU MAY CHECK OVER YOUR WORK ON THIS PART ONLY.

PART 9: NUMERICAL OPERATIONS

*NOTE: This section is not included on paper-and-pencil versions of ASVAB. It is included on the ASVAB computer-adaptive test (CAT) but may be eliminated in the near future. Check with your recruiter for details.

Directions

This is a test to see how rapidly and accurately you can do 50 simple arithmetic computations. Each problem is followed by four answers, only one of which is correct. Decide which answer is correct, then blacken the space on your answer form that has the same number and letter as your choice.

Now look at the four example problems below.

S1. $3 \times 3 =$ Ⓐ Ⓑ Ⓒ Ⓓ

    S1-A   6

    S1-B   0

    S1-C   9

    S1-D   1

The answer is 9, so choice C is correct.

S2. $3 + 7 =$ Ⓐ Ⓑ Ⓒ Ⓓ

    S2-A   4

    S2-B   6

    S2-C   8

    S2-D   10

The answer is 10, so choice D is correct.

S3. $5 - 2 =$ Ⓐ Ⓑ Ⓒ Ⓓ

    S3-A   2

    S3-B   3

    S3-C   1

    S3-D   4

The answer is 3, so choice B is correct.

S4. $9 \div 3 =$ Ⓐ Ⓑ Ⓒ Ⓓ

    S4-A   3

    S4-B   6

    S4-C   9

    S4-D   12

The answer is 3, so choice A is correct.

This is a speed test, so work as fast as you can without making mistakes. Do each problem as it comes. If you finish before time is up, go back and check your work. When the signal is given, you will turn the page and begin with question 1 in Part 9 of your test booklet and answer space 1 in Part 9 of your answer form.

DO NOT CONTINUE UNTIL TOLD TO DO SO.

Numerical Operations

Time: 3 Minutes—50 Questions

1. $2 + 5 =$
   - 1-A   3
   - 1-B   7
   - 1-C   9
   - 1-D   10

2. $18 \div 2$
   - 2-A   3
   - 2-B   6
   - 2-C   9
   - 2-D   11

3. $10 - 8 =$
   - 3-A   2
   - 3-B   9
   - 3-C   16
   - 3-D   18

4. $3 \times 3 =$
   - 4-A   6
   - 4-B   9
   - 4-C   30
   - 4-D   33

5. $1 + 8 =$
   - 5-A   18
   - 5-B   8
   - 5-C   7
   - 5-D   9

6. $9 \times 8 =$
   - 6-A   56
   - 6-B   64
   - 6-C   72
   - 6-D   76

7. $4 \times 5 =$
   - 7-A   20
   - 7-B   24
   - 7-C   28
   - 7-D   30

8. $3 + 7 =$
   - 8-A   37
   - 8-B   21
   - 8-C   10
   - 8-D   4

9. $9 - 5 =$
   - 9-A   7
   - 9-B   14
   - 9-C   12
   - 9-D   4

10. $3 \times 9 =$
   - 10-A   3
   - 10-B   6
   - 10-C   12
   - 10-D   27

11. $50 \div 5 =$
   - 11-A   5
   - 11-B   10
   - 11-C   55
   - 11-C   11

12. $8 - 6 =$
   - 12-A   14
   - 12-B   4
   - 12-C   3
   - 12-D   2

13. $6 \div 3 =$
   - 13-A   3
   - 13-B   2
   - 13-C   18
   - 13-D   24

14. $2 \times 9 =$
   - 14-A   7
   - 14-B   17
   - 14-C   18
   - 14-D   19

15. 4 + 8 =

    15-A   4

    15-B   10

    15-C   12

    15-D   16

16. $7 \times 9 =$

    16-A   45

    16-B   63

    16-C   72

    16-D   75

17. $5 \times 6 =$

    17-A   11

    17-B   13

    17-C   15

    17-D   30

18. 0 + 8 =

    18-A   0

    18-B   1

    18-C   8

    18-D   18

19. 4 + 5 =

    19-A   6

    19-B   1

    19-C   9

    19-D   11

20. $64 \div 8 =$

    20-A   6

    20-B   7

    20-C   8

    20-D   9

21. 7 − 1 =

    21-A   6

    21-B   7

    21-C   8

    21-D   0

22. $2 \times 3 =$

    22-A   5

    22-B   1

    22-C   9

    22-D   6

23. 9 − 7 =

    23-A   6

    23-B   5

    23-C   2

    23-D   4

24. 6 + 8 =

    24-A   16

    24-B   12

    24-C   15

    24-D   14

25. $10 \div 2 =$

    25-A   2

    25-B   5

    25-C   20

    25-D   12

26. $6 \div 3 =$

    26-A   2

    26-B   9

    26-C   12

    26-D   18

27. 5 + 9 =

    27-A   14

    27-B   16

    27-C   17

    27-D   18

28. $7 \div 7 =$

    28-A   49

    28-B   77

    28-C   0

    28-D   1

29. 6 − 6 =

    29-A   0

    29-B   1

    29-C   6

    29-D   12

30. $9 \times 6 =$

    30-A   15

    30-B   54

    30-C   45

    30-D   72

31. 7 + 9 =

31-A	12
31-B	15
31-C	16
31-D	17

32. 5 − 4 =

32-A	9
32-B	20
32-C	3
32-D	1

33. 4 ÷ 4 =

33-A	1
33-B	4
33-C	8
33-D	16

34. 10 − 5 =

34-A	50
34-B	15
34-C	9
34-D	5

35. 7 × 4 =

35-A	21
35-B	28
35-C	36
35-D	42

36. 36 ÷ 6 =

36-A	11
36-B	9
36-C	10
36-D	6

37. 8 × 3 =

37-A	24
37-B	21
37-C	29
37-D	32

38. 2 × 4 =

38-A	6
38-B	2
38-C	16
38-D	8

39. 8 − 1 =

39-A	9
39-B	8
39-C	7
39-D	6

40. 1 + 5 =

40-A	6
40-B	5
40-C	4
40-D	1

41. 90 ÷ 9 =

41-A	9
41-B	10
41-C	11
41-D	12

42. 2 − 2 =

42-A	1
42-B	4
42-C	2
42-D	0

43. 7 + 8 =

43-A	9
43-B	19
43-C	17
43-D	15

44. 4 − 0 =

44-A	1
44-B	4
44-C	5
44-D	8

45. 8 + 3 =

45-A	24
45-B	15
45-C	13
45-D	11

46. 3 − 2 =

46-A	1
46-B	2
46-C	5
46-D	6

47. 5 + 8 =

    47-A   12

    47-B   11

    47-C   13

    47-D   17

48. 3 ÷ 3 =

    48-A   0

    48-B   1

    48-C   3

    48-D   6

49. 9 ÷ 1 =

    49-A   19

    49-B   9

    49-C   10

    49-D   1

50. 4 × 6 =

    50-A   28

    50-B   24

    50-C   23

    50-D   18

STOP!

IF YOU FINISH BEFORE THE TIME IS UP, YOU MAY CHECK OVER YOUR WORK ON THIS PART ONLY.

PART 10: CODING SPEED

NOTE: This section is not included on paper-and-pencil versions of ASVAB. It is included on the ASVAB computer-adaptive test (CAT) but may be eliminated in the near future. Check with your recruiter for details.

Directions

This is a test of 84 items to see how quickly and accurately you can find a number in a table. At the top of each section, there is a number table or "key." The key is a group of words with a code number for each word.

Each question in the test is a word taken from the key at the top. From among the possible answers listed for each question, find the one that is the correct code number for that word.

Look at the sample key and answer the five sample questions below. Note that each of the questions is one of the words in the key. To the right of each question are possible answers listed under the options A, B, C, D, and E.

Sample Questions

Key

| green .... 2715 | man .... 3451 | salt .... 4586 |
| hat .... 1413 | room .... 2864 | tree .... 5972 |

Questions		Options				
		A	**B**	**C**	**D**	**E**
S-1.	room	1413	2715	2864	3451	4586
S-2.	green	2715	2864	3451	4586	5972
S-3.	tree	2715	2864	3451	4586	5972
S-4.	hat	1413	2715	2864	3451	4586
S-5.	room	1413	2864	3451	4586	5972

By looking at the key you see that the code number for the first word, "room," is 2864. 2864 is listed under the letter C, so choice C is the correct answer. The correct answers for the other four questions are choices A, E, A, and B.

This is a speed test, so work as fast as you can without making mistakes.

Notice that Part 10 begins at the top of the next answer form. When you begin, be sure to start with question number 1 in Part 10 of your test booklet and number 1 in Part 10 on your answer form.

DO NOT CONTINUE UNTIL TOLD TO DO SO.

Coding Speed

Time: 7 Minutes—84 Questions

Key

apron........4341	canoe.......1936	earth........9229	germ.........8606	knot.........6157
bridge......3636	date..........2024	face..........5678	jet.............7699	lizard.......5162

Questions		Options			

		A	B	C	D	E
1.	lizard	2024	3636	4341	5163	7699
2.	jet	1936	5163	5678	6157	7699
3.	bridge	1936	3636	4341	7699	8606
4.	face	5678	6157	7699	8606	9229
5.	knot	1936	2024	4341	5163	6157
6.	apron	2024	4341	5163	6157	9229
7.	canoe	1936	3636	4341	5163	5678
8.	date	2024	5163	6157	7699	8606
9.	germ	2024	3636	6157	7699	8606
10.	earth	1936	4341	5163	6157	9229
11.	face	2024	3636	4341	5163	5678
12.	knot	1936	4341	6157	8606	9229

Key

bank.........3029	dinner......8002	farm.........9564	husk.........4488	mule.........9984
candle......5605	eel............2270	hill...........6883	luck..........1654	tube..........7240

Questions		Options			

		A	B	C	D	E
13.	candle	2270	3029	4488	5605	7240
14.	hill	1654	5605	6883	8002	9984
15.	farm	3029	4488	6883	7240	9564
16.	bank	2270	3029	5605	6883	8002
17.	dinner	4488	7240	8002	9564	9984
18.	luck	1654	3029	4488	6883	7240
19.	husk	4488	6883	7240	8002	9564
20.	mule	3029	4488	8002	9564	9984
21.	eel	2270	3029	4488	6883	8002
22.	inner	3029	4488	6883	8002	9984
23.	tube	5605	7240	8002	9564	9984
24.	husk	1654	2270	3029	4488	6883

Key

army 9234	disc 6957	line 1854	pain 2610	rug 5600
coast 4532	land 1620	man 3002	paint 7677	test 8406

Questions			Options		
	A	**B**	**C**	**D**	**E**
25. disc	1620	3002	5600	6957	8406
26. paint	1854	2610	4532	6957	7677
27. line	1620	1854	2610	3002	5600
28. test	1854	4532	6957	8406	9234
29. pain	2610	3002	5600	7677	8406
30. army	1620	2610	3002	6957	9234
31. rug	4532	5600	6957	8406	9234
32. man	3002	4532	6957	7677	8406
33. paint	1620	2610	7677	8406	9234
34. coast	2610	3002	4532	5600	6957
35. land	1620	1854	2610	3002	5600
36. rug	2610	4532	5600	6957	9234

Key

author 6509	cake 2988	fire 1886	hunter 4141	shore 5135
blood........3348	card 7074	frog 9492	pin 8768	time 6852

Questions			Options		
	A	**B**	**C**	**D**	**E**
37. hunter	1886	2988	4141	5135	8768
38. shore	2988	3348	5135	6509	7074
39. frog	3348	4141	6852	8768	9492
40. author	2988	5135	6509	6852	8768
41. blood	1886	3348	4141	6852	7074
42. cake	2988	3348	5135	6509	6852
43. card	1886	4141	7074	8768	9492
44. pin	2988	3348	5135	6852	8768
45. fire	1886	2988	4141	6509	7074
46. time	3348	4141	5135	6509	6852
47. author	1886	3348	4141	6509	6852
48. shore	5135	6509	6852	7074	9492

Key

| book | 3498 | exam | 2412 | hotel | 9804 | navy | 4404 | sea | 7602 |
| boy | 1518 | guard | 5249 | motel | 8940 | pie | 6765 | thing | 5521 |

Questions		Options				
		A	**B**	**C**	**D**	**E**
49. guard		1518	4404	5249	5521	6765
50. exam		1518	2412	5521	7602	9804
51. thing		2412	5521	5249	6765	8940
52. motel		3498	4404	6765	8940	9804
53. sea		5249	6765	7602	8940	9804
54. boy		1518	2412	4404	5521	7602
55. navy		2412	3498	4404	5249	6765
56. book		3498	5249	5521	7602	8940
57. hotel		1518	2412	6765	8940	9804
58. pie		5521	6765	7602	8940	9804
59. navy		4404	5249	5521	6765	7602
60. book		1518	2412	3498	4404	9804

Key

| art | 2679 | crust | 9911 | gas | 1499 | music | 6242 | nature | 7004 |
| basket | 4562 | flag | 4855 | link | 3964 | nation | 5897 | razor | 8282 |

Questions		Options				
		A	**B**	**C**	**D**	**E**
61. basket		1499	4562	4855	5897	6242
62. nation		1499	2679	3964	4855	5897
63. music		4562	6242	7004	8282	9911
64. nature		2679	3964	4855	6242	7004
65. gas		1499	3964	4562	4855	9911
66. ink		1499	2679	3964	5897	6242
67 flag		4562	4855	5897	6242	8282
68. razor		2679	4562	6242	8282	9911
69. art		2679	3964	4855	5897	6242
70. crust		1499	4562	4855	7004	9911
71. nature		2679	5897	7004	8282	9911
72. flag		1499	2679	3964	4562	4855

Key

acorn 4745	camel 8808	ego 2190	halo 3835	steak 6667
bear 1086	desk 7621	fly 9266	star 5704	wax 7512

Questions			**Options**		
	A	**B**	**C**	**D**	**E**
73. steak	3835	4745	5704	6667	7621
74. ego	2190	5704	7512	7621	8808
75. halo	1086	2190	3835	4745	6667
76. fly	4745	5704	7512	8808	9266
77. wax	3835	4745	5704	7512	7621
78. camel	1086	2190	5704	6667	8808
79. bear	1086	2190	6667	8808	9266
80. desk	4745	5704	6667	7512	7621
81. acorn	3835	4745	5704	7621	9266
82. star	1086	2190	3835	4745	5704
83. camel	2190	3835	6667	8808	9266
84. steak	4745	5704	6667	7512	7621

END OF THE EXAMINATION

IF YOU FINISH BEFORE THE TIME IS UP, YOU MAY CHECK OVER YOUR WORK ON THIS PART ONLY.

ANSWER KEY

Use these answer keys to determine how many questions you answered correctly on each part and to list those items that you answered incorrectly or that you are not sure how to answer.

Be certain to review carefully and understand the rationale for arriving at the correct answers for all questions you answered incorrectly, as well as those you answered correctly but are unsure of. This is absolutely essential in order to acquire the knowledge and expertise necessary to obtain the maximum scores possible on the actual ASVAB tests.

Transfer the scores you obtained on each part of the Third ASVAB Specimen Test to the Self-Appraisal Chart appearing on page 24. This will enable you to see the progress made as you continue to prepare for the actual test.

Part 1—General Science

Answer Key				
1. A	2. C	3. B	4. D	5. A
6. D	7. C	8. C	9. B	10. A
11. B	12. B	13. D	14. C	15. D
16. A	17. D	18. C	19. B	20. A
21. C	22. D	23. C	24. C	25. C

Items Answered Incorrectly: ___ ; ___ ; ___ ; ___ ; ___ ; ___ ; ___ ; ___ .

Items Unsure Of: ___ ; ___ ; ___ ; ___ ; ___ ; ___ ; ___ ; ___ .

Total Number Answered Correctly: _____ .

Part 2—Arithmetic Reasoning

Answer Key				
1. B	2. B	3. D	4. B	5. C
6. D	7. D	8. C	9. D	10. B
11. A	12. C	13. D	14. D	15. C
16. C	17. C	18. D	19. B	20. B
21. B	22. D	23. B	24. A	25. C
26. D	27. C	28. D	29. B	30. D

Items Answered Incorrectly: ___ ; ___ ; ___ ; ___ ; ___ ; ___ ; ___ .
Items Unsure Of: _____ ; ____ ; ___ ; ____ ; ___ ; ____ ; ____ ; ___ .
Total Number Answered Correctly: _____ .

Part 3—Word Knowledge

Answer Key				
1. D	2. B	3. C	4. D	5. A
6. D	7. B	8. C	9. A	10. D
11. B	12. B	13. D	14. C	15. A
16. A	17. D	18. B	19. A	20. D
21. D	22. C	23. C	24. C	25. C
26. A	27. B	28. C	29. D	30. C
31. B	32. A	33. D	34. C	35. C

Items Answered Incorrectly: ___ ; ___ ; ___ ; ___ ; ___ ; ___ ; ___ ; ___ .
Items Unsure Of: _____ ; ____ ; ___ ; ____ ; ___ ; ____ ; ____ ; ___ .
Total Number Answered Correctly: _____ .

Part 4—Paragraph Comprehension

Answer Key				
1. B	2. D	3. C	4. D	5. C
6. D	7. A	8. C	9. D	10. C
11. C	12. D	13. A	14. D	15. B

Items Answered Incorrectly: ___ ; ___; ___ ; ___ ; ___; ___ ; ___ ; ___.

Items Unsure Of: _____ ; ____; ___ ; ____; ___ ; ____ ; ____; ___ .

Total Number Answered Correctly: _____ .

Part 5—Mathematics Knowledge

Answer Key				
1. C	2. D	3. C	4. D	5. B
6. B	7. A	8. D	9. B	10. C
11. B	12. D	13. C	14. B	15. B
16. D	17. C	18. B	19. C	20. B
21. B	22. C	23. A	24. B	25. A

Items Answered Incorrectly: ___ ; ___; ___ ; ___ ; ___; ___ ; ___ ; ___.

Items Unsure Of: _____ ; ____; ___ ; ____; ___ ; ____ ; ____; ___ .

Total Number Answered Correctly: _____ .

Part 6—Electronics Information

Answer Key				
1. A	2. C	3. C	4. D	5. D
6. A	7. C	8. D	9. C	10. B
11. B	12. A	13. A	14. D	15. A
16. C	17. D	18. A	19. B	20. D

Items Answered Incorrectly: ___ ; ___ ; ___ ; ___ ; ___ ; ___ ; ___ ; ___ .

Items Unsure Of: _____ ; _____ ; ___ ; _____ ; ___ ; _____ ; _____ ; ___ .

Total Number Answered Correctly: _____ .

Part 7—Auto & Shop Information

Answer Key				
1. A	2. A	3. D	4. C	5. B
6. A	7. D	8. D	9. C	10. A
11. B	12. D	13. C	14. C	15. A
16. C	17. B	18. B	19. B	20. B
21. D	22. B	23. C	24. D	25. A

Items Answered Incorrectly: ___ ; ___ ; ___ ; ___ ; ___ ; ___ ; ___ ; ___ .

Items Unsure Of: _____ ; _____ ; ___ ; _____ ; ___ ; _____ ; _____ ; ___ .

Total Number Answered Correctly: _____ .

Part 8—Mechanical Comprehension

Answer Key

1. A	2. B	3. C	4. C	5. A
6. C	7. C	8. D	9. B	10. D
11. D	12. C	13. D	14. B	15. C
16. C	17. C	18. D	19. A	20. B
21. A	22. C	23. D	24. B	25. C

Items Answered Incorrectly: ___ ; ___; ___ ; ___ ;___ ; ___ ; ___ ;___ .

Items Unsure Of: _____ ; ____; ___ ;____; ___ ;____ ; ____ ; ___ .

Total Number Answered Correctly: _____ .

Part 9—Numerical Operations

Answer Key

1. B	2. C	3. A	4. B	5. D
6. C	7. A	8. C	9. D	10. D
11. B	12. D	13. B	14. C	15. C
16. B	17. D	18. C	19. C	20. C
21. A	22. D	23. C	24. D	25. B
26. A	27. A	28. D	29. A	30. B
31. C	32. D	33. A	34. D	35. B
36. D	37. A	38. D	39. C	40. A
41. B	42. D	43. D	44. B	45. D
46. A	47. C	48. B	49. B	50. B

Items Answered Incorrectly: ___ ; ___; ___ ; ___ ;___ ; ___ ; ___ ;___ .

Items Unsure Of: _____ ; ____; ___ ;____; ___ ;____ ; ____ ; ___ .

Total Number Answered Correctly: _____ .

Part 10—Coding Speed

Answer Key

1. D	2. E	3. B	4. A	5. E
6. B	7. A	8. A	9. E	10. E
11. E	12. C	13. D	14. C	15. E
16. B	17. C	18. A	19. A	20. E
21. A	22. D	23. B	24. D	25. D
26. E	27. B	28. D	29. A	30. E
31. B	32. A	33. C	34. C	35. A
36. C	37. C	38. C	39. E	40. C
41. B	42. A	43. C	44. E	45. A
46. E	47. D	48. A	49. C	50. B
51. B	52. D	53. C	54. A	55. C
56. A	57. E	58. B	59. A	60. C
61. B	62. E	63. B	64. E	65. A
66. C	67. B	68. D	69. A	70. E
71. C	72. E	73. D	74. A	75. C
76. E	77. D	78. E	79. A	80. E
81. B	82. E	83. D	84. C	

Items Answered Incorrectly: ___ ; ___ ; ___ ; ___ ; ___ ; ___ ; ___ ; ___ .

Items Unsure Of: _____ ; ____ ; ___ ; ____ ; ___ ; ____ ; ____ ; ___ .

Total Number Answered Correctly: _____ .

ANSWER EXPLANATIONS

Part 1—General Science

1-A   Fruits have seeds. Tomatoes, cucumbers, and green peppers have seeds. A potato is a tuber.

2-C   The hammer, anvil, and stirrup are the three tiny bones that connect the eardrum with the inner ear.

3-B   Cigarette smoking can speed up the heartbeat.

4-D   The prefix *hypo-* means *below* or *abnormally deficient*. Hypothermia is a condition in which the body's temperature falls well below the normal 98.6°F. If it is very hot and you have nothing to drink, you may become dehydrated and might develop *hyper*thermia, overheating. Another name for rabies is hydrophobia.

5-A   Lightning is most likely to strike the highest object in an area. If you are standing in an open field or at the top of a small hill, you are likely to be the highest object and a good target. If you stand under a tree, lightning might hit the tree and cause it to fall on you. A car is grounded. If you are inside a car that is hit by lightning you will only be frightened. The lightning will be transmitted into the ground by the car.

6-D   The speed of light is about a million times that of sound.

7-C   The Kelvin scale or absolute scale is used in the physical sciences to measure temperature. On this scale, water freezes at 273°K and boils at 373°K.

8-C   Water boils at 212°F and freezes at 32°F. 212° − 32° = 180°.

9-B   As viewed from space, one half of the moon is always illuminated by the sun. However, as the moon changes its position in its orbit around the earth, different amounts of the illuminated side are visible from the earth.

10-A   Rabies is caused by a virus. The other diseases listed are caused by pathogenic bacteria.

11-B   The length of the vector represents the magnitude of the force.

12-B   The "highs" on a weather map are based on barometric pressure. The greater the air pressure, the higher the mercury in the barometer.

13-D   An atom is the smallest part of an element that retains all the properties of the element.

14-C   The action of narcotics is to deaden pain.

15-D   Fungi do not contain chlorophyll, so they cannot produce their own food through photosynthesis. Since fungi must rely for their food upon decaying organic matter, the forest is a hospitable home.

16-A   Coal is formed by the partial decomposition of vegetable matter under the influence of moisture, pressure, and temperature and in the absence of air. If there is coal in Alaska, there must once have been abundant vegetation in Alaska.

17-D Damage to the neck and back is especially dangerous because the spinal cord is so vulnerable. Once the spinal cord is severed, paralysis is inevitable and irreversible, so if there is any question of back or neck injury the person should be moved only by a skilled professional.

18-C Like displaces like.

19-B Vitamin C, contained in citrus fruits, tomatoes, and green vegetables, is also known as ascorbic acid.

20-A Radiation is the process by which energy is transferred in space.

21-C Barometric pressure is expressed in inches. The range is generally from 28 to 31 inches.

22-D Clover serves to return nitrates to the soil through the action of nitrogen-fixing bacteria in nodules on its roots.

23-C The vascular system is the system of vessels for the circulation of blood. The respiratory system is concerned with respiration (breathing) and the endocrine system with enzymes.

24-C Fossils are found chiefly in sedimentary rock. When an organism falls in place and is covered and compressed by sand, mud, or soil, as the sediment hardens into rock, parts of the organism are preserved as fossil.

25-C Milk and milk products such as cheese and butter are high in saturated fat and cholesterol.

Part 2—Arithmetic Reasoning

1-B 3 for 20¢ × 4 = 12 for 80¢

80¢ − 70¢ = 10¢ profit per dozen

10¢ × 6 doz. = 60¢ total profit

2-B 60 ft. = 20 yd. The wall is

4 yd. × 20 yd. = 80 sq. yd.

$10.50 × 80 = $840

3-D $6\frac{1}{2}$ pounds $- 4$ pounds $= 2\frac{1}{2}$ pounds

There are 5 half-pounds in $2\frac{1}{2}$ pounds .

$$\$9.26 + 5(1.06) = \$9.26 + 5.30$$
$$= \$14.56$$

4-B   The whole paper is 9 in. × 12 in. = 108 sq. in. The paper she uses is

$9 \text{ in.} - 1 \text{ in.} - 1 \text{ in.} = 7 \text{ in.} \times 12 \text{ in.} - 1\frac{1}{2} \text{ in.} - 1\frac{1}{2} \text{ in.} = 9 \text{ in.}$ The paper she uses is 7 in. ×

9 in. = 63 sq. in. $\dfrac{63}{108} = \dfrac{7}{12}$ is used for typing.

5-C   2 ft. 9 in. × 4 = 8 ft. 36 in. = 11 ft.

6-D $.2\overline{2}$ = approximately 22%

$$\frac{2}{9} = 9\overline{\smash)2.00}^{\displaystyle .22\overline{2}}$$

$$\begin{array}{r} \underline{18} \\ 20 \\ \underline{18} \\ 2 \end{array}$$

7-D   2 in. = 5 ft.; therefore, $1 \text{ in.} = 2\frac{1}{2} \text{ ft.}$;

$$7\frac{1}{2} \times 2\frac{1}{2} = 18\frac{3}{4} \text{ ft.}$$

8-C $375 is 75% of the original price.

$$\begin{aligned} \text{The original price} &= \$375 \div 75\% \\ &= \$375 \div .75 \\ &= \$500 \end{aligned}$$

9-D $\begin{aligned} \text{Perimeter} &= 2l + 2w \\ &= 2(46 \text{ ft.}) + 2(34 \text{ ft.}) \\ &= 92 \text{ ft.} + 68 \text{ ft.} \\ &= 160 \text{ ft.} \end{aligned}$

$$160 \div 3 = 53\frac{1}{3} \text{ yd.}$$

10-B   First rename the feet as inches. 35 ft. 6 in. = 420 in. + 6 in. = 426 in.

$$426 \div 4 = 106.5 \text{ in. per shelf} = 8 \text{ ft. } 10\frac{1}{2} \text{ in. per shelf}$$

11-A   The team won 2 games and lost 10, so it played 12 games. $\dfrac{2}{12} = \dfrac{1}{6}$.

12-C $600 × .08 = \$48 × 2 = \$96$

13-D
$$\begin{aligned}
.50 × 3 &= \$1.50 \\
.25 × 8 &= \$2.00 \\
.10 × 7 &= \$\ .70 \\
.05 × 6 &= \$\ .30 \\
+.01 × 9 &= \$\ .09 \\
\hline
&\ \ \$4.59
\end{aligned}$$

14-D $\$68 × 40\% = \$27.20$

15-C   Eighteen clerks can do the job in 26 days. Therefore, 1 clerk takes $18 × 26 = 468$ days to do the job. To get the job done in 12 days will take $468 ÷ 12 = 39$ clerks.

16-C   The carton contains $9 × 12 = 108$ folders. $108 - 53 = 55$ remain in carton.

17-C $\$25 ÷ \$4.95 = 5.05$—He could buy 5 ties. $\$4.95 × 5 = \$24.75$. After buying 5 ties the man would still have 25¢ left.

18-D
$$\begin{aligned}
\$20.56 \\
32.90 \\
+20.78 \\
\hline
\$74.24\ ÷\ 2 = \$37.13\ \text{left}
\end{aligned}$$

19-B $15\ \text{lb.} ÷ \dfrac{3}{4} = \dfrac{\overset{5}{\cancel{15}}}{1} × \dfrac{4}{\underset{1}{\cancel{3}}} = 20$ packages

20-B $10.2 + 10.4 + 10 = 30.6 ÷ 3 = 10.2$ seconds

21-B   11 lb., 16 oz. − 9 lb., 9 oz. = 2 lb., 7 oz.

22-D $12\ \text{ft.} × 15\ \text{ft.} = 4\ \text{yd.} × 5\ \text{yd.} = 20\ \text{yd.}^2$

23-B $\$12.50 - \$10.98 = \$1.52$ cost to upgrade the blouse $\$5.00 - \$1.52 = \$3.48$ change

24-A   If you look at the entire problem, you will see that the time between sunrise and sunset was just 8 minutes short of 12 hours $(14 - 6 = 8)$.

$$\begin{aligned}
11\ \text{hrs.}\ 60\ \text{min.} \\
-\qquad 8\ \text{min.} \\
\hline
11\ \text{hrs.}\ 52\ \text{min.}
\end{aligned}$$

25-C   Only 10 boys can play at one time. Therefore, the 30 boys must be divided into 3 groups. Each group can then play 45 min. ÷ 3 = 15 min.

26-D   65¢ − 5¢ for the first day = 60¢ for the other days. 60¢ ÷ 2¢ = 30 other days. The book was 31 days overdue.

27-C   1 lb. = 16 oz.; 2 lb. = 32 oz.;

32 oz. ÷ 2 oz. = 16 slices

28-D $\frac{1}{2}$ cup of spinach = 80 calories

$\frac{1}{2}$ cup of peas = 300 calories

1 cup of peas = 600 calories

$\frac{2}{3}$ cup of peas = 400 calories

$400 \div 80 = 5$ half cups of spinach

$= 2\frac{1}{2}$ cups of spinach

29-B   30 min. for 6 pages; 1 hr. for 12 pages; $126 \div 12 = 10.5$ hrs.

30-D   9 hrs. = 540 mins.; $540 \div 45 = 12$

The night watchman stops at the storage area 12 times during his tour plus once at the beginning of his tour of duty for a total of 13 times.

Part 3—Word Knowledge

1-D   *Superiority* is *excellence.*

2-B   *Absurd* means *irrational, unreasonable,* or *foolish.*

3-C   *Inflammable* means *easily inflamed,* hence *explosive.*

4-D   *Conscious* means *mentally awake* or *aware.*

5-A   To *exhibit* means to *show publicly* or to *display.* Often one exhibits goods that one hopes to subsequently trade or sell.

6-D   To *assume* is to *take for granted* or to *suppose.*

7-B   That which is *counterfeit* is an *imitation made with intent to defraud,* hence *false.*

8-C   That which is done *expertly* is done *skillfully.* It might also be done quickly but not necessarily so.

9-A   *Marshy* means *boggy* or *swampy.*

10-D   *Allegiance* means *devotion* or *loyalty.*

11-B   To *yearn* is to *have a great desire for* or to *be filled with longing.*

12-B   The *summit* is the *top.*

13-D   To *heed* is to *pay attention to* or to *take notice of.*

14-C   *Vigorously* means *forcefully* and *energetically.*

15-A   To *imitate* is to *copy.*

16-A   *Severity* means *seriousness, extreme strictness,* or *harshness.* It does not necessarily imply unfairness.

17-D   That which is *incredible* is *too improbable to believe*.

18-B   *Leisure* is *freedom from pressure*. With a full month, the trip could be leisurely or unhurried.

19-A   *Gratitude* is the *state of being grateful* or *thankfulness*.

20-D   *Familiar* means *well known*. (Think of the word "family.")

21-D   An *acute* pain may well be alarming, but what makes it *acute* is its *sharpness*.

22-C   To be *bewildered* is to be *confused* or *puzzled*.

23-C   The *conclusion* is the *end*.

24-C   An *aroma* is a *pleasing smell* or *fragrance*.

25-B   The prefix *non* means *not*. That which is *not essential* is *unnecessary*.

26-A   To *amplify* is to *enlarge* by adding illustrations or details, in short, to *expand*.

27-B   *Intact* means *unimpaired*, *whole*, or *undamaged*.

28-C   *Potent* means *powerful* or *effective*. The word that means *drinkable* is "potable."

29-D   To *terminate* is to *end*. The *end* of a train line is the *terminus* or *terminal*.

30-C   *Notorious* means *well-known*, generally in an unfavorable sense.

31-B   *Fatal* means *causing death* or *deadly*.

32-A   *Indigent* means *needy* or *poor*. Indigent people might be lazy or homeless, but their indigence is their poverty. Indigent people might also become angry or *indignant*.

33-D   The *technique* is the *method* by which something is done.

34-C   One's *vocation* is one's *occupation* or *calling*.

35-C   That which is *mature* is *fully aged* or *ripe*.

Part 4—Paragraph Comprehension

1-B   The passage states that mechanics must be instructed in safety rules that they must follow for their own protection. This implies that industrial accidents may be due to ignorance of safety rules.

2-D   If the collection letter must show clear organization and show evidence of a mind that has a specific end in view, it should be carefully planned.

3-C   When the activities of an individual come in conflict with the community interest, the individual's rights are no longer considered to be of greatest importance but actually become secondary.

4-D   The passage does not support any of the first three options but states Edison invented the phonograph and motion picture film.

5-C   The last sentence in the passage states that burning wood produces more CO, carbon monoxide, than natural gas does when it burns. CO is the chemical formula for carbon monoxide.

6-D   The key word is "compromise." A railroad line must be built along logical trade and commerce routes even if construction is more expensive.

7-A The survey showed that of all the subjects, typing helped most in business. It was also considered valuable by college students in their schoolwork.

8-C The second sentence states that direct lighting causes glare on the working surface.

9-D The connective "Others, however," with which the second sentence begins implies the converse of the first sentence. Some citizens are public-spirited; others, however, are not.

10-C A laborer who has only one skill may find himself or herself unemployed if that skill is not in demand. A more versatile worker can find a job requiring another skill.

11-C The third sentence states that heating the drill will spoil its temper and cutting edges.

12-D The second sentence states that the drill point must be withdrawn frequently to cool it.

13-A If an employee is injured, no matter how small the injury, he or she should have the injury treated. A small cut not attended to can easily become infected.

14-D Loose or torn clothing should not be worn near moving machinery.

15-B Wearing shoes with open toes can easily lead to foot injuries. Accordingly, they should not be worn.

Part 5—Mathematics Knowledge

1-C $8 \times 8 \times 8 = 512$

2-D $(2x-1)(10) = 70$; divide both sides by 10

$\qquad 2x - 1 = 7$; add 1 to both sides

$\qquad\quad 2x = 8$; divide both sides by 2

$\qquad\qquad x = 4$

3-C The formula to find the circumference of a circle is $2\pi r$. The formula to find the area of a circle is πr^2—the only number that has the same value when multiplied by 2 or squared is 2.

4-D To find what percent one number is of another number, create a fraction by putting the part over the whole. Then convert to a decimal by dividing the numerator by the denominator and change to a percent by multiplying by 100.

$$\frac{R}{1,000} = .001R = .1R\%$$

5-B Right now he gets 120 mi. ÷ 12 gal. = 10 mpg. After carburetor adjustment, he will need 80% of 12, or 9.6 gal., to go 120 miles. He will then get 120 mi. ÷ 9.6 gal. = 12.5 mpg. 12 gal × 12.5 mpg = 150 miles on 12 gal.

6-B Perimeter $= r + r + r + r = 4r$

7-A By definition, a quadrilateral is a parallelogram only if both pairs of its opposite sides are parallel.

8-D $\overline{CD}$ is a hypotenuse, so use the Pythagorean Theorem:

$$CD = \sqrt{CE^2 + ED^2}$$
$$CD = \sqrt{7^2 + 6^2} = \sqrt{49 + 36} = \sqrt{85}$$

9-B $100 \times 5\% = 5$; $5 \times 5\% = .25$

10-C $\dfrac{3}{8}x = 96$

$$3x = 96 \times 8 = 768$$
$$x = 256$$

11-B   6 words per line × 5 lines per inch = 30 words per inch, 30 words per inch × 8 inches = 240 words.

If the article has 270 words and there is space for only 240 words, then 30 words must be deleted.

12-D   Let x = measurement of supplement; $5x$ = measurement of angle. $x + 5x = 180°$; $6x = 180°$; $x = 30°$; $5x = 150°$.

13-C   If $\dfrac{2}{3}$ of the jar is filled in 1 minute, then $\dfrac{1}{3}$ of the jar is filled in $\dfrac{1}{2}$ minute. Since the jar is $\dfrac{2}{3}$ full, $\dfrac{1}{3}$ remains to be filled. The jar will be full in another $\dfrac{1}{2}$ minute.

14-B   The quickest way to answer this question is to try substituting the given values. If $x = 2$, then $2 - 2 = 2 - 2$ is a true statement.

To solve algebraically: $2 - x = x - 2 \,(\text{add } 2, \text{add } x)$
$$4 = 2x \,(\text{divide by} 2)$$
$$2 = x$$

15-B $\dfrac{2}{3}$ of 60 min. = 40 min.
$$5:00 + 40 \text{ min.} = 5:40$$

16-D   Assign arbitrary values to solve this problem:

A square 10 ft. × 10 ft. = 100 sq. ft.

A rectangle 9 ft. × 11 ft. = 99 sq. ft.

$$100 - 99 = 1; \dfrac{1}{100} = 1\%$$

17-C   Diagram this problem:

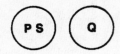

18-B $x + a$

$\underline{x + b}$

$x^2 + ax$

$\underline{+ \quad\quad bx + ab}$

$x^2 + ax + bx + ab$

$x^2 + (a+b)x + ab$

19-C $\dfrac{5}{4}x = \dfrac{5}{4}$

$x = \dfrac{5}{4} \div \dfrac{5}{4} = \dfrac{\overset{1}{\cancel{5}}}{\underset{1}{\cancel{4}}} \times \dfrac{\overset{1}{\cancel{4}}}{\underset{1}{\cancel{5}}} = 1; \; 1 - 1 = 0$

20-B $a^2 - 2ab + b^2 = (a-b)(a-b) = (a-b)^2$

21-B $0.017)\overline{5.100}$ $\overset{300.}{}$

To divide by a decimal, move the decimal point of the divisor to the right until the divisor becomes a whole number. Move the decimal point of the dividend to the right the same number of spaces. Place the decimal point of the quotient directly above the decimal point in the dividend.

22-C   The formula for the area of a circle is πr^2. In this problem, $r^2 = 64$ so $r = 8$. The circle is tangent with the square on all four sides; the radius is exactly $\dfrac{1}{2}$ the length of a side of the square. Each side, then, is 16 units long. The formula for the perimeter of a square is $P = 4s$, so $4 \times 16 = 64$.

23-A   The first step to finding the square root of a number is to pair the digits to each side of the decimal point. Each pair represents one digit in the square root. $\underline{64}\ \underline{04}\ \underline{80}\ \underline{09}$.

24-B   9% of $x =$ 9

     $.09x =$ 9

       $x =$ 100

25-A $\sqrt[3]{64} = 4$ centimeters

Part 6—Electronics Information

1-A   Outdoor boxes and fittings must be weatherproof to withstand any problems caused by moisture.

2-C   A rectifier is a device that converts AC current into DC current by allowing the current to flow in only one direction while blocking the flow of electricity in the reverse direction.

3-C   The starting current of a motor is normally six times greater than its running current.

4-D   Lead acid batteries give off highly explosive hydrogen gas. This is a normal product of the acid reacting with the lead plates when electricity is made. A single spark can explode the gas.

5-D   According to Ohm's law:

$$V = IR; V = 5 \times 20; V = 100 \text{ volts.}$$

6-A   Receptacles in a house are connected in parallel. In parallel circuits, the current increases as more appliances are added but the voltage remains the same. $E_t = E_1 = E_2 = ... E_n I_t + I_1 + I_2 + ... I_n$

7-C   The symbol is a standard one and shows the two conducting surfaces of a capacitor.

8-D   An electric shock is determined by the contact resistance. If a person is standing in water while being shocked, the shock will be very severe because water reduces the amount of resistance and the electricity will flow freely through his body.

9-C   Locknuts are bent so that their metal edges will bite into the terminal board and will require the use of a wrench to loosen them.

10-B   A condenser, or capacitor, is an electrical device that will store and discharge an electrical charge. When the bell is off, the condenser will store electricity. When the circuit is on, the condenser will discharge. This will eliminate arcing.

11-B   Paper is not used in the makeup of a lighting wire because a small electrical charge could set it on fire.

12-A   No electricity flows through a burned-out bulb. However, the voltmeter acts as a bypass around the burned-out bulb and is therefore connected in series. It measures all of the voltage in the circuit. The voltage is 600 volts.

13-A   Silver is a much better conductor than copper. It is not used in wires because it is very expensive.

14-D   A household iron is the only device that depends on a thermostat to control its use. An overheated iron will damage the clothing that it is supposed to press.

15-A   An alternator is a device that is found in automobiles. It is used to produce AC. In a car, the electronic circuitry changes AC to DC.

16-C   An incandescent electric light bulb is a typical light bulb found in the home. When the incandescent bulb, which is rated for 110 volts, is run at 90 volts, it will not burn as brightly. Because the 110-volt capacity is not being used, it will last longer.

17-D   This object is a ground clamp. It will be tightened around a cold water pipe. A grounding wire will be attached to the screw and thus stray electricity will be grounded.

18-A   When a refrigerator motor starts up, it draws considerable current. This takes current away from the bulb. Thicker wires would allow more electricity to pass through, but they would be too expensive and impractical.

19-B   A mil is $\dfrac{1}{1,000}$ of an inch. A circular mil is the area of the cross-section of a wire.

20-D   Electric power is measured in units called watts. A watt is calculated by multiplying voltage by amperage. Watts are measured by a watt-meter.

Part 7—Auto & Shop Information

1-A   Engine bearings hold the crankshaft in place and are lubricated with engine oil. The oil lessens the friction caused by metal rubbing on metal and stops the metal from burning.

2-A   If an engine starts to overheat, you must stop the car immediately. Otherwise, the metal will expand and damage the engine. If you pour anything on an overheated engine, the rapid cooling may cause the block to crack.

3-D   Piston slap occurs when a piston slams into the sides of the cylinder wall as it travels inside the cylinder. The piston rings keep the tight fit necessary between the wall and the piston. Properly ground pistons will move more smoothly.

4-C   Cylinder head torquing, or tightening, is done in a special order so that the head will fit very closely to the block. Otherwise, the head will warp and have vapor leaks.

5-B   Water in the crankcase is usually caused by condensation. A cracked engine block can also cause this condition, but this is not usual.

6-A   The popping sound is likely to be an intermittent supply of gasoline reaching the cylinders. The lack of gas causes the engine to lose power and slow down.

7-D   If the spark plug gap was set closer than required, the spark plugs would fire sooner than necessary. This would cause a rougher idle speed and a longer power stroke.

8-D   The device being described is a voltage regulator. When the battery becomes fully charged, a relay opens up so that the battery doesn't overcharge. A permanently closed voltage regulator will cause overcharging.

9-C   The piston rings form a seal around the piston and the wall of the cylinder. Dirty oil in the crankcase will stop the rings from working properly.

10-A   If an engine loses oil pressure, the car must be stopped immediately. Otherwise, it will overheat and become damaged.

11-B   Nail holes are filled with putty after applying the priming coat, before you apply the finishing coat of paint.

12-D   Although this tool looks like a screwdriver, the head will fit into a hex nut and works like a socket wrench.

13-C   The length of a flat head screw is its entire length.

14-C   If you look at the top of a hammer where it is joined to the handle, you will see either the top of a wooden wedge or the top of a metal wedge. Driving another wedge into the handle will tighten the hammer.

15-A The end grain of a block of wood is sanded crosswise.

16-C The tool is an offset screwdriver. It is used for tightening screws in hard-to-reach places where a regular screwdriver cannot turn in a complete revolution.

17-B A star drill is used to drill into masonry. Then an expansion shield is placed into the hole.

18-B "Skin" forms when air combines with paint. To stop this from happening, pour a thin layer of solvent over the paint. The air will then be prevented from reaching the paint and forming a layer of skin.

19-B Figure B is a keyhole saw used to make curved cuts; A is a backsaw: C is a rip or crosscut saw; and D is a hack saw.

20-B An EZY-out is a reverse threaded drill used to extract broken screws. The other tools suggested would be impractical.

21-D Paint adheres best to a dry surface. If the surface is wet when it is painted on, the moisture becomes trapped. Blistering occurs when the trapped moisture expands and breaks through the paint.

22-B A spoke shave is used to plane a dowel-shaped surface. The other planes are used to smooth flat surfaces.

23-C Figure C is a pipe wrench; A is a crescent or expandable wrench; B is a ratchet wrench; and D is an open-end wrench.

24-D An oil ring expander must be of the vented type. As piston rings heat up, they expand. The vent is necessary to allow for expansion.

25-A A squeegee is a rubber wiper that removes water from a wet window.

Part 8—Mechanical Comprehension

1-A Here, right (R) can be thought of as how a point on the axle would appear to be moving. If gear Z moves to the right, gear Y will move in the opposite direction, to the left; and gear X will move in the opposite direction from gear Y, to the right.

2-B If pipe 2 is open while pipe 1 is closed, then the level will drop to the lowest level of 2, leaving the volume below 2 still filled, having no way to discharge. All other statements are true.

3-C The hand wheel tightens to the left when rotated clockwise since it is a right-handed thread. It goes 1 inch (20 revolutions = 1 inch). It then pulls the threaded block 1 inch in the opposite direction.

4-C The function of A and B in the crankshaft is to counterbalance the weight for smooth piston motion.

5-A The air surrounding a pipe contains water vapor at room temperature. This cold water cools the air in the immediate vicinity, reducing its ability to hold water vapor (warmer air will hold more water than cooler air). The water condenses on the cool pipe as sweat.

6-C Three ropes are supporting tank T. The mechanical advantage (the number of supporting wires holding the load) is 3. The distance must be 3 times the height raised, while the amount of force exerted by the truck will be $\frac{1}{3}$ of the weight of T.

7-C   The slowest points for lever AB are 3 and 7 where the direction reverses and the velocity momentarily becomes zero. The midpoint, 5, represents the maximum speed, as it is halfway between these minimum points.

8-D   A yellow flame means too much fuel or too little oxygen is present during combustion. For complete combustion: fuel + oxygen → carbon dioxide + water. The best answer is to allow more air to enter and mix with the gas.

9-B   Gear A turns in the opposite direction from gear B. A clockwise turn of A results in a counterclockwise revolution of B. Since the distance traversed by A (perimeter = π × diameter = π × 4) is twice that of C (perimeter = π × 2), the speed of C is doubled.

10-D   Each division marks 2 units: 20 units/10 divisions = 2 units/division. The pointer is $3\frac{1}{2}$ divisions above 10 or 2 units/division × $3\frac{1}{2}$ divisions = 7; 7 + 10 = 17.

11-D   The volume of water flowing at points 1, 2, and 3 must be the same because of the conservation of mass: mass in = mass out. Also, since no water is added or removed after point 1, there cannot be any change of volume.

12-C   Gear 1 turns clockwise; gear 2 turns counterclockwise; gears 3 and 4 turn clockwise.

13-D   By the process of elimination, numbers 1 and 3 are not shaped cylindrically and will wobble in the circular hole; number 2 may fall out if the assembly is tilted; but number 4, a cotter pin, will exert the proper tension to remain inside the hole without slipping.

14-B   Because of the ratio, the pinion will rotate 3 times for each rotation of the gear; 300 rotations of the gear will cause 300 × 3 = 900 rotations of the pinion.

15-C $2\frac{1}{2}$ ft. = 30 in.; $\frac{30}{6} = 5$; TMA = 5.

16-C   Begin with part 4, the line upon which the force is directed; part 1 is the next strand; then part 3; and finally, attached to the lower block, is part 2.

17-C   *Step 1:* Pulley X revolves at 100 rpm (given). *Step 2:* Middle pulley (inner) rotates at $100 \times \frac{10}{7}$. (Remember that a larger pulley causes a smaller one to travel faster by the ratio of their diameters.) *Step 3:* Pulley Y travels at $(100 \times \frac{10}{7}) \times \frac{14}{5} = 400$.

18-D   The raft will move in the opposite direction.

Let x = theoretical distance moved.

$10 \times 150 = x \times 500$; $500x = 1500$;

$x = \dfrac{1500}{500} = 3$ feet.

19-A An inclined plane is a sloping, triangular shape, used here as a wedge to force open an axe cut made in the wood.

20-B The bolt thread makes one revolution per eighth of an inch, or has 8 threads in one inch.

21-A Once every second = 60 times a minute. With 10 projection rods on the wheel, the wheel must rotate at 6 rpm to make 60 rod contacts per minute.

22-C The simplest and least expensive thing to do is to change the washer, which may have deteriorated due to excessive wear.

23-D Choice A does not permit air flow through G and S; option B does not permit air flow through S; choice C does not permit air flow through G; choice D is correct.

24-B Wood is an insulator. Silver is a better conductor than steel.

25-C One revolution of the rear wheel causes 10 teeth to rotate completely. But one revolution of the front sprocket causes 20 teeth to rotate completely, making the 10-teeth rear sprocket revolve twice.

Part 9—Numerical Operations

1-B	$2 + 5 = 7$		**21-A**	$7 - 1 = 6$
2-C	$18 \div 2 = 9$		**22-D**	$2 \times 3 = 6$
3-A	$10 - 8 = 2$		**23-C**	$9 - 7 = 2$
4-B	$3 \times 3 = 9$		**24-D**	$6 + 8 = 14$
5-D	$1 + 8 = 9$		**25-B**	$10 \div 2 = 5$
6-C	$9 \times 8 = 72$		**26-A**	$6 \div 3 = 2$
7-A	$4 \times 5 = 20$		**27-A**	$5 + 9 = 14$
8-C	$3 + 7 = 10$		**28-D**	$7 \div 7 = 1$
9-D	$9 - 5 = 4$		**29-A**	$6 - 6 = 0$
10-D	$3 \times 9 = 27$		**30-B**	$9 \times 6 = 54$
11-B	$50 \div 5 = 10$		**31-C**	$7 + 9 = 16$
12-D	$8 - 6 = 2$		**32-D**	$5 - 4 = 1$
13-B	$6 \div 3 = 2$		**33-A**	$4 \div 4 = 1$
14-C	$2 \times 9 = 18$		**34-D**	$10 - 5 = 5$
15-C	$4 + 8 = 12$		**35-B**	$7 \times 4 = 28$
16-B	$7 \times 9 = 63$		**36-D**	$36 \div 6 = 6$
17-D	$5 \times 6 = 30$		**37-A**	$8 \times 3 = 24$
18-C	$0 + 8 = 8$		**38-D**	$2 \times 4 = 8$
19-C	$4 + 5 = 9$		**39-C**	$8 - 1 = 7$
20-C	$64 \div 8 = 8$		**40-A**	$1 + 5 = 6$

41-B	$90 \div 9 = 10$	**46-A**	$3 - 2 = 1$
42-D	$2 - 2 = 0$	**47-C**	$5 + 8 = 13$
43-D	$7 + 8 = 15$	**48-B**	$3 \div 3 = 1$
44-B	$4 - 0 = 4$	**49-B**	$9 \div 1 = 9$
45-D	$8 + 3 = 11$	**50-B**	$4 \times 6 = 24$

Part 10—Coding Speed

There is no way to explain the answers to the Coding Speed questions. If you are still making many mistakes, get more practice by redoing the Coding Speed sections of each of the specimen tests. Write the letter answers on a plain piece of paper.

CHAPTER 7

FOURTH ASVAB TEST BATTERY

ere is your fourth opportunity to take a practice ASVAB test battery. All of your practice and preparation will be evident in your results of this final test battery. Once you have completed the test, review the scores you recorded for each test battery in the Self-Appraisal chart. You can then determine if you feel prepared and confident enough for your test day or if you need further practice.

If you feel confident and prepared, go on to the next chapter of this book for information about how the military calculates test results. This is followed by a section on Military Careers and Enlistment Opportunities, which gives a listing of careers and score requirements.

Here are the guidelines again to help you make the most of this sample test battery:

- Take this test under "real" test conditions (time yourself, take it in a quiet room without distractions, and use the sample answer sheets).
- Time each test carefully and do not go over the time allotted for each section.
- Use the answer keys to get your test scores and to evaluate your performance on each test.
- Record the number of items you answered correctly and incorrectly for each section in the answer chart provided at the end of the battery. Also, record the number of items you want to review further or were unsure about.
- Carefully review and understand the answer explanations to all questions you answered incorrectly.
- Don't forget to review each of the questions that you answered correctly but may not be sure of. This is a necessary step to gain the knowledge and expertise you need to get the highest scores possible on the real ASVAB tests.
- Transfer your scores for each section of the First ASVAB Sample Test Battery to the Self-Appraisal Chart appearing on page 24. This will enable you to track your progress as you continue to prepare for the actual test.
- Use the sample answer sheets provided to record your answers. If you want, you can cut them out to make them easier to use and to simulate actual test conditions.

Specimen Answer Sheet for Answering Parts 1–10
(On the following page)

Part 1: General Science

1. Ⓐ Ⓑ Ⓒ Ⓓ   2. Ⓐ Ⓑ Ⓒ Ⓓ   3. Ⓐ Ⓑ Ⓒ Ⓓ   4. Ⓐ Ⓑ Ⓒ Ⓓ   5. Ⓐ Ⓑ Ⓒ Ⓓ
6. Ⓐ Ⓑ Ⓒ Ⓓ   7. Ⓐ Ⓑ Ⓒ Ⓓ   8. Ⓐ Ⓑ Ⓒ Ⓓ   9. Ⓐ Ⓑ Ⓒ Ⓓ   10. Ⓐ Ⓑ Ⓒ Ⓓ
11. Ⓐ Ⓑ Ⓒ Ⓓ   12. Ⓐ Ⓑ Ⓒ Ⓓ   13. Ⓐ Ⓑ Ⓒ Ⓓ   14. Ⓐ Ⓑ Ⓒ Ⓓ   15. Ⓐ Ⓑ Ⓒ Ⓓ
16. Ⓐ Ⓑ Ⓒ Ⓓ   17. Ⓐ Ⓑ Ⓒ Ⓓ   18. Ⓐ Ⓑ Ⓒ Ⓓ   19. Ⓐ Ⓑ Ⓒ Ⓓ   20. Ⓐ Ⓑ Ⓒ Ⓓ
21. Ⓐ Ⓑ Ⓒ Ⓓ   22. Ⓐ Ⓑ Ⓒ Ⓓ   23. Ⓐ Ⓑ Ⓒ Ⓓ   24. Ⓐ Ⓑ Ⓒ Ⓓ   25. Ⓐ Ⓑ Ⓒ Ⓓ

Part 2: Arithmetic Reasoning

1. Ⓐ Ⓑ Ⓒ Ⓓ   2. Ⓐ Ⓑ Ⓒ Ⓓ   3. Ⓐ Ⓑ Ⓒ Ⓓ   4. Ⓐ Ⓑ Ⓒ Ⓓ   5. Ⓐ Ⓑ Ⓒ Ⓓ
6. Ⓐ Ⓑ Ⓒ Ⓓ   7. Ⓐ Ⓑ Ⓒ Ⓓ   8. Ⓐ Ⓑ Ⓒ Ⓓ   9. Ⓐ Ⓑ Ⓒ Ⓓ   10. Ⓐ Ⓑ Ⓒ Ⓓ
11. Ⓐ Ⓑ Ⓒ Ⓓ   12. Ⓐ Ⓑ Ⓒ Ⓓ   13. Ⓐ Ⓑ Ⓒ Ⓓ   14. Ⓐ Ⓑ Ⓒ Ⓓ   15. Ⓐ Ⓑ Ⓒ Ⓓ
16. Ⓐ Ⓑ Ⓒ Ⓓ   17. Ⓐ Ⓑ Ⓒ Ⓓ   18. Ⓐ Ⓑ Ⓒ Ⓓ   19. Ⓐ Ⓑ Ⓒ Ⓓ   20. Ⓐ Ⓑ Ⓒ Ⓓ
21. Ⓐ Ⓑ Ⓒ Ⓓ   22. Ⓐ Ⓑ Ⓒ Ⓓ   23. Ⓐ Ⓑ Ⓒ Ⓓ   24. Ⓐ Ⓑ Ⓒ Ⓓ   25. Ⓐ Ⓑ Ⓒ Ⓓ
26. Ⓐ Ⓑ Ⓒ Ⓓ   27. Ⓐ Ⓑ Ⓒ Ⓓ   28. Ⓐ Ⓑ Ⓒ Ⓓ   29. Ⓐ Ⓑ Ⓒ Ⓓ   30. Ⓐ Ⓑ Ⓒ Ⓓ

Part 3: Word Kowledge

1. Ⓐ Ⓑ Ⓒ Ⓓ   2. Ⓐ Ⓑ Ⓒ Ⓓ   3. Ⓐ Ⓑ Ⓒ Ⓓ   4. Ⓐ Ⓑ Ⓒ Ⓓ   5. Ⓐ Ⓑ Ⓒ Ⓓ
6. Ⓐ Ⓑ Ⓒ Ⓓ   7. Ⓐ Ⓑ Ⓒ Ⓓ   8. Ⓐ Ⓑ Ⓒ Ⓓ   9. Ⓐ Ⓑ Ⓒ Ⓓ   10. Ⓐ Ⓑ Ⓒ Ⓓ
11. Ⓐ Ⓑ Ⓒ Ⓓ   12. Ⓐ Ⓑ Ⓒ Ⓓ   13. Ⓐ Ⓑ Ⓒ Ⓓ   14. Ⓐ Ⓑ Ⓒ Ⓓ   15. Ⓐ Ⓑ Ⓒ Ⓓ
16. Ⓐ Ⓑ Ⓒ Ⓓ   17. Ⓐ Ⓑ Ⓒ Ⓓ   18. Ⓐ Ⓑ Ⓒ Ⓓ   19. Ⓐ Ⓑ Ⓒ Ⓓ   20. Ⓐ Ⓑ Ⓒ Ⓓ
21. Ⓐ Ⓑ Ⓒ Ⓓ   22. Ⓐ Ⓑ Ⓒ Ⓓ   23. Ⓐ Ⓑ Ⓒ Ⓓ   24. Ⓐ Ⓑ Ⓒ Ⓓ   25. Ⓐ Ⓑ Ⓒ Ⓓ
26. Ⓐ Ⓑ Ⓒ Ⓓ   27. Ⓐ Ⓑ Ⓒ Ⓓ   28. Ⓐ Ⓑ Ⓒ Ⓓ   29. Ⓐ Ⓑ Ⓒ Ⓓ   30. Ⓐ Ⓑ Ⓒ Ⓓ
31. Ⓐ Ⓑ Ⓒ Ⓓ   32. Ⓐ Ⓑ Ⓒ Ⓓ   33. Ⓐ Ⓑ Ⓒ Ⓓ   34. Ⓐ Ⓑ Ⓒ Ⓓ   35. Ⓐ Ⓑ Ⓒ Ⓓ

Part 4: Paragraph Comprehension

1. Ⓐ Ⓑ Ⓒ Ⓓ   2. Ⓐ Ⓑ Ⓒ Ⓓ   3. Ⓐ Ⓑ Ⓒ Ⓓ   4. Ⓐ Ⓑ Ⓒ Ⓓ   5. Ⓐ Ⓑ Ⓒ Ⓓ
6. Ⓐ Ⓑ Ⓒ Ⓓ   7. Ⓐ Ⓑ Ⓒ Ⓓ   8. Ⓐ Ⓑ Ⓒ Ⓓ   9. Ⓐ Ⓑ Ⓒ Ⓓ   10. Ⓐ Ⓑ Ⓒ Ⓓ
11. Ⓐ Ⓑ Ⓒ Ⓓ   12. Ⓐ Ⓑ Ⓒ Ⓓ   13. Ⓐ Ⓑ Ⓒ Ⓓ   14. Ⓐ Ⓑ Ⓒ Ⓓ   15. Ⓐ Ⓑ Ⓒ Ⓓ

Part 5: Mathematics Knowledge

1. Ⓐ Ⓑ Ⓒ Ⓓ   2. Ⓐ Ⓑ Ⓒ Ⓓ   3. Ⓐ Ⓑ Ⓒ Ⓓ   4. Ⓐ Ⓑ Ⓒ Ⓓ   5. Ⓐ Ⓑ Ⓒ Ⓓ
6. Ⓐ Ⓑ Ⓒ Ⓓ   7. Ⓐ Ⓑ Ⓒ Ⓓ   8. Ⓐ Ⓑ Ⓒ Ⓓ   9. Ⓐ Ⓑ Ⓒ Ⓓ   10. Ⓐ Ⓑ Ⓒ Ⓓ
11. Ⓐ Ⓑ Ⓒ Ⓓ   12. Ⓐ Ⓑ Ⓒ Ⓓ   13. Ⓐ Ⓑ Ⓒ Ⓓ   14. Ⓐ Ⓑ Ⓒ Ⓓ   15. Ⓐ Ⓑ Ⓒ Ⓓ
16. Ⓐ Ⓑ Ⓒ Ⓓ   17. Ⓐ Ⓑ Ⓒ Ⓓ   18. Ⓐ Ⓑ Ⓒ Ⓓ   19. Ⓐ Ⓑ Ⓒ Ⓓ   20. Ⓐ Ⓑ Ⓒ Ⓓ
21. Ⓐ Ⓑ Ⓒ Ⓓ   22. Ⓐ Ⓑ Ⓒ Ⓓ   23. Ⓐ Ⓑ Ⓒ Ⓓ   24. Ⓐ Ⓑ Ⓒ Ⓓ   25. Ⓐ Ⓑ Ⓒ Ⓓ

Part 6: Electronics Information

1. Ⓐ Ⓑ Ⓒ Ⓓ   2. Ⓐ Ⓑ Ⓒ Ⓓ   3. Ⓐ Ⓑ Ⓒ Ⓓ   4. Ⓐ Ⓑ Ⓒ Ⓓ   5. Ⓐ Ⓑ Ⓒ Ⓓ
6. Ⓐ Ⓑ Ⓒ Ⓓ   7. Ⓐ Ⓑ Ⓒ Ⓓ   8. Ⓐ Ⓑ Ⓒ Ⓓ   9. Ⓐ Ⓑ Ⓒ Ⓓ   10. Ⓐ Ⓑ Ⓒ Ⓓ
11. Ⓐ Ⓑ Ⓒ Ⓓ   12. Ⓐ Ⓑ Ⓒ Ⓓ   13. Ⓐ Ⓑ Ⓒ Ⓓ   14. Ⓐ Ⓑ Ⓒ Ⓓ   15. Ⓐ Ⓑ Ⓒ Ⓓ
16. Ⓐ Ⓑ Ⓒ Ⓓ   17. Ⓐ Ⓑ Ⓒ Ⓓ   18. Ⓐ Ⓑ Ⓒ Ⓓ   19. Ⓐ Ⓑ Ⓒ Ⓓ   20. Ⓐ Ⓑ Ⓒ Ⓓ

Part 7: Auto & Shop Information

1. Ⓐ Ⓑ Ⓒ Ⓓ   2. Ⓐ Ⓑ Ⓒ Ⓓ   3. Ⓐ Ⓑ Ⓒ Ⓓ   4. Ⓐ Ⓑ Ⓒ Ⓓ   5. Ⓐ Ⓑ Ⓒ Ⓓ
6. Ⓐ Ⓑ Ⓒ Ⓓ   7. Ⓐ Ⓑ Ⓒ Ⓓ   8. Ⓐ Ⓑ Ⓒ Ⓓ   9. Ⓐ Ⓑ Ⓒ Ⓓ   10. Ⓐ Ⓑ Ⓒ Ⓓ
11. Ⓐ Ⓑ Ⓒ Ⓓ   12. Ⓐ Ⓑ Ⓒ Ⓓ   13. Ⓐ Ⓑ Ⓒ Ⓓ   14. Ⓐ Ⓑ Ⓒ Ⓓ   15. Ⓐ Ⓑ Ⓒ Ⓓ
16. Ⓐ Ⓑ Ⓒ Ⓓ   17. Ⓐ Ⓑ Ⓒ Ⓓ   18. Ⓐ Ⓑ Ⓒ Ⓓ   19. Ⓐ Ⓑ Ⓒ Ⓓ   20. Ⓐ Ⓑ Ⓒ Ⓓ
21. Ⓐ Ⓑ Ⓒ Ⓓ   22. Ⓐ Ⓑ Ⓒ Ⓓ   23. Ⓐ Ⓑ Ⓒ Ⓓ   24. Ⓐ Ⓑ Ⓒ Ⓓ   25. Ⓐ Ⓑ Ⓒ Ⓓ

Part 8: Mechanical Comprehension

1. Ⓐ Ⓑ Ⓒ Ⓓ   2. Ⓐ Ⓑ Ⓒ Ⓓ   3. Ⓐ Ⓑ Ⓒ Ⓓ   4. Ⓐ Ⓑ Ⓒ Ⓓ   5. Ⓐ Ⓑ Ⓒ Ⓓ
6. Ⓐ Ⓑ Ⓒ Ⓓ   7. Ⓐ Ⓑ Ⓒ Ⓓ   8. Ⓐ Ⓑ Ⓒ Ⓓ   9. Ⓐ Ⓑ Ⓒ Ⓓ   10. Ⓐ Ⓑ Ⓒ Ⓓ
11. Ⓐ Ⓑ Ⓒ Ⓓ   12. Ⓐ Ⓑ Ⓒ Ⓓ   13. Ⓐ Ⓑ Ⓒ Ⓓ   14. Ⓐ Ⓑ Ⓒ Ⓓ   15. Ⓐ Ⓑ Ⓒ Ⓓ
16. Ⓐ Ⓑ Ⓒ Ⓓ   17. Ⓐ Ⓑ Ⓒ Ⓓ   18. Ⓐ Ⓑ Ⓒ Ⓓ   19. Ⓐ Ⓑ Ⓒ Ⓓ   20. Ⓐ Ⓑ Ⓒ Ⓓ
21. Ⓐ Ⓑ Ⓒ Ⓓ   22. Ⓐ Ⓑ Ⓒ Ⓓ   23. Ⓐ Ⓑ Ⓒ Ⓓ   24. Ⓐ Ⓑ Ⓒ Ⓓ   25. Ⓐ Ⓑ Ⓒ Ⓓ

Part 9: Numerical Operations

1. Ⓐ Ⓑ Ⓒ Ⓓ   2. Ⓐ Ⓑ Ⓒ Ⓓ   3. Ⓐ Ⓑ Ⓒ Ⓓ   4. Ⓐ Ⓑ Ⓒ Ⓓ   5. Ⓐ Ⓑ Ⓒ Ⓓ
6. Ⓐ Ⓑ Ⓒ Ⓓ   7. Ⓐ Ⓑ Ⓒ Ⓓ   8. Ⓐ Ⓑ Ⓒ Ⓓ   9. Ⓐ Ⓑ Ⓒ Ⓓ   10. Ⓐ Ⓑ Ⓒ Ⓓ
11. Ⓐ Ⓑ Ⓒ Ⓓ   12. Ⓐ Ⓑ Ⓒ Ⓓ   13. Ⓐ Ⓑ Ⓒ Ⓓ   14. Ⓐ Ⓑ Ⓒ Ⓓ   15. Ⓐ Ⓑ Ⓒ Ⓓ
16. Ⓐ Ⓑ Ⓒ Ⓓ   17. Ⓐ Ⓑ Ⓒ Ⓓ   18. Ⓐ Ⓑ Ⓒ Ⓓ   19. Ⓐ Ⓑ Ⓒ Ⓓ   20. Ⓐ Ⓑ Ⓒ Ⓓ
21. Ⓐ Ⓑ Ⓒ Ⓓ   22. Ⓐ Ⓑ Ⓒ Ⓓ   23. Ⓐ Ⓑ Ⓒ Ⓓ   24. Ⓐ Ⓑ Ⓒ Ⓓ   25. Ⓐ Ⓑ Ⓒ Ⓓ
26. Ⓐ Ⓑ Ⓒ Ⓓ   27. Ⓐ Ⓑ Ⓒ Ⓓ   28. Ⓐ Ⓑ Ⓒ Ⓓ   29. Ⓐ Ⓑ Ⓒ Ⓓ   30. Ⓐ Ⓑ Ⓒ Ⓓ
31. Ⓐ Ⓑ Ⓒ Ⓓ   32. Ⓐ Ⓑ Ⓒ Ⓓ   33. Ⓐ Ⓑ Ⓒ Ⓓ   34. Ⓐ Ⓑ Ⓒ Ⓓ   35. Ⓐ Ⓑ Ⓒ Ⓓ
36. Ⓐ Ⓑ Ⓒ Ⓓ   37. Ⓐ Ⓑ Ⓒ Ⓓ   38. Ⓐ Ⓑ Ⓒ Ⓓ   39. Ⓐ Ⓑ Ⓒ Ⓓ   40. Ⓐ Ⓑ Ⓒ Ⓓ
41. Ⓐ Ⓑ Ⓒ Ⓓ   42. Ⓐ Ⓑ Ⓒ Ⓓ   43. Ⓐ Ⓑ Ⓒ Ⓓ   44. Ⓐ Ⓑ Ⓒ Ⓓ   45. Ⓐ Ⓑ Ⓒ Ⓓ
46. Ⓐ Ⓑ Ⓒ Ⓓ   47. Ⓐ Ⓑ Ⓒ Ⓓ   48. Ⓐ Ⓑ Ⓒ Ⓓ   49. Ⓐ Ⓑ Ⓒ Ⓓ   50. Ⓐ Ⓑ Ⓒ Ⓓ

Part 10: Coding Speed

1. Ⓐ Ⓑ Ⓒ Ⓓ   2. Ⓐ Ⓑ Ⓒ Ⓓ   3. Ⓐ Ⓑ Ⓒ Ⓓ   4. Ⓐ Ⓑ Ⓒ Ⓓ   5. Ⓐ Ⓑ Ⓒ Ⓓ
6. Ⓐ Ⓑ Ⓒ Ⓓ   7. Ⓐ Ⓑ Ⓒ Ⓓ   8. Ⓐ Ⓑ Ⓒ Ⓓ   9. Ⓐ Ⓑ Ⓒ Ⓓ   10. Ⓐ Ⓑ Ⓒ Ⓓ
11. Ⓐ Ⓑ Ⓒ Ⓓ   12. Ⓐ Ⓑ Ⓒ Ⓓ   13. Ⓐ Ⓑ Ⓒ Ⓓ   14. Ⓐ Ⓑ Ⓒ Ⓓ   15. Ⓐ Ⓑ Ⓒ Ⓓ
16. Ⓐ Ⓑ Ⓒ Ⓓ   17. Ⓐ Ⓑ Ⓒ Ⓓ   18. Ⓐ Ⓑ Ⓒ Ⓓ   19. Ⓐ Ⓑ Ⓒ Ⓓ   20. Ⓐ Ⓑ Ⓒ Ⓓ
21. Ⓐ Ⓑ Ⓒ Ⓓ   22. Ⓐ Ⓑ Ⓒ Ⓓ   23. Ⓐ Ⓑ Ⓒ Ⓓ   24. Ⓐ Ⓑ Ⓒ Ⓓ   25. Ⓐ Ⓑ Ⓒ Ⓓ
26. Ⓐ Ⓑ Ⓒ Ⓓ   27. Ⓐ Ⓑ Ⓒ Ⓓ   28. Ⓐ Ⓑ Ⓒ Ⓓ   29. Ⓐ Ⓑ Ⓒ Ⓓ   30. Ⓐ Ⓑ Ⓒ Ⓓ
31. Ⓐ Ⓑ Ⓒ Ⓓ   32. Ⓐ Ⓑ Ⓒ Ⓓ   33. Ⓐ Ⓑ Ⓒ Ⓓ   34. Ⓐ Ⓑ Ⓒ Ⓓ   35. Ⓐ Ⓑ Ⓒ Ⓓ
36. Ⓐ Ⓑ Ⓒ Ⓓ   37. Ⓐ Ⓑ Ⓒ Ⓓ   38. Ⓐ Ⓑ Ⓒ Ⓓ   39. Ⓐ Ⓑ Ⓒ Ⓓ   40. Ⓐ Ⓑ Ⓒ Ⓓ
41. Ⓐ Ⓑ Ⓒ Ⓓ   42. Ⓐ Ⓑ Ⓒ Ⓓ   43. Ⓐ Ⓑ Ⓒ Ⓓ   44. Ⓐ Ⓑ Ⓒ Ⓓ   45. Ⓐ Ⓑ Ⓒ Ⓓ
46. Ⓐ Ⓑ Ⓒ Ⓓ   47. Ⓐ Ⓑ Ⓒ Ⓓ   48. Ⓐ Ⓑ Ⓒ Ⓓ   49. Ⓐ Ⓑ Ⓒ Ⓓ   50. Ⓐ Ⓑ Ⓒ Ⓓ
51. Ⓐ Ⓑ Ⓒ Ⓓ   52. Ⓐ Ⓑ Ⓒ Ⓓ   53. Ⓐ Ⓑ Ⓒ Ⓓ   54. Ⓐ Ⓑ Ⓒ Ⓓ   55. Ⓐ Ⓑ Ⓒ Ⓓ
56. Ⓐ Ⓑ Ⓒ Ⓓ   57. Ⓐ Ⓑ Ⓒ Ⓓ   58. Ⓐ Ⓑ Ⓒ Ⓓ   59. Ⓐ Ⓑ Ⓒ Ⓓ   60. Ⓐ Ⓑ Ⓒ Ⓓ
61. Ⓐ Ⓑ Ⓒ Ⓓ   62. Ⓐ Ⓑ Ⓒ Ⓓ   63. Ⓐ Ⓑ Ⓒ Ⓓ   64. Ⓐ Ⓑ Ⓒ Ⓓ   65. Ⓐ Ⓑ Ⓒ Ⓓ
66. Ⓐ Ⓑ Ⓒ Ⓓ   67. Ⓐ Ⓑ Ⓒ Ⓓ   68. Ⓐ Ⓑ Ⓒ Ⓓ   69. Ⓐ Ⓑ Ⓒ Ⓓ   70. Ⓐ Ⓑ Ⓒ Ⓓ
71. Ⓐ Ⓑ Ⓒ Ⓓ   72. Ⓐ Ⓑ Ⓒ Ⓓ   73. Ⓐ Ⓑ Ⓒ Ⓓ   74. Ⓐ Ⓑ Ⓒ Ⓓ   75. Ⓐ Ⓑ Ⓒ Ⓓ
76. Ⓐ Ⓑ Ⓒ Ⓓ   77. Ⓐ Ⓑ Ⓒ Ⓓ   78. Ⓐ Ⓑ Ⓒ Ⓓ   79. Ⓐ Ⓑ Ⓒ Ⓓ   80. Ⓐ Ⓑ Ⓒ Ⓓ
81. Ⓐ Ⓑ Ⓒ Ⓓ   82. Ⓐ Ⓑ Ⓒ Ⓓ   83. Ⓐ Ⓑ Ⓒ Ⓓ   84. Ⓐ Ⓑ Ⓒ Ⓓ

PART 1: GENERAL SCIENCE

Directions

This is a test of 25 questions to find out how much you know about general science as usually covered in high school courses. Pick the best answer for each question, then blacken the space on your answer form that has the same number and letter as your choice.

Here are three sample questions.

S1. Water is an example of a   Ⓐ Ⓑ Ⓒ Ⓓ
- S1-A   solid.
- S1-B   gas.
- S1-C   liquid.
- S1-D   crystal.

Now look at the section of your answer sheet labeled Part 1, "Practice." Notice that answer space C has been marked for question 1. Now do practice questions 2 and 3 by yourself. Find the correct answer to the question, then mark the space on your answer form that has the same letter as the answer you picked. Do this now.

S2. Lack of iodine is often related to which of the following diseases?   Ⓐ Ⓑ Ⓒ Ⓓ
- S2-A   Beriberi
- S2-B   Scurvy
- S2-C   Rickets
- S2-D   Goiter

S3. An eclipse of the sun throws the shadow of the   Ⓐ Ⓑ Ⓒ Ⓓ
- S3-A   earth on the moon.
- S3-B   moon on the earth.
- S3-C   moon on the sun.
- S3-D   earth on the sun.

You should have marked choice D for question 2 and choice B for question 3. If you made any mistakes, erase your mark carefully and blacken the correct answer space. Do this now.

Your score on this test will be based on the number of questions you answer correctly. You should try to answer every question. Do not spend too much time on any one question.

When you begin, be sure to start with question number 1 of Part 1 of your test booklet and number 1 in Part 1 on your answer form.

DO NOT CONTINUE UNTIL TOLD TO DO SO.

General Science

Time: 11 Minutes—25 Questions

1. Citrus fruits and tomatoes are good sources for vitamin
   - 1-A   A.
   - 1-B   B.
   - 1-C   C.
   - 1-D   D.

2. If a $33\frac{1}{3}$ rpm phonograph record is played at a speed of 45 rpm, it will
   - 2-A   sound lower-pitched.
   - 2-B   sound higher-pitched.
   - 2-C   give no sound.
   - 2-D   play louder.

3. The chief nutrient in lean meat is
   - 3-A   starch.
   - 3-B   protein.
   - 3-C   fat.
   - 3-D   carbohydrates.

4. On the Celsius temperature scale, each Celsius degree represents what fraction of the temperature range between freezing and boiling points of water?
   - 4-A $\dfrac{1}{180}$
   - 4-B $\dfrac{1}{100}$
   - 4-C $\dfrac{1}{18}$
   - 4-D $\dfrac{1}{10}$

5. When uranium decays, it becomes
   - 5-A   carbon.
   - 5-B   copper.
   - 5-C   lead.
   - 5-D   tin.

6. "Shooting stars" are
   - 6-A   exploding stars.
   - 6-B   cosmic rays.
   - 6-C   planetoids.
   - 6-D   meteors.

7. Two children are seated on a seesaw. The first child, seated 4 feet from the center, weighs 80 pounds. If the second child weighs 40 pounds, how far from the center must that child sit to balance the seesaw?
   - 7-A   1 foot
   - 7-B   2 feet
   - 7-C   8 feet
   - 7-D   16 feet

8. The part of the digestive system in which digested materials are absorbed into the bloodstream is the
   - 8-A   large intestine.
   - 8-B   liver.
   - 8-C   small intestine.
   - 8-D   stomach.

9. Skeletal muscles are joined to bones by tough connective tissue called
   - 9-A   cartilage.
   - 9-B   ligaments.
   - 9-C   muscle fibers.
   - 9-D   tendons.

10. Hearing an echo is most like seeing
    - 10-A   around the corner through a periscope.
    - 10-B   fine print under strong illumination.
    - 10-C   stars at night that are invisible in the daytime.
    - 10-D   one's image in a mirror.

11. Vitamin K is needed for
    11-A   energy release.
    11-B   formation of bones.
    11-C   normal blood clotting.
    11-D   normal metabolism.

12. Refraction of light affects the aim one should take when
    12-A   shooting at a fish that has jumped out of the water.
    12-B   spearing a fish in the water from the bank.
    12-C   spearing a fish under water when one is swimming under water.
    12-D   casting a fly on the surface of the water.

13. The primary reason designers seek to lower the center of gravity in automobiles is to
    13-A   reduce wind resistance.
    13-B   provide smoother riding.
    13-C   increase stability.
    13-D   reduce manufacturing costs.

14. Substances that hasten a chemical reaction without themselves undergoing change are called
    14-A   buffers.
    14-B   catalysts.
    14-C   colloids.
    14-D   reducers.

15. A hip joint is best described as a
    15-A   ball-and-socket joint.
    15-B   gliding joint.
    15-C   hinge joint.
    15-D   pivot joint.

16. AIDS is a disease caused by a
    16-A   bacillus.
    16-B   saprophyte.
    16-C   spirillum.
    16-D   virus.

17. Lack of iodine is often related to which of the following diseases?
    17-A   Beriberi
    17-B   Scurvy
    17-C   Rickets
    17-D   Goiter

18. Why will a given quantity of steam always produce a more severe burn than that produced by the same quantity of boiling water?
    18-A   Steam always penetrates the epidermis.
    18-B   Steam causes the skin to contract and break.
    18-C   Steam always releases more heat per gram than water.
    18-D   Steam always covers more area of the skin.

19. A lead sinker weighs 54 grams in air, 23.8 grams in liquid A, and 28.6 grams in liquid B. From this information, what conclusions can be drawn concerning the densities of the two liquids?
    19-A   Liquid A has a greater density than liquid B.
    19-B   Both liquids are more dense than water.
    19-C   Both liquids are less dense than water.
    19-D   No conclusions can be drawn concerning the densities of the two liquids.

20. After adding a solute to a liquid, the freezing point of the liquid is
    20-A   lowered.
    20-B   the same.
    20-C   raised.
    20-D   inverted.

21. Organisms that sustain their life cycles by feeding off other live organisms are known as

    21-A   parasites.
    21-B   saprophytes.
    21-C   bacteria.
    21-D   viruses.

22. Chemicals that have been pumped into the air by industries cause air pollution. This leads to

    22-A   acid rains that destroy crops and animals.
    22-B   respiratory ailments in animals and people.
    22-C   possible changes in the climate.
    22-D   All of the above

23. A body in space that orbits around another body is known as a

    23-A   moon.
    23-B   planet.
    23-C   satellite.
    23-D   comet.

24. Photosynthesis is the process by which green plants manufacture carbohydrates from

    24-A   oxygen and nitrogen.
    24-B   carbon dioxide and water.
    24-C   oxygen and water.
    24-D   glucose and water.

25. When two or more elements combine to form a substance that has properties different from those of the component elements, that new substance is known as a

    25-A   mixture.
    25-B   solution.
    25-C   alloy.
    25-D   compound.

STOP!

IF YOU FINISH BEFORE THE TIME IS UP, YOU MAY CHECK OVER YOUR WORK ON THIS PART ONLY.

Part 2: Arithmetic Reasoning

Directions

This test has 30 questions about arithmetic. Each question is followed by four possible answers. Decide which answer is correct, then blacken the space on your answer form that has the same number and letter as your choice. Use your scratch paper for any figuring you wish to do.

Here are two sample questions.

S1. A person buys a sandwich for 90¢, soda for 55¢, and pie for 70¢. What is the total cost?

    S1-A $2.00

    S1-B $2.05

    S1-C $2.15   Ⓐ Ⓑ Ⓒ Ⓓ

    S1-D $2.25

The total cost is $2.15; therefore, choice C is the correct answer.

S2. If 8 workers are needed to run 4 machines, how many workers are needed to run 20 machines?

    S2-A   16

    S2-B   32

    S2-C   36   Ⓐ Ⓑ Ⓒ Ⓓ

    S2-D   40

The number needed is 40; therefore, choice D is the correct answer.

Your score on this test will be based on the number of questions you answer correctly. You should try to answer every question. Do not spend too much time on any one question.

Notice that Part 2 begins with question number 1. When you begin, be sure to start with question number 1 in Part 2 of your test booklet and number 1 in Part 2 on your answer form.

DO NOT CONTINUE UNTIL TOLD TO DO SO.

Arithmetic Reasoning

Time: 36 Minutes—30 Questions

1. A fruit picker gets $3.00 an hour plus 72¢ for every bushel over 40 that he picks in a day. If he works 8 hours and picks 50 bushels, how much will he get?

    1-A $29.76
    1-B $30.20
    1-C $31.20
    1-D $31.76

2. How many 36-passenger buses will it take to carry 144 people?

    2-A   4
    2-B   3
    2-C   5
    2-D   6

3. A gallon contains 4 quarts. A cartoning machine can fill 120 one-quart cartons a minute. How long will it take to put 600 gallons of orange juice into cartons?

    3-A   1 minute and 15 seconds
    3-B   5 minutes
    3-C   10 minutes
    3-D   20 minutes

4. A mechanic greased 168 cars in 28 days. What was his daily average of cars greased?

    4-A   5
    4-B   6
    4-C   7
    4-D   8

5. What is the fifth term in the series:

    $$4\frac{1}{2};\ 8\frac{3}{4};\ 13;\ 17\frac{1}{4};\ \underline{\quad}?$$

    5-A $20\frac{3}{4}$
    5-B   21
    5-C $21\frac{1}{2}$
    5-D $21\frac{3}{4}$

6. Three workers assemble 360 switches per hour, but 5% of the switches are defective. How many good (nondefective) switches will these 3 workers assemble in an 8-hour shift?

    6-A   2,736
    6-B   2,880
    6-C   2,944
    6-D   3,000

7. The butcher made $22\frac{1}{2}$ pounds of beef into hamburger and wrapped it in $1\frac{1}{4}$-pound packages. How many packages did he make?

    7-A   15
    7-B   16
    7-C   17
    7-D   18

8. If a car-renting agency charges a fixed rate of $12 per day plus 17¢ per mile, what would the charge be for using a car for 6 days and traveling 421 miles?

    8-A $143.57
    8-B $153.57
    8-C $163.57
    8-D $173.57

9. It cost a couple $27.00 to go out for the evening. Sixty percent of this was for theater tickets. What was the cost for each ticket?

    9-A $7.90
    9-B $8.10
    9-C $10.80
    9-D $16.20

10. Soap, ordinarily priced at 2 bars for $0.66, may be purchased in lots of one dozen for $3.48. What is the saving per bar when it is purchased in this way?

    10-A   4 cents
    10-B   8 cents
    10-C   16 cents
    10-D   19 cents

11. Twenty students contribute $25 each for a Christmas party. Forty percent of the money is spent for food and drinks. How much is left for other expenses?

    11-A $125
    11-B $200
    11-C $300
    11-D $375

12. A pole 24 feet high has a shadow 8 feet long. A nearby pole is 72 feet high. How long is its shadow?

    12-A   16 feet
    12-B   24 feet
    12-C   32 feet
    12-D   56 feet

13. The price of a $250 item after successive discounts of 20% and 30% is

    13-A $125
    13-B $130
    13-C $140
    13-D $180

14. If a laborer works from 7:15 a.m. to 3:45 p.m. with 1 hour off for lunch, his working time equals

    14-A   7 hours
    14-B $7\frac{1}{2}$ hours
    14-C   8 hours
    14-D $8\frac{1}{2}$ hours

15. A home has a tax rate of 2%. If the tax is $550, what is the assessed value of the home?

    15-A $1,100
    15-B $2,750
    15-C $11,000
    15-D $27,500

16. A delivery company employs 6 truck drivers. If each driver travels 250 miles a day, how many miles do all 6 drivers travel in a 5-day work week?

    16-A   750
    16-B   1,500
    16-C   7,500
    16-D   15,000

17. The minute hand fell off a watch but the watch continued to work accurately. What time was it when the hour hand was at the 17-minute mark?

    17-A   3:02
    17-B   3:17
    17-C   3:24
    17-D   4:17

18. A manufacturer has 3,375 yards of material on hand. If the average dress takes $3\frac{3}{8}$ yards of material, how many dresses can he make?

    18-A   844
    18-B   1,000
    18-C   1,125
    18-D   1,250

19. It costs $1 per square yard to waterproof canvas. What will it cost to waterproof a canvas truck cover that is 15¢ × 24¢?

    19-A $20
    19-B $36
    19-C $40
    19-D $360

20. A part-time employee worked a total of $16\frac{1}{2}$ hours during 5 days of the past week. What was this employee's average workday?

    20-A   3 hours
    20-B   3 hours, 15 minutes
    20-C   3 hours, 18 minutes
    20-D   3 hours, 25 minutes

21. A driver traveled 100 miles at the rate of 40 mph, then traveled 80 miles at 60 mph. The total number of hours for the entire trip was

    21-A $1\frac{3}{20}$

    21-B $1\frac{3}{4}$

    21-C $2\frac{1}{4}$

    21-D $3\frac{5}{6}$

22. After an article is discounted at 25%, it sells for $112.50. The original price of the article was

    22-A $28.12
    22-B $84.37
    22-C $150.00
    22-D $152.50

23. A checking account has a balance of $627.04. After writing three checks for $241.75, $13.24, and $102.97, what is the balance remaining in the account?

    23-A $257.88
    23-B $269.08
    23-C $357.96
    23-D $369.96

24. If erasers cost 8¢ each for the first 250, 7¢ each for the next 250, and 5¢ for every eraser thereafter, how many erasers may be purchased for $50?

    24-A   600
    24-B   750
    24-C   850
    24-D   1,000

25. A plane left New York at 3:30 p.m. EST and arrived in Los Angeles at 4:15 p.m. PST. How long did the flight take?

    25-A   7 hours, 15 minutes
    25-B   6 hours, 45 minutes
    25-C   3 hours, 45 minutes
    25-D   3 hours, 15 minutes

26. The toll on the Island Bridge is $1.00 for car and driver and 75 cents for each additional passenger. How many people were riding in a car for which the toll was $3.25?

    26-A   1
    26-B   2
    26-C   3
    26-D   4

27. What is the total cost of 3 sheets of 23¢ stamps, 2 sheets of 50¢ stamps, and 4 sheets of 29¢ stamps if each sheet has 100 stamps?

    27-A $265
    27-B $275
    27-C $285
    27-D $295

28. An employee's net pay is equal to her total earnings less all deductions. If an employee's total earnings in a pay period are $497.05, what is her net pay if she has the following deductions: federal income tax, $90.32; FICA, $28.74; state tax, $18.79; city tax, $7.25; and pension, $1.88?

    28-A $351.17
    28-B $351.07
    28-C $350.17
    28-D $350.07

29. The price of a radio is $31.29, which includes a 5% sales tax. What was the price of the radio before the tax was added?

    29-A $29.80
    29-B $29.85
    29-C $29.90
    29-D $29.95

30. At the rate of 40 words per minute, how long will it take a typist to type a 3,600-word article?

    30-A $1\frac{1}{2}$ hours

    30-B $1\frac{3}{4}$ hours

    30-C   2 hours

    30-D $2\frac{1}{4}$ hours

STOP!

IF YOU FINISH BEFORE THE TIME IS UP, YOU MAY CHECK OVER YOUR WORK ON THIS PART ONLY.

PART 3: WORD KNOWLEDGE

Directions

This test has 35 questions about the meanings of words. Each question has an underlined word. You are to decide which one of the four words in the choices most nearly means the same as the underlined word, then mark the space on your answer form that has the same number and letter as your choice.

Now look at the two sample questions below.

S1. <u>Mended</u> most nearly means   Ⓐ Ⓑ Ⓒ Ⓓ
      S1-A   repaired
      S1-B   torn
      S1-C   clean
      S1-D   tied

Repaired, choice A, is the correct answer. *Mended* means *fixed* or *repaired*. *Torn*, choice B, might be the state of an object before it is mended. The repair might be made by *tying*, choice D, but not necessarily. *Clean,* choice C, is wrong.

S2. It was a <u>small</u> table.   Ⓐ Ⓑ Ⓒ Ⓓ
      S1-A   sturdy
      S1-B   round
      S1-C   cheap
      S1-D   little

Little means the same as *small*, so choice D is the best one.

Your score on this test will be based on the number of questions you answer correctly. You should try to answer every question. Do not spend too much time on any one question.

When you begin, be sure to start with question number 1 in Part 3 of your test booklet and number 1 in Part 3 on your answer form.

DO NOT CONTINUE UNTIL TOLD TO DO SO.

Word Knowledge

Time: 11 Minutes—35 Questions

1. Inform most nearly means
   - 1-A   ask.
   - 1-B   tell.
   - 1-C   heed.
   - 1-D   ignore.

2. Crimson most nearly means
   - 2-A   crisp.
   - 2-B   neatly pressed.
   - 2-C   reddish.
   - 2-D   colorful.

3. Caution most nearly means
   - 3-A   signals.
   - 3-B   care.
   - 3-C   traffic.
   - 3-D   haste.

4. The fog horn sounded intermittently.
   - 4-A   constantly.
   - 4-B   annually.
   - 4-C   using intermediaries.
   - 4-D   at irregular intervals.

5. He told us about a strange occurrence.
   - 5-A   Event
   - 5-B   Place
   - 5-C   Occupation
   - 5-D   Opinion

6. Deception most nearly means
   - 6-A   secrets.
   - 6-B   fraud.
   - 6-C   mistrust.
   - 6-D   hatred.

7. Did the storm cease during the night?
   - 7-A   Start
   - 7-B   Change
   - 7-C   Continue
   - 7-D   Stop

8. The crowd received him with acclaim.
   - 8-A   Amazement
   - 8-B   Applause
   - 8-C   Booing
   - 8-D   Laughter

9. The town will erect the bridge.
   - 9-A   Paint
   - 9-B   Design
   - 9-C   Destroy
   - 9-D   Construct

10. Relish most nearly means
    - 10-A   care.
    - 10-B   speed.
    - 10-C   amusement.
    - 10-D   enjoy.

11. Sufficient most nearly means
    - 11-A   durable.
    - 11-B   substitution.
    - 11-C   expendable.
    - 11-D   appropriate.

12. She will return in a fortnight.
    - 12-A   Two weeks
    - 12-B   One week
    - 12-C   Two months
    - 12-D   One month

13. Flaw most nearly means
    - 13-A   defect.
    - 13-B   mixture.
    - 13-C   surface.
    - 13-D   movement.

14. Impose most nearly means
    - 14-A   disguise.
    - 14-B   escape.
    - 14-C   prescribe.
    - 14-D   purchase.

15. Jeer most nearly means
    15-A   peek.
    15-B   scoff.
    15-C   turn.
    15-D   judge.

16. Alias most nearly means
    16-A   enemy.
    16-B   sidekick.
    16-C   hero.
    16-D   other name.

17. Impair most nearly means
    17-A   direct.
    17-B   improve.
    17-C   weaken.
    17-D   stimulate.

18. Itinerant most nearly means
    18-A   traveling.
    18-B   shrewd.
    18-C   ignorant.
    18-D   aggressive.

19. We were told to abandon the ship.
    19-A   Relinquish
    19-B   Encompass
    19-C   Infiltrate
    19-D   Quarantine

20. Resolve most nearly means
    20-A   understand.
    20-B   decide.
    20-C   recall.
    20-D   forget.

21. Ample most nearly means
    21-A   plentiful.
    21-B   enthusiastic.
    21-C   well shaped.
    21-D   fat.

22. Stench most nearly means
    22-A   puddle of slimy water.
    22-B   pile of debris.
    22-C   foul odor.
    22-D   dead animal.

23. Sullen most nearly means
    23-A   grayish yellow.
    23-B   soaking wet.
    23-C   very dirty.
    23-D   angrily silent.

24. Rudiments most nearly means
    24-A   basic procedures.
    24-B   politics.
    24-C   promotion opportunities.
    24-D   minute details.

25. Clash most nearly means
    25-A   applaud.
    25-B   fasten.
    25-C   conflict.
    25-D   punish.

26. Camaraderie most nearly means
    26-A   interest in photography.
    26-B   close friendship.
    26-C   petty jealousies.
    26-D   arts and crafts projects.

27. His answer was a superficial one.
    27-A   Excellent
    27-B   Official
    27-C   Profound
    27-D   Cursory

28. We admired the exquisite tapestry.
    28-A   Fabric of woven designs
    28-B   Tent
    28-C   Piece of elaborate jewelry
    28-D   Exquisite painting

29. Terse most nearly means
    29-A   concise.
    29-B   trivial.
    29-C   oral.
    29-D   lengthy.

30. She prepared a delicious concoction for us.
    30-A   Combination of ingredients
    30-B   Appetizer
    30-C   Drink made of wine and spices
    30-D   Relish tray

31. <u>Incessant</u> most nearly means
   - 31-A   occasional.
   - 31-B   disagreeable.
   - 31-C   constant.
   - 31-D   noisy.

32. <u>Solidity</u> most nearly means
   - 32-A   unevenness.
   - 32-B   smoothness.
   - 32-C   firmness.
   - 32-D   color.

33. <u>Increment</u> most nearly means
   - 33-A   an improvisation.
   - 33-B   an account.
   - 33-C   an increase.
   - 33-D   a specification.

34. The judge ruled it to be <u>immaterial</u>.
   - 34-A   Unclear
   - 34-B   Unimportant
   - 34-C   Unpredictable
   - 34-D   Not debatable

35. We <u>misconstrued</u> what she had said.
   - 35-A   Followed directions
   - 35-B   Ingenious
   - 35-C   Acting to supervise
   - 35-D   Interpreted erroneously

STOP!

IF YOU FINISH BEFORE THE TIME IS UP, YOU MAY CHECK OVER YOUR WORK ON THIS PART ONLY.

PART 4: PARAGRAPH COMPREHENSION

Directions

This test contains 15 items measuring your ability to obtain information from written passages. You will find one or more paragraphs of reading material followed by incomplete statements or questions. You are to read the paragraph(s) and select the lettered choice that best completes the statement or answers the question.

Here are two sample questions.

S1. From a building designer's standpoint, three things that make a home livable are the needs of the client, the building site, and the amount of money the client has to spend.

According to the passage, to make a home livable Ⓐ Ⓑ Ⓒ Ⓓ

S1-A   the prospective piece of land makes little difference.
S1-B   it can be built on any piece of land.
S1-C   the design must fit the owner's income and site.
S1-D   the design must fit the designer's income.

The correct answer is that the designer must fit the owner's income and site, so choice C is the correct response.

S2. In certain areas, water is so scarce that every attempt is made to conserve it. For instance, on one oasis in the Sahara Desert the amount of water necessary for each date palm tree has been carefully determined.

How much water is each tree given?

S2-A   No water at all   Ⓐ Ⓑ Ⓒ Ⓓ
S2-B   Exactly the amount required
S2-C   Water only if it is healthy
S2-D   Water on alternate days

The correct answer is exactly the amount required, so choice B is the correct response.

Your score on this test will be based on the number of questions you answer correctly. You should try to answer every question. Do not spend too much time on any one question.

When you begin, be sure to start with question number 1 in Part 4 of your test booklet and number 1 in Part 4 on your answer form.

DO NOT CONTINUE UNTIL TOLD TO DO SO.

Paragraph Comprehension

Time: 13 Minutes—15 Questions

1. Numerous benefits to the employer as well as to the worker have resulted from physical examinations of employees. Such examinations are intended primarily as a means of increasing efficiency and production, and they have been found to accomplish these ends.

   The passage best supports the statement that physical examinations
   - 1-A may serve to increase output.
   - 1-B are required in some plants.
   - 1-C often reveal serious defects previously unknown.
   - 1-D always are worth more than they cost.

2. Examination of traffic accident statistics reveals that traffic accidents are frequently the result of violations of traffic laws—and usually the violations are the result of illegal and dangerous driving behavior rather than the result of mechanical defects or poor road conditions.

   According to this passage, the majority of dangerous traffic violations are caused by
   - 2-A poor driving.
   - 2-B bad roads.
   - 2-C unsafe cars.
   - 2-D unwise traffic laws.

3. Complaints from the public are no longer regarded by government officials as mere nuisances. Instead, complaints are often welcomed because they frequently bring into the open conditions and faults in operation and service that should be corrected.

   This passage means most nearly that
   - 3-A government officials now realize that complaints from the public are necessary.
   - 3-B faulty operations and services are not brought into the open except by complaints from the public.
   - 3-C government officials now realize that complaints from the public are in reality a sign of a well-run agency.
   - 3-D complaints from the public can be useful in indicating needs for improvement in operation and service.

4. In a pole-vaulting competition, the judge decides on the minimum height to be jumped. The vaulter may attempt to jump any height above the minimum. Using flexible fiber-glass poles, vaulters have jumped as high as 18 feet $8\frac{1}{4}$ inches.

   According to the passage, pole vaulters

   4-A   may attempt to jump any height in competition.

   4-B   must jump higher than $18' 8\frac{1}{2}"$ to win.

   4-C   must jump higher than the height set by the judge.

   4-D   must use fiber-glass poles.

5. When gas is leaking, any spark or sudden flame can ignite it. This can create a "flash-back," which burns off the gas in a quick puff of smoke and flame. But the real danger is in a large leak, which can cause an explosion.

   According to the passage, the real danger from leaking gas is

   5-A   a flashback.

   5-B   a puff of smoke and flame.

   5-C   an explosion.

   5-D   a spark.

6. A year—the time it takes the earth to go exactly once around the sun—is not 365 days. It is actually 365 days 6 hours 9 minutes $9\frac{1}{2}$ seconds, or $365\frac{1}{4}$ days. Leap years make up for this discrepancy by adding an extra day once every four years.

   The purpose of leap year is to

   6-A   adjust for the fact that it takes $365\frac{1}{4}$ days for the earth to

           circle the sun.

   6-B   make up for time lost in the work year.

   6-C   occur every four years.

   6-D   allow for differences in the length of a year in each time zone.

7. Any business not provided with capable substitutes to fill all important positions is a weak business. Therefore, a foreman should train each man not only to perform his own particular duties but also to do those of two or three positions.

   The paragraph best supports the statement that

   7-A   dependence on substitutes is a sign of a weak organization.

   7-B   training will improve the strongest organization.

   7-C   the foreman should be the most expert at any particular job under him.

   7-D   vacancies in vital positions should be provided for in advance.

8. In the business districts of cities, collections from street letter boxes are made at stated hours, and collectors are required to observe these hours exactly. Anyone using these boxes can rely with certainty upon the time of the next collection.

The paragraph best supports the statement that
   8-A   mail collections in business districts are more frequent during the day than at night.
   8-B   mail collectors are required to observe safety regulations exactly.
   8-C   mail collections are made often in business districts.
   8-D   mail is collected in business districts on a regular schedule.

9. The increasing size of business organizations has resulted in less personal contact between superior and subordinate. Consequently, business executives today depend more upon records and reports to secure information and exercise control over the operations of various departments.

The increasing size of business organizations
   9-A   has caused a complete cleavage between employer and employee.
   9-B   has resulted in less personal contact between superior and subordinate.
   9-C   has tended toward class distinctions in large organizations.
   9-D   has resulted in a better means of controlling the operations of various departments.

10. Kindling temperature is the lowest temperature at which a substance catches fire and continues to burn. Different fuels have different kindling temperatures. Paper catches fire easily because it has a low kindling temperature. Coal, because of its high kindling temperature, requires much heat before it will begin to burn. Matches are tipped with phosphorus, or some other low kindling material, to permit the small amount of heat produced by friction to ignite the match.

The property of phosphorus that makes it ideal for use on matches is
   10-A   its light color.
   10-B   its high kindling temperature.
   10-C   its low kindling temperature.
   10-D   the fact that it contains carbon.

Questions 11 and 12 are based on the following passage.

Racketeers are primarily concerned with business affairs, legitimate or otherwise, and preferably those that are close to the margin of legitimacy. They get their best opportunities from business organizations that meet the needs of large sections of the public for goods and services that are defined as illegitimate by the same public, such as gambling, illicit drugs, etc. In contrast to the thief, the racketeer and the establishments he or she controls deliver goods and services for money received.

11. According to the above passage, racketeering, unlike theft, involves
   11-A   payment for goods received.
   11-B   unlawful activities.
   11-C   organized gangs.
   11-D   objects of value.

12. It can be deduced that suppression of racketeering is difficult because

    12-A   many people want services that are not obtainable through legitimate sources.

    12-B   racketeers are generally engaged in fully legitimate enterprises.

    12-C   victims of racketeers are not guilty of violating the law.

    12-D   laws prohibiting gambling are unenforceable.

Questions 13–15 are based on the passage shown below.

The two systems of weights and measures are the English system and the metric system. The English system uses units such as foot, pound, and quart; the metric system uses meter, gram, and liter.

The metric system was first adopted in France in 1795 and is now used by most countries in the world. In the metric system, the unit of length is the meter, which is one ten-millionth of the distance from the Equator to the North Pole.

The British recently changed their system of weights and measures to the metric system; however, in the United States, there has been much opposition to this change. It would cost billions of dollars to change all our weights and measures to the metric system.

13. According to the passage above, the metric system is used

    13-A   in all of Europe except Great Britain.

    13-B   in almost all countries of the world.

    13-C   in only a few countries.

    13-D   mostly in Europe.

14. The United States has not changed to the metric system because

    14-A   the system is too complicated.

    14-B   the change would be costly.

    14-C   the system is not accurate.

    14-D   it is difficult to learn.

15. The meter is equal to

    15-A   the distance from the Equator to the North Pole.

    15-B $\dfrac{1}{1,000,000}$ of the distance from the Equator to the North Pole.

    15-C $\dfrac{1}{10,000,000}$ of the distance from the Equator to the North Pole.

    15-D $\dfrac{1}{100,000,000}$ of the distance from the Equator to the North Pole.

STOP!

IF YOU FINISH BEFORE THE TIME IS UP, YOU MAY CHECK OVER YOUR WORK ON THIS PART ONLY.

PART 5: MATHEMATICS KNOWLEDGE

Directions

This is a test of your ability to solve 25 general mathematical problems. You are to select the correct response from the choices given. Then mark the space on your answer form that has the same number and letter as your choice. Use the scratch paper that has been given to you to do any figuring that you wish.

Now look at the two sample problems below.

S1. If $x + 6 = 7$, then x is equal to   Ⓐ Ⓑ Ⓒ Ⓓ
    S1-A   0
    S1-B   1
    S1-C   –1

    S1-D $\dfrac{7}{6}$

The correct answer is 1, so choice B is the correct response.

S2. What is the area of this square?   Ⓐ Ⓑ Ⓒ Ⓓ
    S2-A   1 square foot
    S2-B   5 square feet
    S2-C   10 square feet
    S2-D   25 square feet

The correct answer is 25 square feet, so choice D is the correct response.

Your score on this test will be based on the number of questions you answer correctly. You should try to answer every question. Do not spend too much time on any one question.

When you are told to begin, be sure to start with question number 1 in Part 5 of your test booklet and number 1 in Part 5 on your answer form.

DO NOT CONTINUE UNTIL TOLD TO DO SO.

Mathematics Knowledge

Time: 24 Minutes—25 Questions

1. If you subtract $6a - 4b + 3c$ from a polynomial, you get $4a + 9b - 5c$. What is the polynomial?

    1-A $10a - 5b + 2c$
    1-B $10a + 5b - 2c$
    1-C $2a + 13b - 8c$
    1-D $2a + 5b + 8c$

2. $(x + 1)(x + 2) =$

    2-A $x^2 + 2x + 2$
    2-B $x^2 + 3x + 2$
    2-C $x^2 + 2x + 3$
    2-D $x^2 + 3x + 3$

3. If $3x = -5$, then x equals

    3-A $\dfrac{3}{5}$

    3-B $-\dfrac{5}{3}$

    3-C $-\dfrac{3}{5}$

    3-D -2

4. The first digit of the square root of 59043 is

    4-A   2
    4-B   3
    4-C   4
    4-D   5

5. A square is equal in area to a rectangle whose length is 9 and whose width is 4. Find the perimeter of the square.

    5-A   24
    5-B   26
    5-C   34
    5-D   36

6. A square has sides of length 4. What is the length of the diagonal?

    6-A   4
    6-B $4\sqrt{2}$
    6-C   8
    6-D $8\sqrt{2}$

7. If the perimeter of an equilateral triangle is $6n - 12$, what is the length of the base?

    7-A $3(2n - 4)$
    7-B $2(3n - 6)$
    7-C $3n - 6$
    7-D $2n - 4$

8. An angle has a measure twice that of its complement. What is the measure of the angle?

    8-A   30°
    8-B   45°
    8-C   60°
    8-D   75°

9. A man walks once around a regular hexagonal (six-sided) field. If he starts in the middle of a side and follows the contour of the field, he will make 6

    9-A   30° turns.
    9-B   45° turns.
    9-C   60° turns.
    9-D   75° turns.

10. The area of a rectangle 12 feet by 18 feet is equal to

    10-A   8 square yards.
    10-B   24 square yards.
    10-C   36 square yards.
    10-D   72 square yards.

11. Given the formulas $d = rt$ and $A = r + \dfrac{d}{t}$, which formula below correctly expresses the value of A without using t?

    11-A $A = dr$

    11-B $A = r + 2\dfrac{d}{t}$

    11-C $A = 2r + d$

    11-D $A = 2r$

12. Which of the following is a prime number?

    12-A   23
    12-B   27
    12-C   39
    12-D   51

13. The distance in miles around a circular course that has a radius of 35 miles is (use $\dfrac{22}{7}$ for pi)

    13-A   156
    13-B   220
    13-C   440
    13-D   880

14. The expression "3 factorial" equals

    14-A $\dfrac{1}{9}$

    14-B $\dfrac{1}{6}$

    14-C   6

    14-D   9

15. If $a = 2b$ and $4b = 6c$, then $a =$

    15-A $3c$
    15-B $4c$
    15-C $9c$
    15-D $12c$

16. Solve for x: $\dfrac{2x}{7} = 2x^2$

    16-A $\dfrac{1}{7}$

    16-B $\dfrac{2}{7}$

    16-C   2

    16-D   7

17. Solve the following equation for C:

$$A^2 = \dfrac{B^2}{C + D}$$

    17-A $C = \dfrac{B^2 - A^2 D}{A^2 B}$

    17-B $C = \dfrac{A^2}{B^2} - D$

    17-C $C = \dfrac{A^2 + D}{B^2 - D}$

    17-D $C = \dfrac{B^2}{A^2} - D$

18. The perimeter of a rectangle is 90. One side of the rectangle is twice the length of the other side. What is the length of the shorter side?

    18-A   15
    18-B   20
    18-C   25
    18-D   30

19. Which one of the following is correct?

    19-A   Every rhombus is a square.
    19-B   Every rectangle is a square.
    19-C   Every square is a rhombus.
    19-D   Every trapezoid is a rectangle.

20. What is the area, in square inches, of a circle whose radius measures 7 inches? (use $\frac{22}{7}$ for pi)

20-A   22
20-B   44
20-C   154
20-D   616

21. Evaluate the expression $5a - 4x - 3y$ if $a = -2$, $x = -10$, and $y = 5$.

21-A   +15
21-B   +25
21-C   −65
21-D   −35

22. If one book costs c dollars, what is the cost, in dollars, of m books?

22-A $m + c$
22-B mc
22-C $\dfrac{c}{m}$
22-D $\dfrac{m}{c}$

23. If $m\angle 8 = 80°$, $m\angle 2 =$

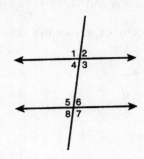

23-A   80°
23-B   100°
23-C   120°
23-D   None of the above

24. Solve for x: $\dfrac{x}{2} - \dfrac{x}{5} = 3$

24-A   2
24-B   3
24-C   52
24-D   10

25. If the radius of a circle is increased by 3, the circumference is increased by

25-A   −3
25-B 3π
25-C 6π
25-D   6

STOP!

IF YOU FINISH BEFORE THE TIME IS UP, YOU MAY CHECK OVER YOUR WORK ON THIS PART ONLY.

PART 6: ELECTRONICS INFORMATION

Directions

This is a test of your knowledge of electrical, radio, and electronics information. There are 20 questions. You are to select the correct response from the choices given. Then mark the space on your answer form that has the same number and letter as your choice.

Now look at the two sample questions below.

S1. What does the abbreviation AC stand for?

1S-A   Additional charge

1S-B   Alternating coil

1S-C   Alternating current

1S-D   Ampere current

The correct answer is alternating current, so choice C is the correct response.

S2. Which of the following has the least resistance?

2S-A   Wood

2S-B   Silver

2S-C   Rubber

2S-D   Iron

The correct answer is silver, so choice B is the correct response.

Your score on this test will be based on the number of questions you answer correctly. You should try to answer every question. Do not spend too much time on any one question.

When you are told to begin, be sure to start with question number 1 in Part 6 of your test booklet and number 1 in Part 6 on your answer form.

DO NOT CONTINUE UNTIL TOLD TO DO SO.

Electronics Information

Time: 9 Minutes—20 Questions

1. The most likely cause of a burned-out fuse in the primary circuit of a transformer in a rectifier is
   - 1-A   grounding of the electrostatic shield.
   - 1-B   an open circuit in a bleeder resistor.
   - 1-C   an open circuit in the secondary winding.
   - 1-D   a short-circuited filter capacitor.

2. The primary coil of a power transformer has 100 turns and the secondary coil has 50 turns. The voltage across the secondary will be
   - 2-A   four times that of the primary.
   - 2-B   twice that of the primary.
   - 2-C   half that of the primary.
   - 2-D   one-fourth that of the primary.

3. The best electrical connection between two wires is obtained when
   - 3-A   the insulations are melted together.
   - 3-B   all insulation is removed and the wires bound together with Friction tape.
   - 3-C   both are wound on a common binding post.
   - 3-D   they are soldered together.

4. Excessive resistance in the primary circuit will lessen the output of the ignition coil and cause the
   - 4-A   battery to short out and the generator to run down.
   - 4-B   battery to short out and the plugs to wear out prematurely.
   - 4-C   generator to run down and the timing mechanism to slow down.
   - 4-D   engine to perform poorly and be hard to start.

5. During a "short circuit," the
   - 5-A   current flow becomes very large.
   - 5-B   resistance becomes very large.
   - 5-C   voltage applied becomes very small.
   - 5-D   power input becomes very small.

6. The main reason for making wire stranded is
   - 6-A   to make it easier to insulate.
   - 6-B   so that the insulation will not come off.
   - 6-C   to decrease its weight.
   - 6-D   to make it more flexible.

7.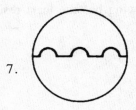

   The oscilloscope image shown above represents
   - 7-A   steady DC.
   - 7-B   resistance in a resistor.
   - 7-C   AC.
   - 7-D   pulsating DC.

8. Voltage drop in a circuit is usually due to
   - 8-A   inductance.
   - 8-B   capacitance.
   - 8-C   resistance.
   - 8-D   conductance.

9. Which of the following sizes of electric heaters is the largest one that can be used in a 120-volt circuit protected by a 15-ampere circuit breaker?

9-A   1000 watts

9-B   1300 watts

9-C   2000 watts

9-D   2600 watts

10. Of the following devices, which one will store an electric charge?

10-A   Capacitor

10-B   Inductor

10-C   Thyristor

10-D   Resistor

11. Of the nonmetallic elements listed below, which one is the best conductor of electricity?

11-A   Mica

11-B   Carbon

11-C   Formica

11-D   Hard rubber

12. If an electric motor designed for use on AC is plugged into a DC source, what will probably happen?

12-A   Excessive heat will be produced.

12-B   It will operate the same as usual.

12-C   It will continue to operate but will not get so warm.

12-D   It cannot be predicted what will happen.

13. Most electrical problems involving voltage, resistance, and current are solved by applying

13-A   Ohm's law.

13-B   Watt's law.

13-C   Coulomb's law.

13-D   Kirchoff's voltage and current laws.

14. If every time a washing machine is started the circuit breaker must be reset, the best solution would be to

14-A   oil the motor in the washer.

14-B   replace the circuit breaker.

14-C   tape the breaker switch closed.

14-D   repair the timing mechanism.

15. Electronic circuits designed to produce high frequency alternating currents are usually known as

15-A   oscillators.

15-B   amplifiers.

15-C   rectifiers.

15-D   detectors.

16. Which of the following devices converts heat energy directly into electrical energy?

16-A   A piezoelectric crystal

16-B   A photoelectric cell

16-C   A steam-driven generator

16-D   A thermocouple

17. One use of a coaxial cable is to

17-A   ground a signal.

17-B   pass a signal from the set to the antenna of a mobile unit.

17-C   carry the signal from a ballast tube.

17-D   carry grid signals in high altitude areas.

18. Which of the following has the least resistance?

18-A   Silver

18-B   Aluminum

18-C   Copper

18-D   Steel

19. In electronic circuits, the symbol shown below usually represents a

19-A   transformer.

19-B   capacitor.

19-C   transistor.

19-D   diode.

20. In electronic circuits, the symbol shown below usually represents a

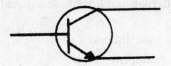

20-A   diode.
20-B   magnetron.
20-C   transistor.
20-D   triode.

STOP!

IF YOU FINISH BEFORE THE TIME IS UP, YOU MAY CHECK OVER YOUR WORK ON THIS PART ONLY.

PART 7: AUTO & SHOP INFORMATION

Directions

This test has 25 questions about automobiles, shop practices, and the use tools. Pick the best answer for each question, then blacken the space on your answer form that has the same number and letter as your choice.

Here are four sample questions.

S1. The most commonly used fuel for running automobile engines is

S1-A   kerosene.

S1-B   benzine.

S1-C   crude oil.

S1-D   gasoline.

Gasoline is the most commonly used fuel, so choice D is the correct answer.

S2. A car uses too much oil when which parts are worn?

S2-A   Pistons

S2-B   Piston rings

S2-C   Main bearings

S2-D   Connecting rods

Worn piston rings causes the use of too much oil, so choice B is the correct answer.

S3. The saw shown above is used mainly to cut

S3-A   plywood.

S3-B   odd-shaped holes in wood.

S3-C   along the grain of the wood.

S3-D   across the grain of the wood.

The compass saw is used to cut odd-shaped holes in wood, so choice B is the correct answer.

S4. Thin sheet metal should be cut with

S4-A   ordinary scissors.

S4-B   a hack saw.

S4-C   tin shears.

S4-D   a jig saw.

Tin shears are used to cut thin sheet metal, so choice C is the correct answer.

Your score on this test will be based on the number of questions you answer correctly. You should try to answer every question. Do not spend too much time on any one question.

When you are told to begin, be sure to start with question number 1 in Part 7 of your test booklet and number 1 in Part 7 on your answer form.

DO NOT CONTINUE UNTIL TOLD TO DO SO.

Auto & Shop Information

Time: 11 Minutes—25 Questions

1. Which of the following devices prevents the generator/alternator from overcharging the battery in an automobile?
   - 1-A   Governor
   - 1-B   Solenoid switch
   - 1-C   Current regulator
   - 1-D   Voltage regulator

2. A torsion bar might be found in the
   - 2-A   transmission.
   - 2-B   distributor.
   - 2-C   speedometer.
   - 2-D   suspension.

3. A black gummy deposit in the end of the tail pipe of an automobile indicates that
   - 3-A   the automobile "burns" oil.
   - 3-B   there is probably a leak in the exhaust manifold.
   - 3-C   the timing is late.
   - 3-D   there are leaks in the exhaust valves.

4. What would be the most probable cause if an automobile has a weak spark at the plugs, "turns over" very slowly, and has dim headlights?
   - 4-A   Weak battery
   - 4-B   Faulty condenser
   - 4-C   Faulty ignition cable
   - 4-D   Worn contact breaker points

5. An automobile engine won't "turn over." If the battery charge is found to be normal, the next test would normally be for
   - 5-A   defective starter motor.
   - 5-B   short-circuited switches.
   - 5-C   faulty battery cable connections.
   - 5-D   defective generator.

6. The generator or alternator of an automobile engine is usually driven by the
   - 6-A   camshaft.
   - 6-B   flywheel.
   - 6-C   fan belt.
   - 6-D   cranking motor.

7. Of the following, which is the most likely cause if an engine is found to be missing on one cylinder?
   - 7-A   A clogged exhaust
   - 7-B   A defective spark plug
   - 7-C   An overheated engine
   - 7-D   Vapor lock

8. If an automobile engine overheats while the radiator remains cold, the difficulty probably lies in
   - 8-A   lack of engine oil.
   - 8-B   a stuck thermostat.
   - 8-C   improper ignition timing.
   - 8-D   an overloaded engine.

9. It is best for an automobile's gas tank to be full or nearly-full to prevent
   - 9-A   gasoline from vaporizing in the fuel lines.
   - 9-B   moisture from condensing in the gas tank.
   - 9-C   drying out of the fuel pump.
   - 9-D   loss of vacuum in the vacuum line.

10. The automotive power train includes all of the following EXCEPT the
    - 10-A   clutch.
    - 10-B   differential.
    - 10-C   steering gear.
    - 10-D   transmission.

11. An automobile handbrake is set tightly and the engine is idling at 30 mph road speed. If you shift into high gear, release the clutch, and the engine continues to run about the same, what would most likely need repair?

    11-A   Clutch
    11-B   Throttle
    11-C   High gear
    11-D   Carburetor

12. The pistons of gasoline engines will sometimes increase in size so that they "stick" in the cylinder. This is often caused by

    12-A   low engine operating temperature.
    12-B   overheating of the engine.
    12-C   worn oil rings.
    12-D   worn compression rings.

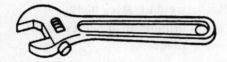

13. The tool shown above is a

    13-A   crescent wrench.
    13-B   monkey wrench.
    13-C   pipe wrench.
    13-D   torque wrench.

14. Concrete is usually made by mixing

    14-A   only sand and water.
    14-B   only cement and water.
    14-C   lye, cement, and water.
    14-D   rock, sand, cement, and water.

15. The set of a saw is the

    15-A   angle at which the handle is set.
    15-B   amount of springiness of the blade.
    15-C   amount of sharpness of the teeth.
    15-D   distance the points stick out beyond the sides of the blade.

16. The principal reason for "tempering" or "drawing" steel is to

    16-A   reduce strength.
    16-B   reduce hardness.
    16-C   increase strength.
    16-D   increase malleability.

17. Sheet metal is dipped in sulfuric acid to

    17-A   clean it.
    17-B   soften it.
    17-C   harden it.
    17-D   prevent it from rusting.

18. The cut of a file refers to the

    18-A   shape of its handle.
    18-B   shape of its edge.
    18-C   kind of metal it is made of.
    18-D   kind of teeth it has.

19. When grinding a good point on a twist drill, it is necessary that

    19-A   the point be extremely sharp.
    19-B   both cutting edges have the same lip.
    19-C   a file be used for the entire cutting process.
    19-D   the final grinding be done by hand.

20. The tool used to locate a point directly below a ceiling hook is a

    20-A   plumb bob.
    20-B   line level.
    20-C   transit.
    20-D   drop gauge.

21. The sawing of a piece of wood at a particular angle, for example 45 degrees, is accomplished by using a

    21-A   jointer.
    21-B   cant board.
    21-C   miter box.
    21-D   binder.

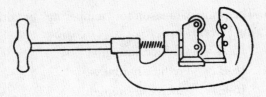

22. The tool above is a
    22-A   marking gauge.
    22-B   knurling tool.
    22-C   threat cutter.
    22-D   pipe cutter.

23. A high-speed grinder operator will check the abrasive wheel before starting the machine because
    23-A   it must be wetted properly before use.
    23-B   if cracked or chipped, it could injure someone.
    23-C   a dry wheel will produce excessive sparks.
    23-D   previous work may have clogged the wheel.

24. When marking wood, an allowance of $\frac{1}{16}$ inch to $\frac{1}{8}$ inch should be made to allow for
    24-A   drying of the wood.
    24-B   absorption of water by wood.
    24-C   the width of the saw.
    24-D   knots in the wood.

25. The tool shown above is used for
    25-A   pressure lubricating.
    25-B   welding steel plate.
    25-C   drilling small holes in tight places.
    25-D   holding small parts for heat treating.

STOP!

IF YOU FINISH BEFORE THE TIME IS UP, YOU MAY CHECK OVER YOUR WORK ON THIS PART ONLY.

PART 8: MECHANICAL COMPREHENSION

Directions

This test has 25 questions about mechanical principles. Most of the questions use drawings to illustrate specific principles. Decide which answer is correct and mark the space on your separate answer form that has the same number and letter as your choice.

Here are two sample questions.

S1. Which bridge is the strongest?

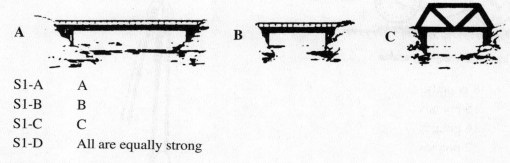

S1-A   A
S1-B   B
S1-C   C
S1-D   All are equally strong

Choice C is correct.

S2. If all of these objects are the same temperature, which will feel coldest?

S2-A   A
S2-B   B
S2-C   C
S2-D   D

Choice B is correct.

Your score on this test will be based on the number of questions you answer correctly. You should try to answer every question. Do not spend too much time on any one question.

When you are told to begin, be sure to start with question number 1 in Part 8 of your test booklet and number 1 in Part 8 on your answer form.

DO NOT CONTINUE UNTIL TOLD TO DO SO.

Mechanical Comprehension

Time: 19 Minutes—25 Questions

1. In the figure shown below, the weight held by the board and placed on the two identical scales will cause *each* scale to read

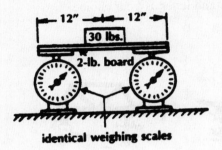

identical weighing scales

1-A   8 pounds.
1-B   15 pounds.
1-C   16 pounds.
1-D   32 pounds.

2. In the figure shown below, the pulley system consists of a fixed block and a movable block. The theoretical mechanical advantage is

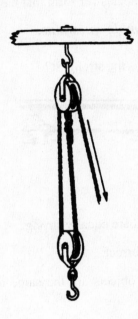

2-A   1
2-B   2
2-C   3
2-D   4

3. A single movable block is being used in the figure shown below. The person is lifting a 200-pound cask with approximately how great a pull (disregard friction, weight of pulley, and weight of line)?

3-A   50-pound pull
3-B   100-pound pull
3-C   200-pound pull
3-D   250-pound pull

4. In the figure shown below, one complete revolution of the sprocket wheel will bring weight W2 higher than weight W1 by

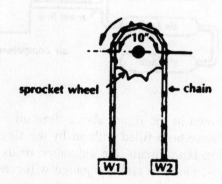

4-A   20 inches.
4-B   30 inches.
4-C   40 inches.
4-D   50 inches.

5. The figure below shows a worm and gear. If the worm rotates slowly on its shaft, the gear will

5-A   turn very slowly.
5-B   turn rapidly.
5-C   oscillate.
5-D   not turn.

6.

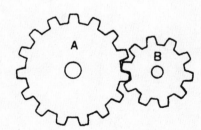

At which point was the basketball moving slowest?

6-A   A
6-B   B
6-C   C
6-D   D

7.

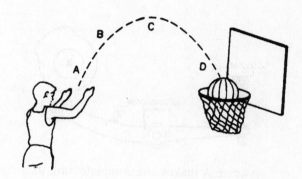

If gear A makes 14 revolutions, gear B will make

7-A   9
7-B   14
7-C   17
7-D   21

8.

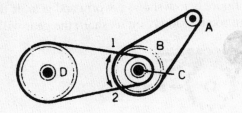

If pulley A is the driver and turns in direction 1, which pulley turns fastest?

8-A   A
8-B   B
8-C   C
8-D   D

9.

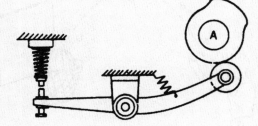

As cam A makes one complete turn, the setscrew will hit the contact point

9-A   once
9-B   twice
9-C   three times
9-D   not at all

10.

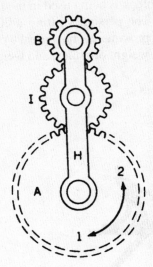

If arm H is held fixed as gear B turns in direction 2, gear

10-A   A must turn in direction 1.
10-B   A must turn in direction 2.
10-C   I must turn in direction 2.
10-D   A must be held fixed.

11.

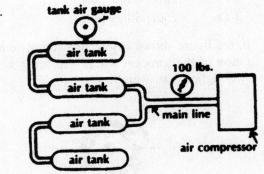

As shown in the figure above, four air reservoirs have been filled with air by the air compressor. If the main line air gauge reads 100 pounds, then the tank air gauge will read

11-A   25 pounds.
11-B   50 pounds.
11-C   75 pounds.
11-D   100 pounds.

12.

A 150-pound man jumps off a 600-pound raft to a point in the water 12 feet away. Theoretically, the raft would move

12-A   12 feet in the opposite direction.

12-B   6 feet in the opposite direction.

12-C   3 feet in the opposite direction.

12-D   1 foot in the opposite direction.

13. Which of the angles is braced most securely?

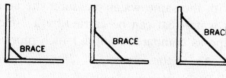

13-A   A

13-B   B

13-C   C

13-D   All are equally braced

14. In order to keep down the inside temperature of an oil tank that is exposed to the sun, the outside of the tank should be painted

14-A   black.

14-B   brown.

14-C   green.

14-D   white.

15.

The amount of gas in the balloons is equal. The atmospheric pressure outside the balloons is highest on which balloon?

15-A   A

15-B   B

15-C   C

15-D   The pressure is equal on all balloons.

16. The difference between the boiling point and the freezing point of water on the Celsius scale is

16-A   0°

16-B   100°

16-C   112°

16-D   180°

17.

Liquid is being transferred from the barrel to the bucket by

17-A   suction in the hose.

17-B   fluid pressure in the hose.

17-C   air pressure on top of the liquid.

17-D   capillary action.

18.

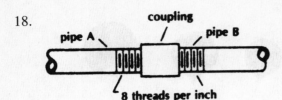

In the figure above, if pipe A is held in a vise and pipe B is turned 4 revolutions with a wrench, the overall length of the pipes and coupling will decrease

18-A $\frac{1}{8}$ inch.

18-B $\frac{1}{4}$ inch.

18-C $\frac{3}{8}$ inch.

18-D $\frac{1}{2}$ inch.

19.

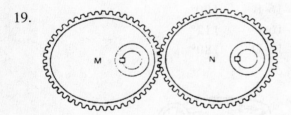

If gear N turns at a constant rpm, gear M turns at

19-A   the same constant rpm as N.
19-B   a faster constant rpm than N.
19-C   a slower constant rpm than N.
19-D   a variable rpm.

20.

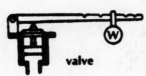

The figure above shows a lever-type safety valve. It will blow off at a lower pressure if weight W is

20-A   increased.
20-B   moved to the right.
20-C   increased and moved to the right.
20-D   moved to the left.

21.

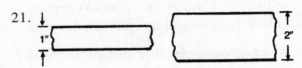

With the same water pressure, the amount of water that can be carried by a 2-inch pipe as compared with a 1-inch pipe is

21-A   the same.
21-B   twice as much.
21-C   3 times as much.
21-D   4 times as much.

22.

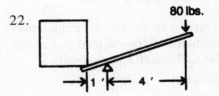

A pry bar is used to move a concrete block. A force of 80 pounds applied as shown will produce a tipping force on the edge of the block of

22-A   80 pounds.
22-B   240 pounds.
22-C   320 pounds.
22-D   400 pounds.

23. In the figure shown below, X is the driver gear and Y is the driven gear. If the idler gear is rotating counterclockwise

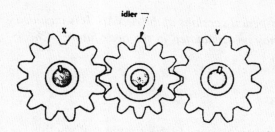

23-A   gear X and gear Y are rotating clockwise.

23-B   gear X and gear Y are rotating counterclockwise.

23-C   gear X is rotating clockwise, while gear Y is rotating counter clockwise.

23-D   gear Y is rotating clockwise, while gear X is rotating counter clockwise.

24.

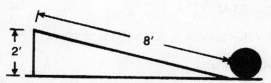

Neglecting friction, what effort is needed to roll a barrel weighing 400 pounds up an incline 8 feet long and 2 feet high?

24-A   50 pounds

24-B   100 pounds

24-C   150 pounds

24-D   200 pounds

25.

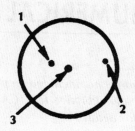

The figure above represents a revolving wheel. The numbers 1 and 2 indicate two fixed points on the wheel. The number 3 indicates the center of the wheel. Of the following, the most accurate statement is that

25-A   point 1 makes fewer revolutions per minute than point 2.

25-B   point 1 will make a complete revolution in less time than point 2.

25-C   point 2 makes more revolutions per minute than point 1.

25-D   point 2 traverses a greater linear distance than point 1.

STOP!

IF YOU FINISH BEFORE THE TIME IS UP, YOU MAY CHECK OVER YOUR WORK ON THIS PART ONLY.

PART 9: NUMERICAL OPERATIONS

NOTE: This section is not included on paper-and-pencil versions of the ASVAB. It is included on the ASVAB computer-adaptive test (CAT), but may be eliminated in the near future. Check with your recruiter for details.

Directions

This is a test to see how rapidly and accurately you can do 50 simple arithmetic computations. Each problem is followed by four answers, only one of which is correct. Decide which answer is correct, then blacken the space on your answer form which has the same number and letter as your choice.

Now look at the four example problems below.

S1. $3 \times 3 =$

     S1-A   6
     S1-B   0
     S1-C   9
     S1-D   1

The answer is 9, so (C) is correct.

S2. $3 + 7 =$

     S2-A   4
     S2-B   6
     S2-C   8
     S2-D   10

The answer is 10, so (D) is correct.

S3. $5 - 2 =$

     S3-A   2
     S3-B   3
     S3-C   1
     S3-D   4

The answer is 3, so (B) is correct.

S4. $9 \div 3 =$

     S4-A   3
     S4-B   6
     S4-C   9
     S4-D   12

The answer is 3, so (A) is correct.

This is a speed test, so work as fast as you can without making mistakes. Do each problem as it comes. If you finish before time is up, go back and check your work. When the signal is given, you will turn the page and begin with question 1 in Part 9 of your test booklet and answer space 1 in Part 9 of your answer form.

DO NOT CONTINUE UNTIL TOLD TO DO SO.

Numerical Operations

Time: 3 Minutes—50 Questions

1. $2 + 3 =$
   - 1-A   1
   - 1-B   4
   - 1-C   5
   - 1-D   6

2. $8 - 5 =$
   - 2-A   4
   - 2-B   3
   - 2-C   2
   - 2-D   1

3. $9 \div 3 =$
   - 3-A   2
   - 3-B   3
   - 3-C   6
   - 3-D   4

4. $4 \div 2 =$
   - 4-A   2
   - 4-B   4
   - 4-C   6
   - 4-D   8

5. $7 \times 3 =$
   - 5-A   4
   - 5-B   10
   - 5-C   12
   - 5-D   21

6. $9 \div 1 =$
   - 6-A   10
   - 6-B   9
   - 6-C   8
   - 6-D   7

7. $18 - 14 =$
   - 7-A   4
   - 7-B   8
   - 7-C   10
   - 7-D   12

8. $2 \times 12 =$
   - 8-A   14
   - 8-B   22
   - 8-C   24
   - 8-D   34

9. $9 - 6 =$
   - 9-A   1
   - 9-B   2
   - 9-C   3
   - 9-D   4

10. $3 \times 2 =$
    - 10-A   1
    - 10-B   4
    - 10-C   5
    - 10-D   6

11. $1 - 1 =$
    - 11-A   2
    - 11-B   3
    - 11-C   0
    - 11-D   1

12. $2 \times 9 =$
    - 12-A   16
    - 12-B   17
    - 12-C   18
    - 12-D   20

13. $9 + 3 =$
    - 13-A   3
    - 13-B   7
    - 13-C   11
    - 13-D   12

14. $8 + 16 =$
    - 14-A   12
    - 14-B   24
    - 14-C   26
    - 14-D   28

15. 9 − 4 =

    15-A   3
    15-B   5
    15-C   6
    15-D   7

16. 10 ÷ 2 =

    16-A   5
    16-B   6
    16-C   8
    16-D   12

17. 17 − 4 =

    17-A   13
    17-B   18
    17-C   21
    17-D   23

18. 3 + 3 =

    18-A   0
    18-B   5
    18-C   6
    18-D   8

19. 4 × 3 =

    19-A   1
    19-B   7
    19-C   12
    19-D   16

20. 8 − 3 =

    20-A   3
    20-B   4
    20-C   5
    20-D   6

21. 7 × 4 =

    21-A   28
    21-B   30
    21-C   32
    21-D   34

22. 5 + 8 =

    22-A   3
    22-B   7
    22-C   12
    22-D   13

23. 20 ÷ 2 =

    23-A   6
    23-B   8
    23-C   10
    23-D   12

24. 15 − 7 =

    24-A   5
    24-B   8
    24-C   10
    24-D   12

25. 6 ÷ 2 =

    25-A   3
    25-B   4
    25-C   5
    25-D   8

26. 7 − 2 =

    26-A   2
    26-B   5
    26-C   6
    26-D   9

27. 10 ÷ 2 =

    27-A   8
    27-B   7
    27-C   5
    27-D   4

28. 1 + 6 =

    28-A   5
    28-B   7
    28-C   8
    28-D   9

29. 4 × 5 =

    29-A   8
    29-B   10
    29-C   16
    29-D   20

30. 7 − 7 =

    30-A   14
    30-B   10
    30-C   1
    30-D   0

31. 5 ÷ 5 =

    31-A   0

    31-B   1

    31-C   10

    31-D   25

32. 5 × 3 =

    32-A   8

    32-B   15

    32-C   18

    32-D   25

33. 16 ÷ 4 =

    33-A   2

    33-B   4

    33-C   6

    33-D   7

34. 7 + 9 =

    34-A   2

    34-B   13

    34-C   16

    34-D   18

35. 15 × 5 =

    35-A   45

    35-B   55

    35-C   65

    35-D   75

36. 4 − 3 =

    36-A   1

    36-B   5

    36-C   7

    36-D   9

37. 7 + 5 =

    37-A   2

    37-B   4

    37-C   8

    37-D   12

38. 27 ÷ 9 =

    38-A   3

    38-B   6

    38-C   12

    38-D   13

39. 6 + 4 =

    39-A   10

    39-B   12

    39-C   14

    39-D   16

40. 10 × 2 =

    40-A   2

    40-B   5

    40-C   12

    40-D   20

41. 4 + 7 =

    41-A   3

    41-B   8

    41-C   11

    41-D   18

42. 8 ÷ 2 =

    42-A   4

    42-B   6

    42-C   8

    42-D   10

43. 12 + 2 =

    43-A   4

    43-B   6

    43-C   10

    43-D   14

44. 3 × 15 =

    44-A   12

    44-B   18

    44-C   35

    44-D   45

45. 25 ÷ 5 =

    45-A   4

    45-B   5

    45-C   6

    45-D   7

46. 30 ÷ 15 =

    46-A   2

    46-B   6

    46-C   15

    46-D   45

47. 7 + 5 =

    47-A   12

    47-B   13

    47-C   14

    47-D   15

48. 3 × 6 =

    48-A   3

    48-B   9

    48-C   15

    48-D   18

49. 9 − 6 =

    49-A   3

    49-B   7

    49-C   15

    49-D   18

50. 4 × 6 =

    50-A   10

    50-B   20

    50-C   24

    50-D   26

STOP!

IF YOU FINISH BEFORE THE TIME IS UP, YOU MAY CHECK OVER YOUR WORK ON THIS PART ONLY.

PART 10: CODING SPEED

NOTE: This section is not included on paper-and-pencil versions of the ASVAB. It is included on the ASVAB computer-adaptive test (CAT), but may be eliminated in the near future. Check with your recruiter for details.

Directions

This is a test of 84 items to see how quickly and accurately you can find a number in a table. At the top of each section, there is a number table or "key." The key is a group of words with a code number for each word.

Each question in the test is a word taken from the key at the top. From among the possible answers listed for each question, find the one that is the correct code number for that word.

Look at the sample key and answer the five sample questions below. Note that each of the questions is one of the words in the key. To the right of each question are possible answers listed under the options A, B, C, D, and E.

Sample Questions

Key

green 2715	man 3451	salt 4586
hat 1413	room 2864	tree 5972

Questions			Options			
		A	B	C	D	E
S-1.	room	1413	2715	2864	3451	4586
S-2.	green	2715	2864	3451	4586	5972
S-3.	tree	2715	2864	3451	4586	5972
S-4.	hat	1413	2715	2864	3451	4586
S-5.	room	1413	2864	3451	4586	5972

By looking at the key you see that the code number for the first word, "room," is 2864. 2864 is listed under the letter C, so C is the correct answer. The correct answers for the other four questions are A, E, A, and B.

This is a speed test, so work as fast as you can without making mistakes.

Notice that Part 10 begins at the top of the next answer form. When you begin, be sure to start with question number 1 in Part 10 of your test booklet and number 1 in Part 10 on your answer form.

DO NOT CONTINUE UNTIL TOLD TO DO SO.

Coding Speed

Time: 7 Minutes—84 Questions

Key

alarm 5050	candle 9311	fortune 2001	knight 1097	oil 4123
button 3916	diver 6898	holiday 8651	match 7299	season 8811

Questions		Options				
		A	**B**	**C**	**D**	**E**
1.	match	2001	3916	5050	7299	8811
2.	holiday	1097	4123	6898	7299	8651
3.	diver	1097	3916	4123	5050	6898
4.	button	3916	6898	7299	8811	9311
5.	alarm	4123	5050	6898	7299	8651
6.	fortune	1097	2001	5050	6898	9311
7.	season	2001	4123	7299	8651	8811
8.	oil	1097	2001	3916	4123	9311
9.	candle	5050	6898	8651	8811	9311
10.	knight	1097	4123	5050	6898	7299
11.	holiday	3916	7299	8651	8811	9311
12.	button	2001	3916	6898	7299	8651

Key

figure 3341	harvest 6400	nature 6445	ruler 8791	tennis 4166
gang 1921	manager ... 2797	peach 7070	signal 9761	wrist 5961

Questions		Options				
		A	**B**	**C**	**D**	**E**
13.	ruler	3341	5961	6400	8791	9761
14.	gang	1921	6445	7070	8791	9761
15.	manager	1921	2797	3341	5961	7070
16.	tennis	3341	4166	6400	7070	8791
17.	wrist	4166	5961	6445	8791	9761
18.	figure	1921	2797	3341	4166	5961
19.	harvest	5961	6400	7070	8791	9761
20.	nature	1921	3341	4166	5961	6445
21.	signal	2797	4166	5961	6445	9761
22.	peach	3341	5961	6400	7070	8791
23.	tennis	1921	3341	4166	5961	6400
24.	manager	2797	4166	5961	8791	9761

Key

costume 5019   guard 3776   knife 7916   officer 9391   ribbon 6591

dime 8117   jelly 4891   liquid 2011   pillow 1511   sword 1171

Questions		A	B	C	D	E
25.	knife	1171	2011	4891	5019	7916
26.	guard	2011	3776	5019	8117	9391
27.	costume	4891	5019	7916	8117	9391
28.	liquid	1171	1511	2011	3776	4891
29.	ribbon	3776	4891	5019	6591	7916
30.	jelly	1511	2011	4891	5019	6591
31.	officer	4891	5019	6591	7916	9391
32.	sword	1171	2011	3776	4891	5019
33.	dime	3776	4891	6591	7916	8117
34.	costume	4891	5019	6591	8117	9391
35.	pillow	1171	1511	2011	3776	4891
36.	guard	3776	4891	6591	7916	8117

Key

artist 3019   enemy 3417   hunter 4697   ruler 7419   umbrella 2499

current 6214   frost 9822   pirate 1347   ticket 5299   whale 8852

Questions		A	B	C	D	E
37.	frost	1347	4697	5299	7419	9822
38.	whale	4697	5299	6214	8852	9822
39.	enemy	2499	3417	4697	5299	6214
40.	pirate	1347	2499	3019	8852	9822
41.	ruler	3019	4697	5299	6214	7419
42.	umbrella	1347	2499	3417	5299	6214
43.	current	3417	5299	6214	7419	8852
44.	hunter	2499	3019	3417	4697	5299
45.	ticket	4697	5299	6214	8852	9822
46.	artist	3019	4697	5299	7419	8852
47.	whale	1347	2499	3417	4697	8852
48.	pirate	1347	5299	6214	7419	9822

Key

| bomb .... 1691 | drill .... 5415 | harbor ..... 4591 | model .... 2009 | record .... 6788 |
| closet .... 8419 | growth ..... 9621 | lawyer ..... 7314 | navy .... 3691 | wave .... 6319 |

Questions		Options				
		A	B	C	D	E
49.	model	1691	2009	4591	6319	7314
50.	record	3691	6319	6788	8419	9621
51.	drill	4591	5415	6319	7314	8419
52.	navy	1691	2009	3691	4591	5415
53.	closet	2009	3691	4591	6788	8419
54.	lawyer	3691	4591	5415	6391	7314
55.	bomb	1691	3691	4591	6788	8419
56.	wave	5415	6319	7314	8419	9621
57.	harbor	1691	2009	3691	4591	6319
58.	growth	3691	4591	5415	7314	9621
59.	record	1691	2009	6788	7314	8419
60.	drill	2009	3691	4591	5415	6319

Key

| auto .... 9619 | energy ...... 3117 | herd .... 7519 | lawn .... 9451 | shovel .... 8321 |
| copper .... 6010 | fork .... 1492 | judge .... 4787 | oven .... 5881 | village .... 2588 |

Questions		Options				
		A	B	C	D	E
61.	copper	3117	4787	5881	6010	7519
62.	energy	1492	2588	3117	8321	9619
63.	herd	4787	6010	7519	9451	9619
64.	judge	2588	4787	5881	6010	8321
65.	village	1492	2588	3117	5881	6010
66.	lawn	2588	3117	4787	7519	9451
67.	shovel	3117	5881	6010	7519	8321
68.	oven	3117	4787	5881	8321	9619
69.	auto	5881	6010	7519	8321	9619
70.	fork	1492	2588	3117	4787	5881
71.	energy	2588	3117	4787	6010	7519
72.	judge	4787	5881	7519	9451	9619

Key

author 9451   donkey 7611   liquid 1152   rake 3829   voice 6284

branch 4390   handle 5497   native 5746   space 8392   wine 2772

Questions		Options A	B	C	D	E
73.	branch	1152	2772	3829	4390	5746
74.	wine	2772	4390	5497	6284	8392
75.	voice	3829	5497	6284	8392	9451
76.	rake	1152	2772	3829	7611	8392
77.	native	4390	5746	6284	7611	9451
78.	donkey	5746	6284	7611	8392	9451
79.	liquid	1152	2772	3829	5497	6284
80.	handle	3829	4390	5497	7611	8392
81.	space	2772	3829	4390	8392	9451
82.	author	1152	2772	3829	7611	9451
83.	voice	2772	4390	5746	6284	7611
84.	rake	3829	5746	7611	8392	9451

ANSWER KEY

Use these answer keys to determine how many questions you answered correctly on each part and to list those items that you answered incorrectly or that you are not sure how to answer.

Carefully review and understand the reasoning for each answer whether you answered it correctly or incorrectly. Note that it is just as important to understand the reasoning for the questions you answered correctly but are unsure of. This will help you gain the knowledge and expertise necessary to obtain the highest score you can on the actual ASVAB tests.

Transfer the scores you obtained on each part of the Fourth ASVAB Specimen Test to the Self-Appraisal Chart appearing on page 24. This will enable you to see the progress made as you continue to prepare for the actual test.

Part 1—General Science

Answer Key				
1. C	2. B	3. B	4. B	5. C
6. D	7. C	8. C	9. D	10. D
11. C	12. B	13. C	14. B	15. A
16. D	17. D	18. C	19. A	20. A
21. A	22. D	23. C	24. B	25. D

Items Answered Incorrectly: _____ ; ____ ; ____ ; ____ ; ____ ; ____ ; ____ ; ____ .

Items Unsure Of: _____ ; ____ ; ____ ; ____ ; ____ ; ____ ; ____ ; ____ .

Total Number Answered Correctly: _____ .

Part 2—Arithmetic Reasoning

Answer Key				
1. C	2. A	3. D	4. B	5. C
6. A	7. D	8. A	9. B	10. A
11. C	12. B	13. C	14. B	15. D
16. C	17. C	18. B	19. C	20. C
21. D	22. C	23. B	24. B	25. C
26. D	27. C	28. D	29. A	30. A

Items Answered Incorrectly: _____ ; ____ ; _____ ; ____ ; ____ ; ____ ; ____ ; ____ .

Items Unsure Of: _____ ; ____ ; ____ ; ____ ; ____ ; ____ ; ____ ; ____ .

Total Number Answered Correctly: _____ .

Part 3—Word Knowledge

Answer Key				
1. B	2. C	3. B	4. D	5. A
6. B	7. D	8. B	9. D	10. D
11. D	12. A	13. A	14. C	15. B
16. D	17. C	18. A	19. A	20. B
21. A	22. C	23. D	24. A	25. C
26. B	27. D	28. A	29. A	30. A
31. C	32. C	33. C	34. B	35. D

Items Answered Incorrectly: _____ ; ____ ; _____ ; ____ ; ____ ; ____ ; ____ ; ____ .

Items Unsure Of: _____ ; ____ ; ____ ; ____ ; ____ ; ____ ; ____ ; ____ .

Total Number Answered Correctly: _____ .

Part 4—Paragraph Comprehension

Answer Key				
1. A	2. A	3. D	4. C	5. C
6. A	7. D	8. D	9. B	10. C
11. A	12. A	13. B	14. B	15. C

Items Answered Incorrectly: _____; ____; ____; ____; ____; ____; ____; ____.

Items Unsure Of: _____; ____; ____; ____; ____; ____; ____; ____.

Total Number Answered Correctly: _____.

Part 5—Mathematics Knowledge

Answer Key				
1. B	2. B	3. B	4. A	5. A
6. B	7. D	8. C	9. C	10. B
11. D	12. A	13. B	14. C	15. A
16. A	17. D	18. A	19. C	20. C
21. A	22. B	23. A	24. D	25. C

Items Answered Incorrectly: _____; ____; ____; ____; ____; ____; ____; ____.

Items Unsure Of: _____; ____; ____; ____; ____; ____; ____; ____.

Total Number Answered Correctly: _____.

Part 6—Electronics Information

Answer Key				
1. D	2. C	3. D	4. D	5. A
6. D	7. D	8. C	9. B	10. A
11. B	12. A	13. A	14. B	15. A
16. D	17. B	18. A	19. D	20. C

Items Answered Incorrectly: _____ ; ____ ; ____ ; ____ ; ____ ; ____ ; ____ ; ____ .

Items Unsure Of: _____ ; ____ ; ____ ; ____ ; ____ ; ____ ; ____ ; ____ .

Total Number Answered Correctly: _____ .

Part 7—Auto & Shop Information

Answer Key				
1. D	2. D	3. A	4. A	5. C
6. C	7. B	8. B	9. B	10. C
11. A	12. B	13. A	14. D	15. D
16. C	17. A	18. D	19. B	20. A
21. C	22. D	23. B	24. C	25. B

Items Answered Incorrectly: _____ ; ____ ; ____ ; ____ ; ____ ; ____ ; ____ .

Items Unsure Of: _____ ; ____ ; ____ ; ____ ; ____ ; ____ ; ____ .

Total Number Answered Correctly: _____ .

Part 8—Mechanical Comprehension

Answer Key

1. C	2. B	3. B	4. C	5. A
6. C	7. D	8. A	9. A	10. B
11. D	12. C	13. C	14. D	15. A
16. B	17. C	18. D	19. A	20. D
21. D	22. C	23. A	24. B	25. D

Items Answered Incorrectly: _____ ; ____ ; ____ ; ____ ; ____ ; ____ ; ____ ; ____ .

Items Unsure Of: _____ ; ____ ; ____ ; ____ ; ____ ; ____ ; ____ ; ____ .

Total Number Answered Correctly: _____ .

Part 9—Numerical Operations

Answer Key

1. C	2. B	3. B	4. A	5. D
6. B	7. A	8. C	9. C	10. D
11. C	12. C	13. D	14. B	15. B
16. A	17. A	18. C	19. C	20. C
21. A	22. D	23. C	24. B	25. A
26. B	27. C	28. B	29. D	30. D
31. B	32. B	33. B	34. C	35. D
36. A	37. D	38. A	39. A	40. D
41. C	42. A	43. D	44. D	45. B
46. A	47. A	48. D	49. A	50. C

Items Answered Incorrectly: _____ ; ____ ; ____ ; ____ ; ____ ; ____ ; ____ ; ____ .

Items Unsure Of: _____ ; ____ ; ____ ; ____ ; ____ ; ____ ; ____ ; ____ .

Total Number Answered Correctly: _____ .

Part 10—Coding Speed

Answer Key				
1. D	2. E	3. E	4. A	5. B
6. B	7. E	8. D	9. E	10. A
11. C	12. B	13. D	14. A	15. B
16. B	17. B	18. C	19. B	20. E
21. E	22. D	23. C	24. A	25. E
26. B	27. B	28. C	29. D	30. C
31. E	32. A	33. E	34. B	35. B
36. A	37. E	38. D	39. B	40. A
41. E	42. B	43. C	44. D	45. B
46. A	47. E	48. A	49. B	50. C
51. B	52. C	53. E	54. E	55. A
56. B	57. D	58. E	59. C	60. D
61. D	62. C	63. C	64. B	65. B
66. E	67. E	68. C	69. E	70. A
71. B	72. A	73. D	74. A	75. C
76. C	77. B	78. C	79. A	80. C
81. D	82. E	83. D	84. A	

Items Answered Incorrectly: ____ ; ___ ; ___ ; ___ ; ___ ; ___ ; ___ ; ___ .

Items Unsure Of: _____ ; ___ ; ___ ; ___ ; ___ ; ___ ; ___ ; ___ .

Total Number Answered Correctly: ____ .

ANSWER EXPLANATIONS

Part 1—General Science

1-C   Citrus fruits and tomatoes prevent scurvy by providing the body with large quantities of vitamin C.

2-B   The greater the number of vibrations per second produced by the sounding object, the higher will be the pitch produced. Playing a $33\frac{1}{3}$-rpm phonograph record at a faster speed (45 rpm) will produce a higher-pitched sound.

3-B   Meat provides much essential protein in the form the body needs. Protein is the principal nutrient in lean meat.

4-B   The freezing point of water is 0°C; the boiling point of water is 100°C. There is a 100° temperature range between the freezing and boiling points of water. $1 \text{ C} = \dfrac{1}{100}$ of this range.

5-C   Uranium decays through a complex series of radioactive intermediates to lead.

6-D   Meteors or "shooting stars" come into the earth's atmosphere from outer space with high velocity. The resistance offered by the earth's atmosphere makes these meteors incandescent in flight.

7-C   To balance the seesaw, the product of the weight and the distance from the weight to the fulcrum must be the same for both sides. Let x = distance from center of seesaw for the second child.

$$4 \times 80 = x \times 40; \, 40x = 320;$$
$$x = \frac{320}{40} = 8 \text{ feet.}$$

8-C   The end products of digestion are absorbed into the blood-stream while traveling through the small intestine.

9-D   Skeletal muscles are joined to bones by tendons. Tendons are so attached that they pull on the bones and make them act like levers.

10-D   An echo is the repetition of a sound caused by the reflection of sound waves. An image is an optical appearance of an object produced by reflection from a mirror.

11-C   Vitamin K is a fat-soluble vitamin needed for normal blood clotting.

12-B   When a beam of light passes obliquely from a medium of one optical density to a medium of another optical density, it is refracted or bent. From the bank, a person viewing a fish under water will find that the fish is not where it appears to be because of the refraction of light traveling from air into water.

13-C The primary reason for lowering the center of gravity in automobiles is to increase stability. Stability is increased largely by lowering the center of gravity and by increasing the width of the automobile.

14-B A substance that changes the rate of a chemical reaction but is itself unchanged at the end of the reaction is called a catalyst.

15-A The hip joint is a ball-and-socket joint that permits circular movement.

16-D The virus that causes AIDS is named human immunodeficiency virus, or HIV.

17-D Goiter is a disease of the thyroid gland, the body's storehouse for iodine. It may be caused by insufficient iodine in the diet.

18-C Steam at 212°F contains much more heat than does the same amount of water at 212°F.

19-A The denser the liquid, the less the weight of the lead sinker. Accordingly, liquid B has less density than liquid A.

20-A The lowering of the freezing point of a solution is generally proportional to the solute particles in the solution. A practical application of this principle is the throwing of salt on a snow- or ice-covered sidewalk to help melt the snow or ice.

21-A Organisms that live on or in the body of other live organisms from which food is obtained are called parasites.

22-D As all the effects listed in choices A, B, and C result from air pollution, choice D (all of the above) is the most inclusive and therefore the best answer.

23-C A satellite is a small body that revolves around a planet. The moon is a satellite that revolves around the planet Earth.

24-B Photosynthesis is the process by which green plants manufacture carbohydrates from carbon dioxide and water in the presence of sunlight and chlorophyll.

25-D Substances are classified as elements or compounds. A compound is a substance composed of the atoms of two or more different elements.

Part 2—Arithmetic Reasoning

1-C $3.00 per hour for 8 hours = $24.00

50 − 40 = 10 bushels

10 bushels @ $.72/bushel = $7.20

$24.00 + $7.20 = $31.20

2-A $\dfrac{144}{36} = 4$ buses

3-D 600 gallons = 2400 quarts

$\dfrac{2400}{120} = 20$ minutes

4-B $\dfrac{168}{28} = 6$ per day

5-C   The interval between each member of the series is $4\dfrac{1}{4}$.

$$17\dfrac{1}{4} + 4\dfrac{1}{4} = 21\dfrac{1}{2}$$

6-A $360 \times 8 = 2,880$ switches/8 hours

$2,880 \times .05 = 144$ defective switches

$2,880 - 144 = 2,736$ good switches

7-D $22\dfrac{1}{2} \div 1\dfrac{1}{4} = \dfrac{45}{2} \div \dfrac{5}{4} = \dfrac{\overset{9}{\cancel{45}}}{\underset{1}{\cancel{2}}} \times \dfrac{\overset{2}{\cancel{4}}}{\underset{1}{\cancel{5}}} =$

18 packages

8-A $\$12 \times 6 = \$72.00$ for daily use

$421 \times .17 = \$71.57$ for mileage charge

$\$72.00 + \$71.57 = \$143.57$

9-B   60% of $\$27.00 = \$16.20$, the cost for 2 tickets; $\dfrac{\$16.20}{2} = \$8.10$, the cost for one

ticket.

10-A   Cost per bar when purchased in small amounts $= \$0.33$; $\dfrac{\$3.48}{12} = \$0.29$, cost

per bar when purchased in lots of one dozen.

$\$0.33 - \$0.29 = \$0.04$, savings per bar

11-C $\$25 \times 20 = \$500$ in contributions

$\$500 \times .40 = \$200$ spent for food and drinks

$\$500 - \$200 = \$300$ remaining for other expenses

12-B   Let $x =$ length of nearby pole's shadow.

$24 : 8 = 72 : x$; $24x = 8 \times 72$;

$$x = \dfrac{8 \times \overset{3}{\cancel{72}}}{\underset{1}{\cancel{24}}} = 24 \text{ feet}$$

13-C $\$250 \times .20 = \$50$; $\$250 - \$50 = \$200$

$\$200 \times .30 = \$60$; $\$200 - \$60 = \$140$

14-B   7:15 to 12 noon $= 4\dfrac{3}{4}$ hours;

12 noon to $3:45 = 3\dfrac{3}{4}$ hours

$4\dfrac{3}{4} + 3\dfrac{3}{4} = 8\dfrac{1}{2}$ hours;

$8\dfrac{1}{2}$ hours -1 hour (lunch) $= 7\dfrac{1}{2}$ hours

15-D   Let $x =$ assessed value of house

$x + .02 = \$550.00$

$x = \dfrac{550}{.02} = \$27,500$

16-C   250 miles a day × 6 drivers = 1,500 miles a day

1,500 miles a day × 5 days = 7,500 miles a week

17-C   The 17-minute mark is $\dfrac{2}{5}$ of the way between 3 and 4 o'clock. $\dfrac{2}{5}$ of $60 = 24$;

24 minutes past 3 o'clock = 3:24

18-B $3375 \div 3\dfrac{3}{8} = 3375 \div \dfrac{27}{8} = 3375 \times \dfrac{8}{27} = 125 \times 8 = 1000$ dresses

19-C $15' \times 24' = 5$ yards × 8 yards = 40 square yards

40 square yards × \$1.00 = \$40.00

20-C $16\dfrac{1}{2}$ hours $= 15$ hours $+ 90$ minutes; $\dfrac{15}{5} =$

3 hours; $\dfrac{90}{5} = 18$ minutes; 3 hours $+ 18$ minutes = 3 hours, 18 minutes

21-D   100 miles @ 40 mph $= 2\dfrac{1}{2}$ hours $= 2\dfrac{3}{6}$ hours

80 miles @ 60 mph $= 1\dfrac{1}{3}$ hours $= 1\dfrac{2}{6}$ hours

$2\dfrac{3}{6}$ hours $+ 1\dfrac{2}{6}$ hours $= 3\dfrac{5}{6}$ hours

22-C

Let $x =$ original price

$x \times .25 = .25x$

$x - .25x = \$112.50$

$.75x = \$112.50$

$x = \dfrac{\$112.50}{.75} = \$150$

23-B $\$241.75 + \$13.24 + \$102.97 = \$357.96$

$\$627.04 - \$357.96 = \$269.08$

24-B $250 \times .08 = \$20.00$; $250 \times .07 = \$17.50$; 500 erasers cost $\$37.50$; $\$50.00 - \$37.50 = \$12.50$

Let $x =$ additional erasers purchased. $x \times .05 = 12.50$;

$x = \dfrac{12.50}{.05} = 250; 500 + 250 = 750$ erasers.

25-C   Time difference between New York and Los Angeles is 3 hours.
4:15 p.m. – 3:30 p.m. = 45 minutes; 3 hours + 45 minutes = 3 hours, 45 minutes for flight time.

26-D   Basic toll = $1.00

$\$3.25 - \$1.00 = \$2.25$ for extra passengers

$\$2.25 \div .75 = 3$

The car holds 1 driver + 3 passengers for a total of 4 people.

27-C   Each sheet contains 100 stamps.

3 sheets of 23¢ stamps cost $69.00

2 sheets of 50¢ stamps cost $100.00

4 sheets of 29¢ stamps cost $116.00

$285.00

28-D   Total earnings in pay period = $497.05

Deduct:

federal income tax	$90.32
FICA	28.74
state tax	18.79
city tax	7.25
pension	+ 1.88
	$146.98

497.05

−146.98

$350.07

29-A   Let $x =$ price of radio before tax was added.

$$x + .05x = \$31.29$$
$$1.05x = 31.29$$
$$x = \frac{39.29}{1.05} = \$29.80$$

30-A $x = \dfrac{3600}{40} = 90$ minutes $= 1\dfrac{1}{2}$ hours

Part 3—Word Knowledge

1-B   *Inform* means to *tell* or to *let someone know something.*

2-C   *Crimson* is a *purplish red color.*

3-B   *Caution* means *care* or *watchfulness.*

4-D   The word *intermittently* means *recurring from time to time.*

5-A   The word *occurrence* is synonymous with *event* or *incident.*

6-B   *Deception* means *fraud* or *subterfuge.*

7-D   The word *cease* means to *stop* or *come to an end.*

8-B   The word *acclaim* is synonymous with *applause* or *approval.*

9-D   The word *erect* means to *build* or *construct.*

10-D   *Relish* means to *like* or *enjoy.*

11-D   *Sufficient* means *adequate, enough,* or *appropriate.*

12-A   The word *fortnight* means *fourteen days* or *two weeks.*

13-A   *Flaw* means *fault* or *defect.*

14-C   *Impose* means to *prescribe* or *dictate.*

15-B   *Jeer* means to *deride, ridicule,* or *scoff*

16-D   *Alias* means an *assumed* or *other name.*

17-C   *Impair* means to *make worse* or *weaken.*

18-A   *Itinerant* means *journeying* or *traveling.*

19-A   The word *abandon* means to *give up* or *relinquish.*

20-B   *Resolve* means to *determine* or *decide.*

21-A   *Ample* means *abundant* or *plentiful.*

22-C   *Stench* means an *offensive smell* or *foul odor.*

23-D   *Sullen* means *morose* or *angrily silent.*

24-A   *Rudiments* means *basic principles* or *procedures.*

25-C *Clash* means to *disagree* or *conflict*.

26-B *Camaraderie* means *comradeship* or *close friendship*.

27-D The word *superficial* is synonymous with *shallow* or *cursory*.

28-A The word *tapestry* means a *fabric woven to produce a design*.

29-A *Terse* means *concise* or *brief*.

30-A The word *concoction* means a *combination of ingredients*.

31-C *Incessant* means *unceasing* or *constant*.

32-C *Solidity* means *firmness* or the *quality of being solid*.

33-C *Increment* means an *addition* or *increase*.

34-B The word *immaterial* means *unimportant*.

35-D The word *misconstrued* means *misinterpreted* or *interpreted erroneously*.

Part 4—Paragraph Comprehension

1-A The passage states that physical examinations are intended to increase efficiency and production and that they do accomplish these ends.

2-A The passage states that traffic violations are usually the result of illegal and dangerous driving behavior.

3-D Complaints frequently bring into the open conditions and faults in operation and service that should be corrected.

4-C The vaulter may attempt to jump any height above the minimum that is set by the judge.

5-C The last sentence in the passage states that the real danger is in a large leak that can cause an explosion.

6-A The time it takes the earth to go around the sun is $365\frac{1}{4}$ days rather than 365 days.

Leap years correct for this discrepancy by adding an extra day once every four years.

7-D The point of the passage is that a business should be prepared to fill unexpected vacancies with pretrained staff members.

8-D See the first sentence in the reading passage.

9-B See the first sentence in the reading passage.

10-C Phosphorus catches fire easily. Therefore, it has a low kindling temperature.

11-A See the last sentence in the reading passage.

12-A From the second sentence in the reading passage, it may be deduced that it is difficult to suppress racketeering because so many people want services that are not obtainable through legitimate sources.

13-B See the second paragraph in the reading passage.

14-B   See the last paragraph in the reading passage.

15-C   A meter is one ten-millionth of the distance from the Equator to the North Pole. One

ten-millionth $= \dfrac{1}{10,000,000}$.

Part 5—Mathematics Knowledge

1-B   Add: $6a - 4b + 3c$

$\qquad \dfrac{4a + 9b - 5c}{10a + 5b - 2c}$

2-B $x + 1$

$\underline{\times x + 2}$

$x^2 + x$

$\underline{+ \quad 2x + 2}$

$x^2 + 3x + 2$

3-B $3x = -5$

$x = \dfrac{-5}{3} = -\dfrac{5}{3}$

4-A   The first step to finding the square root of a number is to pair the digits to each side of the decimal point. If necessary, place 0 to the left of the first digit to form a pair and then solve with a modified form of long division.

$\sqrt{05\,90\,43}$

As the square root of 05 is between 2 and 3, place 2 above the first pair. The first digit of the square root of 59043 is 2.

5-A   Area of rectangle = 9 × 4 = 36. Area of square = 36. Therefore, each side = 6 and the perimeter of the square = 6 + 6 + 6 + 6 = 24

6-B $4^2 + 4^2 = d^2$; 16 + 16 = d^2; 16 × 2 = d^2;

$\sqrt{16} \times 2 = d; d = 4\sqrt{2}$

7-D   An equilateral triangle has 3 equal sides. Therefore, if its perimeter is $6n - 12$, each

side is $\dfrac{6n - 12}{3} = 2n - 4$.

8-C   Let angle of complement = x; let measure of angle = $2x$; $2x + x = 90°$; $x = 30°$; $2x = 60°$

9-C   The sum of the interior angles of a hexagon = $180° (6 - 2) = 180° \times 4 = 720°$. As a hexagon contains 6 angles, $\dfrac{760}{8} = 120°$ = measure of each interior angle. The supplement of $120° = 60°$.

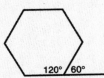

10-B   Area of rectangle = 12 ft × 18 ft = 4 yards × 6 yards = 24 sq. yards.

11-D $d = rt; A = r + \dfrac{d}{t}; A = r + \dfrac{r\cancel{t}}{\cancel{t}}_1;$

$A = r + r; A = 2r.$

12-A   23 is the only option that can be divided only by itself and 1.

13-B   If radius $r = 35$ miles, diameter = 70 miles.

Circumference $= \dfrac{22}{\cancel{7}_1} \times \overset{10}{\cancel{70}} = 220$ miles

14-C $3! = 3 \times 2 \times 1 = 6$

15-A $a = 2b;\ 2a = 4b = 6c;\ a = \dfrac{6c}{2} = 3c$

16-A $\dfrac{2x}{7} = 2x^2;\ 14x^2 = 2x; \dfrac{\overset{7}{\cancel{14}}x^2}{\cancel{2}x}_1 = 1;$

$7x = 1; x = \dfrac{1}{7}$

17-D $A^2 = \dfrac{B^2}{C+D}; A^2(C+D) = B^2;$

$C + D = \dfrac{B^2}{A^2}; C = \dfrac{B^2}{A^2} - D$

18-A   Let x = length of shorter side; let $2x$ = length of longer.

$2x + x + 2x + x = 90; x = 15$

19-C A quadrilateral is a rhombus only if its four sides are equal in length. A square has four equal sides.

20-C Area $= \pi r^2 = \dfrac{22}{7} \times 7^2 = 22 \times 7 = 154$ sq. in.

21-A $5a - 4x - 3y = 5(-2) - 4(-10) - 3(5) = -10 + 40 - 15 = +15$

22-B 1 book costs c dollars; m books $= m \times c = mc$

23-A $\angle 8$ and $\angle 4$ are corresponding angles formed by parallel lines. m$\angle 4 = 80°$. $\angle 4$ and $\angle 2$ are vertical angles and have equal measure. m$\angle 2 = 80°$.

24-D $\dfrac{x}{2} - \dfrac{x}{5} = 3;\ \dfrac{5x}{10} - \dfrac{2x}{10} = 3;\ \dfrac{3x}{10} = 3;$

$3x = 30;\ x = 10$

25-C $C = \pi D = \pi \times 2r$; if radius is increased by 3, $C = \pi \times 2(r + 3)$; $C = \pi \times 2r + 6$

Part 6—Electronics Information

1-D Consider the following filtered rectifier circuit with a short circuit across capacitor A:

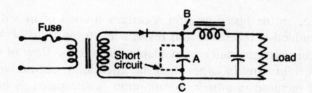

The current at point B, which would ordinarily flow through the load resistor, will now flow through the short circuit to C and back through the transformer. The short circuit has virtually no resistance, causing large currents to flow in both the primary and secondary windings of the transformer. These large currents cause the fuse to burn out.

2-C Voltages are transformed directly as the ratio of the secondary to the primary turns:

$$\frac{\text{VOLTAGE}_{\text{Secondary}}}{\text{VOLTAGE}_{\text{Primary}}} = \frac{\text{TURNS}_{\text{Secondary}}}{\text{TURNS}_{\text{Primary}}}$$

$$\frac{V_S}{V_P} = \frac{T_S}{T_P} = V_S; \frac{T_S}{T_P} \times V_P;\ V_S = \frac{50}{100} V_P = \frac{1}{2} V_P$$

3-D A good electrical connection has as low a resistance as possible. Soldering provides a low resistance path through the connection. It is also a mechanically secure connection.

4-D Resistance in the primary will reduce the current flow and reduce the voltage and current available at the spark plug. A "hot" spark with as high a voltage and current as possible is necessary for easy starting and smooth performance.

5-A   The resistance of a short circuit usually consists of little more than the resistance of the circuit's copper wires since the load has been "shorted" or bypassed. This very low resistance results in very high current flow.

6-D   Wires larger than No. 10 AWG are usually stranded because a solid wire of that diameter is too stiff to make good connections or to "fish" readily through race ways.

7-D   The image shows the current rising and falling from some minimum value indicated by the straight-line portions of the image. The current, therefore, pulses without changing direction. AC involves a reversal of direction.

8-C   Ohm's law; $V = IR$ gives the voltage drop across a resistor. Inductance and capacitance do not produce a voltage drop. Conductance is the reciprocal of resistance. A high resistance has a low conductance.

9-B   Maximum wattage that will cause a 15-ampere breaker to trip is (15 amps) (120 volts) = 1,800 watts. Accordingly, 1,300 watts is the largest heater that will operate without causing the circuit breaker to trip.

10-A   A capacitor contains two conducting surfaces separated by an insulator and can, therefore, store static electrical charges. Caution should be exercised before touching capacitors. They should have their terminals "shorted" before being handled.

11-B   All the other materials are very good insulators. Carbon has some resistance but still conducts more readily than the others. Resistors may contain some carbon.

12-A   The windings in an AC motor are designed to offer a certain amount of impedance, which is a combination of inductive reactance and resistance, to the flow of AC. When DC is applied, only the pure resistance is available to limit the flow of current. Therefore, the direct current flow is larger than the alternating current would be at the same voltage. The increase in power consumption is dissipated as heat.

13-A   Ohm's law describes the relationship between the voltage, current, and resistance in a circuit: $V = IR$. The watts consumed by a circuit are the product of the voltage times the current. One ampere flowing for one second delivers one coulomb of electrical charge. Kirchoff's voltage and current laws concern the way voltages and currents around a circuit can be summed up.

14-B   Since the starting current drawn by the washing machine is usually six times greater than the running current, it is most likely that the circuit breaker is too small to permit the motor to start. Consult the various local laws governing the size of circuit breakers acceptable to permit motors of various ratings to start. These local laws are usually based on the National Electrical Code.

15-A   Oscillators capable of producing high frequency AC may include crystals capable of producing particular frequencies or they may involve electronic components, such as capacitors and inductors, capable of being tuned to various frequencies.

16-D   Thermocouples usually consist of connections between wires of two dissimilar metals. They are frequently calibrated so that the amount of voltage produced can be directly related to the temperature. They are thus capable of measuring temperatures.

17-B   Coaxial cable consists of an inner conducting wire covered with insulation and run inside a concentric cylindrical outer conductor. TV antenna lead-in wires of the 75-ohm variety are examples of coaxial cables. Coaxial cables are used principally to minimize signal loss between antennas and either receiving or transmitting sets.

18-A   All of the materials listed are conductors. Silver is the best, although it is not often used because of its high cost. The moving contacts in motor starters, however, are often made of silver, and it is widely used where low resistance contacts are required.

19-D   The symbol shows a semiconductor diode. These usually contain silicon and some times germanium. They conduct only in the direction shown by the arrow. Currents flowing in the opposite direction meet with high resistance and are effectively blocked. For these reasons, silicon diodes are often used to rectify AC to DC.

20-C   The transistor contains semiconductor material. Two varieties, NPN and PNP, are manufactured. The one shown in the diagram is of the NPN type.

PART 7—AUTO SHOP INFORMATION

1-D   The voltage regulator prevents overcharging the battery by reducing current to the rotating electromagnet as the engine speeds up.

2-D   Torsion bars are used in the suspension to absorb shock by twisting. Coil springs are actually coiled tension bars.

3-A   When an automobile "burns" oil, it means that the engine oil consumption is excessive. This condition is manifested by the formation of a black gummy deposit in the end of the tail pipe.

4-A   The conditions stated indicate that the battery is not properly charged. The conditions are corrected generally by either recharging or replacing the battery.

5-C   A dead battery, defective battery cables, or corrosion between the cables and the battery posts are common causes for failure of an automobile engine to "turn over." If the battery charge is normal, the next best thing to check is the connection between the battery cables and battery posts.

6-C   The generator or alternator is usually mounted at the front of the engine and is linked by a fan belt to the engine's crankshaft pulley.

7-B   Although all of the options may cause an engine to miss, a defective spark plug is the likely cause if the engine misses only on one cylinder.

8-B   If an automobile engine overheats while the radiator remains cold, it is probably a faulty thermostat. The thermostat cuts off the flow of the coolant to the radiator when the engine is cold and allows the coolant to flow to the radiator as the coolant temperature rises. A stuck thermostat prevents this flow to the radiator, resulting in an overheated engine and a cool radiator.

9-B   Moisture enters with the air, especially on damp days. Condensation forms inside the gas tank and collects in the bottom of the tank to form rust or create a thick sludge. Keeping the gas tank as nearly full as possible allows less room for formation of condensation.

10-C   The power train consists of the items used to conduct power from the pistons to the wheels.

11-A   If the clutch slips, the full power of the engine is not transmitted. The clutch needs to be repaired or replaced.

12-B   Pistons expand as the engine warms up. Pistons are designed to fit the cylinders, regardless of whether the pistons are cold or at working temperature. However, when the engine is overheated, the pistons may increase in size to such an extent that they "stick" in the cylinder.

13-A   The tool is an adjustable open-end wrench. One jaw is fixed; the other moves along a slide with a thumbscrew adjustment. The tool shown is also called a crescent wrench.

14-D   Concrete is made by mixing cement, sand, and broken rock with sufficient water to make the cement set and bind the entire mass.

15-D   The set of a saw refers to how much the teeth are pushed out in opposite directions from the sides of the blade.

16-C   Tempering brings steel to the desired hardness and strength.

17-A   Sheet metal is generally cleaned by using an industrial grade of sulfuric acid.

18-D   The cut of a file refers to the kind of teeth it has. It may have single-cut or double-cut teeth. The teeth also have different degrees of fineness.

19-B   In twist drill grinding, it is important to have equal and correctly sized drill-point angles, equal length cutting tips, correct clearance behind the cutting lips, and correct chisel-edge angle. Choice B is the correct answer.

20-A   A plumb bob is a weight, often of lead, used in a line to determine vertical direction.

21-C   A miter box is a device for guiding a handsaw at the proper angle when making a miter joint in wood.

22-D   The tool shown is a pipe cutter. Pipe cutters are used to cut pipe made of steel, brass, copper, wrought iron, and lead.

23-B   The operator should check the abrasive wheel before starting the machine for safety reasons. A cracked or chipped wheel may injure someone.

24-C   The allowance is made for the width of the saw.

25-B   The tool is a welding torch used in making metal-to-metal joints. Welding is generally done with material made of steel.

8—Mechanical Comprehension

1-C   30 lbs. + 2 lbs. = 32 lbs., the total weight equally supported by two scales.

$$\frac{32}{2} = 16 \text{ lbs.,}$$ the reading on each scale.

2-B   The number of parts of the rope going to and from the movable block indicates the mechanical advantage. In this case, it is 2.

3-B   The block is not fixed and the fall is doubled as it supports the 200-lb. cask. Each half of the fall carries one half of the total load, or 100 lbs. The person is lifting a 200-lb. cask with a 100-lb. pull.

4-C   The circumference of the wheel is 20 in. One complete revolution will raise W2 20 in. and lower W1 20 in., a difference of 40 in.

5-A   For every full rotation of the worm shaft, the gear will turn only 22°.

6-C   The vertical component of the momentum of the ball is zero only at position C.

7-D   Gear A has 15 teeth; gear B has 10 teeth.

Let x = number of revolutions gear B will make.

$15 \times 14 = x \times 10$; $10x = 15 \times 14$;

$$x = \frac{15 \times 14}{10}; x = 21.$$

8-A   Pulley A has the smallest circumference and therefore turns the fastest.

9-A   Study the diagram on page 524 and note that with each complete turn of the cam, the setscrew will hit the contact point once.

10-B Gear 1 would turn in direction 1 (opposite that of gear B), and gear A would turn in direction 2 (opposite that of gear I).

11-D The pressure is uniform in the system given. If the main line air gauge reads 100 pounds, the tank air gauge will also read 100 pounds.

12-C Let x = theoretical distance moved in the opposite direction. $12 \times 150 = x \times 600$;

$$600x = 1800; x = \frac{1800}{600\%} = 3 \text{ feet.}$$

13-C As brace C has the greatest area support, it is the most secure.

14-D Of the colors listed, white will reflect the most solar heat, thereby keeping down the inside temperature of the oil tank.

15-A The greater the pressure outside the balloon, the less expansion within the balloon.

16-B Boiling Point = 100°; Freezing Point = 0°; 100° – 0° = 100°

17-C The air pressure on top of the liquid forces the liquid through the hose into the bucket.

18-D If pipe B is turned 4 revolutions and there are 8 threads per inch, the overall length would decrease by 4 threads, or $\frac{1}{2}$ inch.

19-A Gears M and N are eccentric oval gears that are identical in size, shape, and number of teeth. The point of contact of the gears shifts from the right to the left with each revolution. However, if gear N turns at a constant rpm, gear M will turn at the same constant rpm as N.

20-D By reducing the length of the lever arm, you are reducing the effort and will permit the valve to blow off at a lower pressure.

21-D   The amount of water that can leave an outlet depends upon the size or area of the opening. The area of a circular opening is proportional to the radius squared (area = πr^2). Therefore, the 2-inch pipe outlet will carry 4 times the amount of water as will the 1-inch opening. Mathematically,

$$\frac{\text{Area of 2 -inch}}{\text{Area of 1 -inch}} = \frac{\pi 2^2}{\pi 1^2} = \frac{\pi 4}{\pi 1} = 4.$$

22-C   Let x = tipping force. $80 \times 4 = x \times 1 = 320$ pounds

23-A   When two external gears mesh, they rotate in opposite directions. To avoid this, an idler gear is put between the driver gear and the driven gear.

24-B $\text{IMA} = \dfrac{8}{2} = 4; \dfrac{400}{4} = 100$ lbs.

25-D   Number 2 is a greater distance from the center than is number 1. Number 2 would therefore traverse a greater linear distance.

Part 9—Numerical Operations

1-C	$2 + 3 = 5$	**21-A**	$7 \times 4 = 28$
2-B	$8 - 5 = 3$	**22-D**	$5 + 8 = 13$
3-B	$9 \div 3 = 3$	**23-C**	$20 \div 2 = 10$
4-A	$4 \div 2 = 2$	**24-B**	$15 - 7 = 8$
5-D	$7 \times 3 = 21$	**25-A**	$6 \div 2 = 3$
6-B	$9 \div 1 = 9$	**26-B**	$7 - 2 = 5$
7-A	$18 - 14 = 4$	**27-C**	$10 \div 2 = 5$
8-C	$2 \times 12 = 24$	**28-B**	$1 + 6 = 7$
9-C	$9 - 6 = 3$	**29-D**	$4 \times 5 = 20$
10-D	$3 \times 2 = 6$	**30-D**	$7 - 7 = 0$
11-C	$1 - 1 = 0$	**31-B**	$5 \div 5 = 1$
12-C	$2 \times 9 = 18$	**32-B**	$5 \times 3 = 15$
13-D	$9 + 3 = 12$	**33-B**	$16 \div 4 = 4$
14-B	$8 + 16 = 24$	**34-C**	$7 + 9 = 16$
15-B	$9 - 4 = 5$	**35-D**	$15 \times 5 = 75$
16-A	$10 \div 2 = 5$	**36-A**	$4 - 3 = 1$
17-A	$17 - 4 = 13$	**37-D**	$7 + 5 = 12$
18-C	$3 + 3 = 6$	**38-A**	$27 \div 9 = 3$
19-C	$4 \times 3 = 12$	**39-A**	$6 + 4 = 10$
20-C	$8 - 3 = 5$	**40-D**	$10 \times 2 = 20$

41-C	$4 + 7 = 11$	**46-A**	$30 \div 15 = 2$
42-A	$8 \div 2 = 4$	**47-A**	$7 + 5 = 12$
43-D	$12 + 2 = 14$	**48-D**	$3 \times 6 = 18$
44-D	$3 \times 15 = 45$	**49-A**	$9 - 6 = 3$
45-B	$25 \div 5 = 5$	**50-C**	$4 \times 6 = 24$

Part 10—Coding Speed

The answers to the Coding Speed questions you missed can best be obtained by checking the key at the top of each section. If you are still making many mistakes or are not answering most of the questions in the time allotted, get additional practice by redoing the Coding Speed sections in each of the Specimen Tests. Remember, both speed and accuracy are essential. Ascertain and record the correct answer as quickly as you can, then immediately proceed to the next question, and continue working in this manner as accurately and as quickly as you can.

PART III

UNDERSTANDING YOUR TEST RESULTS

YOUR ASVAB RESULTS

Your student ASVAB results are mailed to your school within thirty days after taking the ASVAB. ASVAB results consist of a combined Student Results Sheet and Counselor Summary for each student tested, as well as School Summary Reports.

The Student Results Sheet contains the following information:

- Student identification information (name, grade, social security number, test date, and school)
- Percentile scores for academic composites and all eight tests by same grade/same sex and same grade/opposite sex
- Graphic representation of student same grade/same sex percentile scores showing score bands
- The student's ASVAB Codes and Military Careers Score
- An explanation of percentile scores
- An explanation of score bands
- An explanation of the ASVAB Codes and the Military Careers Score
- An explanation of how to use ASVAB scores for career exploration
- A description of the ASVAB tests
- A brief description of Exploring Careers: The ASVAB Workbook
- An explanation of what information is released, to whom, and for what purposes

Also included is a *Counselor Summary* containing all the information that is provided to the student, plus percentile scores for academic composites and tests by same grade/combined sex. General information of interest to counselors is given on the back of the summary form. This summary can be detached and filed in the student's cumulative record.

If you took the enlistment ASVAB, your recruiter informs you of your scores. The recruiter also explains the breakdown of your scores, including the percentiles, composites, and military scores.

PERCENTILE SCORES

ASVAB scores are reported as percentile scores, which indicate your standing in relation to a national sample of students. Since test results are not exact measures of ability, ASVAB percentile scores are reported within a score band. The score band indicates the range within which your true score probably lies. The ASVAB score report indicates score bands with dashes surrounded by brackets.

When bands for two tests overlap substantially, such as the Paragraph Comprehension and Arithmetic Reasoning tests, for example, it is unlikely that the student has scored better on one than on the other. Where there is little or no overlap, it can be said with more confidence that the student's ability ranking is higher in one area than the other.

Both same grade/same sex and same grade/opposite sex percentile scores are reported. The scores that are most important are those for the student's same grade level and sex. These scores allow you to see your performance compared to that of your peers. The same grade/opposite sex percentiles are reported since men and women tend to perform differently on some ASVAB tests. On those tests that make up the academic composites, the differences are slight. On the more technical tests, the differences are more significant. Men tend to perform better on the Electronics Information test, for example, and women on the coding speed tests. The goal of reporting these differences is for students to determine if they need to gain additional experience through course work or independent study to compete effectively and achieve their career goals.

COMPOSITE SCORES

The composite scores you receive are combinations of results of two or more parts of the ASVAB. The following indicates what each composite score measures and shows the various tests that contribute to each composite score.

ASVAB Codes

Your score report includes two ASVAB Codes, a primary ASVAB Code, and a secondary ASVAB Code. These codes can be used with *Exploring Careers: The ASVAB Workbook* to identify occupations in which workers have aptitude levels similar to your own. ASVAB Codes are based on a five-level reduction of the Academic Ability Composite according to the chart below.

The first number in the ASVAB Code spot is your primary code. It can be used to find the occupations most suited to your aptitude levels. The second number is your secondary code, and it can be used to locate the occupations next most suited to your aptitude levels. Using two ASVAB Codes greatly expands the list of possible occupations to be explored. The codes summarize your level of general ability, and, together with interest inventory results and personal preferences, they can be used to evaluate different occupations as possible career choices.

Primary Code	Academic Ability Percentiles		Secondary Code
1	90–99		2
2	70–89	80–89	1
		70–79	3
3	50–69	60–69	2
		50–59	4
4	30–49	40–49	3
		30–39	5
5	01–29		4

Military Career Score

The Military Career Score is a combination of scores from the Academic Ability, Mechanical Comprehension, and Electronics Information tests. It estimates your likelihood of qualifying for various enlisted occupations described in *Military Careers*, a Department of Defense publication that details occupations available in the military. The Military Career Score is reported in a range between 140 and 240, with a mean of 200. The section in this book entitled *Military Enlisted Occupations and Civilian Counterparts* is a condensed version of enlisted occupations described in *Military Careers* and can be used to estimate your chances of qualifying for such occupations.

Although the military uses sets of composites and scoring slightly different from the student ASVAB composites, most enlistment composites have test content the same as or similar to that of the student ASVAB composites. The two composites both predict successful performance in military technical training courses.

Academic Ability

Academic Ability is a general indicator of future academic success. It is a measure of how well you did on the Verbal Ability and Math Ability sections combined.

$$\begin{matrix} \text{ACADEMIC} \\ \text{ABILITY} \end{matrix} = \begin{bmatrix} \text{WORD} \\ \text{KNOWLEDGE} \end{bmatrix} + \begin{bmatrix} \text{PARAGRAPH} \\ \text{COMPREHENSION} \end{bmatrix} + \begin{bmatrix} \text{ARITHMETIC} \\ \text{REASONING} \end{bmatrix} + \begin{bmatrix} \text{MATHEMATICS} \\ \text{KNOWLEDGE} \end{bmatrix}$$

Scores of tests in brackets are combined and weighted as one unit.

Verbal Ability

Verbal Ability measures your performance on the Word Knowledge and Paragraph Comprehension tests combined. It is a general indicator of ability to learn from written material.

$$\begin{array}{l} \text{VERBAL} \\ \text{ABILITY} \end{array} = \begin{array}{l} \text{WORD} \\ \text{KNOWLEDGE} \end{array} + \begin{array}{l} \text{PARAGRAPH} \\ \text{COMPREHENSION} \end{array}$$

Math Ability

Math Ability measures how well you did on the Arithmetic Reasoning and Mathematics Knowledge tests combined. It is a general indicator of success in future math courses.

$$\begin{array}{l} \text{MATH} \\ \text{ABILITY} \end{array} = \begin{array}{l} \text{ARITHMETIC} \\ \text{KNOWLEDGE} \end{array} + \begin{array}{l} \text{MATHEMATICS} \\ \text{COMPREHENSION} \end{array}$$

Individual Test Scores

Individual test scores that are not used in computing ASVAB Codes—General Science, Auto & Shop Information, Mechanical Comprehension, Electronics Information, Numerical Operations, and Coding Speed—can be used to provide additional direction for career explorations. Scores on individual ASVAB tests that are significantly higher or lower than the rest may point out particular strengths or weaknesses that might be considered in selecting the careers to be explored.

Military Careers Scores

The Military Careers Score may be used with graphs in the book *Military Careers* or with the 50% (50-50) point given for the 127 listed occupations in the section "Military Enlisted Occupations and Civilian Counterparts" to help you estimate your chances of qualifying for enlisted occupations in the military. This score is a combination of the Academic Ability composite scores and the Mechanical Comprehension and the Electronics Information tests. It is reported in a range between 140 and 240, with a mean of 200.

Enlistment processing occurs at Military Entrance Processing Stations (MEPs) and Mobile Examining Team (MET) sites located around the country. ASVAB results are used to determine if you qualify for entry into a service and if you have the specific aptitude level required for job specialty training programs. If you took the ASVAB in high school or postsecondary school, you can use your scores to determine whether you qualify for entry into the military services, provided the scores are not more than two years old.

Armed Force Qualification Scores

The Armed Forces Qualification Test (AFQT) raw score is derived from the raw scores obtained on the ASVAB, as follows:

$$\begin{matrix} \text{AFQT} \\ \text{RAW} = \\ \text{SCORE} \end{matrix} \begin{bmatrix} \text{WORD} & \text{PARAGRAPH} \\ \text{KNOWLEDGE} + \text{COMPREHENSION} \\ \text{RAW SCORE} & \text{RAW SCORE} \end{bmatrix} + \begin{matrix} \text{ARITHMETIC} & \text{MATHEMATICS} \\ \text{REASONING} + \text{KNOWLEDGE} \\ \text{RAW SCORE} & \text{RAW SCORE} \end{matrix}$$

This AFQT Raw Score is then converted into a Percentile Score, which is used to determine eligibility for entrance into the military.

Applicants without prior military service who receive an AFQT percentile score of 10 or higher are eligible for continued processing at a Military Entrance Processing Station. However, the services usually reject those who fail to score in the top three categories. Typically, the services prefer applicants who score in the following categories:

Category	Percentile Score
Category I	93 and over
Category II	65 to 92
Category III	31 to 64

A very limited number of Category IV (Percentile score: 10 to 30) may be accepted under certain circumstances. Final determination of acceptability remains with the services. Also, applicants with prior military service who wish to return to the military are processed for enlistment at the discretion of the service, regardless of AFQT score.

PART IV

MILITARY CAREERS AND ENLISTMENT OPPORTUNITIES

MILITARY ENLISTED OCCUPATIONS AND CIVILIAN COUNTERPARTS*

CHAPTER 9

Besides being the single largest employer in the nation, the military offers the widest choice of career opportunities. Together, the five services offer training and employment in over 2,000 enlisted job specialties. To help you explore the enlisted world-of-work, these specialties are grouped into enlisted occupations. The occupations are organized into twelve groups:

- Human Services
- Media and Public Affairs
- Health Care
- Engineering, Science, and Technical
- Administrative
- Service
- Vehicle and Machinery Mechanic
- Electronic and Electrical Equipment Repair
- Construction
- Machine Operator and Precision Work
- Transportation and Material Handling
- Combat Specialty

This grouping is a convenient reference and index for locating the page numbers of all occupations that relate to a particular broad occupational group. For example, a person interested in the Electronics and Electrical Equipment Repair group may quickly locate the page numbers of all enlisted occupations that fall within this group.

Each enlisted occupation contains a description that includes the following pertinent information:

- Occupational Title—The occupational title names the military occupation.
- Military Service Representation—The military services listed next to the title offer employment and training opportunities in the occupation. Not all services offer every military occupation.
- Typical Tasks—Typical tasks describe the main work activities in the occupation. Some of the activities listed may not apply to all services.

*Condensed from *Military Careers*

- Qualifications—Four separate categories may be listed.
    - *Special Qualifications*—Special qualifications, such as typing ability, fluency in a foreign language, or completion of certain high school courses, must be met to enter certain occupations. This section also identifies combat occupations from which women are excluded by law.
    - *Physical Demands*—Some military occupations place physical demands, such as strength, running, climbing, swimming, clear speech, and special vision or hearing requirements.
    - *Helpful Attributes*—Helpful attributes include interests, school subjects taken, experience, and other personal characteristics that may be helpful for training and working in the military occupation. These are not actual requirements.
    - Military Careers Score at the 50 percent (50-50) point is that score at which you have an even chance of qualifying for a military occupation. Higher Military Careers Scores indicate that you have better than an estimated 50 percent chance of qualifying. Lower Military Career Scores indicate that you have less than an estimated 50 percent chance of qualifying.
- *Civilian Counterparts*—Most military occupations are comparable to one or more civilian occupations because they have similar duties and require similar training. *Civilian Counterparts* identify these civilian occupations and the kinds of companies or organizations in which they are located.

If you have a strong aptitude for a military occupation, you may have a strong aptitude for its civilian counterpart.

Practice for the Armed Forces Test

Military Enlisted Occupations and Civilian Counterparts

ASVAB Occupational Index

Administrative Occupations

Combat Specialty Occupations

Construction Occupations

Electronic and Electrical Equipment Repairer Occupations

Engineering, Science, and Technical Occupations

Health-Care Occupations

Human Services Occupations

Machine Operator and Precision Work Occupations

Media and Public Affairs Occupations

Service Occupations

Transportation and Material Handling Occupations

Vehicle and Machinery Mechanic Occupations

Although not stated, many military occupations require the use of small computers in the performance of duties.

➤ HUMAN SERVICES OCCUPATIONS

Caseworkers and Counselors

Army

Navy

Air Force

Marine Corps

Coast Guard

Typical Tasks

- Interview personnel who request help or are referred by their commanders
- Identify personal problems and determine the need for professional help
- Counsel personnel and their families
- Administer and score psychological tests
- Teach classes on human relations
- Keep records of counseling sessions and make reports to supervisors

Qualifications

Physical Demands

Caseworkers and counselors need to speak clearly and distinctly in order to teach classes and work with personnel who have problems.

Helpful Attributes

Helpful school subjects include health, biology, psychology, sociology, social science, and speech. Helpful attributes include

- Interest in working with people
- Patience in dealing with problems that take time and effort to overcome
- Sensitivity to the needs of others

Civilian Counterparts

Civilian caseworkers and counselors work in rehabilitation centers, hospitals, schools, and public agencies. Their duties are similar to duties in the military. Civilian caseworkers and counselors, however, are usually required to have a college degree in social work, psychology, or counseling. They may be called group workers, human relations counselors, or drug and alcohol counselors.

Military Careers Score at the 50% (50-50) point = 202.

Religious Program Specialists

Army

Navy

Air Force

Typical Tasks

- Assist chaplains in planning and preparing religious programs and activities
- Assist chaplains in conducting religious services
- Prepare religious educational and devotional materials
- Organize charitable and public service volunteer programs
- Maintain relations with religious communities and public service organizations
- Perform administrative duties for chaplains such as scheduling appointments, handling correspondence, maintaining files, and handling finances

Qualifications

Physical Demands

The ability to speak clearly and distinctly is required to enter this occupation.

ARCO ■ ASVAB

Helpful Attributes

Helpful school subjects include English, public speaking, accounting, and typing. Helpful attributes include

- Interest in religious guidance
- Sensitivity to the needs of others
- Knowledge of various religious customs and beliefs
- Ability to express ideas clearly and concisely
- Interest in administrative work

Civilian Counterparts

Civilian religious program specialists manage churches and religious schools. Their duties are similar to those performed by military religious program specialists, including planning religious programs and preparing religious educational materials. They are also called directors of religious activities.

Military Careers Score at the 50% (50-50) point = 197.

➤ MEDIA AND PUBLIC AFFAIRS OCCUPATIONS

Audiovisual Production Specialists

Army

Navy

Air Force

Marine Corps

Coast Guard

Typical Tasks

- Assist producers and directors in selecting and interpreting scripts
- Work with writers in preparing and revising scripts
- Determine the type of presentation needed to convey the message as intended
- Plan and design production scenery, graphics, and special effects
- Help plan the activities of audiovisual production crews
- Operate media equipment and special effects devices

Qualifications

Physical Demands

Normal color vision is required to work with scenery, stage settings, graphics, and other color production aids. The ability to speak clearly is required for some specialties.

Helpful Attributes

Helpful school subjects include graphics, art, speech, and drama. Helpful attributes include

- Interest in creative and artistic work
- Preference for working as part of a team
- Experience in school plays or making home movies

Civilian Counterparts

Civilian audiovisual production specialists work for advertising agencies, radio and television stations, motion picture studios, and educational and training agencies. Their duties are similar to those performed in the military.

Military Careers Score at the 50% (50-50) point = 197.

Graphic Designers and Illustrators

Army

Navy

Air Force

Marine Corps

Typical Tasks

- Produce computer-generated graphics
- Draw graphs and charts to represent budgets, numbers of troops, supply levels, and office organization
- Develop ideas and design posters and signs
- Help instructors to design artwork for training courses
- Draw illustrations of parts of the human body for use in medical training
- Draw cartoons for filmstrips and animation for films
- Make silkscreen prints
- Work with TV and film producers to design backdrops and props for film sets

Qualifications

Physical Demands

- Normal color vision is required to work with paints, watercolors, and other art materials.
- Coordination of eyes and hands is needed to draw sketches.

Helpful Attributes

Helpful school subjects include art, drafting, and geometry. Helpful attributes include

- Interest in artwork or lettering
- Ability to convert ideas into visual presentations
- Neatness and an eye for detail

Civilian Counterparts

Civilian graphic designers and illustrators work for government agencies, advertising agencies, print shops, and engineering firms. They also work for many large organizations that have their own graphics departments. Their duties are similar to military graphics designers and illustrators. They may be known as commercial artists or graphic arts technicians.

Military Careers Score at the 50% (50-50) point = 197.

Interpreters and Translators

Army

Navy

Air Force

Marine Corps

Typical Tasks

- Translate written and spoken foreign language material to and from English, making sure to preserve the original meaning
- Interrogate (question) prisoners of war, enemy deserters, and civilian informers in their native languages
- Record foreign radio transmission using sensitive radios
- Prepare written reports about the information obtained
- Translate foreign documents, such as battle plans and personnel records
- Translate foreign books and articles describing foreign equipment and construction techniques

Qualifications

Physical Demands

Normal hearing and the ability to speak clearly and distinctly are usually required to enter the occupation.

Special Qualifications

Fluency in a foreign language is required in order to enter most specialties within this occupation.

Helpful Attributes

Helpful school subjects include speech and typing. Helpful attributes include

- Interest in foreign languages
- Interest in working with people
- Interest in reading

Civilian Counterparts

Civilian interpreters and translators work for government agencies, embassies, universities, and companies that conduct business overseas. Their work is similar to the work of military interpreters and translators.

Military Careers Score at the 50% (50-50) point = 197.

Motion Picture Camera Operators

Army

Navy

Air Force

Marine Corps

Coast Guard

Typical Tasks

- Set up and operate motion picture equipment including cameras, sound recorders, and lighting
- Operate television cameras in TV studios and remote sites
- Follow script and instructions of film or TV directors to move cameras, zoom, pan, or adjust focus

Qualifications

Helpful Attributes

Helpful school subjects include photography, art and mathematics. Helpful attributes include

- Interest in photography
- Experience in making home movies
- Ability to follow details
- Ability to follow spoken directions

Civilian Counterparts

Civilian motion picture camera operators work for film production companies, TV networks and stations, and government audiovisual studios. Some work as independent film makers. Their duties are similar to military motion picture camera operators.

Military Careers Score at the 50% (50-50) point = 196.

Musicians

Army

Navy

Air Force

Marine Corps

Coast Guard

Typical Tasks

- Play in or lead bands, orchestras, combos, and jazz groups
- Sing in choral groups or as soloists
- Perform for ceremonies, parades, concerts, festivals, and dances
- Rehearse and learn new music when not performing
- Play brass, percussion, woodwind, or string instruments

Qualifications

Special Qualifications

To qualify for a service band, applicants must pass one or more auditions. They must be fairly accomplished musicians and have good music sight-reading ability.

Helpful Attributes

Helpful school subjects include band, music theory, harmony, and other music courses. Helpful attributes include

- Poise when performing in public
- Ability to play more than one instrument
- Ability to sing

Civilian Counterparts

Civilian musicians work for many types of employers including professional orchestras, bands, and choral groups. They work in nightclubs, concert halls, theaters, and recording studios.

Military Careers Score at the 50% (50-50) point = 195.

Photographers

Army

Navy

Air Force

Marine Corps

Coast Guard

Typical Tasks

- Select camera, film, and other equipment needed for the photo assignment
- Determine camera angles, lighting, and any special effects needed
- Take still photos of people, events, military equipment, land areas, and other subjects
- Develop and retouch negatives
- Print and duplicate photos or slides
- Write captions or news articles about the subjects in the photographs

Qualifications

Physical Demands

Normal color vision is required to work with color photography.

Helpful Attributes

Helpful school subjects include photography, art, chemistry, and mathematics. Helpful attributes include

- Interest in photography
- A good eye for composing subjects to be photographed
- Ability to recognize interesting photo subjects

Civilian Counterparts

Civilian photographers work for photography studios, newspapers, magazines, advertising agencies, and large businesses. Some photographers freelance (work independently). Depending on specialty, they may be known as photojournalists, aerial photographers, or still photographers.

Military Careers Score at the 50% (50-50) point = 197.

Radio and Television Announcers

Army

Navy

Air Force

Marine Corps

Coast Guard

Typical Tasks

- Investigate and write news stories
- Choose topics of special interest for broadcast
- Narrate special events broadcasts
- Interview guests
- Assist public affairs officers in responding to inquiries from commercial broadcast media
- Maintain tape, film, and record libraries

Qualifications

Special Qualifications

Basic typing ability is required to enter some specialties in this occupation.

Physical Demands

Radio and television announcers are required to pass a voice audition. A clear speaking ability is also required.

Helpful Attributes

Helpful school subjects include English, journalism, public speaking, and typing. Helpful attributes include

- Ability to write clearly and concisely
- Strong, clear speaking voice
- Interest in music, sports, and current events

Civilian Counterparts

Civilian radio and television announcers work for commercial and public broadcasting firms, as well as other businesses in the entertainment industry. They perform duties similar to their military counterparts.

They are employed as newscasters, disc jockeys, writers, directors, and producers. Civilian radio and television announcers may also work as station managers or supervisors.

Military Careers Score at the 50% (50-50) point = 205.

Reporters and Newswriters

Army

Navy

Air Force

Marine Corps

Coast Guard

Typical Tasks

- Gather information for military news programs and publications
- Write radio and TV scripts
- Develop ideas for news articles
- Arrange and conduct interviews
- Collect information for commercial media use
- Select photographs and write captions for news articles
- Write news releases, feature articles, and editorials

Qualifications

Helpful Attributes

Helpful school subjects include English, journalism, speech, typing, and media communications. Helpful attributes include

- Ability to keep detailed and accurate records
- Interest in researching facts and issues for news stories
- Ability to write clearly and concisely

Civilian Counterparts

Civilian reporters and newswriters work for newspapers, magazines, wire services, and radio and television stations. Their duties are similar to those performed by military reporters and newswriters. However, civilians often specialize in one area of coverage, such as politics, sports, film, or foreign affairs. They may be called copywriters, editors, editorial assistants, or correspondents.

Military Careers Score at the 50% (50-50) point = 205.

➤ HEALTH-CARE OCCUPATIONS

Cardiopulmonary and EEG Technicians

Army

Navy

Air Force

Typical Tasks

- Take patients' blood pressure readings

- Attach electrodes or microphones to the patients' bodies
- Help doctors revive heart attack victims
- Adjust settings and operate test equipment
- Watch dials, graphs, and screens during tests
- Talk to physicians to learn what tests or treatments are needed
- Keep records of test results and discuss them with medical staff
- Operate electrocardiographs, electroencephalographs, and other test equipment

Qualifications

Physical Demands

Normal color vision is required for some specialists in order to set up and monitor equipment.

Helpful Attributes

Helpful school subjects include algebra, chemistry, biology, or related courses. Helpful attributes include

- Interest in electronic equipment
- Ability to follow strict standards and procedures
- Interest in learning how the heart, lungs, and blood work together
- Ability to keep accurate records

Civilian Counterparts

Civilian cardiopulmonary and EEG technicians work in hospitals, clinics, and doctors' offices. Their duties are similar to those performed in the military. They may specialize in either cardiovascular (heart), pulmonary (lungs), or electroencephalograph (brain) testing.

Military Careers Score at the 50% (50-50) point = 197.

Dental Specialists

Army

Navy

Air Force

Coast Guard

Typical Tasks

- Help dentists perform oral surgery
- Prepare for patient examinations by selecting and arranging instruments and medications
- Help dentists during examinations by preparing dental compounds and operating dental equipment
- Clean patients' teeth using scaling and polishing instruments and equipment
- Operate dental X-ray equipment and process X-rays of patients' teeth, gums, and jaws
- Provide guidance to patients on daily care for their teeth
- Perform administrative duties, such as scheduling office visits, keeping patient records, and ordering dental supplies

Qualifications

Physical Demands

Dental specialists must sometimes stand for long periods.

Helpful Attributes

Helpful school subjects include biology and chemistry. Helpful attributes include

- Good eye-hand coordination
- Ability to follow spoken instructions
- Ability to follow detailed procedures
- Interest in working with people

Civilian Counterparts

Civilian dental specialists work in dental offices or clinics. Their work is similar to work in the military. They typically specialize in assisting dentists to treat patients, provide clerical support (dental assistants), or clean teeth (dental hygienists).

Military Careers Score at the 50% (50-50) point = 196.

Medical Laboratory Technicians

Army

Navy

Air Force

Coast Guard

Typical Tasks

- Use lab equipment to analyze specimens (samples) of tissue, blood, and body fluids
- Examine blood and bone marrow under microscopes
- Test specimens for bacteria or viruses
- Draw blood from patients
- Assist in collecting specimens at autopsies (medical examinations of the dead)
- Record and file results of laboratory tests

Qualifications

Helpful Attributes

Helpful school subjects include biology, chemistry, and algebra. Helpful attributes include

- Interest in scientific and technical work
- Ability to follow detailed procedures precisely

Civilian Counterparts

Civilian medical laboratory technicians usually work for privately owned laboratories, hospitals, clinics, or research institutions. They perform duties similar to military medical laboratory technicians.

Military Careers Score at the 50% (50-50) point = 196.

Medical Record Technicians

Army

Navy

Air Force

Coast Guard

Typical Tasks

- Fill out admission and discharge records for patients entering and leaving military hospitals
- Assign patients to hospital rooms
- Prepare daily reports about patients admitted and discharged
- Organize, file, and maintain medical records
- Type reports about physical examinations, illnesses, and treatments
- Prepare tables of medical statistics
- Maintain a library of medical publications

Qualifications

Helpful Attributes

Helpful school subjects include general science and business administration. Helpful attributes include

- Interest in work requiring accuracy and attention to detail
- Ability to communicate well
- Interest in using typewriters and other office machines

Civilian Counterparts

Civilian medical record technicians usually work for hospitals, clinics, and government health agencies. They perform duties similar to military medical record technicians. However, civilian medical record technicians tend to specialize in areas such as admissions ward or outpatient records. Those working in admission or discharge units are called admitting or discharge clerks.

Military Careers Score at the 50% (50-50) point = 197.

Medical Service Technicians

Army

Navy

Air Force

Coast Guard

Typical Tasks

- Examine and treat emergency patients
- Interview patients and record their medical histories
- Take patient temperature, pulse, and blood pressure
- Prepare blood samples for laboratory analysis
- Keep health records and clinical files up to date
- Give shots and medicines to patients

Qualifications

Physical Demands

Medical service technicians may have to lift and carry wounded or injured personnel during emergency situations. Air medical evacuation specialists must pass a special physical exam.

Helpful Attributes

Helpful school subjects include chemistry, biology, psychology, general science, and algebra. Helpful attributes include

- Interest in helping and caring for others
- Ability to communicate effectively
- Ability to work under stressful conditions

Civilian Counterparts

Civilian medical service technicians work in hospitals, clinics, nursing homes, and rehabilitation centers. They perform duties similar to those performed by medical service technicians in the military. Civilian medical service technicians are known for the type of work they do: medical technicians treat victims of accidents, fire, or heart attacks; medical assistants work for physicians and perform routine medical and clerical tasks; medication aides give shots and medicine under the close supervision of physicians; and physician assistants perform routine examinations and treatment for physicians.

Military Careers Score at the 50% (50-50) point = 197.

Nursing Technicians

Army

Navy

Air Force

Typical Tasks

- Provide bedside care in hospitals, including taking the temperature, pulse, and respiration rate of patients
- Serve food and feed patients requiring help
- Bathe and dress patients
- Change bed linens and clean hospital rooms
- Observe patients and inform nurses or doctors if problems develop
- Give medication to patients, under the direction of doctors and nurses

- Drive ambulances and assist doctors and nurses in providing emergency treatment

Qualifications

Physical Demands

Nursing technicians may have to lift and support patients. Air medical evacuation specialists must pass a flight physical exam.

Helpful Attributes

Helpful school subjects include general science, biology, and psychology. Helpful attributes include

- Desire to help others
- Interest in working in the health field
- Ability to follow directions precisely

Civilian Counterparts

Civilian nursing technicians work in hospitals, nursing homes, rehabilitation centers, psychiatric hospitals, or doctors' offices. Their work is similar to duties performed in the military. Those with less than a year of formal training may be called nurses' aides, orderlies, or psychiatric aides. Those who have completed practical nurse training are called practical nurses or licensed practical nurses.

Military Careers Score at the 50% (50-50) point = 196.

Occupational Therapy Specialists

Army

Navy

Air Force

Coast Guard

Typical Tasks

- Interview patients to determine the extent of problems
- Test patients to determine physical and mental abilities
- Assist occupational therapists to plan exercise schedules
- Schedule patients for treatment
- Fit and adjust artificial limbs (prostheses)
- Teach patients new mobility skills
- Set up and maintain equipment, such as exercise machines and whirlpools

Qualifications

Physical Demands

Occupational therapy specialists must sometimes lift and support patients during exercises and treatments.

Helpful Attributes

Helpful school subjects include general science, biology, and psychology. Helpful attributes include

- Interest in working with and helping people
- Patience to work with long-term disabilities
- Ability to communicate effectively

Civilian Counterparts

Civilian occupational therapy specialists work for hospitals, schools, rehabilitation centers, and community mental health centers. They perform duties similar to military occupational therapy specialists. Civilian occupational therapy specialists tend to specialize in the type of patients they serve, such as children, persons who have lost arms or legs (amputees), or the elderly. They may also be called occupational therapy assistants or occupational therapy aides.

Military Careers Score at the 50% (50-50) point = 196.

Operating Room Technicians

Army

Navy

Air Force

Coast Guard

Typical Tasks

- Prepare patients for surgery
- Clean and disinfect operating rooms
- Sterilize instruments
- Prepare surgical supplies and equipment
- Keep count of sponges, needles, and instruments used in surgery
- Pass sterile instruments and supplies to surgeons

Qualifications

Physical Demands

Operating room technicians need sufficient strength to lift and move patients while preparing them for surgery. They must have a normal skin condition to guard against infection.

Helpful Attributes

Helpful school subjects include general science, biology, chemistry, hygiene, and psychology. Helpful attributes include

- Interest in helping others
- Ability to follow spoken instructions
- Ability to work under stressful or emergency conditions

Civilian Counterparts

Civilian operating room technicians work in hospitals, surgical clinics, and emergency medical clinics. Their duties are similar to those performed in the military.

Military Careers Score at the 50% (50-50) point = 196.

Optometric Technicians

Army

Navy

Air Force

Typical Tasks

- Perform screening tests of patients' vision and record results
- Order eyeglasses and contact lenses from prescriptions
- Measure patients for eyeglass frames
- Fit eyeglasses to patients
- Make minor repairs to glasses
- Place eyedrops and ointment into patients' eyes
- Keep records in optometry offices

Qualifications

Helpful Attributes

Helpful school subjects include algebra, geometry, biology, and related courses. Helpful attributes include

- Interest in helping people
- Interest in work requiring accuracy and attention to detail
- Ability to communicate effectively

Civilian Counterparts

Civilian optometric technicians work in private optometry offices, clinics, and government health agencies. They perform duties similar to those performed by military optometric technicians. Optometric technicians are also called optometric assistants.

Military Careers Score at the 50% (50-50) point = 196.

Orthopedic Technicians

Army

Navy

Air Force

Typical Tasks

- Make and apply plaster casts for broken arms and legs
- Construct splints for setting broken bones
- Assemble and adjust traction devices
- Prepare patients for orthopedic surgery
- Assist surgeons during surgery
- Remove casts

Qualifications

Physical Demands

Orthopedic technicians may have to lift and support patients for brief periods.

Helpful Attributes

Helpful school subjects are general science and biology. Helpful attributes include

- Interest in helping others
- Ability to follow instructions precisely
- Ability to work skillfully with the hands

Civilian Counterparts

Civilian orthopedic technicians work in hospitals and clinics. Their work is similar to the work of military orthopedic technicians. They are also known as orthopedic physician assistants or orthopedic assistants.

Military Careers Score at the 50% (50-50) point = 197.

Orthotic Specialists

Army

Navy

Air Force

Typical Tasks

- Design orthotic devices as requested by physicians
- Make plaster casts for injured arms or legs
- Prepare blueprints for parts of braces and supports
- Operate lathes and grinders to make parts from plastic or steel
- Adjust devices to fit patients

Qualifications

Helpful Attributes

Helpful school subjects include biology, shop mechanics, and drafting. Helpful attributes include

- Ability to use hand and power tools
- Interest in work requiring accuracy and attention to detail
- Sensitivity to the needs of others

Civilian Counterparts

Civilian orthotic specialists work in private laboratories. They perform duties similar to those of military orthotic specialists. Civilian orthotic technicians often specialize. Those that fabricate parts using hand and power tools are called orthotic technicians. Those who make casts of body parts and repair or adjust orthotic devices are called orthotic assistants. Those that design orthotic devices and fit them to patients are called orthotists.

Military Careers Score at the 50% (50-50) point = 199.

Pharmacy Technicians

Army

Navy

Air Force

Coast Guard

Typical Tasks

- Read doctor's prescriptions to determine the type and amount of drugs to prepare
- Weigh and measure drugs and chemicals
- Mix ingredients in order to produce prescription medications
- Prepare labels for prescriptions
- Dispense medications to patients
- Keep records of drugs used
- Store shipments and drugs and medications

Qualifications

Physical Demands

Normal color vision is required as is the ability to speak clearly. Some specialties may involve heavy lifting.

Helpful Attributes

Helpful school subjects include algebra, chemistry, biology, physiology, anatomy, and typing. Helpful attributes include

- Interest in body chemistry
- Ability to work using precise measurements and standards
- Ability to follow strict procedures and directions

Civilian Counterparts

Civilian pharmacy technicians work in pharmacies, drug stores, hospitals, and clinics under the direction of pharmacists. They are usually known as pharmacy helpers and generally are not responsible for compounding and dispensing of drugs. They perform simple tasks, such as storing supplies, cleaning equipment, and delivering prescriptions. While military pharmacy technicians generally have more job responsibilities than civilian pharmacy helpers, they do not have the qualifications needed to become civilian pharmacists. Pharmacists must complete a college pharmacy degree program, pass a state board exam, and serve in a pharmacy internship.

Military Careers Score at the 50% (50-50) point = 197.

Physical Therapy Specialists

Army

Navy

Air Force

Coast Guard

Typical Tasks

- Assist physical therapists to plan therapy programs for patients
- Give patients massages and heat treatments
- Help patients to improve their mobility through special exercises
- Teach patients to use artificial limbs, braces, and other such devices
- Care for therapy equipment, such as exercise machines and whirlpools
- Keep records and reports of patients' care and progress

Qualifications

Physical Demands

Physical therapy specialists may have to lift and support patients during exercises and treatment.

Helpful Attributes

Helpful school subjects include biology and physical science. Helpful attributes include

- Interest in working with people
- Patience in working with people whose injuries heal slowly
- Ability to communicate ideas effectively

Civilian Counterparts

Civilian physical therapy specialists work for hospitals, nursing homes, and rehabilitation clinics. They perform duties similar to military physical therapy specialists. Civilian physical therapy specialists usually specialize in the type of patient they work with, such as children, the severely disabled, or the elderly.

Military Careers Score at the 50% (50-50) point = 197.

Radiologic (X-ray) Technicians

Army

Navy

Air Force

Coast Guard

Typical Tasks

- Read requests or instructions from doctors to determine each patient's X-ray needs
- Position patients under radiologic equipment
- Adjust X-ray equipment to the correct time and power of exposure
- Process X-ray pictures
- Prepare and administer radioactive solutions to patients
- Keep records of patient treatment

Qualifications

Helpful Attributes

Helpful school subjects include algebra, biology, and other science courses. Helpful attributes include

- Interest in activities requiring accuracy and attention to detail
- Ability to follow strict standards and procedures
- Interest in helping others

Civilian Counterparts

Civilian radiologic technicians work in hospitals, diagnostic clinics, and medical laboratories. They perform duties similar to military radiologic technicians. They may specialize in various areas of radiology and may be called X-ray technologists or nuclear medicine technologists.

Military Careers Score at the 50% (50-50) point = 196.

Respiratory Therapists

Army

Navy

Air Force

Typical Tasks

- Assist in reviving patients who are no longer breathing or whose hearts have stopped
- Operate and monitor respiratory therapy equipment during treatment
- Observe and record patients' responses to respiratory therapy
- Clean, sterilize, and maintain respiratory therapy equipment
- Instruct patients in breathing exercises to help clear lungs of fluids
- Instruct patients on how to operate home respiratory therapy equipment

Qualifications

Physical Demands

Respiratory therapists may have to lift and position patients for treatments.

Helpful Attributes

Helpful school subjects include general science, chemistry, and biology. Helpful attributes include

- Ability to deal with stressful situations
- Ability to respond quickly to emergencies
- Interest in helping others

Civilian Counterparts

Civilian respiratory therapists work in hospitals and clinics and for ambulance services. Their duties are similar to those of military respiratory therapists. Civilian respiratory therapists may be called inhalation therapists or pulmonary therapists.

Military Careers Score at the 50% (50-50) point = 197.

➤ ENGINEERING, SCIENCE, AND TECHNICAL OCCUPATIONS

Air Traffic Controllers

Army

Navy

Air Force

Marine Corps

Typical Tasks

- Operate radio equipment to issue takeoff, flight, and landing instructions to pilots
- Relay weather reports, airfield conditions, and safety information to pilots
- Use radar equipment to track aircraft in flight
- Plot airplane locations on charts and maps
- Compute speed, direction, and altitude of aircraft
- Maintain air traffic control records and communication logs

Qualifications

Physical Demands

Normal color vision, normal hearing, and a clear speaking voice are required to enter this occupation. Controllers must pass a special physical exam.

Helpful Attributes

Helpful school subjects include English, general mathematics, and typing. Helpful attributes include

- Ability to work under stress
- Skill in math computation
- Ability to make quick, decisive judgments
- Ability to remain alert while performing repetitive tasks

Civilian Counterparts

Civilian air traffic controllers work for the FAA in airports and control centers around the country. They perform duties similar to military air traffic controllers. They may specialize in specific areas, such as aircraft arrivals, departures, ground control, or enroute flights.

Military Careers Score at the 50% (50-50) point = 196.

Broadcast and Recording Technicians

Army

Air Force

Marine Corps

Typical Tasks

- Set up and adjust microphones and tape recorders
- Monitor the level and quality of sound during broadcasts
- Record sound effects and background music for film, radio, and television
- Operate sound mixing boards to control the sound levels from several microphones
- Set up and operate public address systems

Qualifications

Helpful Attributes

Helpful school subjects include audiovisual communications, drama, speech, and photography. Helpful attributes include

- Interest in working with audiovisual equipment
- Ability to work well as a member of a team

Civilian Counterparts

Civilian broadcast and recording technicians work for television and radio studios, motion picture studios, and other media centers. Their work is similar to work in the military. Civilian technicians tend to specialize in particular fields, such as radio, television, motion pictures, or advertising. They may be called sound mixers, recording engineers, or sound cutters.

Military Careers Score at the 50% (50-50) point = 197.

Computer Programmers

Army

Navy

Air Force

Marine Corps

Typical Tasks

- Organize and arrange computer programs into logical steps that direct computers to solve problems
- Draw diagrams and charts illustrating the steps in programs
- Code programs into languages that computers can read
- Test or debug computer programs to see that the desired information is produced
- Prepare detailed instruction sheets for computer operators who run programs
- Review and update old programs as new information is received or changes are needed

Qualifications

Helpful Attributes

Helpful school subjects include math, business administration, and computer science. Helpful attributes include

- Ability to understand math concepts
- Interest in solving problems using rules of logic
- Interest in computers

Civilian Counterparts

Civilian computer programmers work for such organizations as manufacturing firms, banks, data processing organizations, government agencies, and insurance companies. These employers handle large amounts of information that programmers use. Ci-

vilian computer programmers perform duties similar to those in the military.

Military Careers Score at the 50% (50-50) point = 202.

Computer Systems Analysts

Army

Navy

Air Force

Marine Corps

Typical Tasks

- Assist military units to determine their data processing needs
- Develop systems plans, including input, output, and processing steps, and information storage and access methods
- Develop flow charts, documentation, and block diagrams of systems for use by programmers
- Help programmers program, test, and debug computer software
- Make systems secure from unofficial access

Qualifications

Helpful Attributes

Helpful school subjects include geometry, algebra, and computer science. Helpful attributes include

- Ability to solve abstract problems
- Ability to communicate effectively
- Preference for work requiring attention to detail

Civilian Counterparts

Civilians in this field work for a wide variety of employers such as banks, insurance companies, hospitals, large retailers, research firms, manufacturers, and government agencies. Their work is similar to work in the military. They are called programmer/analysts, systems analysts, and systems programmers. Most civilian computer systems analyst jobs require a four-year college degree.

Military Careers Score at the 50% (50-50) point = 201.

Drafters

Army

Navy

Air Force

Coast Guard

Typical Tasks

- Make scale drawings of roads, airfields, buildings, and other military projects from engineers' instructions and sketches
- Draw diagrams for wiring and plumbing
- Identify concrete, lumber, and other materials needed to construct projects
- Compute the cost of materials
- Work with engineers and construction supervisors to change drawings when needed

Qualifications

Special Qualifications

Courses in algebra and geometry are required to enter some specialties in this occupation.

Helpful Attributes

Helpful school subjects include drafting, algebra, and geometry. Helpful attributes include

- Interest in working with drafting equipment
- Ability to print and draw neatly
- Ability to convert ideas into drawings

Civilian Counterparts

Civilian drafters usually work for architectural or engineering firms, government agencies, mining firms, and manufacturing industries. Civilian drafters perform duties similar to military drafters. They usually specialize in a particular type of drafting such as mechanical, electrical, aeronautical, structural, or architectural drafting.

Military Careers Score at the 50% (50-50) point = 196.

Emergency Management Specialists

Army

Navy

Air Force

Marine Corps

Coast Guard

Typical Tasks

- Assist in preparing and maintaining disaster operations plans
- Train military and civilian personnel on what to do in an emergency
- Operate and maintain nuclear, biological, and chemical detection and decontamination equipment
- Conduct surveys to determine needs in the event of an emergency
- Monitor disaster preparedness activities and training operations

Qualifications

Physical Demands

Normal color vision is needed to identify chemical agents.

Helpful Attributes

Helpful school subjects include algebra, chemistry, physics, geometry, and trigonometry. Helpful attributes include
- Ability to communicate effectively
- Ability to plan and organize
- Ability to work calmly under stress

Civilian Counterparts

Civilian emergency management specialists work for federal, state, and local governments including law enforcement and civil defense agencies. They perform duties similar to military emergency management specialists.

Military Careers Score at the 50% (50-50) point = 207.

Environmental Health Specialists

Army

Navy

Air Force

Marine Corps

Coast Guard

Typical Tasks

- Inspect food service, storage, and dining facilities
- Inspect foods for quality and freshness
- Inspect water and waste disposal facilities
- Conduct health and sanitation surveys of living quarters and buildings
- Plan the disposal of radioactive and toxic wastes
- Prepare health inspection reports
- Give hearing exams and monitor noise levels at job sites

Qualifications

Physical Demands

Normal color vision is required to inspect foods for quality and freshness.

Helpful Attributes

Helpful school subjects include algebra, biology, chemistry, and general science. Helpful attributes include
- Interest in gathering information
- Preference for work requiring attention to detail
- Interest in protecting the environment

Civilian Counterparts

Most civilian environmental health specialists work for local, state, and federal government agencies. Their duties are similar to the duties of military environmental health specialists. They may be called food and drug inspectors or public health inspectors.

Military Careers Score at the 50% (50-50) point = 197.

Fuel and Chemical Laboratory Technicians

Army

Navy

Air Force

Coast Guard

Typical Tasks

- Obtain petroleum test samples from storage tanks, barges, and tankers
- Test fuels and oils for water and other contaminants using laboratory equipment
- Analyze chemicals for strength, purity, and toxic qualities

- Perform chemical and physical tests on clothing, food, paints, and plastics
- Keep detailed laboratory records and files

Qualifications

Physical Demands

Normal color vision is required to perform chemical tests. Some specialties may require moderate to heavy lifting.

Helpful Attributes

Helpful school subjects include chemistry and mathematics. Helpful attributes include
- Interest in performing technical work
- Interest in working with chemicals and lab equipment
- Ability to follow detailed procedures

Civilian Counterparts

Civilian laboratory technicians work for petroleum refineries, chemical companies, manufacturing firms, and government agencies. They perform duties similar to military laboratory technicians. Civilian laboratory technicians specialize in particular industries such as petroleum, food processing, or medical drugs. They may be called chemical laboratory technicians or laboratory testers.

Military Careers Score at the 50% (50-50) point = 196.

Intelligence Specialists

Army

Navy

Air Force

Marine Corps

Coast Guard

Typical Tasks

- Study aerial photographs of foreign ships, bases, and missile sites
- Study foreign troop movements
- Operate sensitive radios to intercept foreign military communications
- Study land and sea areas that could become battlegrounds in time of war
- Store and retrieve intelligence data using computers
- Study foreign military codes
- Prepare intelligence reports, maps, and charts

Qualifications

Helpful Attributes

Helpful school subjects include typing, algebra, geometry, trigonometry, and geography. Helpful attributes include
- Interest in reading maps, charts, and aerial photograph
- Interest in gathering information and studying its meaning
- Ability to organize information
- Ability to think and write clearly

Civilian Counterparts

Civilian intelligence specialists generally work for federal government agencies, such as the Central Intelligence Agency or the National Security Agency. Their duties are similar to those performed by military intelligence specialists. The analytical skills of intelligence specialists are also useful in other fields, such as research or business planning.

Military Careers Score at the 50% (50-50) point = 205.

Legal Technicians

Army

Navy

Air Force

Marine Corps

Typical Tasks

- Research court decisions and military regulations
- Process legal claims, appeals, and summonses to appear in court
- Interview clients and take statements
- Prepare trial requests and make arrangements for courtrooms
- Maintain law libraries and trial case files
- Type claims, trial reports, pretrial agreements, and other legal documents
- Prepare military punishment and discharge orders

Qualifications

Some specialties require the ability to type at a rate of fifty words per minute.

Physical Demands

A clear speaking ability is necessary to interview clients.

Helpful Attributes

Helpful school subjects include business mathematics, typing, speech, and shorthand. Helpful attributes include
- Interest in office work
- Ability to use library card catalogs
- Interest in the law

Civilian Counterparts

Civilian legal technicians work for private law firms, banks, insurance companies, manufacturing firms, and government agencies. They perform duties similar to military legal technicians. Civilian legal technicians may also be called legal assistants, paralegal assistants, or legal clerks.

Military Careers Score at the 50% (50-50) point = 203.

Non-Destructive Testers

Navy

Air Force

Typical Tasks

- Inspect metal parts and joints for wear and damage
- Take X-rays of aircraft and ship parts
- Examine X-ray film to detect cracks and flaws in metal parts and welds
- Operate ultrasonic, atomic absorption and other kinds of test equipment
- Conduct oil analysis and heat damage tests in order to detect engine wear
- Prepare inspection reports work

Qualifications

Physical Demands

Normal color vision is required to read color-coded diagrams.

Helpful Attributes

Helpful school subjects include math and metal shop. Helpful attributes include
- Thoroughness and dependability
- Interest in operating test equipment
- Interest in machines and how they work

Civilian Counterparts

Civilian nondestructive testers work for commercial testing laboratories, airlines, aircraft maintenance companies, and industrial plants. They perform duties similar to military nondestructive testers and may be called radiographers.

Military Careers Score at the 50% (50-50) point = 200.

Radar and Sonar Operators

Army

Navy

Air Force

Marine Corps

Coast Guard

Typical Tasks

- Detect and track position, direction, and speed of aircraft, ships, submarines, and missiles
- Plot and record data on status charts and plotting boards
- Set up and operate radar equipment to direct artillery fire
- Monitor early warning air defense systems
- Send and receive messages using radios and electronic communication systems

Qualifications

Special Qualifications

Although there are women radar and sonar operators, some specialties in this occupation are only open to men.

Physical Demands

Specialties involving flying require passing a special physical exam.

Helpful Attributes

Helpful school subjects include geometry, algebra, and science. Helpful attributes include

- Ability to concentrate for long periods
- Interest in working with electronic equipment

Civilian Counterparts

There are no direct Civilian Counterparts to military radar and sonar operators. However, workers in several civilian occupations use radar and sonar equipment in their jobs including weather service technicians, air traffic controllers, ship navigators, and ocean salvage specialists.

Military Careers Score at the 50% (50-50) point = 195.

Radio Intelligence Operators

Army

Navy

Air Force

Marine Corps

Typical Tasks

- Record radio signals coming from foreign ships, planes, and land forces
- Study radio signals to understand the tactics used by foreign military forces
- Tune radios to certain frequencies and adjust for clear reception
- Locate the source of foreign radio signals using electronic direction finding equipment
- Translate Morse code signals into words and type them for review by superiors
- Keep logs of signal interceptions

Qualifications

Physical Demands

Radio intelligence operators may have to sit for long periods and listen to radio transmissions.

Helpful Attributes

Helpful school subjects include math, speech, typing, and foreign languages. Helpful attributes include

- Interest in working with radio equipment
- Interest in finding clues that help answer questions
- Ability to remain alert while doing repetitive tasks
- A long attention span

Civilian Counterparts

Civilian radio intelligence operators work for government agencies like the National Security Agency, the FBI, and the Central Intelligence Agency. They also work in related jobs for private electronics and communications companies. They perform duties similar to military radio intelligence operators and may also be called electronic intelligence operations specialists.

Military Careers Score at the 50% (50-50) point = 197.

Radio Operators

Army

Navy

Air Force

Marine Corps

Coast Guard

Typical Tasks

- Transmit, receive, and log radio messages according to military procedures
- Encode and decode classified messages
- Set up and tune field radio equipment
- Monitor emergency frequencies for distress calls
- Maintain radio and teletype equipment

Qualifications

Physical Demands

Normal color vision, normal hearing, and the ability to speak clearly and distinctly are required to enter this occupation.

Helpful Attributes

Helpful school subjects include typing, English, and speech. Helpful attributes include

- Interest in working with radio equipment
- Interest in learning secret codes

Civilian Counterparts

Civilian radio operators work in airports, harbors, police stations, fire stations, and aboard ships. Their duties are similar to those assigned to military radio operators, although civilian radio operators do not usually work in field units. They may be called airline radio operators, radio officers, or radiotelephone operators, depending on their specialty.

Military Careers Score at the 50% (50-50) point = 193.

Space Systems Specialists

Navy

Air Force

Typical Tasks

- Transmit and verify spacecraft commands using aerospace-ground equipment
- Monitor computers and telemetry display systems

- Analyze data to determine spacecraft operational status
- Repair ground and spacecraft communication equipment
- Assist in preparing spacecraft commands to meet mission objectives
- Operate data handling equipment to track spacecraft

Qualifications

Physical Demands

Normal color vision is required to enter this occupation.

Helpful Attributes

Helpful school subjects include physics, geometry, algebra, and trigonometry. Helpful attributes include

- Interest in operating electronic equipment and systems
- Interest in working as part of a team
- Ability to work with formulas to solve math problems
- Interest in space exploration

Civilian Counterparts

Civilian space systems specialists work for the National Aeronautics and Space Administration (NASA), the U.S. Weather Service, and private satellite communications firms. They perform duties similar to military space systems specialists.

Military Careers Score at the 50% (50-50) point = 198.

Surveying and Mapping Technicians

Army

Navy

Air Force

Marine Corps

Coast Guard

Typical Tasks

- Draw maps and charts using drafting tools such as easels, templates, and compasses
- Understand and use survey measurements
- Compute survey results using mathematical formulas
- Draw land elevations, distances between points, and locations of landmarks on maps
- Build scale models of land areas out of wood, clay, and paper, showing hills, lakes, roads, and buildings
- Piece together aerial photographs of airfields, harbors, and other military sites to form large photomaps

Qualifications

Physical Demands

Good depth perception is required to study aerial photos through stereoscopes.

Helpful Attributes

Helpful school subjects include algebra, geometry, and trigonometry. Helpful attributes include

- Ability to convert ideas into working drawings
- Interest in maps and charts

Civilian Counterparts

Civilian surveying and mapping technicians work for construction, engineering, and architectural firms and government agencies such as the highway department. Their work is used for planning construction projects such as highways, airport runways, dams, and drainage systems. Surveyors and mapmakers are also called cartographers, cartographic technicians, and photogrammetrists.

Military Careers Score at the 50% (50-50) point = 197.

Weather Observers

Army

Navy

Air Force

Marine Corps

Coast Guard

Typical Tasks

- Launch weather balloons to record wind speed and direction
- Identify the types of clouds present and estimate cloud height and television amount of cloud cover
- Take readings of barometric pressure, temperature, humidity, and sea conditions
- Operate radio equipment to receive information from satellites
- Plot weather information on maps and charts
- Forecast weather based on readings and observations

Qualifications

Physical Demands

Normal color vision is required to use color-coded maps and weather charts. Some specialties may involve lifting of heavy weather instruments.

Helpful Attributes

Helpful school subjects include geography, mathematics, and physical science. Helpful attributes include

- Interest in working with formulas, tables, and graphs
- Ability to communicate clearly
- Interest in learning how weather changes
- Interest in gathering and organizing information

Civilian Counterparts

Civilian weather observers work for government agencies (such as the U.S. Weather Service), commercial airlines, radio and television stations, and private weather forecasting firms. They perform duties similar to military weather observers. Civilian weather observers may also be called oceanographer assistants and weather clerks.

Military Careers Score at the 50% (50-50) point = 198.

➤ ADMINISTRATIVE OCCUPATIONS

Accounting Specialists

Army

Navy

Air Force

Marine Corps

Coast Guard

Typical Tasks

- Record details of financial transactions on accounting forms
- Prepare forms for putting payment information into computers
- Audit financial records
- Prepare bills for payment
- Compute cost information on supplies and equipment
- Organize information on past expenses to help plan budgets for future expenses

Qualifications

Special Qualifications

Depending on specialty, entry into this occupation may require courses in mathematics, bookkeeping, or accounting.

Helpful Attributes

Helpful school subjects include mathematics, statistics, business machines, bookkeeping, accounting, and typing. Helpful attributes include

- Ability to work with numbers
- Interest in operating office machines, such as computers, calculators, and bookkeeping machines
- Interest in work requiring accuracy and attention to detail

Civilian Counterparts

Civilian accounting specialists work for all types of businesses and government agencies. They perform duties similar to military accounting specialists. Civilian accounting specialists are also called bookkeepers, accounting clerks, audit clerks, cost clerks, budget clerks, or statistical clerks.

Military Careers Score at the 50% (50-50) point = 203.

Administrative Support Specialists

Army

Navy

Air Force

Marine Corps

Coast Guard

Typical Tasks

- Type letters, reports, requisition (order) forms, and official orders using computer word processing software
- Proofread written material for spelling, punctuation, and grammatical errors
- Organize and maintain files and publications
- Order office supplies
- Greet and direct office visitors
- Sort and deliver mail to office workers
- Schedule training and leave for unit personnel
- Answer phones and provide general information
- Take dictation and make notes of meetings using shorthand or stenotype machines

Qualifications

Helpful Attributes

Helpful school subjects include English, math, shorthand, and typing. Helpful attributes include

- Interest in keeping organized and accurate records
- Preference for office work
- Interest in operating typewriters, word processors, and other office machines
- Ability to organize and plan

Civilian Counterparts

Civilian administrative support specialists work in most businesses, government, and legal offices. They perform duties similar to military administrative support specialists and are called clerk typists, secretaries, general office clerks, administrative assistants, or office managers.

Military Careers Score at the 50% (50-50) point = 197.

Computer Operators

Army

Navy

Air Force

Marine Corps

Coast Guard

Typical Tasks

- Operate computers by entering commands through consoles
- Operate and maintain high speed printers
- Monitor operations and locate causes of problems that occur
- Schedule the flow of jobs with programmers
- Operate specialized computers that calculate position, target weapons, and operate machinery

Qualifications

Helpful Attributes

Helpful school subjects include general math and computer science. Helpful attributes include

- Interest in working with computers
- Ability to follow detailed instructions
- Ability to work quickly and accurately

Civilian Counterparts

Computer operators work for government agencies, computer firms, and all types of businesses. They perform duties similar to military computer operators.

Military Careers Score at the 50% (50-50) point = 194.

Court Reporters

Navy

Air Force

Marine Corps

Coast Guard

Typical Tasks

- Type text from stenotyped records, short hand notes, or taped records of court proceedings
- Prepare records of hearings, investigations, courts-martial, and courts of inquiry
- Prepare legal forms and documents
- Process incoming and outgoing correspondence and maintain legal files
- Maintain the legal calendar, law library, and reference file of pending cases

Qualifications

Physical Demands

Good hearing and clear speech are required to record and read aloud court proceedings.

Special Qualifications

The ability to type at forty words per minute is required to enter some specialties in this occupation.

Helpful Attributes

Helpful school subjects include English, business math, typing, and commercial law. Helpful attributes include

- A good memory
- Ability to listen carefully
- Ability to keep accurate records
- Interest in legal proceedings

Civilian Counterparts

Civilian court reporters often work for government agencies, law firms, or local, state, and federal courts and legislatures. They may be called court clerks or court recorders. They perform duties similar to military court reporters.

Military Careers Score at the 50% (50-50) point = 197.

Dispatchers

Army

Navy

Air Force

Marine Corps

Typical Tasks

- Schedule the use of motor vehicles
- Assign drivers for trucks, buses, and cars
- Determine which vehicles to use based on freight or passenger movement requirements
- Schedule repair and maintenance of vehicles
- Determine transportation routes
- Review requests for using vehicles
- Prepare reports about fuel used, miles driven, and number of vehicles needing repair

Qualifications

Physical Demands

The ability to speak clearly and distinctly is required to enter some specialties in this occupation.

Helpful Attributes

Helpful school subjects include general math, driver's education, and auto mechanics. Helpful attributes include

- Interest in planning and scheduling
- Preference for working with figures

Civilian Counterparts

Civilian dispatchers work for bus lines, trucking firms, police departments, auto repair garages, taxi companies, and motor vehicle dealerships. They perform duties similar to military dispatchers. They usually specialize in either dispatching passenger carriers or freight transports.

Military Careers Score at the 50% (50-50) point = 189.

Flight Operations Specialists

Army

Navy

Air Force

Marine Corps

Coast Guard

Typical Tasks

- Help plan flight schedules and air-crew assignments
- Keep flight logs on incoming and outgoing flights
- Keep aircrew flying records and flight operations records
- Receive and post weather information and flight plan data, such as air routes and arrival and departure times
- Coordinate aircrew needs, such as ground transportation
- Plan aircraft equipment needs for air evacuation and dangerous cargo flights
- Check military flight plans with civilian agencies

Qualifications

Physical Demands

The ability to speak clearly and distinctly is required.

Helpful Attributes

Helpful school subjects include general math and typing. Helpful attributes include

- Interest in work involving computers
- Ability to use typewriters and office machines
- Interest in work that helps others
- Ability to keep accurate records

Civilian Counterparts

Civilian flight operations specialists work for commercial and private airlines and air transport companies. They perform duties similar to military flight operations specialists.

Military Careers Score at the 50% (50-50) point = 196.

Lodging Specialists

Army

Navy

Air Force

Coast Guard

Typical Tasks

- Register personnel and assign them rooms
- Issue courtesy items, such as alarm clocks and towels
- Receive payments and keep financial records
- Operate switchboards to relay calls and provide information to callers
- Keep accurate records on room occupancy
- Arrange hotel accommodations when lodging on base is not available

Qualifications

Physical Demands

Lodging specialists need to have clear speech in order to communicate with guests.

Helpful Attributes

Helpful school subjects include math and bookkeeping. Helpful attributes include

- Interest in meeting and serving people
- Ability to work independently
- Ability to communicate effectively

Civilian Counterparts

Civilian lodging specialists work for hotels or motels. They perform many of the same tasks as military lodging specialists; however, they may specialize as registration clerks, bookkeepers, cashiers, or telephone operators.

Military Careers Score at the 50% (50-50) point = 196.

Maintenance Data Analysts

Army

Navy

Air Force

Marine Corps

Coast Guard

Typical Tasks

- Review maintenance schedules and notify mechanics about the types of service needed

- Compare schedules to records of maintenance work actually performed
- Prepare charts and reports on maintenance activities
- Calculate how many mechanics and spare parts are needed to maintain equipment
- Operate computers and calculators to enter or retrieve maintenance data

Qualifications

Physical Demands

Normal color vision is required to read and interpret maintenance charts and graphs in some specialties. Some specialties require the ability to speak clearly.

Helpful Attributes

Helpful school subjects include general math and algebra. Helpful attributes include

- Interest in working with numbers and statistics
- Preference for work requiring attention to detail
- Ability to use mathematical formulas
- Interest in working with computers

Civilian Counterparts

Civilian maintenance data analysts work for government agencies, airlines, and large transportation firms. They also work for firms with large numbers of machines. They perform duties similar to military maintenance data analysts.

Military Careers Score at the 50% (50-50) point = 197.

Payroll Specialists

Army

Navy

Air Force

Marine Corps

Coast Guard

Typical Tasks

- Compute basic pay and allowances, bonuses, and other payments
- Compute social security, income tax, insurance, and other deductions
- Prepare pay and travel vouchers (checks), earnings and deduction statements, and financial accounts and reports
- Compute travel distances and travel pay allowances
- Prepare, maintain, and audit personnel financial records
- Disburse cash, checks, advance travel pay, and bonds

Qualifications

Helpful Attributes

Helpful school subjects include math, accounting, business machines, and typing. Helpful attributes include

- Interest in working with numbers
- Ability to use typewriters, computers, and calculators
- Preference for work requiring attention to detail

Civilian Counterparts

Civilian payroll specialists work for schools, hospitals, government agencies, and almost every kind of industry and business firm. They perform duties similar to military payroll specialists and are commonly called payroll clerks.

Military Careers Score at the 50% (50-50) point = 197.

Personnel Specialists

Army

Navy

Air Force

Marine Corps

Coast Guard

Typical Tasks

- Organize, maintain, and review personnel records
- Enter and retrieve personnel information using computer terminals
- Assign personnel to jobs
- Prepare organizational charts, write official correspondence, and prepare reports
- Provide career guidance
- Assist personnel and their families who have special needs
- Provide information about personnel programs and procedures to persons in the military

Qualifications

Helpful Attributes

Helpful school subjects include English, speech, and typing. Helpful attributes include

- Ability to follow detailed procedures and instructions
- Ability to compose clear instructions or correspondence
- Interest in working closely with others

Civilian Counterparts

Civilian personnel specialists work for all types of organizations including industrial firms, retail establishments, and government agencies. They perform duties similar to military personnel clerks. However, specific jobs vary from company to company.

Military Careers Score at the 50% (50-50) point = 198.

Postal Specialists

Army

Navy

Air Force

Marine Corps

Coast Guard

Typical Tasks

- Process mail using metering and stamp-cancelling machines
- Weigh packages, using scales, to determine postage due
- Examine packages to ensure they meet mailing standards
- Process and sort registered, certified, and insured mail
- Receive payment for and issue money orders and stamps
- Prepare postal reports and claims for lost or damaged mail

Qualifications

Physical Demands

Postal specialists may have to lift and carry heavy sacks of mail or large packages.

Helpful Attributes

Helpful school subjects include English, math, and typing. Helpful attributes include

- Courteous manner and patience
- Ability to check names and numbers with speed and accuracy
- Preference for work requiring attention to detail

ARCO ■ ASVAB

Civilian Counterparts

Civilian postal specialists work for the United States Postal Service and for private courier or express mail firms. They perform many of the same duties as military postal specialists. They are usually called postal clerks.

Military Careers Score at the 50% (50-50) point = 195.

Recruiting Specialists

Army

Navy

Air Force

Marine Corps

Coast Guard

Typical Tasks

- Interview civilians interested in military careers
- Describe military careers to groups of high school students
- Explain the purpose of the ASVAB (Armed Services Vocational Aptitude Battery) and test results to students and counselors
- Participate in local jobs fairs and career day programs
- Talk about the military to community groups
- Counsel military personnel about career opportunities and benefits

Qualifications

Helpful Attributes

Helpful school subjects include the social sciences, speech, psychology, and English. Helpful attributes include

- Interest in working with youth
- Ability to speak before groups
- Ability to work independently

Civilian Counterparts

Civilian recruiting specialists work for businesses of all kinds searching for talented people to hire. Recruiters also work for colleges, seeking to attract and enroll talented high school students.

Military Careers Score at the 50% (50-50) point = 198.

Sales and Stock Specialists

Army

Navy

Air Force

Marine Corps

Coast Guard

Typical Tasks

- Operate snackbars, laundries, and dry cleaning facilities
- Order and receive merchandise and food for retail sales
- Inspect food and merchandise for spoilage or damage
- Price and mark retail sales items using markers and stamping machines
- Stock shelves and racks for the display of products
- Count merchandise and supplies during inventories
- Record and account for money received and prepare bank deposits

Qualifications

Physical Demands

The ability to speak clearly is required. Sales and stock specialists may have to lift and carry heavy objects.

Helpful Attributes

Helpful school subjects include book-keeping, mathematics, and typing. Helpful attributes include

- Interest in marketing and sales work
- Ability to use cash registers, calculators, and adding machines
- Interest in working with people

Civilian Counterparts

Civilian sales and stock specialists work in many kinds of retail businesses, such as grocery stores and department stores. They perform duties similar to military sales and stock specialists. They may also be called sales clerks or stock clerks.

Military Careers Score at the 50% (50-50) point = 194.

Shipping and Receiving Specialists

Army

Navy

Air Force

Marine Corps

Coast Guard

Typical Tasks

- Prepare shipping papers for goods to be shipped
- Choose the kind of transport and route
- Calculate shipping costs based on the shipping rates of commercial carriers
- Pack, crate, weigh, and mark goods for shipment
- Load and unload crates using forklifts, hand trucks, and conveyers
- Inspect goods received for damage
- Check shipping papers and goods received to make sure the correct type and amount of goods were shipped

Qualifications

Physical Demands

Shipping and receiving specialists may need to lift and carry heavy crates. Normal color vision, good eyesight, and normal hearing may be required for some specialties.

Helpful Attributes

Helpful school subjects include math and typing. Helpful attributes include

- Interest in operating forklifts and conveyers
- Preference for a combination of physical and office work
- Ability to keep detailed records and operate office equipment

Civilian Counterparts

Civilian shipping and receiving specialists work in business or government warehouses and stockrooms. They perform duties similar to military shipping and receiving specialists. They may also be called shipping and receiving clerks or cargo agents.

Military Careers Score at the 50% (50-50) point = 188.

Stock and Inventory Specialists

Army

Navy

Air Force

Marine Corps

Cost Guard

Typical Tasks

- Locate and catalog stock usually using microfiche viewers
- Verify the quantity and description of stock received
- Give special handling to medicine, ammunition, and other delicate supplies
- Select the correct stock for issue
- Load, unload, and move stock using equipment, such as forklifts and hand trucks
- Keep records on incoming and outgoing stock
- Prepare storage space

Qualifications

Physical Demands

Stock and inventory specialists may have to lift and carry heavy boxes of ammunition and other supplies. Normal color vision is required for specialties that handle color-coded parts, supplies, and ammunition.

Helpful Attributes

Helpful school subjects include math, bookkeeping, accounting, business administration, and typing. Helpful attributes include

- Ability to keep accurate records
- Preference for physical work
- Interest in operating forklifts and other warehouse equipment

- Preference for work requiring attention to detail

Civilian Counterparts

Civilian stock and inventory specialists work for factories, parts departments in repair shops, department stores, and government warehouses and stockrooms. They perform duties similar to military stock and inventory specialists. Civilian stock and inventory specialists may also be called stock control clerks, parts clerks, or storekeepers.

Military Careers Score at the 50% (50-50) point = 192.

Telephone Operators

Army

Navy

Air Force

Marine Corps

Typical Tasks

- Operate different types of telephone switch boards
- Install and operate switchboards in the field
- Patch long distance calls through ex changes
- Respond rapidly to emergency calls
- Receive and deliver messages or battle commands
- Maintain switchboard equipment

Qualifications

Physical Demands

Normal color vision, hearing, and the ability to speak clearly are required. Operators must often sit for long periods.

Helpful Attributes

Helpful school subjects include speech and mathematics. Helpful attributes include

- Ability to remain calm in an emergency
- Good organizational skills
- Interest in working with switchboards
- Patience and courtesy
- Ability to follow spoken instructions

Civilian Counterparts

Civilian telephone operators work for telephone companies, police stations, telephone-answering services, and many businesses. They perform duties similar to military telephone operators but do not install equipment. Civilian operators usually specialize as central office operators, long distance operators, or directory assistance operators. They may also be called PBX operators, switchboard operators, or telephone-answering service operators.

Military Careers Score at the 50% (50-50) point = 193.

Trainers

Navy

Air Force

Marine Corps

Coast Guard

Typical Tasks

- Prepare course outlines and materials to present during training
- Select training materials, such as textbooks and films
- Teach classes and give lectures, either in person, over closed circuit TV, or on video tape
- Work with students individually when necessary
- Test and evaluate student progress

Qualifications

Physical Demands

Trainers must be able to speak clearly and distinctly.

Helpful Attributes

Helpful school subjects include public speaking. Helpful attributes include

- Interest in teaching
- Ability to communicate effectively, in writing and speaking
- Interest in counseling and promoting human relations

Civilian Counterparts

Civilian trainers work for vocational and technical schools, high schools, colleges, businesses, and government agencies. Their duties are similar to those performed by military trainers. Civilian trainers may be called teachers, instructors, or training representatives.

Military Careers Score at the 50% (50-50) point = 200.

Transportation Specialists

Army

Navy

Air Force

Marine Corps

Coast Guard

Typical Tasks

- Arrange for passenger travel via plane, bus, train, or boat
- Arrange for shipment and delivery of household goods

- Find the least expensive and most direct shipping routes for cargo
- Prepare transportation requests and shipping documents
- Check-in passengers and baggage before military transport flights
- Serve as military airplane flight attendants
- Inspect cargo for proper packing, loading, and marking

Qualifications

Helpful Attributes

Helpful school subjects include mathematics, English, and typing. Helpful attributes include

- Interest in arranging travel schedules
- Interest in using adding machines, computers, and typewriters
- Interest in serving people

Civilian Counterparts

Civilian transportation specialists work for airlines, shipping firms, and commercial freight lines. They perform duties similar to military transportation specialists. Civilian transportation specialists may also be called travel clerks, reservation clerks, or transportation agents.

Military Careers Score at the 50% (50-50) point = 195.

➤ SERVICE OCCUPATIONS

Corrections Specialists

Army

Navy

Air Force

Marine Corps

Typical Tasks

- Stand guard at gates, cellblocks, or on towers
- Search inmates and cells for contraband (illegal goods)
- Search vehicles entering and leaving correctional facilities
- Participate in informal counseling sessions with inmates
- Investigate prisoner disturbances
- Inspect facilities to see if they are clean and safe
- Perform fire and riot control duties

Qualifications

Special Qualifications

Some specialties have minimum age and height requirements.

Helpful Attributes

- Interest in safeguarding and caring for others
- Ability to remain calm under pressure

Civilian Counterparts

Civilian corrections specialists work in city and county jails, federal and state prisons, reformatories, and other correctional facilities. They perform duties similar to military corrections specialists. They may be called guards, corrections officers, or deputy guards.

Military Careers Score at the 50% (50-50) point = 188.

Detectives

Army

Navy

Air Force

Marine Corps

Coast Guard

Typical Tasks

- Investigate crimes against the U.S. (espionage and treason) and against government property (sabotage)
- Help special agents investigate possible terrorist activities
- Investigate criminal activities (theft, assault, drug selling)
- Interview witnesses and question suspects, sometimes using polygraph (lie detector) machines
- Help with ballistic (bullet movement) and forensic (police lab) studies for clues
- Testify at trials

Qualifications

Physical Demands

Normal color vision is required.

Helpful Attributes

Helpful school subjects include foreign languages, chemistry, speech, and government. Helpful attributes include

- Interest in law enforcement and crime prevention
- Willingness to perform potentially dangerous work
- Interest in gathering and analyzing information

Civilian Counterparts

Civilian detectives work in federal, state, and local intelligence and law enforcement agencies. Some work as self-employed private detectives. Civilian detectives perform duties similar to military detectives. They may be called plain-clothes officers, homicide detectives, private investigators, or undercover agents.

Military Careers Score at the 50% (50-50) point = 201.

Firefighters

Army

Navy

Air Force

Marine Corps

Coast Guard

Typical Tasks

- Operate pumps, hoses, and extinguishers
- Force entry into aircraft, vehicles, and buildings in order to fight fires and rescue personnel
- Drive fire-fighting trucks and emergency rescue vehicles
- Give first aid to injured personnel
- Inspect aircraft, buildings, and equipment for fire hazards
- Teach fire protection procedures
- Repair fire fighting equipment and fill fire extinguishers

Qualifications

Physical Demands

Good vision without glasses and a clear speaking voice are required to enter some specialties in this occupation. Firefighters have to climb ladders and stairs. They must also be able to lift and carry injured personnel.

Helpful Attributes

Helpful school subjects include health and general science. Helpful attributes include

- Ability to remain calm under stress
- Willingness to risk injury to help others
- Ability to think and act decisively

Civilian Counterparts

Civilian firefighters work for city and county fire departments, other government agencies, and industrial firms. They perform duties similar to those performed by military firefighters including rescue and salvage work.

Military Careers Score at the 50% (50-50) point = 190.

Food Service Specialists

Army

Navy

Air Force

Marine Corps

Coast Guard

Typical Tasks

- Order, receive, and inspect meat, fish, fruits, and vegetables
- Prepare standard cuts of meat using cleavers, knives, and band-saws
- Cook steaks, chops, and roasts
- Bake or fry chicken, turkey, and fish
- Prepare gravies and sauces
- Bake breads, cakes, pies, and pastries
- Serve food in dining halls, hospitals, field kitchens, or aboard ship
- Clean ovens, stoves, mixers, pots, and utensils

Qualifications

Physical Demands

Food service specialists may have to lift and carry heavy containers of food-stuffs and large cooking utensils.

Helpful Attributes

Helpful school subjects include home economics, math, accounting, and chemistry. Helpful attributes include

- Interest in cooking
- Interest in working with the hands

Civilian Counterparts

Civilian food service specialists work in cafes, restaurants, and cafeterias. They also work in hotels, hospitals, manufacturing plants, schools, and other organizations that have their own dining facilities. Depending on specialty, food service specialists are called cooks, chefs, bakers, butchers, or meat cutters.

Military Careers Score at the 50% (50-50) point = 188.

Military Police

Army

Navy

Air Force

Marine Corps

Typical Tasks

- Patrol areas on foot, by car, or by boat
- Interview witnesses, victims, and suspects in the course of investigating crimes
- Collect fingerprints and other evidence
- Arrest and charge criminal suspects
- Train and walk with police dogs
- Testify in court
- Guard entrances and direct traffic

Qualifications

Physical Demands

Normal hearing and a clear speaking voice are usually required in order to enter this occupation. Some specialties have minimum height requirements.

Helpful Attributes

Helpful school subjects include government and speech. Helpful attributes include

- Interest in law enforcement and crime prevention
- Ability to remain calm in stressful situations
- Ability to think and react quickly

Civilian Counterparts

Civilian police officers generally work for state, county, or city law enforcement agencies. Some work as security guards for industrial firms, airports, and other businesses and institutions. They perform duties similar to military police.

Military Careers Score at the 50% (50-50) point = 202.

➤ VEHICLE AND MACHINERY MECHANIC OCCUPATIONS

Aircraft Mechanics

Army

Navy

Air Force

Marine Corps

Coast Guard

Typical Tasks

- Service and repair helicopter, jet, and propeller aircraft engines
- Inspect and repair aircraft wings, fuselages (bodies), and tail assemblies
- Service and repair aircraft landing gear
- Repair or replace starters, lights, batteries, wiring, and other electrical parts

Qualifications

Physical Demands

Some specialties require moderate to heavy lifting. Normal color vision is required to work with color-coded wiring.

Helpful Attributes

Helpful school subjects include math and shop mechanics. Helpful attributes include

- Interest in work involving aircraft
- Interest in engine mechanics
- Ability to use hand and power tools

Civilian Counterparts

Civilian aircraft mechanics work for aircraft manufacturers, commercial airlines, and government agencies. They perform duties similar to military aircraft mechanics. They may also be called airframe or powerplant mechanics.

Military Careers Score at the 50% (50-50) point = 198.

Automobile Mechanics

Army

Navy

Air Force

Marine Corps

Typical Tasks

- Troubleshoot problems in vehicle engines, electrical systems, steering, brakes, and suspensions
- Tune and repair engines using engine test equipment
- Replace clutches, brakes, transmissions, and steering assemblies
- Repair auto pollution control equipment
- Replace starters, water pumps, and fuel pumps
- Establish and follow schedules for maintaining vehicles
- Keep records of repairs made and parts used

Qualifications

Physical Demands

Normal color vision is required for some specialties to work with color-coded wiring and to read diagrams.

Helpful Attributes

Helpful school subjects include auto mechanics and industrial arts. Helpful attributes include

- Preference for doing physical work
- Interest in troubleshooting mechanical problems
- Interest in automobile engines and how they work

Civilian Counterparts

Civilian automobile mechanics work for service stations, repair garages, and auto dealers. They perform duties similar to military automobile mechanics. Civilian mechanics may also be called garage mechanics, carburetor mechanics, transmission mechanics, or radiator mechanics depending on their specialty.

Military Careers Score at the 50% (50-50) point = 190.

Automotive Body Repairers

Army

Navy

Air Force

Marine Corps

Typical Tasks

- Pound out dented panels and fenders using mallets, hammers, and pry bars
- Weld damaged body parts and frames
- Straighten fenders, doors, hoods, and frames to their original shape and position
- Replace damaged body parts including bumpers, body panels, and radiators
- Refinish bodies using body fillers, primers, and paints
- Cut and install safety glass in windows
- Keep accurate records of parts and supplies and repairs made

Qualifications

Physical Demands

Automotive body repairers may have to lift heavy parts and move heavy tools and equipment. They sometimes have to stoop, kneel, and work in cramped positions. Normal color vision is required to match paint colors and set and adjust welding torches.

Helpful Attributes

Helpful school subjects include auto mechanics, auto body repair, and industrial arts. Helpful attributes include

- Preference for doing physical work
- Ability to use hand and power tools
- Interest in working with cars and trucks

Civilian Counterparts

Civilian automotive body repairers work in auto body shops and repair garages. They perform duties similar to military automotive body repairers.

Military Careers Score at the 50% (50-50) point = 190.

Divers

Army

Navy

Marine Corps

Coast Guard

Typical Tasks

- Inspect and clean ship propellers and hulls
- Patch damaged ship hulls using underwater welding equipment
- Patrol the waters below ships at anchor
- Salvage (recover) sunken equipment
- Assist with underwater construction of piers and harbor facilities
- Survey rivers, beaches, and harbors for underwater obstacles
- Use explosives to clear underwater obstacles

Qualifications

Physical Demands

Divers must be good swimmers and physically strong.

Helpful Attributes

Helpful school subjects include shop mechanics and building trades. Helpful attributes include

- Interest in underwater diving
- Ability to stay calm under stress
- A high degree of self-reliance

Civilian Counterparts

Civilian divers work for oil companies, salvage companies, underwater construction firms, and police or fire rescue units. They perform duties similar to divers in the military.

Military Careers Score at the 50% (50-50) point = 197.

Engine Mechanics

Army

Navy

Air Force

Marine Corps

Coast Guard

Typical Tasks

- Troubleshoot engine problems using engine analyzers and other test equipment
- Adjust and repair ignition, fuel, electrical, and steering systems
- Remove engines using hoists and jacks
- Replace pistons, rings, and valves
- Repair and replace clutches and transmissions
- Lubricate engines and other vehicle parts
- Keep records of repairs made and parts used

Qualifications

Physical Demands

Engine mechanics may have to lift heavy engine parts, tools, and equipment.

Helpful Attributes

Helpful school subjects include industrial arts and auto mechanics. Helpful attributes include

- Interest in finding out why engines do not work and choosing the correct method of repair
- Preference for physical work
- Ability to use hand and power tools
- Ability to accurately interpret charts and diagrams

Civilian Counterparts

Civilian engine mechanics usually work for garages, service stations, construction firms, and truck or bus companies. They perform duties similar to military engine mechanics. They are also called truck, bus, or diesel mechanics.

Military Careers Score at the 50% (50-50) point = 190.

Heating and Cooling Mechanics

Army

Navy

Air Force

Marine Corps

Coast Guard

Typical Tasks

- Install and repair furnaces, boilers, and air conditioners
- Recharge cooling systems with refrigerant gases
- Install copper tubing systems that circulate water or cooling gases
- Install air ducts and floor vents
- Replace compressor parts, such as valves, pistons, bearings, and electrical motors on refrigeration units
- Repair thermostats and electrical circuits

Qualifications

Physical Demands

Heating and cooling mechanics may have to lift or move heavy equipment. They are often required to stoop, kneel, and work in cramped positions. Normal color vision is required for locating and repairing color-coded wiring.

Helpful Attributes

Helpful school subjects include science, math, and shop mechanics. Helpful attributes include

- Ability to use hand and power tools
- Interest in working on machines
- Interest in solving problems

Civilian Counterparts

Civilian heating and cooling mechanics work for contractors that install home furnaces and air conditioners or firms that repair refrigerators and freezers in homes, grocery stores, factories, and warehouses. Heating and cooling mechanics in civilian life often specialize more than those in the military. They may be called heating, air conditioning, refrigeration, or climate control mechanics.

Military Careers Score at the 50% (50-50) point = 197.

Heavy Equipment Mechanics

Army

Navy

Air Force

Marine Corps

Coast Guard

Typical Tasks

- Locate engine problems using test equipment
- Place engines and transmissions in bulldozers and other heavy equipment using hoists and jacks
- Adjust or replace engine and transmission parts using power and hand tools
- Repair brake, steering, and electrical systems
- Inspect bearings, gears, and other parts for wear
- Replace or repair hydraulic arms or shovels and grader blades
- Repair tank turrets

Qualifications

Physical Demands

Heavy equipment mechanics may have to lift heavy parts and tools.

Helpful Attributes

Helpful school subjects include auto mechanics and industrial arts. Helpful attributes include
- Preference for doing physical work
- Interest in locating and repairing mechanical problems
- Interest in working with repair tools

Civilian Counterparts

Civilian heavy equipment mechanics work for construction equipment dealers, farm equipment companies, and state highway agencies. They perform duties similar to military heavy equipment mechanics. They may also be known as construction equipment mechanics and endless track vehicle mechanics.

Military Careers Score at the 50% (50-50) point = 190.

Marine Engine Mechanics

Army

Navy

Air Force

Coast Guard

Typical Tasks

- Repair and maintain shipboard gasoline and diesel engines
- Locate and repair machinery parts including valves and piping systems
- Repair ship propulsion machinery
- Repair and service hoisting machinery and ship elevators
- Repair refrigeration and air conditioning equipment on ships
- Repair engine-related electrical systems

Qualifications

Physical Demands

Normal color vision is required to work with color-coded diagrams and wiring.

Helpful Attributes

Helpful school subjects include shop mechanics. Helpful attributes include
- Interest in fixing engines and machinery
- Ability to use hand and power tools
- Preference for doing physical work

Civilian Counterparts

Civilian marine engine mechanics work in many industries including marine transportation, commercial fishing, and oil exploration and drilling. They perform duties similar to military marine engine mechanics.

Military Careers Score at the 50% (50-50) point = 197.

Powerhouse Mechanics

Army

Navy

Air Force

Coast Guard

Typical Tasks

- Install generating equipment, such as gasoline and diesel engines, turbines, and air compressors
- Repair and maintain nuclear power plants
- Inspect and service pumps, generators, batteries, and cables
- Tune engines using hand tools, timing lights, and combustion pressure gauges
- Diagnose (troubleshoot) engine and electrical system problems
- Replace damaged parts, such as fuel injectors, valves, and pistons

Qualifications

Special Qualifications

Algebra course work is a requirement for nuclear power plant specialties. Nuclear specialties are open only to men.

Physical Demands

Powerhouse mechanics may have to lift and move heavy electrical generators or batteries. Normal color vision is required to work with color-coded wiring and cables.

Helpful Attributes

Helpful school subjects include shop mechanics and math. Helpful attributes include

- Interest in repairing machines and equipment
- Preference for doing physical work
- Interest in nuclear power

Civilian Counterparts

Civilian powerhouse mechanics work for a wide variety of employers, such as utility and power companies, manufacturing companies, and others that operate their own power plants. They perform duties similar to military powerhouse mechanics.

Military Careers Score at the 50% (50-50) point = 197.

Riggers

Army

Navy

Marine Corps

Coast Guard

Typical Tasks

- Splice wire and rope cables to make slings and block-and-tackle devices
- Assemble rigging devices, such as cranes and winches
- Select the correct cables, ropes, pulleys, and winches for the size and weight of loads
- Attach grappling devices (for holding cargo) to cranes or winches
- Give hoisting directions to crane and winch operators
- Guide cargo being moved using guide ropes

Qualifications

Physical Demands

Riggers need strength and endurance in order to work with heavy equipment and material.

Helpful Attributes

- Ability to work closely with others as a member of a team
- Attention to safety requirements
- Preference for doing physical work

Civilian Counterparts

Civilian riggers work in shipyards and dockyards. They also work for large construction companies and cargo and pleasure cruise shiplines. Civilian riggers perform duties similar to military riggers. They may also be called crane riggers, hook tenders, slingers, and yard riggers.

Military Careers Score at the 50% (50-50) point = 190.

➤ ELECTRONIC AND ELECTRICAL EQUIPMENT REPAIRER OCCUPATIONS

Aircraft Electricians

Army

Navy

Air Force

Marine Corps

Coast Guard

Typical Tasks

- Troubleshoot aircraft electrical systems using test equipment
- Repair or replace defective generators and electric motors
- Inspect and maintain electrical systems
- Replace faulty wiring
- Solder electrical connections
- Repair or replace instruments, such as tachometers, temperature gauges, and altimeters
- Read electrical wiring diagrams

Qualifications

Physical Demands

Normal color vision is required to work with color-coded wiring.

Helpful Attributes

Helpful school courses include math and shop mechanics. Helpful attributes include

- Interest in solving problems
- Interest in electricity and how electrical equipment works
- Ability to work with hand tools

Civilian Counterparts

Civilian aircraft electricians work mainly for airlines and aircraft maintenance firms. They may also work for aircraft manufacturers and organizations that have fleets of airplanes or helicopters. Their duties are similar to those of military aircraft electricians.

Military Careers Score at the 50% (50-50) point = 202.

Computer Equipment Repairers

Army

Navy

Air Force

Marine Corps

Typical Tasks

- Install computers and other data processing equipment
- Inspect data processing equipment for defects in wiring, circuit boards, and other parts
- Test and repair data processing equipment using electrical voltage meters, circuit analyzers, and other special testing equipment
- Locate defective data processing parts using technical guides and diagrams

Qualifications

Physical Demands

Specialties that involve flying require passing a special physical exam. Normal color vision is required to work with color-coded wiring.

Helpful Attributes

Helpful school subjects include math and electronic equipment repair. Helpful attributes include

- Interest in working with electrical and electronic equipment

Civilian Counterparts

Civilian computer equipment repairers work for computer manufacturers, repair services, and other businesses with large computer facilities. They perform duties similar to military computer equipment repairers. They may also be called computer service technicians.

Military Careers Score at the 50% (50-50) point = 208.

Electrical Products Repairers

Army

Navy

Air Force

Marine Corps

Coast Guard

Typical Tasks

- Maintain, test, and repair electric motors in many kinds of machine, such as lathes, pumps, office machines, and kitchen appliances
- Inspect and repair electrical, medical, and dental equipment
- Inspect and repair electric instruments, such as voltmeters
- Replace worn gaskets and seals in watertight electrical equipment
- Maintain and repair portable electric tools, such as saws and drills
- Maintain and repair submarine periscopes

Qualifications

Physical Demands

Normal color vision is required to work with color-coded wiring.

Helpful Attributes

Helpful school subjects include math, electricity, and shop mechanics. Helpful attributes include

- Ability to use tools
- Interest in electric motors and appliances
- Interest in solving problems

Civilian Counterparts

Civilian electrical products repairers work in many industries including hospitals, manufacturing firms, and governmental agencies. They also work in independent repair shops. They perform duties similar to military electrical products repairers. They may be called electric tool repairers, electrical instrument repairers, electromedical equipment repairers, or electric motor repairers.

Military Careers Score at the 50% (50-50) point = 199.

Electronic Instrument Repairers

Army

Navy

Air Force

Marine Corps

Coast Guard

Typical Tasks

- Test meteorological and medical instruments, navigational controls, and simulators using electronic and electrical test equipment
- Read technical diagrams and manuals in order to locate, isolate, and repair instrument parts
- Replace equipment parts, such as resistors, switches, and circuit boards

Qualifications

Physical Demands

Normal color vision is required to work with color-coded wiring.

Helpful Attributes

Helpful school subjects include math and electronic equipment repair. Helpful attributes include

- Interest in working with electronic equipment
- Interest in solving problems
- Attention to detail

Civilian Counterparts

Most civilian electronic instrument repairers work for manufacturing, medical research, and satellite communications firms or commercial airlines. They may also work for government agencies, such as the Federal Aviation Administration, the National Aeronautics and Space Administration, or the National Weather Service. They perform the same kind of duties as military instrument repairers. They are called electronics mechanics, dental equipment repairers, or biomedical equipment technicians, depending on their specialty.

Military Careers Score at the 50% (50-50) point = 208.

Electronic Weapons Systems Repairers

Army

Navy

Air Force

Marine Corps

Coast Guard

Typical Tasks

- Install electronic components (parts) in weapons systems
- Test and adjust weapon firing, guidance, and launch systems using electronic test equipment, calibrators, and other precision instruments
- Maintain electronic weapons systems on a regular schedule
- Repair and maintain missile mounts, platforms, and launch mechanisms using hand and power tools
- Clean and lubricate gyroscopes, sights, and other electro-optical fire control components
- Prepare inspection, maintenance, and other repair reports and logs

Qualifications

Special Qualifications

Although there are women weapons systems repairers, some specialties in this occupation are open only to men.

Physical Demands

Some specialties involve moderate to heavy lifting. Normal color vision is required to read color-coded charts and diagrams.

Helpful Attributes

Helpful school subjects include science and math. Helpful attributes include

- Interest in working with electronic or electrical equipment
- Ability to do work requiring accuracy and attention to detail

Civilian Counterparts

Civilian electronics weapons systems repairers work for firms that design, build, and test electronic weapons systems for the military. They perform duties similar to military electronics weapons systems repairers. They may also be called electronic mechanics, avionics technicians, or missile facilities repairers.

Military Careers Score at the 50% (50-50) point = 198.

Line Installers and Repairers

Army

Navy

Air Force

Marine Corps

Coast Guard

Typical Tasks

- Erect utility poles
- Operate mechanical lifts ("cherry pickers") or climb poles to attach conductors and insulators
- String overhead communications and electric cables between utility poles
- Install streetlights and airfield lighting systems
- Operate mechanical plows to dig trenches for underground cables
- Splice and seal cables to keep them watertight
- Install and adjust telephone switch-boxes, electrical transformers, and voltage regulators

Qualifications

Physical Demands

Line installers and repairers have to climb utility poles and work from heights. They have to lift and work with heavy wires and cables. Normal color vision is required to work with color-coded wires.

Helpful Attributes

Helpful school subjects include math and shop mechanics. Helpful attributes include

- Ability to work as a member of a team
- Ability to use hand and power tools
- Preference for working
- Preference for doing physical work

Civilian Counterparts

Civilian line installers and repairers work for telephone and power companies. They perform duties similar to military line installers and repairers. They may specialize in certain areas, such as line installing, cable splicing, or cable testing.

Military Careers Score at the 50% (50-50) point = 194.

Ordinance Mechanics

Army

Navy

Air Force

Marine Corps

Coast Guard

Typical Tasks

- Load nuclear and conventional explosives and ammunition on aircraft, ships, and submarines
- Inspect and maintain mounted guns, bomb release systems, and missile launchers
- Repair and maintain tank weapons and fire control systems
- Repair and maintain artillery, naval gun systems, and infantry weapons
- Check the accuracy of radar sighting systems
- Assemble and load explosives
- Defuse unexploded bombs

Qualifications

Physical Demands

Ordnance mechanics may have to carry artillery shells and other ordnance.

Helpful Attributes

Helpful school subjects include general science and shop mechanics. Helpful attributes include

- Interest in working with guns and explosives
- Ability to remain calm under stress
- Ability to maintain concentration

Civilian Counterparts

There are no direct civilian counterparts for many of the military ordnance mechanics specialties. However, there are many occupations that are related—for example, civilian work for government agencies and private industry doing ordnance research and development. Others work for police or fire departments as bomb-disposal experts. Some also work as gunsmiths or work for munitions manufacturers and firearms makers.

Military Careers Score at the 50% (50-50) point = 194.

Photographic Equipment Repairers

Army

Navy

Air Force

Marine Corps

Typical Tasks

- Adjust and repair camera shutter mechanisms, focus controls, and flash units
- Maintain and repair aerial cameras mounted in airplanes
- Maintain aerial sensors that detect foreign military activities
- Maintain and repair motion picture cameras and sound recording equipment
- Repair photoprocessing equipment, such as enlargers, film processors, and printers
- Diagnose problems in all types of cameras

Qualifications

Physical Demands

Normal color vision is required to work with color-coded wiring.

Helpful Attributes

Helpful school subjects include math and science. Helpful attributes include

- Interest in solving problems
- Ability to use repair tools

Civilian Counterparts

Civilian photographic equipment repairers work for photographic laboratories, engineering firms, and government agencies. They perform duties similar to those performed in the military. Depending on specialty, they may also be called camera repairers, motion picture equipment machinists, or photographic equipment technicians.

Military Careers Score at the 50% (50-50) point = 198.

Power Plant Electricians

Army

Navy

Air Force

Marine Corps

Coast Guard

Typical Tasks

- Maintain and repair motors, generators, switchboards, and control equipment
- Maintain and repair power and lighting circuits, electrical fixtures, and other electrical equipment
- Detect and locate ground, open circuits, and short circuits in power distribution cables
- Connect emergency power to the main control board from an emergency switchboard
- Operate standard electrical and electronic test equipment
- Read technical guides and diagrams to locate damaged parts of generators and control equipment

Qualifications

Special Qualifications

Although there are women power plant electricians, some specialties in this occupation are open only to men.

Physical Demands

Normal color vision is required to work with color-coded wiring.

Helpful Attributes

Helpful school subjects include electrical and electronic theory, math, and technical drawing. Helpful attributes include

- Ability to use hand and power tools
- Interest in working with large machinery
- Interest in electricity

Civilian Counterparts

Civilian power plant electricians often work for construction companies, manufacturers, and utility companies. They perform duties similar to military power plant electricians.

Military Careers Score at the 50% (50-50) point = 198.

Precision Instrument Repairers

Army

Navy

Air Force

Marine Corps

Typical Tasks

- Calibrate weather instruments, such as barometers and thermometers
- Repair gyrocompasses
- Adjust and repair weapon-aiming devices, such as range finders, telescopes, periscopes, and ballistic computers
- Calibrate engineering instruments, such as transits, levels, telemeters, and stereoscopes
- Calibrate and repair instruments used in aircraft
- Repair watches, clocks, and timers
- Calibrate electrical test instruments

Qualifications

Physical Demands

Normal color vision is required to work with color-coded wiring and repair manuals.

Helpful Attributes

Helpful school subjects include math, science, electronics, and shop mechanics. Helpful attributes include

- Interest in machines and how they work
- Ability to solve mechanical problems
- Ability to work with tools

Civilian Counterparts

Civilian precision instrument repairers work for firms that manufacture or use precision instruments. These include manufacturing firms, airlines, machinery repair shops, maintenance shops, and instrument makers. Civilian precision instrument repairers perform duties similar to military precision instrument repairers. They may also be called instrument mechanics or calibration specialists.

Military Careers Score at the 50% (50-50) point = 198.

Radar and Sonar Equipment Repairers

Army

Navy

Air Force

Marine Corps

Coast Guard

Typical Tasks

- Test radar systems using electronic and electrical test equipment
- Monitor the operation of air traffic control, missile tracking, air defense, and other radar systems to make sure there are no problems
- Repair sonar and radar components (parts) using soldering irons and other special hand and power tools
- Install receivers, transmitters, and other components using technical manuals and guides
- Read wiring diagrams, designs, and other drawings to locate components of radar equipment

Qualifications

Special Qualifications

Although there are women radar and sonar equipment repairers, some specialties in this occupation are open only to men.

Physical Demands

Specialties involving flying require passing a special physical exam. Normal color vision is required to work with wiring.

Helpful Attributes

Helpful school subjects include math and physics. Helpful attributes include

- Interest in working with electrical and electronic equipment
- Ability to apply electronic principles and concepts

Civilian Counterparts

Civilian radar and sonar equipment repairers work for engineering firms, the federal government, or aircraft and military hardware manufacturers. They perform duties similar to military radar and sonar equipment repairers. They may also be called communications technicians.

Military Careers Score at the 50% (50-50) point = 205.

Radio Equipment Repairers

Army

Navy

Air Force

Marine Corps

Coast Guard

Typical Tasks

- Maintain, test, and repair radio equipment in broadcasting and relay stations, tanks, ships, and airplanes
- Maintain, repair, and replace circuitry, frequency controls, and other radio parts using special hand and power tools
- Adjust, tune, and gauge microwave, satellite, aircraft, and other radio equipment using electronic testing equipment
- Locate and isolate defective parts of radio equipment using technical guides and diagrams

Qualifications

Special Qualifications

Although there are women radio equipment repairers, some specialties in this occupation are open only to men. However, this policy is being reevaluated and women may be admitted.

Physical Demands

Normal color vision is required to work with color-coded wiring.

Helpful Attributes

Helpful school subjects include algebra and radio and TV repair. Helpful attributes include

- Interest in working with electrical and electronic equipment
- Interest in solving problems

Civilian Counterparts

Civilian radio equipment repairers often work for firms that design and make air and space, communications, and electronic equipment. They may also work for the federal government. They perform duties similar to military radio equipment repairers. They may be called radio repairers, radio mechanics, or radio technicians.

Military Careers Score at the 50% (50-50) point = 201.

Ship Electricians

Navy

Coast Guard

Typical Tasks

- Install wiring for lights and equipment
- Troubleshoot electrical wiring and equipment using test meters
- Inspect and maintain devices that distribute electricity throughout ships, such as circuits, transformers, and regulators

- Monitor and maintain electrical devices connected to the ship's main engines or nuclear reactors
- Repair motors and appliances

Qualifications

Special Qualifications

Nuclear specialties require successful completion of high school algebra and are open only to men. However, this policy is being reevaluated and women may be admitted.

Physical Demands

Normal color vision is required to work with color-coded wiring.

Helpful Attributes

Helpful school courses include math and shop mechanics. Helpful attributes include

- Interest in electricity and how electrical machines work
- Interest in solving problems
- Ability to use tools

Civilian Counterparts

Civilian ship electricians work for shipbuilding and dry dock firms and shipping lines. They perform duties similar to military ship electricians. Other civilian electricians, such as building electricians and electrical product repairers, also perform similar work. Civilian nuclear power plant electricians perform duties similar to ship electricians who work with nuclear plants on ships and submarines.

Military Careers Score at the 50% (50-50) point = 203.

Telephone Technicians

Army

Navy

Air Force

Marine Corps

Coast Guard

Typical Tasks

- Diagnose the cause of equipment failure
- Install interior wiring and switching equipment
- Connect telephones and switchboards
- Check telephone equipment using test meters
- Repair or replace broken equipment
- Repair short circuits in wiring
- Read wiring diagrams to determine installation steps

Qualifications

Physical Demands

Telephone technicians may have to work from ladders or on tall utility poles. Normal color vision is required to work with color-coded wiring and diagrams.

Helpful Attributes

Helpful school courses include math, electricity, and shop mechanics. Helpful attributes include

- Ability to use hand tools
- Interest in solving problems
- Interest in learning how telephone systems work

Civilian Counterparts

Most civilian telephone technicians work for telephone companies. They perform duties similar to military telephone technicians, although they usually specialize in either installation or repair. They may be called central office repairers, PBX repairers, central office installers, station installers and repairers, or telephone maintenance mechanics, depending on specialty.

Military Careers Score at the 50% (50-50) point = 198.

➤ CONSTRUCTION OCCUPATIONS

Blasting Specialists

Army

Navy

Air Force

Marine Corps

Typical Tasks

- Determine the amount of explosives required for each job
- Transfer explosives from magazines (storage) to blasting areas
- Determine the placement of explosives for the safest and most efficient result
- Drill holes in rock, tree stumps, or structures at the proper depth and spacing
- Select explosives and assemble charges, fuses, and blasting caps
- Place explosives in drilled holes and detonate using electric detonators
- Oversee the storage of explosives
- Keep records of explosives used

Qualifications

Physical Demands

Some specialties require that workers have no history of heart or vascular problems because of the stress of working with explosives. Normal hearing and color vision are required to work with explosives.

Helpful Attributes

Helpful school subjects include science and math. Helpful attributes include

- Emotional stability
- Ability to stay calm under pressure
- Ability to observe strict safety procedures

Civilian Counterparts

Civilian blasting specialists work for construction companies or rock quarries. They perform duties similar to military blasting specialists and are commonly called blasters.

Military Careers Score at the 50% (50-50) point = 197.

Bricklayers and Concrete Masons

Army

Navy

Air Force

Marine Corps

Typical Tasks

- Build foundations and walls with brick, cement block, or stone
- Set masonry in correct position using mortar
- Cut and shape masonry using power saws, chisels, and hammers
- Mix and pour concrete to form footings, foundations, and floor slabs
- Finish surfaces of poured concrete using finishing tools, such as floats, screeds, and edgers
- Plaster inside walls and ceilings
- Set ceramic tile on walls and floors

Qualifications

Physical Demands

Bricklayers and concrete masons work with heavy materials. Sometimes, they are required to climb and work from ladders and scaffolds.

Helpful Attributes

- Preference for doing physical work
- Ability to work with blueprints
- Preference for working outdoors

Civilian Counterparts

Civilian bricklayers and concrete masons work for construction firms and as independent contractors. They perform duties similar to military bricklayers and concrete masons. They may also be called brick-masons, stonemasons, cement masons, or cement finishers.

Military Careers Score at the 50% (50-50) point = 190.

Building Electricians

Army

Navy

Air Force

Marine Corps

Coast Guard

Typical Tasks

- Install and wire transformers, junction boxes, and circuit breakers using wire cutters, insulation strippers, and other hand tools
- Read blueprints, wiring plans, and repair orders to determine wiring layouts or repair needs
- Cut, bend, and string wires and conduits (pipe or tubing)

- Inspect power distribution systems, shorts in wire, and faulty equipment using test meters
- Repair and replace faulty wiring and lighting fixtures
- Install lightning rods to protect electrical systems

Qualifications

Physical Demands

Normal color vision is required to work with color-coded wiring and circuits.

Helpful Attributes

Helpful school subjects include science and math. Helpful attributes include

- Ability to use hand tools
- Preference for doing physical work
- Interest in electricity

Civilian Counterparts

Civilian building electricians usually work for building and electrical contracting firms. Some work as self-employed electrical contractors. They perform duties similar to military building electricians.

Military Careers Score at the 50% (50-50) point = 198.

Carpenters

Army

Navy

Air Force

Marine Corps

Coast Guard

Typical Tasks

- Erect wood framing for buildings using hand and power tools, such as hammers, saws, levels, and drills
- Lay roofing materials, such as roofing felt and asphalt, tile, and wooden shingles
- Install plasterboard and paneling to form interior walls and ceilings
- Lay wood and tile floors and build steps, staircases, and porches
- Operate precision power tools, such as drill presses, table saws, and lathes
- Build temporary shelters for storing supplies and equipment while on training maneuvers

Qualifications

Physical Demands

Carpenters may have to lift and carry heavy building materials, such as lumber and plasterboard. Also, they may have to climb and work from ladders and scaffolding.

Helpful Attributes

Helpful school subjects include math, woodworking, and industrial arts. Helpful attributes include

- Preference for physical work
- Ability to use woodworking tools
- Interest in construction work

Civilian Counterparts

Civilian carpenters usually work for construction or remodeling contractors, government agencies, utility companies, or manufacturing firms. Other carpenters are self-employed contractors. Civilian carpenters perform duties similar to military carpenters. Civilian carpenters often specialize in finish or rough carpentry or cabinetmaking.

Military Careers Score at the 50% (50-50) point = 190.

Paving Equipment Operators

Army

Navy

Air Force

Marine Corps

Typical Tasks

- Operate rock crushers and other quarry equipment to make gravel
- Operate mixing plants to make batches of concrete and asphalt
- Spread asphalt and concrete with paving machines
- Operate pavement rollers to smooth asphalt surfaces
- Inspect pavement for damage or wear
- Patch worn pavement
- Take samples and test asphalt or concrete quality

Qualifications

Physical Demands

Some specialties require heavy lifting.

Helpful Attributes

Helpful school subjects include science and shop mechanics. Helpful attributes include

- Preference for working outdoors
- Interest in working with large machines and equipment

Civilian Counterparts

Civilian paving equipment operators work for construction companies, paving contractors, and state highway agencies. They perform duties similar to military paving equipment operators.

Military Careers Score at the 50% (50-50) point = 190.

Plumbers and Pipe Fitters

Army

Navy

Air Force

Marine Corps

Coast Guard

Typical Tasks

- Plan layouts of pipe systems using blueprints and drawings
- Bend, cut, and thread pipes made of lead, copper, and plastic
- Install connectors, fittings, and joints
- Solder or braze pipe and tubing to join them
- Install sinks, toilets, and other plumbing fixtures
- Troubleshoot, test, and calibrate hydraulic and pneumatic systems
- Keep accurate records of tasks completed and materials used

Qualifications

Physical Demands

Plumbers and pipe fitters have to lift and carry heavy pipes and tubes.

Helpful Attributes

Helpful school subjects include math and shop mechanics. Helpful attributes include

- Preference for doing physical work
- Ability to work with detailed plans

Civilian Counterparts

Civilian plumbers and pipe fitters usually work for mechanical or plumbing contractors or as self-employed contractors. Some plumbers and pipe fitters work for public utilities. Civilian plumbers and pipe fitters perform duties similar to those performed in the military.

Military Careers Score at the 50% (50-50) point = 190.

Well Drillers

Army

Navy

Typical Tasks

- Select drilling sites
- Erect and position derricks (towers for supporting drilling equipment)
- Drill wells using drilling rigs
- Study drilling core samples to find the best places to drill
- Test well water for purity
- Repair drill bits, drilling rigs, and related equipment

Qualifications

Physical Demands

Well drillers may have to lift and carry heavy equipment, such as drill bits and casings. Normal color vision is required to enter this occupation.

Helpful Attributes

Helpful school subjects include general science and geology. Helpful attributes include

- Preference for working outdoors
- Interest in working with machines and equipment

Civilian Counterparts

Civilian well drillers work for independent water well drillers and construction contractors. They perform duties similar to military well drillers.

Military Careers Score at the 50% (50-50) point = 191.

ARCO ■ ASVAB

➤ MACHINE OPERATOR AND PRECISION WORK OCCUPATIONS

Boiler Technicians

Navy

Coast Guard

Typical Tasks

- Operate main and auxiliary boilers
- Operate the steam turbines that generate power for the ship
- Maintain the heat source, high pressure fittings, and other boiler parts
- Operate and maintain automatic boiler controls
- Repair valves, pumps, and forced-air blowers
- Align fuel, water, and air piping systems using hand and power tools
- Test water and fuel for quality and purity

Qualifications

Physical Demands

Boiler technicians may have to lift or move heavy pumps, air-blowers, and other equipment. They may have to stoop and kneel and work in awkward positions while repairing boilers.

Helpful Attributes

Helpful school subjects include metal shop and math. Helpful attributes include

- Interest in working with machines and equipment
- Preference for doing physical work
- Ability to work in confined areas

Civilian Counterparts

Civilian boiler technicians, called boilermakers, work for shiplines, boiler repair shops, or factories. They perform duties similar to military boiler technicians. Boiler technicians also build and install boilers, as well as operate and repair them. Besides shipping, boilers are used in buildings and factories for steam heat and power.

Military Careers Score at the 50% (50-50) point = 197.

Clothing and Fabric Repairers

Army

Navy

Air Force

Marine Corps

Typical Tasks

- Inspect and mark items received for repair
- Repair tents, covers, and other canvas equipment
- Mend worn or damaged fabric and rubber goods
- Measure and mark uniforms for alterations
- Alter and repair uniforms
- Operate and maintain sewing machines

Qualifications

Helpful Attributes

- Ability to sew by hand or with machines
- Interest in work requiring accuracy and attention to detail

Civilian Counterparts

Civilian clothing and fabric repairers work for retail clothing stores, tailor shops, and firms that manufacture covers for boats, cars, and other equipment. Some clothing and fabric repairers work for laundries or dry cleaning shops. Civilian clothing and fabric repairers perform duties similar to military clothing and fabric repairers. Depending on specialty, civilian clothing and fabric repairers may also be called menders, canvas repairers, alteration tailors, or garment fitters.

Military Careers Score at the 50% (50-50) point = 190.

Compressed Gas Technicians

Navy

Air Force

Marine Corps

Typical Tasks

- Operate valves to control the flow of air through machinery that compresses or liquefies gases
- Remove impurities, such as carbon dioxide, from gases
- Fill storage cylinders with compressed gas
- Test cylinders for leaks using pressure gauges
- Operate dry ice making plants
- Maintain compressed gas machinery

Qualifications

Physical Demands

Normal color vision is usually required to enter this occupation.

Helpful Attributes

- Interest in working with machines
- Preference for doing physical work

Civilian Counterparts

Civilian compressed gas technicians work for a wide range of industrial companies and processing plants, especially distilling and chemical firms They perform duties similar to military compressed gas technicians. They may also be called oxygen plant operators, compressed gas plant workers, or acetylene plant operators.

Military Careers Score at the 50% (50-50) point = 194.

Dental Laboratory Technicians

Army

Navy

Air Force

Coast Guard

Typical Tasks

- Read instructions from dentists to make dentures, braces, and other dental devices
- Make dentures or crowns using molds made from teeth impressions
- Grind and polish dentures to match natural teeth and to fit properly in a patient's mouth
- Match the color of artificial teeth to natural tooth color following prescription orders from dentists
- Harden and cure new dentures in high temperature ovens
- Construct, repair, and align metal braces and retainers
- Order, store, and issue lab supplies

Qualifications

Physical Demands

Normal color vision is required to match color of artificial teeth with natural tooth color.

Helpful Attributes

Helpful school subjects include biology and chemistry. Helpful attributes include

- Ability to use precision tools and instruments
- Interest in working in a laboratory setting
- Interest in work requiring attention to detail

Civilian Counterparts

Civilian dental laboratory technicians normally work for small, privately owned dental laboratories. However, some are employed in large dental offices. They perform duties similar to military dental laboratory technicians. However, civilian technicians often specialize in one of five dental areas: full dentures, partial dentures, crowns and bridges, ceramics, or orthodontics (tooth straightening).

Military Careers Score at the 50% (50-50) point = 196.

Machinists

Army

Navy

Air Force

Marine Corps

Typical Tasks

- Study blueprints or written plans of the parts to be made
- Set up and operate lathes to make parts such as shafts and gears

- Cut metal stock using power hacksaws and bandsaws
- Bore holes using drill presses
- Shape and smooth parts using grinders
- Measure work using micrometers, depth gauges, and calipers

Qualifications

Helpful Attributes

Helpful school subjects include math, general science, metal working, and mechanical drawing. Helpful attributes include

- Preference for working with the hands
- Interest in making things and finding solutions to mechanical problems
- Ability to apply mathematical formulas

Civilian Counterparts

Civilian machinists work for factories and repair shops in many industries, including the electrical product, automotive, and heavy machinery industry. They perform duties similar to military machinists.

Military Careers Score at the 50% (50-50) point = 198.

Opticians

Army

Navy

Typical Tasks

- Calculate the correct lens size and thickness from written prescriptions
- Grind and polish lenses using power grinders and polishers
- Smooth lens edges using hand or power tools
- Dye lenses to prescribed tints and apply lens coatings for protection
- Harden lenses using heat treating equipment

- Assemble eyeglass frames and lenses using optical tools
- Fit and adjust glasses for eye care patients

Qualifications

Special Qualifications

Successful completion of high school algebra is required to enter some specialties in this occupation.

Helpful Attributes

Helpful attributes include
- Ability to follow detailed instructions
- Ability to do precise work
- Interest in working with one's hands

Civilian Counterparts

Civilian opticians work for optical laboratories and retail opticians. They perform duties similar to military opticians. They may also be called ophthalmic laboratory technicians.

Military Careers Score at the 50% (50-50) point = 196.

Photoprocessing Specialists

Army

Navy

Air Force

Typical Tasks

- Develop film "negatives" by using a series of chemical and water baths
- Produce prints from negatives
- Operate developing machines that make prints from film
- Monitor the flow of film and printing paper through automated processors
- Operate photo enlargers
- Maintain photographic lab equipment

Qualifications

Physical Demands

Normal color vision is required to produce accurate color prints.

Helpful Attributes

Helpful school subjects include chemistry and photography. Helpful attributes include
- Interest in photography and photoprocessing
- Interest in chemistry
- Ability to do work requiring accuracy and attention to detail

Civilian Counterparts

Civilian photoprocessing specialists work for large commercial photograph developers, portrait and studio labs, newspaper and magazine publishing companies, and advertising agencies. They perform duties similar to military photoprocessing specialists. They may also be called film developers, automatic print developers, or print controllers.

Military Careers Score at the 50% (50-50) point = 189.

Power Plant Operators

Army

Navy

Air Force

Marine Corps

Coast Guard

Typical Tasks

- Monitor and operate control boards to regulate power plants
- Operate and maintain diesel generating units to produce electric power

- Monitor and control nuclear reactors that produce electricity and power ships and submarines
- Operate and maintain stationary engines, such as steam engines, air compressors, and generators
- Operate and maintain auxiliary equipment, such as pumps, fans, and condensers
- Inspect equipment for malfunctions

Qualifications

Special Qualifications

Successful completion of high school algebra is required for nuclear power plant specialties, Nuclear specialties are open only to men. However, this policy is being reevaluated and women may be admitted.

Physical Demands

Power plant operators lift heavy parts or tools when maintaining power plants.

Helpful Attributes

Helpful school subjects include math and shop mechanics. Helpful attributes include
- Interest in working with large machinery
- Interest in nuclear power

Civilian Counterparts

Civilian power plant operators work for power companies, factories, schools, and hospitals. They perform duties similar to military power plant operators.

Depending on the specialty, power plant operators may also be called boiler operators, stationary engineers, nuclear reactor operators, or diesel plant operators.

Military Careers Score at the 50% (50-50) point = 197.

Printing Specialists

Army

Navy

Air Force

Marine Corps

Typical Tasks

- Reproduce printed matter using offset or lithographic printing processes
- Prepare photographic negatives and transfer them to printing plates using copy cameras and enlargers
- Prepare layouts of artwork, photographs, and text for lithographic plates
- Produce brochures, newspapers, maps, and charts
- Bind printed material into hardback or paperback books using binding machines
- Maintain printing machines

Qualifications

Physical Demands

Normal color vision is required to enter some specialties in this occupation.

Helpful Attributes

Helpful school subjects include shop mechanics. Helpful attributes include
- Preference for doing physical work
- Interest in learning about printing

Civilian Counterparts

Civilian printing specialists work for commercial print shops, newspapers, insurance companies, government offices, or businesses that do their own printing. They perform duties similar to military printing specialists. They may be called offset printing machine operators, lithograph press operators, offset duplicating machine operators, lithograph photographers, or bindery workers.

Military Careers Score at the 50% (50-50) point = 194.

Sheet Metal Workers

Navy

Air Force

Marine Corps

Coast Guard

Typical Tasks

- Read blueprints and lay out work on sheet metal
- Cut metal using shears or tin snips
- Bend metal using breaks or bending rolls
- Solder, weld, rivet, or screw sheet metal parts together
- Smooth seams and edges with files or grinders
- Measure work with calipers, micrometers, and rulers

Qualifications

Physical Demands

Normal color vision is needed for locating and marking reference points on sheet metal.

Helpful Attributes

Helpful school subjects include math, mechanical drawing, and metal working. Helpful attributes include

- Ability to use hand and power tools
- Preference for doing physical work
- Interest in making and repairing things

Civilian Counterparts

Civilian sheet metal workers work for air conditioning contractors, metal repair shops, or construction companies. They perform duties similar to those performed by sheet metal workers in the military. However, civilians usually specialize in certain areas, such as making heating and air conditioning ducts, gutters, or metal roofs.

Military Careers Score at the 50% (50-50) point = 190.

Shipfitters

Army

Navy

Coast Guard

Typical Tasks

- Inspect hulls, hatches, and decks for leaks
- Weld or rivet metal plates onto hulls and decks in order to repair damage
- Repair the walls (bulkheads) that separate ship compartments
- Repair holes in small boats by applying fiberglass mixtures
- Smooth patches to match hull shape using hand tools, such as files and sanders
- Apply paint to seal and protect repair work
- Repair hatches and watertight doors

Qualifications

Physical Demands

Shipfitters may have to lift heavy steel plates. They may have to work in crouching or kneeling positions. Normal color vision is required to adjust welding equipment and to match paints.

Helpful Attributes

- Preference for doing physical work

- Ability to use hand and power tools
- Ability to remain calm in emergencies
- Preference for working outdoors

Civilian Counterparts

Civilian shipfitters work for shipyards, dry dock repair firms, or other marine servicing companies. They tend to specialize by size of craft. They perform duties similar to military shipfitters and may also be called marine services technicians.

Military Careers Score at the 50% (50-50) point = 197.

Survival Equipment Specialists

Army

Navy

Air Force

Marine Corps

Coast Guard

Typical Tasks

- Inspect parachutes for rips and tangled lines
- Pack parachutes for safe operation
- Repair life rafts and load them with emergency provisions
- Test emergency oxygen regulators on aircraft
- Stock aircraft with fire extinguishers, flares, and survival provisions
- Train crews in the use of survival equipment

Qualifications

Physical Demands

Normal color vision is required to work with color-coded wiring and repair charts.

Helpful Attributes

Helpful school subjects include shop mechanics and science. Helpful attributes include

- Interest in working for the safety of others
- Ability to do work requiring accuracy and attention to detail

Civilian Counterparts

Civilian survival equipment specialists work for commercial airlines, parachute rigging and supply companies, survival equipment manufacturing firms, and some government agencies. They perform duties similar to military survival equipment specialists. Those who specialize on parachutes are called parachute riggers.

Military Careers Score at the 50% (50-50) point = 192.

Water and Sewage Treatment Plant Operators

Army

Navy

Air Force

Marine Corps

Coast Guard

Typical Tasks

- Operate pumps to transfer water from reservoirs and storage tanks to treatment plants

- Add chemicals and operate machinery that purifies water for drinking or cleanses it for safe disposal
- Test water for chlorine content, acidity, oxygen demand, and impurities
- Regulate the flow of drinking water to meet demand
- Clean and maintain water treatment machinery
- Keep records of chemical treatments, water pressure, and maintenance

Qualifications

Physical Demands

Normal color vision is needed to examine water for acidity and impurities.

Helpful Attributes

Helpful school subjects include chemistry, math, and shop mechanics. Helpful attributes include

- Interest in working with mechanical equipment
- Interest in chemistry and pollution control

Civilian Counterparts

Civilian water and sewage treatment plant operators work for municipal public works and industrial plants. Their work is similar to military water and sewage treatment plant operators. Civilian plant operators usually specialize as water treatment plant operators, waterworks pump station operators, or wastewater treatment plant operators.

Military Careers Score at the 50% (50-50) point = 190.

Welders

Army

Navy

Air Force

Marine Corps

Coast Guard

Typical Tasks

Welders in the military perform some or all of the following duties:

- Select welding equipment, torch tips, and fill rods based on the type of welding to be done
- Weld, braze, or solder metal parts together
- Forge and repair small items and tools
- Connect piping
- Cut away unneeded metal using arc (electric) welders or acetylene (gas) torches
- Clean metal surfaces before welding
- Operate automatic welding machines to connect metal parts

Qualifications

Physical Demands

Normal color vision is required for setting and adjusting torches.

Helpful Attributes

Helpful school subjects include shop mechanics, metal working, and mechanical drawing. Helpful attributes include

- Preference for doing physical work
- Good eye-hand coordination

Civilian Counterparts

Civilian welders work in many settings, including welding shops, pipeline companies, ship builders, and aircraft manufacturing plants. They perform the same basic duties as welders in the military.

Military Careers Score at the 50% (50-50) point = 190.

➤ TRANSPORTATION AND MATERIAL HANDLING OCCUPATIONS

Air Crew Members

Army

Navy

Air Force

Marine Corps

Coast Guard

Typical Tasks

- Operate aircraft communication and radar equipment
- Operate and maintain aircraft defensive systems
- Operate helicopter hoists to lift equipment and personnel from land and sea
- Operate and maintain aircraft in-flight refueling systems

Qualifications

Special Qualifications

Although there are women air crew members, some specialties in this occupation are open only to men.

Physical Demands

Air crew members must be in excellent physical condition and pass a special physical exam in order to qualify for flight duty. They must be mentally sound and have normal hearing.

Helpful Attributes

Helpful school subjects include mathematics and mechanics. Helpful attributes include
- Interest in flying
- Ability to work under stress
- Ability to work as a team member

Civilian Counterparts

There are no direct civilian equivalents to military air crew members. However, some of the skills gained in the military could be useful in civilian government and private agencies that provide emergency medical services. Also, weight and load computation skills are useful for civilian air transport operations.

Military Careers Score at the 50% (50-50) point = 200.

Aircraft Launch and Recovery Specialists

Navy

Marine Corps

Typical Tasks

- Operate consoles to control launch and recovery equipment, including catapults and arresting gear

- Operate elevators to transfer aircraft between flight and storage decks
- Install and maintain visual landing aids
- Test and adjust launch and recovery equipment using electric and mechanical test equipment and hand tools
- Install airfield crash barriers and barricades
- Direct aircraft launch and recovery operations using hand or light signals
- Maintain logs of airplane launches, recoveries, and equipment maintenance

Qualifications

Special Qualifications

This occupation is open only to men. However, this policy is being reevaluated and women may be admitted.

Physical Demands

Normal color vision is required to work with color-coded parts and the wiring of launch and recovery equipment.

Helpful Attributes

Helpful school subjects include shop mechanics. Helpful attributes include
- Interest in working on hydraulic and mechanical equipment
- Ability to use hand tools and test equipment
- Interest in aircraft flight operations

Civilian Counterparts

There are no direct civilian counterparts to military aircraft launch and recovery specialists. However, many of the skills learned are relevant to jobs performed by ground crews at civilian airports.

Military Careers Score at the 50% (50-50) point = 194.

Cargo Specialists

Army

Navy

Air Force

Marine Corps

Coast Guard

Typical Tasks

- Load supplies into trucks, transport planes, and railroad cars using forklifts
- Load equipment such as jeeps, trucks, and weapons aboard ships using dockyard cranes
- Pack and crate boxes of supplies for shipping
- Inspect cargo for damage
- Plan and inspect loads for balance and safety
- Check cargo against invoices to make sure the amount and destination of materials is correct

Qualifications

Physical Demands

Cargo specialists must lift and carry heavy cargo.

Helpful Attributes

Helpful school subjects include general office and business mathematics. Helpful attributes include
- Interest in working with forklifts and cranes
- Preference for physical work

Civilian Counterparts

Civilian cargo specialists work for trucking firms, air cargo companies, and shipping lines. They perform duties similar to military cargo specialists. Depending on specialty, they may also be called industrial truck operators, stevedores, longshoremen, material handlers, or cargo checkers.

Military Careers Score at the 50% (50-50) point = 198.

Construction Equipment Operators

Army

Navy

Air Force

Marine Corps

Typical Tasks

- Drive bulldozers, roadgraders, and other heavy equipment to cut and level earth for runways and roadbeds
- Lift and move steel and other heavy building materials using winches, cranes, and hoists
- Dig holes and trenches using power shovels
- Remove ice and snow from runways, roads, and other areas using scrapers and snow blowers

Qualifications

Physical Demands

Normal color vision is required to identify colored flags and stakes.

Helpful Attributes

Helpful school subjects include shop mechanics. Helpful attributes include

- Interest in operating heavy construction equipment
- Preference for working outdoors

Civilian Counterparts

Civilian construction equipment operators work for building contractors, state highway agencies, and other large scale construction firms. They perform duties similar to military construction equipment operators. Civilian construction equipment operators may also be known as operating engineers or heavy equipment operators.

Military Careers Score at the 50% (50-50) point = 190.

Flight Engineers

Navy

Air Force

Marine Corps

Coast Guard

Typical Tasks

- Inspect aircraft before and after flights, following preflight and post-flight checklists
- Plan and monitor the loading of passengers, cargo, and fuel
- Assist pilots in engine start-up and shutdown
- Compute aircraft load weights and fuel distribution
- Compute fuel consumption using airspeed data, charts, and calculators
- Monitor engine instruments and adjust engine controls following pilot orders
- Check fuel, pressure, electrical, and other aircraft systems during flight
- Inform pilot of aircraft performance problems and recommend corrective action

Qualifications

Special Qualifications

Although there are women flight engineers in the military, some specialties in this occupation are open only to men.

Physical Demands

Flight engineers, like pilots and navigators, have to be mentally alert and physically sound to perform their job. They must be in top physical shape and pass a special physical exam to qualify for flight duty.

Helpful Attributes

Helpful school subjects include general mathematics and shop mechanics. Helpful attributes include

- Skill in using wiring diagrams and maintenance manuals
- Interest in working with mechanical systems and equipment
- Strong desire to fly
- Ability to work as a member of a team

Civilian Counterparts

Civilian flight engineers work for passenger and cargo airline companies. They perform the same duties as in the military.

Military Careers Score at the 50% (50-50) point = 198.

Petroleum Supply Specialists

Army

Navy

Air Force

Marine Corps

Coast Guard

Typical Tasks

- Connect hoses and valves and operate pumps to load petroleum products into tanker trucks, airplanes, ships, and railroad cars
- Test oils and fuels for pollutants
- Repair pipeline systems, hoses, valves, and pumps
- Check the volume and temperature of petroleum and gases in tankers, barges, and storage tanks
- Prepare storage and shipping records
- Store and move packaged petroleum products using forklifts

Qualifications

Physical Demands

Petroleum supply specialists may have to perform moderate to heavy lifting.

Helpful Attributes

Helpful school subjects include shop mechanics and business math. Helpful attributes include

- Interest in working with machines and equipment
- Ability to follow spoken instructions
- Preference for physical work

Civilian Counterparts

Civilian petroleum supply specialists work for oil refineries, pipeline companies, and tanker truck and ship lines. They may also refuel airplanes at large airports. They perform many of the same duties as military petroleum supply specialists.

Military Careers Score at the 50% (50-50) point = 192.

Quartermasters and Boat Operators

Army

Navy

Air Force

Coast Guard

Typical Tasks

- Direct the course and speed of boats
- Consult maps, charts, weather reports, and navigation equipment
- Pilot tugboats when towing and docking barges and large ships
- Operate amphibious craft during troop landings
- Maintain boats and deck equipment
- Operate ship-to-shore radios
- Keep ship logs

Qualifications

Physical Demands

Quartermasters and boat operators may have to stand for several hours at a time. They must be able to speak clearly. Some specialties require normal depth perception and hearing.

Helpful Attributes

Helpful school subjects include mathematics. Helpful attributes include

- Ability to work with mathematical formulas
- Interest in sailing and navigation
- Ability to follow detailed instructions and read maps

Civilian Counterparts

Civilian quartermasters and boat operators may work for shipping and cruise lines, piloting tugboats, ferries, and other small vessels. They perform duties similar to military quartermasters and boat operators. Depending on specialty, they may also be called tugboat captains, motorboat operators, navigators, or pilots.

Military Careers Score at the 50% (50-50) point = 196.

Seamen

Army

Navy

Air Force

Coast Guard

Typical Tasks

- Operate hoists, cranes, and winches to load cargo or set gangplanks
- Operate and maintain on-deck equipment and ship rigging
- Supervise firefighting and damage control exercises
- Handle lines to secure vessels to wharves or other ships
- Stand watch for security, navigation, or communications
- Supervise crews painting and maintaining decks and sides of ships

Qualifications

Physical Demands

Seamen may have to climb ships' rigging and perform work at heights. Their work often involves moderate to heavy lifting.

Helpful Attributes

Helpful school subjects include mathematics and shop mechanics. Helpful attributes include

- Ability to work closely with others
- Interest in sailing and being at sea
- Preference for physical work

Civilian Counterparts

Civilian seamen work primarily for shipping companies, sometimes called the Merchant Marine. They also work for cruise shiplines. They perform many duties similar to military seamen. They are called able seamen, deckhands, or boatswains.

Military Careers Score at the 50% (50-50) point = 196.

Truck Drivers

Army

Navy

Air Force

Marine Corps

Coast Guard

Typical Tasks

- Read travel instructions to determine travel routes, arrival dates, and types of cargo
- Make sure vehicles are loaded properly
- Check oil, fuel, and other fluid levels and tire pressure
- Drive vehicles over all types of roads, traveling alone or in convoys
- Keep records of mileage driven and fuel and oil used
- Wash vehicles and perform routine maintenance and repairs

Qualifications

Physical Demands

Normal color vision is required to read road maps.

Helpful Attributes

Helpful school courses include driver education. Helpful attributes include

- Interest in trucks and truck driving
- Interest in mechanics

Civilian Counterparts

Civilian truck drivers work for trucking companies, moving companies, bus companies, and businesses with their own delivery fleets. They perform duties similar to military truck drivers. They may specialize as tractor-trailer truck drivers, tank truck drivers, heavy truck drivers, or bus drivers.

Military Careers Score at the 50% (50-50) point = 189.

➤ COMBAT SPECIALTY OCCUPATIONS

Artillery Crew Members

Army

Navy

Marine Corps

Coast Guard

Typical Tasks

- Determine target location using computer or manual calculations
- Set up and load artillery weapons

- Prepare ammunition, fuses, and powder for firing
- Fire artillery weapons according to instructions from artillery officers
- Clean and maintain artillery weapons
- Drive trucks and self-propelled artillery

Qualifications

Special Qualifications

This occupation is open only to men. However, this policy is being reevaluated and women may be admitted.

Physical Demands

Artillery crew members must have physical stamina to perform strenuous activities for long periods without rest. They are also required to have normal color vision to identify color-coded ammunition and to read maps and charts.

Helpful Attributes

- Ability to remain calm under stress
- Ability to work as a member of a team
- Interest in cannon and rocket operations
- Ability to perform a wide variety of duties

Civilian Counterparts

Although the job of artillery crew member has no equivalent in civilian life, the close teamwork, discipline, and leadership experiences it provides are helpful in many civilian jobs.

Military Careers Score at the 50% (50-50) point = 190.

Combat Engineers

Army

Marine Corps

Typical Tasks

- Construct trails, roads, and temporary shelters
- Erect floating or prefabricated bridges
- Lay and clear mine fields and booby traps
- Construct field fortifications, such as bunkers and gun emplacements
- Erect camouflage and other protective barriers for artillery and troop positions
- Load, unload, and move supplies and equipment using planes, helicopters, trucks, and amphibious vehicles
- Construct airfields and perform ground traffic control duties
- Participate in combat operations as infantrymen

Qualifications

Special Qualifications

This occupation is open only to men. However, this policy is being reevaluated and women may be admitted.

Physical Demands

Combat engineers must meet very demanding physical requirements. They need agility and balance and must be able to perform strenuous physical activities over long periods of time. Combat engineers must lift and move heavy objects. Some specialties require good swimming abilities.

Helpful Attributes

Helpful school subjects include mathematics, general science, and industrial arts. Helpful attributes include

- Ability to use hand and power tools
- Ability to think and remain calm under stress
- Preference for working outdoors

Civilian Counterparts

Although the job of combat engineer has no direct equivalent in civilian life, experience as a combat engineer is related to occupations in several civilian fields. These include the logging, mining, construction, shipping, and landscaping industries. Civilians in these jobs are called forestry aides, loggers, blasters, and construction workers.

Military Careers Score at the 50% (50-50) point = 190.

Infantrymen

Army

Marine Corps

Typical Tasks

- Operate, clean, and store automatic weapons, such as rifles and machine guns
- Parachute from troop transport airplanes while carrying weapons and supplies
- Fire armor-piercing missiles from hand-held antitank missile launchers
- Carry out scouting missions to spot enemy troop movements and gun locations
- Operate two-way radios and signal equipment to relay battle orders
- Drive vehicles mounted with machine guns or small missiles
- Perform hand-to-hand combat drills that involve martial arts tactics
- Set firing angles and fire mortar shells at targets
- Dig foxholes, trenches, and bunkers for protection against attacks

Qualifications

Special Qualifications

This occupation is open only to men. However, this policy is being reevaluated and women may be admitted.

Physical Demands

The infantry has very demanding physical requirements. Infantrymen must perform strenuous physical activities, such as marching while carrying equipment, digging foxholes, and climbing over obstacles. Infantrymen need good hearing and clear speech to use two-way radios and good night vision and depth perception to see targets and signals.

Helpful Attributes

- Readiness to accept a challenge and face danger
- Ability to stay in top physical condition
- Interest in working as a member of a team

Civilian Counterparts

Although the job of infantrymen has no equivalent in civilian life, the close teamwork, discipline, and leadership experiences it provides are helpful in many civilian jobs.

Military Careers Score at the 50% (50-50) point = 190.

Special Operations Forces

Army

Navy

Air Force

Marine Corps

Typical Tasks

- Go behind enemy lines to recruit, train, and equip friendly forces for guerilla raids
- Carry out demolition raids against enemy military targets, such as bridges, railroads, and fuel depots
- Clean mine fields, both underwater and on land
- Conduct missions to gather intelligence information on enemy military forces

- Conduct offensive raids or invasions of enemy territories
- Destroy enemy ships in coastal areas using underwater explosives

Qualifications

Special Qualifications

This occupation is open only to men. However, this policy is being reevaluated and women may be admitted.

Physical Demands

The special operations forces have very demanding physical requirements. Good eyesight, night vision, and physical conditioning are required to reach mission objectives by parachute, over land, or underwater. Also required is excellent hand-eye coordination to detonate or deactivate explosives. In most instances, special operations forces team members are required to be qualified divers, parachutists, and endurance runners.

Helpful Attributes

Ability to work as a team member
- Readiness to accept a challenge and face danger
- Ability to stay in top physical condition
- Ability to remain calm in stressful situations

Civilian Counterparts

Although the job of special operations forces team member has no equivalent in civilian life, training in explosives, bomb disposal, scuba diving, and swimming may be helpful in such civilian jobs as blaster, police bomb disposal specialist, diver, or swimming instructor. The discipline and dependability of special operations forces are assets in many civilian occupations.

Military Careers Score at the 50% (50-50) point = 200.

Tank Crew Members

Army

Marine Corps

Typical Tasks

- Drive tanks or amphibious assault vehicles in combat formation over roadways, rough terrain, and in heavy surf
- Operate target sighting equipment to aim guns
- Load and fire guns
- Operate two-way radios and signaling equipment to receive and relay battle orders
- Gather and report information about terrain, enemy strength, and target location
- Perform preventive maintenance on tanks, guns, and equipment
- Read maps, compasses, and battle plans

Qualifications

Special Qualifications

This occupation is open only to men. However, this policy is being reevaluated and women may be admitted.

Physical Demands

Tank crew members must be in good physical condition and have exceptional stamina. They must be able to work inside the confined area of a tank for long periods of time. Good vision and normal color vision are required in order to read maps, drive vehicles around obstacles, and locate targets.

Helpful Attributes

Helpful attributes include
- Ability to work as a member of a team
- Readiness to accept a challenge and face danger

- Ability to follow direction and execute orders quickly and accurately

Civilian Counterparts

Although the job of tank crew member has no equivalent in civilian life, the close teamwork, discipline, and leadership experiences it provides are helpful in many civilian jobs.

Military Careers Score at the 50% (50-50) point = 190.

CHAPTER

ENLISTED OPPORTUNITIES IN THE UNITED STATES MILITARY *

The military is the largest employer of high school graduates entering the work force full-time. Each year, over 200,000 young men and women, most of whom are recent high school graduates, join the enlisted forces of the Army, Navy, Air Force, Marine Corps, and Coast Guard.

Besides being the largest employer in the nation, with total employment of over 1.4 million enlisted men and women, the military offers the widest choice of career opportunities. Together, the five services offer training and employment in more than 2,000 enlisted job specialties, which have been grouped into military occupations in this book.

More than three fourths of all military occupations have counterparts in the civilian world of work. For example, air traffic controller, aircraft mechanic, computer programmer, dental hygienist, and electronic technician occupations exist in both the military and civilian work force.

GENERAL ENLISTMENT QUALIFICATIONS

The general qualifications for military enlistment are listed in the chart on page 655. The specific requirements may vary depending on the individual service.

Service Obligation

Joining the military involves entering into a legal contract called an enlistment agreement. The service agrees to provide a job, pay, benefits, and occupational training. In return, the enlisted member agrees to serve for a certain period of time, which is called the service obligation. The standard service obligation is eight years, which is divided between active military duty and reserve duty. Depending on the enlistment program selected, enlisted members spend between two and six years on active duty, with the balance of the eight-year obligation period spent in reserve status.

* Condensed from *Military Careers*

Enlistment Programs

Enlistment programs vary by service. The services adjust the programs they offer to meet changing recruiting needs. Major enlistment options include cash bonuses for enlisting in certain occupations and guaranteed choice of job training and assignments. Currently, all services also offer a Delayed Entry Program (DEP), an option that is used by many high school students who wish to enlist now but wait before entering into active duty. By enlisting under the DEP option, you can delay entry into active duty for up to one year. High school students often enlist under the DEP during their senior year and enter a service after graduation. Other qualified applicants choose the DEP program because the job training they want is not currently available but will be within the next year.

General Enlistment Qualifications*

Age	Must be between 17 and 35 years. Consent of parent or legal guardian required if 17.
Citizenship Status	Must be either (1) U.S. citizen or (2) an immigrant alien legally admitted to the U.S. for permanent residence and possessing immigration and naturalalization documents.
Physical Condition	Must meet minimum physical standards listed below to enlist. Some military occupations have additional physical standards.

Height—	For males:	Maximum—6'8"
		Minimum—5'0"
	For females:	Maximum—6'8"
		Minimum—4'10"

Weight—There are minimum and maximum weights, according to age and height, for males and females.

Vision—There are minimum vision standards.

Overall Health—Must be in good health and pass a medical exam. Certain diseases or conditions may exclude persons from enlistment—for example, diabetes, severe allergies, epilepsy, alcoholism, and drug addiction.

Education	High school graduation is desired by all services and is a requirement under most enlistment options.
Aptitude	Must make the minimum entry score on the ASVAB (Armed Services Vocational Aptitude Battery). Minimum entry scores vary by service and occupation.
Moral Character	Must meet standards designed to screen out persons likely to become disciplinary problems. Standards cover court convictions, juvenile delinquency, arrests, and drug use.
Marital Status and Dependents	May be either single or married.
Waivers	On a case-by-case basis, exceptions (waivers) are granted by individual services for some of the above qualification requirements.

Each service sets its own enlistment standards.

Enlistment Contracts

The enlistment contract specifies the enlistment program you select. It contains the enlistment date, term of enlistment, and other options such as a training program guarantee or a cash bonus. If the service cannot meet its part of the agreement (for example, to provide a specific type of job training), then you are no longer bound by the contract. If you accept another enlistment program, a new contract is written.

High School Graduates

The military encourages young people to stay in school and graduate. Research has shown that high school graduates are more likely to adjust to military life and complete an initial tour of duty. Therefore, the services accept very few non-high school graduates.

ENLISTING IN THE MILITARY

There are four basic steps to the enlistment process. A summary is listed below. For detailed information about the enlistment process, including information about basic training, military pay and benefits, refer to *Guide to Joining the Military* (ARCO 2001).

Step 1: Talking with a Recruiter

If you are interested in enlistment with a particular military service, you must talk with a recruiter from that service. Recruiters can provide detailed information about the employment and training opportunities in their service, as well as answer specific questions about service life, enlistment options, and other topics. They can also provide details about their service's enlistment qualification requirements.

If you decide to apply for entry into the service and the recruiter identifies no problems (such as a severe health problem), the recruiter will examine your educational credentials. You will then be scheduled for enlistment processing.

Step 2: Qualifying for Enlistment

Enlistment processing occurs at over 60 Military Entrance Processing Stations (MEPS), located around the country. At the MEPS, you take the ASVAB if you have not already done so and receive medical examinations to determine if you are qualified to enter the service. The ASVAB is also administered at Mobile Examining Team (MET) sites.

ASVAB results are used to determine if you qualify for entry into a service and whether you have the specific Military Careers Score required to enter job specialty training programs. If you took the ASVAB at your school, you can use your scores to determine if you qualify for entry into the military services, provided the scores are not more than two years old. Applicants with current ASVAB scores are not required to take the ASVAB a second time.

Step 3: Meeting with a Service Classifier

A service classifier is a military career information specialist who helps you select military occupations. For example, if you were applying for entry, the classifier informs you of service job training openings that match your aptitudes and interests. The classifier enters your ASVAB scores into a computerized reservation system. Based on your scores, the system shows the career fields and training you qualify for and when job training will be available.

After discussing job training options with the classifier, you select an occupation and schedule an enlistment date. Enlistment dates may be scheduled for up to one year in the future to coincide with job training openings. This option is called the Delayed Entry Program (DEP).

Following selection of a military training program, you sign an enlistment contract and take the oath of enlistment. If you choose the DEP option, you return home until your enlistment date.

Step 4: Enlisting in the Service

After completing enlistment processing, applicants who select the immediate enlistment option receive their travel papers and proceed to a military base for basic training. Those who select the Delayed Entry Program option return to the MEPS on their scheduled enlistment date. At that time, applicants officially become "enlistees" (also known as "recruits") and proceed to a military base.

In the uncommon event that your guaranteed training program is not available on the reserved date, you have three options:
1. Make another reservation for the same training and return at a later date to enter the service.
2. Select another occupation and job training option.
3. Decide not to join the service and be free from any obligation.

MILITARY TRAINING

The military operates one of the largest training systems in the world. The five services sponsor nearly 300 technical training schools offering more than 10,000 separate courses of instruction.

The military generally provides four kinds of training to its personnel:
1. Recruit training
2. Job training
3. Advanced training
4. Leadership training

Recruit Training

Recruit training, popularly called basic training or "boot camp," is a rigorous orientation to the military. Depending on the service, recruit training lasts from six to thirteen weeks and provides a transition from civilian to military life. The services train recruits at selected military bases across the country. Where an enlistee trains depends on the service and the job training to be received. Through basic training, recruits gain the pride, knowledge, discipline, and physical conditioning necessary to serve as members of the Army, Navy, Air Force, Marine Corps, and Coast Guard.

Upon reporting for basic training, recruits are divided into groups of 40 to 80 people. They then meet their drill instructor, receive uniforms and equipment, and move into assigned quarters.

During basic training, recruits receive instruction in health, first aid, and military skills. They also improve their fitness and stamina by participating in rigorous daily exercises and conditioning. To measure their conditioning progress, recruits are tested on sit-ups, push-ups, running, and body weight.

Recruits follow a demanding schedule throughout basic training; every day is carefully structured with time for classes, meals, physical conditioning, and field instruction. Some free time (including time to attend religious services) is available to recruits during basic training. After completing basic training, recruits normally proceed to job training

Job Training

Through job training, also called technical or skill training, recruits learn the skills they need to perform their job specialties. The military provides its personnel with high-quality training because lives and mission success depend on how well people perform their duties. Military training produces highly qualified workers, and, for this reason, many civilian employers consider military training excellent preparation for civilian occupations.

The type of job specialty determines the length of training. Most training lasts from 10 to 20 weeks, although some nuclear specialties require over one year of training.

Military training occurs both in the classroom and on the job. Classroom training emphasizes hands-on activities and practical experience, as well as textbook learning. For example, recruits who will be working with electronic equipment practice operating and repairing the equipment, in addition to studying the principles of electronics.

At their first assignments, enlisted members continue to learn on the job. Experienced enlisted members and supervisors help servicemen and servicewomen further develop their skills. In addition, the military offers refresher courses and advanced training to help military personnel maintain and increase their skills. As personnel advance in rank, they continue their training with leadership and management courses.

The Army, Navy, and Marine Corps offer apprenticeship programs for some job specialties. These programs consist of classroom and on-the-job training that meet U.S. Department of Labor apprenticeship standards. After completing an apprenticeship program, personnel receive a Department of Labor apprenticeship certificate. To military commanders and civilian employers, these certificates demonstrate that the worker has acquired specific skills and qualifications.

Advanced Training

Hundreds of advanced training courses have been developed by the services to improve the technical skills of the enlisted workforce. These courses offer instruction in skills not covered in initial training. Advanced training also includes courses covering new or additional job-related equipment. Advanced training is especially important in high-technology areas where military technicians are constantly exposed to newer and more sophisticated equipment. Other advanced courses provide instruction in supervising and managing the daily operations of military units, such as repair shops or medical facilities.

Some advanced training involves classroom training, but the services also provide enlisted members with a wide choice of self-study correspondence courses. Some are general courses and address most duties of a job; others are designed to cover highly complex tasks or job-related skills. Self-study courses are particularly important to individual career advancement.

DUTY ASSIGNMENT

Leadership Training

Each service has schools and courses to help supervisors be more effective in managing the day-to-day operations of their units. These classes are designed primarily for noncommissioned officers. Courses include instruction in leadership skills, service regulations, and management techniques needed to train and lead other servicemembers.

The five services have similar systems for assigning personnel to jobs. Each system is designed to satisfy the staffing needs of the particular service. At the same time, the services attempt to meet the desires of the individual service member and provide opportunities for career development. The duty assignment process determines where enlisted personnel work, how often they move, and the opportunities open to them.

All services require their members to travel. Enlisted personnel are stationed in each of the 50 states and in countries all over the world. They are routinely reassigned after two-, three-, or four-year tours of duty. To many people, this is one of the attractive parts of service life, and many men and women join for the opportunity to travel, live in foreign countries, and see different parts of the United States.

Pay and Benefits

Military personnel in all five services are paid according to the same pay scale and receive the same basic benefits. Military pay and benefits are set by Congress, which normally grants a cost-of-living pay increase once each year. In addition to pay, the military provides many of life's necessities, such as food, clothing, and housing, or pays monthly allowances for them. The following sections describe military pay, allowances, and benefits in more detail.

Enlisted Pay Grades

Enlistees can progress through nine enlisted pay grades during their careers. Pay grade and length of service determine a servicemember's pay. Figure 1 illustrates the insignia for the ranks in each service and their accompanying pay grade.

New recruits begin at pay grade E-1, except in some services, where a few who have certain technical job skills enter at a higher pay grade. Within six months, enlistees usually move up to E-2. Within the next six to twelve months, the military promotes enlistees to E-3 if job performance is satisfactory and other requirements are met. Promotions to E-4 and above are based on job performance, leadership ability, promotion test scores, years of service, and time in the present pay grade. Promotions become more competitive at the higher pay grades.

Incentives and Special Pay

The military offers incentives and special pay (in addition to basic pay) for certain types of duty. For example, incentives are paid for submarine and flight duty. Other types of hazardous duty with monthly incentives include parachute jumping, flight deck duty, and explosives demolition. In addition, the military gives special pay for sea duty, diving duty, special assignments, duty in some foreign places, and duty in areas subject to hostile fire. Depending on the service, bonuses are also paid for entering certain occupations.

Allowances

Most enlisted members, especially in the first year of service, live in military housing and eat in military dining facilities free of charge. Those living off base receive quarters (housing) and subsistence (food) allowances in addition to their basic pay. In 1997, the monthly housing allowance ranged from $202 to $659, depending on pay grade and number of dependents. The food allowance ranged from $249 to $329 per month, depending on living circumstances. Because allowances are not taxed as income, they provide a significant tax savings in addition to their cash value.

Employment Benefits

Military personnel receive substantial benefits in addition to their pay and allowances. While they are in the service, enlisted members' benefits include health care, vacation, legal assistance, recreational programs, educational assistance, and commissary-exchange (military store) privileges. Families of servicemembers also receive some of these benefits. The chart below contains a summary of these employment benefits.

Figure 1 Insignia of the United States Armed Forces

Rank Level	Army		Navy / Coast Guard		Air Force		Marines	
E-1	Private	(no insignia)	Seaman Recruit (SR)		Airman Basic	(no insignia)	Private (Pvt)	(no insignia)
E-2	Private		Seaman Apprentice (SA)		Airman		Private First Class (PFC)	
E-3	Private First Class		Seaman (SN)		Airman First Class		Lance Corporal (LCpl)	
E-4	Specialist							
	Corporal		Petty Officer Third Class (PO3)		Senior Airman		Corporal (Cpl)	
E-5	Sergeant		Petty Officer Second Class (PO2)		Staff Sergeant		Sergeant (Sgt)	
E-6	Staff Sergeant		Petty Officer First Class (PO1)		Technical Sergeant		Staff Sergeant (SSgt)	
E-7	Sergeant First Class		Chief Petty Officer (CPO)		Master Sergeant		Gunnery Sergeant (GySgt)	
					Master Sergeant with first sergeant status			

Basic Pay

The major part of an enlistee's paycheck is basic pay. Pay grade and total years of service determine an enlistee's pay. Figure 2 lists annual basic pay for each pay grade as of 2002. Cost-of-living increases generally occur once a year.

Figure 2. Basic Pay—Effective January 1, 2002

PAY GRADE	YEARS OF SERVICE Under 2	Over 2	Over 3	Over 4	Over 6	Over 8	Over 10	Over 12	Over 14	Over 16	Over 18	Over 20	Over 22	Over 24	Over 26
E-9	N/A	N/A	N/A	N/A	N/A	N/A	3423.90	3501.30	3599.40	3714.60	3830.40	3944.10	4098.30	4251.30	4467.00
E-8	N/A	N/A	N/A	N/A	N/A	2858.10	2940.60	3017.70	3110.10	3210.30	3314.70	3420.30	3573.00	3724.80	3937.80
E-7	1986.90	2169.00	2251.50	2332.50	2417.40	2562.90	2645.10	2726.40	2808.00	2892.60	2975.10	3057.30	3200.40	3292.80	3526.80
E-6	1701.00	1870.80	1953.60	2033.70	2117.40	2254.50	2337.30	2417.40	2499.30	2558.10	2602.80	2602.80	2602.80	2602.80	2602.80
E-5	1561.50	1665.30	1745.70	1828.50	1912.80	2030.10	2110.20	2193.30	2193.30	2193.30	2193.30	2193.30	2193.30	2193.30	2193.30
E-4	1443.60	1517.70	1599.60	1680.30	1752.30	1752.30	1752.30	1752.30	1752.30	1752.30	1752.30	1752.30	1752.30	1752.30	1752.30
E-3	1303.50	1385.40	1468.50	1468.50	1468.50	1468.50	1468.50	1468.50	1468.50	1468.50	1468.50	1468.50	1468.50	1468.50	1468.50
E-2	1239.30	1239.30	1239.30	1239.30	1239.30	1239.30	1239.30	1239.30	1239.30	1239.30	1239.30	1239.30	1239.30	1239.30	1239.30
E-1	1105.50	1105.50	1105.50	1105.50	1105.50	1105.50	1105.50	1105.50	1105.50	1105.50	1105.50	1105.50	1105.50	1105.50	1105.50

Note: E-1 with less than 4 months service = 1022.70

SUMMARY OF EMPLOYMENT BENEFITS FOR ENLISTED MEMBERS

Vacation	Leave time of thirty days per year
Medical, Dental, and Eye Care	Full medical, hospitalization, dental, and eye-care services for enlistees and most health-care costs for family members
Continuing Education	Voluntary educational programs for undergraduate and graduate degrees or for single courses, including tuition assistance for programs at colleges and universities
Recreational Programs	Programs include athletics, entertainment, and hobbies: Softball, basketball, football, swimming, tennis, golf, weight training, and other sports
	Parties, dances, and entertainment
	Club facilities, snack bars, game rooms, movie theaters, and lounges
	Active hobby and craft clubs and book and music libraries
Exchange and Commissary Privileges	Food, goods, and services are available at military stores, generally at lower costs than regular retail stores.
Legal Assistance	Many free legal services are available to assist with personal matters.

Retirement Benefits

The military offers one of the best retirement programs in the country. After 20 years of active duty, personnel may retire and receive a monthly payment equal to 40 percent of their average basic pay for their last five years of active duty. Those who retire with more than 20 years of service receive higher pay. Other retirement benefits include medical care and commissary-exchange privileges.

Veterans' Benefits

Veterans of military service are entitled to certain veterans' benefits set by Congress and provided by the Department of Veterans Affairs. In most cases, these include guarantees for home loans, hospitalization, survivor benefits, educational benefits, disability benefits, and assistance in finding civilian employment.